CONCORDIA
Springfield, Ill.
G 2 UPE
BOOK STORE
$ 5.10

COMMENTARY ON THE GOSPEL OF LUKE

The New
INTERNATIONAL COMMENTARY
on the
NEW TESTAMENT

COMMENTARY ON THE GOSPEL OF LUKE

by

NORVAL GELDENHUYS

B.A., B.D., Th.M.

*Former Elsie Ballot Scholar at Princeton Theological Seminary
and at Cambridge University*

Foreword by F. F. Bruce

WM. B. EERDMANS PUBLISHING COMPANY

GRAND RAPIDS   MICHIGAN

WM. B. EERDMANS PUBLISHING COMPANY
GRAND RAPIDS, MICHIGAN, U.S.A.
ALL RIGHTS RESERVED

First published 1951
Reprinted 1952
Reprinted 1954
Reprinted 1956
Reprinted 1960

PHOTOLITHOPRINTED BY CUSHING - MALLOY, INC.
ANN ARBOR, MICHIGAN, UNITED STATES OF AMERICA
1960

Dedicated to my Father and Mother who were the first to lead me to love the Gospel Story; and to Professor Dr. E. P. Groenewald of the theological faculty of Pretoria University, South Africa, whose inspiring lectures and guidance made the study of the New Testament an ever greater joy to me.

GENERAL FOREWORD

With the publication of this *Commentary on the Gospel According to Luke* the *New International Commentary on the New Testament,* which was announced in 1946 as a seventeen-volume project, begins to pass from promise to reality. Other volumes are in preparation and there is good hope that they will appear with some regularity.

The Commentary has been undertaken to provide earnest students of the New Testament with an exposition that is thorough and abreast of modern scholarship and at the same time loyal to the Scriptures as the infallible Word of God. The urgent need for such a series has been widely recognized and expressed in recent years by ministers and other leaders who are occupied with the study of the Bible and are concerned to foster a deeper understanding of its message among Christians today.

The plan is being realized through the cooperation of scholars in Europe, South Africa and America whose Christian convictions are of a distinctly Reformed expression. While we recognize our Christian unity with brethren in other streams of Christendom, and freely acknowledge our indebtedness to them, we believe that we can contribute to the need of the Christian Church most significantly if the Commentary possesses the specific character and integration provided by the Reformed Faith.

Although, then, the volumes will necessarily reflect the Reformed viewpoint of the contributors, it is our judgment that the result need not be a mere repetition of a tradition, and still less a subjection of Scripture to a preconceived dogmatic system of thought. Since the Bible is acknowledged as being the Word of God, that Word must have the right of way at all times. The goal is to set forth the message of the New Testament, not a modernization of it. On this basis there may be the fervent hope and prayer that these commentaries, rather than being obscurantist in their thrust, will make for some definite progress in the march of the truth of God.

With a view to meeting the needs of Christians generally the expositions proper as well as the Introductions to the several volumes are written exclusively in English. Since, moreover, the expositions will be free of Greek and Hebrew terms and of the more technical aspects of interpretation, the work will appeal to the untrained student of the Bible.

At the same time the Commentary has in view the needs of ministers and others who desire a scholarly exposition of the original text of Scripture that takes account of contemporaneous discussions. To achieve this second goal, without jeopardy to the primary objective, the following two provisions have been adopted: (1) The expositions proper, though written in English, are prepared on the basis of a thorough study of the Greek text, including an evaluation of the textual problems which are especially significant for the interpreter and taking account of the most scholarly exegetical literature. (2) Supplementing the expositions, the more technical aspects, including grammatical, textual and historical problems, appear in footnotes and special notes or appendices. These notes are intended to contribute to the goal of providing a thorough exposition of the New Testament rather than to treat exhaustively the more technical questions.

Although the expositions are based upon the Greek of the New Testament, an English text is printed with a view to enhancing the usefulness and practicality of the Commentary. The text in this volume is that of the Revised Version of 1881.

That the first volume in the series should be contributed by Norval Geldenhuys is particularly fitting in view of his special part in the development of the idea of the Commentary. In the fall of 1945 he called to extend greetings from his former professor, Dr. E. P. Groenewald of Pretoria University, who had been a fellow-student of mine in Amsterdam, and in the course of the conversation began to speak of the significant work in the New Testament field being carried on by Groenewald and others in his native country. At once the hope of recruiting a corps of scholars who might collaborate in the production of such a Commentary as had been taking shape in my mind brightened measurably. As time went on there was further encouragement as scholars in Great Britain, Holland, and America, in addition to South Africa, indicated their willingness to cooperate in such an undertaking. To Mr. Geldenhuys one must also credit the initiative of approaching Mr. Willian B. Eerdmans, Sr., on the subject of the publication as well as of arousing the interest of Marshall, Morgan & Scott of London.

The special foreword by Professor Bruce calls attention to some of the particular qualifications of Mr. Geldenhuys as an expositor. As the volume goes forth it will speak for itself, and it will speak with no uncertain sound. May many know the truth more fully and do it more perfectly because of this volume!

N. B. STONEHOUSE,

Philadelphia, Pa., *General Editor*
April 1, 1951

FOREWORD

IT IS arguable that too many commentaries on books of the Bible
have been written by people in academic life. The Bible is not
really an academic book—although it is pre-eminently worthy of
academic study. It deals from first to last with the most urgently
practical issues of human life. And for that reason those whose
daily work brings them face to face with these issues are best
qualified to understand and interpret the Bible.

Mr. Geldenhuys is such a man. He has, of course, a fine
academic equipment, to which Cambridge, Princeton and
Pretoria have made their distinctive contributions. His acquaintance with the literature of his subject is obviously wide and
scholarly. But he is more than a scholar. Practically every page
of this commentary reveals him as preacher, pastor and theologian.

That a minister of the Divine Word should write a commentary
on one of the Gospels is as it should be. For the Gospels consist
essentially of the written deposit of the apostolic preaching, and
are most fittingly expounded by those whose chief business in life
is the proclamation of the good news which the apostles proclaimed. The Third Evangelist, indeed, displays more of a bio-
graphical interest in the life of Jesus than do the other three; but
the basis of his work is none the less surely the primitive Christian
message.

Our author, as befits a minister of the Dutch Reformed Church
of South Africa, makes that message stand out plainly, and re-
preaches it in the course of his exegesis. The practical application
of the lessons of each section of the Gospel to his readers bespeaks
a faithful pastor, well experienced in the cure of souls; and if the
Reformed theologian is also in evidence, may it not be claimed
in justification that Reformed theology is Biblical theology, and
must therefore be present whenever the Scriptures are expounded?

Mr. Geldenhuys manifests a healthy scepticism of some parts of
the critical stock-in-trade of academic Biblicists like the writer of
this Foreword. It probably does us good to be invited to take our
theories out and see what they look like in the light of daily life.
At any rate it is salutary to remember that, as a very distinguished
member of our own order once said, " source-criticism in the New

7

Testament is largely guess-work ". But Mr. Geldenhuys shows no obscurantist antagonism to all such criticism just because it is criticism; he recognises, for example, Luke's dependence on Mark. Perhaps, however, it is necessary that he should so repeatedly and emphatically expose the fallacy of the tacit assumption sometimes made that Jesus could never have said the same thing twice!

The turning-point in Luke's record comes in his ninth chapter, with the narrative of the transfiguration of Jesus and " the fulfilment of the days of his being taken up ". Instead of ascending to heaven in His glorified body from the holy mount at that moment, Jesus with fixed purpose came down again to the plain and set His face in the direction of Jerusalem. One of the most valuable features of Mr. Geldenhuys's exegesis of this Gospel is the way in which he traces first the progressive self-revelation of Jesus' divine glory up to its full manifestation on the mount of transfiguration, and then the successive stages on the way to the cross, the shadow of which grows more ominous and dark the nearer He approaches it, until in resurrection He emerges triumphantly on the other side.

Mr. Geldenhuys has already published a work on the third Gospel in his native Afrikaans. The present work, however, is no mere translation of the Afrikaans commentary. But the access which he naturally has to the writings of Dutch scholars who are not so familiar to us in the British Isles enables him to make references to them which add to the interest of the present work. The text of the Gospel printed here is that of the British Revised Version, but those who can read the original will find this commentary all the more useful if they keep a Greek Testament ready to hand.

I have much pleasure in commending this work to Bible students who appreciate a commentary which calls for time and thought, and not least to those who, like the author himself, are actively engaged in the ministry of the Word.

F. F. BRUCE,
*Rylands Chair of Biblical Criticism
and Exegesis, University of Manchester*

AUTHOR'S NOTE

For the sake of readers of this commentary who do not read Greek the text of the Gospel is printed in the English of the Revised Version of 1881. Our expositions are, however, based upon the Greek text (as exhibited in Nestle's latest edition). In most of the places where the Nestle text differs from the *Textus Receptus* which underlies the English Authorised Version we have, in our footnotes, tried to indicate why Nestle's text is to be preferred as representing the original more faithfully. Only in a few instances do we disagree with Nestle's text.

LIST OF CONTENTS

INTRODUCTION

I

THE AUTHOR OF THE GOSPEL

IT IS generally recognised to-day that the author of the third Gospel was also the writer of the book of Acts. This is borne out by the following considerations: (1) The Gospel, as well as Acts, is dedicated to a certain Theophilus (Luke i. 3; Acts i. 1). (2) In Acts i. 1 the writer refers to " the former treatise " written by him. From his brief reference to the contents of " the former treatise " it is evident that the third Gospel is meant. (3) In language, style and vocabulary of the original Greek there is such an unmistakable similarity between the Gospel and Acts that no doubt remains as to both books being the work of the same author.[1]

From the preface of Luke (i. 1–4) it appears that the writer does not claim to have been an eyewitness of the life and work of Jesus. He declares, however, that he possessed first-hand sources of information for writing his account.[2] He was in close personal contact with hearers and eyewitnesses of Christ and had knowledge of efforts that had already been made to arrange in narrative form the facts concerning Him (i. 1, 2).

The following peculiar phenomenon in the narrative in Acts brings us yet another step nearer in our endeavour to identify the writer of Luke and Acts: the account of the occurrences described in Acts is related throughout[3] up to xvi. 9 in the third person. But at xvi. 10 there is a sudden change-over to the first person plural. Thus in xvi. 8 we still read: " And they[4] [Paul and his fellow-travellers] passing by Mysia came down to Troas." But in xvi. 10 f.

---

[1] For the detailed evidence of this cf. Howkins, *Horae Synopticae*, pp. 174–93. Cf. also Plummer, *St. Luke* (I.C.C.), pp. lii lxiii, for a complete list of words and expressions used throughout in Luke and Acts but nowhere else, or very seldom, in the rest of the New Testament.

[2] See W. Manson, *The Gospel of St. Luke*, p. xxvii.

[3] The Western text, however, already uses the first person at Acts xi. 28, where it reads ἦν δὲ πολλὴ ἀγαλλίασις · συνεστραμμένων δὲ ἡμῶν ἔφη εἰς ἐξ αὐτῶν ὀνόματι Ἄγαβος (" and there was much rejoicing. And when *we* were gathered together, one of them, Agabus by name, said . . .").

[4] The italics are mine.

15

(after mention was made in xvi. 9 of Paul's vision of the Macedonian who prayed him to come over to Macedonia) the narrative suddenly resumes: " And when he had seen the vision, straightway *we*[1] sought to go forth into Macedonia, concluding that God had called *us* for to preach the gospel unto them. Setting sail therefore from Troas, *we* made a straight course to Samothrace . . ."

The obvious explanation of this phenomenon is that the writer of the book joined the Apostle Paul and his party at Troas and now accompanied them as fellow-traveller on the first missionary journey to Europe. He was, however, too reserved and modest to make express mention of his joining the party and in his narrative merely changes over from the third to the first person (plural) to indicate when he, too, was with Paul.

The first person plural is used up to xvi. 17, but after that again the third person plural (e.g. in xvii. 1). Apparently, therefore, the writer did not accompany Paul from Philippi to Thessalonica, Berea and the other places visited by him on his second and on the greater portion of his third missionary journey. But when Paul on his third journey was again on his way back to Jerusalem, the writer once more joined Paul's travelling party at Philippi (xx. 5) and remained a member of the party until they arrived in Jerusalem (from xx. 5 to xxi. 17 " we " and " us " are used throughout in the narrative).

After xxi. 17 the first person plural does not occur again before xxvii. 2. From the latter verse it is maintained until near the end of the book, so that the writer was with Paul on his voyage (as a prisoner) to Rome, where he arrived together with him (xxviii. 16).

From all this it is obvious that the writer of Luke and Acts was a fellow-traveller and friend of Paul. It is also generally recognised that those portions of Acts in which the first person plural is used, owing to the freshness and accuracy with which the occurrences therein are described, undoubtedly constitute the narrative of a personal eyewitness and hearer.[2]

Now it has been asserted in some quarters[3] that, while the portions in the first person plural were written by a fellow-traveller of Paul, the other portions of Acts and the third Gospel were written by a different person. The thorough-going investigations of Hawkins[4] and Harnack[5] have, however, proved conclusively that the language, style and vocabulary of the parts in the first person plural correspond so closely to those of the Gospel and of

---

[1] The italics are mine.
[2] Cf. Major, I. W. Manson and Wright, *The Mission and Message of Jesus*, p. 352.
[3] Windisch, *Beginnings of Christianity*, part ii, pp. 329 ff.
[4] *Horae Synopticae*, 2nd ed., pp. 182–9.
[5] *Luke the Physician*, pp. 26 ff.

the rest of Acts, that the identity of authorship must be upheld.[1]

We therefore conclude that the author of Luke and Acts was an intimate friend and fellow-worker of the Apostle Paul.

In proceeding to examine the epistles of Paul to attempt to discover the identity of this fellow-traveller of his who is at the same time the author of Luke and Acts, we do not find any express indications in this respect. Paul in his epistles does name different persons who often accompanied him on his journeys, but does not indicate who the writer is.

Fortunately, from very early times in the history of the Christian Church there exists straightforward evidence that Luke[2] was Paul's fellow-traveller who wrote the Gospel and Acts.[3] The anti-Marcionite Prologue to the Third Gospel (between A.D. 160 and 180), which survives in both Greek and Latin, gives the following account:

" Luke was an Antiochian of Syria, a physician by profession. He was a disciple of the apostles and later accompanied Paul until the latter's martyrdom. He served the Lord without distraction [or 'without blame'], having neither wife nor children, and at the age of eighty-four he fell asleep in Boeotia, full of the Holy Spirit. While there were already Gospels previously in existence—that according to Matthew written in Judaea and that according to Mark in Italy—Luke, moved by the Holy Spirit, composed the whole of this Gospel in the parts

[1] If the portions in the first person plural had been taken by a later writer from the journal of a fellow-traveller of Paul and had been worked up by the writer in his own style (as is professed by Cadbury, Windisch and others), he would assuredly also have altered the first person plural to the third person plural. Cf. also the words of Clogg, *Introduction to the New Testament*, p. 228: " The diary passages are among the most vivid in the book, and do not seem to have been edited." Cf. also Harnack, *The Date of Acts and the Synoptic Gospels*, p. 12.

[2] That the name " Lukas " is the abbreviated form of " Lukios " is generally accepted (cf. Deissmann, *Light from the Ancient East*, p. 435). Zahn, however, thinks it is the abbreviation of Lucanus (*Introduction to the New Testament*, iii, p. 5).

[3] Cf. Jülicher-Fascher, *An Introduction to the New Testament*, p. 330.

It has even been argued that the original form of the Western text explicitly mentioned Luke as the author of Acts. In 1913 J. R. Harris argued, on the strength of an Armenian " catena " on Acts, based chiefly on Ephrem Syrus and Chrysostom, that the original Western text of Acts xx. 13 ran: " But I Luke, and those who were with me, went on board." (See *Expository Times*, xxiv, p. 530, quoting from *The British Friend*, April 1913.) This argument was strengthened in 1921, when the Mechitarist (Armenian) Fathers in Vienna published the Armenian translation of Ephrem's commentary on Acts, and these very words were found at xx. 13. F. C. Conybeare renders them by the Latin " ego Lucas et qui mecum intravimus navem " in *The Beginnings of Christianity*, iii, p. 442. If this argument could be accepted, the evidence for Lucan authorship would be pushed back as early as A.D. 100 or thereabout, when the Western text seems to have taken shape. But the argument is too slender to bear any weight, and the " reading " may simply have been Ephrem's own paraphrase of the Biblical text.

about Achaia. In his prologue he makes this very point clear, that other Gospels had been written before his, and that it was necessary to expound to the Gentile believers the accurate account of the [divine] dispensation, so that they should not be perverted by Jewish fables, nor be deceived by heretical and vain imaginations and thus err from the truth. And so right at the beginning he relates for us the nativity of John—a most essential matter, for John is the beginning of the Gospel, being our Lord's forerunner and companion both in the preparation of the Gospel and in the administration of baptism and the fellowship of the Spirit. This ministry [of John] had been mentioned by one of the Twelve Prophets [i.e. Malachi]. And afterwards the same Luke wrote the Acts of the Apostles."

Commenting on this evidence, Jülicher-Fascher's *Einleitung in das Neue Testament* (7th ed., 1931) remarks: " We should possess an exceptionally circumstantial and favourable tradition about Luke's Gospel if we might trust the anti-Marcionite Prologue to the Gospel " (p. 312). There seems to be no good reason to doubt the reliability of the Prologue. Composed as it was at a time when the Marcionite dispute was very much alive, its author was not likely to make statements which the opposite side could readily refute.[1]

Then Irenaeus[2] states (about A.D. 185) that Luke is the author of the third Gospel as well as of Acts. Justin Martyr (about A.D. 150) apparently also knew that Luke was the author.[3] The Canon of Muratori (about A.D. 195) states that the physician Luke wrote the third Gospel and makes mention of the fact already stated that he had never seen Jesus in the flesh.

Clement of Alexandria,[4] Origen,[5] Tertullian[6] and all[7] the later church fathers also agree that Luke, the physician, was the author of our third Gospel.

Tradition, therefore, is in complete accord that Luke, the physician, is the author of Luke and Acts. Accordingly it is generally accepted that there exists no reason why these data of

---

[1] The character and date of the anti-Marcionite Prologues to the Gospels was brought to the attention of scholars by Dom Donatien DeBruyne in 1928, in the *Revue Bénédictine* for July of that year (vol. 40, no. 3). His arguments speedily won the support of Harnack in *Sitzungsberichte der preussischen Akademie der Wissenschaften*, Phil.-hist. Klasse, 24 (1928), and since then the view that the Prologues are to be dated between the dates of Papias and Irenaeus has been generally accepted, with one or two notable dissenting voices.

[2] *Adv. Haeres*, iii, 1 and 2.

[3] Cf. Creed, *The Gospel according to St. Luke*, p. xiii.

[4] *Strom.*, i, 21

[5] Cf. Eusebius, *Historia Ecclesiastica*, vi, 25, 3.

[6] *Contra Marc.*, iv, 2.

[7] Cf. Eusebius, *op. cit.*, iii, 24, 5; Jerome, *De Viris Illustribus*, vii.

the ancient writers should be questioned.[1] As Streeter and others rightly declare, it would be historically inexplicable why tradition should ascribe the third Gospel to Luke if he had not really been the author of it. For it was part of a decided tendency to ascribe the writing of books and epistles to the apostles or to others of the most important eyewitnesses. It is, therefore, unthinkable that the Gospel should have been ascribed to Luke, who had not been an eyewitness of Jesus' life and work, unless he was known to have been the real author.

If we now go back to the data in the New Testament, we find that the statements made by the ancient church fathers as to the authorship of Luke and Acts fit in admirably with the New Testament data. For note the following:

Paul in three different places in his epistles calls Luke a companion of his. Thus, e.g., in Colossians iv. 14 he writes: " Luke, the beloved physician, and Demas, greet you." It is clear from the context here that Luke was of Gentile descent (cf. iv. 10–14).[2]

In Philemon Paul calls Luke one of his fellow-labourers (Philem. 24).

In 2 Timothy iv. 11 Paul, shortly before his martyrdom, writes the affecting words: " Only Luke is with me."

Now we know that all three of these[3] epistles in which Paul speaks of Luke being with him were written by Paul during his captivities in Rome.[4] Their evidence, therefore, fits in beautifully with the data of Acts, already mentioned, according to which it is evident that the author of Luke and Acts accompanied Paul when he was taken as a captive to Rome.

Accordingly everything points to the fact that the beloved physician of Colossians iv. 14 is the author of the third Gospel and of Acts.

The statement by numerous church fathers and by Paul that Luke was a physician is also corroborated in the Gospel and in Acts. In 1882 W. K. Hobart, in *The Medical Language of St. Luke*, defended the thesis that the third Gospel and Acts are permeated by the medical terminology current during the first century. Harnack, Zahn and Moffatt also, after a careful sifting of Hobart's data, came to the conclusion that the author of Luke and

---

[1] The attempts of Cadbury, Windisch and others who try to ignore the traditional data and who do not accept the authorship of Luke are effectively refuted by Streeter, *Four Gospels*, pp. 542 ff.

[2] Cf. Plummer, *op. cit.*, pp. xviii–xix.

[3] 2 Timothy was probably written during his second captivity in Rome., i.e. just before his execution (cf. Eusebius, *Historia Ecclesiastica*, ii, 22, 6).

[4] Duncan, Deissmann and a number of other scholars who have tried to prove that the imprisonment letters were written from Ephesus and not from Rome have not been able to establish their case.

Acts was a physician. Later on Cadbury,[1] who is exceptionally critical and unwilling to assume Luke to have been the author of the Gospel and of Acts, maintained that the so-called medical words and terms in Luke and Acts also occur in non-medical writers like Lucian and Josephus and that in those days there existed no noticeable difference between the technical and non-technical language.

Cadbury is right to the extent that the language of Luke and Acts does not *of itself prove* that the author was a physician. Nevertheless the fact remains that the language and terminology of Luke and Acts are of such a nature that they *corroborate*[2] in a striking manner the tradition that the author was Luke the physician. The following may be cited as a number of examples of medically tinted language and terminology from Luke: Luke iv. 38 describes the disease of Peter's mother-in-law as a " great fever ", while Mark merely describes it as " fever ". Now it is a well-known fact that medical writers of those times were accustomed to describe fever as a " small " or as a " great " fever.[3]

Luke v. 12 describes the leper as " a man full of leprosy ", while Mark and Matthew merely say " a leprous man ". Here also the expression of Luke is typically medical, as is evident from the writings of Hippocrates.[4]

In the same way the precise manner in which Luke describes different cases of disease (e.g. xiii. 11, viii. 42, vi. 18, xiii. 32; Acts vi. 22, ix. 33, etc.) fits in with the fact that he was a physician.[5]

Taking all the data into consideration, one cannot but come to the conclusion that, although the language and style do not *per se* prove that the author of the books was a physician, the statement by Paul[6] in Colossians iv. 14, and the unanimous assertions of the

---

[1] *The Style and Literary Method of Luke*, pp. 39–72.

[2] Plummer, Moffatt, Creed and several others also favour this view.

[3] Cf. Creed, *op. cit.*, p. xx.

[4] *ibid.*

[5] It seems probable that Luke, even after he became a companion of Paul, continued with his practice as a physician. "It is also possible that he rendered valuable services as a physician to the apostle himself, who was often severely ill " (Zahn, *Introduction to the New Testament*, English transl., vol. iii, p. 1). This would make it clear why Paul calls Luke " the beloved physician " (Col. iv. 14). For would he have called him so if he had discarded his practice as physician years before? And by calling him the *beloved* physician, does that not point to personal gratitude Paul felt towards him for services rendered to him by his physician companion?

[6] That the Luke of Colossians, iv. 14 is the same as the author of Acts (and so of the Gospel) " is completely established by the content [of Acts], the thoroughly Pauline conception of Christianity, the accurate acquaintance with Paul's fortunes and the central rôle which is accorded to Paul" (Ed. Meyer, *Ursprung und Anfränge des Christentums*, i, p. 3). Only a companion of Paul, and a very close companion at that, could and would have written the book of Acts, in which so much prominence is given to the apostle.

ancient church fathers that Luke was a physician, are clearly corroborated by the nature of the contents of the books.[1]

The statement of the anti-Marcionite Prologue,[2] which also occurs in Eusebius[3] and Jerome,[4] that Luke, the author of the Gospel, was of Gentile descent and a former inhabitant of Antioch, also finds corroboration in the Gospel and Acts. With regard to the Gentile descent of the author, the books, e.g., show signs throughout that they were written for Gentiles by a person who himself was of Gentile descent. This is evident from such facts as that (a) the citations in Luke and Acts from the Old Testament are made from the Septuagint (Greek) translation and not from the Hebrew;[5] (b) in the Gospel the Lord is addressed not as " Rabbi " but by the Greek titles *Didaskalos* (" Teacher ") and *Epistates* (" Master "); in other instances Hebrew names are avoided, or superseded by Greek names or paraphrases (e.g. in iv. 2, xxii. 40, xxiii. 33, and others); in the few cases where a Hebrew name is indeed retained an explanation of the name is added (e.g. Acts iv. 36); (c) the author, unlike Matthew and Mark, never makes Jesus use Aramaic words, and only very occasionally the typically Jewish " amen " (" verily "); (d) the author is free from all Jewish particularism.

That Luke was possibly a native of Antioch finds support in the reading of the Codex Bezae (a witness to the Western text) in Acts xi. 28, which makes mention of the joy which " we " (the Christians of Antioch) experienced from the visit of certain persons from Jerusalem. Although this version is perhaps not original,[6] it nevertheless shows that the view had already existed at an early period that Luke was a resident of Antioch.

The fact that Luke relates such an exceptionally large number of particulars in Acts (cf. Acts xi. 19-27, xiii. 1, xiv. 19, 21, 26, xv. 22-5, xviii. 22) regarding the earliest history of the Christian congregation at Antioch also points to the possibility that he was an inhabitant of this town and had there at a relatively early period passed over from paganism to Christianity.[7]

Jerome, about A.D. 400, wrote the following concerning Luke: " Luke, a medical man from Antioch, was not ignorant of the Greek language; he was a follower of Paul and a companion in

---

[1] Cf., for a fuller exposition, Harnack, *Luke the Physician*, pp. 175-98; and Ramsay, *Luke the Physician*, p. 16.

[2] See quotation already made from Prologue.

[3] *Historia Ecclesiastica*, iii, 4.

[4] *De Viris Illustribus*, vii.

[5] Cf. Jülicher-Fascher, *Einleitung in das Neue Testament*, pp. 315 ff.

[6] Streeter, *op. cit.*, p. 533, however, prefers this Western text reading.

[7] Cf. Major, T. W. Manson and Wright, *op. cit.*, p. 252; also Creed, *op. cit.*, p. xxi; and Streeter, *ibid.*

all his journeyings, and wrote the Gospel. Paul said regarding him: ' We send[1] with him the brother whose praise in the Gospel is through all the churches.' And to the Colossians (he wrote): ' Luke, the beloved physician, salutes you '; and to Timothy (he wrote): ' Luke alone is with me.' He [Luke] also published another excellent volume named by the title: Acts of the Apostles " (*De Viris Illustribus*, vii).[2] And Eusebius, nearly a hundred years earlier, had written: " Luke, who was by race an Antiochian and a physician by profession, was long a companion of Paul, and had careful conversation with the other apostles, and in two books left us examples of the medicine for souls which he had gained from them."[3]

[1] Cf. 2 Corinthians viii. 18. Zahn is inclined to agree with Origen and Jerome on this point, that Paul did in this verse refer to Luke (cf. his *Introduction to the New Testament*, Engl. transl., iii, p. 6). Cf. the Collect for St. Luke's Day in the Book of Common Prayer.

[2] Jerome says further that Luke wrote the Acts in Rome and that he wrote this second book as an eyewitness. Then he relates that the remains of Luke, together with those of the apostle Andrew, were brought (from Bithynia, probably) to Constantinople in the twentieth year of Constantine (thus about 333) and buried there. For other traditions concerning Luke cf. Eusebius, *Historia Ecclesiastica*, iii, 4, 6. The so-called *Syriac Martyrdom of Luke* " contains nothing of historical tradition " (Zahn, *ibid*. p. 8).

[3] *Historia Ecclesiastica*, iii, 4.

II

SOURCES DRAWN UPON BY LUKE

AFTER what we have been able to note as facts in the previous section concerning Luke, the author of the third Gospel and of Acts, it is clear that he was in a specially favourable position to acquire the very best first-hand knowledge concerning Christ and the history of the first Christians.

He was not, indeed, as has already been mentioned, an eyewitness of Jesus' life on earth, but he had the best opportunity of acquiring, by means of the communications of eyewitnesses and hearers, a clear account of the occurrences connected with our Lord.

He was for many years in the most intimate contact with Paul, who in turn came in contact with numerous eyewitnesses of Jesus' life, death, resurrection and ascension (e.g. with Peter, James and others).

Besides, Luke himself was also in personal contact with eyewitnesses. For this he had especially valuable opportunities during the years A.D. 57–9 when he was with Paul in Palestine (especially at Caesarea and Jerusalem) (Acts xxi.–xxvii. 2). In Jerusalem he was present at Paul's interviews with James, the brother of Jesus (Acts xxi. 18 ff.). At that time he also had the privilege of making acquaintance with the elders and with many of the other members of the congregation of Jerusalem.[1] Many of these had been eyewitnesses of at least some of the events in the life of Jesus.[2] On the strength of what we know concerning the personality of Luke we feel convinced that he would have availed himself fully of this and other opportunities of collecting, as far as possible, unadulterated, firsthand knowledge concerning Christ. As an educated man, versed in the art of writing, he would most probably, from an early date after he became a Christian, have made notes of the information received by him.

During his stay at Jerusalem he would probably also have made use of the opportunity of personally visiting the " holy places ",

[1] Cf. Zahn, *Introduction to the New Testament*, part iii, pp. 51 ff.
[2] Cf., e.g., Paul's statement in 1 Corinthians xv. 6, where he relates that the majority of the five hundred persons to whom Jesus had appeared after His resurrection were then still alive as living witnesses.

23

like Golgotha, the garden of Gethsemane and other places and buildings connected with the life of Jesus. For he was no stock or stone (as he is represented by some critics with their exaggerated source-theories), devoid of all interest in such particulars regarding the life of Him in whom he saw his Lord and Saviour. We feel convinced that one of the most fundamental errors that many critics have committed in the past, and are still to some extent committing, in their theories in connection with the origin of the Gospels is that they have not adequately taken into account the fact that the writers of the Gospels were *men*—and normal men at that—who made full use of the splendid opportunities they had of acquiring firsthand knowledge concerning Jesus.[1]

The following facts also show in what favourable circumstances Luke found himself for acquiring reliable information concerning Jesus and the history of the first Christians. In Acts xxi. 8–10 we read how Luke stayed, together with Paul, in the house of Philip the evangelist and tarried there many days. There they were visited by the Christian prophet Agabus of Judaea (Acts xxi. 10). Formerly, on the journey from Troas to Philippi, Luke had travelled along with the well-known Christian leader Silas, originally a member of the Jerusalem church (Acts xv. 22, 27, 40, xvi. 10).

It is, moreover, noteworthy that Luke was very intimately associated with Mark. The latter is the author of the second Gospel and had himself very probably been an eyewitness of at least some events in the life of Jesus. In any case he was an intimate follower of Peter, and it is generally recognised that his Gospel is mainly a rendering of Peter's preaching concerning Jesus. Luke had been together with this Mark, at least in Rome during Paul's captivity in that city. This is evident from Colossians iv. 10, 14 and Philemon 24, where Mark is mentioned along with Luke as one of the persons with Paul.

Luke, therefore, had numerous firsthand sources of information concerning the Saviour through his personal association with eye-witnesses and with other persons who had been in close contact with eyewitnesses.

In his preface to the Gospel (i. 1–4) it appears, moreover, that, apart from the data which he had received verbally from " eye-witnesses and ministers of the word ", he also had at his disposal written accounts of the history of the Lord. He does not inform us

---

[1] One cannot but take a stand, for instance, against the manner in which Streeter supposes Luke to have composed his Gospel in such a measure of dependence on written sources as though he himself possessed no independent knowledge acquired directly from eyewitnesses.

who committed these accounts to writing. However, it goes without saying that numbers of Christians who could write would from early times have begun to commit to writing information concerning Christ.[1] It is indeed true that " the Church of Christ had no need of a written Gospel so long as the hearers and eye-witnesses lived in her midst and so long as she had the living word of the apostles, chosen by Christ and guided by the Holy Ghost in all truth " (J. A. C. van Leeuwen, *Markus*, introd., para. 2). But, as Dr. van Leeuwen himself continues: " It is quite possible that the apostles and first evangelists themselves felt the need of written notes and availed themselves of these for their preaching. It is even highly probable that for this purpose various events in the life of the Lord, various data from His preaching, were committed to writing " (*ibid.*). Especially as the first disciples began to fall away through death, the need of committing the stories and words to writing would inevitably have grown bigger. Accordingly Luke, during his journeys and his association with fellow-Christians, very likely came across attempts to commit the tales to writing.

Now he states in his preface, addressed to Theophilus, that it seemed good to him also, " having traced the course of all things from the very first, to write (the story of Jesus) unto thee in order, . . . that thou mightest know the certainty of those things wherein thou hast been instructed " (i. 3, 4).

Thus, as stated by himself and borne out by the contents of his Gospel, he started, in an accurate and systematic manner, to compose an orderly account concerning Christ from all the data at his disposal in written form and otherwise.

Precisely how much use was made by him of the written data which he received from others, and to what extent he was already in possession of the necessary information through oral communications, cannot now be ascertained.

In any case it seems fairly certain that in composing his Gospel he made use to a great extent of the Gospel of Mark, which had already been written. It was quite natural for him to do so, for, as we have already seen, he was in intimate contact with Mark, and he was aware of the fact that the Gospel of Mark was based on the authoritative data of Peter.

In this connection the words of Paul to Timothy (2 Tim. iv. 11, 13) are of interest: " *Only Luke is with me. Take Mark*, and

---

[1] In view of the fact that Deissmann and others have shown how generally the art of writing was practised at that time, it would be hazardous to presume, as most critics do, that the narratives concerning Jesus were for the first thirty years or longer exclusively oral traditions. Cf. also Ramsay, *Luke the Physician*, p. 99.

bring him with thee, for he is profitable to me. . . . The cloke that
I left at Troas with Carpus, when thou comest, bring with thee,
and the books, but especially the parchments."[1]

These words, written in Rome about A.D. 64–5, probably during
a second[2] (and last) captivity of Paul in that city, involuntarily
raise the question as to whether Luke was not then, with the
help and perhaps under the guidance of Paul, engaged upon
some kind of writing. For this reason Paul requests that Mark
(who had probably already written his Gospel by that time)
should be brought to him, " for he is profitable to me " (2 Tim.
iv. 11), and also asks that the books and parchments should be
brought.

If we are correct in our surmise in connection with the words,
namely that Luke with the help of Paul was engaged[3] upon the
composition (or upon preparatory work for the composition) of the
third Gospel and/or Acts, this will explain why in the old church
tradition it was sometimes asserted that,[4] just as the Gospel of Mark
represents the preaching of Peter, so the Gospel of Luke represents Paul's preaching.[5] Nothing can, however, be stated here
with certainty, and the matter merely remains an interesting possibility. Also, in view of the use made by Luke of the Gospel of
Mark when writing the third Gospel, it is a remarkable fact that
Paul in his last epistle before his martyrdom in the space of two
short sentences refers to Luke, to Mark and to books and parchments.

According to the majority of modern critics Luke, in addition
to drawing upon Mark as a source, also made use of the so-called
" Q " document—a document which scholars have attempted to
isolate from the material common to the first and third Gospels
which is not found in Mark. As this material consists for the most
part of sayings of our Lord, many have connected it with the
" Logia of our Lord ", which, according to the second-century

---

[1] The italics are mine.

[2] See our discussion *infra* near the end of section iii of our Introduction.

[3] In the circumstances in which they were situated, e.g. Paul's expectation of his
end at any moment, it is obvious that far-seeing leaders like Paul and Luke would
realise the necessity of committing to writing the events concerning Jesus as well as
concerning the life and work of the first apostles and of Paul himself before the
impending storm should break.

[4] Irenaeus, *Adv. Haeres*, iii. 1, 1; cf. Origen in Eusebius, *Historia Ecclesiastica*, vi, 25, 4.

[5] We cannot here investigate the statement by critics that the Gospel of Luke and
Acts, and the epistles of Paul on the other hand, breathe such a different spirit that
any connection between Luke and Paul in the composition of his works should be
impossible. Suffice it to state that the epistles of Paul throughout assume the data in
the Gospel. And in instances such as the rendering of the history of the institution
of the Holy Communion in 1 Corinthians xi and in the Gospel of Luke there are
unmistakable indications of a close connection between Paul and Luke.

Christian writer Papias, Matthew " compiled in the Hebrew (or Aramaic) speech ".[1] In Great Britain several scholars have accepted the view propounded by B. H. Streeter[2] and amplified by V. Taylor[3] that Luke first composed a shorter Gospel, to which they give the name " Proto-Luke ", consisting of " Q ", together with other material, not found in the other Gospels, which Luke acquired from a variety of sources, written and oral. Into this " Proto-Luke " he inserted, at a later date, blocks of material from Mark's Gospel, thus producing the third Gospel as we now know it. According to Streeter and Taylor, where Luke already had in " Proto-Luke " an account of something told in Mark, he preferred to retain his original account, the outstanding example of this preference being found in the Passion Narrative. The " Proto-Luke " theory has been powerfully and attractively argued, especially by Taylor, but it falls a little short of proof, and has not won the approval of many scholars outside these islands.

More recently there has been a recrudescence of the view, popular in some quarters in the nineteenth century, that Luke's Gospel as we now have it dates from the middle of the second Christian century. This theory, formerly associated with the Baur school in Germany and with the anonymous work *Supernatural Religion* in this country, has been revived by an American scholar, J. Knox, in his *Marcion and the New Testament* (1942). Knox's view is that the canonical Luke was based on an earlier work (lacking much of the peculiarly Lukan material[4]), on which the heresiarch Marcion also based his "Gospel" (c. A.D. 140), and that Marcion's "Gospel" resembled this earlier work far more closely than the canonical Luke does. The canonical Luke, he argues, is a post-Marcionite writing, compiled along with the Acts of the Apostles with the

[1] It should be mentioned, however, that some scholars, like J. H. Ropes in *The Synoptic Gospels* (1934), J. Chapman in *Matthew, Mark and Luke* (1937), and M. S. Enslin in *Christian Beginnings* (1938), maintain that Luke derived his " Q " material not from any such hypothetical document but from the first Gospel itself. It is difficult on this assumption to account for the manner in which Luke distributes his " Q " material throughout his Gospel.

[2] *The Four Gospels* (1924), pp. 199 ff. Streeter had already sketched his theory in the *Hibbert Journal* for 1921; but the idea that Luke combined " Q " with his special material before adding the Markan material seems to have been first suggested in 1891 by Paul Feine in *Eine vorkanonische Überlieferung des Lukas in Evangelium und Apostelgeschichte*.

[3] *Behind the Third Gospel* (1926).

[4] Thus with regard to the Nativity narratives of the first two chapters of the canonical Luke, described by W. Sanday as " the most archaic thing in the whole volume " of New Testament writings, Knox brings forward " considerations suggesting a later date for this part than for most of the rest of the Gospel "; these narratives, he thinks, are " wonderfully adapted . . . to show the nature of Christianity as the true Judaism and thus to answer one of the major contentions of the Marcionites ".

express purpose of refuting Marcion's doctrines. The " Proto-Luke " envisaged in this reconstruction is radically different from the Streeter-Taylor " Proto-Luke ".

But the historical and geographical background of the twofold canonical work Luke-Acts is distinctively first-century, as the researches of W. M. Ramsay made abundantly clear. On these grounds alone such a theory as Knox's cannot commend itself at this time of day, to mention no others.

As regards the other theories mentioned, however, many of them (especially the Streeter-Taylor " Proto-Luke " theory[1]) contain features of suggestiveness and value, but we must remember that source-criticism in the New Testament is for the most part hypothetical, and we can come to no definite conclusion. J. H. Ropes summed up the measure of our certainty in the following words, which are as true to-day as when they were written in 1934:

" That Mark, in substantially its present form, was drawn on by Matthew and Luke for the greater part of their narrative of events and incidents, can be regarded as an achieved result of Synoptic criticism, and can be used without scruple as the basis of modern study. But it is surprising, and a little mortifying to scholarship, to have to admit that this fundamental conclusion is the only assured result of the vast amount of incessant labour which has been expended on the so-called Synoptic Problem in the whole of the past hundred years and more " (*The Synoptic Gospels*, p. 92).

We can, nevertheless, state with absolute certainty that Luke had at his disposal an exceedingly large number of firsthand sources of information, written as well as oral.[2] By sifting and arranging the most reliable data available to him, Luke was able, under the guidance of the Holy Spirit promised by Christ to His followers to remind them of His words and deeds and to lead them into the full truth (John xvi. 26), to commit to writing the story " of all that Jesus began both to do and to teach " in our third Gospel[3]

---

[1] Outside the British Isles the majority of students of Gospel criticism still assume that Luke used Mark as his first and main source and then added data from " Q " and other sources. See Creed, *op. cit.*, p. lviii.

[2] For a convincing refutation of the theory, still propounded by a few scholars, that Luke drew upon Ebionite sources, see Plummer, *St. Luke*, introd., para. 3, and James Orr, *Neglected Factors in the Study of the Early Progress of Christianity*, pp. 103–7.

[3] He performed this task so well that even the illustrious German historian, Eduard Meyer (who was by no means an apologist), declared that Luke must be given " a prominent place among the most significant historians of world-history " (*Ursprung und Anfänge des Christentums*, i, p. 3).

—a writing styled by Renan " the most beautiful book that was ever written ".[1]

---

[1] For further critical theories of Luke's sources cf. B. S. Easton, *The Gospel According to St. Luke*, pp. xiii–xxxiv; A. M. Perry, *The Sources of Luke's Passion-Narrative*; Jülicher-Fascher, *Einleitung in das Neue Testament*, pp. 320 ff.; B. Weiss, *Die Quellen des Lk.-Evangeliums*; Creed, *The Gospel According to St. Luke*, introd., ch. iii; E. W. Parsons, *A Historical Examination of some non-Markan Elements in Luke*. The large degree of divergence in the views expressed apart from Luke's undoubted dependence on Mark indicates what a considerable element of speculation enters into this source-criticism.

III

TIME AND PLACE OF WRITING

DURING the second half of the second century the Gospel of Luke was already generally known and regarded as authoritative.[1]

Justin (about A.D. 150) made abundant use of this Gospel in his writings.[2] From this it appears that by the middle of the second century the Gospel of Luke already occupied a recognised place as an authoritative writing concerning Jesus. Accordingly it must have been written at least several years previously.

Other facts pointing to Luke's having been written and having become known already before the turn of the second century are the following: When Marcion (about A.D. 140) composed his heretical " Gospel ", he mainly used the Gospel of Luke.[3] The gnostics Basilides and Valentinus, who flourished between about A.D. 120–40, also knew the Gospel,[4] carrying the witness to the existence of the Gospel still further back.

Probably during the same period the writer of the apocryphal " Gospel according to Peter ", too, made use of Luke (about A.D. 130).[5] Also the *Didache*, parts of which were probably written between A.D. 80 and 120, shows (at any rate in its existing text) dependence on Luke.[6]

Finally there is the high probability that when the Gospel of John was written (about A.D. 90) Luke was already regarded at Ephesus as a recognised standard work on the life of Jesus.[7] From this it is clear that Luke was written at least before A.D. 90.

---

[1] By Tertullian, Clement of Alexandria, Irenaeus, Tatian and numerous others.

[2] e.g. *Dial.* 78, 88, 100, 103, 105, 106.

[3] Marcion expunged from the Gospel all Jewish and Old Testament references and everything that was not in keeping with his own doctrine. The first two chapters were omitted altogether, as was most of chapter iii and the temptation-narrative of chapter iv. The first verse of Marcion's Gospel was based on Luke iii. 1 and iv. 31, " In the fifteenth year of Tiberius Caesar Jesus came down to Capernaum " (came down, that is to say, directly from heaven). See W. Sanday, *The Gospels in the Second Century* (1876), pp. 204 ff.; and for a contrary argument the book by J. Knox, mentioned on p. 27 of the present work.

[4] Cf. Creed, *op. cit.*, p. xxvii, and Plummer, *op. cit.*, p. xv.

[5] Cf. Creed, *op. cit.*, p. xxvi.

[6] Cf. Plummer, *op. cit.*, p. lxxvi.

[7] See argumentation in this connection in Streeter, *op. cit.*, pp. 407 ff., and also Creed, *op. cit.*, p. xii.

Against such an early dating of Luke the objection is raised in some quarters[1] that Luke shows a certain degree of dependence on Josephus' *Antiquities* (published about A.D. 94). This objection, however, is based on extremely weak grounds, and most critics reject[2] the view that Luke made use of the *Antiquities*.

It is to-day accepted by many scholars[3] that Luke was written about A.D. 85. The principal reasons advanced against assigning an earlier date to the writing of Luke are the following:

In Mark xiii. 14 we find the words of Jesus: " But when ye shall see the abomination of desolation, spoken of by Daniel the prophet, standing where it ought not (let him that readeth understand), then let them that be in Judaea flee to the mountains." In Luke xxi. 20, 21, where the same prophetic discourse of the Lord is rendered, we read, however: " And when ye shall see Jerusalem compassed with armies, then know that the desolation thereof is nigh. Then let them which are in Judaea flee to the mountains."

On the strength of this it is asserted that Luke purposely altered the more obscure words of Mark in Mark xiii. 14 because the destruction of Jerusalem was already an accomplished fact. The words in Luke are, therefore, so they[4] declare, not the actual words of Jesus, but a *vaticinium post eventum*. This is, however, an extremely subjective way of reasoning, which loses all its force if we note the following facts. It appears throughout that Luke, as a Gentile Christian (i.e. not a Jewish Christian) is writing his Gospel for Gentile readers (who were not conversant with Jewish terms and ideas). Obviously, therefore, he would not put in his Gospel

---

[1] e.g. Schmiedel in *Encyclopaedia Biblica*, under " Lysanias " and " Theudas ".

[2] The case for Luke's dependence on Josephus is given most fully in M. Krenkel's *Josephus und Lukas* (1894). Some of the arguments are linguistic, and their weakness has been demonstrated on statistical grounds by J. de Zwaan in *The Beginnings of Christianity*, vol. ii, pp. 81 f. Of the arguments based on subject-matter, the outstanding one with reference to the third Gospel is the mention of Lysanias, tetrarch of Abilene, in Luke iii. 1 (see note on p. 142). This mention has been thought due to Luke's misreading of *Antiquities* xix. 5., 1, where Claudius is said to have bestowed on Herod Agrippa I in A.D. 41 "Abila, that had belonged to Lysanias," or of *Antiquities*, xx, 7, 1, where Agrippa II receives in A.D. 53 " Abila, that had been the tetrarchy of Lysanias ". The only Lysanias elsewhere mentioned by Josephus bore the title " king " and was killed in 36 B.C. (*Antiquities* xv, 4, 1). But there is inscriptional and numismatic evidence for a later Lysanias who bore the title " tetrarch " and flourished at the time indicated in Luke iii. 1; see Schürer's *History of the Jewish People*, I, ii, pp. 335 ff.; Ramsay, *Bearing of Recent Discovery on the New Testament*, pp. 297 ff.; Meyer, *Ursprung und Anfänge*, i, pp. 47 ff. (where Luke's reference to Lysanias is described as " entirely correct "); A. H. M. Jones, *The Herods of Judaea*, pp. 69, 208. Arguments for the dependence of passages in Acts on Josephus (especially the reference to Theudas in Acts v. 37) are equally unconvincing. The fact is, as Schürer has said: " Either Luke had not read Josephus, or he had forgotten all about what he had read " (*Zeitschrift für wissenschaftliche Theologie*, 19 (1876), p. 582). See also Streeter, *op. cit.*, p. 557; Creed, *op. cit.*, p. xxiii; Clogg, *op. cit.*, p. 237.

[3] Cf. Jülicher-Fascher, *Einleitung in das Neue Testament*, p. 314.

[4] Streeter, *op. cit.*, p. 540; Enslin, *Christian Beginnings*, p. 411.

31

the Jewish expression " the abomination of desolation ", as it would have been quite incomprehensible to his readers of Gentile origin. For this reason he gives the prophecy of the Lord in words that are more intelligible to his readers. Since his Gospel was intended mainly for Roman readers, he would certainly not designate the Roman forces, or the Roman leader who was to invade the country, by such a term as " the abomination ".

The expression " abomination of desolation " in Matthew and Mark is indeed taken by many as indicating the anti-Christ. But it seems to us that in the prophetical discourse it was used as the general designation of a hostile force threatening[1] the Holy Land and more especially Jerusalem, the Holy City.

Essentially the words in Luke xxi. 20, therefore, convey the same idea as those in Mark xiii. 14. The form in which Luke renders the words of Jesus is thus by no means a proof that he wrote his Gospel after the destruction of Jerusalem in A.D. 70. The contention[2] that Mark xiii. 14 could not already before A.D. 70 have been properly rendered in the form as given by Luke xxi. 20 is contradicted by the historical fact that the Christians of Jerusalem, when the first Roman armies were threatening the city, in obedience to the words of the Master left everything behind and fled to Pella, the modern[3] Kherbit-el-Fahil, beyond the river Jordan.[4] They thus understood our Lord's words in the sense of Luke xxi. 20. Accordingly there is no need to date the writing of these words in Luke after A.D. 70.

Also the fact that Matthew (written, according to the majority of the critics who date Luke later than A.D. 70, only about A.D. 85) used the same words as Mark xiii. 14 in his rendering of Jesus' prophecy (Matt. xxiv. 15) shows the invalidity of the above forms of reasoning. For to the question why Matthew, unlike Luke, did not also change the prophecy, no conclusive answer has as yet been given.[5]

To adduce Luke's omission of the words of Mark, " let him that readeth understand ", as a further proof that Luke wrote after A.D. 70, is also inadmissible. For Luke writes for readers in Rome, or at any rate for readers far from Jerusalem; the warning that

---

[1] Cf. Rackham, *The Acts of the Apostles*, introd., para. 5.
[2] e.g. of Luce, *St. Luke*, p. xxiv.
[3] Cf. Morton, *In the Steps of the Master*, p. 26.
[4] Cf. Eusebius, *Historia Ecclesiastica*, iii, 32.
[5] C. C. Torrey (*Documents of the Primitive Church* (1941), pp. 20 ff.) argues that Luke's form of the prophecy is original, being based on such an Old Testament passage as Zechariah xiv. 2, and that it was replaced by the reference to the " abomination of desolation " during the crisis of A.D. 40, caused by Caligula's demand to set up his image in the temple. But this view involves more difficulties than the one adopted above.

they should take notice of Jesus' words so as to flee in time, therefore, did not refer to them, and accordingly Luke, as an intelligent writer, omits these words.

The contention that Jesus would not have prophesied the destruction of Jerusalem so definitely and expressly as appears in Luke does not carry any weight.[1] For then also His words in Mark xiii. 2 should be regarded as written after A.D. 70. And these words are a prophecy as explicit as that in Luke xix. 42–4 and xxi. 20. Nevertheless the majority of critics who date Luke after A.D. 70 accept the fact that Mark was written before A.D. 70. How can it then consistently be held that Luke xxi. 20 could not also have been written before A.D. 70?

From all this it is perfectly clear that in the words of Jesus in Luke concerning the destruction of Jerusalem there is not the slightest proof that the third Gospel was written after A.D. 70.[2]

Herewith the most important argument[3] for fixing the date of the writing of Luke as after A.D. 70 falls away.

Secondary arguments for assigning a later date to Luke are the following: While Luke in his preface makes mention of many attempts made to commit the story of Jesus to writing, it is contended that therefore he most probably wrote after A.D. 70, seeing that (according to them) there had not been so many attempts before A.D. 70. But again we have to state that this argument is of a subjective nature. What conclusive proofs exist that during the forty years or so from the time of the Ascension to the destruction of Jerusalem numerous attempts had not been made to commit the history of Jesus to writing? Most of the critics themselves admit that already at that time there existed at least two writings, namely Mark and the so-called document " Q ". Why could there not have been others besides these two?

It is also claimed, in favour of assigning a later date to Luke, that, since Mark was probably not written until about A.D. 60 and since Luke made use of Mark, he therefore must have written considerably later. In view of the fact already mentioned, that, according to Colossians iv, Philemon and 2 Timothy, there was a

---

[1] Cf. Luce's admission at Luke xix. 41–4.

[2] For a detailed demonstration of this cf. Harnack, *The Date of Acts and the Synoptic Gospels*, pp. 90 ff.

[3] Besides this argument K. and S. Lake in *An Introduction to the New Testament* (p. 49) mention the argument in connection with Luke's alleged dependence on Josephus as the only additional argument of much importance for assigning a late date to Luke. Even men like Creed do not accept the contention (advanced mostly by men of the older liberal school of critics like Krenkel, *Josephus und Lukas* (1894), Schmiedel, and others) that Luke was dependent on the writings of Josephus (*St. Luke*, p. xxiv). So this argument for a late date of Luke also falls to the ground. See p. 31.

33

close relation between Luke and Mark, we wish to state emphatically that there is no reason why Luke should not have written his Gospel until several years after Mark had written his. It is quite possible that Luke could, even within the first few weeks after Mark had written his Gospel, have borrowed it from him to use it for the composition of his own Gospel.

The arguments in favour of a later date for Luke, based on allegations[1] such as, e.g., that Luke xxiv. 39–42 manifests anti-docetic traits and therefore should date from a period at the end of the first century, are far-fetched and inconclusive.

Taking everything into consideration, we are compelled to come to the conclusion that thus far no convincing proof has been brought forward that Luke was written only after A.D. 70.[2]

However, we also wish to state at once that no definite proof can be adduced for assigning a date prior to A.D. 70. Nevertheless the following facts seem to point in that direction.[3]

Acts, as has already been shown, was written after Luke. It has never yet been proved conclusively that Acts was written after A.D. 70.[4] On the contrary, several considerations would seem to plead in favour of an earlier date. Thus Acts ends at the captivity of Paul in Rome where he is awaiting his trial before the emperor. If Luke, when he wrote the book, knew *either* that Paul was discharged after his first trial, and after another missionary journey was again arrested and imprisoned and this time condemned to death (probably after the outbreak of the Neronian persecution in A.D. 64), *or* (as others hold) that Paul's two years' detention in Rome of Acts xxviii. 30 were followed by his conviction and execution, would he have made no reference to these facts? The atmosphere of optimism at the end of Acts suggests that the Neronian persecution was still in the future at the time of writing. And if Acts had been written after the destruction of Jerusalem in A.D. 70, we should have expected some hint of the writer's knowledge of this event to colour the language in which throughout Acts the Jews are denounced for their recalcitrance. But there is no such hint. Furthermore, Luke mentions that the prophecy of Agabus (xi. 28) had been fulfilled; why, then, is no single reference made in Acts or in Luke to the fulfilment of Jesus' prophecy concerning the destruction of Jerusalem? Remember, too, that no epistles or portions of epistles of Paul were included in

---

[1] E.g. that of Enslin, *op. cit.*, p. 412.

[2] The same would, in my opinion, apply to the date of the writing of Matthew.

[3] Blass, Harnack, Allen and others have drawn attention to these facts.

[4] Especially after it has been shown that there was no ground for the statements that Luke made use of the *Antiquities* of Josephus (cf. Creed, *St Luke*, p. xxiv), there is no strong argument in favour of assigning a late date to Acts.

Acts; in point of fact, Luke betrays no knowledge of them. Does this not point to the fact that Luke was still in personal contact with the apostle and in consequence does not yet value his epistles as highly (especially as an intimate companion of Paul) as he would certainly have done had Paul already been dead for several years?[1]

Now we realise that different answers have been given to these questions. No single one of these answers is, however, conclusive, and in view of all the facts we are compelled to leave open the possibility that Acts was written before A.D. 70.[2] And with this there is obviously connected the possibility that Luke was written still earlier (several months or a year or even a number of years earlier than Acts).[3] It is difficult to assess the worth of the statement of the anti-Marcionite Prologue (see p. 17) that Luke wrote his Gospel in Greece (Achaia). It is not impossible. Jerome, in the preface to his commentary on Matthew, says that Luke's Gospel was written " in parts of Achaia and Boeotia ", but in *De Viris Illustribus* he concludes that Acts was written in Rome. Possibly Luke wrote part of his twofold history in Rome and completed or published it in Greece.[4] The evidence is inadequate to lead us to a positive conclusion.

[1] Cf. Clement of Rome's *Epistle to the Corinthians*, v, 7; Eusebius, *Historia Ecclesiastica*, ii, 22; Muratorian Canon, for statements regarding Paul's release from his first Roman imprisonment, followed later by his second imprisonment and death. A careful discussion of the reliability of these statements is given by Zahn in his *Introduction to the New Testament*, ii, pp. 54 ff. Cf. also Lietzmann, *Beginnings of the Christian Church*, p. 146.

[2] Detailed arguments for the early date of both the Lukan writings are to be found in Harnack, *Date of the Acts and Synoptic Gospels*; Allen and Grensted, *Introduction to the New Testament*, p. 62; Rackham, *The Acts of the Apostles*, introd., para. 5.

[3] There exists no reason why a long period should be supposed to have elapsed between the writing of the Gospel of Luke and the writing of Acts, although Hawkins, *Horae Synopticae* (2nd ed., pp. 177 ff.), on linguistic evidence places Luke " at a considerably earlier date than Acts ".

[4] In Greek minuscules sometimes Rome and sometimes Greece are named as the place where the Gospel was written (cf. Zahn, *Introduction to the New Testament*, Eng. trans., iii, p. 8).

IV

LANGUAGE, STYLE AND VOCABULARY OF LUKE

WE HAVE already referred to the well-known verdict of Renan in which he declares that the Gospel of Luke is the most beautiful book ever written. He undoubtedly intended this to apply to the book as a whole—including contents, language and style taken together.

But apart from the contents of the Gospel, the work ranks as one of very high standard merely regarded from a literary point of view in the original Greek. And indeed it is almost universally admitted that Luke is the most literary author in the New Testament.[1]

The idyllic charm, homely earnestness, simplicity and purity, and the deep, devotional spirit characterising the stories concerning the birth of John and that of Jesus, are unsurpassed. These stories as well as others in the Gospel of Luke have indeed done more than anything else in the world to inspire painters and other artists to create masterpieces of art. The statement in the tradition of later centuries that Luke was a painter and that he painted Mary, the Mother of Jesus, is probably incorrect. But none the less Luke may with justice and *par excellence* be styled the " painter in words ". His description of the various personalities in the Gospel is so simply realistic and at the same time so sublime that throughout the centuries it has set to work tens of thousands of artists.

Something very striking in Luke's language and style is his literary versatility. We find, for instance, that he commences his Gospel with an accurately balanced sentence written in irreproachable, pure, literary Greek. After the preface, however, in the description of the nativities of John and Jesus he immediately switches over to a Hebraistically tinted language corresponding to

---

[1] Cf. Creed, *op. cit.*, pp. lxxvi ff; and Grieve, in his introduction to Luke in Peake's Commentary. Jülicher-Fascher declares that the Prologue of Luke proves that the author is a man of " higher rhetorical training. He has complete command of language " (*Einleitung in das Neue Testament*, p. 319). In another place Jülicher-Fascher declares that some of Luke's descriptions " are among the most precious pearls of narrative art " (*ibid.*, p. 321).

that of the Septuagint, the Greek translation of the Old Testament. This transition from the one kind of style to the other shows that Luke is consciously an artist. He could, had he chosen, have retained throughout the distinguished literary style with which he had commenced. But in order to adapt his style better to the nature of the events that had taken place in a Jewish environment, he changes to a more Hebraistic diction[1] in the description of such events.

The contention[2] that the Hebraistically tinted stories in Luke were originally separate written documents which Luke incorporated in his Gospel cannot be proved. On the contrary, those stories also bear such unmistakable imprints of Luke's characteristic language, style and vocabulary that they were undoubtedly written by Luke himself, at any rate in their Greek form. As Howard[3] rightly contends: " The Hebraic phraseology [of these Infancy stories] is beyond question, but there is nothing that lies beyond the range of composition by one who was steeped in the diction of the Greek version of the Psalter."[4]

In his descriptions of stories with a Jewish background Luke is Semitising throughout, but in stories with a Greek background (as repeatedly occur in Acts) he writes in a purely Greek style.[5] His Greek style may be explained from the fact that he was of Gentile origin and spoke Greek and that as a physician he was, moreover, an educated man. However, the fact that he was also at home in a Hebraistic style may be explained mainly from the use that he made throughout of the Greek Septuagint translation of the Old Testament, which is through and through Hebraistic. In this way he became expert in the characteristic Septuagint style.[6] We should also bear in mind that Jesus and His disciples themselves spoke Aramaic and that the earliest traditions concerning Him were circulated either in Aramaic or in translations made by persons who spoke Aramaic. By these means Luke would have come in contact with another class of Semitising language and style forms.[7]

---

[1] Creed, *op. cit.*, para. v; Plummer, *op. cit.*, para. vi.

[2] Cf. C. C. Torrey, *The Composition and Date of Acts; The Four Gospels*, p. 263; *Our Translated Gospels*, p. ix.

[3] *Grammar of New Testament Greek*, vol. ii, pp. 482–3.

[4] Ed. Meyer, *Ursprung und Anfänge des Christentums*, i, pp. 8 f., held the same view (cf. our footnote at i. 4).

[5] Plummer, *op. cit.*, p. xlix.

[6] Creed, *op. cit.*, para. v.

[7] *Ibid.* In speaking of Semitisms in New Testament Greek, we must remember that they are of two quite different kinds. The Hebraisms are mainly due to the literary influence of the Septuagint; the Aramaisms are mainly due to the oral archetype of the words of Christ and His apostles. It is usually pretty easy for a reader familiar with Hebrew, Aramaic and Greek to say whether a reasonably long piece

His mastery of the Greek language is evident from the freedom of his constructions and from the exceptional wealth of his vocabulary. In his two writings he has a larger vocabulary than any other New Testament writer and uses about eight hundred words which occur nowhere else in the New Testament.[1]

of translation-Greek from a Semitic tongue is from Hebrew or Aramaic. There are striking differences between Hebrew and Aramaic idiom, especially in matters of syntax. On the whole question reference should be made to the cautious and masterly work by Matthew Black, *An Aramaic Approach to the Gospels and Acts* (Oxford, 1946).

[1] For full particulars in connection with his language, style and vocabulary, cf. Plummer, *op. cit.*, para. vi; Creed, loc. cit.; Hawkins, *Horae Synopticae*.

V

THE HISTORICAL TRUSTWORTHINESS
OF LUKE

ONE OF the most phenomenal changes that have taken place in the field of New Testament studies during the past years is that relating to the criticism of the historical reliability of Luke as author. In 1902 Weizsächer still declared that the historical value of Acts " shrinks until it reaches a vanishing point ".[1] Yet another writer stated that " apart from the ' we '-sections no statement [in Acts] needs immediate acceptance on the mere ground of its presence in the book ".

By eminent critics Luke was regarded as a hopeless, unreliable author, especially from the time of F. C. Baur and his Tübingen school.

Towards the end of the last century and during the first part of the present century, however, the researches of men like Ramsay,[2] Harnack,[3] Hawkins[4] and Deissmann[5] brought to light masses of surprising facts that have confirmed the historical accuracy of the statements in Luke and Acts which were formerly condemned as fictitious. In consequence, a complete change-over has been brought about in the opinions concerning the historical trustworthiness of the works of Luke.

A detailed discussion of this matter belongs rather to the introduction to Acts. Suffice it for us to refer to the works of the scholars mentioned and to quote a few passages from one of these works.

After doing research work for many years in the regions where the events described by Luke (particularly in Acts) were enacted, Ramsay stated unambiguously that "Luke's history is unsurpassed in respect of its trustworthiness ".[6]

---

[1] *Apostolic Age*, p. 106.

[2] See his works, *St. Paul the Traveller and Roman Citizen, The Bearing of Recent Discovery on the Trustworthiness of the New Testament*, etc.

[3] *Beiträge zur Einleitung in das Neue Testament* (three volumes of this work have been translated into English under the titles *Luke the Physician, The Acts of the Apostles* and *The Date of Acts and the Synoptic Gospels*).

[4] *Horae Synopticae*, pp. 15 ff., 27 ff., and especially 174 ff.

[5] *Light from the Ancient East* (Eng. trans.).

[6] *The Bearing of Recent Discovery*, p. 80.

Summing up, he wrote: " Luke is a historian of the first rank; not merely are his statements of fact trustworthy; he is possessed of the true historic sense; he seizes the important and critical events and shows their true nature at greater length, while he touches lightly or omits entirely much that was valueless for his purpose. In short, this author should be placed along with the very greatest of historians."[1]

These words are especially important as coming not from an apologist or theologian but from a recognised authority in the field of archaeology.[2]

Professor Otto Piper has thus rightly declared: " Wherever modern scholarship has been able to check up on the accuracy of Luke's work the judgment has been unanimous: he is one of the finest and ablest historians in the ancient world."[3]

[1] *Op. cit.*, p. 222.

[2] In Maurice Jones's work, *The New Testament in the Twentieth Century* (pp. 227 ff.), there is a skilful summary of the research results that prove the historical trustworthiness of Luke. The recent booklet of F. F. Bruce, *Are the New Testament Documents Reliable?*, also gives a valuable summary of the facts with references to the authorities.

[3] " The Purpose of Luke " in *The Union Seminary Review*, Nov. 1945, vol. lxvii, no. 1.

VI

THE AIM OF THE GOSPEL OF LUKE

IN HIS preface Luke himself states the immediate purpose of his book. He addresses it to Theophilus[1] in order that he may know the certainty of those things wherein he was instructed (i. 4). Luke, however, did not intend the Gospel merely for Theophilus, but undoubtedly wrote it for Gentile converts in general.[2] It was not his purpose to write an apologetic[3] or controversial work, but he desires to show, especially to Gentile Christians, on what firm historic facts their faith is based.[4]

He therefore intended his Gospel as a historical work. In his preface to the Gospel and from the nature of his writings it is abundantly clear that he was gifted not merely with an artistic temperament but also with a historical and scientific aptitude. This is evident *inter alia* from the fact that, unlike any other New Testament writer, he constantly refers to the relation between the history of Jesus and the first Christians and that of the Jewish and Roman world of the time (cf., e.g., his time-notes in ii. 1 f. and iii. 1 f.).

His statement in i. 3 that he composed his narrative " in order " is clearly corroborated in the Gospel. As far as possible he gives indications of time (i. 5, 26, 36, 56, 59, ii. 42, iii. 23, ix. 28, xxii. 1, 7, etc.) and lets most of his stories follow in chronological order.[5] Where he does not do this, he nevertheless maintains a logical and artistic unity in his descriptions.[6]

[1] See exegesis of i. 3.
[2] Cf. Zahn, *Introduction to the New Testament*, Eng. trans. iii, p. 44.
[3] We cannot accept the view of Streeter and others that Luke's books are apologetic writings to make the Roman authorities favourably disposed towards the Christians. If Luke did have apologetic objects in view, these were of quite subsidiary importance.
[4] What was written by E. F. Scott in *Harvard Theological Review*, in April 1926, pp. 143 ff., to refute the allegations that the Gospels are theological polemic writings still remains true. He declares *inter alia* that " their historical interest is not to be placed third or fourth, but first ".
[5] It is often asserted that where he gives indications of time with stories that occur also in Mark (but in the latter without such indications) Luke is himself fabricating artificial datings. We reject this because the indications of time are, e.g., natural and fitting throughout. Luke undoubtedly collected information as far as possible from eyewitnesses and others, also as to the exact chronological order of the events, and was therefore able in numerous places to supplement Mark.
[6] iv. 1, 38, 40, vii. 1, 18, 24, xxii. 66, xxiv. 13, etc. Cf. Plummer, *op. cit.*, p. xlvii.

41

Whilst being a historically-scientific work, the Gospel of Luke is, however, no biography in the usual sense.

In the first place he did not attempt to include in his book even all the important data. He would, moreover, not have been able to do this, seeing that the length of the Gospel as it is almost exceeds the limits of a writing on a parchment roll.[1] Nevertheless his Gospel is the most complete and comprehensive of all four Gospels. Several of the most beautiful stories[2] concerning Jesus and of the most thrilling parables[3] of the Lord occur only in Luke.

In the second place Luke relates the historical events and words in his Gospel not merely for the sake of historical writing. For his motive (as is the case with all the Gospel writers) is practical and religious; and for this reason his books are written in a simple, popular style. He wrote his Gospel not merely to write a beautiful story, to afford pleasure to his readers or to satisfy curiosity, and not even just for the sake of giving instruction. He wrote with the object of convincing, converting, saving and spiritually edifying his fellow-men. What he puts before us is not merely " the reasonableness or the truth of ethical and spiritual ideas, nor even the holiness and beauty of a life, but the testimony of a religious society to One in whom redemption has been experienced, and for whom faith, obedience, love and worship are unqualifiedly claimed ".[4] Quite naturally, therefore, all attempts to classify this Gospel (and the same applies to the three other Gospels) under the ordinary types of literature are doomed to failure. " According to their *form*, as literature, they fall under no category along with other writings; that is owing to their *contents* that determine the form."[5] Just as Jesus Christ is utterly unique[6] in the history of mankind, unique in His being, words and works as well as in His death, resurrection and ascension, so also the Gospel of Luke (together with the three other Gospels) is absolutely unique in the whole of the world's literature.

The Gospel was written " out of faith unto faith " in order to hold up Jesus as Lord and Redeemer. The contents of the book should, therefore, be viewed in this light.

[1] Kenyon reckons that the length of the parchment roll required by Luke for his Gospel was approximately thirty feet.

[2] E.g. stories of Jesus' nativity and childhood-days; the raising of the son of the widow of Nain, etc.

[3] E.g. that of the Good Samaritan, the Rich Fool, the Fig-tree, etc.

[4] W. Manson, *op. cit.*, p. xii.

[5] J. A. C. van Leeuwen, *op. cit.*, para. 2.

[6] Read in this connection, e.g., Carnegie Simpson's famous *The Fact of Christ*.

VII

SPECIAL CHARACTERISTICS OF THE GOSPEL

IN A manner which distinguished it from the other Gospels, the third Gospel depicts Jesus as the Divine Physician who came to seek and to save what is lost. While, e.g., Matthew lays more emphasis on the fact that Jesus came as the Fulfiller of the Old Testament prophecies, the Gospel of Luke shows us in the first place how Jesus came as Redeemer. Thus it is pointed out, even before His birth, that Mary was charged to name Him " Jesus " (i.e. " Saviour "). In Mary's hymn of praise the redeeming work of God is lauded, and in the message of the angels to the shepherds it is stated that in the city of David has been born " a Saviour, which is Christ the Lord " (ii. 11). When Simeon holds the little Child in his arms in the temple he praises the Lord because he had seen (ii. 30) " the *salvation* which God prepared ". And in the first public announcement made by Jesus Himself concerning His mission (iv. 16–32) His work as *Redeemer* and Divine Physician is again emphasised.

The fundamental quality of Jesus which Luke wishes to show us is, therefore, that He has come as Saviour, as Redeemer. In the other Gospels, too, attention is drawn to this, but in Luke it occupies the most central position.

Luke, in addition, lays more stress on the fact that Jesus came to accomplish a *universal* redemption. He depicts Christ not so much as the Messiah of the Old Testament but as the Redeemer of the whole world. Time and again the point is stressed in this Gospel that Jesus offers forgiveness and redemption to all—freely and independently of the privileges of a particular race, generation or merit. Admission to the Kingdom is open to Samaritans (ix. 51–6, x. 30–7, xvii. 11–19) and pagans (ii. 32, iii. 6, 38, iv. 25–7, vii. 9, x. 1, xxiv. 47) as well as to the Jews (i. 33, ii., 10); to publicans, sinners and outcasts (iii. 12, v. 27–32, vii. 37–50, xix. 2–10, xxiii. 43) as well as to respectable people (vii. 36, xi. 37, xiv. 1); to the poor (i. 53, ii. 7, vi. 20, vii. 22) as well as to the rich (xix. 2, xxiii. 50); and to women as well as to men. So universal and all embracing, according to the Gospel, is the redeeming work of Christ!

For this reason Luke shows throughout the design of his book that the coming of Jesus is by no means merely an event in the history of the Jewish nation, but a world event. Thus Luke again and again points out the relation between the Gospel events and the great world-movements of that time—e.g. he connects the birth of Jesus with the reign of the Roman Emperor Augustus, and the beginning of the preaching of John, the forerunner of Christ, he dates as " in the fifteenth year of the reign of Tiberius Caesar, Pontius Pilate being governor of Judaea, and Herod being tetrarch of Galilee, and his brother Philip tetrarch of the region of Ituraea and Trachonitis, and Lysanias tetrarch of Abilene, in the high-priesthood of Annas and Caiaphas " (iii. 1–2). The Gospel history is to Luke of international, world-wide importance and " all flesh shall see the salvation of God " (iii. 6).

In his genealogy of Jesus Luke carries back His descent not only as far as Abraham, as is done by Matthew, but past Abraham, and even past Adam up to God (iii. 38). By this means, also, he emphasises the universal significance of Jesus.

Then the Gospel further stresses the fact that Jesus' work of redemption is not only intended for all people, and indeed for the whole world, but that He brings salvation in soul and in body, for time and eternity. Even more so than the other Gospels Luke depicts Jesus as the Redeemer who takes an interest in man's spiritual as well as physical state and who is mighty to heal in soul and in body.

Luke describes a large number of incidents to show how all-embracing is Jesus' power to redeem—how large numbers of different types of people, people in different circumstances, with different needs, were all saved by the redeeming work of Christ.

This work of salvation, as the Gospel emphasises, was carried out by Jesus mainly by means of personal expressions of friendship. In Luke Jesus is not only the Great Physician, but also the self-sacrificing Friend who shows friendship towards the poor as well as the rich, towards the highly honoured as well as towards the despised publicans and sinners, and even towards fallen women.

Especially to Jesus' saving and uplifting work amongst women an important place is assigned in the Gospel. In Luke is shown, as nowhere else, what a totally different attitude Jesus assumed towards women in contrast with the contemptuous attitude which Jews[1] as well as pagans manifested towards them.[2]

[1] In a recognised portion of the Jewish liturgy the men thank God that they are not women.

[2] For further remarks on the prominent and honoured part played by women in the Gospel of Luke we may refer to Ramsay, *Was Christ Born at Bethlehem?*, pp. 83–90; Harnack, *Luke the Physician*, pp. 153 ff.; Plummer, *op. cit.*, pp. xlii ff.

Another characteristic of Luke is the intimate and homely atmosphere pervading the whole book. In the Gospel Jesus is mostly shown in houses—speaking to publicans at table; as guest in the home of Mary and Martha; together with the men of Emmaus at table, and so on.

In all this, Luke's depiction of Jesus is by no means of a sentimental nature. On the contrary, he emphasises to the same extent the severity and power in Jesus' attitude towards sin and falsehood and towards the works of the Evil One.

The most fervent passion of the best Greek idealism and philosophy was for the perfecting of human personality. The educated Greek sought for the ideal, the perfect individual. Thus Luke found in Jesus the Person who realised all his ideals and who completely excelled the highest Greek ideals. For this reason he depicts in his Gospel the personality of Jesus especially from this point of view, and shows by means of numerous facts concerning Him that *as Man* He fulfils to the highest and most absolute extent the ideal of perfection—in love and severity,[1] in tenderness and might, in humility and in fearlessness, in wisdom and in all other virtues of character. He also especially emphasises Jesus' perfect attitude towards God—and in this manner he points out, more than all the other Gospels, what a prominent place prayer to the Father occupied in the life of Jesus.[2]

In his stressing of the perfection of Jesus as Man, Luke in his Gospel also just as emphatically depicts His perfect Deity. He is completely Man—born of a woman, He passes through the ordinary human development from child to adult (ii. 52), He needs food, rest, friendship, prayer—but He is also Christ the Lord (ii. 11). And as Lord, as the Son of Man, and as the Christ of God (ix. 20) He is the Divine Redeemer who has come to seek and to save what is lost (ix. 56).

---

[1] E.g. at the purification of the temple.

[2] The Gospel of Luke can rightly be termed " the Gospel of prayer " because of the central place given by it to the subject of prayer.

VIII

MAIN DIVISIONS OF LUKE'S GOSPEL

THE CONTENTS of the Gospel of Luke may be classified as follows:

(1) The Preface (i. 1–4).
(2) The nativity and childhood years of John the Baptist and of Jesus (i. 5–ii. 52).
(3) The preaching of John the Baptist (iii. 1–20).
(4) Jesus' Baptism and Temptation (iii. 21–iv. 13).
(5) The ministry of Jesus especially in Galilee (iv. 14–ix. 50).
(6) Jesus and His disciples on their way to Jerusalem (ix. 51–xix. 44).
(7) The last days in Jerusalem, the Crucifixion and Burial (xix. 45–xxiii. 56).
(8) The appearances of the resurrected Christ and His Ascension (xxiv. 1–53).

From the above it appears that Luke *in broad outline*[1] composed his Gospel very systematically. In this manner he carried out his resolution, as stated in his preface, to write the narrative of Jesus " in order ".

[1] Not, however, in sub-divisions and smaller particulars (as will appear abundantly in the exposition of the book). It was not his purpose to give a finely elaborated biography of Jesus, but to proclaim the Gospel, the glad tidings, concerning the Redeemer.

IX

BIBLIOGRAPHY

THE FOLLOWING are some of the more important commentaries on the Gospel of Luke:

J. Baljon, *Com. op het Evangelic van Lukas* (Utrecht, 1908).
H. Balmforth, *The Gospel According to St. Luke* (Oxford, 1930).
J. M. Creed, *The Gospel According to St. Luke* (Macmillan, 1942).
B. S. Easton, *The Gospel According to St. Luke* (T. & T. Clark, Edinburgh, 1926).
J. A. Findlay, *The Gospel According to St. Luke* (S.C.M. Press, 1937).
S. Greydanus, *Het Heilig Evangelic naar de Beschrijving van Lukas* (2 vols., Amsterdam, 1940).
A. J. Grieve, *St. Luke* in *Peake's Commentary* (revised ed., Nelson, 1936).
F. Godet, *Commentary on the Gospel of Luke* (T. & T. Clark, 1879).
Fr. Hauch, *Das Evangelium des Lukas* (Leipzig, 1934).
Jamieson, Fausset and Brown, *St. Luke* in *Critical and Explanatory Commentary on the Bible* (Eerdmans, 1935).
E. Klostermann, *Das Lukas Evangelium* (2nd completely revised ed., 1929) in the series *Handbuch zum Neue Testament*.
H. K. Luce, *St. Luke* (Cambridge, 1933).
A. Loisy, *L'Évangile selon Luc* (Paris, 1924).
M. J. Lagrange, *Évangile selon Saint Luc* (Paris, 1921).
G. Campbell Morgan, *The Gospel According to Luke* (Revell, 1931).
W. Manson, *The Gospel of Luke* (in *The Moffatt New Testament Commentary*, 1930).
A. Plummer, *Gospel According to St. Luke* (5th ed., I.C.C., T. & T. Clark, 1922).
Rengstorf and Büchsel, *Das Evangelium nach Lukas* (in *Das Neuen Testament Deutsch*).
Lonsdale Ragg, *St. Luke* (*Westminster Commentary*, 1925).
A. Schlatter, *Das Evangelium des Lukas* (Stuttgart, 1931).
Strack and Billerbeck, *Das Evangelium nach Lukas* (vol. ii in *Kommentar zum Neuen Testament aus Talmud und Midrasch*, München, 1924).
J. Wellhausen, *Das Evangelium Lucae* (Berlin, 1904).

A. Wright, *The Gospel According to St. Luke in Greek* (Macmillan, 1900).

J. Weiss, *Lukas* (in *Die drei älteren Evangelien*), revised by W. Bousset (1917).

Theodore Zahn, *Das Evangelium des Lucas* (Leipzig, 1913).

The following are a number of books that are important in the study of Luke's Gospel:

I. Abrahams, *Studies in Pharisaism and the Gospels* (Cambridge, series i, 1917; series ii, 1924).

W. Arnot, *The Parables of Our Lord* (London, 1893).

R. Bultmann, *Die Geschichte der synoptischen Tradition* (Göttingen, 1921).

G. A. Buttrick, *The Parables of Jesus* (New York, 1928).

F. C. Burkitt, *The Gospel History and its Transmission* (Edinburgh, 1906).

A. B. Bruce, *The Parabolic Teaching of Christ* (3rd ed., New York, 1900).

F. F. Bruce, *Are the New Testament Documents Reliable?* (London, 1943).

F. Bertram Clogg, *An Introduction to the New Testament* (London, 1937).

J. Chapman, *Matthew, Mark and Luke* (Longmans, 1937).

C. J. Cadoux, *The Historic Mission of Jesus* (Lutterworth, 1941).

H. J. Cadbury, *The Making of Luke-Acts* (Macmillan, 1927).

G. Dalman, *The Words of Jesus* (Eng. trans., Edinburgh, 1909).

G. Dalman, *Jesus-Jeshua* (Eng. trans., London, 1929).

G. Dalman, *Sacred Sites and Ways* (Eng. trans., London, 1934).

A. Deissmann, *Light from the Ancient East* (Eng. trans., London, 1927).

C. H. Dodd, *The Parables of the Kingdom* (London, 1936).

Martin Dibelius, *The Message of Jesus* (Eng. trans., 1939).

A. Edersheim, *Life and Times of Jesus the Messiah* (2 vols., 1900).

Douglas Edwards, *The Virgin Birth in History and Faith* (London, 1941).

M. S. Enslin, *Christian Beginnings* (London, 1938).

F. J. Foakes-Jackson and K. Lake (ed.), *The Beginnings of Christianity* (Macmillan, 1920—especially vol. i).

A. Huck, *A Synopsis of the First Three Gospels* (ed. of Hans Leitzmann, 1935).

A. Harnack, *Luke the Physician* (Eng. trans., 1907).

A. Harnack, *The Date of Acts and the Synoptic Gospels* (Eng. trans., 1911).

J. C. Hawkins, *Horae Synopticae* (2nd ed., Oxford, 1909).

Jülicher-Fascher, *Einleitung in das Neue Testament* (7th ed., Tübingen, 1931).

A. Jülicher, *Die Gleichnisreden Jesu* (2nd ed., Tübingen, 1910).

Flavius Josephus, especially his *Antiquities* and *The Jewish War* (many translations and editions, e.g. Loeb Classical Library edition).

Maurice Jones, *The New Testament in the Twentieth Century* (3rd ed., London, 1934).

N. Levison, *The Jewish Background of Christianity* (Edinburgh, 1932).

K. and S. Lake, *An Introduction to the New Testament* (London, 1938).

H. D. A. Major, T. W. Manson and C. J. Wright, *The Mission and Message of Jesus* (Macmillan, 1940).

J. Moffatt, *Introduction to the Literature of the New Testament* (3rd ed., Edinburgh, 1918).

G. F. Moore, *Judaism in the First Centuries of the Christian Era* (2 vols., 1927).

C. G. Montefiore, *The Synoptic Gospels* (2nd ed., Macmillan, 1927).

J. Gresham Machen, *The Virgin Birth of Christ* (2nd ed., 1932).

Ed. Meyer, *Ursprung und Anfänge des Christentums* (3 vols., Berlin, 1921–3).

E. R. Micklem, *Miracles and the New Psychology* (Oxford, 1922).

Rudolf Otto, *The Kingdom of God and the Son of Man* (Eng. trans., 1943).

E. W. Parsons, *A Historical Examination of Some Non-Markan Elements in Luke* (Chicago, 1914).

A. T. Olmstead, *Jesus in the Light of History* (New York, 1942).

A. M. Perry, *The Sources of Luke's Passion Narrative* (Chicago, 1920).

W. M. Ramsay, *Luke the Physician* (London, 1908) and *Was Christ born at Bethlehem?* (1898).

A. E. J. Rawlinson, *The New Testament Doctrine of the Christ* (Longmans, 1929).

Alan Richardson, *The Miracle Stories of the Gospels* (S.C.M. Press, 1942).

C. A. Anderson Scott, *Living Issues in the New Testament* (Cambridge, 1933).

E. Schürer, *Geschichte des jüdischen Volkes im Zeitalter Jesu Christi* (3 vols., 3rd ed., Leipzig, 1901–9).

A. Schweitzer, *The Quest of the Historical Jesus* (Eng. trans., London, 1910).

V. H. Stanton, *The Gospels as Historical Documents* (Cambridge, vol. i, 1903; vol. ii, 1909).

B. H. Streeter, *The Four Gospels* (Macmillan, 1924).
Vincent Taylor, *Behind the Third Gospel* (Oxford, 1926).
Vincent Taylor, *Jesus and His Sacrifice* (Macmillan, 1937).
R. C. Trench, *Notes on the Parables of Our Lord* (14th ed., London, 1882).
B. Weiss, *Die Quellen des Lukas-evangeliums* (Stuttgart, 1907).
Th. Zahn, *Einleitung in das Neue Testament* (2 vols., 2nd ed., Leipzig, 1900). (Translated into English under title: *Introduction to the New Testament* [3 vols., T. & T. Clark, 1909].)
Abott-Smith, *Manual Greek Lexicon of the New Testament* (3rd ed., 1937).
F. Blass, *Grammar of New Testament Greek* (Macmillan, 1905).
W. Bauer, *Wörterbuch zum Neuen Testament*.
G. Kittel, *Theologisches Wörterbuch zum Neuen Testament*.
W. F. Moulton and A. S. Geden, *A Concordance to the New Testament* (1897).
J. H. Moulton, *A Grammar of New Testament Greek* (2 vols., vol. ii completed by W. F. Howard, 1919).
Grimm-Thayer, *Greek-English Lexicon of the New Testament* (4th ed., 1901).
H. Cremer, *Biblisch-Theologisches Wörterbuch der Neutestamentlichen Gräzität* (10th ed. by Julius Kögel, 1915).

Furthermore, the most important commentaries on the other Gospels, standard works on the theology of the New Testament, and the best books on the life of our Lord, are indispensable in an intensive study of the Gospel of Luke.

EXPOSITION

THE GOSPEL ACCORDING TO
ST. LUKE

PREFACE

i. 1–4

1 Forasmuch[1] as many have taken in hand to draw up a narrative concerning those matters[2] which have been ful-
2 filled[3] among us,[4] even as they delivered[5] them unto us, which from the beginning[6] were eyewitnesses and ministers
3 of the word,[7] it seemed good to me also,[8] having traced the course of all things accurately from the first, to write unto thee in order,[9] most excellent Theophilus; that thou mightest
4 know[10] the certainty[11] concerning the things wherein thou wast instructed.[12,13]

For its simplicity, modesty and terseness, this is a model preface for a historical work. It is something unique in the Gospel writings. For nowhere else does a Gospel writer address his readers in the first person or communicate his intentions beforehand. The preface to the fourth Gospel is a religious and philosophical contemplation of the Word become flesh, and thus differs completely from this prologue of Luke. The latter, however, shows agreement with the prefaces of classical historians like Herodotus, Thucydides and Polybius, and also with those of medical writers of antiquity like Dioscorides.

1 Luke here gives a kind of justification of his undertaking to set forth a written declaration of the Gospel narrative. For " it was a daring thing, and at first somewhat of an innovation, to propose to substitute writings for the spoken word on which the church had hitherto depended " (W. Manson, *The Gospel of Luke*). Originally the Christians had clung to the living word as communicated to them by the apostles and other hearers and eyewitnesses of the Gospel story. But as the church extended further and the apostles passed away one by one, there arose a more and more urgent need of authoritative written renderings of the facts on

51

which the Christian faith is based. As an educated and far-seeing man, Luke had a strong sense of this need. That was his reason for undertaking the great task. And in order to justify his action, he refers to the well-known fact that many had already taken in hand to set forth a narrative " of those things which have been fulfilled among us ". His reference to the attempts made by these persons is by no means intended to designate their work as unreliable or a failure. At most he signifies thereby that for his purpose something is still wanting in their writings. He does not tell us who are the authors of the forerunners of his Gospel. To-day, however, it is generally accepted that Mark, the writer of the second Gospel, was one of these authors.

2   But although he does not mention the names of his predecessors, he here declares that their writings are based on the communications of those who " from the beginning were eye-witnesses and ministers of the word ". The latter expression refers to the apostles, who were all eyewitnesses of Jesus, and the first reliable preachers of the glad tidings. Luke, therefore, lays special emphasis on the fact that those writings are by no means the collecting of legends or mere human gossip, but the written rendering of what had really happened and had been communicated by authoritative witnesses. Here, therefore, we have to deal not with fabricated fables but with the written reproduction of the tradition of the apostles. This statement of Luke is corroborated by the evidence which dates from the earliest times of Christianity, to the effect that Mark, who is one of Luke's predecessors, wrote his Gospel mainly as a report of Peter's preaching (Eusebius, *Historia Ecclesiastica*, iii, 39). Luke himself also joins the ranks of those who are not themselves eyewitnesses but to whom the stories were handed down by original eyewitnesses. In the Introduction (pp. 23 ff.), we referred to the splendid opportunities which Luke had as a companion of Paul to obtain at Jerusalem and elsewhere firsthand information concerning Jesus and the earliest history of the Christian congregations. As Plummer rightly states: " The modest position claimed by the writer is evidence of his honesty. A forger would have claimed to be an eyewitness, and would have made no apology for writing " (*op. cit.*).

3   Here he states that, whilst the attempts of his predecessors to give to the Gospel history a written form made him courageous enough also to compose a written account of the facts, his own attempt bears special characteristics. In the first place, he declares that (in contrast, e.g., with Mark) in his investigation he had gone back to the course of events right at the commencement of the Gospel history. We therefore find in his Gospel that he does

not, as Mark did, begin only with Jesus' public actions, but starts off with the announcement of the nativity of His predecessor, John the Baptist. In the second place, Luke states, he investigated " all things ". He had, therefore, examined all available data with a fixed purpose in order to be able to give as detailed a rendering as might be necessary. By this, however, he does not mean that he included all the information in his Gospel. He did, indeed, investigate all things, but selected therefrom only those data which (under the guidance of the Holy Ghost) he considered necessary for the composition of his narrative, which naturally was not intended to be too circumstantial. That Luke indeed strove to attain a necessary measure of completeness is evident from the fact that his Gospel is the most comprehensive of all four Gospels. Many of the most beautiful stories, parables and words of Jesus which are to-day familiar to us occur only in Luke. In the third place, he examined everything *carefully*, so that his investigation was not made superficially or too hurriedly. Through long periods (during his travels along with Paul and also at other times) he made thorough researches concerning the Gospel stories so that he was able to set forth the actual course of events. He collected and studied all available written renderings of words and works of Jesus; wherever the opportunity was presented to him he discussed the Gospel stories with persons who possessed firsthand knowledge concerning Him; and during his stay in Jerusalem (see Introduction, p. 23) and in other parts of Palestine he collected as much information as possible concerning the buildings and places connected with the history of Christ. This is all clearly evidenced by the contents of the third Gospel. Although in the previous century attacks upon the historical trustworthiness of Luke were launched from numerous quarters, more thorough-going researches have proved time and again that Luke is amazingly accurate in his writings. In the fourth place, he states that it was his object to compose the narrative of the occurrences " in order ", so that he tried to give not merely a collection of incidents and sayings but an orderly account. By this he does not mean that he intended to relate everything in strict chronological order, but that it was his purpose to write a narrative which would form a connected whole. From a study of the Gospel it is abundantly clear that his object was realised.

In his preface Luke addresses himself to Theophilus. As he calls him " most excellent ", it is probable that Theophilus was a real person and indeed one of high official rank. Most probably he was a procurator or governor in some province or other of the Roman Empire. Since Luke in the beginning of Acts merely calls him "Theophilus", Zahn and others think that he had in the meantime become a Christian. There are also all kinds of other conjectures in regard to him. Perhaps he may, e.g., have been a prominent personage in Antioch. Streeter suggests that he may have been Titus Flavius Clemens, heir-presumptive of the Emperor Domitian, in which case Theophilus ("dear to God" or "lover of God") would be a pseudonym. Undoubtedly Theophilus was "a man of distinction and probably also of wealth. This may be deduced from this dedication. Moreover, it might be concluded that Theophilus would see to the publication and dissemination of this Gospel narrative and would bear the expense of it" (Greydanus). It was in those times an acknowledged practice to dedicate a book to some or other important person—the book being at the same time meant for a wider circle of readers (cf. Jülicher-Fascher, *Einleitung in das Neue Testament*, p. 314).

4 Luke was aware of the fact that in the case of Theophilus (and others of his kind) there existed a need of reliable and comparatively full information regarding the Gospel story. Theophilus, it is true, had already received oral instruction. However, his knowledge concerning Christ is still too incomplete and is not based on sufficiently firm grounds. For this reason Luke addresses his writing to him so that he may learn the truth with full certainty. "The work does not merely prove or authenticate what Theophilus has already learnt; rather it conveys in a permanent and assured form what he has previously learnt in a less systematic manner" (Creed, *in loc.*). It is a historic fact that when Luke wrote his Gospel there existed among many educated persons of the time a strong desire for firmly established truth in the field of religion. The various philosophic systems left them unsatisfied, the popular pagan religions filled them with repugnance and they yearned for trustworthy knowledge concerning religious matters. To such a seeker after well-established truth Luke addresses himself, and through him to all other persons who feel the need of knowing the glad tidings with full certainty. It is Luke's earnest desire that as regards their knowledge of the Gospel they shall have firm ground beneath their feet.

These four verses form one single sentence in the original Greek. It is constructed in the classical manner, with principal and dependent clauses, subordinate connection of sentences and participial construction. Thus it is proved that Luke was able to write in classical style. Where in the rest of his Gospel he does not continue in this style but in the Hebraising style of the Greek translation of the Old Testament, in Greek which reflects

Aramaic idiom, or in the daily colloquial style of that time, he does not do so through his inability to write classical Greek. " This he did, as we may now suppose, intentionally and in order to bring the narrative to the foreground as clearly as possible without concealing it behind fine language forms and in beautiful linguistic ornaments of skilful sentence constructions which might distract the attention from the contents " (Greydanus). Luke does not desire to obtrude himself and his literary skill, but wishes to let the Lord Jesus remain alone in the foreground in the description of His appearance and self-revelation in word and act, in suffering and triumph.

In his preface Luke expressly declares that he himself guarantees the truth of the Gospel narrative. It is, indeed, the unique characteristic of the Christian religion that it is based on definite historical facts and not on speculations or theories. Spiritually we cannot live on uncertainties or half-truths. All other religions and philosophic systems rest on human speculations and figments. That is why they contradict each other so radically in practically every important matter and afford no true satisfaction for the deepest yearning of the human heart. In Christianity, however, we see how God throughout many centuries has dealt effectively with man and has spoken to him—at first to prepare him for the coming of Christ and finally in and through the Lord Jesus Himself. While all other religions are thus only a manifestation of the struggle of humanity in its deep longing to know and enjoy divinity, we find in the Word of God the history of how the living God in His saving grace entered into the life of mankind, seeking to save those that are lost. Luke, therefore, justly emphasises the historical trustworthiness of the data of the Gospel narrative.

It is important to note that, although Luke is an inspired Biblical writer, he makes it quite clear in his preface that he made use of all available human means and methods so as to present an exact and well-arranged account of the occurrences. The men called by the Lord to write the Bible books were not used by Him as mere automatons. He selected persons who, through their natural, God-given gifts and training, under the guidance of the Holy Ghost, were suited to their special task. God always respects the independence of personality given by Him to those whom He has called. The Spirit of God does not despise human means, but recognises and blesses them. That is why it is only when we recognise the human element in the Bible that we are able to discover more clearly what is divine in it. But God always led, formed and inspired the Biblical writers in such a manner that

what they composed was truly the Word of God—not human uncertainties but facts and divine truths. For this reason we also
" may know the certainty of those things wherein we have been
instructed ".

¹ '*Επειδήπερ* is a classical Greek word which occurs nowhere else in
the New Testament or in the LXX. Plummer calls it " a stately compound, suitable for a solemn opening ". We may translate it by
" forasmuch as, inasmuch as ". It points to something that is a well-
known fact, for motivating or justifying " some action or other that is
to be or has been named " (Greydanus).

² Luke here uses *πρᾶγμα* instead of *ῥῆμα*, and in this way makes it
clearer that it is here not a question of mere narratives, but of actual
historical facts, i.e. of things that have really taken place.

³ *πεπληροφορημένων*, in connection with persons, may mean " surely
believed " or " fully persuaded " (Rom. iv. 21). But here, where
πράγματα are mentioned, *πληροφορεῖν* is synonomous with *πληροῦν*.
Here the events are thought of as completed, and hence fit to be the
subject of a historical narrative. The correct translation is thus " which
have been fulfilled amongst us ". The perfect participle passive is used
here to indicate the permanent state after the completed action. The
expression also points to the fact that in Jesus the divine promises of the
Old Dispensation have been fulfilled and that a new era has been
inaugurated. The fullness of the saving purpose of God has been
revealed and the glad tidings must be proclaimed.

⁴ *ἐν ἡμῖν* here does not mean " within us ", but " among us "
(the Christians). However, the facts had not occurred only among the
Christians, and Luke and many others had not themselves been eyewitnesses thereof. The events had nevertheless taken place in the
circle of Christ's followers, and all believers in Christ are in a special
way connected with the facts. In addition, there exists a close unity
between the actual eyewitnesses and all other Christians. The events
may, therefore, be correctly described as facts fulfilled " among us ".

⁵ *παρέδοσαν* does not necessarily mean that this had taken place
only orally.

⁶ *ἀπ' ἀρχῆς* refers to the. beginning of Christ's ministry (John
xv. 27).

⁷ That *τοῦ λόγου* should be taken only together with *ὑπηρέται* is
clear from the context in which it occurs. *αὐτόπται* refers to the
πράγμαται of verse 1, and *τοῦ λόγου* is not Christ the Word, but
the word, i.e. the preaching, of the Gospel (cf. Ed. Meyer, *Ursprung
und Anfänge des Christentums*, i, p. 5). The apostles not only beheld
Christ in His appearance, preaching and manner of life, but are also
ὑπηρέται whose vocation it is to preach what they have seen and
heard.

⁸ With *ἔδοξε κἀμοί* he places himself on the same line with the
persons mentioned in verse 1. The aorist here (*ἔδοξε*) may be the

Greek epistolary aorist, in which the writer puts himself in the position of the reader; or it may simply mean that before setting pen to paper he had taken the decision to write thus.

[9] καθεξῆς does not necessarily point only to chronological order, but to context, linking up and systematic co-ordination. He aimed, therefore, not merely at chronological order, but also at logical and artistic arrangement. Wherever the demands of the last two considerations made it necessary, he did not confine himself to time-sequence in his narrative (cf. iv. 16). None the less he substantially conformed to the chronological order, as is abundantly clear from the Gospel.

[10] ἐπιγνῷς expresses the definiteness and sureness of the knowledge, with special reference to the trustworthiness of the information imparted; here, says J. A. Robinson (*Ephesians*, p. 250), " we have the word used with good effect to indicate the discernment of a particular point in regard to things already known ".

[11] τὴν ἀσφάλειαν indicates the absolute certainty, the truthfulness of the report concerning the πράγματα, the history of Jesus. This does not merely point to intellectual conviction, but to security and stability. " With full certainty " would be a good rendering of the sense of the word. Luke, therefore, intends that the faith of his readers should rest upon unshakable historical grounds.

[12] κατηχεῖν originally means " to sound in the cars ", and then " to teach by word of mouth " or merely " to instruct "; but sometimes also (in the passive) " to be informed through rumours " (Acts xxi. 21, 24). This last is the sense suggested by Greydanus here; he does not think that this is the technical sense of ecclesiastical religious instruction, as in the case of a candidate for baptism. Ed. Meyer, however (*op. cit.*, i, p. 7), takes the view that Theophilus was already instructed as a believer. II. J. Cadbury (*The Beginnings of Christianity*, ii, pp. 508 f.), on the other hand, says that in view of the use of the word to denote either accurate or inaccurate information " probably a neutral translation—'heard '—is safest " in this place. In any case, Luke's words indicate that certain things are wanting in Theophilus's knowledge of the Gospel story. He desires to supplement what is lacking and to make Theophilus realise how unshakable is the historical foundation on which the Christian faith rests.

[13] On the classical style of Luke's preface Ed. Meyer remarks: " The prologue proves that the author possesses the customary literary culture of Hellenistic-Roman times and claims a place for his work in literature " (*op. cit.*, i, p. 8). He rejects the idea that Luke, or parts of Luke, may have been translated from Aramaic originals, and declares " His work is from the very outset conceived and written in Greek " (p. 9). The Semitising character of many parts of the Gospel he ascribes to the fact that Luke was steeped in the diction of the Septuagint version of the Old Testament, " and in his style, far from avoiding this leaning to the Septuagint, he has actually aimed at it, and many of his narratives are formed on the pattern of the Greek

57

Bible " (*ibid.*). We are convinced that in taking this stand on the matter Meyer does justice to the facts of the situation as regards the Hebraistic element in Luke's Greek. The Aramaising element is due, of course, to the fact that our Lord and His apostles spoke in Aramaic (see above on " Language, Style and Vocabulary of Luke " in the Introduction, pp. 36 ff.).

NATIVITY OF JOHN ANNOUNCED

i. 5–25

5   There was in the days of Herod, king of Judaea,[1] a certain priest named Zacharias, of the course of Abijah,[2] and he had a wife of the daughters of Aaron, and her name was Elisa-
6 beth. And they were both righteous[3] before God, walking in all the commandments and ordinances of the Lord blame-
7 less. And they had no child, because that Elisabeth was barren, and they both were *now* well stricken in years.[4]
8   Now it came to pass, while he executed[5] the priest's office
9 before God in the order of his course, according to the custom of the priest's office, his lot was to enter into the
10 temple[6] of the Lord and burn incense. And the whole multi-tude of the people were praying[7] without at the hour of
11 incense. And there appeared unto him an angel of the Lord
12 standing on the right side of the altar of incense. And Zacharias was troubled when he saw *him*, and fear fell upon
13 him. But the angel said[8] unto him, Fear not, Zacharias: because thy supplication is heard, and thy wife Elisabeth
14 shall bear thee a son, and thou shalt call his name John. And thou shalt have joy and gladness,[9] and many shall rejoice[10]
15 at his birth. For he shall be great in the sight of the Lord, and he shall drink[11] no wine nor strong drink; and he shall be filled with the Holy Ghost, even from his mother's womb.
16 And many of the children of Israel shall he turn[12] unto the
17 Lord their God.[13] And he shall go before his face in the spirit and power[14] of Elijah, to turn the hearts of the fathers to the children, and the disobedient *to walk* in the wisdom of the just; to make ready for the Lord a people prepared *for*
18 *him*. And Zacharias said unto the angel, Whereby shall I know this? for I am an old man, and my wife well stricken
19 in years. And the angel answering said unto him, I am Gabriel,[15] that stand in the presence of God; and I was sent to speak unto thee, and to bring thee these good tidings.[16]
20 And behold, thou shalt be silent and not able to speak, until the day that these things shall come to pass, because thou believedst not my words, which shall be fulfilled in their
21 season. And the people were waiting[17] for Zacharias, and
22 they marvelled while he tarried in the temple. And when he came out, he could not speak unto them: and they perceived that he had seen a vision in the temple: and he continued

23 making signs unto them, and remained dumb. And it came to pass, when the days of his ministration[18] were fulfilled, he departed unto his house.

24 And after these days Elisabeth his wife conceived;[19] and
25 she hid herself five months, saying, Thus hath the Lord done unto me in the days wherein he looked upon *me*, to take away my reproach among men.

With the history related in these verses, we already stand on the threshold of the supremely important period in the history of mankind—that period of approximately thirty-three years during which the incarnate Son of God was on this earth of ours as Man among men. The appearance and activity of Jesus on earth is the central and most important event of all time. Everything that had gone before had led up to it. And everything that has followed upon it is connected therewith.

The history of John the Baptist and his parents forms the link between the revelation of God in the Old Testament period and that in the New Testament period. " Here we see all the things of the past economy, and this remarkable man, John, linking up that past with that which was to come. The old and the new are seen to be a continuous movement in the programme of God. Sharp the break in many ways between the old and the new on the level of humanity's experience; but in the economy of God everything moved forward " (Morgan, *in loc.*).

For a period of about four hundred years after the appearance of the last Old Testament prophets, no further direct divine revelation had been given to the chosen people of God. The voice of prophecy had been silent, for the Old Testament revelation had been finally rounded off. Everything was now in readiness for the second and last phase in the progress of the divine revelation. This time God was to turn not merely to a chosen group but to the whole world. " But when God begins a new work, He does not scornfully break with the instrument by which the past work has been effected. As it is from the seclusion of a convent that in the middle ages He will take the reformer of the church, so it is from the loins of an Israelitish priest that He now causes to come forth the man who is to introduce the world to the renovation prepared for it. The temple itself, the centre of the theocracy, becomes the cradle of the new covenant, of the worship in spirit and in truth. There is, then, a divine suitability in the choice both of the actors and theatre of the scene which is about to take place " (Godet, *in loc.*).

Although Luke begins his Gospel with the announcement of the nativity of John the Baptist, he is here also, as in his whole Gospel, engaged in depicting Christ, i.e. in everything that he recounts he presents in a clear light who Christ is. He narrates the story of John only in so far as it points to Christ.

5 With this verse Luke commences his real narrative. In i. 5–iii. 38 he then first describes the coming of the Lord into the world and the preparatory work of John. The history of the nativity of John has been taken up along with the history of Jesus' nativity because there is the closest connection between the two, since John is Christ's forerunner.

The words with which he here commences his narrative place the dawn of Christianity in impressive contrast with the political conditions existing at the time. John, the morning star that announces the dawn of the new dispensation, appears just at the moment when the reign of Herod, King of Judaea from 40 to 4 B.C., approaches its tragic and hopeless end. This Herod is the one who is called " the Great ". He was an Idumaean by descent, but professed the Jewish religion. Although he was called king, this was merely by grace of the Romans on whom he was largely dependent. Outwardly his reign had been crowned with considerable success. He had especially achieved much fame through the numerous beautiful buildings erected by him. He had also been responsible for the rebuilding of the temple in Jerusalem. On the other hand, he had polluted the Jewish land by the erection of temples in honour of pagan gods and through the institution of pagan games. His reign was, in addition, deeply stained with blood. He acted with relentless cruelty towards any sign of opposition to his sovereignty. His last years especially were characterised by bloody family horrors. He regarded his own family with so much distrust that he caused several of them to be done to death. Finally in 4 B.C. he died, unmourned by his own kin and hated by the Jewish nation.

The expression " in the days of Herod " thus points to a dark, ominous and calamitous period in the history of the Jewish nation. Against this gloomy background Luke now gives the history of the dawn of the new day in the life of humanity—the coming of Christ, which was prepared by the advent of John the Baptist.

Since the time of David (1 Chron. xxiv) the priests had been divided into twenty-four orders. The order of Abijah was the eighth. After the banishment only a few orders existed. But the surviving priests were again divided into twenty-four orders with the original names. Thus Zacharias was a priest who belonged to the order or course of Abijah. He was married to Elisabeth, who was also of priestly descent. To be a priest and to be married to a priest's daughter was considered to be a double and special distinction. Of an excellent woman it was often said: " She deserves to be married to a priest." In this way John was, in the fullest sense of the word, of honoured, priestly origin. The name of his father, Zacharias, means: " The Lord remembers (viz. His covenant) "; and his mother's name, Elisabeth, means: " My God is an oath (i.e. my God is the absolutely Faithful One) ". These names, therefore, given to them in the providential ruling of God, are pregnant with meaning, especially here where we stand at the portals which lead to the full revelation of God in Christ.

6 Zacharias and Elisabeth fully came up to the expectation of the ideal of Israelitish piety. Both were righteous and upright, as it was God's will that they should be. They led a strictly religious and moral life, and this they did not merely in so far as they were seen by men but " before God ". They asked, therefore, not what men thought of them but how God judged them. This, of course, does not imply that they were quite sinless. The quality of their life was, however, of such a kind that it presents to us a clear contrast with the general spirit of the period. The purest Jewish piety kept its flame bright in their consecrated and noble conduct before God. John, therefore, was sprung from parents in whom the highest form of Old Testament piety was personified. In his parentage, as well as in himself, he represented the perfect form of the old Jewish religion and fulfilled its highest calling by pointing to the One that was to come.

7 Over the life of the married couple there hung a great sorrow. Although already far advanced in age, they were still childless. For a Jewish married couple childlessness was a double sorrow because this would rule them out as potential parents or ancestors of the expected Messiah. The case of this couple seemed particularly hopeless as Elisabeth was not only barren but both were already far advanced in years. However sore their affliction was, they nevertheless (verse 6) did not allow the disappointed hope to embitter their lives and to estrange them from God. They nobly accepted the trial with inward resignation and persevered faithfully in the service of God.

8, 9 There were some thousands of priests at the time, and it was arranged that each course should in turn send a number of priests to the temple for a week to execute their office there. In this particular week it was the turn of the course of Abijah, and Zacharias was one of the priests of that course who had to serve. Each day the lot was cast to assign the various duties of the priests for the day. As there were so many priests, it was not allowed that a priest should burn incense more than once in his lifetime. On that particular day the lot had fallen upon Zacharias and he had to attend to the burning of the incense. This incense-offering had to be brought twice a day—early in the morning and again at about three o'clock in the afternoon (Exod. xxx. 7, 8). Thus Zacharias had entered the temple after the lot had fallen upon him. The actual temple-building or sanctuary proper consisted of the holy place and the holy of holies. Into the latter apartment only the high priest was allowed to go (and that but once a year, on the Great Day of Atonement), while the officiating priests might enter the holy place. (For a detailed description of the temple service cf. Edersheim: *The Temple: Its Ministry and Service in the Time of Christ.*)

10 Three times a day there were public gatherings for prayer in the temple court or square outside the actual sanctuary. The first and last of these prayer gatherings coincided with the morning and afternoon incense-offering. While Zacharias was engaged in presenting the incense-offering on the golden altar in the holy place, a great multitude of the people were praying in the outer temple court. After everything had been prepared for the incense-offering, all the other priests had left the holy place and only Zacharias waited there for the sign of the sacerdotal president that it was " the time of the incense-offering ". When the signal was given, he immediately offered the incense on the altar. As soon as the people saw the ascending smoke of the incense-offering, which was the symbol of true consecration to God, they fell down before the Lord and spread out their hands in silent prayer. For several minutes there followed a dead silence in the temple sanctuary and in the surrounding temple-building and courts. To Zacharias, as to every other priest, this was one of the most solemn experiences of his whole life—especially since the privilege of offering the incense, as we have seen, fell to the lot of a priest only once in his lifetime.

11 During these moments of impressive silence there suddenly appears to Zacharias an angel of the Lord. He had not seen the angel approach, but all at once he notices him on the right side, the side of honour, of the golden altar on which he was engaged in offering the incense.

12 Zacharias's natural reaction, when during the solemn moments he suddenly saw the heavenly messenger, was to be agitated and overcome with fear.

13 But he had no need to fear, the angel assured him, for his prayer had been heard. Zacharias was standing there as representative of the people and, together with the devout ones among them, he was praying for the spiritual redemption of Israel.

63

It cannot be clearly ascertained whether the angel is referring to the prayer of Zacharias as representative of the people or to his prayer for a son that had naturally been uttered by him on many previous occasions. But probably he refers to the prayer of Zacharias for the salvation of his people, i.e. for their redemption by the Messiah. For it does appear that the angel speaks of the prayer in which Zacharias was at that moment engaged. And it is extremely improbable that, while as consecrated priest he had to act on behalf of the people, he would think of his own interests and not of theirs. In addition, he and his wife were already so far advanced in years and had been so long without a child that most probably they had already ceased to pray about the matter. What the angel meant, therefore, was that his prayer for the coming of the Messiah was heard and that therewith a great privilege was to be conferred on him and his wife. Elisabeth was to bear him a son who would act as a predecessor and harbinger of the coming Redeemer. God, therefore, was also going to answer their former prayers for a child, although it had seemed for long as though He was unwilling to do so. The son whom Elisabeth was to bear him, so the angel further declared, was to be called John. The name John, according to Hebrew etymology, means " The Lord is merciful " or " the gracious gift of God ". This name, therefore, refers to the grace of God that was going to descend upon the people. It was characteristic of the acts of God with Israel that He often caused to be given, to those called by Him, names that carried a suitable meaning, as also in this instance. To the significant names of John's parents is now added the significant meaning of his own name. By this means it is indicated that the grace of God, soon to be revealed in the Redeemer whose coming is to be prepared by John, is the outcome of His remembrance of His Covenant and of His absolute faithfulness.

14 Not only his parents, but also many others will rejoice at his nativity. Especially since God for so many centuries had sent no more prophets to the people, the coming of John as prophet will bring great joy among the devout.

15 His birth will be a matter of rejoicing, because he " shall be great in the sight of the Lord "—great in the highest sense of the word. For what one is in the sight of God is what one is in reality. He is to drink neither wine nor any other kind of strong drink; he will not require the stimulation so caused, for he will be constantly full of the Holy Ghost and receive from Him the necessary strength and inspiration for fulfilling his life's calling. During Old Testament times the Holy Ghost descended upon people temporarily and fitted them for some task or other, and then departed again.

John, however, will be permanently filled with the Holy Ghost from the very commencement of his life.

16 Israel was, through its sins, again and again estranged from God. And it was one of the functions of a true prophet to call the people back to the ways of righteousness to serve God (Jer. iii. 7, 10; Ezek. iii. 19; Dan. ix. 13). John, then, so the angel declares, is to turn many of his people to God. Because he will be great in the sight of the Lord and strengthened by the Holy Ghost, he will be able to accomplish this.

17 He will do much more than an ordinary prophet. As a special prophet he will go before the Lord who reveals Himself in the Messiah and will prepare the way for Him. For what was prophesied in the last book of the Old Testament, in Malachi, will be fulfilled in John. In Malachi iii. 1 is written: " Behold, I send my messenger, and he shall prepare the way before me: and the Lord, whom ye seek, shall suddenly come to his temple, even the messenger of the covenant, whom ye delight in, behold, he cometh, saith the Lord of hosts." " The messenger of the covenant " refers constantly throughout the Old Testament to Christ before His incarnation. Malachi iii. 1 therefore expressly prophesies that before Christ the Lord appears to His people He will send a messenger ahead to prepare the way before Him. In Malachi iv. 5, 6 we read: " Behold, I will send you Elijah the prophet before the great and terrible day of the Lord come. And he shall turn the heart of the fathers to the children, and the heart of the children to their fathers; lest I come and smite the earth with a curse." That these words do not refer exclusively to the time of the final Consummation, but in the first place to the time of the incarnation of Christ, appears from the fact that Jesus Himself said of John that he was the prophet Elijah who was to come. The incarnation and appearance of Christ had already brought a " great and terrible day " into the life of the Jewish people, because by it the people were sifted. And when the majority refused to accept Him, the judgments of God smote the people in an unparalleled manner, until Jerusalem and the whole of the Jewish national existence in Palestine were totally destroyed in A.D. 70. The angel then declares that John will appear as the prophet who will work like an Elijah. He will be, as it were, a reincarnation of that fearless prophet of old. His traits of character would, therefore, also be like those of Elijah, marked by strength and not by weakness. Just as Elijah had often been in the deserts, thus, too, it was with John; and just as his predecessor had pronounced divine judgment on sinners without respect of persons, so also did John. Indeed, if we compare the two characters with one another, it becomes clear that in the whole of the Holy Scriptures there are no two persons who bear a greater resemblance to one another than Elijah and John the Baptist. What Malachi, and now centuries later the angelic messenger, prophesied concerning the predecessor of Christ was thus completely confirmed.

Where the messenger declares that John will turn the hearts of the fathers to the children, he points again to the words of Malachi iv. 6. These words imply that there had been a turning away of the hearts of the fathers from their children but that they will again become affectionate towards them. Here we have, therefore, a reference to the re-establishment of the correct relation between fathers and children. Several expositors take these words to have a literal meaning. Probably there is a reference here to the re-establishment of broken family ties, but the words of the messenger include a great deal more. John will call people to repentance and by this means the dissensions in homes will be removed after a thorough renunciation of sin. But his call includes far more. With Greydanus we imagine the case to be as follows. By " fathers " the pious ancestors of Israel are meant. They are, as it were, filled with aversion towards their descendants who have fallen into ungodliness. Now John, through the power of the Holy Ghost, will bring it to pass that many of these descendants will be converted to God and will thus give up their sinful ways. And in this manner they will win back the affection of their pious ancestors. The meaning is, therefore, that John will bring the present rebellious generation into religious harmony with the upright ones of former times. It will be his task to reunite and consolidate Israel on the basis of the devotion of the forefathers. And by thus turning " the disobedient to the disposition of righteous ones " he will prepare a people that is spiritually alert and expectant, ready for the kingdom of the Lord which is at hand.

18 The glorious promises of the angel, however, sound incredible to Zacharias. For how, indeed, can Elisabeth bear him a son since both of them are already so far advanced in years and Elisabeth, moreover, is barren? He feels that his doubts are justified and asks for a sign which shall prove the truth of the prophecy.

19 His doubts are, however, not justified, for had he not himself often read in the Old Testament how God had given Isaac as a son to the barren wife of the aged Abraham, and how Samuel was given as a son to a formerly barren woman? In former times, indeed, signs had been given, without reproach or punishment, to people like Abraham (Gen. xv) and Gideon (Judges vi) who had asked for them in the same manner. But they still lived in the twilight period of the divine revelation and had not

66

had as many opportunities as Zacharias to know God in His might and mercy. On him, therefore, there rests a greater responsibility, and his unbelief merits chastisement.

In contrast with the words of Zacharias, " I am an old man ", the angel declares: " I am Gabriel, that stand in the presence of God; and I was sent to speak unto thee, and to bring thee these glad tidings." In this manner the angel points out to him the foolishness of his doubts. For he draws attention to his dignity as a divine messenger. He is not merely one amongst numbers of equals, but Gabriel, who stands in the immediate presence of God. Accordingly it is a special favour accorded to Zacharias that God sends such a special messenger to him. How can he then still doubt the truth of his words? For by this attitude he distrusts not only him but the Almighty Lord who sent him.

In the Holy Scriptures the veil which conceals the invisible world of angels from us is again and again drawn away. Thus 2 Kings vi. 17 makes us realise that God surrounds His children, as it were, with a camp of celestial forces for their protection. In Matthew xviii. 10 the Lord says: " See that ye despise not one of these little ones; for I say unto you, that in heaven their angels do always behold the face of my Father which is in heaven." Thus again and again in the Word of God angels and angelic forces are mentioned in a most natural manner. On the other hand, no detailed particulars are given concerning them. For indeed the Word of God is the message of salvation and not a textbook to satisfy human curiosity on all possible subjects.

Only two angels are mentioned by name in the canonical books of the Bible, Gabriel and Michael. Gabriel means " man of God "; and Michael, " who is like God? " Critics here ask the sarcastic question whether Hebrew is spoken in heaven. These names are, however, symbolical in order to indicate what are the special functions of these celestial personalities. When we speak to anybody, we do it in such a way that he is able to understand us. So also when God reveals heavenly truths to man He does so in the language of human beings, in such a manner that it is intelligible to them. Thus Gabriel, according to the name he bears and his description as one who stands in the presence of God, is the mighty messenger of God. Therefore, throughout the Holy Scriptures, he appears as the one who brings good tidings from God to man (Dan. viii. 16, ix. 21; Luke i. 19, 26). Michael, again, as his name indicates, is the destroyer of everyone who dares to aspire to equality with God or to resist Him (Dan. x. 13, 21, xii. 1; Jude 9; Rev. xii. 7). Thus Gabriel is the one that builds up and Michael the one that overthrows. In the case of Michael the justice and

67

judicial activity of God plays its part, while in Gabriel's case the grace and redeeming activity of the Lord is in the foreground. In extra-biblical Jewish writings and legends the exact opposite is the case, which proves that the Bible does not borrow from Jewish or other fables (cf. Plummer, *in loc.*).

20 Because Zacharias, notwithstanding the fact that God had through His mighty heavenly messenger brought him the glad tidings, did not believe, a sign will indeed be given to him, but at the same time the sign will serve as chastisement for his unbelief. He will from that moment be dumb until the promised son has been born. This chastisement, however, serves to cleanse him from his unbelief. Although he doubted the words of Gabriel, they will nevertheless come true in due time because God will bring them to pass.

21 While Zacharias underwent his overwhelming experience in the sanctuary, the people without began anxiously to wonder why he was so long in coming forth. It was customary that the priest, who offered the incense alone in the sanctuary, should appear as soon as possible after the prayers had been offered up, to prevent anxiety among the people. For they were afraid that the priest might for some reason or other be struck dead by the judgment of God in such a holy place, or that an unusual divine phenomenon might befall him.

22 When Zacharias at last comes out, the people immediately perceive that he has undergone some remarkable experience. It was part of the temple procedure that after the priest had offered the incense and the prayers were over he should come forth from the holy place. From the steps leading to the court where the worshipping people stood, the officiating priest had then to pronounce over them the priestly blessing of Numbers vi. 24–6, the other priests repeating it after him. When Zacharias came out, the multitude waited in vain for the pronouncement of the blessing. Zacharias, who had to take the lead in this, remained dumb and beckoned in an agitated manner. His agitation and continued silence immediately caused the multitude to realise that something extraordinary had happened to him. From his whole attitude and the solemnity of the preceding moments they concluded that he had seen a supernatural vision.

23 As soon as the rest of the week of service in the temple was accomplished, Zacharias went back to his house. This was not in Jerusalem, in the Ophel quarter where many of the priests lived, but probably in a village in the mountainous region to the south of Jerusalem (verse 39).

24, 25 Before long the words of the angel began to be fulfilled

68

and Elisabeth became pregnant. Thereupon she withdrew from public life for a period of five months. Various explanations are given as to why she did so. That it was not in order to hide her pregnancy goes without saying since it was precisely during the first five months that others would most probably not notice it. It is more likely that Elisabeth purposely sought retirement in order to glorify her God in silence with grateful worship for the miracle accorded to her and her aged husband. She would naturally also long for quietness in order to meditate calmly upon the glorious event that had befallen her husband in the temple and upon her supernatural pregnancy. For Zacharias would naturally communicate to his wife in writing all about his experiences in the temple. Especially when she saw that the promises were beginning to be fulfilled she would doubtless believe and deeply ponder every word that Zacharias had communicated to her in connection with the angel's prophecy concerning her expected son. Owing to the miraculous character of what had happened she would very naturally seek silence and seclusion during the first months. With whom outside her home could she have discussed the supernatural, holy matters? For would not outsiders, during those first five months, have considered it ridiculous if she had told them that she, who had been childless all these years, had received the promise that a son would be born to her and that, in addition, he would be the predecessor of the Messiah? How could she, especially since her husband had come back deaf and dumb from Jerusalem, go her ordinary way and move about in public life as usual? Everything was so radically important and supernatural that she could not but seek retirement. Where, therefore, Creed and others declare that they can see no reason why Elisabeth should hide herself for the five months, they betray a regrettable lack of capacity for entering into her real circumstances. It would be the most natural thing in the world for her to seek quietness during that time. And only after the fifth month, when it would be indisputably clear that the angel's words were going to be fulfilled, would she begin to end her retirement and inform her neighbours and relations, without fear of ridicule, that God had done, and was still going to do, great and wonderful things for her and her husband.

The history of the revelation of God as presented in the Bible is the history of the supernatural and divine, which is brought into relation with, and acts upon, what is natural and human. What is exceptional to man is ordinary to God. What is supernatural in the eyes of man is natural to God. This we perceive quite clearly in the manner in which Luke describes this history of Zacharias and Elisabeth. He writes from the divine point of view. Thus, e.g., he does not argue the question of the existence of angels, but describes in a most natural manner how God sent His heavenly messenger to Zacharias. The supernatural is here written down as the natural, and the exceptional as the usual. Everything that is supernatural in the Word of God is supernatural because it is above and outside our human understanding. Human considerations in this connection are, therefore, of no decisive importance. We accept it, not because we can understand or prove it by means of human comprehension, but because the living God has thus revealed it—knowing that what seems impossible for us is possible for Him, and that " the secret things belong unto the Lord our God; but the things that are revealed belong unto us and to our children " (Deut. xxix. 29).

[1] Ἰουδαίας here stands for the Jewish land in a wider sense and therefore includes also Samaria and Galilee (Acts ii. 9, x. 37).

[2] For a detailed exposition of the division of the priests into various classes and of their various functions cf. Strack-Billerbeck, " Das Evangelium nach Lukas " in vol. ii of their Kommentar zum N.T. aus Talmud und Midrasch (München, 1924), in loc.; or E. Schürer, History of the Jewish People in the Time of Christ (Eng. trans.), division II, vol. i (1885), pp. 207–305.

[3] δίκαιοι originally (Ezek. xviii. 5 ff.) had the meaning of "righteous" in the highest sense of the word. But gradually it came to denote not much more than the careful performance of ceremonial acts. The addition ἐναντίον τοῦ θεοῦ (a Hebraistic expression) here, again gives to δίκαιοι its original meaning.

[4] Levites had to give up their ministration at the age of sixty. But priests served as long as possible. " Old age did not render the priests unfit for service " (Strack-Billerbeck, in loc.).

[5] Ἐγένετο δὲ is a Hebraism used more frequently by Luke than by any other Gospel writer. For a detailed exposition of the various constructions with which he uses it cf. Plummer, in loc.; J. H. Moulton, Prolegomena, p. 233.

[6] ναός is used for the actual temple sanctuary consisting of the holy place and the holy of holies, while ἱερόν (ii. 27) refers to the whole complex of buildings on the temple hill. For an account of the religious ceremonies, etc., in the temple cf. Schürer, op. cit., II, i, pp. 273 ff.; Edersheim, The Temple and Its Service in the Time of Jesus the Messiah; and Strack-Billerbeck, op. cit., at i. 10.

[7] προσεύχεσθαι is the common word for prayer, which includes supplication, invocation, praise and thanksgivings.

[8] Here he does not use ἐλάλησεν (which has reference to the sound or the tone), but εἶπεν, which points rather to the content of what is said.

70

⁹ ἀγαλλίασις denotes jubilant utterance of rejoicing.

¹⁰ χαρήσονται is the future of certainty; it indicates that it will be a sincere, deep joy which will be outwardly revealed in a spontaneous manner.

¹¹ It cannot be definitely asserted that these words mean that John will be a Nazirite in the full sense of the word (as stated by Strack-Billerbeck, *in loc.*). More probable is the opinion of M. J. Lagrange that John occupies his own place and belongs neither to the Nazirites nor to the priests, although he has certain qualities in common with both.

¹² The call of John will not be merely to outward fulfilling of·the law, but to regeneration, conversion, purification, moral renewal. He will take up the burden of many Old Testament prophets who had a deep, morally religious conception of the demands of God's word and the fulfilment of His law. ἐπιστρέψει indicates that he will cause them to change for the better in religious conviction and life-conduct, as God uses him to that end.

¹³ It will be a turning to God in conviction, thought and act.

¹⁴ While πνεῦμα here indicates the internal driving power, δύναμις points to the expression or revelation of it.

¹⁵ Whilst in the Holy Scriptures only the angels Gabriel and Michael are mentioned by name, this is quite different in later Judaism (cf. Strack-Billerbeck, *in loc.*). The matter-of-factness of the Bible did not satisfy them, and under Persian influence, especially, they came to believe in many more angelic beings, with special names and functions. Godet rightly declares (*in loc.*) in this connection: " History does not advance from the complicated to the simple." What is taught in the Word of God concerning angels is, therefore, not the fruit of Persian or other influence. On the contrary, the extra-biblical, fantastic opinions are the degeneration of the original truths of revelation. For this reason they present such a sharp contrast to the sober data of the Holy Scriptures. If we think here of the angel Gabriel's message to Zacharias, we agree that " there is not a word in this speech of the angel which is not at once simple and worthy of the mouth into which it is put. It is not after this fashion that man makes heaven speak when he is inventing; only read the apocryphal writings! " (Godet, *in loc.*).

¹⁶ εὐαγγελίσασθαι. Here for the first time in the Gospel narrative appears the word which ere long will be so frequently used. In the LXX it was used for the announcement of any good tidings (2 Sam. i. 20), but especially for announcements in connection with the Messiah (Isa. xl. 9, lii. 7, lx. 6, lxi. 1). Henceforth it will be more and more used in the Gospel stories in the sense of the glad tidings preached in connection with Christ Jesus.

¹⁷ ἦν ὁ λαὸς προσδοκῶν. The periphrastic imperfect (ἦν προσδοκῶν instead of προσεδόκει) is here used to indicate the constant and long-continued watch.

¹⁸ λειτουργία was used in classical Greek of the various forms of public service which well-to-do citizens had to perform at their own expense. In Biblical Greek it was, however, used in connection with

priestly ministry (Heb. viii. 6) and also in connection with the service to the poor (2 Cor. ix. 12; Phil. ii. 30).

[19] συνέλαβεν—Luke alone in the New Testament uses this word in the sense of " to become pregnant ". This is, however, the common meaning of the word in the writings of medical authors of that time. The number of expressions used by Luke to refer to pregnancy is almost as large as the number used by Hippocrates (Plummer, *in loc.*).

SPECIAL NOTE

THE SUPERNATURAL ELEMENTS IN THIS NATIVITY STORY

With regard to the constant attacks on the credibility of Luke where he describes events such as those in verses 5–25, we wish only to remark that the attitude adopted by commentators towards such Biblical stories forms part of their whole opinion of God and His revelation to man. He who believes that God is really the Almighty Creator and Preserver of the whole creation will have no difficulty in believing that He has intervened miraculously in the course of human history. Such a person realises that, although God as a God of order will not act " contrary to nature ", or violate His own laws, nevertheless, where it is necessary for His glory and for the spiritual well-being of mankind, He acts in a supernatural manner, by bringing into play higher laws than those with which we as human beings are familiar. Especially with the coming of Christ into the world it is the most natural thing that God Almighty should by these supernatural means announce and display the greatest of all events in the history of mankind—the incarnation of Christ for the salvation of the lost.

Historically and psychologically it is impossible that legends should so soon have been included in the Gospel of Luke. He was not only himself able to collect firsthand knowledge concerning all the data in his book, but several of his first readers were persons who still stood in the closest relation to the Gospel events. It was only later on, when there was no longer such an intimate contact with firsthand sources of information, that the curiosity of some persons caused attempts to be made to supplement the actual events by means of various fantastic figments. The apocryphal gospels, which possibly began to appear towards the end of the first century A.D., mark the time when some began to leave the pure paths. A comparison between the soberly written and sublime stories of the New Testament Gospels and the absurd and fantastic stories of the apocryphal writings of later times immediately shows the unbridgeable chasm existing between the divinely inspired works of the Biblical writers and the uninspired works. (M. R. James, *The Apocryphal New Testament*, gives the texts of the apocryphal writings in Eng. trans.)

Everything pleads in favour of the trustworthiness of the Gospel stories. This particularly applies to this first story related by Luke.

The style of the narrative is so sober and simple that we cannot but exclaim: " No person invents stories in this manner! " Accordingly when Dr. Luce, for example, declares concerning these and the other stories in i. 5–ii. 52: " These beautiful stories are the imaginative poetry of devotion rather than the sober prose of history " (*in loc.*), this is only the outcome of his aprioristic opinion that such stories cannot be true. He cannot, however, adduce a single *proof* to show why the stories are not historical. Especially after what Luke himself has declared in his preface about the accurate manner in which he investigated matters, the burden of proof falls on those who doubt the truth of his stories. Luke offers these events not as poetical speculations, but as pure history, and as such we accept them, rejoicing in the grand and glorious manner in which God acted in the history of mankind when the time came for the coming of His Son.

THE ANNOUNCEMENT OF THE NATIVITY
OF JESUS

i. 26–38

26 Now in the sixth month the angel Gabriel was sent from
27 God unto a city of Galilee,[1] named Nazareth, to a virgin
betrothed to a man whose name was Joseph, of the house of
28 David,[2] and the virgin's name was Mary. And he came in
unto her, and said, Hail thou that art[3] highly favoured, the
29 Lord *is* with thee.[4] But she was greatly troubled at the saying,
and cast in her mind what manner of salutation this might
30 be. And the angel said unto her, Fear not, Mary: for thou
31 hast found favour with God. And behold,[5] thou shalt conceive in thy womb, and bring forth a son, and shalt call his
32 name JESUS.[6] He shall be great, and shall be called the Son
of the Most High: and the Lord God shall give unto him
33 the throne of his father David:[7] and he shall reign over the
house of Jacob[8] for ever; and of his kingdom[9] there shall be
34 no end.[10] And Mary said unto the angel, How shall this be,
35 seeing I know[11] not a man? And the angel answered and
said unto her, The Holy Ghost shall come upon thee, and
the power of the Most High shall overshadow thee: wherefore also that which is to be born shall be called[12] holy, the
36 Son of God.[13] And behold, Elisabeth thy kinswoman, she also
hath conceived a son in her old age: and this is the sixth
37 month with her that was called barren. For no word from
38 God shall be void of power.[14] And Mary said, Behold, the
handmaid of the Lord; be it unto me according to thy word.
And the angel departed from her.

In these verses we have an amazing story—mysterious and
glorious! For here is described how God sent a celestial being to
the earth with the tidings of the impending incarnation of His Son,
Jesus, the Saviour of the world.

26, 27 During the sixth month, after the angel had appeared
to Zacharias in the temple (verses 5–25), he was again sent by God
to the earth. This time, however, he was sent not to Jerusalem
again but to the Galilean village of Nazareth. This village was
situated about seventy miles to the north-east of Jerusalem in a
hollow valley of a mountain on the northern side of the plain of
Jezreël or Esdraëlon. It was surrounded by hills on all sides except

on the southern side, so that it could not be seen from the surrounding territory. The village is still in existence to-day, and is known as En-Nasirah. It is at present inhabited by some ten thousand persons—two-thirds of whom are Christians and one-third Mohammedans, but no Jews (these latter purposely avoid the village). From the hills around Nazareth one has a very extensive view in all directions. " Winding in and out among the hills the great highways from Egypt to Damascus, from Jerusalem to the north, could clearly be seen in the New Testament times, white ribbons of road now floating in the dust of merchant caravans, now glittering with the diamond-headed spears of soldiery. Towering skyward in the distance were three of the most noted mountains in Scripture—the rounded dome of Tabor, Hermon's snowclad peak, and the historic heights of Carmel " (S. L. Caiger, *In His Steps*, p. 639).

To this Galilean village Gabriel was sent to the virgin Mary, and here Jesus afterwards spent His childhood days and grew up to Manhood.

The virgin was still unmarried but engaged to a man named Joseph, a descendant of David. At that time an engagement was regarded as a definite promise of mutual fidelity and its violation was looked upon as adultery (cf. Deut. xxii. 13 ff., 23 ff.).

28, 29 The angel greets her and calls her " highly favoured ". By this he does not mean, as Roman Catholics teach, that she is " full of favour " in the sense that she will be able to *confer* favour, but that she has *received* favour. God had given her His free and uncaused grace in a unique measure by choosing her as mother of His Son. Mary is naturally very much agitated by the words of the angel. By her reaction to his greeting she shows that she is modest and sober-minded. She is agitated by the words of the angel because she feels that such a greeting is not suited to her. However, she shows no hysterical excitement on account of the angel's word, for, as Luke declares, she considered it in her mind.

30-3 The heavenly bearer of glad tidings again reassures the agitated Mary with the words: " Fear not! ", the same words used by him to reassure Zacharias (verse 13). As the reason why she need not fear, he declares that God regards and treats her as the special object of His favour. She need not, therefore, be afraid on account of her humble station and personal unworthiness. God has chosen her in His mercy to bring forth a Son who is to be called Jesus. In Hebrew the name means: " The Lord is salvation." Because Luke is writing for Gentile Christian readers who have no knowledge of Hebrew, he does not refer to the etymological meaning of the name as does Matthew, who writes for Jewish Christians (Matt.

75

i. 21). The Son, therefore, in the highest sense of the word (for God Himself commands that this name shall be given to Him) will be the One through whom He will accomplish redemption, salvation, blessedness. Like John (verse 15), Jesus also will be " great ". But His greatness will bear a quite different character. Of John it was foretold: " He shall be great in the sight of the Lord." But of Jesus it is declared: " He shall be great, and shall be called the Son of the Most High." His greatness will therefore excel everything. In Greek the words are merely " Son of Highest ", without the articles, in order to indicate the absolute uniqueness and highness of His divine Sonship. To Him, as the One exalted above all, God will give the throne of His father David. " Throne " occurs in this place as symbol of supreme power. To Him, therefore, shall be given the royal might and sovereignty promised in the Old Testament to the Messiah-king of the lineage of David (2 Sam. vii. 14; Ps. ii. 7, lxxxix. 26, 27). His sovereignty will, however, not be a passing, earthly sovereignty, but a spiritual and everlasting one, not over an earthly people but over the spiritual Israel. Christ will reign unto all eternity, although a change in the manner of His sovereignty may set in when the whole of creation is brought back to full submission to God, when all things shall be subdued unto Him (1 Cor. xv. 24–8) and when Satan with his satellites shall have been banished from His presence (Rev. xx. 11–15).

34 The announcement of the angel is still too overwhelming and incomprehensible to Mary. Yet she does not, like Zacharias, doubt its veracity. She does not ask for a sign to prove the truth of the words, but asks for further information. She believes that what he has declared as God's messenger is going to happen. But she does not understand how it will be realised, and therefore asks: " How shall this be, seeing I know not a man? " According to the original Greek, Mary's words do not express doubt; but overwhelmed by the incomprehensible grandeur of the announcement, she merely enquires as to the manner in which that which has been promised will take place.

35 In the reply of the angel we notice the parallelism which among the Hebrews always indicates the expression of sublime sentiments and poetical style. The angel in his reply deals with one of the deepest and holiest mysteries, and for this reason his words are here exalted to a song. In a tender and chaste manner he declares in the song the fact of the impending pregnancy of the virgin Mary through divine influence. The Holy Ghost will come upon Mary and overshadow her with His power, through which she will become pregnant. In the original Greek the reading is

76

" Holy Ghost " without the article to indicate that here there is a reference to the Holy Ghost according to His creative operation or power. " The power of the Most High " is thus used as synonymous with it. Like a cloud, the symbol of the divine presence in which God appears (Exod. xl. 34; Num. ix. 15), the power of the Highest shall overshadow her. " Wherefore also," the angel declares further, " that which is to be born shall be called holy, the Son of God." It should be noted that he does not say that through His conception by the Holy Ghost Jesus will *become* the Son of God. No; as a result of this supernatural conception He will, in His humanity, reveal Himself as a divine Being; and for this reason, too, He will be acknowledged as such and will be called Son of God.

The angel in these words does not merely announce that the incarnation of Jesus will take place through the direct influence of the Holy Ghost, but also expressly declares that He who will through Him be begotten as Man will be free from all taint of sin— He will be the Holy One. It was necessary for the Redeemer to be " born of a woman " (Gal. iv. 4) so that He should be of the same nature as those whom He came to save. But it was just as imperative that He should be perfectly holy, since no sinful being can accomplish reconciliation for the sins of others. The angel, as God's messenger, clearly emphasises the glorious fact that both these requirements will be fulfilled in the case of Jesus.

36 What the angel had communicated to Mary was something tremendous. She exercised the faith required on her part to accept the truth of it. The angel now informs her that Elisabeth, who is already advanced in years, has also conceived a son. This fact serves to strengthen her faith still more and to make her realise better the reality of the impending event. In addition, the words of the angel are a hint to Mary to pay a visit to Elisabeth, who is related to her. By coming in contact with her who also (though to a lesser extent) had been favoured by God, she will be enabled to accommodate herself better to the marvellous happenings announced concerning her.

37 Everything that has been announced is possible, for with God nothing is impossible—even the stupendous miracle of the incarnation of His Son—and His word is self-fulfilling (cf. Isa. lv. 11).

38 The message from God that was brought to Mary by the angel was no command. It was merely an announcement of what He was going to do. Mary submits herself completely to God's will so announced. She does so in a few words which are at the same time simple and sublime: " Behold, the handmaid of the

77

Lord; be it unto me according to thy word." This was no trivial matter to her. On the one hand the highest honour ever given to a woman had been conferred on her by the Lord—to become the mother of the Son of God. But on the other hand Mary was placed in an extremely difficult and even mortally dangerous position. For she clearly realised how radically it would influence her social position and especially her relation to Joseph if she should become pregnant before her marriage. Now it is alleged by some that what is described in Matthew i. 18–23 conflicts with what is here recorded by Luke. For, they declare, Mary would surely have informed Joseph of the angel's message. Our answer is, however, that everything goes to show that this was precisely what the quiet, modest Mary would not do (ii. 51). In addition to this, Joseph, if he had not received the revelation described in Matthew i. 18–23, would most assuredly not have believed her— however pious and good he may have been. We are therefore compelled to agree with Plummer that under existing circumstances " she would prefer to leave the issue with regard to Joseph in God's hands " (*in loc.*). And God did not disappoint her, as we learn from Matthew i. 18.

After Mary's words of surrender and devotion to God the angel left her. In the delicacy and sobriety of the Bible story no unnecessary details are given. Thus the fact and the moment of the conception itself are not narrated. The veil over the miraculous is not lifted. In accordance with the sacred story, the emphasis should here be placed on the submissiveness and faith of Mary.

In the tidings brought from God by the angel to Mary we have an impressive testimony to the divine greatness of Jesus—a greatness wholly different from that of any human being: in respect of His existence as Man He will be of unique origin (verse 35). Born of the virgin Mary through the overshadowing of the power of the Most High, He will be—as He eternally is—the only-begotten Son of God (verse 32). His God-given name (verse 31) will be Jesus (i.e. Saviour). Therefore He is the One who will appear as the divine Redeemer. Unlike all other human beings, He will be wholly without sin. He will be the Holy One in an absolute sense (verse 35). Therefore He will also be the divine King who will reign over His spiritual kingdom unto all eternity (verse 34).

---

[1] Where Luke here describes Nazareth as a " city of Galilee ", it indicates that he is writing for Gentile readers to whom the Jewish land is not very well known. Various critics (cf. Major, *Mission and*

Message of Jesus, pp. 262–3) allege that Luke here contradicts Matthew. While Luke declares that the announcement took place in Nazareth and in his stories assumes throughout that Mary and Joseph were both resident there, it is alleged that Matthew maintains that they lived in Bethlehem and owned a house there. However, it remains a puzzle to us how they can find this in Matthew's narrative. In his description of the announcement to Joseph Matthew makes no mention of the place where it happened. Why could it not have been Nazareth? Nowhere in Matthew i and ii is it alleged that Mary and Joseph originally came from Bethlehem or had a house there. The contention that Matthew and Luke contradict one another is, therefore, unfounded.

² ἐξ οἴκου Δαυείδ—these words have sometimes been taken in conjunction with παρθένον, but without justification, as is shown by the grammatical construction of the sentence. From this it does not, however, follow that Mary was not also of Davidic descent. Verses 32 and 69 of this chapter have no sense unless she is also a descendant of David. That Mary was necessarily of the house of Aaron because this was the case with Elisabeth by no means follows from the statement (verse 36) that she was related to her. For, as Creed admits: " Of course it might be supposed without inconsistency that Mary was in reality of Davidic descent on her father's side and was related to Elisabeth by her mother " (*in loc.*).

³ χαῖρε κεχαριτωμένη—the Vulgate translates this by " *Ave, gratia plena* ". Roman Catholic expositors take this to mean that Mary is full of gifts of grace and accordingly appears between God and man as mediator to dispense gifts. It is, however, clear from the context that Mary is merely the *recipient* of the favour of God in that He had chosen her to become the mother of Jesus. As Bengel pithily remarks (*in loc.*): " Non ut mater gratiae, sed ut filia gratiae " (" not as the mother of grace, but as the daughter of grace ").

The well-known hymn " Ave Maria " was written under the inspiration of these words in verse 28. The first two parts of the hymn date from the earliest times and are purely Biblical. But the third portion, in which the words " Holy Mary, Mother of God, pray for us sinners " occur, was added only in the fifteenth century and in 1568 declared by Pope Pius V to be authoritative (cf. Plummer, *in loc.*).

⁴ These words do not give us any right to elevate Mary practically to divine Mediator as the Roman Catholics do. Yet we realise anew that the crown and glory of all motherhood is apportioned to her. Although she was also a sinner, in need of redemption (she herself calls God her Saviour in verse 47), nevertheless amongst all women the highest honour has been accorded her.

⁵ By καὶ ἰδού the extraordinary character of the announcement is emphasised.

⁶ The name means " The Lord saves " and hence also "the One through whom the Lord saves ". In its various Hebrew forms (Joshua, Jehoshua, Jeshua, etc.) the name was given to many Jewish sons— often as an utterance of the parents' longing that their child might be

the expected Messiah, or at least a leader and champion of Israel, like the great Joshua. Here, however, it is God's command that this name should be given to Christ. Accordingly He will be the real "Redeemer"—the Fulfiller of the age-long expectations of the pious in Israel.

7 Δαυειδ τοῦ πατρὸς αὐτοῦ—these words tell us expressly that Mary was a descendant of David. For how else could David be called the father of Him who was to be born out of her without the agency of a husband? There is here no mention of Joseph, or of her future marriage with him.

8 Where hereafter mention is made of the eternal kingdom of Christ it is obvious that it is not the earthly "house of Jacob" that is meant here, but His people in a spiritual sense.

9 βασιλεία here indicates not a territory but the Lord's activity in kingly rule, His sovereignty to which there shall be no end.

10 The old Latin MS. " b " stands alone in leaving out verse 34. And yet Streeter, Harnack, Luce and others argue, on the ground of this omission and other considerations, that this verse together with a few others that teach the fact of the " virgin birth " are interpolations. However, they have no clear grounds for this. Creed rejects this attempt to exclude the " virgin birth " from the original text of Luke (cf. his arguments, in loc.). Also cf. Major, *The Mission and Message of Jesus*, p. 262.

11 γινώσκω is here used in the sense of the Hebrew יָדַע (yāda‘), as it occurs in Genesis xix. 8, etc., of sexual relationship. The verb is here used in the present tense and not in the future as though Mary were taking an oath to remain a virgin forever, as Roman Catholics and others maintain.

The following words of Plummer still retain their importance: " The words are the avowal of a maiden conscious of her own purity; and they are drawn from her by the strange declaration that she is to have a son before she is married " (in loc.). Nevertheless his last few words should perhaps be amended to " to have a son without the intervention of a man ". For we should note that Mary is here talking not merely of Joseph but of all men. Apparently, therefore, she felt intuitively that the angel means a conception without the intervention of a man, and now she utters her amazement at this and asks the angel how such a miraculous event is to take place. For a brief summary of the various critical explanations of these words, cf. Klostermann, in loc.

12 κληθήσεται is stronger than ἔσται, and indicates that He not only is the Son of God but will also be called and acknowledged as such.

13 υἱὸς θεοῦ without articles, so as to express more strikingly the unique quality of His divine Sonship.

14 οὐκ ἀδυνατήσει . . . πᾶν ῥῆμα. The construction is Semitic, but the double negative serves to emphasise all the more strongly the omnipotence of God.

MARY'S VISIT TO ELISABETH

i. 39-45

39 And Mary arose in these days and went into the hill
40 country[1] with haste, into a city of Judah;[2] and entered into
41 the house of Zacharias and saluted Elisabeth. And it came
to pass, when Elisabeth heard the salutation of Mary, the
babe leaped in her womb; and Elisabeth was filled with the
42 Holy Ghost;[3] and she lifted up her voice with a loud cry, and
said, Blessed *art* thou among women, and blessed *is* the fruit
43 of thy womb.[4] And whence is this to me, that the mother of
44 my Lord should come unto me? For behold, when the voice
of thy salutation came into mine ears, the babe leaped in my
45 womb for joy. And blessed *is* she that believed; for there shall
be a fulfilment of the things which have been spoken to her
from the Lord.

At the end of the day when twilight falls, and again at the
beginning of a new day when the lustre of the rising sun becomes
visible, the beautiful song of the birds is heard in the open. Accordingly it does not surprise us that in the twilight of the Old
Testament dispensation and in the morning splendour of the New
Testament dispensation we hear various persons, favoured by God,
bursting forth in song. It is striking that Luke alone, the educated
and artistically disposed Greek, has committed to writing the songs
of Elisabeth, Mary, Zacharias and Simeon and the hymn of the
angels. " Luke, the artist, has gathered and collected, under the
guidance of the Holy Ghost, the stories which reveal the fact that
when Jesus came into the world poetry expressed itself and music
was reborn " (Morgan, *in loc.*). This fact agrees with Luke's
whole disposition and with his thorough method of research
(verses 1-4) by which he was enabled to ascertain the course of the
whole of the Gospel history from the very beginning. No one but
the sensitive and sympathetic physician, Luke, was so obviously
the right person to collect the data written down in i. 5-ii. 52.
And with what unsurpassed beauty was it granted him to reproduce this!

39, 40 Mary at once reacted to the angel's suggestion (verse
36) that she should visit Elisabeth. That she undertook the
journey fairly soon is evident from the fact that the angel in verse

D

36 declared that the pregnancy of Elisabeth was already in the sixth month, and in verse 56 it is stated that Mary, who returned just before the birth of John (verse 57), had remained with Elisabeth for some three months. The contention of some expositors that Mary's journey to Elisabeth was caused by Joseph's intention to put her away privily, or by the distrustful attitude shown towards her by the inhabitants of Nazareth, is therefore altogether without foundation. According to the context of the story, Mary departed on her journey to Elisabeth within a few days after the visit of the angel, and consequently no one, not even Joseph, could so soon have conceived the idea that she was pregnant. Only after her return from Elisabeth would Joseph have noticed it, and then, when he was engaged in devising plans to put her away privily without bringing her before the tribunal for supposed infidelity, God sent the angel to him to inform him of the truth (Matt. i. 18–25).

So Mary went in the very first place to Elisabeth. Apart from the fact that the angel had, as it were, given her the hint to go to her, it is obvious that she would have felt the urge to go to someone who had also been miraculously blessed. In her own environment she would naturally not yet be able to discuss with anyone the sacred experiences that had befallen her. In Elisabeth, however, she would find an understanding person.

After a journey of some four or five days Mary arrived at the house of Zacharias in a village in the hilly region to the south of Jerusalem.

41, 42 When Mary salutes her, Elisabeth's unborn babe leaps for joy, through the incomprehensible working of the Spirit of God, to salute the Son of God who has been conceived in the virgin's womb by the power of that same Spirit. Though it is a natural phenomenon for an unborn child frequently to make movements during the sixth month of pregnancy, the movement made by him was nevertheless extraordinary. And as Godet remarks: " At the sudden leaping of this being who she knows is compassed about by special blessing, the veil is rent. The Holy Spirit, the prophetic Spirit of the old covenant, seizes her, and she salutes Mary as the mother of the Messiah " (*in loc.*).

Elisabeth is tremendously thrilled by the unexpected and magnificent revelation and calls out excitedly: " Blessed art thou among women! " which is another expression for " Blessed art thou above all other women! "

43–5 Through the supernatural enlightenment of the Holy Ghost Elisabeth recognises in Mary the mother of the promised Redeemer whom she calls " my Lord " (cf. Ps. cx. 1). Joyfully and wholeheartedly she acknowledges that a much greater honour has been conferred on Mary than on her.

But Elisabeth shows no sign of jealousy. In humility of heart she utters her amazement that she is so privileged as to be visited by the mother of her Lord. She rejoices, together with her babe, in the greatness of the coming Redeemer. And she beatifies Mary because she, unlike her own husband, believed what had been promised her and consequently had not been afflicted with dumbness or some other chastisement.

In her salutation and beatification of Mary, Elisabeth is so inspired that we unmistakably hear the sounds of a hymn in these words (cf. Plummer, *in loc.*). Thus she is the first songstress of the dawning new era.

Elisabeth nobly and voluntarily placed herself in the background and acknowledged unreservedly and joyfully that her younger relative had received infinitely more honour than she. The gift of God to herself she accepted in grateful worship. But when she meets Mary, to whom a still greater gift has been given, she does not become jealous or unsympathetic. She humbles herself and sings to the honour of the all-excelling privileged one among women who is to become the Mother of her Lord. Because she was filled with the Holy Ghost, she was capable of such special magnanimity. Whilst jealousy would have darkened her life, her humble attitude opened for her the gates to true, deep and jubilant joy. He who elevates himself is constantly engaged in wrecking his own life. But he who is sincerely humble finds richness of life and happiness.

[1] ἡ ὀρινή was the usual description of the hilly regions of Judaea to the south of Jerusalem, in contrast with the plains (Plummer, *in loc.*).

[2] Ἰούδα; because it is here used in contradistinction with Galilee, Judaea in the narrower sense is meant. Attempts to ascertain precisely which village in Judaea is meant have thus far been unsuccessful. The manner of expression indicates that it was an unimportant place.

[3] ἐπλήσθη πνεύματος ἁγίου ἡ Ἐλισάβετ. No article is used here with πνεῦμα because the reference is to the working of the Holy Ghost that completely inspires and subjugates Elisabeth. This prophetic action of the Spirit differs completely from the outpouring of and the filling with the Holy Ghost on and from Pentecost (Acts ii), seeing that it is only temporary and again recedes.

[4] By these words it is clearly indicated that, although begotten by the Holy Ghost, Jesus, according to His human nature, was really born of the flesh and blood of Mary, and is therefore truly Man.

MARY'S HYMN OF PRAISE

46   And Mary[1] said,
My soul[2] doth magnify the Lord,

47   And my spirit[3] hath rejoiced in God my Saviour.[3]

48   For he hath looked upon the low estate of his handmaiden:
For behold, from henceforth all generations shall call me
blessed.

49   For he that is mighty hath done to me great things;
And holy is his name.[4]

50   And his mercy is unto generations and generations
On them that fear him.

51   He hath shewed[5] strength[6] with his arm;
He hath scattered[7] the proud in the imagination of their
hearts.[8]

52   He hath put down princes from *their* thrones,
And hath exalted them of low degree.

53   The hungry he hath filled with good things;[9]
And the rich he hath sent empty away.

54   He hath holpen Israel his servant,
That he might remember mercy

55   (As he spake unto our fathers)
Toward Abraham and his seed for ever.[10]

56   And Mary abode with her about three months, and returned
unto her house.[11]

Mary began to utter praises not when the angel Gabriel brought her the wonderful tidings, but when a woman like herself called her " mother of my Lord " (verse 43). The message of the angel at once assumed for her a living shape when Elisabeth, in whom the promises of the Lord had already been unmistakably realised, saluted her with beatifications. Her spontaneous reaction to this is to sing this beautiful hymn. From the first word of her hymn of praise in the Vulgate translation, this hymn is known as the " Magnificat ". From the earliest times it has been used in the praises of the Christian church.

In its form as uttered by Mary it is a beautiful lyrical poem. It is remarkable how genuinely Hebrew it is in thought and manner of expression, in extolling praise and in worship. It is almost wholly made up of Old Testament quotations. There is an especially close connection between it and the song of Hannah, the mother of Samuel. Nevertheless the hymn of Mary is essentially different from the triumphal song of Hannah. While Mary sings her happiness with deep humility and holy reserve, Hannah completely surrendered herself to a feeling of personal triumph over her enemies. Where Mary borrowed expressions from the Old Testament, she gives to the consecrated words a deeper meaning and a higher application. The prophets had often done the same with the words of their predecessors under the guidance of the Holy Ghost.

In discussing this hymn of praise, some critics have asked whether Mary had her Old Testament open before her when she uttered the song. They forget that all pious Israelites from their childhood days knew by heart songs from the Old Testament and often sang them in the home circle and at celebrations. Mary was steeped in the poetical literature of her nation, and accordingly her hymn also bears the unmistakable signs of it.

Elisabeth uttered her beatification in great excitement ("she lifted up her voice with a loud cry ", verse 42). Mary's hymn, however, breathes a spirit of greater calm. The deeper the joy, the more restful is the heart. Mary's panegyric is far grander than that of Elisabeth, but more controlled. A regal majesty reigns throughout the hymn of praise. It strikes us that Mary in this hymn does not utter a single direct word in connection with the Son promised to her. Nevertheless she assumes throughout that He has indeed been promised her. Her whole hymn is inspired by this fact.

46-8 This first strophe of the hymn, in which Mary describes her personal emotions and experiences, is marked by a restful, dignified tone. She first sings of the worshipful gratitude of her own heart to God, her Saviour. Then she gives the reason for her rejoicing: God had so richly favoured her, His handmaiden, notwithstanding her humbleness of person (as a simple inhabitant of Nazareth), that from henceforth she will always be called blessed.

49, 50 Here her hymn becomes more animated where she sings of God's glorious deeds of redemption and of His omnipotence and holiness and His mercy continually shown to those that fear Him. To " fear " God means to cherish reverence and respect for Him—not to be afraid, but to honour Him lovingly by avoiding what is contrary to His will and by striving after what pleases Him.

51-3 With these words her hymn reaches its climax, where she sings of the mighty reversal of things which in principle has already been accomplished by the entrance of God upon the course of history and in the life of mankind, through the coming Messiah, her promised Son. In God's choice of two persons of humble life like herself and Elisabeth she sees the powerful revolutionary principle according to which God is going to renew everything through the Messiah. This principle entails a complete reversal of all human opinions of greatness and insignificance. The proud, those who exalt themselves and take no account of God, He puts down—beaten by His mighty arm. The powers that be, oppressors who tyrannise over the poor and lowly, are deprived of their power and high standing, while those who are truly humble are exalted to great things. The hungry, those who realise their own need and yearn for spiritual food, are blessed. But the rich, those who are self-satisfied and proud, are shamed in the imagination of their hearts.

Because this working of God had already commenced in Mary and Elisabeth, and because its continuation is so absolutely assured through the promises concerning the coming Redeemer, Mary throughout uses the past tense in these verses. The reversal in human relationships and existence has already begun and will be perfectly completed. (In the course of the past nineteen centuries these words have already been wonderfully fulfilled. But only at the final Consummation will they find their perfect accomplishment.)

54, 55 In this last strophe of the hymn the song of praise again passes away in calm restfulness. This practically forms its " Amen! " Here she points out that everything of which she has sung earlier in the hymn is the outcome of the fact that God is true to His promises of salvation through a coming Redeemer, made from of old to Abraham and his descendants.

56 After spending about three months with Elisabeth and Zacharias, Mary returned to Nazareth. She and Elisabeth had naturally during this period been meditating together and discussing and rejoicing in the miraculous things promised to them and already in the course of fulfilment. Undoubtedly they also communicated to Zacharias in writing, because he was still deaf and dumb (cf. verse 62), the essentials of Mary's experience. This would explain how he was able to sing the words of verses 67–79 immediately after regaining his speech—he had for several months already meditated over all the wonderful things communicated to him and Mary.

That Mary did not wait before returning until after the birth of John may partly be explained by the fact that she knew that this event would cause a huge concourse of people, and she would naturally prefer not to be there then.

In this hymn of praise Mary sings gloriously of the all-excelling perfections of God: His divine power (verses 49, 51), His holiness (verse 49), His mercy (verse 50), and His faithfulness (verses 54, 55). In the fact that He is engaged in fulfilling His promises concerning the Messiah King and Redeemer, she sees all these divine perfections revealed. For it is only through the incarnation of Jesus that we learn with full certainty to know God in His omnipotence, holiness, mercy and faithfulness. Without this we all would have lived forever in the pitch-dark night of spiritual ignorance. For even the Old Testament revelation gives to us assured knowledge concerning God only in the light of the actual incarnation of Christ.

What Mary sang of God's workings of mercy and power through the dawning of the Messianic times has in every respect become historically true. From the beginning Christ has acted in a revolutionary manner on the life and history of mankind. For without Him individual and social life is based on principles which are totally opposed to the right foundations for true life. As far as His influence has extended, and is still extending, a reversal in that connection is brought about for the redemption of man and society.

---

[1] Instead of Μαριάμ the following have *Elisabeth*: the Old-Latin translations " a ", " b " and the later Italian text " 1 ", a number of MSS. of Irenaeus (*Adv. Haeres.*, iv, 7, 1) and a few other unimportant texts. This comparatively insignificant textual evidence has been used by Creed, Harnack, Blass, Loisy and others to reject the authenticity of the reading (Μαριάμ) of all the existing Greek MSS. and practically all the translations. Some textual critics then defend the reading " Elisabeth ", but the majority maintain that the original reading was merely καὶ εἶπεν (" and she said ") and that, therefore, the hymn of praise should be ascribed to Elisabeth, who was the speaker in the previous verses. The parallels between the " Magnificat " and the song of Hannah are thought to support the ascription of the former, like the latter, to a woman who had become a mother after prolonged childlessness. The textual evidence is, however, too strongly in favour of Μαριάμ. If originally the reading had been only καὶ εἶπεν, why is there no better textual evidence to support it? There is not a single word in the hymn of praise that is not naturally fitting in the mouth of Mary in the circumstances described in verses 39–56. On the other hand, it is extremely improbable that Elisabeth, after her words in verses 42–5, would immediately proceed to sing her own favour and

would declare: " from henceforth all generations shall call me blessed ". Taking everything into consideration, there is no reason whatever for denying the hymn to Mary (for a detailed argument cf. Gresham Machen's classic work, *The Virgin Birth of Christ*, chap. iv).

[2] ψυχή and πνεῦμα are here used synonymously and serve to describe the speaker according to her intrinsic existence. Thus Mary here declares that she whole-heartedly and from the depths of her inner being magnifies and glorifies God.

[3] These words show that there is no room here for the dogma that Mary was immaculately conceived and personally sinless, for she also calls God her Saviour.

[4] καὶ ἅγιον τὸ ὄνομα αὐτοῦ. The last three words, according to general Biblical usage, denote the Lord Himself in the revelation of His divine holiness. ἅγιον is used here not in a moral sense but in the sense of being " exalted " (cf. Klostermann, *in loc.*).

[5] ἐποίησεν. The aorist here and in the sentences that follow should most probably be taken in its ingressive force, and thus would point to the fact that God in His choice of Mary and Elisabeth had already begun the revolutionary reversal of things described here.

[6] κράτος = " power ", an irresistible force, to which all must bow. Here the reference is to an act in which the irresistible power finds expression.

[7] διεσκόρπισεν refers to a struggle in which the enemy is driven apart and scattered. Here mention is made of the acts of God in an anthropomorphic manner, in the regular idiom of the Old Testament (cf. Exod. xv. 6; Ps. xcviii. 1; cxxxvi. 12; Isa. li. 9).

[8] " Heart " is used in the Bible to indicate the pivot of human life in its fullest extent with regard to man's thoughts, desires and emotions.

[9] The reference is not merely or mainly to bodily and material needs but to spiritual hunger.

[10] Not all descendants according to the flesh, but his true seed (John viii. 39, 44, 56; Rom. ix. 7–8)—first of all Christ, and then all who belong to Him (Gal. iii. 16).

[11] For a terse refutation of doubts which have been cast upon the historicity of Mary's visit to Elisabeth we refer our readers to Plummer (digression at i. 56).

THE NATIVITY OF JOHN THE BAPTIST

i. 57–66

57 Now Elisabeth's time was fulfilled that she should be
58 delivered; and she brought forth a son. And her neighbours
   and her kinsfolk heard that the Lord had magnified his
59 mercy towards her; and they rejoiced with her. And it came
   to pass on the eighth day,[1] that they came to circumcise the
   child; and they would have called him Zacharias, after the
60 name of his father. And his mother answered and said, Not
61 so; but he shall be called John.[2] And they said unto her,
62 There is none of thy kindred that is called by this name. And
   they made signs[3] to his father, what he would have him
63 called. And he asked for a writing tablet,[4] and wrote, saying,
64 His name is John. And they marvelled all. And his mouth
   was opened immediately, and his tongue *loosed*, and he spake,
65 blessing God. And fear[5] came on all that dwelt round about
   them: and all these sayings were noised abroad throughout
66 all the hill country of Judaea. And all that heard them laid
   them up in their heart, saying, What then shall this child be?
   For the hand of the Lord was with him.

Less than a year previously it had appeared to the aged
Zacharias and Elisabeth an utter impossibility that their prayers
for a child, uttered in former years when they still had a measure
of hope, would ever be answered. But what is impossible with
man can be made possible through the power of God. And for
this reason their longing is eventually gratified by the birth of
a son.

57, 58 Shortly after Mary's departure the promised son is born
to Zacharias and Elisabeth. Their neighbours and kindred, on
account of the extraordinary occurrence, join in unrestrained rejoicing with the aged couple.

59–61 In accordance with the direction of the Law, his circumcision took place on the eighth day. The neighbours and
kindred who were present then desired to call him after his father,
as was the general Jewish custom (Josephus, *Vita*, i). Elisabeth,
who had in written form (cf. verse 63) found out from her dumb

husband what had happened to him in the temple and what the angel had commanded with regard to the name of the son, firmly refuses to have him called Zacharias and tells them that his name is to be John. Thereupon they raise the objection that no one amongst her kindred is called by that name.

62, 63 Because Elisabeth remains firm in this, they turn to the deaf and dumb Zacharias (" they make signs " to him). After they had handed him a writing tablet (a flat piece of wood covered with a film of wax, on which letters might be traced with a stylos or stiletto, at that time commonly used for occasional writing purposes), he writes on it. He does not write, " We have decided to call him John ", or, " You must call him John ", but, " His name is John ". It is a settled thing. God had through His angel given him this command and therefore his name *is* John and nothing else. This firm attitude of Zacharias as well as that of Elisabeth surprises those present. What could have influenced the aged couple, they must have wondered, to be so firm in insisting that this particular name should be given to the son?

64 After Zacharias's obedience to the command of God the chastisement that had come upon him on account of his unbelief was removed. And immediately he began to praise God with his recovered speech.

65, 66 The extraordinary occurrences in connection with the nativity and naming of John made a deep impression on the people in the surrounding districts, the hilly regions to the south of Jerusalem. Many of them silently wondered and discussed with others what the son was going to become one day. And " the hand of the Lord was with him ", i.e. he was constantly supported by the power of the Lord, who preserved, led and strengthened him so that he might be fitted for his life's work.

" His name is John." These are the key-words in this portion. Throughout the history of the divine revelation, as it is committed to writing in the Holy Scriptures, we see what special value is attached by God to the names given to persons. We think, e.g., of the various names of God Himself (e.g. " I am what I am "), which express so wonderfully His divine perfections and virtues. Abram's name was changed by God to Abraham, Jacob's name to Israel, and so on, because they had to have names with a meaning fitting in better with their circumstances.

It is natural, therefore, that when the New Dispensation was on the point of commencing, the leading characters had to be called by special significant names. Thus we have Zacharias—God remembers His covenant; Elisabeth—God is the absolutely faithful One; John—God is merciful, or the gift of the mercy of God; and finally Jesus—God saves, or the divine Saviour.

[1] By some writers (e.g. Montefiore) it has been asserted that Luke is mistaken here, for, they declare, it was the Jewish custom to give the name just after birth. But even Loisy and Lagrange contend that the name (officially at least) was given only at the circumcision when (as at the baptism of Christian children) the child was incorporated (although as a minor) in the community (cf. Luce, *in loc.*). Some account of name-giving among the Jewish people in general is given by Strack-Billerbeck at i. 59.

[2] The statement by Creed (*in loc.*) and others that the narrative assumes that Elisabeth was also supernaturally informed what the name of the son should be is superfluous and unlikely. It is impossible that Zacharias should not, during the long months, have communicated to his wife (in writing, naturally) the message and commands of the angel. Besides, the amazement of those present should be ascribed not to the fact that Zacharias and Elisabeth were in agreement, but to the remarkable firmness with which both insisted that the son had to be called definitely by that name and by no other.

[3] ἐνένευον. The imperfect tense indicates the continuance of the action. This means that they did not merely beckon to Zacharias but "made signs" to him. From this it appears that he was deaf and dumb. "Communication with a dumb man by means of sign-language had legal validity according to the *halakhah* [Rabbinical legal tradition]" (Strack-Billerbeck, *in loc.*).

[4] πινακίδιον—"The tablets which were used for writing were made of wood, as early as Numbers xvii. 17 f.; Ezck. xxxvii. 16, 20" (Strack-Billerbeck, *in loc.*).

[5] "Fear" also in the sense of "terror", or numinous awe, at the marvels that they had witnessed.

ZACHARIAS'S HYMN OF PRAISE

i. 67–80

67 And his father Zacharias[1] was filled with the Holy Ghost, and prophesied,[2] saying,

68 Blessed *be* the Lord, the God of Israel;
For he hath visited[3] and wrought redemption for his people,

69 And hath raised up a horn[4] of salvation for us
In the house of his servant David[5]

70 (As he spake by the mouth of his holy prophets which have been since the world began),

71 Salvation from our enemies, and from the hand of all that hate us;

72 To shew mercy towards our fathers,
And to remember his holy covenant;

73 The oath which he sware unto Abraham our father,

74 To grant unto us that we being delivered out of the hand of our enemies
Should serve him without fear,

75 In holiness and righteousness before him all our days.

76 Yea and thou, child,[6] shalt be called the prophet of the Most High:
For thou shalt go before the face of the Lord to make ready his ways;

77 To give knowledge of salvation unto his people
In the remission of their sins,[7]

78 Because of the tender mercy[8] of our God,
Whereby the dayspring[9] from on high[10] shall visit us,

79 To shine upon them that sit in darkness and the shadow of death;
To guide our feet into the way of peace.

80 And the child grew,[11] and waxed strong in spirit, and was in the deserts[12] till the day of his shewing unto Israel.

From the first word of the hymn of Zacharias in the Latin translation, it has been since early times called the " Benedictus ". While Mary's hymn of praise is modelled on Hannah's song and the Psalms, we find in Zacharias's song a closer resemblance to the prophetic writings of the Old Testament. The " Magnificat " breathes a regal spirit and the " Benedictus " a sacerdotal one.

The one is as fitting in the mouth of the daughter of David as the other in the mouth of the priest Zacharias.

In this hymn of praise Zacharias, as it were, gathers together the echoes of the Old Testament period and fuses them to a new outpouring of jubilant hope and faith.

There is an intimate connection between the name of his son and the contents of his hymn of praise. He wrote on the tablet, " His name is John ". " John " means " God is merciful ". And Zacharias's whole hymn is practically a song in praise of God's glorious acts of salvation, which are the outcome of His mercy.

The hymn may be divided into two main parts, namely verses 67-75 and verses 76-9.

67 Luke does not state at precisely what period Zacharias uttered the words. Probably it was relatively soon after he regained his speech. After the long months of dumbness and the glorious fulfilment of the promises which God had brought him through Gabriel, it was a most natural thing for him to give utterance in a hymn of praise to his jubilant rejoicing in the goodness of God. Filled with the Holy Ghost, like the prophets of old, he sang the hymn. For this reason it is no ordinary hymn, but one which bears an exceptionally rich and deep significance.

68, 69 He utters the praise of God because after so many centuries He has again visited His people and revealed Himself to them in saving acts. In these two verses he celebrates, in general terms, the salvation which the Lord had already begun to carry out in principle. In the salvation he probably sees a liberation of Israel also from political bonds. But nevertheless the principal meaning of these words, uttered under the inspiration of the Holy Ghost, is salvation from the guilt and power of sin. In verse 69 it is stated that this salvation will be accomplished by means of a Saviour. Just as the power of an animal is, as it were, concentrated in its horn, so all the redeeming power of God that was promised to the house of David will be concentrated in the Messiah-Redeemer. For this reason Christ is here referred to as " a horn of salvation in the house of David ". That Zacharias in this verse does not refer to the birth of John but to the coming Christ (whose nativity, as Zacharias knew after Mary's stay of three months in his house, had already been promised to Mary) is evident *inter alia* from the words " in the house of David ", for John was not a descendant of David, unlike Jesus.

70 This will happen in accordance with the promises of God, uttered by Him through His prophets of old. Edersheim, in his work *Prophecy and History in Relation to the Messiah*, gives more than four hundred Messianic prophecies in the Old Testament. But even apart from all the definite prophecies in it, the whole of the Old Testament points to Christ (cf. Luke xxiv. 27).

71-3a In a typically Old Testament manner the full salvation which God will accomplish through the Messiah is described in earthly political terms. That these words should, however, be taken chiefly in a spiritual sense appears from the words of Zacharias in verses 77–80. In this, therefore, we have an indication given by the Holy Ghost Himself that the Old Testament prophecies and promises regarding Christ are to be taken by us not in a literal and materialist sense but in a spiritual sense. His kingdom is not a kingdom of this world (John xviii. 36).

73b-5 The ultimate aim of redemption from the forces of sin and darkness by Christ is that God should be served by the godly, without hindrance and in righteousness and holiness. Although there may be a reference here to political liberation as well, something far more glorious is meant: the whole-hearted service of the Lord in complete freedom from all bonds of sin, guilt, punishment, curse, Satan and destruction.

76, 77 While Zacharias has thus far sung of the redemption which God has already wrought in principle through the Messiah and will further bring to completion, he refers in these two verses to the part which his son John will play as predecessor of the Messiah. He will go before the face of the Lord to make His ways straight. The ways of the Lord are the paths along which He wishes to come to impart His salvation to man (John i. 23). And because God comes to men whose hearts and inmost natures and attitudes towards life are receptive for His manifested salvation, it follows that John's task as forerunner of Christ will be to bring people to the right attitude through the power of God. This attitude will mainly consist in this, that men will be brought to a realisation and confession of sin and will long and hunger for the Messiah-Redeemer. Thus John will proclaim to his people the arrival of redemption, a redemption which does not consist in external political liberation (at least in the first instance) but in forgiveness of sins. He himself will not accomplish the redemption; the Messiah will do this. John will merely give notice to the people that it is coming and that it takes the form of salvation from the guilt and power of sin through the work of the Messiah. In this manner, then, he will prepare the people for the work of Christ. This preparation was most necessary because the people as a whole (with few exceptions) at that time had an altogether wrong opinion concerning the redemption to be brought about by the Messiah. They regarded the expected Messiah as a worldly ruler whose great task would be to free the people from the yoke of Rome. Thus they took an earthly and material view of the Messianic redemption and had no conception of their own spiritual need—they regarded themselves as the righteous ones and the Romans as " Gentiles " and " dogs " who were to be defeated by the Messiah and driven from the Holy Land. Therefore it was necessary that John, the forerunner of Christ, should summon the people to a realisation of guilt and to a confession of sins, and should make as many of them as possible see that the real redemption needed by them was deliverance from the power of their spiritual enemies—sin and the forces of darkness, so that they might escape from the wrath of God.

78 Zacharias in this verse points to the fount and origin of the stream of blessings of which he spoke in the preceding verses— the tender mercy of God. Clothed in this tender mercy, says Zacharias, the ascending Light, the Messiah, " hath visited us " (A.V.). Thus the fulfilment of the prophecy had already commenced and was already there in principle. The representation of the Messiah as the " dayspring " fits in with the words of Isaiah ix. 2 and lx. 1 and especially with Malachi iv. 2 where God declares: " Unto you that fear my name shall the sun of righteousness arise with healing in his wings."

79 The purpose of the visitation of Christ as the dayspring is to shine on those who are sitting in darkness and in the shadow of death. The original metaphor here refers to a party of travellers who, before reaching their destination, have been overtaken by the darkness of a pitch-black night and are now sitting terrified and powerless and expect any moment to be overwhelmed and killed by wild beasts or enemies. But all at once a bright light appears to show them the way, so that they reach their destination safely where they enjoy rest and peace. These words, therefore, point to the awful darkness and misery prevailing among mankind before the coming of Christ. Powerless, panic-stricken and threatened by deadly enemies, mankind finds itself in black darkness. But through the coming of Christ a bright light appears —the darkness is dispelled and those who avail themselves of His light are able to see clearly the path leading to peace. By the path of peace is meant the way of forgiveness of sins, of reconciliation to God through the redeeming work of Jesus, the Messiah-Redeemer—a way which leads to real peace and safety.

80 To conclude the story of John's nativity, Luke records that the boy grew in body, and waxed strong in the spirit.

Probably from about his twentieth year until the time when he began his public career he remained in the desert parts of Judaea, to the west of the Dead Sea, undergoing preparation for his task.

No more striking description of our Lord's work can be given than that He shines upon us with His divine light and leads us on the path of peace. Out of darkness—the symbol of estrangement from God, of ignorance, impurity and misery—He, the Sun of righteousness, leads us through His work of reconciliation along the way everlasting—the path of light and peace. When Zacharias, under the guidance of the Holy Ghost, uttered his hymn of praise, a terrible spiritual darkness prevailed in the world. Despair and pessimism were the key-note of the inner life of mankind (for a gripping characterisation of those conditions cf. *Five Stages of Greek Religion*, by Prof. Gilbert Murray, chap. iv). Even to-day, wherever the light of Christ has not yet penetrated, there prevails the same spiritual darkness. And notwithstanding all the external show and dynamic power of modern mankind, there is everywhere manifest a weariness of life, a pessimism, as deepest key-note of the inner life of those who live without Christ. Through Christ the estrangement from God, the spiritual ignorance, enslavement to sin and the feeling of futility are replaced by intimate communion with God, by true knowledge of the deepest truths of life, by inner freedom and richness of life—a consciousness of vocation which makes life worth while.

[1] Some critics (e.g. Major, *The Mission and Message of Jesus*, p. 265) allege that the hymn of praise that follows is not fitting in the mouth of Zacharias, because in it there is only an incidental treatment of the work of his son John, while the Messiah occupies a central place in it. This view is, however, mistaken. Zacharias, who as a pious Israelite had already long looked forward to and prayed for the coming of the Messiah, would, especially under the influence of the Holy Ghost, naturally have rejoiced, above all, over the coming of the Messiah— a coming which had already become a reality through the promise to Mary (a promise of which, as we have already seen, he had undoubtedly been informed). After he had, as it were, been cut off from his fellow-men for so many months as a deaf and dumb person and thus had special opportunities for deepened spiritual reflection on all the miraculous things that God had brought upon him and his wife and later on also upon Mary, the words of the hymn of praise are just what we might expect of him. Purified by these deep experiences and enlightened by the Holy Ghost, he saw the coming of the

Messiah and the preparatory nature of the work of John in the right perspective.

² To prophesy (προφητεύειν) does not merely mean to make predictions, but to speak as the mouthpiece of God, to proclaim His counsel, in which predictions might or might not be included.

³ ἐπεσκέψατο—the prophetic past tense (as in Old Testament Hebrew), to express the certainty of the matter and also the fact that it had already commenced.

⁴ The metaphor of a " horn " has no connection with the horns of the altar or of the soldier's helmet, but with those of a bull. It therefore symbolises not safety and dignity, in the first place, but power. " The pictorial expression *qeren*, a symbol of strength in the Old Testament (LXX κέρας), has also remained current in Rabbinical Hebrew " (Strack-Billerbeck, *in loc.*).

⁵ These words prove that Zacharias knew Mary to be a descendant of David, for there is no reference to Joseph here. When Mary was with Zacharias and Elisabeth, she was not yet married to Joseph, and they had as yet no assurance that he would not put her away.

⁶ καὶ σὺ δέ, παιδίον. By καὶ and δέ connection is indicated, but also contrast. From this it appears that in the previous verses there was no question of John, but of the Messiah to whom he stands in a certain relation, but only as forerunner. By merely calling him " child " and not " my child ", Zacharias shows that in the light of John's high vocation he has put into the background the fact of his personal relation to him.

⁷ ἐν ἀφέσει ἁμαρτιῶν αὐτῶν should, according to the context, be taken together with σωτηρίας (Plummer, *in loc.*).

⁸ σπλάγχνα really means " entrails " and thus indicates the profound depth of the mercy: in Hebrew idiom the affections are seated not in the heart (as in our speech) but in the bowels.

⁹ ἀνατολή refers to the sprouting of grass or to the rising of the sun. But from verse 79 it appears that it has a concrete meaning here, and in conjunction with Malachi iv. 2 and Isaiah lx. 1-2 it refers to Christ, the Sun of righteousness (Creed, *in loc.*). " In the LXX ἀνατολή is a rendering of Hebrew *tsemach*, " branch ", " shoot ", " sprout ". Since *tsemach* was accepted by the Synagogue as a Messianic title, in accordance with Zechariah iii. 8, vi. 12, ἀνατολή in Luke. i. 78 is also intended to denote the Messiah " (Strack-Billerbeck, *in loc.*).

¹⁰ ἐπεσκέψατο (aorist) is here probably the original reading, although many authorities have the future ἐπισκέψεται, which is the reading followed by the R.V.

¹¹ ηὔξανεν—the imperfect indicates the progressive growth (here in a physical sense).

¹² ἐν ταῖς ἐρήμοις. The plural indicates that he did not continually remain in the same place. It is sometimes alleged that John was influenced by the sect of the Essenes that was also somewhere in the deserts of Judaea, probably near the Dead Sea. This cannot,

however, be proved. On the contrary, John is essentially different from the Essenes: he preached the coming of Christ, while they wanted to have nothing to do with Him; he strove to purify his fellow-countrymen from their errors and sins, while they constantly avoided society; he preached social righteousness, while they were in favour of rigid seclusion and asceticism as the road to redemption.

THE NATIVITY OF JESUS

1 Now it came to pass in those days, there went out a decree[1] from Caesar Augustus, that all the world[2] should be enrolled.
2 This was the first[3] enrolment made when Quirinius was
3 governor of Syria.[4] And all went to enrol themselves, every
4 one to his own city.[5] And Joseph also went up from Galilee, out of the city of Nazareth, into Judaea, to the city of David, which is called Bethlehem, because he was of the house and
5 family of David; to enrol himself with Mary, who was
6 betrothed to him,[6] being great with child.[7] And it came to pass, while they were there, the days were fulfilled that she
7 should be delivered. And she brought forth her firstborn[8] son; and she wrapped him in swaddling clothes, and laid him in a manger,[9] because there was no room for them in the inn.

Throughout the centuries God had so led the course of history that everything was now prepared for the coming of His Son. The preparatory Old Testament revelation had been completed long ago; the weary, longing spirit of mankind was in dire need of His coming; His forerunner, John, had already been born; the "fulness of time" had arrived. And at last the promised Redeemer, whose coming had been looked forward to with so much heartfelt yearning, is born. In a few verses—written simply, in a matter-of-fact and natural way—Luke here relates the tremendous and all-important event. The extreme simplicity of the narrative forms the strongest contrast to the stupendous significance of the occurrence that is recounted.

1-3 Here Luke indicates the historical circumstances that brought Joseph and Mary to Bethlehem. Caesar Augustus had decreed that all the world, i.e. the whole of the Roman Empire, should be taxed. This Caesar reigned from 30 B.C. to 19th August, A.D. 14. After he had, by political astuteness and military strength, put an end to the terrible civil wars which had raged for many years throughout the Roman world and to all resistance that was offered to him, he reigned for forty-four years as absolute monarch over the Roman Empire. Through a peaceful and mild rule he gave to the world a period of unprecedented outward calm and to his huge empire a permanent organisation which

99

afterwards facilitated the spread of Christianity. In this, and also in the fact that through his command (verse 1) the prophecy of Micah v. 1 was fulfilled, he was an instrument in the all-guiding hand of God. Ere long, however, the successors to this Roman emperor (e.g. Nero) were to act most violently, as instruments in the power of the Evil One, against the Christian church, but even then still under the permissive will of God.

In such a census as had been commanded by Augustus the name, occupation, property and kindred had to be entered in the public registers. In this instance the census probably took place with a view to the levying of taxes. The Jews were exempted from military service, but were at that time tributary to the Romans, although they nominally had their own king, Herod the Great.

Luke describes this taxing as " the first " and states that it took place when Quirinius was governor of Syria. He calls it " the first enrolment " to distinguish it from the well-known enrolment in A.D. 6 of which he makes mention in Acts v. 37. Of this " first enrolment " we have no other direct mention outside the New Testament. There is, however, no cogent reason why doubt should be cast on Luke here. There is inscriptional evidence. Quirinius was governor of Syria for some time in the first decade B.C. as well as from A.D. 6 to 9.

The genuineness of the statement that everyone had to go into his own city to be enrolled has also been strikingly confirmed. It was a characteristic feature of Augustus's action towards a subject people that he gave every consideration to their national customs. Especially since he had the enrolment made through Herod, who ruled as king of the Jews, it goes without saying that the Jewish custom was followed to let the inhabitants go to their original native city for the taxings.

4, 5 Thus it came about that Joseph, who was of the house of David, had to go to Bethlehem. Here David had been born about a thousand years previously. Originally the town had been called Efratha (Gen. xxxv. 19). At the present time the place is called Beth-Lahm and is inhabited by about eight thousand people— mostly Christians. It is situated about six miles to the south of Jerusalem.

That Joseph, a carpenter, knew his Davidic lineage and could prove it is something quite natural. The Jews from earliest times kept their genealogical tables in order with amazing fidelity.

At a Roman census a woman also had to pay taxes, but it was not necessary for her to go and do so in person. There were, however, several considerations that made it necessary for Joseph to take Mary with him to Bethlehem. Because the time was already close at hand when she was to be delivered of her first-born, Joseph did not want to leave her behind in Nazareth, since she would probably, when the child came to be born, be treated with insult and distrust, as the people knew that she had been married to Joseph for considerably less than nine months (cf. i. 56). It is also possible that Joseph and Mary knew that according to Micah v. 1 the Messiah would be born in Bethlehem and that both accordingly decided to go there. At that time it was generally accepted among the religious Jews that the promised Redeemer was to be born in Bethlehem. In Micah v. 1 this is expressly foretold. The fact that, according to Matthew ii. 22, Joseph intended to return from Egypt to Judaea, and only after the warning by the angel decided to go to Nazareth, also indicates that Joseph and Mary knew that the Messiah was to come from Bethlehem.

Luke still speaks of Mary as " betrothed " to Joseph, although it appears in Matthew that Joseph had already married her (after her return from Elisabeth). He does this to show that although they were already married they were still all the time living merely as espoused persons (Matt. i. 25) and that she was pregnant not through him but through the overshadowing of the Holy Ghost.

6, 7 On account of the great concourse of people who had come to Bethlehem by reason of the taxing, there was no room for them in the inn. And although Mary's critical situation was clear to all, no one gave up accommodation to her and Joseph. The result was that they had to take up their lodging in a " stable ", a place where animals were kept. The early church father, Justin Martyr (c. A.D. 150), states that this " stable " was a cave. About A.D. 330 Constantine the Great caused a church to be built over this cave, which according to some experts was most probably the real place of the nativity. Justinian, some time later, rebuilt this as a more beautiful building, and the church which to-day still stands over the cave is mainly the same as the one erected there at that time, about one thousand six hundred years ago.

These two verses, then, proclaim that at last there had taken place the greatest and most glorious event in the whole history of mankind—the Redeemer was born, the Son of God became Man, so as to be able to become the Saviour of the world. He had left the glory of the Father and humbled Himself to be born as a human child in the most lowly circumstances. And . . . He was laid in a manger.

Although the Christian church commemorates the birth of Jesus on 25th December, we do not know for certain on what day the Saviour was born. The Bible does not give us any data concerning this, and also in the writings of the first centuries A.D. we find no definite indication as to the day on which He was born. We also do not know why the church specially chose 25th December as the day for commemorating the birth of Jesus. Some are of the opinion that the idea was to supplant the pagan Mithras birth-feast by a purely Christian celebration. Christmas was for the first time celebrated in Rome in 354, in Constantinople in 379, and in Antioch in 388. Since then it has found general acceptance in Christendom.

Whether 25th December is really the birth-date of Jesus, as some people still maintain, or not makes no essential difference to the significance of the day to all believers throughout the length and breadth of the world. For it is the great event itself that is commemorated and not the day as such.

The fact that Luke gives no particulars concerning the exact date of Jesus' nativity is an example of the fact already noticed, that the Gospel was not written as an ordinary complete biography, but as a " preaching " concerning Christ as Redeemer and Lord.

What the inhabitants of Bethlehem did in their ignorance is done by many to-day in wilful indifference—they refuse to make room for the Son of God. They give no place to Him in their feelings, their affections, their thoughts, their views of life, their wishes, their decisions, their actions, or their daily conduct. And thus they deny themselves the greatest privilege of all and incur the greatest loss to their lives.

---

[1] δόγμα is derived from δοκεῖν, " to seem ", " to think ", " to decide ", and may mean: opinion, philosophical view, a decision or ordinance, a command or decree. The nature of a δόγμα is according to the authority behind it. Here the meaning is, therefore, an authoritative decree (of the emperor).

[2] πᾶσαν τὴν οἰκουμένην (" all the inhabited world ") was the common expression used to signify the whole of the Roman Empire (Creed, in loc.).

[3] πρώτη distinguishes this enrolment from the one mentioned by Luke in Acts v. 37 (the same as is mentioned by Josephus). The fact that Luke does not there call it " the second enrolment " but merely " the enrolment " points to the fact that this enrolment (probably on account of the disturbances attending it, etc.) was the enrolment most commonly known. That Luke should confuse the census of A.D. 6 with the one mentioned by him in verse 2, as is alleged, e.g., by Guignebert (Jesus, p. 101), is impossible, for Luke, by calling this enrolment " the

first " or " the former ", clearly distinguishes it, from the later one which he mentions in Acts v. 37.

⁴ ἡγεμονεύοντος τῆς Συρίας Κυρηνίου does not necessarily mean that Quirinius was *governor* or *legate* over Syria, but only that he was invested with official authority (Plummer, *in loc.*). The possibility is thus left open that, while some other person was at that time the *legate* over Syria, Quirinius was there at the same time to carry out a certain official charge. That such was indeed the case appears from the data to which we have already referred (cf. also C. M. Cobern, *The New Archaeological Discoveries*, p. 538). The suggestion of J. W. Jack and B. S. Easton that *Saturninus* should be read here instead of *Quirinius* is unnecessary. (Saturninus was legate of Syria from 8 to 6 B.C.)

⁵ Cf. the parallel instance in Egypt, discussed by Deissman, *Light from the Ancient East*, pp. 270 ff.

⁶ A few versions (the Old Latin and the Sinaitic Syriac) read here only τῇ γυναικὶ αὐτοῦ without τῇ ἐμνηστευμένη αὐτῷ. J. Weiss, E. Klostermann, Creed and others accept this reading as original, and some (e.g. J. Weiss) allege that by these words our Lord's conception by the Holy Ghost is denied. The textual-critical evidence in favour of τῇ ἐμνηστευμένη αὐτῷ is, however, overpowering. The longer reading on which the A.V. (" his espoused wife") is based is a fusion of the other two readings. The reason why Luke still describes Mary as " betrothed " to Joseph has already been given by us in the exposition at verse 5.

⁷ οὔσῃ ἐγκύῳ. The participle οὔσῃ denotes not a mere fact, but the reason for what has been previously mentioned (Plummer, *in loc.*). Joseph took Mary with him *because* she was great with child (cf. our exposition at verse 5).

⁸ πρωτότοκον most naturally suggests that she had more children later on. The Gospels also mention the fact that Jesus had brothers and sisters (Matt. xiii. 55, 56; John vii. 35, etc.) and even give the names of his brothers (James, Joses, Simon and Judas, cf. Matt. xiii. 55). The Roman Catholic opinion that Mary bore no further children cannot be maintained, for then we should have expected here μονογενῆ (only-begotten) and not πρωτότοκον (first-born).

⁹ Th. Zahn writes in connection with these words: " That Mary herself, without the assistance of other women (which could not have remained unmentioned) wrapped her new-born child in swaddling clothes, and that she cradled Him in a manger, are both statements which give the impression of great poverty, in which the King's Son was born " (*in loc.*). " The birth itself is mentioned in the briefest and most general manner, so different from what we find later [in the Apocryphal Gospels] " (Klostermann, *in loc.*).

SPECIAL NOTE

THE ENROLMENT UNDER AUGUSTUS

Against the historical genuineness of Luke's statements concerning the enrolment numerous objections have been raised. E. Schürer, at the beginning of the present century, mentioned the following objections: (1) History knows nothing about a general imperial census in the time of Caesar Augustus. (2) Joseph could not be compelled by a Roman enrolment decree to travel to Bethlehem, and still less Mary to accompany him. (3) A Roman census could not be held in Palestine during the reign of King Herod. (4) Josephus knows nothing about such a census and regards the census of A.D. 6 or 7 as an innovation which caused Jewish resistance. (5) A census held under Quirinius could not take place in the time of Herod, since Quirinius was not yet governor of Syria at the time.

Since the time when the trustworthiness of Luke's data was called in question by Schürer much new light has been thrown on the matter, especially in the works of W. M. Ramsay (*Was Christ Born in Bethlehem?*, *The Bearing of Recent Discoveries on the Trustworthiness of the New Testament*); A. Deissmann (*Licht vom Osten*, Eng. trans. *Light from the Ancient East*); C. M. Cobern (*The New Archaeological Discoveries*); W. Lodder (*Die Schätzung des Quirinius bei Flavius Josephus*, and his later work *Historische Nevenfiguren uit het Nieuwe Testament*, 1938); H. Holzmeister (*Chronologia Vitae Christi*, 1933); G. J. D. Aalders (*Het Romeinsche imperium en het Nieuwe Testament*, 1938); Th. Zahn (especially *Grundriss der Geschichte des Lebens Jesu*, 1928).

In the light of more recent research we give the following brief answers to the five objections of E. Schürer (which are still the main objections brought, as, e.g., by Creed, *in loc.*) against Luke's statements:

(1) Although no express mention of this enrolment has been found outside the New Testament and Christian writers, this does not by any means prove that Luke's statement is incorrect. For numerous important events are mentioned, e.g. in the works of Josephus, which are not mentioned elsewhere and yet no one will allege that all such statements of his are false. Why, then, in the case of Luke, who has been proved to be throughout more trustworthy than Josephus, should a confirmation of his statements first have to be found in the works of Josephus or elsewhere before accepting them as the truth? A general enrolment such as described by Luke is historically very probable because it is a well-known fact that Augustus was working throughout for a more effective centralisation and organisation of his empire. For this purpose an enrolment would be necessary. W. M. Ramsay and others have shown that during the first century A.D. a census was held regularly every fourteen years or so, and that one was probably held at the time of the birth of Jesus.

(2) A notice of C. Vibius Maximus, a prefect of Egypt (A.D. 104), which has been discovered (A. Deissmann, *Light from the Ancient East*, pp. 270 ff.) shows that the manner of enrolment described by Luke agrees with what was also the custom in Egypt. All who are away from home are instructed to return to their ordinary abodes for the enrolment. In our statement at verse 5 we have already pointed out the reasons why Mary accompanied Joseph.

(3) Here, also, Schürer is in error. For it is generally acknowledged that Herod the Great was not king over Palestine in the full sense of the word. He was only a vassal king under overlordship of the emperor. Josephus even relates that during the last years of his reign Augustus demanded an oath of fidelity from all Jews (cf. W. Manson, *in loc.*). It is, therefore, quite natural that he also decreed a general taxing of the inhabitants of Palestine. He would, however, have left Herod at liberty to arrange the census according to the acknowledged Jewish customs. Especially during the last months of Herod's rule it was very natural for Augustus to have decreed that an enrolment should be held also in Palestine, since on account of Herod's age and illness it was clear to him that he was not going to live long and that preparations should be made in connection with the future rule of Palestine (cf. Plummer, *in loc.*).

(4) Although Josephus makes mention of the taxing during the time (about A.D. 6) when Quirinius was governor of Syria after Herod's death (*Antiquities*, xviii), he nowhere states that this was the first census. He does, however, allege that it created a disturbance among the Jews. This may nevertheless be explained from the fact that, while the census in the time of Herod was held according to Jewish customs because Augustus was still leaving to Herod a great measure of freedom in the management of affairs in Palestine, this later taxing (shortly after Palestine had come under direct Roman rule) was much more a form of Roman suppression and domination. This is clearly evident from the description of it given by Josephus (*Antiquities*, xviii, 1). It was for this reason that it gave rise to opposition, and not because it was the first taxing (as is wrongly maintained by Guignebert, *Jesus*, p. 100).

(5) It must, indeed, be admitted that Quirinius became governor in A.D. 6 (if the statement by Josephus in this connection is correct). But it is fairly generally accepted that outside the New Testament there are proofs enough that Quirinius had already at an earlier period been acting in an official capacity in Syria (cf., e.g., Deissmann, *op. cit.*, pp. 5–6). Dr. Major, in *The Mission and Message of Jesus* (p. 267), admits that " a critical examination of the evidence supports the view that Quirinius occupied an official position in Syria at this earlier date ".

" The evidence for two Syrian governorships of Quirinius," says Professor W. M. Calder (*Classical Review*, vol. 41, 1927, p. 151), " is conclusive (Lapis Tiburtinus and Lapis Venetus); the evidence for a census in Judaea during his first governorship is Luke ii. 1–5, taken in conjunction with Matthew ii, and supported by the analogy of Kietis in A.D. 36 (Tacitus, *Annals*, vi, 41)." (Note how a classical scholar, unlike many theologians, regards the evangelists as respectable historical authorities in their own right!) It is not certain whether Quirinius's earlier governorship should be dated between 10 and 7 B.C. or from 3 to 2 B.C. The former date was maintained by Ramsay, who argued that during these years Quirinius acted as extraordinary imperial legate for certain military purposes in the joint province of Syria and Cilicia, while the civil governor was Sentius Saturninus— during whose period of office (8–6 B.C.) Tertullian informs us that Christ was born (*Adv. Marc.*, iv, 19). In that case the census will have been instituted during Quirinius's legateship, though probably not completed (especially in Palestine) until a year or two afterwards. If his first governorship of Syria was from 3 to 2 B.C., it was not an extra-ordinary but a regular appointment, and Luke's meaning will be that the census, begun a year or two earlier (while Herod the Great, who died in 4 B.C., was yet alive), was completed and the returns sent to Rome during his governorship. In neither case need Quirinius have actually held the census, nor does Luke say that he did; his mention of Quirinius is simply intended to indicate the date of the census, and consequently of the Holy Nativity. See further F. G. Kenyon, *Classical Review*, vol. 7 (1893), p. 110; T. Corbishley, *Klio*, vol. 29 (1936), pp. 81 ff.

In recent times the following argument is also adduced against the trustworthiness of Luke's data. A number of inscriptions, dated by Creed and others as from the period 7–6 B.C., show that, while the imperial government was in possession of lists with the names of the Roman citizens in the province of Cyrene, they did not possess lists of the names of the Greek inhabitants. This would go to prove, it is alleged (Creed, *St. Luke*, p. 29), that there was no imperial decree to have all the inhabitants of the empire taxed. But such reasoning is far-fetched. That they did possess lists of the names of the Roman citizens points to the fact that there had indeed been a census. Why there were no lists of the names of the Greek inhabitants we are unable to explain in view of the meagre data at our disposal. In any case, we cannot infer from this that the census as related by Luke did not take place.

Taking all facts into consideration, we may confidently assert that no one has yet succeeded in *proving* that Luke is mistaken. On the contrary, according as our knowledge of the historical circumstances of those times has increased, the accuracy and trustworthiness of Luke's statements have become more clearly evident.

SPECIAL NOTE

THE VIRGIN BIRTH

Right through the centuries until practically the beginning of the nineteenth century the whole Christian church accepted the fact that Jesus was born of a virgin without the intervention of a man. And it was taken up in all the great confessions of the church. Thus the words of the Apostolic Confession of Faith of the universal Christian church had on innumerable occasions resounded across the world ever since the earliest times: " I believe . . . in Jesus Christ . . . conceived by the Holy Ghost, born of the Virgin Mary." And these words found (and still find) a deep echo in the heart of every regenerated child of God.

The conviction that Jesus was born of a virgin who had been over-shadowed by the Holy Ghost was not a later development of Christian thought, but existed from the beginning. And in the church of the first centuries there were only two inferior and degenerate sects that denied the fact of the virgin birth—those Gnostics who denied it because they also denied His Birth from a woman and His true humanity; and the Ebionites who denied His divinity.

But although the whole of Christian tradition is so unanimous about it, many modernists (and even a few writers of fairly conservative view-point) have in our day attacked the belief in it and have tried to over-throw it. As a rule they argue as follows. In the New Testament the story of the virgin birth is found only in Matthew and Luke; Mark and John do not mention it at all and the rest of the New Testament is also silent about it; in the Gospels Jesus is frequently mentioned as the son of Joseph and Mary; and even Matthew and Luke, it is alleged, often contradict one another in their stories of the nativity. They then ascribe the origin of the belief in the virgin birth to what is called by them a wrong application of Old Testament prophecies such as Isaiah vii. 14 or to the influence of pagan myths.

In our exposition of Luke i and ii we have already drawn attention to the baselessness of many of these objections, so that we shall here limit ourselves to a brief treatment of those not dealt with formerly.

Instead of Matthew and Luke really contradicting one another in this matter (as is alleged), we find on carefully comparing the two Gospels that, although they have evidently drawn their data from various sources (Matthew from a source or sources reproducing the events from the viewpoint of Joseph and his family, and Luke from a source or sources reproducing the history from the standpoint of Mary), they are really in agreement on all the main points and further supplement and explain one another. Thus both state that Jesus was born during the last days of Herod; that celestial messengers announced His impending birth; that He was conceived by the overshadowing of the

Holy Ghost; that His mother was a virgin; that Mary was betrothed to Joseph, a man of the house of David; that the nativity took place at Bethlehem; and that God had sent angelic messengers to announce His coming as the Redeemer, and for this reason ordained that He should be named Jesus.

What powerful and impressive evidence is unanimously borne by these two Gospels to the fact that Jesus as the Holy Son of God was born of a virgin!

How trivial are the seeming contradictions (which on closer investigation all disappear) in comparison with the unambiguous announcement by Matthew and Luke of the virgin birth!

Should any one ask why Mark does not mention the fact that Jesus was conceived of the Holy Ghost, we may just as well ask why he does not describe Jesus' birth, for this is also omitted by him. It is quite arbitrary to interpret the fact that Mark makes no mention of the virgin birth as an argument against its actual occurrence. Mark omits many other particulars which are described in the other Gospels. He is concerned to record in writing the primitive apostolic preaching (particularly as publicly announced by Peter), in which the birth of Christ, and especially the peculiarly holy, private and intimate circumstances attending it, found no place. John is more concerned with the eternal pre-existence of the Divine Word who became flesh, and while he does not enlarge on the manner of the incarnation, his language reflects the fact of the virgin birth.

But although in the other New Testament books the fact of the virgin birth is not expressly mentioned, it is nevertheless assumed throughout as a recognised fact. Just consider the numerous expressions in the Gospel of John that point to the fact that Jesus is the Son of God who descended from heaven. Or take Paul's words in Romans v where he calls Christ the new Head of reborn humanity, and writes in 1 Corinthians xv. 47: " The first man is of the earth, earthy: the second man is of heaven " (cf. also Gal. iv. 4 " When the fulness of the time came, God sent forth his Son, born of a woman "). Never could such things have been written concerning Jesus if He had not come into the world in some such manner as is so clearly described by Matthew and Luke. " He came from God, all the apostles believed, in a *sense* in which no other came; does it not follow that He came in a *way* in which no other came? " (James Denney, *Studies in Theology*, p. 64).

In connection with the two theories mentioned, as to how the belief in the virgin birth might have originated, no single fact has as yet been adduced to prove either. On the contrary, the supporters of these theories continue to contradict to and to cancel each other out, thereby revealing their inability to refute the historical fact of the virgin birth. The only reason why they have recourse to their contradictory theories is that as a result of subjective considerations they are unwilling to believe in such a miraculous event. He, however, who believes in the Almighty Creator and knows that God came in Christ to the world to save doomed humanity, knows that the virgin birth is not only a historical reality, but that it obviously had to happen thus that the Son of God who had chosen for the sake of guilty humanity to live on earth in humbled human form, to suffer and to die, was conceived of the Holy Ghost and born of the virgin—truly God and truly Man—as our Substitute and divine Redeemer. [1]

[1] It is, of course, possible to believe in the incarnation without believing in the virgin birth, just as it is possible to believe in the virgin birth, as Muslims do, without believing in the incarnation. But it is most natural that a supernatural event—the incarnation—should take place in a supernatural way—the virgin birth—and that it did so take place is the testimony of Scripture and of the historic Christian faith. For a detailed refutation of all objections against the historical fact of the virgin birth we refer our readers to James Orr, *The Virgin Birth*; J. Gresham Machen, *The Virgin Birth of Christ*; and Douglas Edwards, *The Virgin Birth in History and Faith*.

THE SHEPHERDS OF BETHLEHEM

8 And there were shepherds[1] in the same country abiding in
9 the field, and keeping[2] watch by night over their flock. And
an angel of the Lord stood by them, and the glory[3] of the
Lord shone round about them: and they were sore afraid.
10 And the angel said unto them, Be not afraid; for behold, I
bring you good tidings of great joy which shall be to all the
11 people: for there is born to you this day in the city of David
12 a Saviour, which is[4] Christ the Lord. And this *is* the sign
unto you; Ye shall find a babe wrapped in swaddling clothes,
13 and lying in a manger. And suddenly there was with the
angel a multitude of the heavenly host praising God, and
saying,
14 Glory to God in the highest,
And on earth peace among men in whom he is well
pleased.[5]
15 And it came to pass, when the angels went away from
them into heaven, the shepherds said one to another, Let us
now go even unto Bethlehem, and see this thing that is come
16 to pass, which the Lord hath made known unto us. And they
came with haste, and found both Mary and Joseph, and the
17 babe lying in the manger. And when they saw it, they made
known concerning the saying which was spoken to them
18 about this child. And all that heard it wondered at the
19 things which were spoken unto them by the shepherds. But
Mary kept all these sayings, pondering them in her heart.
20 And the shepherds returned, glorifying and praising God for
all the things that they had heard and seen, even as it was
spoken unto them.

This story excels by reason of its unaffected simplicity. In it we
hear throughout the sound of sober, historical truth. It is like a
charming idyll. But although it may claim poetical beauty, it is
by no means merely the product of poetical imagination or the
forming of legends. Its reserved sobriety forms a sharp contrast to
all apocryphal and legendary versions of the occurrences in later
times. All attempts made to explain the narrative of the shepherds
as an imitation of extra-Biblical stories have failed. In this narrative
Luke recounts in a sober and life-like manner, events of a beautiful
and miraculous nature, but at the same time actual history.

After the event of universal and eternal significance had taken place—the incarnation of the Son of God—we are not surprised that God should announce and illuminate it by means of celestial beings and miraculous phenomena, although Christ was born in humble circumstances. But it is noteworthy that these heavenly visions and miracles were not given to the world as a whole, but to a small group of simple shepherds and to a few wise men from the East (Matt. ii). All of this fits in perfectly with the course of the revelation and work of redemption of God through Christ Jesus.

8 Somewhere in the fields near Bethlehem, where David many centuries before had also kept sheep (1 Sam. xvii. 34, 35), a small group of shepherds were keeping watch over their sheep. Apparently they had driven their separate flocks together in the open and were keeping watch during the night over the collected flock.

9 To this assembled group of simple shepherds, who were probably pious men who also longed for the coming of the promised Messiah, there suddenly appeared an angel of the Lord. In addition the radiating glory of God's majesty became visible to them as it had appeared to Moses at the burning bush, to the Israelites in the pillar of fire in the desert, and to the worshippers in the tabernacle or temple, or as it would later on become visible to the three disciples on the mountain of transfiguration. Overcome by the unexpected and supernatural occurrence, fear came upon the shepherds.

10, 11 But again the first words of the celestial being are: "Fear not!" While it is natural that man should be afraid when the invisible, the unknown, suddenly becomes visible to him, the angel, now that Christ has been born, comes with the words: "Fear not!" He does not, however, leave it at that, but gives the reason why they need have no fear. He brings to them the glorious tidings that in Bethlehem, the city of David, on that day, the promised Messiah has at length been born. The hope of the centuries has been fulfilled. For this reason the tidings are joyful to them and to all the people—to all who have looked forward to His coming, to every true member of the people of God. He who has been born is "the Saviour", the One who saves from all dangers, need, sin, and death, who safeguards against all disasters and destruction, and who gives blessedness in the fullest sense of the word. But He is also "Christ, the Lord", the Anointed One, the Messiah of God who is also God Himself. The name "Christ" refers to Him as the Fulfiller of the promises of God and as the One who has been anointed by God as the Great Prophet, Priest and King —the divine Saviour. And as such He Himself is also "the Lord".

12 The angel does not expressly command them to go to the Child, but takes it for granted that they will. However, he informs them how they may find out who the Child is—they will find Him, not surrounded by splendour and outward glory, but as a little Child wrapped in swaddling clothes and lying in a manger. He gives them this sign, not in order that they may through this be able to believe the truth of his words (the humble circumstances in which the Child finds Himself would perhaps have exactly the opposite effect); but they already believe what has been told them, and now he merely explains how they may recognise Him. No other new-born babe in Bethlehem would be lying in a manger like this.

13 Coming from the depths of the invisible world of celestial beings, there is all at once a great host of angels with the angel who brought the tidings. It is their heavenly calling and pleasure to glorify God continually. And now also they praise Him there around the group of shepherds chosen by God to be the beholders of this celestial glory.

14 In words intelligible to the shepherds (see at i. 13–25) the host of angels sing a hymn of praise on the nature, the significance and the consequences of the event concerning which the heavenly messenger brought tidings to the shepherds:

" Glory to God in the highest,
  And on earth peace,
  Among men who are the objects of God's good pleasure! "

What has happened, the birth of the Redeemer, is the outcome and revelation of the glory of God, for in the coming of Christ the zenith of the divine Self-revelation has been reached. Therefore to God belongs the honour and the glory and to Him who is in highest heaven all praise should be accorded for the event.

The birth of the Christ bears the richest significance to the world—it brings peace, real peace on earth. When Christ was born, some form of external peace (the " pax Romana ") did prevail. But, as was declared by Epictetus, the pagan thinker of the first century, " while the emperor may give peace from war on land and sea, he is unable to give peace from passion, grief and envy. He cannot give peace of heart, for which man yearns more than even for outward peace ". Through the coming of Christ, however, as the angels sing, true peace will come on earth. Here in the first place is meant peace with God and a peace given by God through Christ. And when the inner harmony is there because the human soul has peace with its Lord, peace also spontaneously comes about in mutual relations between human beings.

It is the work of Christ to bring peace into all human relations—in man's relation to God, to himself (his own feelings, desires, and the like), to his life's circumstances (calamities and trials), and to his fellow-men. According as Christ is honoured and is given admission to human lives, to that extent the peace on earth, which He came to bring, becomes a glorious actuality. In so far as people live outside Him, the earth remains in a state of disorder and strife without real peace.

The third phrase of the song should probably read: " among men who are the objects (or recipients) of God's good pleasure "— not " good will toward men " (A.V., rendering an inferior text), nor " among men in whom he is well pleased " (the attempt of the R.V. to render the better text), nor yet " among men of good will" (a popular modern phrase). The good pleasure or good will proceeds from God, not men. The meaning is that peace on earth will in the highest instance become a reality among those who are blessed by the good-will and gracious favour of God, those redeemed in Christ, those ordained to full salvation as children of God.

15 The host of angels had appeared unexpectedly and suddenly, but (as is indicated by the original Greek) they departed gradually so that the shepherds could see them ascending to heaven. By this means they could better realise the actuality of what had happened, the message, their appearance and song. As a result, there is no question of doubt with them concerning the truth of the tidings brought by the celestial messenger. They know that the event has actually taken place and realise that it is the Lord who has sent them the tidings through the angel.

16 So they make haste to go to Bethlehem. Whether they left their flock under the care of one or more of them or under the direct protection of God we do not know. We also do not know whether they reached the Child the same night or only the following morning and whether they found Him at once or first had to search about for a long time. The Word of God is silent here, as elsewhere, about many details which are relatively unimportant. In any case, they found Joseph and Mary and, lying in the manger, the Holy Child. What a tremendous contrast it must have been to them—the miraculousness of the announcement of the nativity and now the poor and humble circumstances in which they find Him!

17 Just as these simple shepherds are the first persons to whom the glad tidings concerning the birth of Christ are communicated, so in turn they are the first proclaimers of the event to others. It is probable that their flock was intended for offerings in the temple, as flocks for this purpose were kept in the vicinity of Bethlehem (cf. Edersheim, *Life and Times of Jesus*, i, p. 189). In this case they would ere long have gone to Jerusalem and would there also have told the whole story to the pious people who were awaiting the coming of the promised Messiah. In this manner they would have prepared persons like Simeon and Anna (verses 25–40) for their welcoming of the Christ-child.

18, 19 While Luke does not state what results the initial surprise at the words of the shepherds had in the case of the other listeners, he makes express mention of the fact that Mary kept all these things and pondered them in her heart. The story told by the shepherds concerning the tidings and the appearance and song of the celestial beings was to her yet another link in the golden chain of miraculous happenings that had commenced on the day when the angel Gabriel brought her the news that she would become the mother of the Messiah. Every one of these events made her realise better the divine glory of her Son. An extremely superficial objection is raised here by some critics (e.g. Luce, *in loc.*), to the effect that if Mary had really lived through these occurrences and taken them to heart she would not have acted as described in Mark iii. 20–35. Was Mary, then, a perfect being who immediately, perfectly and permanently grasped the full significance of the angels' tidings, the supernatural conception, and so forth? Would she not, as a fallible mortal, also sometimes through the years (as was likewise the case with John the Baptist) have times of doubt and uncertainty? This 19th verse is a clear indication that it was Mary herself who in later years related this story (probably to Luke himself, or else to some person or group of persons standing in intimate relation to her, who afterwards communicated it to Luke in speech or writing). Dr. W. Sanday[1] and many more of the most sober and learned expositors of the Scriptures agree that Luke received from Mary, directly or indirectly, practically all the data related by him in the first two chapters of the Gospel. As we have shown in the Introduction, he had splendid opportunities of acquiring such first-hand information.

20 After the shepherds had thus found the Child in the circumstances which had been described by the angels, they went back and glorified and praised God as the Source of everything that had happened.

The first message sent to mankind after the birth of Jesus was that which the angel brought to the shepherds: " Fear not! " And the reason why they should not be afraid at his appearance

[1] *Outlines of the Life of Christ*, p. 193; *The Life of Christ in Recent Research*, p. 266.

out of the invisible world and the revelation of God, is that the angel is bringing the glad tidings of the birth of the Redeemer, Christ the Lord. The incarnation of the Son of God is indeed still the only foundation upon which real fearlessness towards the invisible, the unknown, the divine may be based. Without the coming of Christ we should have had no assurance that God really exists as a personal God, perfect in love and mercy, and we should still have been overcome with fear as regards the invisible, the hereafter, the divine and eternal. But thanks be to God that His Son gave Himself to the world in condescending love and became Man, bringing a perfect revelation of God as the Holy and Merciful Lord. Ever since the incarnation of Jesus all tidings from the Higher World are " good tidings of great joy " for those who through Him are at peace with God. For the child of God the invisible and eternal can no longer have any terror, because the Christ who has come out of the unseen world and has returned to it and now fills the whole universe is his Redeemer and Lord.

[1] " Shepherds were despised people. They were suspected of not being very careful to distinguish 'mine' and 'thine'; for this reason, too, they were debarred from giving evidence in court " (Strack-Billerbeck, in loc.).

[2] φυλάσσειν indicates to guard vigilantly so as to protect against dangers.

[3] δόξα (Hebrew כָּבוֹד—kābhōdh) here stands for the radiating, brilliant splendour or majesty of God (Greydanus, in loc.): probably the Shekinah is to be understood.

[4] A few MSS. have Χριστὸς Κυρίου (the Lord's Anointed), but the MS. evidence for Χριστὸς Κύριος is too strong and unanimous to permit us to regard it as an alteration of the former. The angel declares that the Redeemer is Christ (the Anointed) and Lord, and not simply " the anointed Lord " (as B. Weiss has it).

[5] The textual-critical evidence is in favour of εὐδοκίας (genitive) and not εὐδοκία (nominative) on which the A.V. rendering is based (" good will toward men "). But even so, it is the divine good will that is meant here, and not the human quality indicated in the popular expression " men of good will ".

THE CIRCUMCISION AND DEDICATION OF JESUS AND THE STORY OF SIMEON AND ANNA

ii. 21–40

21 And when eight days were fulfilled for circumcising him, his name was called JESUS, which was so called by the angel before he was conceived in the womb.

22 And when the days of their[1] purification[2] according to the law of Moses were fulfilled, they brought him up to Jerusa-
23 lem, to present him to the Lord[3] (as it is written in the law of the Lord, Every male that openeth the womb shall be
24 called holy to the Lord), and to offer a sacrifice according to that which is said in the law of the Lord, A pair of turtledoves,
25 or two young pigeons. And behold,[4] there was a man in Jerusalem, whose name was Simeon;[5] and this man was righteous and devout, looking for the consolation of Israel:[6]
26 and the Holy Spirit was upon him. And it had been revealed unto him by the Holy Spirit,[7] that he should not see death,
27 before he had seen the Lord's Christ. And he came in the Spirit into the temple: and when the parents[8] brought in the child Jesus, that they might do concerning him after the cus-
28 tom of the law, then he received him into his arms, and blessed God, and said,

29   Now lettest thou thy servant depart, O Lord,[9]
      According to thy word, in peace;
30   For mine eyes have seen thy salvation,
31   Which thou hast prepared before the face of all peoples;
32   A light for revelation to the Gentiles,
      And the glory of thy people Israel.

33 And his father and his mother were marvelling[10] at the things
34 which were spoken concerning him; and Simeon blessed them, and said unto Mary his mother, Behold, this *child* is set for the falling and rising up of many in Israel; and for a
35 sign[11] which is spoken against; yea and a sword[12] shall pierce through thine own soul; that thoughts out of many
36 hearts may be revealed. And there was one Anna, a prophetess, the daughter of Phanuel, of the tribe of Asher (she was of a great age, having lived with a husband seven
37 years from her virginity, and she had been a widow even for fourscore and four years), which departed not from the temple, worshipping with fastings and supplications night

38 and day. And coming up at that very hour she gave thanks
  unto God, and spake of him to all them that were looking
39 for the redemption of Jerusalem. And when they had
  accomplished all things that were according to the law of the
  Lord, they returned into Galilee, to their own city Nazareth.
40   And the child grew, and waxed strong,[13] filled with wisdom: and the grace of God was upon him.

In these verses we see in what strikingly intimate relation the
incarnate Son of God stands to the Old Covenant. The whole of
the Old Testament revelation was a preparation for the coming of
Christ and for the full revelation of God in Him. And when the
fulfilment has set in with the birth of Christ, the things of the Old
Covenant are not recklessly cast aside. From the very outset the
New Testament revelation in Christ is most closely joined to that
of the Old.

21   God sent His Son in the likeness of sinful flesh (Rom. viii. 3).
In all things He had to become like His brothers (Heb. ii. 17).
When the fulness of the time had come, God sent forth His Son,
born of a woman, *born under the law*, to redeem them that were
under the law (Gal. iv. 4). Thus it is that He who is Himself
without sin or guilt and who has been conceived of the Holy
Ghost must nevertheless also perform all the obligations of the Law
and fulfil all righteousness (Matt. iii. 15). The circumcision and
purification customs after a birth had reference to the state of
sin in which each human being is born and to the purification
therefrom by blood-sprinkling and sacrifices. Where, therefore,
Jesus, the stainless and Holy One, undergoes these things, this is
not on His own account, but it serves as a sign that He voluntarily
places Himself under the Law and takes upon Himself the obligations of His people so as to procure their redemption. He takes
upon Himself their impurity and guilt and therefore He undergoes
circumcision and later on also the baptism by John. Along this
road He moves to undertake the work of redemption. The name
Jesus (" Jehovah the Saviour ") given to Him at the circumcision
in obedience to the command of God (i. 31) indicates this fact
forcibly. That is why Luke lays so much emphasis on this
designation.

22-4   The correct reading of the first words here is (as in R.V.)
" after the days of *their* purification according to the law of Moses
were accomplished ". This refers to the provisions of Leviticus
xii. A woman was regarded as ceremonially impure for forty days
after the birth of a son. Because her " impurity " was connected

117

with the birth of a child, the child is also involved in it, and therefore the original reading is " *their* purification ". Through this also the Saviour undergoes humiliation. For the sake of the redemption of His people, He takes their impurity upon Himself also in this connection.

After the forty days two " purification " sacrifices—a lamb as burnt-offering and a pigeon as sin-offering—had to be brought. But in the case of poor persons a pigeon could also be sacrificed in the place of the lamb. Because Joseph and Mary were poor, they brought two pigeons to be sacrificed in the temple at Jerusalem. The sacrifices symbolised that the sacrificer deserved death, but that the sacrificial animal is loaded with the guilt and death-penalty and for the sake of the sacrificer enters upon death to set him free from his guilt of sin. According to Exodus xiii a sacrifice had always to be offered for a first-born to symbolise the fact that the death-penalty lay on him and had to be taken away through the sacrifice. This sacrifice is brought in the case of Jesus because He has taken upon Himself the death-penalty of the sinful people for whose salvation He became Man.

Apart from the bringing of the sacrifices, Joseph and Mary also brought Jesus to the temple to present Him to the Lord (verse 22), to consecrate Him to the service of God. And whilst the consecration of first-born babes was but too often unrealised in later life, in the case of Jesus it was completely fulfilled. Right from the very beginning until the end He served God perfectly and glorified Him by His voluntary and complete devotion.

This visit of Joseph and Mary with the Child to Jerusalem probably preceded the visit of the Wise Men from the East (Matt. ii), for after the warning in connection with Herod they would probably not have come to Jerusalem. And would they, after receiving the costly gifts from these men, have sacrificed only two pigeons?

25 Notwithstanding the general low spiritual condition of the Jewish people at that time there were nevertheless (as always) genuinely pious and upright ones who served God faithfully and who (especially during the years before and around the coming of Jesus) looked forward with great yearning to the coming of the Messiah. They were expecting " the consolation of Israel "—the salvation to come through the Messiah. One of this group of faithful people in Jerusalem was the devout Simeon. He was constantly under the influence of the prophetic working of the Holy Ghost.

26 Through direct revelation by the Holy Ghost it was announced to him that he would not die before he had beheld the promised Redeemer with his own eyes.

27, 28 Under the guidance of the Spirit he came into the temple just before Joseph and Mary arrived there with the Child. Whether he had already heard from the shepherds or from someone else about the miraculous circumstances of the birth of Jesus we do not know. In any case, God had revealed to him that the Child, no matter how humble and poor His parents were, was truly the Messiah. So he takes Him in his arms and praises God in the beautiful hymn which was later on to become known in the Church as the " Nunc dimittis ".

29–32 Simeon's brief hymn of praise, owing to its restrained ecstasy and intense clarity, is as beautiful as any of the psalms of praise in the Old Testament. The thought underlying its wording is of a slave who is instructed by his master to keep watch through the long, dark night on a high place to wait for the rising of a special star and then to announce it. After wearisome hours of waiting he at last sees the star rising in all its brightness. He announces it and is then discharged from keeping watch any longer.

Simeon had been instructed to await the rising of the " Sun of righteousness " (Mal. iv. 2), the Star of the house of Jacob. At last, now that the Child is in his arms, he has beheld the redemption of God incarnate in Christ Jesus. So he knows that God now lets him depart in peace and discharges him from the task of further watching.

God's salvation, he declares, is one that He has prepared before the face of all people—and therefore it will be observed not by a few pious persons, or by the nation of Israel only, but by " all peoples ". Everyone will see the work of redemption. The plan of salvation embraces all mankind.

The people of Israel and the nations are enveloped in spiritual darkness, but the deliverance brought by God in Christ is there to dissipate the darkness. In the place of the darkness, which is the symbol of ignorance, sin and misery, this redemption will bring to all nations light, the symbol of life, growth, knowledge and happiness. Then the nations will realise what glorious privileges God has granted to Israel in the course of the centuries, but especially through the birth of Jesus from their midst.

33 Although Joseph and Mary had already known, through the tidings of the angel (i. 26–38 and Matt. i. 20), through the supernatural conception and through the words of the shepherds, that the Child was the promised Messiah, they still did not grasp the full significance of all these things. For this reason the acts and words of the pious Simeon, that cast a new and bright light on His greatness, cause deep amazement. Simeon's words especially, regarding the universal purport and significance of the redemption wrought by God through Jesus, bring to Joseph and Mary a clearer perception of the divine majesty of the Child. But even after this the full significance of it all could not be realised by them, and again and again we notice how even Mary wavers and becomes confused through human weakness (e.g. Mark iii. 21).

34 After the hymn of praise, Simeon acknowledges that God has conferred on Joseph and Mary a glorious privilege, and prays for blessings on them (as is indicated by the Greek word translated by " to bless "). After this he addresses Mary, and for the first time in the Gospel history the coming struggle and suffering are referred to. Jesus, Simeon declares, will be like a stone over which some will trip and fall and perish, but by which others will be enabled to arise and be saved. In order to fall, it must be assumed that a person is first standing. So these words mean that those who imagine themselves to be strong and high, who rely on their own merit and power, will come to woeful ruin and undoing, because in their pride they do not realise their own need and doom and do not take refuge in Christ. But the humble ones, those who bend low at His feet with confession of sin and faith in Him, will be raised up by His mighty arm to eternal life.

No one will be able to take up a neutral attitude towards Him. He will serve as a clear sign by which God makes known to man that everyone in himself is doomed and guilty and that there is salvation for the penitent only in Christ. But many will refuse to accept the sign and to seek salvation through Him; they will contradict the sign and resist Him. This will bring about their everlasting fall. This resistance to the Redeemer reached its climax in the Crucifixion and we know what judgments of God afterwards overtook the Jewish people. Their resistance brought them to a fall and they forfeited their special place as the chosen people of God.

35 The resistance of the people to Jesus will be so frightful that Mary, His mother, will be overtaken by the deepest sorrows. Portents of this during His childhood years no doubt already began to make good the prophecies. When during His public appearance He was treated by the Jewish authorities with growing hate, envy and persecution, she experienced ever-increasing grief. But it was especially when He was nailed to the cross that the " sword pierced through her soul ". She is, therefore, rightly called *Mater Dolorosa* (Mother of Sorrows) and represented as such in Christian art.

The crisis which the coming of Christ will bring about will cause " the thoughts of many hearts to be revealed ". This means that God, who already knows the secret inclinations of the heart of man, will so bring it about that the appearance of Christ will cause a clear division between those who really serve Him and those who are hostile to Him. Through the acceptance or rejection of Christ it will become clear what is really everyone's real bent and bias is, what he thinks of himself (whether he is humble or arrogant), and what he thinks of God (whether he really loves Him and is devoted to Him or not).

36, 37 Yet another of the pious people in Israel is led by God to the Child in the temple. She is Anna, the prophetess, one through whom God gave revelations, like Deborah (Judges iv. 4) and Huldah (2 Kings xxii. 14). She is of the tribe of Asher, one of the ten so-called lost tribes. This shows, as also appears from other references in the Scriptures, that after the carrying away of the ten tribes some of them, nevertheless, returned to full membership of the Jewish people.

This Anna had been married only seven years when she became a widow and remained unmarried for the rest of her long life. It is possible, but not certain, that a room was given to her in one of the buildings on the temple-hill to live in. In any case, she was exceptionally faithful in attending all services in the temple and spent much time in fasting and prayer.

38 She was also one of those who looked and longed for the coming of the promised Redeemer. And when she found the Child, and her eyes were opened to the fact that He was the Christ, she spoke with gratitude and praise of God as the Faithful One who fulfilled His promises. And she spoke about the Child, especially to the group of righteous people in Jerusalem who were also looking forward to the redemption of God that He would bring through the Messiah. For this reason the coming of Jesus became known in a comparatively wide circle—but only among those faithful souls who had earnestly hoped for His coming.

39 Luke does not mention the visit of the Wise Men of the East or of the flight of Joseph and Mary to Egypt. (Matt. ii). It was, however, not his purpose to record everything that happened. We assume (according to the account in Matt. ii) that Joseph and Mary after their visit to the temple returned to Bethlehem and there went to live in a house (Matt. ii. 11). This may be perhaps explained from the fact that they felt, especially after their conversations with such pious people like Simeon and Anna (who undoubtedly spoke much more to them than Luke has recorded), that the Messiah-child ought to grow up in Bethlehem, the city of David. There the Wise Men of the East visited them. Afterwards they fled to Egypt, and when, for the above-mentioned reason, they wished to return to Bethlehem, after the death of Herod, they were warned by God to go back to Nazareth (Matt. ii).

Luke does not give these particulars (though he does not contradict them), but merely mentions the fact that after these days they again went to Nazareth.

40 In this short verse the history of twelve years of the life of Jesus is told. As a true human Child He passed through a process of physical and spiritual growth and increase. This verse expressly tells us that the intellectual, moral and spiritual growth of Jesus as a Child was just as real as His physical growth. He was completely subject to the ordinary laws of physical and intellectual development, except that in His case there was nothing of the influence of sin or shortcoming. Physically and spiritually He grew up perfectly as no one before or after Him. He was truly Man, but a perfect Man, even in childhood. " His was a perfect humanity developing perfectly, unimpeded by hereditary or acquired defects. It was the first instance of such a growth in history. For the first time a human infant was realising the ideal of humanity " (Plummer, *in loc.*). His physical and spiritual development was the most beautiful of all time, because it was perfect. Only later on, when He appeared in public and had to walk upon the *via dolorosa*, the path of sorrows, did that which was prophesied concerning Him in Isaiah liii. 3 begin to be fulfilled. And through all the years of growth and increase in true wisdom the grace of God, His guiding, protecting and supporting love and power, rested upon the Child. There was no partition-wall between Him and God, because He was perfect in all things.

Simeon uses exceptionally striking words where he declares to Mary: " Behold, this child is set for the fall and rising again of many in Israel; and for a sign which shall be spoken against; yea, a sword shall pierce through thy own soul, that the thoughts of many hearts may be revealed."

Jesus is the Inescapable One—sooner or later everyone *must* take up a position with regard to Him and must choose for or against Him. A man's attitude towards Him reveals and defines the real quality of his character. It is not an outward " doing good " or a " good life " that counts before God and reveals the deepest inclination and character of a man; what really matters is his attitude towards Christ. On this, and on this alone, the eternal weal or woe of everyone depends. He who in his pride of self-satisfaction despises Christ thereby dooms himself to everlasting ruin. But he who humbles himself under His mighty arm is raised up by Him to everlasting salvation.

[1] Textual-critical evidence is here in favour of the reading αὐτῶν and not αὐτοῦ.

[2] καθαρισμός here implies the removal of those things that interfere with communion with God. The Jewish purification laws, as expounded by the Rabbis, are detailed by Strack-Billerbeck, in loc.

[3] τῷ κυρίῳ. Here God is referred to as God of the Covenant (κύριος is used as translation of Yahweh, Jehovah).

[4] Various critics allege that these stories concerning the welcoming of the Messiah-child are legends formed under the influence of stories of the welcoming of the Buddha-child. A comparison of the Buddhist stories, including all their senseless and ridiculous representations, with the sober, unaffected Gospel stories is sufficient to prove the hollowness and far-fetchedness of these allegations. Even radical expositors like Bultmann and Clemen reject this theory of dependence (cf. Creed, in loc.).

[5] The name " Simeon " was very common, and therefore any attempts to identify this Simeon with Simeon the father of Hillel are far-fetched and precarious.

[6] " Consolation of Israel " is a comprehensive expression for the fulfilment of the Messianic hope (cf. Strack-Billerbeck, in loc.).

[7] A detailed exposition of the Old Testament doctrine of the Holy Spirit and of subsequent Jewish opinions regarding His operation is given by Strack-Billerbeck, in loc.

[8] τοὺς γονεῖς. Again and again these words are adduced as a so-called " proof " that Luke here made use of a source which did not accept the virgin birth of Jesus. This is, however, quite unwarranted, for as Godet rightly states: " The word parents is simply used to indicate the character in which Joseph and Mary appeared at this time in the temple and presented the child " (in loc.). Also cf. Plummer (in loc.), and Baljon (in loc.).

[9] Only a few times in the Scriptures is Δεσπότης ("absolute master of a slave ") used as a designation for God. Here Simeon uses it to acknowledge thereby that the Lord possesses absolute right over him, so that he is in an absolute sense His property.

[10] Strauss's contention (subsequently repeated by Loisy, Bultmann, Creed, Luce, and many others) that this " marvelling " on the art of Joseph and Mary proves that they knew nothing of former angels' tidings or of a supernatural conception, is founded on a superficial

review of the facts (see our explanation at verse 33 and cf. Plummer, *in loc.*).

[11] σημεῖον indicates a phenomenon which cannot escape notice, of which cognisance must be taken, and through which something else is made known.

[12] ῥομφαία is a broadsword.

[13] ηὔξανεν καὶ ἐκραταιοῦτο refers to physical development in stature and strength.

THE CHILD JESUS IN THE MIDST
OF THE DOCTORS

41 And his parents[1] went every year to Jerusalem at the feast
42 of the passover. And when he was twelve years old,[2] they
43 went up after the custom of the feast; and when they had
fulfilled the days, as they were returning, the boy Jesus tarried
44 behind in Jerusalem; and his parents knew it not; but
supposing him to be in the company, they went a day's
journey; and they sought for him among their kinsfolk and
45 acquaintance: and when they found him not, they returned
to Jerusalem, seeking for him. And it came to pass, after
three days they found him in the temple, sitting in the midst
of the doctors, both hearing them, and asking them ques-
47 tions:[3] and all that heard him were amazed at his under-
48 standing and his answers. And when they saw him, they were
astonished: and his mother said unto him, Son,[4] why hast
thou thus dealt with us?[5] behold, thy father and I sought
49 thee sorrowing. And he said unto them, How is it that ye
sought me? wist ye not that I must be in my Father's
50 house? And they understood not the saying which he spake
51 unto them.[6] And he went down with them, and came to
Nazareth; and he was subject[7] unto them: and his mother
kept all *these* sayings in her heart.
52 And Jesus[8] advanced in wisdom and stature,[9] and in favour
with God and men.

The apostolic preaching about Jesus dealt chiefly with His
public ministry, from His baptism by John onwards, and His
crucifixion and resurrection. Of these events the apostles had
themselves been personal witnesses. But only gradually did particulars concerning His birth and childhood years become known—
chiefly through the information given by Mary herself (as every
now and then appears from the contents of the stories in Luke
i and ii).

Apart from the history of the twelve-year-old Jesus in the temple
as told by Luke nothing further is related in the Gospels concerning His life as a boy or a young man (except, of course, the
general statements in verses 40 and 51–2). This reserve of the
Gospels, however, did not satisfy the curiosity of later generations,

with the result that we find in the apocryphal Gospels and other extra-Biblical writings all sorts of stories concerning Jesus' doings and sayings as a Child. Most of these stories are, however, so fantastic and childish and give such an unnatural and distorted representation that they cannot by a long way be compared with the contents of the four Gospels. We at once realise what an unbridgeable gulf exists between the canonical Gospels (written under the inspiration of the Holy Ghost by personal witnesses or by persons who had firsthand information at their disposal), and the apocryphal writings (which are the fruit of fabrications and legends).

41 Joseph and Mary were accustomed to attend the Passover in Jerusalem every year. Although the Lord had commanded in Exodus xxiii. 17 and Deuteronomy xvi. 16 that the Israelites should go to the sanctuary for all the three principal festivals, it gradually became a fairly common practice for Jews outside Jerusalem to go only at the Passover.

42 Whether Jesus had already gone with His parents to Jerusalem at an earlier date we do not know. In any case, Luke relates that He did go when He was twelve years old. That was probably in order to be prepared for the ceremony of the following year, when He would be permitted as a young Jewish boy to join the religious community as a responsible member—i.e. as " son of the commandment " (*Bar Mitzvah*). This important event takes place when the the Jewish boy is thirteen.

43, 44 After the seven festival days (Exod. xiii. 6) were over, Joseph and Mary left Jerusalem, together with others attending the festival from Nazareth and its environs, and were on their way back to their homes. It is possible that it was the custom in those days that when a company of festival pilgrims went on their return-journey the women went on ahead with the younger children and the men followed them. The bigger boys then travelled either along with the fathers or with the mothers. Joseph, therefore, may have thought, when he did not notice Jesus, that He was with Mary, and Mary probably thought that He was with Joseph. In addition, it was a definite custom that in the evening, after the day's journey, the whole of the travelling company came together for the night at a place previously arranged. At the end of the day's journey Joseph and Mary then noticed to their consternation that Jesus was not with the company and must thus have remained behind in Jerusalem. From all this it appears that they had a great deal of confidence in the young child. They knew that He would be where He ought to be, so that, when they left Jerusalem, they had not definitely ascertained whether He was with the party of travellers. Only in the evening, when they necessarily had to seek Him as the family groups came together for the night, did they discover that He was not there. Accordingly there can be no question of their having neglected Him. The whole occurrence may be explained, on the one hand, from the fact that they had the fullest confidence in Him and knew that He would be where He ought to be, and on the other hand from the fact that they did not realise that on His first definite attendance at the festival in the temple and acquaintance with the doctors He would naturally tarry in the temple as long as possible. While knowing that He would be where He ought to be, they nevertheless did not realise that in those circumstances He would inevitably be in His " Father's house ", the temple.

45-7 The next morning Joseph and Mary at once went back to Jerusalem, then already distant a day's journey. Consequently they arrived there only that night and could not find Him until the following day (the third day after their departure from Jerusalem). They then discovered that He had remained behind in the temple and was sitting in one of the courts where a number of Jewish doctors had gathered together for disputations among themselves as they were accustomed to do after such a festival. He listened to the disputations and then asked some questions on certain matters, and sometimes questions were put to Him in turn. According to the custom of that time, pupils had to receive instruction in this manner—by asking and answering questions. Jesus here appeared not as a teacher (as the apocryphal writings represent Him), but as a pupil, nor yet as a child who wanted to show that he knew better than his instructors (for then they would not have marvelled at Him, verse 47). However, His unaffected questions and answers to their questions showed so many proofs of exceptional insight and lucid intelligence that the doctors marvelled at it. With the Child Himself, however, there was no boasting, self-conceit, arrogance or self-exaltation.

48 Mary, His mother, was especially full of anxious concern during the period of about two days since their discovery that Jesus was not with them. Accordingly she is the first to give utterance in words to her inward emotion. She does so in words that give evidence of her deep motherly affection and her anxiety at the same time: " Son, why hast thou thus dealt with us? Behold, thy father and I have sought thee sorrowing."

This anxiety on the part of Joseph and Mary does not by any means indicate that they did not know (as we are informed by the stories in Luke i and ii) that He was the Messiah. Their genuinely human uneasiness only shows that they did not yet fully and constantly realise that since He was in reality the Christ of God there was therefore no need for them to be anxious about His welfare. Indeed, it was only after Jesus' resurrection and the outpouring of the Holy Ghost at Pentecost that Mary realised fully who her Son was. And not until then would she be capable of really seeing in the true light the announcements of the angels, the supernatural conception, and so forth.

49 Jesus' reply is no reproof, but an utterance of amazement. From this it may be deduced that He was not uneasy when He had not seen His parents for some days and that His human consciousness had no suspicion that they were anxious about Him. Completely devoted as He was to His earthly parents, He was, nevertheless, especially since He began to grow older, exceptionally self-reliant and strong in personality. In His answer He especially expresses surprise that they had not known where to find Him and had sought Him so anxiously. How was it—that was what His question really amounted to—that when they missed Him they had not at once realised that He had to be busy in the temple about the concerns of His Father, about the revelation, knowledge and service of God? Reverting to Mary's words " *thy father* and I ", Jesus here in a special sense calls God His Father because He, and not Joseph, is His real Father.

It is remarkable that the first words of Jesus quoted in the Gospel narrative are these words in which He so clearly refers to His divine Sonship, and in which He points to His life's vocation to be about His Father's business—to serve and glorify Him in all things and at all times. The words indicate a divine inevitability: Jesus *must* be busy with the interests of His Father. With Him it is, however, not a case of external compulsion—His whole nature yearns to serve and obey His Father voluntarily. This divine calling of His is to such a degree of the very first importance that even His most intimate earthly relations must be subordinated to it. To the Child Jesus all this is quite natural and obvious, and so He is amazed that Joseph and Mary did not realise it.

50 Again it is evident how thoroughly human Mary and Joseph are in the restrictedness of their insight into the nature and vocation of the Child. As W. Manson correctly remarks: " The words in which He expresses himself have . . . an unfathomable quality passing his parents' comprehension " (*in loc.*).

51 It was in accordance with His divine Sonship that He was engaged in His Father's business in the temple with the teachers of God's law, and it was genuinely and naïvely childlike that under the circumstances He had never thought that His parents would be uneasy. But when they came to fetch Him, He went voluntarily, without demurring, with them to Nazareth and was subject unto them, for this also was the will of His heavenly Father.

The last sentence of this verse again points to the fact that Luke obtained all these particulars directly or indirectly from Mary herself. She was the only one who could tell what is related here.

52 As Luke in verse 40 gives in a single sentence, pregnant with meaning, a summary of the life, growth and development of Jesus from His birth to His twelfth year, so in this verse he again gives a beautiful summary of the subsequent eighteen years or so of His life until He began to appear in public. What was done by Him during all these years is not known to us in detail. From other data in the Gospels it appears, however, that He grew up in a fairly large family—Mary and Joseph had quite a number of sons and daughters after His birth (cf. Mark vi. 3). We also know that Joseph was a carpenter and that Jesus helped him in this work. During the years after the happenings in the temple and before our Lord's appearance in public, Joseph died; and as far as can be ascertained from the allusions in the Gospels and in the early church fathers Jesus after this took the place of Joseph as provider for His mother and His younger brothers and sisters (Mark vi. 3). Thus He continued in the work of carpentry until the beginning of His public appearance. A carpenter's trade in those days included the erection of houses, the making of all kinds of furniture and household requirements, and the construction of such agricultural implements as ploughs and yokes. Indeed, in the words and parables of Jesus we find many traces of His intimate knowledge of these things. Thus, e.g., He spoke about houses built on sand or upon a rock; of a person who " turns his hand to a plough "; of the taking up of His yoke—a yoke which is easy and thus makes the load light; and so on.

But whatever was precisely done and experienced by Jesus during these years, we know from this verse that " Jesus increased in wisdom and stature, and in favour with God and man ". He passed through a natural but perfect spiritual and physical development. At every stage He was perfect for that stage. But there is a big difference between the perfection of a child and that of an adult—the difference between perfect innocence and perfect holiness. Therefore it is stated that Jesus *increased* in wisdom and stature and thus also in favour with God and man. According to His human nature and character, He grew and developed in such a manner that His life and condition were at all times in full agreement with God's will. Thus the creative idea of God was for the first time realised completely—Jesus was a perfect Man in soul and body. Adam and Eve were also created in perfection, but their spiritual perfection before the fall was merely the perfection of innocence. In order to possess the perfection of holiness, they had voluntarily and deliberately to choose good and reject evil, but, alas, they did not do so. Jesus, however, chose rightly, without any external pressure, completely and voluntarily, to serve His Father, and never gave way to temptation. And thus in Him was realised in every respect the perfect creative ideal of God. Accordingly God could in an absolute sense show Him His favour and reveal His pleasure in Him.

And because He associated as an absolutely perfect human being, spiritually as well as physically, with the people in Nazareth and elsewhere in Palestine, they could not but feel attracted towards Him. His body, not having been disfigured by sin, was in the highest sense beautiful and attractive, the expression of His eyes pure and exalted like the mirror of His spotless and noble soul. His whole human personality was without any defect or injury of whatever kind. So Luke declares that He " increased in favour " with man as well as with God. According as He came to a fuller and more adult development, both physically and spiritually, He was more and more highly esteemed and loved by His fellow-men.

Thus it was through all the years until He began to appear in public. Then it was that the unavoidable crisis foretold by Simeon arose, for then the Son of God, by exercising His Messianic vocation, openly exposed the low condition of the inner life of the people. And this led to sides being taken for or against Him. Those who loved the darkness more than the light resisted Him and His divine claims, so that from henceforth He was no longer in favour with the people as a whole. His *via dolorosa* began with His public appearance and ere long the words of Isaiah liii would be fulfilled.

But, as is expressly shown in verse 52, before these clashes came, He was One who enjoyed the highest respect and affection of people who knew Him. And God gave His approval to this, for He Himself also showed Him His favour and pleasure—" He was in favour with God ".

In these verses we have seen Jesus in His perfection, physically and spiritually, as Child and later on as grown-up Man (verse 52), and also in His consciousness of the fact that God is His Father. It is blessed to know that every believer is accepted in Him as a beloved child of God; that in and through Him, the Son of God, we also may call His Father our Father—not in the same sense

as He is His Father, in an eternal and unique relationship within
the Godhead, but, nevertheless, in a very real and unending sense,
for no one can wrest us from His arms.

In addition, we have the blessed knowledge that, because we
have been accepted in Him as the beloved children of God, we,
with glorified and heavenly bodies, shall also hereafter partake of
His perfection as Man. He came to save us *as complete human beings,
in soul and body alike.*

[1] In civil law and in the language of everyday life Joseph was the
father of Jesus. For this reason Luke could speak of His " parents".
This does not, however, contradict the fact that in reality Joseph was
not His father.

[2] Major in *The Mission and Message of Jesus* (*in loc.*) maintains that it
was at the age of twelve that a Jewish boy became a " son of the commandment ", which entails his being henceforth himself responsible for
his religious life and must himself fulfil the obligations in connection
therewith. Strack-Billerbeck, however, who speak on such matters
with much weightier authority, state with truth that this took place
only at the age of thirteen, and that here Jesus went to the Passover
only in preparation. " The legal obligation to be present at the pil-
grimage-festivals in Jerusalem, did not begin for Jesus until a year
later " (*in loc.*). Religiously a boy became of age on his thirteenth
birthday, but in a civil sense only on his twentieth birthday (*in loc.*).

[3] It is generally admitted that it was a custom for the pupil to ask
and to answer questions. " The asking of questions by the pupil
formed an essential element in the ancient Jewish method of instruction " (Strack-Billerbeck, *in loc.*).

[4] τέκνον is the form of address indicating love and reproof.

[5] E. Klostermann maintains (*in loc.*) that the anxiety and reproving
attitude of Mary make the stories of Luke i and ii untrue. He declares
that if she had realised that He was the Messiah she would not have
acted thus. In this he is mistaken, for Mary was a fallible mortal with
imperfect insight, and did not always completely realise the full significance of what had happened or been made known to her.

[6] Montefiore, E. Klostermann, F. Hauch, Creed, Luce and others
allege that this verse definitely shows that Joseph and Mary knew
nothing of the virgin birth of Christ. These words, however, do not in
the least justify such an opinion. Joseph and Mary (as we have already
shown in numerous places), learned only gradually what was contained
and conveyed in Jesus' Messiahship. And when Jesus in His answer to
Mary so expressly pointed to the fact that God is His Father, and that
it is His vocation to be in His Father's house or about His business, it
still sounded incomprehensible to them. These words in verse 50 are
indeed one of the numerous indications of the historical accuracy and
lifelikeness of the Gospel of Luke. He who invents stories or writes

down legends will not so faithfully record the genuinely human weakness and shortcomings of Joseph and Mary. It has been rightly said concerning this story: " This fine, tender picture, in which neither truth to nature, nor the beauty which that implies, is violated in a single line . . . cannot have been devised by human hands, which, when left to themselves, were always betrayed into coarseness and exaggeration as shown by the apocryphal Gospels" (Keim, in Plummer, *in loc.*).

[7] ἦν ὑποτασσόμενος. This periphrastic form emphatically points to the continuous character of His subjection.

[8] By means of the various words used by Luke to describe the Saviour, βρέφος (a new-born babe) in verse 16, παιδίον (a young child) in verse 40, παῖς (a boy) in verse 43, and 'Ιησοῦς (Jesus, the Saviour) in verse 52, he indicates our Lord's development to maturity.

[9] ἡλικία here means bodily stature, physical growth. See note on xii. 25.

THE PREACHING OF JOHN THE BAPTIST

1 Now in the fifteenth year of the reign of Tiberius Caesar,[1] Pontius Pilate being governor of Judaea, and Herod being tetrarch[2] of Galilee, and his brother Philip tetrarch of the region of Ituraea and Trachonitis, and Lysanias tetrarch of

2 Abilene,[3] in the high-priesthood of Annas and Caiaphas,[4] the word of God came unto John[5] the son of Zacharias in the

3 wilderness. And he came into all the region round about Jordan, preaching[6] the baptism of repentance[7] unto

4 remission of sins; as it is written in the book of the words of Isaiah the prophet,[8]

> The voice of one crying in the wilderness,
> Make ye ready the way of the Lord,
> Make his paths straight.

5   Every valley shall be filled,
> And every mountain and hill shall be brought low;
> And the crooked shall become[9] straight,
> And the rough ways smooth;

6   And all flesh[10] shall see the salvation of God.

7 He said therefore to the multitudes that went out to be baptized of him, Ye offspring of vipers, who warned you to

8 flee from the wrath to come? Bring forth therefore fruits worthy of repentance, and begin not to say within yourselves, We have Abraham to our father: for I say unto you, that God is able of these stones to raise up children unto

9 Abraham. And even now is the axe also laid unto the root of the trees: every tree therefore that bringeth not forth

10 good fruit is hewn down, and cast into the fire. And the mul-

11 titudes asked him, saying, What then must we do? And he answered and said unto them, He that hath two coats, let him impart to him that hath none; and he that hath food, let him

12 do likewise. And there came also publicans to be baptized,

13 and they said unto him, Master, what must we do? And he said unto them, Extort no more than that which is appointed

14 you. And soldiers also asked him, saying, And we, what must we do? And he said unto them, Do violence[11] to no man, neither exact *anything* wrongfully;[12] and be content with your wages.

15 And as the people were in expectation, and all men reasoned in their hearts concerning John, whether haply

16 he were the Christ; John answered saying unto them all, I

indeed baptize you with water; but there cometh[13] he that is
mightier than I, the latchet of whose shoes I am not worthy
to unloose: he shall baptize you with the Holy Ghost[14] and
17 *with* fire:[15] whose fan is in his hand, thoroughly to cleanse his
threshing-floor, and to gather the wheat into his garner;
but the chaff he will burn up with unquenchable fire.[16]
18   With many other exhortations therefore preached he good
19 tidings unto the people; but Herod the tetrarch, being
reproved[17] by him for Herodias his brother's wife, and for all
20 the evil things which Herod had done, added yet this above
all, that he shut up John[18] in prison.

We are now approaching the narrative of Jesus' public ministry.
Luke introduces this with a brief account of the ministry of John
the Baptist, which served to prepare the way for Jesus. He
describes the work and preaching of John only in so far as it is of
preparatory significance for the public appearance and work of
Christ. He therefore gives no detailed account of the career or of
the preaching of John, but only a general outline of his work as the
forerunner of the Redeemer.

1, 2 As an author with historical aptitude, Luke gives an exceptionally full chronology for the commencement of John's
public appearance. He does this because, on account of the preparatory nature of his work, it is really also the time-indication for
the beginning of the public appearance of Jesus (which commenced only about six months later); Luke is chiefly concerned
throughout to let the full light fall upon Christ. Here he states
that the divine charge to John to act openly as the forerunner
of Christ was given " in the fifteenth year of Tiberius Caesar ".
Tiberius was emperor from the death of Caesar Augustus in A.D.
14 (on 19th August) until A.D. 37. Some consider that his
fifteenth year is reckoned here from the time when he was
appointed co-ruler of the provinces by his step-father Augustus in
A.D. 11–12. But no example is produced of his regnal years being
counted from any other epoch than his actual accession. According to the Roman reckoning, this would make his fifteenth
year A.D. 28–9. But in Syria the reigns of monarchs were reckoned
according to a method retained from the days of the Seleucid
dynasty, by which a new regnal year started in September-
October. Tiberius's second year would by this computation have
started in September-October of A.D. 14, although in fact he had
donned the purple only a month earlier; and his fifteenth year
would be deemed to start in September-October of A.D. 27.

As a further indication of the time Luke states that Pontius

Pilate was then procurator of Judaea, Herod tetrarch of Galilee, his brother Philip tetrarch of the region of Ituraea and Trachonitis, and Lysanias tetrarch of Abilene.

Pontius Pilate was procurator of Judaea from A.D. 26–36; Herod Antipas, son of Herod the Great, ruled as tetrarch over Galilee and Perea from 4 B.C. until A.D. 39, when he was dismissed from his post by Caligula as a result of his attempt to change his title from " tetrarch " to the higher one of " king "; Philip, son of Herod the Great and Cleopatra, was the best of the Herod family, and ruled from 4 B.C. to A.D. 34 as tetrarch over a region that *inter alia* included Ituraea and Trachonitis; Lysanias (the younger) ruled over Abilene, to the north of Philip's territory. It was formerly considered that it was a historical error on the part of Luke to mention Lysanias as ruling over Abilene at that time. Inscriptions have, however, been discovered which prove that while several years previously (about 36 B.C.) one Lysanias ruled over Abilene as king, another Lysanias (probably a descendant of the former one) later governed the same territory as tetrarch (cf. our exposition in the footnotes).

After indicating the chronology by reference to secular rulers, Luke proceeds to state that the events took place in " the high-priesthood of Annas and Caiaphas ". Annas was really high priest from A.D. 6 to 15 (when he was dismissed from his post by Valerius Gratus, the Roman governor). In practice, however, he still retained and exercised a considerable share of the high-priestly power, especially during the high-priesthood of Caiaphas, his son-in-law, and of a number of his own sons. Luke's uncommon expression ἐπὶ ἀρχιερέως ῎Αννα καὶ Καϊάφα, " Annas and Caiaphas being high priest " (singular and not plural), thus indicates the real state of affairs: although the Romans had deposed Annas, and Caiaphas was the official high priest, Annas nevertheless in reality still exercised some high-priestly authority.

All these chronological data, taken together, show that John was called to appear as forerunner of Christ in public between the years A.D. 26 and 29. Probably the exact year was A.D. 27.

By mentioning the names of the various secular and spiritual leaders, Luke not only assigns a date to the public appearance of John and especially of Jesus (a few months after John), but by this means also depicts the political and religious relations and circumstances in Palestine at that time—the milieu in which the ministry of John and Jesus took place. This list of names points to dark conditions. In the first place it makes us think of the administration of Tiberius which was characterised by severity and cruelty. It was shortly before the date indicated here that Tiberius went into semi-retirement on the island of Capri,[1] leaving affairs in Rome in the hands of his unscrupulous and despicable favourite Sejanus, until the latter's ambition o'ervaulted itself and compassed his ruin in the year A.D. 31. " In the reign of Tiberius Caesar " reminds us of the moral degeneration and political chaos in the Roman Empire, which in the course of time brought about its downfall.

In the second place the names show us the Holy Land under the domination of a pagan power that arbitrarily divided the country up and placed it under different rulers (most of whom were also moral degenerates and maladministrators). In the third place, especially, the expression " during the high-priesthood of Annas and Caiaphas " points to the chaos which had set in even in sacred matters—the religious life of God's people—as a result of the pagan domination by which high priests were arbitrarily deposed and supplanted by others.

During a period when conditions in the world and in Palestine were dark and desperate, God at length called John to come forth in public as forerunner of the Deliverer. It was not on his own initiative or at his own discretion that John commenced his preaching and preparatory work. It was the word of God that came to him: God commissioned him in a clear and personal manner and also gave him the necessary equipment to undertake the work.

3 After several centuries during which no prophet of God had appeared among Israel, John was commanded by God to give up his secluded life in the desert and act as His mouthpiece. Because baptismal ministration would accompany his preaching, he had to appear in the vicinity of water and was accordingly led to the banks of the Jordan. He probably mostly appeared in the environs of Jericho. Luke gives a particularly brief summary of John's work in the words: " he preached the baptism of repentance for the remission of sins ". This means that he called the people to repentance and then baptized those who confessed their sins and gave indications that they desired to lead a different and better life, in the assurance that God grants pardon to those who sincerely repent. So the baptism is the outward sign and seal that God has forgiven their sins. John himself could not impart this forgiveness; God alone can give it, and only to true penitents. The baptism is merely the outward symbol of the washing away of sin

---

[1] The picture drawn by Tacitus and Suetonius of the private vices of Tiberius should not be accepted uncritically; these writers depend largely on sources biased against Tiberius. Soured and embittered as he later became, not without reason, he was in his earlier years a capable and equitable ruler.

through forgiveness. John performed this work in preparation for the appearance of Jesus, the Messiah. Although various ceremonial ablutions were known among Israel, the baptism of members of the chosen people was something quite new; for this reason John was called " the Baptist "—for his appearance as baptizer was something exceptional. Proselytes had to submit to baptism on entering the Jewish fold, but that true-born Jews should be urged to undergo this initiatory rite implied that hereditary membership of the nation of Israel was in itself useless, or at least insufficient. Which (as verse 8 makes plain) was exactly what John desired to convey. The striking language of Zechariah xiii. 1 and Ezekiel xxxvi. 25 f. is specially appropriate to John's ministry.

4-6 The appearance and preaching of John are the fulfilment of what had been prophesied concerning him in the Old Testament, e.g. in Isaiah xl. 3 ff. Although the words in Isaiah referred in the first place to the redemption which God brought to the people with the return from exile, they nevertheless point in their fullest sense to the appearance of the great forerunner of Christ. So John is a voice of one who is calling, he is the one through whom God speaks and summons the people to be prepared for His coming in Jesus, the Saviour and Lord. The way of the Lord that has to be prepared is the way along which He desires to come in order to bring redemption. Accordingly the preparing of the way refers to the fact that the inclination and life of the people have to be changed to such an extent that they will be ready to receive His redemption. What is crooked must be made straight—where man has deviated from the well-beaten ways of God as revealed in His Word and thus followed crooked ways, he has to return to the straight paths. Along the road of lowly humiliation, repentance, confession and calling upon God man will receive His salvation. What is wanting must be supplied and what is in the way must be broken down (as pride and self-satisfaction). Thus John performed the work of preparation forcefully by appealing to the people to turn to God and have a clear outlook on the things that matter. This preparatory work was particularly necessary, not only because the people as a whole were morally and spiritually degenerate, but also because they had so many false, man-made opinions concerning the expected Messiah. With few exceptions the Jews of that time expected an earthly, political Messiah who should release them from their pagan oppressors. They had no realisation of their own sinfulness and of their need of a Messiah who, above all, was to bring a spiritual deliverance. John, therefore, had to point out to them their spiritual need and the true nature of the Messiah whom they should expect. In verses 4b–5a we read what God commands and in verses 5b–6 He declares what will assuredly happen. The way *shall* be ready for the coming of God (through the Redeemer) and all flesh shall see His redemption as it finds form in the Messiah. Nothing will prevent Him. Everything is prepared for His coming. He will come and all will see Him. This does not, however, mean that all will be saved by Him. His coming will mean redemption to those that are prepared, but doom to His adversaries.

7-9 In verse 7 and the following verses Luke describes in brief outline how John fulfilled the prophecies concerning him (those mentioned in the preceding verses and also those made in various parts of Luke i and ii)—how he prepared the way for the coming Redeemer.

The appearance of John, according to the Gospel narrative as well as the account given by the Jewish historian Josephus, attracted the attention of the whole Jewish nation. This may be explained from the fact that after so many centuries he was the first one who appeared as a messenger of God with evident divine authority and holy conviction. It is also certain that, even before his public appearance and as a result of the supernatural events which took place before, during and after his birth (Luke i), he was regarded by a large number of his fellow-countrymen who had heard of these things (i. 65, 66) as an exceptional person. So when after his calling he began to appear openly, and especially when he announced that the coming of the Messiah was close at hand and that the people must prepare themselves for His coming through repentance and baptism, the Jews came to him in multitudes.

Of the many admonitions addressed by John to the multitudes (verse 18), Luke mentions only a few. But what he mentions is typical and representative of the general trend of his preaching. In these words we hear John addressing the people in fearless and pointed terms—drawing their attention to their sins and calling them to true repentance. He warns and threatens them as he announces the approaching judgment on those who refuse to turn to God. He does not even hesitate to address them (according to Matt. iii. 7 it was especially the Pharisees and Sadducees) as a " brood of vipers ". In these words he draws attention to their tortuous behaviour—they live in self-satisfaction and sin and now they desire, without true conversion and by a merely external participation in the baptism, to protect themselves against the impending judgment. He summons the people to whole-hearted repentance, after which they must have themselves baptized as an outward sign of their acknowledgment of their spiritual impurity, so that the baptism may be to them a sign and seal of the forgiveness granted by God to the meek. But when he notices that they fix their eyes only on the outward ceremony with no inward contrition on account of their sins and no deep change of heart, he calls to them: " Ye offspring of vipers, who hath warned you to flee from the wrath to come? "—like snakes hastening to escape when the grass which sheltered them has been set on fire behind them. Thereafter (verse 8) he warns them not to rely on their natural descent from Abraham, but to see to it that their repentance is genuine. Outward ceremonies and carnal descent will not save them from the coming wrath of God against sin— wrath which, because they rejected Jesus, came down upon Jews of Palestine in an unparalleled manner in A.D. 70, and which in the final instance will be poured out at the end of the age. In His promises to Abraham, John declares, God is not bound to his descendants in the flesh: unless they are true children of Abraham in a spiritual sense, the wrath will come upon them and God will show His salvation among other nations to true, spiritual children of Abraham.

There must be no postponement of repentance on the part of his hearers, for the axe is already being laid to the root of the trees— the judgment is on the point of being executed on those who remain unrepentant.

10, 11 Alarmed at his urgent words, the multitude ask what they shall do. They thought that they had to do something special, but John replies that they must do what lies to their hand and carry out the well-known demands of God—show true neighbourly love.

12, 13 Even " publicans ", Jews who, as agents of Caesar or Herod, collected customs duties and were hated and despised by the people, came to John asking what they should do to escape the wrath to come. And again John replies that they must live lives of neighbourly love in their particular profession. He does not demand that they should give it up, but that they should show the genuineness of their repentance by never abusing their position and by never extorting excessive taxes for their own enrichment.

14 He also does not forbid the soldiers (probably persons who assisted the publicans in the collection of taxes) to be soldiers, but makes the inexorable demand that they, too, should exercise neighbourly love in their particular circumstances. They have to be content, he declares, with their wages, and not extort money from the people with whom they have to deal through violence, terrorisation, or false accusation.

15, 16 Thus far Luke has shown how John through his earnest and urgent appeal for whole-hearted and practical repentance was engaged in preparing the people for the coming of the Messiah. He now relates how John, when the people began to wonder whether he was the Messiah, expressly and unconditionally placed himself in the background and pointed to Christ, the One who was coming, as the promised Redeemer.

John then points out that, no matter how important and necessary his preparatory work and baptismal ministration are, they are of quite subordinate value in comparison with the work of the coming Messiah. He can only administer the outward baptism, but Christ will bring about the inward purification and renewal. He will administer the true baptism (with the Holy Ghost and with fire)—a baptism which gives inwardly what is outwardly symbolised by the baptism in water. Just as fire consumes what is destructible and thus works in a purifying and cleansing manner, so the Messiah will through the Holy Ghost consume sin and the sinners in so far as they cling to sin. In this way those who persist in sin will be destroyed, but those who sincerely confess their sins and flee to Him for refuge will be purified from sin to their own salvation, and delivered from its penalty and power.

So divinely great and exalted is the coming Messiah, John declares, that he is not even worthy to be His slave—one who unlooses his master's shoe-laces or carries his shoes to him (Matt. iii. 11).

17 The coming of the Redeemer will not mean salvation for all—He will sift and separate men like one who with a pitchfork or winnowing-fan tosses in the air the already threshed-out wheat on the threshing-floor so that the chaff may be separated from the wheat, the chaff being blown away while the wheat falls on the floor. So those receiving baptism must see that their repentance is genuine so that they may be truly saved. While most of the Jews of that time thought that the Messiah was going to visit only the heathen with His judgment and that they themselves would be privileged above all others, John declares plainly that judgment will overtake all who are not prepared for His coming through a true change of heart.

18 This verse proves that Luke included in his Gospel only a few typical pronouncements of John.

Although John with so much poignant earnestness called the attention of the Jews to their sins and to the impending judgment, Luke nevertheless declares that he "preached good tidings unto the people". John's preaching is thus a true proclamation of the Gospel because he announces that the Messiah is coming who, while He will visit the unrepentant with His judgment, brings forgiveness of sins and inward renewal and purification through the Spirit to all who truly turn to God and sincerely await His coming and take refuge in Him.

19, 20 Because Luke is, above all, engaged in depicting the revelation of God through Christ, he gives extremely few details of John's biography. Here he merely mentions the fact that John in his preaching of repentance did not even shrink from charging Herod Antipas, the ruler of Galilee and Perea, with his sinful life, and thus warning him and calling him, too, to repentance. In particular he reproved Herod for the crime committed by him in persuading the wife of his half-brother Philip (who lived as a private person somewhere in the East) to leave her husband (together with her daughter Salome) and to marry him. This sinful act cried to heaven, especially since he put away his own wife, the daughter of Aretas IV of Arabia, and also because his marriage to Herodias was incest, as her husband, his brother, was still alive.

John continued to reprove Herod fearlessly, until he was cast into prison by this degenerate ruler and was finally beheaded through the contrivance of Herodias (ix. 7-9). Josephus also describes (*Antiquities*, xviii, 5, 2) the ministry of John the Baptist and the fact that he was thrown into prison and beheaded by Herod. In the main his description agrees with that of the Gospels. From his account we see that, while the real reason for Herod's hatred towards John was that mentioned by Luke (the Baptist's reproof of his sinful life), he tried to justify his action by declaring that John had such great influence that it would be dangerous to set him free—he would easily be able to lead the people into insurrection. Because Josephus writes for Roman readers, he mentions only this consideration and not the more deep-seated one mentioned by the Gospels.

Before the Saviour began His public appearance for the redemption of souls and the establishment of His kingdom, God so ordered it that John the Baptist first appeared with his powerful message of repentance. First, men had to be shown their terrible spiritual plight, the fact that they stood before God full of sin and guilt, and that they should repent without delay. They were to realise that they were in danger of being visited by the judgment of God and that it was in vain for them to rely on their own dignity of descent or of outward piety.

This preaching of repentance must always be an inherent element in the Gospel-preaching of the church. Firstly, the sinfulness of sin should be pointed out, as well as God's wrath against it, followed by the inexorable demand for true repentance, and then there should be a summons to have faith in Jesus, the Saviour. Without the preaching of the need for repentance the message of the church would degenerate into sentiment. The Biblical balance between the two sides of the preaching of the Gospel must be preserved.

[1] Thus far no one has yet been able to prove with any degree of finality whether Luke reckons the reigning years of Tiberius from A.D. 11 to 12 when he became co-regent, or from A.D. 14 when he became emperor. B. Weiss, Zahn, and Greydanus prefer the former date (although we have no other example of reckoning Tiberius's regnal years from this point), while E. Meyer, E. Klostermann, Creed and A. Plummer are in favour of the latter. For a detailed discussion with bibliography cf. Greydanus, *in loc.*, or Holzmeister, *Chromologia Vitae Christi*, 1933, pp. 55 ff.; G. Ogg, *Chronology of the Public Ministry of Jesus* (1940), pp. 170 ff.

[2] τετραάρχης originally referred to a ruler over a fourth part of a land. "But it had come to be used as a general term for a subordinate native ruler" (Creed, *in loc.*).

[3] It was acknowledged years ago by E. Schürer and E. Meyer that Luke's reference to Lysanias is perfectly correct. To-day it is practically admitted by all that at that time a younger and less famous Lysanias did rule over Abilene (cf. Creed, *The Gospel According to St. Luke*, Additional Notes, pp. 307–9).

[4] Annas was high priest from A.D. 6 to 15 (deposed by the Roman governor) and Caiaphas from A.D. 18 to 36. But, as Luce admits, "(a) the high-priesthood appears to have been regarded by the Jews as a life office in spite of official deposition, (b) Annas was a man of great power and influence, and Caiaphas was his son-in-law. It is not, therefore, surprising that Annas should have continued in power in spite of Caiaphas's official appointment, and that Luke should have described them as joint holders of the office" (*in loc.*).

W. Manson, too, writes: "Annas was high priest only from A.D. 6 to 15, but as he was succeeded by various members of his family, the best known being Caiaphas, who held office from A.D. 18 to 36, he exercised unofficial powers which were practically equivalent to full status" (*in loc.*). And A. T. Olmstead says of Annas: "He generally contrived to remain the power behind the high-priestly throne" (*Jesus in the Light of History*, p. 50).

When, therefore, E. Meyer writes that Luke's expression "is, of course, incorrect", and Creed speaks of "Luke's misapprehension" (*in loc.*), they do so in spite of all indications that Luke was better informed than his modern critics in this matter as in others.

[5] ἐγένετο ῥῆμα θεοῦ ἐπὶ Ἰωάννην is an Old Testament expression used particularly of the prophets, indicating claim to divine inspiration.

[6] κηρύσσειν (from κῆρυξ, " herald ") means in the New Testament " to proclaim openly ", and in particular " to proclaim the Gospel ", the idea of " proclaiming as a herald in order to prepare for the coming of the Lord " being also contained in the word where it is used here in connection with John the Baptist.

[7] μετάνοια represents the Aramaic תוב (tûbh) = Hebrew שוב (shûbh) " to turn ", which refers to the turning away from sin and turning back to God, and also to an inward change as revealed in deeds.

[8] Isaiah xl. 3–5.

[9] ἔσται placed before its subject with emphasis to indicate the certainty of the matter. Whatever happens, God will see that everything is prepared for the coming of Christ.

[10] σάρξ here refers to mankind as fallen creatures, with the need to be redeemed (Plummer, in loc.).

[11] διασείειν = to rob with violence (Creed, in loc.).

[12] συκοφαντεῖν = " to show figs by shaking the tree " and then, figuratively, " to rob through false accusations or intimidation " (Plummer, in loc.).

[13] ἔρχεται (present) indicates the fact that He is already coming.

[14] In Acts xix. 1–6 we meet with disciples of John who had never yet heard of the baptism with the Holy Ghost. Some scholars (e.g. T. W. Manson, The Mission and Message of Jesus, p. 333) conclude from this that John did not speak these words reported by Luke. But what right have they to allege this? These disciples may have been absent when John uttered those words (although he did so on several occasions), or they may have found his words unintelligible and soon forgotten them, or their contact may have been not with John himself but with some of his disciples.

[15] Creed writes here: " For ' Baptism by fire ' the thought of fire as a testing as well as a destructive force seems required, as in 1 Corinthians iii. 13 " (in loc.).

[16] Schlatter says with regard to these words of John: " The comparison of the Coming One's activity with what takes place on the threshing-floor gives the speech a powerful conclusion, for it presents the two manifestations of divine sovereignty, grace and wrath, as a unity " (Evangelium des Matthäus, at iii, 12).

[17] ἐλεγχόμενος (present participle passive) refers to the continuity of the rebuke.

[18] For a thorough refutation of the idea that John was influenced by the syncretistic Mandaean movement cf. Lietzmann, Beginnings of the Christian Church, pp. 52 f.

SPECIAL NOTE

THE BAPTISM OF JOHN

In the pagan, Graeco-Roman world ceremonial purifications by means of ablutions were commonly known. But as Creed rightly states: " It would be quite fanciful to look for any direct influences from these quarters upon the historical beginnings of the Christian rite " (*op. cit.*, p. 310).

Although in the Old Testament there are examples of ceremonial " washings in water " (Lev. xi–xv), there is no mention of " baptism ". Proofs exist, however, that in the time of the New Testament, before the destruction of Jerusalem, the Jews administered a baptism for proselytes (cf. Abrahams, *op. cit.*, 1st series, p. 37).[1] Nevertheless the baptism of John was essentially new in the life of the Jewish people, because (1) his baptism was one of " repentance for the remission of sins " and not merely a ceremonial purification, (2) it is intended for all Jews and not merely for proselytes, (3) it is in preparation for the coming of the Greater One.

Because his baptism was something new and special, John was called " the Baptist " *par excellence*.

Josephus (*Antiquities*, xviii, 5, 2) also describes the appearance and baptismal ministration of John. The genuineness of this paragraph in Josephus is generally accepted (Creed, *op. cit.*, p. 311). His account differs from that of the Gospels with regard to the following points: (1) he makes no mention of John's relation to Christ, (2) he represents John's preaching in such a manner as though he regarded the baptism as an object in itself and not as a sign of repentance and a seal of forgiveness of sins.

These differences, as well as the few others that exist, may be explained from the fact that Josephus writes as a Jew and to a circle of pagan readers. So A. T. Olmstead rightly declares that Josephus " gives the preaching in terms of Greek philosophy " (*op. cit.*, p. 54), and what he considers as not too appropriate for his readers, he just omits or alters. Accordingly there is nothing in Josephus's rendering that proves Luke's data to be untrustworthy. On the contrary, it affords indeed a striking confirmation of the historicity of the Gospel narrative.

[1] See also H. H. Rowley, " Jewish Proselyte Baptism and the Baptism of John " in *Hebrew Union College Annual*, vol. 15 (1940), pp. 313 ff. The Jewish proselyte-baptism ceremonially " washed away the uncleanness from the heathen on entering Judaism, and grafted them with ceremonial purity on to the people of God " (Lietzmann, *Beginnings of the Christian Church*, p. 51). In the case of John's baptism, however, there was no ceremonial or sacramental character attached to it (*ibid.*, p. 52), but it was of religious-ethical significance in preparing the people for the coming of the Christ. It " is a single action which signifies that the baptized initiate has gone over to the sphere of the life of righteousness " (*ibid.*, p. 49), and is so prepared to meet the coming Messiah.

JESUS BAPTIZED

(Cf. Matt. iii. 13–17; Mark i. 9–11; John i. 31–4)

iii. 21–22

21 Now it came to pass, when all the people were baptized,
that, Jesus also having been baptized, and praying, the
22 heaven[1] was opened, and the Holy Ghost descended in a
bodily form,[2] as a dove, upon him and a voice came out of
heaven,[3] Thou art my beloved[4] Son; in thee I am well
pleased.[5]

The years of perfect and unhampered growth and development,
physical and spiritual (i. 52), were past; Jesus had attained to
maturity as a Man and was now in the full prime of His human
life (iii. 23). John the Baptist had already made great progress
with his preparatory work. The time was now ripe in every respect
for Jesus to leave the ordinary life in Nazareth and to appear in
public as the Messiah. Before doing this, however, He first goes
to John to be baptized by him. The three other Gospels give us
more particulars in connection with the occurrence than Luke
gives. He does not actually relate the baptism itself, but tells what
God did and said just after the baptism. To Luke the important
question is not how the baptism took place or what was done or
said by John, but what God revealed concerning the Person and
Nature of Jesus on this occasion, right at the commencement of
His public appearance.

21 According to the first words of this verse, Jesus, before going
to John, first waited until the great mass of the Jewish people had
had their baptism completed. This does not mean that all had by
this time already been baptized. In vii. 30 Luke states that the
Pharisees and lawyers did not get themselves baptized, and in
John iii. 23 we learn that John still continued to baptize even after
Jesus had been baptized. But nevertheless it is clear from this
verse (verse 21) that the great majority of the people had then
already been baptized. The procession to John had become a
popular movement, as we know also from Josephus. The vast
majority had already had themselves baptized and finally, when
for a short time there was apparently no one else with John,

Jesus also went and was baptized by him. The occurrence was to Jesus one of tremendous significance: by subjecting Himself to the baptism, He finally and openly took the sin of mankind upon Him and placed Himself on the altar for the sake of the redemption of the guilty ones. He Himself had no need to be baptized, but He offers Himself as the Substitute and Representative of sinful mankind and so He, the Sinless One, also undergoes this humiliation. Through this He shows his solidarity with the guilty human race for whose salvation He came. He who is Himself without sin takes upon Himself the sins of mankind in order to bring about reconciliation and redemption.

So, because the baptism of Jesus meant to Him the final acceptance of the work of redemption which would have to be completed through suffering and death, it was a most momentous occurrence. For this reason He was now praying as He often did subsequently before or during important moments in the course of His ministry.

And while He was thus engaged in communion with God through prayer, " the heaven was opened ". Here, as so often in the Word of God, we stand before the humanly incomprehensible, the unfathomable divine. But although we are unable to form an idea of the " opening of the heaven ", it undoubtedly indicates that, after Jesus had now offered Himself so completely and voluntarily as the Substitute and Redeemer, God gave to His human consciousness a perfect revelation of the majesty and glory of the Father, and of the fact that He was the Son of God in an absolute sense.

22 And when the heaven was opened the Saviour (and also John—John i. 32) saw the Holy Ghost descending upon Him in the shape of a dove. As formerly it had pleased the Triune God to reveal Himself in a visible shape (e.g. the cloud and fire during Israel's desert journeys, and the divine light in the holy of holies), and as the Holy Ghost later on, on the Day of Pentecost, descended upon the first Christians in the visible shape of tongues of fire, so He here reveals Himself in the shape of a dove. In the Scriptures a dove symbolises purity, innocence and loveliness. So when the Holy Ghost here descends upon Jesus in the shape of a dove, this symbolises the nature of that holy and lovely Spirit and the everlastingness and completeness of His descent upon Him. This, of course, does not mean that the Lord Jesus was not previously full of the Holy Ghost or that He was not conceived by the Holy Ghost, but merely indicates that He had now been equipped by the Holy Ghost with all *official* gifts to appear *openly* as Messiah and Redeemer. At the time of His conception by the Holy Ghost it was a question of the forming and development of His human nature, but at the baptism it is a question of the public declaration of His Messiahship and His equipment with the gifts necessary for this official and public fulfilling of His vocation as the Christ of God.

What God has made known through the opening of the heaven and the descent of the Spirit, He confirms and completes through a voice from heaven, saying: " Thou art my beloved Son; in thee I am well pleased." On two other occasions (on the mount of transfiguration and in John xii when Jesus was already standing under the shadow of the cross) God spoke with a voice from heaven in confirmation of the true Sonship of Jesus.

Where God here declares that Jesus is His beloved Son, this does not merely refer to the fact that He was conceived by the Holy Ghost. The reference is to His Eternal Sonship. From all eternity He is, in an absolute and unique sense, the only-begotten Son of God.

The words " in thee I am well pleased " are also all-embracing. From eternity to eternity God is well pleased in Him. But nevertheless the reference here is in a special sense to the pleasure of God in Him who in every respect carried out His will throughout the approximately thirty years that He had lived as perfect Man on earth before the baptism, and also especially as the One who voluntarily and completely, through His submission to baptism, took upon Himself the work of redemption—and trod the path of suffering leading to Golgotha.

This opening of the heaven, the descent of the Holy Ghost in a visible shape, and the voice from heaven, were to Jesus the final assurance from God that He was indeed His Son and the anointed Messiah, and that God wholly approved of His assumption of the work of redemption. To John, again, it was the unambiguous proclamation that Jesus was truly the promised Redeemer, the " Mightier One ".

In Isaiah lxiv. 1 the prophet called out: " Oh that thou wouldest rend the heavens, that thou wouldest come down! " In the story of the baptism of Jesus we see how God answered the sighings of the centuries and did indeed open the heavens, as we read in Mark i. 10. The heavens are opened to Jesus as our Representative and Substitute, and thus we have the divine assurance that every impediment and wall of partition that might hinder our return to God have been removed by Him. In Christ Jesus heaven has been opened to us—the way has been paved for us to go to the Father's eternal home as His beloved children, saved by our Redeemer.

¹ τὸν οὐρανόν here stands for the real heaven, the eternal abode of God.

² There is here no contradiction of what is related by Matthew, Mark and John (as has often been alleged). Luke does indeed expressly emphasise the " bodily shape ", but the other Gospels by no means deny it. They nowhere declare that what was seen by Jesus and John was entirely visionary. " There must have been something visible, namely, the shape of a dove. Otherwise they would also not have spoken of a dove " (Greydanus, in loc.). Greydanus rightly asks why, if God could appear in human form (Gen. xviii. 2, xix. 1), the Holy Ghost could not just as well appear in the shape of a dove, in all its rich symbolism.

³ A few MSS. ("D", "a", "b") and patristic citations, representing the " Western " text, have, instead of σὺ εἶ ὁ υἱός μου ὁ ἀγαπητός, ἐν σοὶ εὐδόκησα, the words of Psalm ii. 7 υἱός μοῦ εἶ σύ, ἐγὼ σήμερον γεγέγνηκά σε.

Numerous expositors (e.g. W. Manson, Zahn, Klostermann, Harnack, Moffatt, Streeter) accept this variant reading as the original. The majority then explain the alteration of the text from the fact that copyists regarded these words as a contradiction of the reality of the virgin birth of Jesus. With this, however, we cannot agree. The MS. evidence is overwhelmingly strongly in favour of the reading followed by us and it can be easily understood that, owing to the similarity of the first part of Psalm ii. 7 to the words in verse 22, a few copyists who knew Psalm ii. 7 by heart substituted the words of the psalm for the words in verse 22. It is, on the other hand, difficult to understand how the vast majority of copyists could of set purpose have altered the well-known words of the psalm (which were regarded as Messianic), represented as spoken by God from heaven. Even Creed admits that the variant reading " may well be due to assimilation to the text of the psalm " (in loc.).

But even if the words of the psalm were originally in verse 22, they by no means contradict the fact of the conception of Jesus by the Holy Ghost, and they do not teach any adoptionist Christology. " It is God who speaks here. And God's to-day is not a temporary to-day of a few hours, but an eternal unchangeable to-day " (Greydanus). If Luke did indeed write these words, it is obvious that he saw no contradiction in them of the other data in his Gospel.

Taking everything into consideration, we do not, however, feel convinced that the variant reading is the original one.

⁴ ὁ ἀγαπητός " may bear the well-attested meaning of ' only ', ' unique ' " (Creed, in loc.), representing the Hebrew yāchīd. Gustaf Dalman (The Words of Jesus, p. 281), after having shown that there is no difference in meaning between " the beloved Son " and " the only-begotten Son ", declares: " The position of the only Son is, in these cases (in the Gospels) as in Psalm ii, regarded as a lawful standing which confers a right to claim the entire household property. In the case of the Son of God the reference can only be to the sovereignty of

the world, and to such a sovereignty as would be exercised not by a Jewish emperor but by a divine Sovereign ''. These words from God at the baptism of Jesus thus unequivocally proclaim our Lord's absolute authority (cf. Foerster's illuminating article in Kittel's *Theologisches Wörterbuch zum Neuen Testament*, under ἐξουσία, on the authority of Christ, the Lord, as proclaimed and revealed in the New Testament).

[5] εὐδόκησα is the *timeless* aorist (Plummer, *in loc.*).

THE GENEALOGICAL TABLE OF JESUS

(Cf. Matt. i. 1-17)

iii. 23-38

23 And Jesus himself,[1] when he began[2] *to teach*, was about
thirty years of age, being the son (as was supposed[3]) of
24 Joseph,[4] the *son* of Heli,[5] the *son* of Matthat, the *son* of Levi,
25 the *son* of Melchi, the *son* of Jannai, the *son* of Joseph, the *son*
of Mattathias, the *son* of Amos, the *son* of Nahum, the *son* of
26 Esli, the *son* of Naggai, the *son* of Maath, the *son* of Mattathias,
27 the *son* of Semein, the *son* of Josech, the *son* of Joda, the *son* of
Joanan, the *son* of Rhesa,[6] the *son* of Zerubbabel,[7] the *son*
28 of Shealtiel, the *son* of Neri, the *son* of Melchi, the *son* of Addi,
29 the *son* of Cosam, the *son* of Elmadam, the *son* of Er, the *son* of
Jesus, the *son* of Eliezer, the *son* of Jorim, the *son* of Matthat,
30 the *son* of Levi, the *son* of Symeon, the *son* of Judas, the *son* of
31 Joseph, the *son* of Jonam, the *son* of Eliakim, the *son* of Melea,
the *son* of Menna, the *son* of Mattatha, the *son* of Nathan, the
32 *son* of David, the *son* of Jesse, the *son* of Obed, the *son* of Boaz,
33 the *son* of Salmon, the *son* of Nahshon, the *son* of Amminadab,
the *son* of Arni, the *son* of Hezron, the *son* of Perez, the *son* of
34 Judah, the *son* of Jacob, the *son* of Isaac, the *son* of Abraham,
35 the *son* of Terah, the *son* of Nahor, the *son* of Serug, the *son* of
36 Reu, the *son* of Peleg, the *son* of Eber, the *son* of Shelah, the
son of Cainan, the *son* of Arphaxad, the *son* of Shem, the *son*
37 of Noah, the *son* of Lamech, the *son* of Methuselah, the *son* of
Enoch, the *son* of Jared, the *son* of Mahalaleel, the *son* of
38 Cainan, the *son* of Enos, the *son* of Seth, the *son* of Adam, the
son of God.[8]

Thus far Luke has dealt mostly with people and matters that had
a preparatory significance for the appearance of Jesus. Now,
however, he is about to relate the public activity of the Lord. All
subordinate personalities are now to be relegated to the background and henceforth he proceeds to place Jesus, the Central
Figure in the divine drama, completely in the foreground of his
narrative, as it should be. For this reason he regards this as the
suitable place to record the genealogical table.

23 He first states (and he, the physician, is the only one of the
New Testament historians to do so) at what age Jesus began His
public career—namely when He was about thirty years old.

He then follows this up by giving the genealogical table.

There is nothing strange in it that the genealogical table of Jesus existed at that time. Under the guiding hand of God the Jews preserved their genealogical tables with remarkable accuracy through all the centuries before the birth of Jesus and also during the first century after His birth (cf. the numerous genealogical tables in the Old Testament). Ever since the earliest times the lineage lists were compiled and preserved as accurately as possible. After their return from the Babylonian exile the Jews again thoroughly fixed their genealogical tables by committing them to writing and bringing them up to date, and this was continued until the time of Josephus. In his *Autobiography* (para. 1) Josephus states that he reproduces his genealogical table as he found it " in the public records ". And in his work *Against Apion* (i) he relates how Jews—even those who lived outside Palestine—sent the names of their children to Jerusalem to be officially recorded.

It is also well known that the famous Rabbi Hillel at about the time of the appearance of the Saviour was able to prove his Davidic descent from the public registers.

Especially would persons like Joseph and the family of Mary, who were of Davidic descent, preserve their genealogical tables with special care because the Old Testament prophesied that the Messiah would be born of the house of David. Apart from the public registers, numbers of Jewish families kept private family trees in their homes and handed them down from generation to generation.

Thus Luke, probably through the instrumentality of Mary herself, or of persons intimately connected with her, obtained possession of the genealogical table of Mary's father Heli and committed it to writing in his Gospel. However, because it was not customary (among the Romans as well as among the Jews) to insert the name of a woman in a lineage list, he added the words " (as was supposed) the son of Joseph ". He was not afraid that his readers would get the impression that the genealogical tree was that of Joseph and not that of Mary, for in Luke i and ii he had pointed out expressly that Jesus was solely the son of Mary and not of Joseph and Mary. Why should he then reproduce the long family tree of Joseph which ends with the words " which was the son of Adam, which was the son of God " if he has already informed his readers that Jesus is in fact not Joseph's son but that uninformed people only " supposed so "? In the case of Matthew matters are entirely different. There he expressly reproduces the family tree of Joseph himself (and for this reason it naturally differs to such an extent from that given by Luke). He does so because Jesus was in the eye of the Jewish law the legitimate descendant of Joseph. For although He had no earthly father Joseph was nevertheless married to His mother and this established the legal relationship. Matthew writes for Christians of Jewish descent and they (especially those who could not yet understand the fact of the virgin birth) would have liked to know whether the man who was known as the father of Jesus was really of Davidic descent. With a view to the ministering to unbelieving Jews who before their conversion would naturally not attach any credence to Jesus' conception by the Holy Ghost, it was particularly necessary that Matthew should draw attention to the fact that Joseph, Jesus' *legal* father, was himself of Davidic descent.

But since Luke writes for Romans and Greeks with whom the Davidic origin of Jesus was no matter of topical interest, it was unnecessary for him to reproduce the genealogical table of Joseph.

Above all he wanted to show that Jesus, as regards His actual human descent, is through David, Abraham, and finally Adam, the Son of God. For this purpose the genealogical table of Joseph would have been of no use to him. For he specifically desires to prove the solidarity of Jesus with the human race, and of what benefit would it be to him to give the family tree of one who is not actually the father of Jesus?

That Matthew gives the family tree of Joseph and Luke that of Mary also fits in beautifully with the contents of the first chapters of their Gospels. For Matthew throughout gives the antecedents (announcement of the birth, the birth itself, the childhood years) as seen from the standpoint of Joseph, while in Luke we feel from beginning to end that we are concerned with the course of events from Mary's point of view. Matthew evidently obtained his data through persons who were closely connected with Joseph and to whom he had already before his death communicated the stories (probably his sons, as, e.g., James and Judas). Luke, on the other hand, obtained his information either from Mary or from intimate acquaintances of hers.

A conclusive proof that Mary was indeed of Davidic origin is the fact that the Jewish opponents of Christianity in the first centuries never denied the Davidic origin of Jesus. Since they knew the Christian claim that He was only the son of Mary, they would certainly have attacked His Messiahship on that ground, if they knew or even surmised that He was not a descendant of David.

24-38 While Matthew, who is writing for Jewish readers, begins with Abraham and then carries the genealogy down through David as far as Joseph and after that names Mary as the mother of

Jesus, Luke commences with Jesus and carries the family tree back as far as Adam, whom he then calls " the son of God " (because God had created him directly in His own image). That Luke does this fits in beautifully with the whole spirit of his Gospel. For he has his eye throughout on the universal, all-embracing significance of Jesus. For this reason, in the family tree, he draws attention very expressly to the fact that Christ (through Adam) is, in His manhood, related to the whole human race. As the second Adam, born of a woman but conceived of the Holy Ghost, His coming and appearance have a universal significance—not only for Israel but for the whole world.

In this genealogical table of Jesus we see His unity with all mankind. Therein we have, therefore, a powerful incentive to mission work in the fullest sense of the word: Jesus as Redeemer belongs not merely to a special nation or nations or to privileged groups of people but to all mankind. So the clarion call comes, " Go ye then, and make disciples of all the nations! "

[1] αὐτός, with emphasis, to accentuate the fact that it is He, the One of whom the foregoing has been related, who is henceforward the grand Subject of our narrative.

[2] After ἀρχόμενος we must understand διδάσκειν (Plummer, in loc.).

[3] ὡς ἐνομίζετο cannot here mean: " according to legitimate calculation ", seeing that the family tree goes back not only to David but to God, but should be taken in the sense, " as was supposed by them ", thus indicating that Joseph was not the real father of Jesus. From this it also follows that the genealogical table is not that of Joseph but of Mary, for otherwise it would have been of no value for the purpose for which Luke recorded it, namely, to show that Jesus is linked up with the whole human race through Adam.

The contention by Creed and others that ὡς ἐνομίζετο was inserted by Luke in the original genealogical table to prevent its clashing with what he had recorded concerning the virgin birth of Jesus is without any foundation. For the reason why Luke wrote these words here along with the name of Joseph in this family tree of Jesus through Mary, we refer to our exposition at verse 23.

[4] It is noteworthy that Luke has no τοῦ before Joseph as he has before every other name in the list. By this he shows that Joseph's name is not really part of the list. " By the omission of the article Joseph's name is separated from the genealogical chain and accorded a place of its own " (F. Rienecker, Praktisches Handkommenter zu Lukas Evangelium, 1930, p. 302). This had previously been pointed out by Godet (in loc.). That Jesus, therefore, according to this (if we take " as was supposed, of Joseph " as a parenthesis), is called the son of Heli, while Heli was

His grandfather, is not surprising. In Jewish lineage lists " son " was often used also in the sense of " grandson " or even " descendant " (cf. Matt. i. 8 where several names are omitted between Joram and Ozias; also cf. Dan. v. 11).

5 The Miriam, daughter of Eli, who is referred to in the Talmud (*Chagigah* 77d), has in all probability nothing to do with Mary the mother of Jesus, as is made plain in Strack-Billerbeck (*in loc.*). Godet, accepting the identification, asked: " From whence have the Jewish scholars derived this information? If from the text of Luke, this proves that they understood it as we do; if they received it from tradition, it confirms the truth of the genealogical document Luke made use of " (*in loc.*). As it is, however, this imagined confirmation proves unreal. It is true that we have no example in the old church fathers and of the other oldest Christian writers before the fifth century (see Creed, *in loc.*), where it is stated that Luke gives the genealogical table of Mary. This, however, proves nothing, for the earliest data in connection with the whole problem we only find in Julius Africanus (about A.D. 200). What most likely happened was that in the earliest times the true interpretation of Luke's genealogical table was generally known, so that no problem arose at first. Only when towards the end of the second or the beginning of the third century there was no longer any first-hand connection with the apostles and their contemporaries and first successors did the genealogical data begin to give trouble. See the Additional Note on p. 155.

6 Rhesa is probably not a personal name, but the Aramaic word for " prince " in the emphatic state (*rêshâ*), introduced originally as a title of Zerubbabel. The sense would then be: " Joanan, the son of Prince Zerubbabel, the son of Shealtiel." Zerubbabel, who was appointed governor of Judaea for a short time after the return from exile, would have the title " prince " as the heir of the kings of Judah. If this emendation is justified, it suggests that Luke was indebted to an Aramaic source for this genealogical table.

7 The names Zerubbabel and Shealtiel occur also in Matthew's genealogical list (Matt. i. 12). But there Shealtiel is called the son of Jechoniah (Jehoiachin), while Luke calls him the son of Neri. This may possibly be explained from the fact that Jechoniah had no child of his own (Jer. xxii. 30), and so Shealtiel, the son of Neri, was regarded as his legitimate heir (cf. Plummer, *in loc.*). For a detailed exposition cf. Plummer, *in loc.*, and Godet, *in loc.* However, matters are rendered difficult in this connection through the fact that there is a considerable difference of readings in the Old Testament genealogical tables in which we find the names of Shealtiel and Zerubbabel. No one, however, is in a position to charge either Matthew or Luke with error here. There are different possible explanations as to why their lists make contact in Shealtiel and Zerubbabel and then again separate as far as David (e.g. as a result of levirate marriages, adoption of heirs, and the like). Matthew and Luke both had excellent opportunities of access to the right genealogical tables.

[8] This is the climax to which the genealogical table leads up, and this is also the main purpose of Luke's inclusion of the genealogical table in his Gospel—to show that Jesus according to His human descent is one with all mankind.

Additional Note: Many of the problems arising out of this genealogical table and its relation to the Matthaean list are dealt with in a characteristically able manner by J. Gresham Machen in *The Virgin Birth of Christ*, pp. 203 ff. Dr. Machen, however, preferred the view that " Matthew gives the *legal* descendants of David—the men who would have been legally the heir to the Davidic throne if that throne had continued—while Luke gives the descendants of David in that particular line to which, finally, Joseph, the husband of Mary, belonged. There is nothing at all inherently improbable in such a solution. When a kingly line becomes extinct, the living member of a collateral line inherits the throne. So it may well have been in the present case " (*op. cit.*, p. 204).

THE TEMPTATION

(Cf. Matt. iv. 1–11; Mark i. 12, 13)

iv. 1–13

1 And Jesus, full of the Holy Spirit, returned from the
2 Jordan, and was led by the Spirit in the wilderness[1] during
forty days, being tempted[2] of the devil.[3] And he did eat
nothing in those days: and when they were completed, he
3 hungered. And the devil said unto him,[4] If thou art the Son
4 of God, command this stone that it become bread. And
Jesus answered unto him, It is written, Man shall not live
5 by bread alone. And he led him up,[5] and shewed him all
6 the kingdoms of the world[6] in a moment of time. And the
devil said unto him, To thee will I give all this authority, and
the glory of them: for it hath been delivered unto me; and to
7 whomsoever I will I give it. If thou therefore wilt worship
8 before me, it shall all be thine. And Jesus answered and said
unto him, It is written, Thou shalt worship the Lord thy God,
9 and him only shalt thou serve. And he led him to Jerusalem,
and set him on the pinnacle[7] of the temple, and said unto
him, If thou art the Son of God, cast thyself down from
10 hence:[8] for it is written,

He shall give his angels charge concerning thee, to
guard thee:

11 and,

On their hands they shall bear thee up,
Lest haply thou dash thy foot against a stone.

12 And Jesus answering said unto him, It is said, Thou shalt not
tempt[9] the Lord thy God.
13 And when the devil had completed every temptation,[10] he
departed from him for a season.[11]

Because Christ Jesus came as our Redeemer, " it behoved him
in all things to be made like unto his brethren, that he might be a
merciful and faithful high priest in things pertaining to God, to
make propitiation for the sins of the people. For in that he himself
hath suffered being tempted, he is able to succour them that are
tempted " (Heb. ii. 17, 18).

As real Man, Jesus could really be tempted, and from His
childhood days until the end of His earthly career He was exposed

156

to all the temptations that every human being has to contend with —except, however, those temptations that come from within as a result of the inward original taint or of the influence of former sins. Owing to His intrinsic spotlessness, temptations in His case could only come from the outside. Plummer rightly observes in this connection that " the fact that the solicitations came wholly from without, and were not born from within, does not prevent that which was offered to Him being regarded as desirable. The force of a temptation depends, not upon the sin involved in what is proposed, but upon the advantage connected with it. And a righteous man, whose will never falters for a moment, may feel the attractiveness of the advantage more keenly than the weak man who succumbs; for the latter probably gave way before he recognised the whole of the attractiveness; or his nature may be less capable of such recognition. In this way the sinlessness of Jesus augments His capacity for sympathy: for in every case He felt the full force of temptation " (*in loc.*). And Westcott remarks at Hebrews ii. 18: " Sympathy with the sinner in his trial does not depend on the experience of sin, but on the experience of the strength of the temptation to sin, which only the sinless can know in its full intensity. He who falls yields before the last strain."

If we bear these considerations in mind we shall realise that the Saviour experienced the violence of the attacks of temptation as no other human being ever did, because all others are sinful and therefore not able to remain standing until the temptations have exhausted all their terrible violence in assailing them.

Now the Lord Jesus did not have to endure temptations only during the forty days in the wilderness and the few other times referred to in the Gospels. For in Hebrews iv. 15 it is expressly stated that He " was in all points tempted like as we are ". Therefore He was tempted as Child, as Youth, and as full-grown Man just like every ordinary human being—except for temptations from within. To Adam also, the first man, the opportunity was given to choose between good and evil while his inward nature was still intact. In his case also, the temptation came from without. And yet he fell, with all the fatal results of that Fall. Christ, however, who had come as Head of the new humanity, was victorious over all the attacks of the powers of darkness. Throughout His earthly life He triumphed over all temptations, although they came upon Him with incomparable ruthlessness. Accordingly the temptations during the forty days in the wilderness and His triumph over them are merely an example of what He experienced and attained throughout His life on earth.

Nevertheless the temptations in the wilderness were special

temptations. They were not merely intended to tempt Jesus as Man, but to attack Him as the Messiah. This is evident from the fact that the temptations came immediately after His baptism when He had finally taken upon Himself His vocation as Saviour, and when God, by means of the heavenly voice, had given His approval to His decision and conduct, and had also equipped Him for carrying out this vocation by the special impartation of the Holy Ghost in all His fullness.

These temptations were, therefore, not the ordinary temptations such as Adam, the head of the old fallen humanity, had also to endure, but the special temptations which Jesus as Head of the new humanity had to experience. " And it is not simply a question here, as in our conflicts, whether a given individual shall form part of the kingdom of God; it is the very existence of this kingdom that is at stake. Its future sovereign, sent to found it, struggles in close combat with the sovereign of the hostile realm " (Godet, *in loc.*).

If Jesus had here (or indeed at any other time) lost in the conflict, God's whole plan of redemption in Him would have been defeated. As the Anointed One from heaven He had come to face the whole empire of evil and darkness in the person of Satan, the ruler of that empire.

1, 2 As the Ideal Man—perfectly developed in soul and body (ii. 52), full of the Holy Ghost and thus in the most intimate fellowship with the Father—Jesus, after His return from Jordan immediately after His baptism, is led in the wilderness by the Spirit. Fully equipped with all gifts for the execution of His calling as Messiah, the divine Redeemer, He is for forty days tempted of the devil. The conflict with the prince of the forces of darkness demands His attention and powers to such a degree that, although for days on end He had taken no food, it was only at the end of that period that He was conscious of hunger. The sense of physical need had been supplanted throughout by the violence of the spiritual conflict. Exhaustion followed upon this long period of wrestling and fasting, and it was now, at the end of the forty days, that the enemy came with his overwhelming attacks. When the Son of Man had been physically and spiritually exhausted to the utmost, the conflict with the Evil One reached its climax. After Christ had rejected the temptations, the proof had been furnished that, although He had found Himself in the most unfavourable circumstances when the devil launched his most ruthless attacks against Him, He was nevertheless victorious. What a contrast this forms with Adam, who fell although he was living at that time under the most favourable circumstances!

Since the Saviour, even under these extremely difficult and dangerous conditions, conquered as Man, it is a proof that man's fall into sin " was not due to any defect or inadequate equipment of that nature (as God created it), but to the subject of that nature, to man himself, who led his nature wrongly. By the temptations of the Lord and His firmness against all temptation, even the severest, there had thus to be brought to light God's right, man's guilt, sin's culpability, Satan's criminality " (Greydanus, *in loc.*).

3 The evil one realised in what a famished condition Jesus now found Himself and he assails Him precisely in this connection. By his first words (" If thou art the Son of God ") he attempts to put doubt into His mind: God had acknowledged Him at the baptism as His Son. How can this be reconciled with the fact that He has now already been in the wilderness for forty days, without food, forsaken and exhausted? How does He know, in the face of all outward signs to the contrary, that He is really the Son of God?

He then also attempts to incite Jesus to dissatisfaction, impatience and self-will. Why should He undergo such privation any longer—while He has the power of making bread even of the stones? Why should He deny Himself and submit to the laws of an ordinary human existence and so run the risk of starvation if He is able to change all by an authoritative utterance? This temptation of the evil one is thus directed against the chief requisites for the execution of His calling as Messiah: His consciousness of His vocation, His faith in God and His self-renunciation.

4 The Saviour, however, repels the temptation unconditionally. He had come to the wilderness under the guidance of the Holy Ghost and had lived there all the time under His guidance. Accordingly He knows that it is the will of His Father for Him to be thus foodless and famished. He does not doubt His love in this matter and He knows that His Father will in His own good time see that He again receives the food that He needs. However, before the Spirit leads Him to do it, He is not going to leave the wilderness. And still less will He abuse His divine gifts to make bread for Himself out of stones through an authoritative utterance, for this would be an act of insubordination and want of faith towards His Father. He does not desire wilfully to put an end to the privations that God has called upon Him to endure.

So Jesus replies with a quotation from God's Word (Deut. viii. 3) and resists the wily seductions of the devil. In these words He declares that He and every person are, ultimately, not dependent on bread, but on God, the giver and supporter of all life. According to the context in which these words occur in Deuteronomy, the reference is to the fact that in man's life everything depends on God: He is able, in a supernatural manner (as by means of the manna in the desert), to support man's life, and without His blessing even an abundance of material means will be of no avail. Everything depends on His authoritative word and blessing. Accordingly Jesus will not be perturbed and make bread from stones, but will persist with faith in God. He knows that His Father will not leave Him in the lurch. It is His meat, above all, to do the will of God (John iv. 34). It is not material interests but the relation to God that is of most importance. First the kingdom of God must be sought and then the other necessary things will also be added in His time and according to His will. Therefore Jesus, with the fullest confidence in and love for His Father, however exhausted He may be in body, will wait until the Father Himself guides His ways so that He may again receive the necessary bodily sustenance. In the meantime He will continue fasting in the wilderness. In Matthew iv. 11 we see that God did not put Jesus' faith to shame, but after He had finally repelled the devil sent angels to serve Him and to provide Him with what was needful.

5 God permits the devil to take the Saviour—in thought (we are probably to understand)—to a high mountain and to bring before His vision all the kingdoms of the world in one moment of time.

6, 7 The devil knows that Jesus came to the world to found the Messianic kingdom and to be the Head thereof. Now he declares that if only Jesus will worship him, he will give Him all the kingdoms of the world with all their glory. So he proposes that Jesus should found the Messianic kingdom by making a compromise with him. Then He will be able to achieve His aim without any struggle and suffering. He can make the offer, the devil declares, because all the kingdoms of the world have been delivered unto him and he has the power to give them to whomsoever he will. In these words Satan appears in his true colours, as the arch-deceiver and the aspirant after the power and glory which belong only to God. It is, indeed, true that by God's permission the kingdoms of the world (in so far as sin rules in the hearts and lives of the leaders and also of the individual members of the nations) have been delivered to him. Thus Jesus Himself spoke of him as the prince of this world (John xii. 31, xiv. 30, xvi. 11). But He did not mean it in an absolute sense as the arch-deceiver himself pretended. Only to the extent that mankind surrender themselves in sin to the evil one does God permit him to rule over the world of men, but nevertheless always under His highest and final overruling, so that everything in the end leads to His glory. God never lets the reins slip out of His hands. It remains true that " the earth is the Lord's and the fulness thereof, the world and they that live therein ". Even the powers of darkness cannot act without His *permissive* will. Moreover, the devil cannot deliver the world's kingdoms into the power of whomsoever he chooses, as he declared in the second temptation. God Himself is, in the final instance, the establisher and dispenser of worldly power (cf. Dan. iv. 17, etc.; John xix. 11; Rom. xiii. 1).

With his deceitful half-truths and cunning offer, Satan hazarded this assault against Jesus, especially in connection with the method and way by which He had to establish His kingdom, namely by attempting to lead Him to a compromise and to cause Him to bid farewell to the path of suffering.

8   This was probably the last temptation (as in Matthew) and not the second one (Luke does not profess to relate all details chronologically). Accordingly Jesus not only repels the temptation here, but commands Satan to go away. Once more Jesus beats off the crafty assault by referring to a pronouncement of God in the Old Testament (Deut. vi. 13). Here, as throughout the Gospels, we see how Jesus acknowledges the absolute authority of the Word of God and maintains it as guiding principle of His life as Man. What is written therein gives to Him the final, conclusive answer. So He does not argue with the devil, but again and again repels him unconditionally by means of a single pronouncement from God's Word.

Here He completely rejects the proposal of the devil that He should by way of compromise gain dominion over the world by the aid of the Evil One. Jesus' kingdom is not of this world (John xviii. 36, 37) and He refuses to acquire a kingdom for Himself by the worldly methods of sin, external violence, earthly power and glory. He chooses of set purpose to establish and build up the eternal kingdom of God along the road of self-denying love, struggling with spiritual weapons, suffering, and at last sacrificial death, in complete devotion and obedience to His Father. He has no desire to gain the kingdom for himself but for His Father, for He alone must be worshipped and served.

Just as the devil at the first temptation linked up his seductions with Jesus' legitimate and natural longing for food, so he here joined it to His legitimate desire for power—a desire which was very natural in His case as Messiah. Jesus, however, refuses entirely to seek for food and power along illegitimate paths and with wrong motives.

In His rejection of this temptation Jesus also repudiated the Jewish conception of an earthly Messiah and thus He ensured His own rejection by the majority of the Jews. And by refusing to choose Satan as leader or ally, He finally chooses the way of utter conflict with the powers of darkness, and the way of suffering and death.

9-11 Again God permits Jesus to be tempted in a special manner. The devil takes Him to a high pinnacle of the temple— again, no doubt, in thought—and again attempts to raise doubts in Jesus by commencing with the words: " If thou art the Son of God." He tries to induce Him to put God to the test in an idle and self-willed manner by casting Himself down from the temple. For, as Satan declares, it is written that God will preserve Him by means of His angels. He quotes the words of Psalm xci. 11, 12, but omits the words " in all thy ways ". In this manner he uses the quotation to make it appear as though Jesus would be fully justified in risking His life arbitrarily and then expecting God to protect Him.

It should be noted that the rabbis identified the person addressed by God in Psalm xci with the Messiah. The Midrash, known as *Pesiqta Rabbati* (162a), records a traditional belief that Messiah would manifest himself standing on the roof of the temple. The part of the temple indicated in the temptation narrative may have been the part overlooking the " Royal Colonnade "—which Josephus (*Antiquities*, xv, 11, 5) describes as looking down a precipitous descent into the Kidron valley, the height being so great as to make the spectator dizzy.

The object of this temptation was to seduce Jesus to test the faithfulness of God in a purely arbitrary manner and to expect of Him a spectacular intervention for His safety. Satan thus wants to tempt the Saviour to fanaticism—a sin of which many Jews at that time, and especially during the Roman-Jewish war, were guilty (their fanatical bigotry was indeed the main reason why the war ended with such terrible results for them). The conception of the promised Messiah accepted by many Jews, was in many respects that of a fanatical earthly leader (like Theudas or Judas the Galilean).

12 Jesus, however, again firmly repels the suggestion of the devil that He should test the faithfulness of God by exposing Himself to danger in a self-willed, unlawful manner and then expecting God to preserve Him. He does not for a moment waver in His trust in God and is not going to put Him to the test—for, indeed, he who tests God in this fashion proves thereby that he does not trust Him completely. Our Lord does not point out to the devil his omission of the words " in all thy ways ", nor does He argue with him, because He knows that he is false and full of deceit. So He again turns him away uncompromisingly with a single pronouncement from God's Word. He quotes the words of Deuteronomy vi. 16: " Ye shall not tempt the Lord your God " (changing the plural number to the singular). " To tempt " here means " to subject to a test or trial ", or perhaps " to see how far one can go with someone ".

In this manner Jesus rejects all self-will, self-seeking, self-display and fanaticism as being incompatible with God's Word and God's will.

13 The Greek of this verse may be understood as follows: " When the devil had ended every possible kind of temptation, he departed until a suitable time." In every possible way that he could think of he assailed the Saviour, but without avail. So he departed when vanquished, but not for good. Again and again he renewed his attacks on Jesus on suitable occasions (cf. xi. 13 and Mark viii. 32–33), even through Peter. But it was especially when the Lord on the eve of the crucifixion wrestled in Gethsemane that Satan attacked Him in person and with all the power and savagery of hell in a desperate attempt to overcome Him before He finally triumphed in His death on the cross over all the powers of darkness and confirmed His victory through the resurrection and ascension.

In the account of Jesus' temptations in the wilderness we see the prince of the forces of darkness in all his fiendish cunning and determination intent upon causing the failure of God's plan of redemption. But we thank God that we also see how our Redeemer, even under the most adverse circumstances (spiritually as well as physically) emerges from the conflict as the spotless and Holy One as well as triumphant Conqueror. And how wonderful it is to know that this conflict and victory of His took place not merely for His own sake but also, as our Leader and Representative, for our sake. Therefore we know that through Him we also are conquerors and that we must display this fact in practice for the glory of God.

---

[1] ἤγετο ἐν τῷ πνεύματι ἐν τῇ ἐρήμῳ. He was led *in* (ἐν) the wilderness and not merely *to* the wilderness, and not merely by (ὑπό) the Holy Ghost, but in (ἐν) Him. He was thus guided throughout in the wilderness by the Spirit, equipped with His fullness and enjoying the closest communion with God. For this reason He was

victorious. God never intended that any one should wrestle with evil without the power of the Spirit. Indeed, in the sight of God no man is really a normal person unless he is filled with the Holy Ghost and lives by His power. As the Ideal and Perfect Man, Jesus was completely at one with the Spirit. Armed thus, He won the battle.

² πειραζόμενος—the present participle, to indicate the persistence of the temptations throughout the forty days.

³ διάβολος—the Greek equivalent of Hebrew *sātān*, " adversary " —means " slanderer ", and refers to the fact that Satan tries to calumniate the devout before God (as in Job i–ii) and on the other hand to calumniate God before man (as in the temptation in Paradise and in the temptations of Jesus where Satan casts reflections on the faithfulness of God). He is constantly trying to make men accept false representations of God.

⁴ Conservative expositors differ on the question whether Satan appeared in visible form or not. In our opinion, no conclusive answer can be given. In any case, the Gospels tell us that Satan was personally and actually present. Whether this was in a visible shape or only in a spiritual sense makes no difference to the real nature of the case. It is nowhere stated that he was visible. Schlatter and Plummer side with those who accept a spiritual presence, while Greydanus is in favour of a visible presence in human shape.

⁵ There is again a difference of opinion as to whether this was visionary or actual, though in the nature of the case the former view seems more probable, as also in the account of the following temptation.

⁶ τῆς οἰκουμένης here means the inhabited world (cf. Heb. i. 6; Rev. xvi. 14) and not simply the Roman Empire, as in ii. 1.

⁷ πτερύγιον really means " a little wing ", and then anything resembling a little wing. Here the reference is probably to a high part of the temple jutting out like a little wing (Abbot Smith, *Greek Lexicon of the New Testament*).

⁸ Plummer's conception that the idea of this temptation is that Jesus must do something spectacular before the priests and the people is rejected by Schlatter (*in loc.*) and also by Greydanus (*in loc.*)—probably rightly.

⁹ ἐκπειράζω = " to try ", " to test ". Here it means to put the character and power of God to the test.

¹⁰ πάντα πειρασμὸν = " every temptation ", possibly meaning all kinds of temptations.

¹¹ ἄχρι καιροῦ—literally, " until a time " (i.e. until a suitable time).

JESUS IS DRIVEN FROM NAZARETH

iv. 14–32

14 And Jesus returned in the power of the Spirit into Galilee:
and a fame went out concerning him through all the region
15 round about. And he taught in their synagogues, being
glorified of all.

16 And he came to Nazareth,[1] where he had been brought up:
and he entered, as his custom was, into the synagogue on the
17 sabbath day, and stood up to read. And there was delivered
unto him the book of the prophet Isaiah. And he opened the
book, and found the place where it was written,[2]

18 The Spirit of the Lord is upon me,
Because he anointed[3] me to preach good tidings to the
poor:
He hath sent me[4] to proclaim release to the captives,
And recovering of sight to the blind,
To set at liberty them that are bruised,[5]
19 To proclaim the acceptable year of the Lord.[6]
20 And he closed the book, and gave it back to the attendant,
and sat down: and the eyes of all in the synagogue were
21 fastened on him. And he began to say unto them, To-day
22 hath this scripture been fulfilled in your ears. And all bare
him witness, and wondered at the words of grace which proceeded out of his mouth: and they said, Is not this Joseph's
23 son? And he said unto them, Doubtless ye will say unto me
this parable,[7] Physician, heal thyself: whatsoever we have
heard done at Capernaum, do also here in thine own country.
24 And he said, Verily[8] I say unto you, No prophet is acceptable
25 in his own country. But of a truth I say unto you, There were
many widows in Israel in the days of Elijah, when the
heaven was shut up three years and six months, when there
26 came a great famine over all the land; and unto none of them
was Elijah sent, but only to Zarephath, in the land of Sidon,
27 unto a woman that was a widow. And there were many
lepers in Israel in the time of Elisha the prophet; and none
28 of them was cleansed, but only Naaman the Syrian. And
they were all filled with wrath in the synagogue, as they
29 heard these things; and they rose up, and cast him forth out
of the city, and led him unto the brow of the hill whereon
their city was built, that they might throw him down head-
30 long. But he passing through the midst of them went his way.

31 And he came down to Capernaum, a city of Galilee. And
32 he was teaching them on the sabbath day: and they were
astonished at his teaching; for his word was with authority.[9]

From iv. 14 to ix. 50 Luke describes Jesus' ministry in Galilee.
The contents of vi. 20–viii. 4 do not occur at all in Mark (who
gives a much shorter account of Jesus' life). On the other hand,
Luke, for some reason or other, omits everything described in Mark
vi. 45–viii. 26. We notice throughout that, although Luke gives a
more detailed account of the story of Jesus, he nevertheless makes
a definite choice of what to include and what to omit.

When comparing the contents of Luke with those of John, we
see again how Luke (like the other Synoptists) omits numerous
details, especially in connection with Jesus' earliest public
ministry in Judaea. He nowhere declares that the incident
described by him in verses 14–32 is Jesus' first public appearance
after His baptism and the temptations in the wilderness. In fact, it
is clear from various details in his narrative that he assumes that
a great deal had already preceded this visit in Nazareth (cf.
verse 23).

The reason why Luke in recounting Jesus' public ministry
commences with the visit to Nazareth is linked up with the whole
framework of his Gospel. He depicts Jesus as the One who came
as God's Anointed to bring salvation not only to the Jews but to all
who believe in Him. For this reason it is especially appropriate
that he should begin with the story of Jesus' preaching and
rejection in Nazareth, for in this episode we observe Him so
clearly as the Anointed Redeemer who does not consider Himself
bound to bring the glad tidings to the Jews only.

14, 15 In these two introductory verses Luke gives a general
characterisation of Jesus' actions during that period in Galilee. He
particularly notes the fact that His appearance caused a tremendous sensation and that He was at that time still in very high
favour with the people.

16, 17 After His previous appearance in Galilee (verse 23)
and in Judaea (John i. 35–iv. 44) Jesus at length came again to His
old home-city of Nazareth, where He had grown up. By that time
the inhabitants of the little town had already heard many rumours
of Jesus' fame in Capernaum and elsewhere. During the thirty
years or so that He was in Nazareth the inhabitants knew and
honoured Him as the Perfect Man (ii. 52). But at that time He had
not yet performed any miracles or openly proclaimed His Messiahship. For this reason, after they had heard of His growing fame,

they were curious to see Him again personally and to hear Him. If Mark vi. 1–6 and Matthew xiii. 53–8 describe the same visit of the Saviour to Nazareth, we should picture to ourselves the course of events more or less as follows. A few days before the Sabbath Jesus had come there, healed only a few sick (Mark vi. 5) owing to the sceptical attitude of the inhabitants (the old acquaintances of a great person are but too often his keen critics and slow to believe in his greatness). For the time being, however, they had not yet clashed with Him, but adopted a waiting attitude until the Sabbath.

As He had been accustomed to do from His youth, Jesus on this occasion also went to the synagogue on the Sabbath. Someone else probably read the prescribed portion from the Law (the first five books of the Old Testament) in Hebrew and the official interpreter (*methurgeman*) translated it into Aramaic. After that, Jesus stood up as a sign that it was His wish to officiate for the rest of the service. It was customary to give such an opportunity in the synagogue to visiting rabbis; and especially as all were curious to hear Jesus, the head of the synagogue caused the book of the prophet Isaiah to be delivered to Him from which a portion had next to be read. Whether Jesus looked for a special portion that He wished to read or whether His eye immediately fell upon it we do not know; but probably it was the lesson from the Prophets (the *haphtarah*) appointed for that Sabbath.

18, 19 He then read a number of verses from Isaiah lxi. 1, 2 with a single phrase from Isaiah lviii. 6 that fitted in with the portion read first. As far as we know, He read in Hebrew and translated into Aramaic, the common spoken language at that time (see exposition at verse 21). G. Dalman finds reflections of the traditional Aramaic paraphrase (*Targum*) in the present passage in Luke.

20 After this He closed the book (since it was a parchment roll, the meaning is that He rolled it up again), and gave it back to the " servant " (*ḥuzzan*) who was subordinate to the head of the synagogue. Then, as was the custom, He seated Himself on the small platform intended for the purpose and proceeded to deliver His message by way of expounding the portion that had been read. Out of respect for the Word it was customary for the reader to stand while he was reading, but when a rabbi addressed the hearers in the synagogue he had to do so sitting. With the Jews the addresses or sermons were more in the nature of instructions than public orations.

So, after Jesus had sat down, the eyes of all (the old acquaintances in Nazareth) were fastened on Him expectantly.

21 We do not know everything that Jesus said: Luke merely gives a brief account of the main theme of His words. It amounted to a declaration by Him that the words which He had read to them had finally come to fulfilment—in His own person. By this He really announced that He was the One anointed by God with the Spirit to proclaim the glad tidings to the poor. God had sent Him to heal those who were broken-hearted and found themselves in spiritual distress; to proclaim deliverance to those who were captives in the power of sin and in spiritual wretchedness; to give back to the spiritually blind the power of sight; to cause those who were downcast and inwardly bruised to go forward in triumph; and thus to "proclaim the acceptable year of the Lord", i.e. to announce the Messianic age—the period ushered in by His appearance, in which God will grant His salvation to His people.

22 The words of the Lord were uttered with such graciousness, power and conviction that the first reaction on the part of the hearers was particularly favourable and they testified to His ability. But then came the turning-point when they reflected that, after all, He was only the son of Joseph whom they had already known as an ordinary person. And so their initial enthusiasm was chilled into indifference and scepticism.

23 Jesus immediately observed their unsympathetic and sceptical attitude and said that they would undoubtedly quote to Him the proverb: "Physician, heal thyself!" But a moment ago Jesus declared that He was anointed to give deliverance to the poor, the bruised, the captive, the blind, and the like. Now He knows that the hearers in Nazareth demand that He shall first give evidence that He has improved His own position and circumstances—for is He not a simple former inhabitant of Nazareth who Himself has had to struggle against poverty and difficult conditions? And if it is indeed true that He has performed so many miracles in Capernaum, let Him first reveal His miracle-working power in His home-town of Nazareth. Why, then, does He not first see to it that indisputable proofs be here given of the genuineness of His claims?

24-7 The reason why they do not also acknowledge Him as in other parts of Galilee is the well-known circumstance that an exceptional person is never recognised and treated as a great man by those who know him well. All kinds of factors, such as envy, contribute to this. To prove that this is always the case Jesus refers to the instances of Elijah and Elisha, who also did not meet with the necessary acknowledgment among their own people and were consequently sent by God to pagans to bring His salvation to them.

By this means Jesus proclaims plainly that unless the inhabitants of Nazareth and the Jewish people as a whole are going to accept Him as the promised Messiah He will turn to the heathen.

He refuses to comply with their demand to prove the genuineness of His claims through displays of power and sensational miracles. They were not desirous of salvation in their request for a revelation of His power, but did so with motives which were anything but holy, and which resulted in His refusal.

28 The indifference and unbelief of the Nazarenes were stimulated to blind hate through the plain words of the Lord, just as the Jews afterwards became enraged at Paul's statements of the same tenor, that God would give to the heathen the salvation which the Jews despised (Acts xiii. 46, 50; xxii. 21, 22).

29 Nazareth was (as it still is) situated in a hollow, high up against the slopes of a mountain, in such a manner that it is enclosed on three sides by more elevated portions of the mountain. The Jews, after they had driven Jesus out of the synagogue and the town, brought Him to one of the mountain peaks to throw Him down the cliffs.

30, 31 It was not yet the time for Jesus to lay down His life, and so He makes use of His divine power to foil the wicked plans of the Nazarenes to take His life. How He actually did this we are not told. In any case, He departed unscathed and again came to Capernaum on the shore of the Lake of Galilee and went on with His work.

32 As before (verse 15), His words find acceptance and the hearers are astonished at the power and authority of His teaching. Whilst the Jewish rabbis and scribes had spoken only by appealing to the traditions of their predecessors, Jesus spoke with a unique freshness and consciousness of His calling, based on the fact that He was the Son of God and thus possessed divine authority. The authority of the words of Jesus was the authority of absolute truth. For these reasons it was said of Him: " Never man spake like this man! " (John vii. 46).

No one will ever be able to do much for mankind unless he has a deep realisation of the terrible need of the human race. An imperfect insight into the actual needs and misery of man results in giving inadequate prescriptions for finding relief. Now it is characteristic of the Saviour's preaching that He referred in a remarkably plain manner to the unfathomable spiritual need of mankind. This appears especially in the words of Isaiah which He quoted in the synagogue at Nazareth and to which He attached the deepest meaning. He points to the condition of man as one of spiritual poverty, broken-heartedness, captivity, blindness and mutilation. This spiritual distress is caused by the sin of mankind. For sin makes man inwardly poor, sows destruction in his heart and life, makes him a captive in its stranglehold, makes him spiritually blind so that he loses all vision and all power of clear judgment, and crushes his personality.

How necessary and glorious, therefore, are the words of the Lord by which He assures us that He came not merely to *preach* a solution of the problem but to *bring* the deliverance Himself, yea even to *be* the Redeemer in His own person. Through Him God's work of redemption is actualised.

---

[1] It was held by Augustine in his day that this incident is the same as the one described in Matthew xiii. 53–8 and Mark vi. 1–6. The majority of expositors agree with this. Because it fitted in so well with Luke's scheme, he placed it first without thereby pretending that it was also chronologically first (see verse 23). The Nazareth sermon announced the programme of the Kingdom of God so clearly that Luke removed it from its Markan sequence to place it in the forefront of his account of Christ's ministry. The idea of Creed (*in loc.*) that Luke purposely expanded Mark's shorter rendering editorially in this manner without having actually had the data for his further details is entirely groundless. There is no contradiction between Luke and the other Gospels in connection with Jesus' visit to Nazareth (cf. our explanation at verses 16, 17).

[2] Strack-Billerbeck say that it has not been possible to ascertain whether as early as the time of Jesus certain prescribed portions from the Prophets had to be read on the different Sabbaths; there is good evidence, however, that it was so.

[3] ἔχρισέν (aorist) = " He anointed " (once and for all), i.e. at the baptism.

[4] ἀπέσταλκέν με (perfect) = " He has sent me " (and as a result I am now here). ἀποστέλλω differs from πέμπω (the usual word for " send ") in that in many cases, and almost always in the New Testament, it has the subsidiary idea of being sent with delegated authority, as representative of the one who sends. Cf. for a thorough demonstration of this the article of Rengstorf on ἀποστέλλω in Kittel's *Theologisches Wörterbuch zum Neuen Testament*.

[5] Why this sentence from Isaiah lviii. 6 is added here we do not know. It is known that it was not necessary to read only consecutive verses, but to omit portions if the reader so desired. But it is not certain whether it was permitted in the time of Christ even to turn back the scroll. No definite decision can be made regarding this matter, and we cannot say that our Lord could *not* have turned back to Isaiah lviii. 6.

[6] Because ἐνιαυτόν is qualified by κυρίου, it is not an ordinary year, but the whole of the period of salvation which God inaugurates with the appearance of the Messiah.

[7] παραβολή is derived from παραβάλλειν, which means " to lay side by side ", " to compare ", and thus refers to a figure taken from daily life and teaching a spiritual truth. Such a figure of speech may be worked out in detail as in some of Jesus' parables, or may be a brief, gnomic statement, as here.

[8] ἀμήν (" verily ") is here used to emphasise and affirm the seriousness of the words that follow. It is derived from the Hebrew אָמֵן ('āmēn) which means something which is true, firm, steadfast, or faithful, and thus calls attention to the veracity of what is said.

[9] Reitzenstein interprets ἐξουσία here wrongly in a quasi-magic sense (cf. Creed, in loc.). The word here means " authority and power over " (cf. Foerster, " ἐξουσία, ", in Kittel's Theologisches Wörterbuch zum Neuen Testament).

CURE OF THE MAN POSSESSED OF A DEVIL IN CAPERNAUM

(Cf. Mark i. 23-8)

iv. 33-7

33 And in the synagogue there was a man, which had a spirit
34 of an unclean devil; and he cried out with a loud voice, Ah!
what have we to do with thee,[1] thou Jesus of Nazareth? art
thou come to destroy us? I know thee who thou art, the
35 Holy One of God.[2] And Jesus rebuked him, saying, Hold
thy peace, and come out of him. And when the devil had
thrown him down[3] in the midst, he came out of him, having
36 done him no hurt.[4] And amazement came upon all, and they
spake together, one with another, saying, What is this word?[5]
for with authority and power he commandeth the unclean
37 spirits, and they come out. And there went forth a rumour
concerning him into every place of the region round about.

The Son of God came out of the invisible, eternal, divine world
for the purpose of destroying the works of the devil (1 John iii. 8).
This was fully realised by the members of the kingdom of the evil
one (Mark i. 24, v. 7; Luke iv. 34). Accordingly it goes without
saying that the power of darkness would attempt everything to
conquer Christ or at any rate to hamper Him as much as possible.
Especially after the Saviour had so decisively repelled the devil's
temptations in the wilderness, the evil one brought all possible
manner of hellish rage to bear on Christ and tried to oppose
the establishment of His kingdom. Demon-possession was one of
the means used by the kingdom of darkness in this struggle. The
proximity and the rage of Satan and his satellites were clearly
reflected in this. In order to be truly the Redeemer, Jesus had
also to engage in strife with demon-possession and to prove that
He had indeed overcome the power of the evil one. This is the
reason why in the Gospels numerous instances are described where
Jesus delivered demon-possessed persons. Luke realised the
importance of this matter and therefore he relates at this early
stage in his Gospel a striking example of how Jesus triumphed
over the forces of demons by casting out an evil spirit.

33, 34 The silence in the Capernaum synagogue while Jesus was busy giving instruction there, or had probably just ended His instruction, was suddenly interrupted by a man who began to cry out with a loud voice. He was possessed of " a spirit of an unclean demon ", and was indeed so dominated by him that he shouted out as the mouthpiece of the demon: " Ah! what have we to do with thee, thou Jesus of Nazareth? " This is not an exclamation of surprise but of terror and dismay. In the presence of the Holy One the demon is convicted by the knowledge that for him and his kind only destruction is waiting. He knows and recognises Christ as the Holy One of God, and therefore cries out, shuddering with terror.

35 Jesus does not reason with the evil spirit but immediately rebukes him and commands him to hold his peace and forthwith to come out of the man who was his unhappy victim. Although he has openly admitted that Jesus is the Holy One of God, Jesus would have nothing to do with him and delivers the man from his domination. In his desperate rage the demon threw the man down, but Jesus' manifestation of power was so perfect that He even prevented the man from being in any way hurt.

36, 37 This proof of His divine authority and power filled those present with amazement. Never before had they seen such a manifest overthrow of the powers of darkness. The result was that rumours concerning Jesus' unique power were spread everywhere in the vicinity.

Horrible growths vegetating in darkness become shrivelled up and die when exposed to the bright sunlight. This is also the case in the spiritual field. Where the light of the Pure One, Christ Jesus, falls, the impure powers that thrive in darkness disappear.

[1] τί ἡμῖν καὶ σοί; a Hebraism, used to indicate that two parties have nothing to do with each other.
[2] Plummer correctly observes: " It was not in flattery that the evil spirit thus addressed Him but in horror. From the Holy One he could expect nothing but destruction " (in loc.). The final destruction of the power of the evil one will be carried out only at the final Consummation. In principle the power of darkness has, however, already been overcome and convicted.
[3] and [4] ῥίπτειν and βλάπτειν are regarded by Hobart as definitely medical terms (Medical Language of Luke, p. 2).
[5] λόγος. Possibly the reference is here particularly to the command of Jesus that the evil spirit must come out of the man.

SPECIAL NOTE

DEMON-POSSESSION

In the New Testament demon-possession means that a person is dominated by the spirit of a demon and tormented by him. It is noteworthy that it is distinguished (especially in the Gospel of the physician, Luke) from cases of ordinary sickness, insanity ("lunacy"), leprosy, blindness, lameness, deafness and other natural defects and diseases (cf., e.g., Matt. iv. 23, 24, viii. 16, x. 8; Mark vi. 13; Luke iv. 40, vii. 21, 22). Accordingly this was not merely an ordinary form of mental disease as some writers have alleged, but a special phenomenon which was particularly frequent during Jesus' earthly sojourn and thus was directly connected with His coming to destroy the power of darkness.

That the unclean spirits were personal beings is evident from what is related about their leaving a possessed person, talking or crying out, possessing knowledge concerning Jesus, as well as other supernatural knowledge—showing fear, and the like.

Demon-possession is, therefore, not merely a mental state in which someone suffers from a delusion or is subjected to some subjective disturbance of the world of ideas. Neither is it only a kind of physical disease, although spiritual and physical disease often accompany it (e.g. Matt. xii. 22, xvii. 15; Mark ix. 18).

It is noteworthy that Jesus nowhere speaks of forgiveness of sins or of purification-sacrifices that have to be brought after His curing of such cases (as He did in some cases of physical illness). Those possessed are depicted throughout as unfortunate sufferers who by no fault of their own are dominated by evil spirits and who, when the spirits are cast out by Jesus, accept their deliverance with joy and gratitude (Mark v. 18–20, Luke viii. 2).

It should also be observed that nowhere in the Old Testament (except in 1 Sam. xvi. 14 ff. and 1 Kings xxii. 22 ff. where something similar occurs) is demon-possession mentioned, and that outside the Gospels it is referred to only twice in the New Testament (Acts xvi. 16 ff., xix. 13 ff.). From this it is clear that *demon-possession is a phenomenon which occurred almost exclusively, but then to be sure on an amazing scale, during Jesus' appearance on earth and to a lesser extent during the activity of the apostles.* For the reason why this is so we refer the reader to the introduction preceding the exposition of verses 33–7.

Although demon-possession after that time no longer occurs on such a devastating and noticeable scale, the absolute form of demon-possession will appear at the end of the age in the Antichrist and in his followers (2 Thess. ii. 9; Rev. xiii. 2 ff., xvii. 8 ff.). But then also Christ will triumph and finally put an end to the evil one and all his powers of darkness (Rev. xvii. 14).

For an illuminating discussion see Otto Borchert, *The Original Jesus,* pp. 410 f. (*special note on demon-possession*); cf. also John L. Nevius, *Demon Possession and Kindred Themes* (New York, 1895); W. M. Alexander, *Demonic Possession* (Edinburgh, 1902); W. O. E. Oesterley, " Demoniacal Possession ", in Hastings' *Dictionary of Christ and the Gospels*, vol. i, p. 438; A. R. Short, *Modern Discovery and the Bible* (London, 1943), pp. 89 ff.

THE HEALING OF SIMON'S MOTHER-IN-LAW AND OTHER WORKS OF JESUS

(Cf. Matt. viii. 14–17; Mark i. 29–31)

iv. 38–44

38 And he rose up from the synagogue, and entered into the house of Simon.[1] And Simon's wife's mother was holden
39 with a great fever;[2] and they besought him for her. And he stood over her, and rebuked the fever; and it left her: and immediately she rose up and ministered unto them.
40 And when the sun was setting, all they that had any sick with divers diseases brought them unto him; and he laid his
41 hands on every one of them, and healed them. And devils also came out from many, crying out, and saying, Thou art the Son of God. And rebuking them, he suffered them not to speak, because they knew that he was the Christ.
42 And when it was day, he came out and went into a desert place: and the multitudes sought after him, and came unto him, and would have stayed him, that he should not go
43 from them. But he said unto them, I must preach the good tidings of the kingdom of God[3] to the other cities also: for therefore was I sent.
44 And he was preaching in the synagogues of Galilee.[4]

In the foregoing portions Luke has shown Jesus as the One equipped with the Holy Ghost as Son of God and the Messiah (at the baptism); as the Conqueror over the temptations of the evil one (in the wilderness); as the One who spoke with final authority and who possessed divine power over men (at Nazareth and Capernaum); as the One who has power to cast out evil spirits (the case in the synagogue at Capernaum); and he now shows us how Jesus came also to deliver man from physical diseases.

The Saviour came to save man as man, in soul and body alike. For this reason He acted throughout as the great Physician of bodily ailments.

38, 39 In 1 Corinthians ix. 5 it appears that Peter was married; and one of the early Christian writers, Clement of Alexandria, tells that his wife helped him in ministering to women (*Stromata*, iii, 6).

176

Now his mother-in-law, who was staying with him in his house at Capernaum, was seriously ill with fever. From the accurate description in this verse we learn unmistakably that the narrator is the physician Luke. After Jesus had been consulted about her, he healed her so completely by an authoritative word that, although she was suffering from a great fever (always an exhausting sickness), she immediately arose and waited on them. Here nothing is said about Peter's wife. Although she may have been there, her mother could nevertheless have ministered to them, especially as a proof of her gratitude.

40, 41 The instances of casting out demons and of healing mentioned by Luke were no exceptional cases. This is evident from what is related in these verses. The Jewish days commenced and ended with the setting of the sun. That was the reason why the inhabitants of Capernaum waited on that day (which was a Sabbath) until sunset (when the Sabbath ended) and then brought their sick and demon-possessed people to Jesus. Although the Saviour had already been through a long and fatiguing day, He still continued until a late hour with His self-sacrificing service. He laid His hands upon the sick, one by one, and healed them, and with His word of power cast out the demons from many who were possessed. The evil spirits again showed that they knew Him as the Anointed Son of God, but Jesus did not suffer them to speak. He wanted no proclamation of His Messiahship through them, the spirits of hell, with whom He has nothing in common.

42 Early in the dawn the Lord left the city unnoticed to go and seek quietness after all the exertion and activities among the masses on the previous day. The multitude, however, went to seek Him and insisted that He should stay with them.

43 However much sympathy He may have felt for the needy multitude, He did not accede to their request. His task at Capernaum was completed and He had to obey the will of His Father and to proceed to other cities, there to preach by word and deed the glad tidings of the kingdom of God. This was His divine calling and He could not restrict His works of mercy and His teachings to one place only.

44 So He went to other places in Galilee and continued His work.

While Jesus is here depicted as the great Physician of the human body as well as of the soul, we must remember that no one has the right to-day to demand that He should heal every disease and this always, or in most cases, without the use of medicine. He is still the

G

177

Almighty and Merciful Physician who is able to heal any illness without such aids where He so desires. It is, however, clear from God's Word that it is not always His will to heal diseases. With a perfect plan in view, He permits even some of His most faithful followers to endure unspeakable afflictions, sometimes even unto death. It is also clear from God's Word that the normal way of healing is that of using medicines (all being gifts of God's mercy) with the prayer that the Lord may give His blessing on them where such is His will.

The case of Jesus' healings during His sojourn on earth is something quite different from what obtains at the present time. He performed the work of healing as a revelation of His love for and sympathy with suffering mankind, and also as a proof that He was really the Messiah and that He came to deliver man in soul and body. The healings effected by the apostles were also of a special nature and were intended to confirm the genuineness of their claims as the founders of the church. No one may, therefore, to-day attempt to imitate the Lord Jesus or the apostles. But, of course, there should in every case of illness be a humble and believing looking up to God in prayer. And where such is His will, He will heal through medicines, or in special cases even without them. But we should never prescribe to God how He is to act. The perfect healing in soul and in body, achieved by Jesus for all believers, will become full reality only to His coming, when the faithful will live and rule along with Him in risen and glorified bodies. Before that Day no believer has the right to demand perfect healing just as he has no right to expect that he will be exempted from all other afflictions of life and from death. It is, indeed, everyone's duty to watch over the well-being of his body to the best of his ability, and to pray in faith that to himself and to others shall be given that measure of recovery and health that is in accordance with the will of our Heavenly Father, who always acts in wisdom and love. And the beautiful and assured prospect always remains that Christ Jesus, who during His public ministry acted as the Perfect and Almighty Physician, will one day cause all the faithful on the New Earth to share fully in the rich inheritance of complete salvation in soul and body.

---

[1] Simon was formerly from Bethsaida (John i. 44) but moved to Capernaum.

[2] Galen and other ancient medical writers distinguished between cases of fever as $\mu\varepsilon\gamma\acute{a}\lambda o\iota$ and $\sigma\mu\iota\varkappa\varrho o\acute{\iota}$. Where Luke describes the case of Simon's mother-in-law by $\mu\varepsilon\gamma\acute{a}\lambda\wp$, where this is not done by Mark

and Matthew, it is an indication of his medical knowledge (Hobart, *op. cit.*, p. 3).

[3] See Special Note below on " The Kingdom of God ".

[4] Probably *Judaea* (so R.V. margin) is the correct reading here: it is to be understood in the wider sense, as equivalent to " Palestine " (cf. i. 5).

SPECIAL NOTE

THE KINGDOM OF GOD

The kingdom of God (ἡ βασιλεία τοῦ θεοῦ) first indicates the ruling activity of God and then the divine rule in its saving operation on the one hand and in its judicial action on the other hand. Then it also refers to the field where the rule of God is exercised and finally to the divine rule as it will at the end of time be fully realised and exist through eternity. βασιλεία may mean " dominion ", " royal sovereignty ", " royal territory ", " kingdom ", and even " royal majesty " (cf. Abbot-Smith, *Manual Greek Lexicon of the New Testament*).

Of special importance is Dalman's exposition of the meaning of " the kingdom of God " (*The Words of Jesus*, pp. 91-139). He states *inter alia*: " No doubt can be entertained that both in the Old Testament and in Jewish literature מַלְכוּת [*malkûth*] (βασιλεία), when applied to God, means always the ' kingly rule ', never ' the kingdom ' as if it were meant to suggest the territory governed by Him " (p. 94). Cf. Psalm xxii. 29, ciii. 19, cxlv. 11, 12, 13; Obadiah 21. Also cf. Schweitzer, *Mystery of the Kingdom of God*; Rudolf Otto, *The Kingdom of God and the Son of Man* (especially pp. 53-7); K. L. Schmidt in G. Kittel's *Theologisches Wörterbuch zum Neuen Testament*, article on " βασιλεία "; P. Feine, *Theologie der Neuen Testament*, pp. 92-117; Greydanus (*in loc.*); Stevens, *Theology of the New Testament*, pp. 27 ff.; C. H. Dodd, *Parables of the Kingdom*, pp. 34-80; T. W. Manson, *The Teaching of Jesus*, pp. 116 ff.; A. N. Wilder, *Eschatology and Ethics in the Teaching of Jesus*, pp. 35 ff., 172 ff.; James Moffatt, *The Theology of the Gospels*, pp. 53, 56, 109; C. J. Cadoux, *The Historic Mission of Jesus*, pp. 107-14; Gloege, *Reich Gottes*, pp. 49-51; Strack-Billerbeck, i, pp. 172 ff.; E. F. Scott, *The Kingdom of God*; Hughes, *The Kingdom of Heaven*; Vincent Taylor, *Jesus and His Sacrifice*, pp. 6-11; Maurice Jones, *The New Testament in the Twentieth Century*, pp. 103 ff.

THE MIRACULOUS DRAUGHT OF FISHES

1 Now it came to pass,[1] while the multitude pressed upon
him and heard the word of God, that he was standing by the
2 lake[2] of Gennesaret; and he saw two boats standing by the
lake: but the fishermen had gone out of them, and were
3 washing their nets. And he entered into one of the boats,
which was Simon's, and asked him to put out a little from
the land. And he sat down and taught the multitudes out of
4 the boat. And when he had left speaking, he said unto
Simon, Put out into the deep, and let down your nets for a
5 draught. And Simon answered and said, Master,[3] we
. toiled all night, and took nothing: but at thy word I will let
6 down the nets. And when they had this done, they inclosed
a great multitude of fishes; and their nets were breaking;
7 and they beckoned unto their partners in the other boat, that
they should come and help them. And they came, and
8 filled both the boats, so that they began to sink.[4] But Simon
Peter, when he saw it, fell down at Jesus' knees, saying,
9 Depart from me; for I am a sinful man, O Lord.[5] For he was
amazed,[6] and all that were with him, at the draught of the
10 fishes which they had taken; and so were also James and
John, sons of Zebedee, which were partners with Simon.
And Jesus said unto Simon, Fear not; from henceforth thou
11 shalt catch men. And when they had brought their boats to
land, they left all, and followed him.

In the previous chapter Luke depicted the Lord Jesus in His
self-revelation as the Messiah of God, as the One who repelled
the temptations of the evil one, who spoke with absolute authority,
cast out unclean spirits and healed physical diseases. In chapter
v he continues to portray the Saviour in His revelation of power.
Here in verses 1-11 he shows how He is also the Almighty Disposer
of the fish of the lake and how He is recognised and followed by
His disciples as a unique Person.

1-3 Luke does not say anything here as to when this event
took place. From the data of the other Gospels it appears that it
was probably quite early during the Galilean ministry, but after
the Lord's first meeting with Peter, John, Andrew and others

(John i. 35–52). It was also after the first call of Peter and the others to be disciples of Jesus (Matt. iv. 18 ff., Mark i. 16 ff.). From this it becomes clear that, although they had followed Jesus at the first call, they did not yet follow Him in a complete and unconditional manner. They were still, at least for part of the time, engaged in their trade as fishermen until the final choice was made to leave all and follow Jesus (v. 11).

On a certain morning, then, Jesus was on the shore of the lake of Gennesaret near Capernaum (for Simon lived there). As a result of His fame at that time, a great multitude had already collected around Him there early in the morning to listen to His teaching. In order to be able to address the multitude more effectively, the Lord entered into Peter's ship—one of two that were lying by the shore of the lake. (The other probably belonged to the sons of Zebedee.) He then asked Peter to push out a little from the land, and from there He taught the multitude out of the ship.

4-7 After finishing His teaching, He commands Peter to launch out from the shore into the deep and to fish there. Peter raises the objection that they had already toiled all the night to catch fish but had been unsuccessful. (According to verse 2 they were already washing their nets to put them away.) The best time for fishing with nets was during the dark night and the worst time was during the morning with the glistening rays of the sun on the waters. But although everything appears to be so unfavourable for fishing, and although Peter and his companions are exhausted after the sleepless and fatiguing night on the lake, the group of fishermen, under Peter's leadership, nevertheless obey Jesus' command. They had already seen many of Jesus' miracles and been impressed by His preaching. So they obey Him, although all circumstances pleaded against it.

Contrary to all human expectation, they catch so many fish in the nets they have let down that they are compelled to call in the assistance of their partners in the other ship. And even then both ships are filled to the utmost with the fish that have been caught.

8-10 All were astonished at the revelation of Jesus' power even over the fishes of the lake—that He could bring about the draught in such a supernatural manner. Peter, who was always the most impulsive one among them, forgets the danger in which the overloaded ships are placed and falls down at the Saviour's feet with the words: " Depart from me; for I am a sinful man, O Lord! "

Peter had already previously seen many revelations of power on the part of the Lord. Although these had impressed him and even made him agree to follow Jesus, this revelation of His power of disposal over the fishes of the lake spoke to him in a very special manner. For he was a fisherman by trade and knew how humanly impossible it was to catch fish successfully in the lake in the early morning hours. The Lord's revelation of power in the field of Peter's own particular calling—the trade of a fisherman—consequently made a very powerful impression on him. That is why it was precisely after this event that he fell down before the Saviour under an overwhelming sense of His superhuman, divine glory and with a deep realisation of his own utter sinfulness. This realisation of sin in Peter's case may perhaps have to be attributed to the fact that, after he had previously begun to follow Jesus, he had again left Him and returned to his old profession, and that he had now come to a profound realisation of the foolish sinfulness of his former half-heartedness.

In any case, this event formed a tremendous turning-point in Peter's life. His exclamation reminds us of Job's words, " now mine eye seeth thee. Wherefore I abhor myself, and repent in dust and ashes " (Job xlii. 5, 6), and also of Isaiah's words after he had seen the glory of God: " Woe is me! for I am undone! " (Isa. vi. 5). When Peter, through Jesus' revelation of power, began to see Him in His divine majesty, this immediately brought him instinctively to realise his own sinfulness. The first natural reaction of a person under such circumstances is to feel that one cannot exist before the Holy One, and therefore Peter cried out impulsively: " Depart from me, O Lord! " This, however, does not mean that it was his permanent, definite desire that the Lord should really leave him.

The Saviour understood Peter's state of mind and therefore He immediately replied with the reassuring words: " Fear not; from henceforth thou shalt catch men." Instead of having, through fear and despondency, to give up the idea of being a disciple of Jesus, he receives from the Saviour the assurance that he will in future be a successful follower of Him.

11 From the nature of the case it follows that the multitude of fishes were first properly dealt with and disposed of. Jesus would not have let them catch the fish to be cast into the sea again or to be wasted. Undoubtedly the Lord allowed them to divide and sell the fishes and to provide for their dependants before commencing to follow Him continuously. Through the miraculous draught of fishes the Saviour thus taught them that He was able to provide for them and their dear ones. It was a valuable lesson to them that if they obeyed Him and entrusted themselves to Him He would provide for them and their families even with regard to temporary needs.

After this wonderful occurrence Peter and the others who were with him (Andrew, James and John) finally chose to forsake all and follow Jesus.

By our Lord's words in verse 10, " from henceforth thou shalt catch men ", it is clear that we should also understand this event symbolically in connection with evangelisation. So the message comes to the church " to launch out into the deep and there to cast the net of the Gospel ". In spite of all failures in the past, the church of Christ must again and again renew its energetic attempts under His guidance to gather in souls for His kingdom, and must do this not merely in the " shallow waters " but in the " deep water "—not only in the vicinity of settled ecclesiastical life, but also among the great masses of people where the need is so great. When the church is obedient in this, " men will be caught "—her work will bear fruit.

[1] This story is by no means the same as that in Matthew iv. 18–22 and Mark i. 16–20. The points of agreement between Luke's story and those of Matthew and Mark may be explained from the fact that Peter and his partners lived at Capernaum as fishermen and were often engaged in their calling on the shore of the lake. For this reason Jesus probably often found them there. Their decision to follow Him wholly and unconditionally was not taken just all of a sudden; there had already been meetings with Jesus and a certain amount of following Him as His disciples after the events related in Matthew iv. 18–22 and Mark i. 16–20. All this, however, was only preparatory to what takes place in verses 1–11. The fact that this occurrence is not related by Matthew and Mark is no argument against its historicity. Not one of the Gospels professes to give a full account of all things. There are numbers of possible explanations why Matthew and Mark relate that first call and are silent about that of verses 1–11.

Wellhausen and Bultmann maintain that the narrative of Luke is his own creation, with didactic objects in view, and that John xxi is a readaptation of it. In diametrical opposition to this, another fairly radical critic declares that " the Johannine version gives a more natural and, presumably, a more original setting " (Creed, *in loc.*). Harnack, again, thinks that Luke and John borrow their accounts from the alleged " lost end " of Mark (*Luke the Physician*, p. 227). E. Klostermann regards the stories in Luke and John as " Petrine legends " (*in loc.*). W. Manson, on the other hand, regards the stories of John and Luke as " different settings of the same tradition " (*in loc.*).

For all these divergent views (which, indeed, contradict and cancel each other) there is no valid ground. Why could not the occurrence of verses 1–11 have taken place as well as that of John xxi? The points of agreement between them are perfectly natural, while the differences are so far-reaching that the supposition of a common source or literary dependence is impossible. In neither of the stories is there a single detail that would make it appear unhistorical. " There is nothing improbable in two miracles of a similar kind, one granted to emphasise and illustrate the call, the other the recall, of the chief apostle " (Plummer, in loc.). Since no single proof can be advanced against the historicity of the stories, the burden of proof continues to rest on those who refuse to accept the stories as true. And the inclination to regard all stories with a few points of agreement as variations in the rendering of the same occurrences is utterly unwarranted.

2 Luke does not speak of the " sea " of Galilee as do the other Gospels that follow the popular manner of speaking, but refers to it accurately as the " lake ". The lake of Gennesareth (or sea of Galilee) is seven miles wide and thirteen miles long. It is situated six hundred feet below sea-level, among mountains and hills, and presents a fine sight. In Jesus' time it was practically surrounded by busy towns and villages and there was a lively trade in fish.

3 ἐπιστάτα—only used by Luke in the New Testament. He avoids the non-Greek word ῾Ραββεί which occurs so often in the other Gospels (cf. Creed, in loc.). " The form ἐπιστάτα, . . . alongside διδάσκαλε, is merely a Greek synonym for the latter, and both are to be traced back to the Aramaic רַבִּי [Rabbi] " (Dalman, The Words of Jesus, p. 336).

4 Klostermann's objection (in loc.) that if the ship was so full Peter would not have fallen down before Jesus is extremely weak and far-fetched. He does not take into consideration the violent emotion by which Peter was overwhelmed.

5 Κύριε. " The address need not mean more than ' sir ', cf. John xx. 15; but here the word must carry its full force of ' Lord '. It expresses a feeling of awe, not suggested by ἐπιστάτα " (Creed, in loc.). This change in the form of address (cf. verse 5) is in full harmony with the change of circumstances—while " Master " (verse 5) refers to someone whose commands must be obeyed, " Lord " points to Someone whose majesty and holiness occasion moral anguish in the sinner (cf. Plummer, in loc.).

6 W. Manson rightly states that " the impression wrought by Jesus was profoundly inward and moral. The disciples are stirred to the depths of their nature by the transcendent qualities of the character of Jesus, and there begins for them what can only be called a reintegration of personality round a new centre " (in loc.).

THE HEALING OF A LEPER

(Cf. Matt. viii. 1–4; Mark i. 40–5)

v. 12–16

12   And it came to pass, while he was in one of the cities,
 behold, a man full of leprosy:[1] and when he saw Jesus, he fell
 on his face, and besought him, saying, Lord, if thou wilt,
13 thou canst make me clean. And he stretched forth his hand,
 and touched him, saying, I will; be thou made clean. And
14 straightway the leprosy departed from him. And he
 charged him to tell no man:[2] but go thy way, and shew thyself
 to the priest, and offer for thy cleansing, according as
15 Moses commanded, for a testimony unto them. But so much
 the more went abroad the report concerning him: and
 great multitudes came together to hear, and to be healed of
16 their infirmities. But he withdrew himself in the deserts,
 and prayed.

Jesus revealed Himself not only as the Almighty Disposer over
the fish of the lake by causing the miraculous draught of fishes to
happen; He is also the Almighty Physician, who even heals the
humanly incurable disease, leprosy.

12   Again Luke does not state when the occurrence took place
or in what time-relation it stands to the foregoing. Chronological
order in all details is, from his point of view, not essential, but what
does matter is a properly arranged account of Jesus' Self-revelation.
In Matthew viii. 1 ff. it is placed immediately after the sermon
on the mount. In a city somewhere in Capernaum a leper came to
Jesus, although it was against the Law that he should come into a
city or near healthy persons (Lev. xiii). By some means or other he
had heard of Jesus' healing miracles and he believed whole-
heartedly that He was able to heal his leprosy. So when he came
to Jesus he immediately fell down before Him and besought Him
to heal him. Apparently he did not yet know the Lord's mercy,
for he says: " if thou wilt ". Or are these words the expression of
his deep humility and submission to His will? He does not want to
demand a cure and to prescribe to Jesus what He must do.

13   In Jesus' attitude to the Sabbath laws He lived up to the
principle that in cases of conflict the law of love and pity should

receive precedence over the ceremonial laws. Here, too, we see the same principle. It was against the ceremonial laws to touch a leper. And nevertheless Jesus did so in this case because pity demanded it. Jesus thus showed that it was truly His will to cleanse the leper and that He is the Almighty One who can heal even this incurable and infectious disease.

14 Jesus does not want the multitudes at this stage to become too enthusiastic about His miraculous works, because it may possibly lead to their proclaiming Him as earthly Messiah. He therefore charges the cleansed man to tell none of the general public how he has been cleansed. But nevertheless he must obey the precept of the Law (Lev. xiv) and show himself to the priest and make the appropriate offering for his cleansing so that he may be pronounced ceremonially clean. The priests will thus have evidence that Jesus does not disregard the ceremonial laws where they do not clash with the law of love, and also that He is indeed the Messiah who heals even leprosy.

15 In Mark i. 45 we read that the cleansed man did not obey Jesus' command and that he spread the news far and wide among the masses how miraculously he had been healed by Him. He did this out of gratitude towards Him, but nevertheless it was against His will, and the action had injurious results (Mark i. 45). Luke does not expressly mention this, but indicates in general terms that great multitudes came together to Him to hear His teachings and to be healed by Him.

16 As so often in his Gospel, Luke again calls attention to the fact that Jesus repeatedly withdrew to seek quiet and to enjoy communion with God in prayer.

Leprosy is presented in God's Word as the symbol of sin. So this story of how Jesus cleansed the man full of leprosy brings a powerful message of His desire and power to cleanse from sin. He who in humility and with confession of sin falls down before Him in faith also hears the glorious words: " I will: be thou clean! "

---

[1] πλήρης λέπρας. While the other evangelists merely state that he was leprous, Luke the physician gives the more accurate description. Creed remarks that " πλήρης is frequently used in Greek medical writers of disease " (*in loc.*), in the sense " infected ".

[2] In other circumstances, where there was no danger that the masses would develop a dangerous form of enthusiasm, Jesus did in fact command persons whom He had healed to proclaim publicly that He had done so (cf. viii. 39).

HEALING A MAN WITH A PALSY

(Cf. Matt. ix. 1–8; Mark ii. 3–12)

v. 17–26

17 And it came to pass on one of those days, that he was teaching; and there were Pharisees and doctors of the law sitting by, which were come out of every village of Galilee and Judaea and Jerusalem: and the power of the Lord was
18 with him to heal.[1] And behold, men bring on a bed a man that was palsied: and they sought to bring him in, and to
19 lay him before him. And not finding by what *way* they might bring him in because of the multitude, they went up to the housetop,[2] and let him down through the tiles[3] with
20 his couch into the midst before Jesus. And seeing their[4]
21 faith, he said, Man, thy sins are forgiven thee. And the scribes and the Pharisees began to reason, saying, Who is this that speaketh blasphemies? Who can forgive sins, but
22 God alone?[5] But Jesus perceiving their reasonings, answered
23 and said unto them, What reason ye in your hearts? Whether is easier, to say, Thy sins are forgiven thee; or to say, Arise
24 and walk? But that ye may know that the Son of man hath power[6] on earth to forgive sins (he said unto him that was palsied), I say unto thee, Arise, and take up thy couch, and
25 go unto thy house. And immediately he rose up before them, and took up that whereon he lay, and departed to his
26 house, glorifying God. And amazement took hold on all, and they glorified God; and they were filled with fear, saying, We have seen strange things to-day.

Luke continues his portrayal of Christ and shows how He was not merely able to control the forces of nature, to perform healings and the like, but that He has the right and the power to forgive sins—a right and power which belong only to the Almighty.

17 Once more the chronological setting of this event is indefinite. Mark puts it very early in the ministry of Jesus, recording it as the first of a series of " paradigms " (ii. 1–iii. 6) or illustrative stories used in the apostolic preaching. Matthew (ix. 2 ff.) places the occurrence at Capernaum after Jesus had returned from the land of the Gergesenes where He had delivered

187

a man possessed by demons (Matt. viii. 28). As appears from John v. 16, the Lord had already come into conflict with the Jewish authorities and they wanted to slay Him. So it was quite natural that Pharisees and doctors of the law (see Special Note, p. 189) should have gone to Capernaum from Jerusalem and elsewhere to observe all His doings carefully. While they were thus watching Him with suspicion, Jesus again revealed Himself as the divine Physician.

18, 19 A number of men who had firm faith in Jesus' healing power tried to bring a paralysed man to Him. The house in which He was had, however, so many people in it that they could not make their way through the multitude. Nevertheless they are determined to take their friend to Jesus. So they climb on to the roof of the house, make an opening in the roof and let down the palsied man with the couch on which he is lying so that he is placed before Jesus.

20 The men had an exceptional faith in Jesus, otherwise they would never had taken all the trouble. The Lord, through His perfect insight into human life, realised immediately that the sickness of the paralytic was closely connected with the sin of which he was guilty. For this reason He first comes down to the root problem and says: " Man, thy sins are forgiven thee! " In other cases Jesus showed plainly that He did not accept the opinions that were current at the time, to the effect that all cases of physical disease were associated with sin (cf. John ix. 3). In this particular case, however, sin did indeed lie at the root of the paralysis.

21 Because God alone has the right and power to forgive sin, Jesus through His action clearly revealed that He is one with God. Nevertheless the Pharisees and scribes, instead of recognising this, accuse Him of blasphemy.

22-4 In a certain sense it is easy to say: " Thy sins are forgiven thee! " for no one is able to prove that it is not true. But when a paralysed man is told to " Rise up and walk! " there must come real healing, or otherwise it is obvious to all that the words possess no value. In this sense it is therefore more difficult to say it. So Jesus orders the paralysed man to rise up and go home. And so, through the revelation of His omnipotence in visible things, His power in the invisible realm—to forgive sins—is also proved. (See Special Note on " The Son of man ", p. 352.)

25, 26 The onlookers realised how humanly hopeless the condition of the paralysed man was, so that his instantaneous cure by Jesus causes great amazement. They could not but acknowledge that this was a work of God and that Jesus in some way or other stood in a special relation to God.

What a challenging example is given to us by these men who, without counting the cost, were so determined to take their paralysed friend to Jesus! And it still remains the holy vocation of the faithful to take to the Saviour those who are spiritually paralysed through the stranglehold of sin. And where He finds real faith in Himself, the Saviour repeats His word of power: " Man, thy sins are forgiven. Rise up and walk."

¹ The correct reading here is αὐτόν (singular) and not αὐτούς (plural), which would give the meaning: " There was power from God to heal *them*." The sense is therefore: " There was power from God so that *He* (Jesus) could effect cures."

² Many houses in Palestine had stairs leading from the outside up to the roof.

³ Luce and others declare that " Luke transforms the Palestinian clay-roofed house into a Roman house with a tiled roof " (*in loc.*). It is, however, unnecessary to deduce this from the single word κεράμων. With all the Gentile influence in Palestine at that time, why could not some Jewish homes have had tiled roofs? Mark (ii. 4) says they " uncovered " the roof and " dug " through it.

⁴ As appears from the fact that Jesus forgives the sins of the man, the reference is here to the faith of the paralysed man himself as well as that of the men who brought him (cf. Plummer, *in loc.*). Zahn and Schlatter are probably incorrect in stating that only the men who brought the paralytic are included in " their ".

⁵ That God could and did freely forgive sins was well known: the scribes and Pharisees criticised Jesus on the ground " that he claimed to himself the exclusive prerogative of God " (Montefiore). True, but He claimed it rightly.

⁶ ἐξουσία here means " power " as well as " authority ", " right " and " ability " (cf. note at iv. 32).

SPECIAL NOTE

PHARISEES AND DOCTORS OF THE LAW

(*a*) *Pharisees.*

The name Pharisees is probably derived from the passive participle of the Hebrew verb *pārash* (פָּרַשׁ), which means " to separate ", and thus they are referred to as " the separated ones ". Immediately after the return from the Babylonian exile we see the development in the Jewish national life of the tendency that eventually leads to the definite formation of the Pharisaic party. Under the leadership of Ezra the pious ones among those that returned made sure of a thorough knowledge of the Law of God as incorporated in the Old Testament books that had already been written. In a painstaking manner they aimed at a conscientious fulfilment of the law and guarded against all foreign influences. It was their ideal that Israel should live as a " separated " people with God as their only King.

The attitude of Antiochus Epiphanes (about 168 B.C.), who attempted to make Israel pagan by force, gave a tremendous impetus to this movement. While the priestly party co-operated with the foreign tyrants, the *chasidim* (" pious ones ") ranged themselves on the side of the Maccabees, who joined issue against the foreigners. During this time there was a progressively strong endeavour to keep the Law of God pure and to ward off all foreign influences. After the initial successes of the Maccabean uprising regained religious freedom for the nation, the *chasidim* discontinued active participation in the struggle with secular weapons. And when in the time of John Hyrcanus (135–105 B.C.) the political leaders of Israel again sought to link up with foreign nations, the *chasidim* of set purpose opposed this tendency, and at least since then they were called the Pharisees (" separated ones ") and more and more formed a distinct party. The priest-rulers of the Maccabean dynasty even adopted violent measures against them, but their influence grew to such an extent that since the reign of Alexandra (76–67 B.C.) they gained the lead and practically dominated the whole of the national life. This influence they retained even after the Romans had subjugated Palestine in 63 B.C. And owing to the antipathy of the people against the Herodian rulers (from 37 B.C.) their influence grew at an increasing pace among the masses of the people, so that in the time of Christ they were the recognised leaders to whom the people looked up for guidance in almost every sphere of life.

According to Josephus (*Antiquities*, xvii, 1, 1), the Pharisaic party at that time consisted of some six thousand full members, but, in addition, had practically all the ordinary Jews as their admirers. The actual members of the party were persons who lived in a most conscientious manner according to the precepts of the Law as interpreted by their scribes (or doctors of the law).

Their characteristic views were : (1) The people must live according to the Law of God (which according to them also included the oral interpretations and regulations handed down by tradition) and must be free from all foreign influence and aim at a theocratic form of government.

(2) They fixed their hopes on the coming Messiah, whom they represented as an earthly ruler who would deliver them from their pagan oppressors.

(3) They attached a special value to the oral traditions and expositions of the Law and in particular observed numerous ceremonial laws in connection with the distinction between " pure " and " impure " and in connection with the observance of the Sabbath. Through the many subtle provisions of the oral law their zeal for the Law often degenerated into superficiality and formality. While observing outward provisions

of the Law very painstakingly, they violated the real spirit of God's laws in many instances and fell into hypocrisy. This was the case especially in the time of the Lord when they had already for a long time been the " people's party " and had in various ways become degenera-ate. It was for this reason that Christ took up such a severe attitude towards them and exposed their inconsistency. In their pride and self-righteousness they exalted themselves above the ordinary people and laboured under the delusion that through their outward obser-vance of the Law they would receive rich rewards from God. Blinded through their spiritual degeneration, they rejected Jesus and, as Professor J. A. C. van Leeuwen writes, " the wickedness of their self-righteous hearts is full-grown when in the name of the Law they reject Him who is the fulfiller of Law and prophecy " (*trans.* from *Christelijke Enc.* under " Fariseërs "). For further details cf. E. Schürer, *Gesch. d. jüd. Volkes*, J. Wellhausen, *D. Pharisäer u.d. Sadducäer*, A. Schlatter, *Gesch. Israels*, G. F. Moore, *Judaism*, and Strack-Billerbeck, *op. cit.*

(*b*) *Doctors of the Law.*

This word indicates the same persons as the " scribes " (cf. Strack-Billerbeck, *in loc.*). They were learned persons whose vocation it was to study the Law (written and oral), and to expound and teach it. Because among the Jews at that time the study of the Scriptures con-sisted mainly of a study of the Law, the " scribes " were also called " doctors of the law ". The vast majority of them belonged to the Pharisaic party. But not all Pharisees were scribes or doctors of the Law. The doctors of the Law among the Pharisees thus had as their vocation the study of the provisions of the Law, handing it down and expounding what they themselves and all other Pharisees had to observe with practical precision. They were subject to the same spiri-tual blindness as the Pharisaic party as a whole, and consequently the majority of them rejected Jesus (see bibliography *supra* under note on " Pharisees ").

THE CALL OF LEVI

(Cf. Matt. ix. 9–13; Mark ii. 14–17)

v. 27–32

27 And after these things he went forth, and beheld a
publican, named Levi,[1] sitting at the place of toll, and said
28 unto him, Follow me. And he forsook all, and rose up and
29 followed him. And Levi made him a great feast in his
house:[2] and there was a great multitude of publicans and of
30 others that were sitting at meat with them. And the Pharisees and their scribes murmured against his disciples, saying,
Why do ye eat and drink with the publicans and sinners?[3]
31 And Jesus answering said unto them, They that are whole
32 have no need of a physician; but they that are sick.[4] I am
not come[5] to call the righteous but sinners to repentance.[6]

In the previous portion we saw how Jesus exercised the divine
authority and power even to forgive sins. Here we observe how He
came for the express purpose of calling sinners to repentance and
reshaping their whole life in such a manner that they should follow
Him as His disciples.

27 Levi, who was also called Matthew (Matt. ix. 9), and after
whom our first Gospel is named, was a tax-collector (" publican ")
in the service of Herod Antipas (in whose kingdom Capernaum
was situated). Along the main road between Acre, on the
Mediterranean Sea, and Damascus, in the north, that went past
Capernaum, Levi was sitting in his custom-house to collect for
Herod the customs on the goods transported by that road. Like
all " publicans ", he himself annually received a considerable sum
of money and was therefore most probably rich. But because he
and his fellow-" publicans " were collaborators with the foreigner
or hirelings of the despised Herod they were held in contempt by
the Jews and regarded as outcasts and outrageous sinners.

Matthew (Levi) had no doubt heard and seen a good deal of
Jesus in Capernaum and felt particularly drawn to Him. Jesus
knew that he was ripe for such a call, and so, when He walked
past him, He commanded him to follow Him as His disciple.

28, 29 Levi immediately obeyed Jesus' words, left everything

192

at the custom-house and followed Him. Because he was eager that his fellow-" publicans " and other acquaintances should also have the opportunity of getting acquainted with Jesus and becoming His disciples, he prepared a great feast for the Lord in his house and invited them to it.

30-2 While the feast was in progress some of the scribes and Pharisees came there also (cf. Matt. ix and Mark ii), probably uninvited, for the purpose of observing Jesus' doings. In answer to their objection to His eating along with publicans and sinners, the Lord says that it was precisely in order to call sinners to repentance that He had come, for " they that are whole have no need of a physician, but they that are sick ". Jesus does not mean by this that the scribes and Pharisees are not also sinners. Elsewhere in the Gospel it appears that He also went to eat with them, and taught and reproved them (vii. 36, xi. 37, xiv. 1). Here, however, the justification of His association with " publicans " and sinners is dealt with. From the words of the Saviour it further appears that those who in their self-complacency imagine themselves to be righteous and spiritually healthy will have no part in the salvation brought by Him. But those who know themselves as sinners will find that He has come to call and heal them. In His attitude towards sinners Jesus was quite different from the Jewish religious leaders who thought it beneath their dignity to mix with sinners and to seek to save them. The best ones among them did allow sinners to come to them to seek a better life, but they never went to fallen ones to try to reclaim them.

The highest vocation of the church of Christ always remains to call sinners to repentance to the glory of God. The church must never be satisfied to preach to " respectable " people only, but should continually be engaged in evangelising those who have fallen into sin or who religiously are outsiders. If Jesus came not to call the righteous but sinners to repentance, this is also the supreme function of His church.

---

[1] A comparison with Matthew ix. 9 makes it clear that Levi is the same person as Matthew.

[2] Since the great feast was held in his own house, it proves that he was a well-to-do person.

[3] The Talmudical tractate *Berakoth* (43) expressly states that the disciples of the scribes may have no table communion (W. Manson, *in loc.*) with the '*Am-ha-'arets* (" the people of the land ", those who do not know or observe the Law).

[4] W. Manson rightly observes: " Over against the Pharisaic idea of salvation by segregation Jesus sets up the new principle of salvation by association " (*in loc.*).

[5] Of Jesus alone it may be said in real and literal sense that He *came* to the world, for He existed from eternity before His incarnation.

[6] Montefiore and Abrahams allege that the Jewish synagogues always stood open for repentant sinners, but admit that there is no example of a Jewish religious leader who (like Jesus) went to seek sinners to call them to repentance (cf. Creed, *in loc.*). " Jesus did not avoid sinners, but sought them out: this was a new and sublime contribution to the development of religion and morality " (Montefiore).

WHAT FASTING MEANS

(Cf. Matt. ix. 14–17; Mark ii. 18–22)

v. 33–9

33 And they said unto him, The disciples of John fast often,
and make supplications;[1] likewise also the *disciples* of the
34 Pharisees; but thine eat and drink.[2] And Jesus said unto
them, Can ye make the sons of the bridechamber[3] fast,
35 while the bridegroom is with them? But the days will come;
when the bridegroom shall be taken away[4] from them, then
36 will they fast[5] in those days.[6] And he spake also a parable
unto them; No man rendeth a piece from a new garment
and putteth it upon an old garment; else he will rend the
new,[7] and also the piece from the new will not agree with the
37 old. And no man putteth new wine into old wine-skins;
else the new wine will burst the skins, and itself will be
38 spilled, and the skins will perish. But new wine must be put
39 into fresh wine-skins. And no man having drunk old *wine*
desireth new:[8] for he saith, The old is good.

Luke has already shown us the unique authority and power of
Jesus and His unique attitude towards the outcasts from Jewish
society—calling them to repentance with a love that seeks them
out. He now shows how Jesus Himself expressly taught that the
form of religion which He preaches and calls into being, is quite
different from that of the followers of John and of the Pharisees.

33 We know from John iii. 26 how envious some of the disciples of John were of Jesus; and those of them who did not listen
to their leader's declarations concerning Him took up a critical
attitude towards Him and His disciples. So some of them come
(Matt. ix. 14) and want to know why His disciples do not also
"fast often and make supplications" like themselves and the
disciples of the Pharisees. (See Special Note on "Fasting",
p. 198).

34, 35 Jesus replies by asking whether it is morally possible
for them to compel the children of the bridechamber (His disciples) to fast while the bridegroom (Jesus Himself) is still with
them. But the days will come when He will be forcibly taken away

195

from them, and then they will spontaneously abstain from food and drink through the grief that overcomes them. Thus we have here Jesus' first reference to the fact of His approaching death (by the expression " taken away ", He suggests that it will be a violent one). In the first instance the Lord here refers to the time from His arrest until His resurrection—then the disciples will of their own accord and without compulsion fast as a result of the grief in their hearts. In a lesser sense the reference is also to the time from His resurrection until the pouring out of the Holy Ghost when He again returned to His followers in the Spirit. So we may not interpret the Lord's words (as the Roman Catholic Church does) as a command that Christians must fast regularly. The words refer only to the time when He had been " taken away " and when the disciples fasted of their own accord because they could not eat or drink owing to the grief in their hearts. After His resurrection and His return through the Holy Ghost, He came to be near and with His followers until the end of the world (Matt. xxviii. 20), and therefore every believer is called upon to be joyful in Him and not to fast in sorrow. A joyful, healthy spiritual discipline indeed always remains the characteristic of a true follower of Christ.

36 In order to indicate still further how very different the religious life is which He brings to His followers, Jesus tells two parables. In them He teaches that, just as it is foolish to mutilate a new garment by tearing from it a piece to repair an old garment, it is equally foolish to mutilate the new way of life taught and called into existence by Him for the sake of the old, obsolete forms of religion such as those of the followers of John and of the Pharisees. Patching up an old garment with a piece of a new garment not only disfigures the new garment, but also causes the old garment to become more ragged than ever, for the new piece has still to shrink and will then pull the old threadbare garment to pieces. Just as fatal will it be to adapt the principles of Jesus to the old systems.

37, 38 These truths are here presented still more clearly. New wine which has the power to ferment cannot be put into old, stretched leathern bottles, for the fermenting wine will cause the bottles to burst and thus the wine as well as the bottles will be lost. But when the wine is put into new, elastic wineskins, both will be preserved. In like manner it is fatal to attempt to preserve the vigorous, new form of divine worship, which Jesus brought, in the old, obsolete forms of religion of the disciples of John and of the Pharisees. Jesus' new way of life also demands new forms of worshipping God. There must be no mixing of the old with the new. There is indeed the closest connection between the Old and the New Dispensation, but only in the sense of preparation and fulfilment, shadow and reality. And now that Jesus has come as the Fulfiller of the promises of the Old Covenant, everything has been made new and no room is left for the old ceremonial, shadowy forms of divine worship. The new spirit existing in the religion of the New Covenant demands new forms of expression. So Jesus does not allow His disciples to act like those of John and of the Pharisees.

39 In these words our Lord explains why the followers of the old forms of religion are not immediately inclined to accept the new forms which He brings. Just as one who is accustomed to drink old wine has no taste for new wine, so those who are accustomed to the old form of divine worship have no taste for the new form of religious life taught and inaugurated by Him. This aversion to His new way was what led to the Saviour's being crucified by the persevering adherents of the old Jewish religion.

Just as the new forms of religion brought by Jesus could not tolerate any compromise with the old forms, so it is also with the new life which every regenerated person finds in Christ. The acceptance of this new life demands the renunciation of all forms of the old life of sin and unbelief. There must be no mixing with the former kind of life to which a man was accustomed before his conversion. Jesus desires and is able to make everything new in the life of the believer.

---

[1] δέησις = supplication, arising out of a sense of need.

[2] Here the reference is not to special feasting but merely to " not fasting " as contrasted with " fasting ".

[3] τοὺς υἱοὺς τοῦ νυμφῶνος—a Hebraism, indicating the wedding-guests who are most closely connected with the bridegroom (Plummer, *in loc.*). Cf. Judges xiv. 11.

[4] ἀπαρθῇ suggests a violent removal by death.

[5] The change is noteworthy from " make . . . fast " in verse 34 to " will . . . fast ". No outward compulsion will be necessary.

[6] Jesus' words here refer to the time from his arrest and crucifixion until His return by the Holy Ghost at Pentecost. Only in a secondary sense are subsequent times of stress referred to.

[7] This detail does not occur in Matthew and Mark, but does not clash with their account (as Creed, *in loc.*, alleges). Luke is here more complete than they are. The piece torn out of the new garment here definitely refers to the freedom of the Lord's disciples to refrain from fasting. If this liberty be taken away from them, their whole new

education will be impeded. On the other hand, if this liberty not to fast be forced upon the old system, it will create chaos there without producing salvation.

[8] The point at issue here has nothing to do with the comparative merits of old and new wine, but refers to the predilection for old wine in the case of those who are accustomed to drink it.

SPECIAL NOTE

FASTING

In the Old Testament fasting is ordered only on the Great Day of Atonement as a definite institution (Lev. xvi. 29, where " afflict your souls " also includes " fasting "). But fasting was also practised voluntarily as a sign of mourning (2 Sam. i. 12), at times of disaster and national calamities (Neh. i. 4), as a sign of repentance for sin (1 Kings xxi. 27), and the like. Thus originally it bore a rich religious significance. During the Babylonian exile, as a result of the lack of the sacrificial services, the opinion arose more and more that fasting was a meritorious work that would be rewarded by God. Thus the practice of fasting assumed an increasingly outward and formal character and lost much of its religious value. For this reason the prophets during and after the exile took such drastic action against it. True fasting, they proclaimed, consisted not in abstaining from food and drink but in renouncing sin (Zech. vii. 5 ff.). Still the degeneration grew apace, so that in the time of Jesus it had become a fixed practice with the Pharisees and many other Jews to fast regularly twice a week (Luke xviii. 12) with much outward display and hypocrisy (Matt. vi. 16, ix. 14).

Jesus' attitude towards fasting briefly amounts to this, that He rejects it as a religiously meritorious ceremony bearing a compulsory, ceremonial character; but He practised it Himself at times and permits it as a voluntary form of spiritual discipline (Matt iv. 2, vi. 16–18).

It was as such a voluntary religious practice that the first Christians observed fasting (Acts ix. 9, xiii. 2, 3, xiv. 23). But after the third century it degenerated in many cases to an obligatory and supposedly meritorious formality as it is still to be met with today among Roman Catholics, Jews and Mohammedans.

JESUS IS LORD OF THE SABBATH

(Cf. Matt. xii. 1–8; Mark ii. 23–8)

vi. 1–5

1 Now it came to pass on a sabbath,[1] that he was going
through the cornfields; and his disciples plucked the ears of
2 corn, and did eat, rubbing them in their hands. But certain
of the Pharisees said, Why do ye that which it is not lawful
3 to do on the sabbath day? And Jesus answering them said,
Have ye not read even this, what David did, when he was
4 an hungred, he, and they that were with him; how he
entered into the house of God,[2] and did take and eat the
shewbread, and gave also to them that were with him; which
5 it is not lawful to eat save for the priests alone?[3] And he said
unto them, The Son of man is lord of the sabbath.

Luke still continues to set forth the contents of his Gospel
narrative in such a manner that we see Jesus more and more
clearly as the One who reveals Himself as the Messiah, the
Redeemer of the world. In the last portion of chapter v the Lord
taught that He had brought a complete renewal of the religious
forms and their application. And now He shows that this also
applies to the keeping of the Sabbath.

1, 2   On a certain sabbath Jesus and His disciples were walking
through the cornfields. The disciples were hungry and plucked
some of the ears, rubbed them in their hands and ate the grain.
According to Deuteronomy xxiii. 25 it was lawful to pluck ears in
the cornfields of others. But according to the rigid opinions of the
Pharisees the behaviour of the disciples was in conflict with the
Sabbath laws. According to them, the plucking and rubbing of
the ears was precisely the same as harvesting and threshing and
therefore was forbidden on the Sabbath. At that time the rigid
observance of the Sabbath was one of the main constituents of the
Jewish religion. Apart from the principles in connection with the
keeping of the Sabbath in the Old Testament, the doctors of the
law laid down literally thousands of subtle provisions of what was
commanded and especially of what was forbidden on the Sabbath.

199

Thus the keeping of the Sabbath had degenerated into deadly formalism. For this reason they clashed as they did with Jesus' free, spiritual attitude towards the Sabbath.

3, 4 In this reply Jesus lays down the principle that no ceremonial provision must stand in the way of providing for the essential needs of life. The spirit of the Sabbath observance must not lead to an unnecessary burden being imposed on those who keep it. Just as the conduct of David (1 Sam. xxi) was not against the spirit of the divine Sabbath laws, so likewise the behaviour of Jesus' disciples on the Sabbath (verse 1) is not sinful, because the eating of the corn-ears was necessary for their physical well-being.

These words do not, however, mean that in the keeping of the Sabbath attention should be paid only to the physical needs of man. Throughout the Gospels it is clear that the Lord taught that the Sabbath should be consecrated to God, and acted accordingly. It is therefore fitting that on the day of rest man should so disentangle himself from ordinary activities that he may be able to serve and glorify God to the best of his ability. For this reason also Jesus regularly attended divine service in the synagogues on the Sabbath. He, however, rejected all outward, man-made formalism in connection with observance of the day.

5 Here Jesus expressly declares that as the Messiah, the Son of Man, He has plenary power to appoint in what spirit and in what manner the Sabbath should be kept. In later days the church—guided, we may well believe, by the Spirit of Jesus—changed the day on which the weekly rest was observed (the seventh day) to the first day (the day of His resurrection from the dead), as a symbol of the fact that the Old Covenant of Works had given place to the New Covenant of Mercy and Liberty. In place of the old rigid Sabbath observance He introduced the new spiritual Sabbath-rest. Thus the deepest purpose of the original Sabbath commandment was realised by Him. For this reason it is fit and proper that Christians should dedicate the first day of every new week to Him in a special sense; while it remains true that the Christian has not one holy day in the week, but seven.

In straightforward language Jesus taught that the observance of the Sabbath should never degenerate into dead, outward formalism which constitutes a stumbling-block to the full development of the life of the believer.

Christians are thus to observe the Lord's day not in the slavish, rigid spirit of the Pharisees (who were but too often tainted with hypocrisy), but in newness of heart and life, as those who are, through Christ, the beloved children of God.

[1] δευτεροπρώτῳ ("second-first", R.V. margin; "the second sabbath after the first", A.V.) should probably be inserted here; its omission by so many of the best textual authorities may be due to ignorance of its meaning. It is "presumably a technical expression of the Jewish calendar" (E. Klostermann, *in loc.*). We cannot be sure what it meant, though Strack-Billerbeck are probably right in taking the term to indicate "a Sabbath which comes second in a series of Sabbaths, the numbering of which begins with the first Sabbath. . . . The situation of Luke vi. 1, the time when the corn was ripe, requires us to think of a series of Sabbaths which lay in the neighbourhood of the Passover. At this time the days and weeks were in fact numbered, according to Leviticus xxiii. 15 f., and so were the Sabbaths between Easter and Whitsuntide. So the 'second-first' Sabbath would mean the second Sabbath after the 15th Nisan, the 'first Sabbath' being that which fell in Passover week itself. The numbering of the days between Easter and Whitsuntide began on the evening of the 15th Nisan with the commencement of the 16th Nisan" (*in loc.*).

Greydanus is also of the opinion that it was approximately Easter-time, since the corn was ripe in the ears. "It would then probably have been the first Easter after that of John ii. 13 ff., preceding that mentioned in John vi. 4. By that time the Lord had been working in public for about a year, namely first for eight months in Judaea, cf. John ii. 13–iv. 35, and next for four months in Galilee, cf. John iv. 35, 43" (Greydanus, *in loc.*).

[2] The sanctuary at Nob (1 Sam. xxi. 1).

[3] Even Montefiore speaks in connection with Jesus' attitude towards the Sabbath of "the greatness and originality of Jesus", and then continues: "His teaching is an excellent counterbalance to that casuistic minuteness which is the danger of legalism. It is emancipating: it allows one to breathe freely" (*The Synoptic Gospels*, vol. i, pp. 63–4).

HEALING OF THE MAN WITH THE
WITHERED HAND

(Cf. Matt. xii. 4–14; Mark iii. 1–12)

vi. 6–11

6   And it came to pass on another sabbath, that he entered
into the synagogue and taught: and there was a man there,
7 and his right[1] hand was withered. And the scribes and the
Pharisees watched[2] him, whether he would heal on the
8 sabbath;[3] that they might find how to accuse him. But he
knew their thoughts; and he said to the man that had his hand
withered, Rise up, and stand forth in the midst. And he
9 arose and stood forth. And Jesus said unto them, I ask you,
Is it lawful on the sabbath to do good,[4] or to do harm? to
10 save[5] a life,[6] or to destroy[7] it? And he looked round about
on them all, and said unto him, Stretch forth thy hand. And
11 he did *so*: and his hand was restored. But they were filled
with madness;[8] and communed one with another what they
might do to Jesus.

In the former portion Jesus, as Lord of the Sabbath, taught that
observance of the Sabbath should not rest on subtle, rigid
regulations. And now He shows what *must* be positively done on
the Sabbath.

6, 7   While Jesus was teaching in a synagogue on a certain
Sabbath, where there was a man with a withered hand, the
Pharisees and scribes watched Him closely. Their enmity against
Him was already stimulated to such an extent that they were of
set purpose seeking a pretext to accuse Him and to procure His
death.

8   The Lord was fully aware of their evil disposition. But instead of being afraid and proceeding carefully so as to avoid any
act of healing, He actually commands the man to arise and to
stand ·in the midst so that all may see him. In the sharpest contrast to the secretiveness of the spies, Jesus acts perfectly openly
so that all may know His attitude in the matter.

9, 10   While the man with the withered hand is standing
there, the Lord asks: " What is lawful on the sabbath—to do good

or to do evil; to save life or to destroy it? " It was the recognised opinion of the Jews at that time that only in a case of deadly peril could a sick person be treated medically on the Sabbath.

The man with the withered hand was not in peril of his life, but still, the withered hand was a great handicap in his life—it impeded his way to full joy of living and full usefulness. Accordingly Jesus, who rejects all man-made Sabbath regulations, regards it as sinful to leave such a man any longer in his pitiable condition while the opportunity is there to heal him. It is in agreement with the will of God that he should be healed even though it be on the Sabbath. What is indeed unlawful on the Sabbath is to attempt to slay an innocent person, as the Pharisees and scribes were engaged in doing by watching Jesus with murderous intent.

As Lord of the Sabbath, who acts in unison with the intentions of God, Jesus then, after looking at His critics and spies with holy indignation but also with sorrow (cf. Mark iii. 5), commanded the man to stretch out his powerless, withered hand; and immediately the hand was perfectly healed.

11 Instead of seeing in His revelation of divine power the genuineness of His claims and believing in Him, His persecutors now became more fanatical than ever in their determination to compass His death (cf. Mark iii. 6).

Christian believers should on the Lord's day not simply avoid dead formalism and rigid lack of freedom, nor should they merely devote it to rest. Jesus' words and actions teach us quite plainly that we should every Lord's day (and indeed on every other day) place ourselves wholly at His disposal to perform works of love and mercy wherever and in whatever way it may be possible. We may not consecrate the day of rest in a merely passive manner, but must be active in His service and thus through Him be of use to those who suffer and need help, spiritually as well as physically.

---

[1] Only Luke the physician gives this detail, that it was the man's right hand.

[2] παρετηροῦντο = " watch narrowly, especially with sinister intent " (Plummer, *in loc.*).

[3] " To heal on the Sabbath is permitted in case of imminent danger of life; but where there is no danger in delay it is unconditionally forbidden "—this was the doctrine of the Pharisees (cf. Strack-Billerbeck, at Matt. xii. 10).

[4] To refuse to do good is sinful and therefore not lawful on the Sabbath. W. Manson has well said: " Nothing could better illustrate

the uncompromising positiveness of Jesus' whole conception of moral obligation than the issue here formulated. Jesus will recognise no alternative to the doing of good except the doing of evil. The refusing to save life is tantamount to the taking of it. Thereby He invalidates at one stroke the do-nothing attitude, which, under cover of the principle of not working on the Sabbath, his contemporaries mistook for obedience to the will of God " (*in loc.*).

[5] σῶσαι (to save, to preserve): everything conducive to true life and happiness is included here.

[6] ψυχή here stands for the whole man—physically and spiritually.

[7] ἀπολέσαι (to destroy): everything that obstructs and destroys true life and true happiness.

[8] ἀνοίας—" The phrensy or loss of reason which is caused by extreme excitement " (Plummer, *in loc.*).

CHOOSING THE TWELVE APOSTLES

(Cf. Matt. x. 1–4; Mark iii. 13–19)

vi. 12–16

12 And it came to pass in these days, that he went out into the
mountain to pray; and he continued all night in prayer to
13 God. And when it was day, he called his disciples: and he
chose from them twelve,[1] whom also he named apostles;[2]
14 Simon, whom he also named Peter, and Andrew his brother,
15 and James and John, and Philip and Bartholomew, and
Matthew and Thomas, and James *the son* of Alphaeus, and
16 Simon which was called the Zealot, and Judas[3] *the son* of
James, and Judas Iscariot,[4] which was the traitor;

Luke thus far has described the mighty self-revelation of the Lord
Jesus as the divine Messiah. In addition, he has shown how the
Jewish religious leaders and also many of the ordinary members of
the people rejected His claim to the Messiahship and became
more and more filled with hatred against Him. The ancient
chosen people as a whole firmly refused to accept Him as their
promised Redeemer. So the new people of God must be called
into being out of the faithful " remnant " among the Jews. And
thus Luke describes how Jesus next chose twelve apostles to be the
founders of His congregation.

12 One of the most striking characteristics of Jesus as Man is
His intimate communion with His Father in prayer. Again and
again, especially in the Gospel of Luke, we read that He sought
the place of silence in order to pray. Here we are told that before
choosing the apostles He spent a whole night in prayer, alone on
a mountain. The step which He was about to take was a very
momentous one. The whole future of His Church depended,
humanly speaking, on the choice to be made by Him. His choice
must be in perfect agreement with the will of His Father. That
was the reason why He spent so many hours in praying to Him.
How incomprehensible and paradoxical to our human intellect is
the fact that He, according to God's will, should also choose Judas,
who would subsequently become His betrayer! Was this not also
a special reason why the Saviour spent such a long time in prayer?

13 Towards daybreak He called to Him the disciples, the group of persons who followed Him, and chose from their number twelve who should be His followers in a special sense. To distinguish them from the wider group of adherents, He called them apostles (i.e. persons sent with a special charge and with special authority from Him).

14-16 The list of names of the apostles also appears in Acts i. 13; Matthew x. 2-4 and Mark iii. 16-19. In all four lists Peter's name stands first because he was the recognised leader among apostles. In John i. 45 a certain Nathanael is mentioned, but the name of Bartholomew does not occur there. The other Evangelists mention Bartholomew but not Nathanael, so that by these two names the same person is probably indicated. This may be explained from the fact that Bartholomew is not a personal name but a patronymic—it merely indicates the person as son of Tholomai (=Ptolemy). His real name was therefore Nathanael.

Matthew is also sometimes called Levi (cf. v. 27 with Matt. ix. 9). And Judas, the son of James, is the same as Thaddeus (Mark iii. 18); he is the "Judas not Iscariot" of John xiv. 22.

Judas Iscariot is always mentioned last in the lists.

The Saviour, who is God as well as perfect Man, spent a whole night in prayer to the Father before He had to make an important choice. How much more urgently necessary it is for us, as erring mortals full of failings, to have the closest communion with Him in constant prayer!

[1] J. Weiss alleges that the idea of the "twelve apostles" is a later creation of the church in order to make it correspond to the twelve tribes of Israel. But even Harnack, Loisy, E. Meyer and Creed reject this and uphold the historicity, at least, of the fact that at a certain stage in His ministry Jesus appointed the twelve to be His most intimate followers.

[2] The Aramaic form used by Jesus for "apostle" was probably שָׁלִיחַ (shālīach) and points to the fact that they were sent with a definite charge and clothed with authority, and therefore speak and act in the name and on the authority of their Sender (cf. Rengstorf's article on "ἀποστέλλω" and "ἀπόστολος" in Kittel's *Theologisches Wörterbuch zum Neuen Testament*).

[3] That there were two apostles by the name of Judas also appears from John xiv. 22.

[4] Judas's surname of Iscariot probably indicates that he was a man from Kerioth: he thus seems to have been the only Judaean among the twelve.

THE SERMON ON THE MOUNT

(Cf. Matt. v-vii)

17 and he came down with them, and stood on a level place, and a great multitude[1] of his disciples, and a great number of the people from all Judaea and Jerusalem, and the sea coast of Tyre and Sidon, which came to hear him, and to be healed
18 of their diseases; and they that were troubled with unclean
19 spirits were healed. And all the multitude sought to touch him: for power came forth from him, and healed *them* all.
20 And he lifted up his eyes on his disciples, and said, Blessed[2]
21 *are* ye poor:[3] for yours is the kingdom of God.[4] Blessed *are* ye that hunger[5] now: for ye shall be filled. Blessed *are* ye that
22 weep now: for ye shall laugh. Blessed are ye, when men shall hate you, and when they shall separate you *from their company*, and reproach you, and cast out your name[6] as
23 evil,[7] for the Son of man's sake. Rejoice in that day, and leap *for joy*: for behold, your reward is great in heaven: for in
24 the same manner did their fathers unto the prophets. But woe[8] unto you that are rich![9] for ye have received your
25 consolation. Woe unto you, ye that are full now! for ye shall hunger. Woe *unto you*, ye that laugh[10] now! for ye shall
26 mourn and weep. Woe *unto you*, when all men shall speak well of you! for in the same manner did their fathers to the false prophets.
27 But I say unto you which hear, Love your enemies, do good
28 to them that hate you, bless them that curse you, pray for
29 them that despitefully use you. To him that smiteth thee on the *one* cheek offer also the other;[11] and from him that taketh
30 away thy cloke withhold not thy coat also.[12] Give to every one that asketh thee; and of him that taketh away thy goods
31 ask them not again.[13] And as ye would that men should do
32 to you, do ye also to them likewise.[14] And if ye love them that love you, what thank have ye? for even sinners love
33 those that love them. And if ye do good to them that do good to you, what thank have ye? for even sinners do the same.
34 And if ye lend to them of whom ye hope to receive, what thank have ye? even sinners lend to sinners, to receive again
35 as much. But love your enemies,[15] and do *them* good, and lend, never despairing;[16] and your reward shall be great, and

ye shall be sons of the Most High:[17] for he is kind toward the
36 unthankful and evil. Be ye merciful, even as your Father is
37 merciful. And judge not, and ye shall not be judged: and
condemn not, and ye shall not be condemned: release, and
38 ye shall be released: give, and it shall be given unto you;
good measure, pressed down, shaken together, running over,
shall they give[18] into your bosom. For with what measure ye
mete it shall be measured to you again.
39 And he spake also a parable unto them, Can the blind
40 guide the blind? shall they not both fall into a pit? The
disciple is not above his master: but every one when he is
41 perfected shall be as his master.[19] And why beholdest[20] thou
the mote that is in thy brother's eye, but considerest not the
42 beam that is in thine own eye? Or how canst thou say to thy
brother, Brother, let me cast out the mote that is in thine eye,
when thou thyself beholdest not the beam that is in thine own
eye? Thou hypocrite, cast out first the beam out of thine
own eye, and then shalt thou see clearly to cast out the mote
43 that is in thy brother's eye. For there is no good tree that
bringeth forth corrupt fruit; nor again a corrupt tree that
44 bringeth forth good fruit.[21] For each tree is known by its
own fruit. For of thorns men do not gather figs, nor of a
45 bramble bush gather they grapes. The good man out of the
good treasure of his heart bringeth forth that which is good;
and the evil *man* out of the evil *treasure* bringeth forth that
which is evil: for out of the abundance of the heart his mouth
speaketh.
46 And why call ye me, Lord, Lord, and do not the things
47 which I say? Every one that cometh unto me, and heareth
my words, and doeth them, I will shew you to whom he is
48 like: he is like a man building a house, who digged and went
deep, and laid a foundation upon the rock:[22] and when a
flood arose, the stream brake against that house, and could
49 not shake it: because it had been well builded. But he that
heareth, and doeth not, is like a man that built a house upon
the earth without a foundation; against which the stream
brake, and straightway it fell in; and the ruin of that house
was great.

On a certain day (cf. John vii. 40–7) the high priests and the
Pharisees sent officers to arrest Jesus. When they came back without Him and their masters asked them why they had not brought
Him, the only answer that they could give was: " Never man
spake like this man." They could not help perceiving the utter
difference between Jesus and all other teachers. His words were
uniquely original, full of authority and perplexingly deep in
content. Especially when one reads His sermon on the mount, it

is almost impossible not to exclaim with those servants of old: "Never man spake like this man!"

In chapters iv and v Luke gives an account of the progressive Messianic self-revelation of Jesus. He continues this in the first eleven verses of chapter vi and finally shows in verses 12–16 how the Lord chose the twelve apostles as the founders, the first institutors of the congregation of God's new people. In the sermon on the mount the Messianic self-revelation continues to proceed majestically, for in it He acts with absolute authority as Announcer of "the laws of the kingdom". He proclaims this not on the ground of someone else's authority, and does not even say as the prophets of the Old Testament did: "Thus saith the Lord." No, in a way in which no man ever spoke before He speaks with a final, personal, divine authority. He is one with the Father and therefore He declares that the weal or woe of human life in the last analysis depends on the attitude adopted towards Himself and His words (cf. especially verses 22, 46–9).

From this it is clear how mistaken those persons are who praise the sermon on the mount as the only true kernel of Christendom and who yet refuse to believe in Jesus' divinity. In the sermon on the mount He does not only present an unsurpassed exposition of principles of behaviour but He really lays explicit claim to final divine authority and thus to unity with the Father.

17–19 If we assume, together with the majority of expositors, that verses 17–49 reproduces the same sermon (though greatly abbreviated) as Matthew v, vi and vii, the events were probably as follows. Great multitudes had collected the previous evening (Matt. v. 1) to come to Jesus. He then went to spend the night in prayer on the mountain (vi. 12). Early in the morning He called the disciples to Him, chose the twelve apostles (vi. 12) and then descended for some distance along the mountain until He came to a level place on the slope of the mountain.[1] There He sat down (Matt. v. 1) and then the apostles and disciples came to sit around Him and a great multitude also assembled there in a wider circle. So there were three groups of persons: the apostles, the wider circle of disciples (persons who were at that time His faithful adherents) and the ordinary multitude.

---

[1] "The Lord Jesus and His companions went up the gentle slope from Capernaum till the top of the ridge was reached. There the twelve were chosen, and the sermon was preached on the level a little way lower down. Matthew walked up with the crowd, and to him it was certainly a hill. Luke came over from Caesarea to view the scene he was to describe, and was impressed with the 'level place' on which he looked down from the Roman highway on the adjoining height" (W. M. Christie, *Palestine Calling* [1939], p. 35).

20 After Jesus had performed many cures He commenced His sermon on the mount (so called because He delivered it on the slope of the mountain). In the first place He addressed His disciples (including the apostles) and pronounced the beatitudes. By speaking specifically to his followers and by declaring: "Blessed be *ye* poor " He made it evident that He does not beatify—or we may render the word "congratulate "—all persons who are poor as regards material possessions, but specifically those that follow Him. The reference is, therefore, to persons who do not seek their wealth and life in earthly things, but who acknowledge their own poverty and come to Him to seek real life. Where outward poverty leads anyone to realise his utter dependence on God and to walk humbly with his Lord, such a person will be blessed—in measure even in this life, and more abundantly in the next, he may expect rich and glorious fullness of spiritual life and joy. The "poor " of this type *are* already members of His kingdom, for Jesus does not say "yours *will* be " but "yours *is* the kingdom of God ". But only at the final consummation will they enjoy the full abundance of their inheritance as participants in His kingdom.

21 So also those who are spiritually hungry, those who realise their own unworthiness and need and who yearn for the fullness of life which He brings, will receive the blessing—the congratulation —of the Lord. And those who mourn deeply in sorrow over the sins of their own hearts and the dishonouring of the Lord by the world will receive real comfort and joy.

22, 23 When unbelieving men hate and despise His adherents, besmirch their good name and persecute them because they are faithful to Him, the Son of Man, they should regard this as a great privilege and as a cause of exceeding joy. For it will be to them the proof that they are living in true fellowship with their Lord, since all genuine prophets of God were thus ill-treated by the ungodly. For them rich blessings are waiting.

24-6 Jesus next addresses those persons who do not follow Him, but who in self-righteousness and pride revel only in earthly possessions. Again He means not all the outwardly rich but the type of persons who seek their life and happiness only or primarily in material things, who do not realise their souls' need and do not acknowledge their dependence on God. They are so self-exalted and so rich in their own eyes that they do not flee to Him, and thus remain spiritually poor and lost. Because they labour under the delusion that they have no need of Him, they will starve spiritually. And because in this life they take their pleasure only in earthly things, they will ere long (already in this life but in an absolute sense in the hereafter) experience the results of their inner emptiness and lack of real happiness. Spiritual darkness and hopeless sorrow will be their portion. Yes, even although they may enjoy the greatest degree of popularity among unbelievers, this will not endow them with real life. On the contrary, when people are lauded by the unbelieving world, this really proves that such persons are not at peace with God—for only false prophets are popular with unbelieving mankind. He who leads a truly holy life will come into collision with the sins of the ungodly and so fall into disfavour with them. How clearly this was proved in the case of Jesus, who was in every respect perfect in His human life! The unbelieving Jews repudiated Him, but subsequently, when false Messiahs arose, some of them enjoyed an amazing popularity among the masses so that they even rebelled against the Romans, with fatal results.

27 Jesus' words in verses 20–6 referred to the qualifications of those who are admitted as members of His kingdom and to the fate of those who, on account of their life and attitude, will have no share in His salvation. And now, from verses 27 to 45, He announces the principles according to which the members of His kingdom must live in their relations with their fellow-men. It is noteworthy that the Lord here addresses all the hearers (" you which hear ") and not only the disciples. This makes it clear that, although the principles (verses 27–45) are, in the first instance, binding on the members of His kingdom, they hold good for all. Everyone is under the obligation to practise what Jesus here lays down as absolute demands. He who does not do so is guilty before God. The root of all the instructions is genuine love, and that not merely as an emotional or passive sentiment, but as an active realisation in all the practical circumstances of life (" love " and " do good "): and this not only with regard to well-disposed persons but even towards those who are hostile.

The Jews limited the divine commandment to love one's neighbour (Lev. xix. 18) by regarding only fellow-Jews as their neighbours (and then only those who were looked upon by them as worthy fellow-countrymen). Jesus, however, rejects this false limitation completely and commands that even one's enemies should be treated with affection and good-will.

28–30 In these three verses the Lord gives practical examples of the manner in which love must be practised towards one's enemies. They must wish and pray for blessings on those who curse and insult them. Even if such persons treat them unjustly and commit acts of violence against them, no revenge should be taken, but an attitude of perfect love should be maintained. Enmity on the part of others must always stimulate us to greater manifestations of love. Naturally the Lord does not enjoin a weak and sentimental attitude towards evildoers; He teaches that hatred should never be repaid with hatred but with true, unselfish love. And genuine love under the guidance of Christ will always do what is best for the enemy. Love knows no bounds except love itself. Therefore firm action may and should be taken against those who do evil whenever this is necessary for the sake of the honour of God and of the highest well-being of the sinning ones themselves. These pronouncements of the Lord must not be wrested from the context of His teachings and life as a whole, but should be understood in their light. What Jesus here commands is no weak, complaisant attitude, which confirms the evildoers in their wickedness. (Cf., e.g., Jesus' attitude towards the soldier who struck Him in the face [John xviii. 23]—in accordance with the claims of real love, He rebuked the irresponsible soldier.) The "offering of the other cheek", the command "not to forbid to take the coat also", the "giving to every man that asketh" and the prohibition of "asking again what has been taken away"—all this should be viewed in the light of the general principle that there should be a constant endeavour, in a spirit of sincere love, to bring the guilty to repentance and to conquer evil by good. And even where severe measures have to be taken, this should be done only from motives of genuine love. But the Christian throughout must be prepared to deny himself to the utmost and to place his own interests completely in the background.

31 Jewish spiritual leaders and a few other persons had, before the time of Jesus, already pronounced this golden rule, but only in a *negative* form (what you do not want others to do unto you do not unto them). The Saviour, however, commands this in a positive sense. In this manner He determines, in a more absolute form than anyone else before Him, and in a concise maxim, how we should act towards our fellow-men.

32-4 In these verses Jesus points out why an attitude of perfect love should be adopted even towards one's enemies. The test of real love is that it should be unselfish—self-interest must play no part in it. Therefore the genuineness or unreality of a man's love will especially appear in his attitude towards those who are evilly disposed to him. There is nothing particularly praiseworthy in our being well-disposed to those who love us and treat us well. Even those who live in sin are generally inclined to be kind to their benefactors.

35 Accordingly a man, in order to be really acceptable before God, must love his *enemies* and must prove this in practice by doing them good. He who does so will prove thereby that he is truly a child of God. For *He* is perfect in His love even towards those who are ungrateful and rebellious towards Him. And those who live in pure communion with Him will reveal the same attitude, being reborn as His children, and so possessing the divine nature.

36-8 They must be not only well-disposed towards their enemies, but must be merciful to them just as their Heavenly Father is merciful—and must take pity on all people. In particular they should reveal this spirit in the matter of judging their fellow-men. For he who judges or condemns his fellow-man, inculpates himself. Only God knows and understands every person in all his circumstances and conditions, and only He has in the final instance the right to judge as to the guilt or innocence of any person, and to condemn where His salvation has been rejected. No human being has the power or the right to this. By His words the Lord does not prohibit the administration of justice in law-courts or the distinction between good and evil, but He does forbid the attitude of those people who want to appoint themselves in God's place as judges over their fellow-men and to judge and condemn right and left. According to the light we possess we must distinguish between good and evil and in His power first combat the evil in ourselves and then in others. But we are never to encroach upon God's right to judge and to condemn. We must avoid all censoriousness and revengefulness, and forgive those who have sinned against us. This is not a ground upon which we shall earn forgiveness from God, but a means by which our lives will be opened for receiving His grace.

As a further expression of mercy, we must give to everyone who is needy, and we must do so in conformity with the highest demands of love, so that it may be to the honour of God and profitable to the one who is in need. To the generous giver will be liberally given—in full in eternity, but even in measure in this life, as God so ordains it. All the blessings which a person receives here and will receive hereafter are gifts of grace from God, not founded upon man's merits. But, nevertheless, the Lord also teaches that there will be conformity between the measure of "reward" and the faithfulness of the person concerned (cf. Matt. xxv. 31–46).

39, 40 It is extremely difficult to decide what connection exists between these verses and the foregoing portion of the sermon. Luke, as already stated, gave a very brief version of the sermon. Much of what Jesus said in explanation of His words that have been committed to writing does not appear here, and consequently we cannot state with absolute certainty what He referred to in these verses. In any case, He emphasises the folly of an attempt by one who is himself still blind to act as a guide to others, and the disastrous consequences of following a blind leader. Because a pupil is dependent upon the guidance given to him by his master, he must see to it that he chooses the right master. For this reason the hearers must leave their old leaders and masters (the Pharisees and scribes) who are blind and lead them to the precipice. In verses 47–9 the Saviour teaches that they must choose Him as their leader and teacher. Then, and only then, will all be well with them, for He is the Way, the Truth, and the Life.

41, 42 Here Jesus warns against an attitude and behaviour specially characteristic of those spiritually blind leaders of the Jewish people of that time against whose guiding influence He had already given warning. Whilst they themselves were spiritually blind (no one can see with a beam in his own eye), they conducted themselves as the leaders of the people, who judged their fellow-countrymen and desired to teach them a better way of life. Such action is unconditionally condemned by the Lord, who lays it down as an absolute rule that he who wants to reform others must first, with the utmost severity, place his own life under the divine search-light and reform it thoroughly. Only then will he have the ability and right (and also the duty) to guide his fellow-men to greater purity of life.

43–5 To illustrate why only he who himself is reformed is able to reform others, Jesus tells the parable of the good and the corrupt tree. This teaches that the deeds one does and the influence one exercises form part of one's character and personality. As a man is in his own inward self, in his deepest being, so will he also act. The nature of his personality will determine the nature of his acts and the quality of his influence. The person who is inwardly bad, will say evil things and do them, too, and will exercise an evil influence. But as the good tree bears good fruit, the kind of fruit corresponding to the species and nature of the tree, so the person who is inwardly good will say and do good things and exercise a wholesome influence. These are indestructible laws. For this reason it is impossible for one who himself is still bad to attempt to improve others. First his own life should be reshaped to real righteousness and holiness.

46–9 This forms the latter portion of the sermon on the mount, and in this portion Jesus indicates what a fatal end awaits those who do not obey His words, and on the other hand what a blessed future is theirs who are obedient.

It will benefit no one to honour Him merely by word of mouth (verse 46) while they do not do His bidding.

But he who comes to Him, surrenders himself to His Lord, follows Him as Guide, listens to His words, and carries them out in practical life, will reap the richest benefit. Just as surely as a house which is built with its foundations firmly fixed upon a rock will brave all storms, so surely will those whose life is governed by obedience to Christ's teachings emerge triumphantly from all storms—afflictions, temptations and the like in this life and at the end the Last Judgment. So there awaits them the greatest salvation, here and hereafter.

But just as surely as a house without a firm foundation will suffer a disastrous fall through the force of the floods, so surely will those who listen to His words but do not obey them come to a fatal crash—even in this life when the storms of life overwhelm them, but irretrievably at the Last Judgment.

What an amazing climax was here reached by Jesus' sermon! No wonder that we read in Matthew vii. 28, 29: " And it came to pass, when Jesus ended these words, the multitudes were astonished at his teaching: for he taught them as one having authority, and not as their scribes."

Never before or after Jesus did anyone lay down such high standards of how one should live in thought and action towards God and one's fellow-men. His law is nothing less than absolute perfection in love. No human being in this life has ever perfectly fulfilled this demand or will ever here be able to do so. But, God be praised, the Saviour Himself accomplished this perfectly in actual practice. He is not only our perfect Lawgiver but also our perfect Example. And He longs to shape us, too, in true righteousness and love through His Spirit. According as we place ourselves more and more at His disposal and live in His power, more and more do we reflect His image and are enabled in our daily life to fulfil more and more the principles of the sermon on the mount. What a revolutionary and blessed metamorphosis of the life of mankind would be brought about if everyone were to live according to His law of love!

[1] T. W. Manson's statement (*Mission and Message of Jesus*, p. 339) that Matthew assumes that only Jesus' disciples were present and not also a multitude as Luke teaches, may have some support in Matthew v. 1, if we interpret it to mean that Jesus ascended the mountain to avoid the multitudes and be alone with His disciples; but in

Matthew vii. 28 it is clear that the multitudes heard the sermon on the mount.

² μακάριος = fortunate, happy, blessed (in an all-embracing sense). " It is to the faithful Christian that poverty, hunger, sorrow, and unpopularity are real blessings; to others they may be mere sterile suffering " (Plummer, *in loc.*).

³ πτωχοί—" In the Judaism of the last two centuries B.C. the term was practically a synonym for *Ḥāsīd*, i.e. ' saintly ' or ' pious ' in the best sense " (T. W. Manson, *op. cit.*, p. 339). In the Psalms (e.g. xl. 18, lxxii. 2-4) we note how the terms " the poor " or " the wretched " already bear a spiritual significance (cf. Creed, *in loc.*)—not " poor " in the literal sense, but those who (often through the refining brought by outward poverty) live under a deep realisation of their dependence on God. The fact that His disciples bade farewell to their earthly possessions and were at any rate inwardly free from them, in order to follow Him, proved that they possessed this quality.

⁴ Here in the sense of the salvation brought by it. " Salvation ", " eternal life ", and " the Kingdom of God " are largely synonymous in the New Testament.

⁵ " The hunger and the tears here alluded to are not exhausted or even properly explained by reference to outward conditions, for in Israel it is known that man does not live by bread alone, and sorrow goes deeper than to the sense of earthly want. The hunger is for God, for the vindication of divine justice, for conformity to the divine will. The tears are for the tragedy of sin, for the evil wrought by alienation from God in Israel and the world " (W. Manson, *in loc.*). And he rightly continues: " But it is not to the bitter but to those whom the sorrows of earth move to genuine tears that the joy of the Realm of God is promised."

⁶ τὸ ὄνομα ὑμῶν. Here the followers of Jesus themselves are meant " in or according to their life's revelation, as they are known and make themselves known, namely as Christians " (Greydanus, *in loc.*).

⁷ πονηρός alludes to that which causes trouble, sorrow or injury.

⁸ οὐαί with dative to indicate that some frightful woe is coming upon them. In the mouth of Jesus it expresses lament, not denunciation: " Alas for you! "

⁹ Here again it is not all the rich in a literal sense that are meant. The cases of Nicodemus and Joseph of Arimathea prove that rich persons are not *ipso facto* excluded from the kingdom, but only those who are worldly-minded and self-exalted.

¹⁰ γελῶντες. Here the meaning is not " laugh " in the literal sense, but the utterance of worldly-mindedness, indifference, and self-satisfaction. T. W. Manson rightly observes concerning these persons: " They lack nothing except the things that really matter " (*op. cit.*, p. 341).

¹¹ Jesus was here addressing ordinary individuals and not representatives of the government, who are put there by God to maintain order and to administer justice (cf. Rom. xiii).

[12] " The issue would be nudism, a sufficient indication that it is a certain spirit that is being commended to our notice not a regulation to be slavishly carried out " (T. W. Manson, *op. cit.*, p. 343).

[13] " Love knows no limits but those which love itself imposes. When love resists or refuses, it is because compliance would be a violation of love, not because it would involve loss or suffering " (Plummer, *in loc.*; cf. also his words at verses 29, 30).

[14] For Jewish forms of the golden rule (in a negative form) cf. Dalman, *Jesus-Jeshua* (Eng. trans., p. 226), and also Strack-Billerbeck (at Matt. vii. 3). And for parallels among other nations of the time before Christ cf. Creed (*in loc.*). Among no nation in the pre-Christian era has an example been found of the golden rule in a positive form as it was uttered by Jesus. For a positive formulation of the Golden Rule in extant non-Christian Jewish literature we have to wait till the time of Maimonides.

[15] The liberal-minded Jewish scholar Montefiore (in his *Rabbinic Literature and Gospel Teachings*, pp. 103 ff.) says that, although Jesus is unique in His pronouncement that one must love one's enemies, He did not carry it out in practice in His attitude towards His enemies. He has, however, no ground for his statement. Jesus did indeed relentlessly expose the inconsistency of the Pharisees and others, but it was in accordance with the highest demand of love that He had to call their attention to their sins and to warn their adherents in order to bring as many as possible to repentance. He accepted invitations to Pharisees' homes and did not neglect them. Nowhere did He harm a single enemy of His and even on the cross He prayed for those who crucified Him: " Father, forgive them ! " (Cf. T. W. Manson, *op. cit.*, pp. 344-5.)

[16] μηδὲν ἀπελπίζοντες. Plummer (*in loc.*) supports the R.V. rendering " never despairing ". But this would be at variance with verse 34. The A.V. translation: " hoping for nothing again ", " without expecting anything in return ", is, therefore, the best (cf. Creed, *in loc.*; so also Greydanus, *in loc.*).

[17] ὑψίστου occurs as a proper name for God only in Luke and Acts. " It was a term admirably fitted to form a bridge between Judaism and the higher Greek religion " (T. W. Manson, *op. cit.*, 347).

[18] δώσουσι, " they will give ", the indefinite third person plural active, here used probably as in the rabbinical writings as " a way of referring to God " (T. W. Manson, *op. cit.*, p. 348).

[19] A similar passage in Matthew x. 24 f. (in a different context) runs: " A disciple is not above his master. . . . It is enough for the disciple that he be as his master." T. W. Manson (*The Teaching of Jesus* [1931], p. 239) suggests the following as the underlying Aramaic original of both passages:

lēth shĕwilyā rab min rabbēh
missath li-shĕwilyā di-yĕhē shĕwē lĕ-rabbēh—

with a double play on *rabbā* (" great " and " teacher ") and *shĕwilyā* (μαθητής and κατηρτισμένος). " This playing upon words is a not uncommon feature in Old Testament prophecy: and it need, therefore, cause us no surprise to find it in the teaching of Jesus."

20 κατανοεῖς " expresses prolonged attention and observation. Careful consideration of one's own faults must precede attention to those of others " (Plummer, *in loc.*).

21 T. W. Manson here says: " The material here given by Luke [verses 43–5] is split up and incorporated with other material in Matthew " (*op. cit.*, p. 351). But why should such a mechanical and historically improbable manner of writing be assumed in Matthew's case? Jesus would probably have used the same figures on other occasions as well (some of which are mentioned by Matthew), so that Matthew and Luke may give independent traditions of words of Jesus spoken at different times.

22 Matthew vii. 24 has only the words " built his house upon a rock ". This, however, by no means excludes Luke's statement that first the ground was dug to lay the foundation upon the rock. So Matthew and Luke by no means contradict one another here as many critics allege. Luke merely gives the figure in a more complete form.

THE CENTURION OF CAPERNAUM

Luke vii. 1–10

1 After[1] he had ended all his sayings in the ears of the people, he entered into Capernaum.

2 And a certain centurion's[2] servant,[3] who was dear unto

3 him, was sick and at the point of death. And when he heard concerning Jesus, he sent unto him elders[4] of the Jews, asking

4 him that he would come and save his servant. And they, when they came to Jesus,[5] besought him earnestly, saying,

5 He is worthy that thou shouldest do this for him: for he

6 loveth our nation, and himself built us our synagogue.[6] And Jesus went with them. And when he was now not far from the house, the centurion sent friends to him, saying unto him, Lord, trouble not thyself: for I am not worthy that thou

7 shouldest come under my roof:[7] wherefore neither thought I myself worthy to come unto thee: but say the word, and

8 my servant shall be healed. For I also am a man set under authority,[8] having under myself soldiers: and I say to this one, Go, and he goeth; and to another, Come, and he

9 cometh; and to my servant, Do this, and he doeth it. And when Jesus heard these things, he marvelled at him, and turned and said unto the multitude that followed him, I say unto you, I have not found so great faith, no, not in Israel.

10 And they that were sent, returning to the house, found the servant whole.[9]

Luke is still engaged in describing the progressive self-revelation of Christ. Here he gives an example of how He heals a dying man through His divine power even while He is far removed from him.

1 These words show that the sermon on the mount in chapter vi must be regarded as a unity and also that Jesus delivered it not only in the hearing of His disciples but also of the whole assembled multitude. After the conclusion of the sermon on the mount He descended from the mountain and went back to Capernaum.

2, 3 A servant of a pagan centurion or non-commissioned officer in the forces of Herod Antipas was at the point of death. The centurion was particularly attached to the servant, and when he heard how Jesus had healed other sick people he sent elders of the Jews to Him to ask Him to come and heal the servant.

Because he himself was a Gentile, he thought that the Jewish leaders would have more influence with Jesus.

4, 5 The centurion was extremely well-disposed towards the Jews and had even built a synagogue for them in Capernaum at his own expense, so the Jewish leaders acceded to his request.

6–8 When the centurion heard or himself saw that Jesus had agreed to come and was already approaching his house he sent word by some friends of his that the Lord should not take the trouble of proceeding any farther on the way to his house. At first he had caused Jesus to be asked to come to his house, but now, on the one hand, he is filled with such a deep realisation of his own unworthiness, and on the other hand he has such a living and powerful faith in Christ, that he sends Him this message. He believes that, just as he, a man with authority, is obeyed by his subordinates, just so surely will the authoritative utterance of Christ be fulfilled even though He is not present where the sick person is.

9 When we bear in mind the parallel account in Matthew viii. 5–13, we must picture to ourselves that after the centurion had sent his friends to Jesus he also went to Him himself. Owing to the seriousness of the circumstances and his inner urge to go to Jesus himself, notwithstanding his feeling of unworthiness, he overcame his initial hesitation. Luke emphasises the fact that the centurion sent friends, while Matthew only states that the centurion went to Jesus. And so the two Gospels supplement each other.

Our Saviour was and is truly Man; therefore it was possible for Him to marvel at the exceptional faith of the centurion. Such a strong faith as the pagan centurion revealed—a faith greater than He had up to that time found among the Jewish people—was something new to Him.

10 Luke still relates the occurrence from the point of view of the messengers and declares that when they came to the house of the centurion the servant was already healed. Matthew, again, gives the story in the light of the centurion's own contact with Jesus.

The centurion of Capernaum strikingly revealed the two indispensable requirements for receiving real blessing: he was deeply humble and he had a whole-hearted faith in Christ. To-day this is still the only way to receive the divine blessings—we must realise our own utter unworthiness, but at the same time cherish a steadfast faith in Christ Jesus, our Lord.

---

[1] Ἐπειδή—the only place in the New Testament where it is used in a temporal sense = " after ".

[2] As a result of the antipathy of the Jews towards the Herod dynasty they were compelled to keep pagan soldiers in their service (cf. Schlatter, *in loc.*).

[3] Matthew here uses παῖς ("boy" or "servant"), while Luke expressly calls him a servant, δοῦλος (literally "slave").

[4] πρεσβυτέρους, without the article, indicates an indefinite number of the local Jewish leaders—who consisted mostly of the older people.

[5] Loisy, Wendland and Klostermann maintain that Matthew's version of the occurrence is the original one and that Luke expanded it, perhaps under the influence of the story of Jairus. But why suppose this? Neither of the Gospels pretends to reproduce all the particulars. Matthew relates in more general terms the fact that the centurion asked Jesus to heal his servant, while Luke gives the detail that the centurion first approached Jesus through the elders. This by no means excludes the possibility that afterwards he also went to him himself.

The suggestion of Creed and others that Luke for the sake of symbolism altered the original story is altogether at variance with Luke's statement in i. 1–4 and is devoid of proof. What we certainly may assume is that Luke describes the incident in such detail because in it he sees another proof that the salvation brought by Christ was intended for Gentiles as well as for Jews.

[6] A similar instance where a pagan official helped with the building of a Jewish synagogue is described in an Egyptian inscription of the second century B.C. (Dittenberger, *Orient. Graec. Inscr. Sel.*, 96). The article τήν before συναγωγήν suggests that there was at that time only one synagogue at Capernaum. Some time ago the ruins of a synagogue were found where old Capernaum was situated. Some have supposed this to be the synagogue of Jesus' time, but much more probably it is to be dated " around A.D. 200 or later, since all the earlier Jewish synagogues appear to have been destroyed by Titus during the Jewish war and by Hadrian after the second-century rebellion of Bar Cochba. Even so, it is probable that the Capernaum synagogue stands on the site and follows the plan of an earlier synagogue or of earlier synagogues and therefore may be safely regarded as a reconstruction of the one in which Jesus himself taught " (J. Finegan, *Light from the Ancient Past* [1946], p. 228).

[7] " The man's humility and faith prevail over his anxiety as soon as he sees that the first deputation has succeeded, and that the great Rabbi and Prophet is really coming to him " (Plummer, *in loc.*).

[8] The whole reasoning of the centurion points to the certainty of the result, apart from the actual presence of Jesus in person. His faith is greater than that of people who desire to see visible or tangible signs before they can believe.

[9] The identification of this occurrence (recorded in verses 1–10) with the healing of the nobleman's son in John iv. 46 ff. is far-fetched and unnecessary.

THE SON OF THE WIDOW OF NAIN

vii. 11–17

11 And it came to pass soon afterwards,[1] that he went to a city called Nain; and his disciples went with him, and a
12 great multitude. Now when he drew near to the gate of the city, behold, there was carried out one that was dead, the only son of his mother, and she was a widow: and much
13 people of the city was with her. And when the Lord[2] saw her, he had compassion on her, and said unto her, Weep not.
14 And he came nigh and touched the bier:[3] and the bearers stood still. And he said, Young man, I say unto thee, Arise.
15 And he that was dead[4] sat up,[5] and began to speak. And he
16 gave him to his mother. And fear took hold on all: and they glorified God, saying, A great prophet is arisen among us:
17 and, God hath visited his people. And this report went forth concerning him in the whole of Judaea,[6] and all the region round about.

Jesus was not only able to heal a dying person from a distance by His authoritative word, but even called back the dead to life. Luke here gives a striking example of the revelation of this kind of power by Christ. Because only Luke describes this incident, many critics have denied its historicity. But many miracles were performed by Jesus that are not described in detail (cf. iv. 23, 40, 41, vi. 18, 19, xii. 37, xxi. 25) and in vii. 22 the Lord Himself implies that He had on several occasions raised the dead.

11, 12 Not long after the healing of the centurion's servant Jesus was followed by His disciples and a great multitude on the way to Nain—a place to the south of Capernaum and about two miles to the west of Endor. It was situated at a high elevation against the slopes of the Little Hermon and still exists to-day as a small village called Nein. Tombs in the rock have been found before the eastern gate of the village along the road leading to Capernaum. Thus we can picture to ourselves fairly vividly how Jesus, with His disciples and the others who were following Him, met the sombre funeral procession near the gate. The procession probably consisted partly of hired mourners and musicians with flutes and cymbals.

13, 14 The widowed mother, according to the usual custom, would probably be walking in front of the bier on which her son was carried. So it was natural that Jesus should first address and comfort her before He touched the bier and made the bearers halt. As an act of love and sympathy with the mourning mother, Jesus, without first requiring faith from her or anyone else, commanded the young man to return to life and rise up from his bier.

15 Because Jesus is the Lord of life and death and possesses all power over the invisible realm to which the spirit of the deceased youth had already departed, the young man's spirit is again joined to his body in obedience to the Lord's command. Out of His deep sympathy with the widowed mother Jesus does not ask the youth to follow Him but gives him back to his mother.

16, 17 The raising of the dead youth was so manifestly a work of divine power performed through Jesus that those present acknowledged that He must therefore be a great prophet in whom God, after many generations which had heard no prophetic voice, had once again visited His people. This testimony to Christ was spread far and wide.

In this story the Saviour's sympathy with the sorrowing and His absolute divine power over the invisible spirit-world are gloriously revealed. We see Him here as the loving Comforter, the Victor over death, and the Reuniter of separated dear ones. What He did here for the widowed mother and son He will one day do for all the faithful in a perfect and final form. He will bring full comfort, He will raise all His people in incorruptibility, and will reunite us, in the heavenly realm, with our loved ones who have died in Him.

---

[1] τῷ ἑξῆς. Although the textual evidence for τῷ and τῇ is here equally strong, τῷ is very probably the original reading, as it is a more uncommon usage than τῇ in Luke and Acts. Consequently we must understand χρόνῳ after τῷ ἑξῆς, and then it does not indicate a specific day as τῇ ἑξῆς ἡμέρᾳ (" the next day ") would indicate, but only the fact that this incident took place not long after the previous one.

[2] ὁ κύριος. The expression is typical of Luke. Here it is of special significance because in the story Jesus as Lord of Life banishes death and sorrow. Against the view expressed by W. Bousset in *Kyrios Christos* that the title " Lord " ascribed to Jesus is of Gentile origin, see the valuable article by W. Foerster on Κύριος in Kittel's *Theologisches Wörterbuch zum Neuen Testament*. It has been aptly said: " The

title *the Lord* which Luke employs in verse 13 has peculiar fitness in this context, where Jesus appears clothed with that exalted power over life and death by which He becomes the object of His church's faith and worship " (T. W. Manson, *in loc.*).

[3] τῆς σοροῦ. Here an open coffin is meant.

[4] Strauss long ago pointed out how unsatisfactory the theories are, that the young man was only in a coma (cf. Plummer, *in loc.*).

[5] ἀνεκάθισεν occurs in the Bible elsewhere only in Acts ix. 40, but is often found in medical writers (Klostermann, *in loc.*).

[6] Not the province of Judaea, but the whole of the Jewish land, practically = Palestine (see notes on i. 5, iv. 44).

SPECIAL NOTE

JESUS' RAISING OF THE DEAD

All four Gospels bear testimony to the fact that Jesus raised the dead, and the earliest Christian tradition also testifies to this unanimously (cf., e.g., Eusebius, *Historia Ecclesiastica*, iv; Justin, *Apol.* i; Origen, *Against Celsus*, ii). Quadratus, one of the first apologists, states in the only extant portion of his defence of Christianity (addressed to Hadrian in A.D. 125): " The persons who were healed and those who were raised from the dead by Jesus were not only seen when they were healed and raised, but were always present also afterwards; and not merely during the time that the Saviour walked upon the earth—but after His departure also they were still there for a considerable time, so that some of them lived even until our times " (quoted by Eusebius, *Historia Ecclesiastica*, iv). Paul also called attention to the fact (in 1 Cor. xv) that great numbers of the witnesses of Christ's victory over the grave and death were still alive at the time when he was writing.

Therefore he who rejects the Gospel stories of Jesus' resurrection and of His raising others from the dead does so in conflict with the available historical evidence inside and outside the New Testament.

JOHN THE BAPTIST SENDS TWO
DISCIPLES TO JESUS

(Cf. Matt. xi. 1–19)

vii. 18–35

18 And the disciples of John told him of all these things.[1]
19 And John[2] calling unto him two of his disciples sent them to
the Lord, saying, Art thou he that cometh, or look we for
20 another?[3] And when the men were come unto him, they
said, John the Baptist hath sent us unto thee, saying, Art
21 thou he that cometh, or look we for another? In that hour
he cured many of diseases and plagues and evil spirits; and
22 on many that were blind he bestowed sight. And he answered and said unto them,[4] Go your way, and tell John
what things ye have seen and heard; the blind receive their
sight,[5] the lame walk, the lepers are cleansed, and the deaf
hear, the dead are raised up, the poor have good tidings
23 preached to them.[6] And blessed is he, whosoever shall find
none occasion of stumbling in me.

24 And when the messengers of John were departed, he began
to say unto the multitudes concerning John, What went ye
out into the wilderness to behold? a reed shaken with the
25 wind? But what went ye out to see? a man clothed in soft
raiment? Behold, they which are gorgeously apparelled, and
26 live delicately, are in kings' courts. But what went ye out to
see? a prophet? Yes, I say unto you, and much more than a
27 prophet. This is he of whom it is written,

[7]Behold, I send my messenger before thy face,
Who shall prepare thy way before thee.

28 I say unto you, Among them that are born of women[8] there is
none greater than John:[9] yet he that is but little in the king-
29 dom of God[10] is greater than he.[11] And all the people when
they heard,[12] and the publicans, justified God, being bap-
30 tized with the baptism of John. But the Pharisees and the
lawyers[13] rejected for themselves[14] the counsel of God, being
31 not baptized of him. Whereunto then shall I liken the men
32 of this generation, and to what are they like? They are like
unto children that sit in the marketplace,[15] and call one to
another; which say, We piped unto you, and ye did not
33 dance; we wailed, and ye did not weep. For John the
Baptist is come eating no bread nor drinking wine; and ye

34 say, He hath a devil.[16] The Son of man is come eating and
   drinking;[17] and ye say, Behold, a gluttonous man, and a
35 winebibber, a friend of publicans and sinners! And wisdom[18]
   is justified of all her children.[19]

Luke here continues to show how Jesus reveals His divine greatness and glory. He does so by calling attention to the miracles performed by Him and by declaring that John, *because he is His forerunner*, is the greatest of all prophets. From this it follows that
Christ Himself is immeasurably greater still—that He is indeed
the son of God. For no one could speak as Jesus is here described
as speaking unless He were God.

18, 19 After disciples of John the Baptist brought their master
a report about the works and attitude of Jesus, John sends two of
his disciples to ask Him whether He is really the promised
Messiah or whether they must expect someone else. John was
already in prison (cf. Matt. xi. 2), and things began to appear
incomprehensible to him. He had expected that Christ would
speedily destroy the powers of darkness and judge the unrighteous.
But instead of doing this, He leaves him, His forerunner, helpless
in prison; and it is clear to John that even the Jewish people did
not follow Him on a great scale and did not believe in Him. All
these things make John impatient and dissatisfied, and even cast
shadows of doubt over his mind.

Because John was a fallible man, he could quite well entertain
these questionings even after all the former clear signs and proofs
of Jesus' divine Messiahship that had been given to him by God.

20-2 When the disciples of John came to ask Him the
question, Jesus was again busy performing many works of mercy
through healing. He continues with this for a considerable time
and only then answers the question. His answer amounts to this:
that they must tell John that He is busy performing divine works
of power, of love and mercy and not of judgment and destruction.
He makes the blind see again, the lame walk, the deaf hear, the
lepers clean, and He even raises the dead. In addition, He uses
the opportunities when multitudes had collected around Him to
preach the glad tidings to them. By mentioning all this, Jesus
wants to remind John of Isaiah xxxv. 5–6 and lxi. 1 ff., where all
the works which He is constantly doing are mentioned as the
blessings to be given to the people in the Messianic time. Thus by
His acts Jesus proves that He is indeed the Promised One.

23 In these words Jesus warns John not to reject or condemn
Him because of a wrong idea concerning what He has to do and

concerning the kind of methods He should adopt in His work. He is the Divine Messiah who does the right things in the right way and at the right time. In this pronouncement Jesus lays claim in a most unmistakable manner to absolute divinity.

24 After the departure of the messengers Jesus puts a number of rhetorical questions to His hearers, to which He expects no answers. By these questions and by His own answers thereto He proclaims the greatness of John, His forerunner. By His first question He points out that John is an unwavering, determined man—one who could not be moved by the opinion or influence of men to be unfaithful to his divine calling. For no one and for nothing did he flinch from accomplishing his vocation. His question by means of the two messengers was not a revelation of instability on his part, but of dissatisfaction with Jesus' methods and the outcome of an imperfect conception of His character and work.

25 The second question to which again a negative answer must be given, together with the words following upon it, gives the hearers a clear idea of the Baptist's attitude as a prophetic preacher of repentance who denied himself to the utmost for the sake of making his message most effective. He denied himself all earthly comforts and luxury and appeared in the rough garments which were appropriate to his vigorous call to repentance.

26 He is a prophet, but also much more than a prophet, because he did not only prophesy concerning the Messiah's coming, but also saw Him personally, pointed Him out to others, and helped to prepare them for the Messianic advent through his preaching and baptism.

27 Yes, he is the messenger written of in Malachi iii. 1 who was sent out in advance of Christ to prepare the way of God and of His only-begotten Son; he was sent to call the people to a change of heart and life, so that they should be eager and ready to accept Jesus and obey Him as the promised Messiah.

28 And because John is His immediate precursor, he is the greatest of all prophets; while the Old Testament prophets could only see and proclaim a shadowy likeness of Christ, John saw Him himself and personally pointed Him out as the Messiah of God.

But although he, as last envoy of the Old Covenant, is nearest to Christ and thus the most important of all, he takes a lower place than even the most insignificant member of the New Covenant. He belonged to the period of preparation and had not yet learned to know Jesus as the Crucified One, as the Risen Redeemer, and as the One who through His Spirit makes His habitation in the believer's heart and life. He will indeed, in common with all other saints of the times before Christ's sacrificial death, share fully in the redemption and blessings achieved by Him, but as regards his place in the unfolding of the divine revelation which culminated in Christ, he still belongs to the preparatory stage and is therefore in this respect less than the most insignificant believer of the New Dispensation—the period which began with the drawing near of the beneficent dominion of God in the coming and redeeming work of Jesus. By declaring in these words the relation men bear to Him as the absolute touchstone of true greatness, the Saviour at the same time declares that He Himself is the greatest of all, the Messenger of the Covenant of Malachi iii. 1, and therefore God Himself (in Mal. iii the Messenger of the Covenant is also called *The Lord*). For this reason He has the right to apply the words of Malachi iii to Himself.

29, 30 Here the Lord points out the difference in the attitude of the ordinary Jews and the Jewish leaders towards the preaching of John. When the common people and the " publicans ", the outcasts, had heard him, they justified God. That is to say, they acknowledged that before God they were guilty and worthy of condemnation and that He was fully justified in demanding from them confession of sins and true repentance, not in word only, but outwardly and publicly by undergoing the baptism of John. On the part of God the baptism then serves as a sign and seal that He forgives the repentant.

The Pharisees and lawyers, however, mostly refused to be baptized and thus rejected the counsel of God concerning them. To their own undoing, they made His plan of redemption worthless so far as they themselves were concerned.

31-4 These words of Jesus should not be taken as an allegory but merely as a parable by which the Lord wishes to indicate the nature and quality of the Jewish leaders and other members of the people who refuse to listen to Him or to John. They are, He says, just like two groups of children who reproach each other because when the one group piped to the other in order that they might be joyful and " play at weddings " they refused to dance; and when they sang a song of lamentation to them to make them " play at funerals " they did not weep. Just as foolishly wilful and intractable are those people who objected to John because as a preacher of repentance he led an ascetic life, and also to Jesus because He led a normal, natural life, and associated even with the " publicans " and sinners. In this way Jesus showed how that self-willed and refractory generation did not know what it really wanted and was dissatisfied with whatever was offered to it.

35 But whatever attitude and behaviour may be adopted by the foolish Jewish leaders and others, wisdom is recognised and honoured by all her children in whatever form she appears. He who loves God and believes in Him observes, accepts and honours His wisdom as revealed through John, the preacher of repentance; but especially as revealed supremely in Christ, the Son of Man.

When John the Baptist became dissatisfied with the Saviour's methods of work, Jesus did not change His methods but continued in the same way and, in addition, expressly informed John that this and this alone was His method of work. What a lesson for the church of Christ when the Biblical methods of living and working are criticised, not to agree to compromises but to continue faithfully with the work as His Word ordains and to give the critics to understand that this and this alone is the method according to which she intends to work. And the method is the practising of mercy and the preaching of the glad tidings—and therefore a spiritual method, with no recourse to outward compulsion or force such as has been and still is advocated in some quarters.

What a serious charge in verse 30: they rejected the counsel of God against themselves—they refused to believe the message sent by God and to accept His offered salvation!

---

[1] περὶ πάντων τούτων refers to the preaching and miracles of Jesus since He commenced to appear in public after His baptism.

[2] Some critics, such as Strauss, Creed and Luce, allege that this attitude on the part of the Baptist is to be explained from the fact that he only began to believe at that time that Jesus was the Christ. So they reject the Gospel testimonies that John had already much earlier (at the baptism) received the divine assurance that Jesus was the Messiah. This inference is, however, quite arbitrary and does violence to the whole of the Gospel narrative. They have no real grounds for their contention. Even if John's attitude has to be viewed as the outcome of doubt and not merely of impatience, it is indeed very natural that he, the lonely prisoner, should begin to let doubts enter his mind under the existing circumstances (see exposition at verse 19).

[3] For various explanations of John's attitude here cf. Plummer (*in loc.*).

[4] Reitzenstein suggests that Jesus' words here were influenced by the Mandaean texts. This is, however, too far-fetched and is accepted practically by no one (cf. Creed, *in loc.*).

[5] " The healing of all diseases was expected to accompany the time of the Messianic salvation. It was assumed that Messiah would restore to His people Israel all those blessings which were lost by Adam's fall; among these, of course, was included the removal of sickness and death " (Strack-Billerbeck at Matt. xi. 5).

[6] Plummer remarks at this portion of the verse: " This was the clearest sign of His being the Christ (Isa. lxi. 1), as He himself had declared at Nazareth (iv. 18–21). His miracles need not mean more than that He was 'a great Prophet'. . . . But it was a new thing that the poor, whom the Greek despised and the Roman trampled on, and whom the priest and the Levite left on one side, should be invited into the kingdom of God (iv. 20) " (in loc.).

[7] Here, as in Matthew xi. 10 and Mark i. 2, Malachi iii. 1 is not quoted verbally—either from the Massoretic or LXX texts; note in particular the change of " me " into " thee ". Nevertheless the meaning of Malachi iii. 1 is correctly given, as mention is there also made of the " Messenger of the Covenant " (Christ before His incarnation) who is One with God and yet distinct from Him. The form of the text given in these Gospel quotations may have been that of a primitive Christian " Testimony Book ".

[8] ἐν γεννητοῖς γυναικῶν = human beings as distinct from God and angels. Here the reference is especially to man's weakness, mortality and sinfulness. From the context in which Jesus says this and from the nature of the case it goes without saying that He does not include Himself under the ordinary human beings. He is truly Man, but without sin and One with God. Rendell Harris's idea that Jesus meant Himself by " he that is least in the kingdom of God " is unconvincing.

[9] These words " presuppose on Jesus' part not merely the highest estimate of John—but a consciousness of the finality of his own mission to Israel " (T. W. Manson, in loc.).

[10] ἡ βασιλεία τοῦ θεοῦ. The emphasis here is on the realm and community within which the divine rule is exercised in the New Dispensation inaugurated by Jesus. See p. 179.

[11] " He is a servant, they are sons; he is the friend of the Bridegroom, they are His spouse " (Plummer, in loc.).

[12] πᾶς ὁ λαὸς ἀκούσας. According to the context we should understand after ἀκούσας " the preaching of John " and translate: " When all the people and the publicans heard John's preaching they . . ." These words form part of what Jesus said on this occasion. Then we have a connected address of our Lord running from verse 24b to verse 35.

[13] " By not submitting to baptism, they made God's will for men's salvation inoperative, so far as they themselves were concerned " (Klostermann, in loc.).

Greydanus (in loc.) states of βουλή that it is " a determination of the will, counsel or plan, resting upon deliberation or consideration, and hence something different from θέλημα (xii. 47, xxii. 42), which means ' will ' or ' command ' or ' order '. Here βουλή does not refer to the eternal decree of God (Eph. i. 1), which cannot be broken or put aside by the creature, but to God's dispensing of salvation as it is revealed in John's mission and work ". Plummer remarks: " Free will enables each man to annul God's purpose for his salvation " (*in loc.*); and Maclaren declares: " Of all the mysteries of this inexplicable world, the deepest, the mother-mystery of all, is, that given an infinite will and a creature, the creature can thwart the infinite. . . . The possibility is mysterious; the reality of the fact is tragic and bewildering " (*Expositions of Holy Scripture, in loc.*). We are here face to face with the paradox of the divine Sovereignty and human responsibility—a paradox which no human mind can ever solve.

14 εἰς ἑαυτούς should be taken together with ἠθέτησαν and not with βουλή, " and therefore does not mean God's counsel for them or for their benefit, but as directed against themselves, i.e. [they nullified it] to their own disadvantage or destruction " (Greydanus, *in loc.*).

15 What Jesus says in connection with the children in the market-place should not be explained allegorically in all its details as Plummer and others attempt to do. " The Lord merely takes an example from child life, in order to bring to light, by means of a single feature of it, the attitude of the Jews towards the work of John and of Himself " (Greydanus, *in loc.*). This complaint of the children quoted by Jesus, as has often been pointed out, forms in Aramaic a poetical couplet with parallelism, rhythm, and rhyme:

> chōlēlnā lĕkhōn wĕ-lā raqqēdhtōn
> 'ailēlnā lĕkhōn wĕ-lā 'arqēdhtōn.

16 " John's inspiration and asceticism implied something more than human: the Jews prefer to ascribe it to possession by a demon rather than the power of God " (Luce, *in loc.*).

17 ἐσθίων καὶ πίνων = not merely the regular use of food and drink, but also taking part in the normal social life (John ii. 2).

18 ἡ σοφία, the wisdom of God as revealed in His plan of salvation. It may even be taken as a personification of God Himself as is often done in Hebrew literature (cf. Luce, *in loc.*). There is, however, no need to suppose that our Lord is here quoting from a book. He is stating a fact in his own words.

19 τέκνων αὐτῆς refers to those born of the wisdom of God, a wisdom which is active in the plan of salvation. Thus the regenerated children of God, the true believers, are meant. In Matthew xi. 19 ἔργων is used instead of τέκνων. Essentially it amounts to the same, for the children reveal their character and nature in their " works " and in their " works " they show that they " justify " (acknowledge, accept and honour) the wisdom of God, as revealed in His work of salvation— with special reference here to His activity through John and in Jesus.

THE SINFUL WOMAN WHO ANOINTED JESUS' FEET

vii. 36–50

36 [1]And one of the Pharisees desired him that he would eat with him.[2] And he entered into the Pharisee's house, and sat
37 down to meat. And behold, a woman which was in the city,[3] a sinner;[4] and when she knew that he was sitting at meat in the Pharisee's house, she brought an alabaster cruse
38 of ointment, and standing behind at his feet, weeping, she began to wet his feet with her tears, and wiped them with the hair of her head,[5] and kissed his feet,[6] and anointed them
39 with the ointment. Now when the Pharisee which had bidden him saw it, he spake within himself, saying, This man, if he were a prophet, would have perceived who and what manner of woman this is which toucheth him, that she is a
40 sinner. And Jesus answering said unto him, Simon, I have somewhat to say unto thee. And he saith, Master, say on.
41 A certain lender had two debtors: the one owed five hundred
42 pence, and the other fifty. When they had not *wherewith* to pay, he forgave them both. Which of them therefore will
43 love[7] him most? Simon answered and said, He, I suppose,[8] to whom he forgave the most. And he said unto him, Thou
44 hast rightly judged. And turning to the woman, he said unto Simon, Seest thou[9] this woman? I entered into thine house, thou gavest me no water for my feet: but she hath wetted my feet with her tears, and wiped them with her hair.
45 Thou gavest me no kiss: but she, since the time I came in,
46 hath not ceased to kiss my feet. My head with oil[10] thou didst not anoint: but she hath anointed my feet with oint-
47 ment.[11] Wherefore I say unto thee, Her sins, which are many, are forgiven; for she loved much:[12] but to whom little
48 is forgiven, *the same* loveth little.[13] And he said unto her, Thy
49 sins are forgiven.[14] And they that sat at meat with him began to say within themselves, Who is this that even forgiveth sins?
50 And he said unto the woman, Thy faith hath saved thee;[15] go in peace.[16]

Thus far Luke has for the most part been shedding light on Jesus' progressive self-revelation of His divine power and sympathy for the suffering. We have seen Him more and more clearly as the Messiah, the Christ of God. In this part Luke proceeds with

232

his portrayal of Christ and lets us see Him exercising His divine and redeeming love for sinners. Here again it is evident that Luke in his Gospel especially brings out the fact that Jesus came to seek and to save those that are lost.

36-8 On a certain day (Luke does not indicate when) our Lord was invited by a Pharisee to eat with him in his house. From what follows in the narrative it is clear that he did this not through love of Him or because he believed in Him but at best out of curiosity or even for the purpose of spying upon Him. Although Jesus was aware of this, He nevertheless accepted the invitation because He loved Simon, too, and longed to call him to repentance.

But while He was at table, a notoriously sinful woman, who had probably just recently come to know the saving power of Jesus, came into the house uninvited. It was something unheard of that a sinner like herself should venture to enter the house of a Pharisee. However, she was so contrite and repentant because of her former sinful life, and on the other hand so grateful and attached to Christ who had come into her life as Redeemer, that she put aside all her fears, and not only entered the house but even went up to the table where the Pharisee was reclining with his guests, and kneeled at the feet of Jesus. In the East it is customary for all taking part in a repast to take off their sandals and to lean towards the table in a recumbent position, with their feet stretched out backwards. So it was easy for this sinful woman, whose name is not given, to wash His feet with her tears and to wipe and anoint them.

39 The critical Pharisee sees in Jesus' attitude, when He permits the weeping sinner to honour Him thus, a " proof " that He can be no prophet. For, according to his self-righteous ideas, no true prophet would allow such a thing. On the contrary, a true prophet would not only know her for a sinner but would avoid her for that very reason.

40-2 Although Simon, the Pharisee, gives no utterance to his thoughts, the Lord knows what is going on in his heart and asks him which person would out of gratitude show the greatest love—one to whom much has been forgiven or one to whom little has been forgiven? Simon doubted the genuineness of Jesus' calling because he regarded Him as unable to read the woman's character. By His question to him, however, the Saviour shows that not only could He read her character but that He could even fathom Simon's innermost thoughts.

43-7 The Pharisee replies that he to whom much is forgiven will love most. Jesus declares that he has answered correctly and

233

then proceeds to apply practically to the woman's case the principle which the Pharisee himself has admitted as true. By pointing out to Simon his neglect even of the customary marks of honour towards Him, He made it clear that he had not invited Him in the right spirit. In contrast with his loveless attitude, the sinful woman had showered exceptional marks of honour and affection upon Him. Therefore, says Jesus, it is clear that she has experienced forgiveness of her sins—which were many. It is because she is conscious not only of the magnitude of her sins but also of the glorious fact that her sins are forgiven that she acts towards Him with such inward contrition and outward esteem and affection. From the whole context of the story—the parable, the question in verses 41–2, and the Saviour's express statement here (before verse 48) that her sins *are forgiven*—it is clear that the woman had already accepted Him as Redeemer (probably not long before, whether as one among the multitudes who had listened to His teaching, or as one whom He had addressed personally).

Her touching marks of honour towards Him are the outcome of the sense of forgiveness which had already become her share. Her abundant love is therefore not the *cause* of her receiving forgiveness, but the result as well as the proof of her having received forgiveness of many sins.

48–50 Although her sins had already been forgiven, she was nevertheless still regarded by others as a notorious sinner. For this reason Jesus now openly declares that her sins *are* forgiven. And when those present were amazed at His making such a pronouncement, He reiterated His confirmation of the fact that she has become a new redeemed person. He declares to her that it was through her faith that she received forgiveness. And then, in front of all, He says to her: " Go in peace! " Her sins are forgiven, she is saved, she has become a new person, and therefore she, the former despised sinner, can and must depart in peace.

All real love towards Christ must be preceded by a deep consciousness of our own sinfulness and unfitness for acceptance before the Holy God and by the assurance that for Jesus' sake our sins, however great they may be, are forgiven.

Love of the Lord that is not founded upon these two foundations cannot be genuine or permanent.

---

[1] This story is not to be regarded as a variant of the story recorded in Matthew xxvi. 7–13, Mark xiv. 3–9 and John xii. 1–11, for the

following reasons. The similarity between the two stories is not exceptional. Similar occurrences may have taken place on several occasions. The name of Simon also gives no ground of proof, as it was a name of very frequent occurrence at that time (in the New Testament about a dozen different Simons are mentioned, and Josephus makes mention of about twenty).

The attitude and disposition of the Simon mentioned in chapter vii are totally different from what we read in Matthew xxvi and Mark xiv. In Luke it is the critical Pharisee, in Matthew and Mark a cleansed leper (Matt. xxvi. 6). In Luke the occurrence takes place probably in Galilee; in Matthew, Mark and John in Bethany. In Luke the chief actor is an unknown sinful woman; in Matthew and John the well-known Mary of Bethany.

It is, therefore, quite arbitrary when Creed, for example, declares: " This narrative is regarded by Luke as a variant to the story of the anointing in Mark xiv. 3 f., for he has omitted the latter narrative from his version of the Passion " (*in loc.*). Luke indeed shows throughout that from the vast storehouse of facts he had gathered in connection with the life of Jesus he chooses only those events which, under the guidance of the Holy Ghost, he regards as the most important in view of the design and purpose of his Gospel. He, like the other evangelists, does not by any means attempt to give a complete account of the Saviour's life.

Other critics (e.g. Strauss and Baur) have accused Luke of confusion in connection with the story of the anointing. But Plummer rightly observes: " The narrative betrays no confusion: everything is clear and harmonious. The conduct both of Jesus and of the woman is unlike either fiction or clumsily distorted fact. His gentle severity towards Simon and tender reception of the sinner are as much beyond the reach of invention as the eloquence of her speechless affection " (*in loc.*).

² Creed's statement that " the behaviour of the Pharisee, who first invites Jesus to his table and then, for some reason unexplained, neglects the ordinary duties of hospitality is unconvincing " (*in loc.*), displays surprising failure to appreciate the actual situation. For what is more natural than that one of the Pharisees who was critical and antagonistic towards Christ should nevertheless invite Him for the purpose of tripping Him up over some utterance or other at table, or out of mere curiosity because He had already found so many adherents among the masses? And is it not obvious that such a person, especially from fear that his fellow-Pharisees might suspect him of too much friendliness towards Christ, would receive Him rather coldly and perhaps even discourteously? And if it be asked why Jesus nevertheless accepted the invitation of such a person, the answer is that He did not go only to those who were well-disposed towards Him. We must not forget that He had come to save Pharisees as well, for He loved them, too, and longed for a change in their lives. Although He associated with notorious sinners and " publicans " to call them to repentance, He did

not neglect the other kind of people, the " respectable " ones. His was no one-sided ministry.

³ Although it is customary in the East for persons to enter the dining-room uninvited, to seat themselves all round against the walls and to converse with those at table, it was, nevertheless, unheard of for such a notorious sinner to enter the house of a Pharisee. So she probably needed much courage and determination to do it. Schlatter rightly says: " The passionateness with the woman pays honour to Jesus, the flood of tears and the manner of her anointing Him, which exceeded all measure and condemned convention, show clearly that deep sorrow had arisen for the woman out of her guilt and shame " (in loc.). And to this should be added that, above all, it reveals her deep gratitude and love for Him who has become her Saviour.

⁴ According to Strack-Billerbeck, " by γυνὴ ἁμαρτωλός a prostitute is specially to be understood " (in loc.).

⁵ " Among the Jews it was a shameful thing for a woman to let down her hair in public; but she makes this sacrifice " (Plummer, in loc.).

⁶ The kissing of the feet was at that time a recognised sign of deep reverence, especially towards honoured teachers.

⁷ From this it is quite clear that from Jesus' point of view the whole question is that of the love which is the outcome of receiving forgive-ness, and not of love which deserves or brings about forgiveness of sins. This is especially clear if we " contemplate the debt, not as an objective, but as a subjective debt,—not as so many outward transgressions and outbreaks of evil, but as so much consciousness of sin; which we know is nowise in proportion to a man's actual and positive violations of God's law " (Trench). Plummer too, states: " The love and gratitude of those who have had debts remitted to them depends upon their estimate of the amount which has been remitted to them rather than upon the actual amount " (in loc.).

⁸ ὑπολαμβάνω = " I suppose ". The word indicates that the Pharisee answers with " an air of supercilious indifference " (Plummer, in loc.).

⁹ βλέπεις κτλ is " formally a question, but really a command to consider the woman more carefully " (Klostermann, in loc.). Simon has to be made to see that, although she was a notorious sinner, she is so no longer—her tribute of love proves that her sins are forgiven and that she is saved.

¹⁰ ἐλαίῳ = with olive oil (very cheap in Palestine, where olive trees grew in abundance).

¹¹ μύρου = expensive ointment.

¹² Roman Catholic exegetes regard these words as a powerful proof-text for their doctrine of contritio caritate formata, because Jesus is alleged to declare thereby that the tribute of love deserves forgiveness. This explanation is, however, untenable, for the following reasons. We have to read Jesus' words in their context. We then find that in the question-parable of verses 41–2 He has just taught that remission of debt pro-duces great love (and not vice versa). We see, further, that the Lord,

immediately after the words " her sins, which are many, are forgiven, for she loved much ", continues: " but to whom little is forgiven, the same loveth little " (and not " he who has loved little, receives little forgiveness ").

If anyone says: " The woman is very sad for she is weeping in a pathetic manner ", it certainly does not mean that her weeping caused her grief. On the contrary, the outward act (weeping) is the result and expression of the inward state of grief.

So also by the words " her sins, which are many, are forgiven; for she loved much " Jesus means that, since she has shown her love for Him by her outward actions in a clearly genuine and earnest manner, it is quite evident from this that she inwardly possesses the assurance of forgiveness of sins.

When Grieve (like many others) declares that the previous parable " hardly fits the scene " (*Peake's Commentary, in loc.*), and Creed (*in loc.*) calls the words of verse 47 " the false antithesis ", it is the outcome of a superficial exegesis, and of failure to envisage the actual circumstances. And it is unnecessary, following C. C. Torrey, to suppose that our Greek text is due to a misreading of an original Aramaic which really means: " She whose many sins are forgiven will love much, but he to whom little is forgiven will love little " (*Our Translated Gospels* [1936], pp. 100 f.).

[13] These words prove, finally, that the Roman Catholic exegesis of this verse is incorrect; for Jesus does not say here: " for he who has loved little, has only received little forgiveness ". The Pharisee, in his self-righteousness, considered that he required forgiveness from God for only a few sins, and for this reason his love for Him was so slight.

[14] The teaching and conduct of Jesus had already previously brought her to repentance and conversion and to an assurance of forgiveness, and this assurance inspired her with love and gratitude. " Jesus now confirms her assurance and publicly declares her forgiveness. He thus lends His authority to rehabilitate her with society " (Plummer, *in loc.*).

[15] Her faith in Him and in the grace of God is meant. Again we see that Jesus does not say " thy love hath saved thee ", but " thy faith " — not because " faith " is a merit, but because it is her faith that appropriates the forgiveness which grace has bestowed.

[16] πορεύου εἰς εἰρήνην. The present imperative indicates the permanency of this state of peace—peace with God, and peace in the heart because all her sins are forgiven. Here the common Hebrew formula (" go in peace ") is used in its deepest and most comprehensive sense.

THE WOMEN WHO MINISTERED UNTO JESUS OF THEIR SUBSTANCE

viii. 1-3

1 And it came to pass soon afterwards, that he went about through cities and villages,[1] preaching[2] and bringing the
2 good tidings of the kingdom of God, and with him the twelve, and certain women which had been healed of evil spirits and infirmities, Mary that was called Magdalene,[3]
3 from whom seven devils[4] had gone out, and Joanna the wife of Chuza Herod's steward,[5] and Susanna,[6] and many others, which ministered unto them of their substance.

In the first half of this chapter we see the Lord, above all, as the Bearer of the glad tidings of the kingdom (verse 1), who knew beforehand that His words would have different effects (verses 4-15) but who none the less commanded that the light of the Gospel should shine (verses 16, 17) and that everyone should listen to His words in a right frame of mind (verse 18). Those who hear His words and do them stand in the closest relation to Him (verses 19-21).

In these first three verses (verses 1-3) we see Him as the Preacher of the Gospel, and learn that His material requirements were met by a large number of well-to-do women who had been healed by Him.

1 Jesus did not confine Himself to only a few cities in Galilee (where He was then working), but with uninterrupted progress visited one city and village after another, announcing the glad tidings of the kingdom of God by His preaching and by all His doings. During these journeys the twelve disciples now followed Him constantly.

2, 3 But there followed Him also a group of women who were intimately attached to Him as the result of blessings received from Him. Many of them were well-to-do women who served the Master out of their substance. Ever since the time that Jesus bade farewell to His carpenter's shop in order to appear constantly in public as the Messiah and Redeemer, He was poor—altogether without possessions. He never made use of His divine power to provide for Himself. He, the Son of God, humbled Himself so deeply that He was willing to be served with earthly means necessary for His support at the hands of a small group of women whom He had healed.

These women, or several of them at least, continued throughout the rest of Jesus' public ministration, until His crucifixion, to follow and serve Him. And when all His disciples (except the beloved disciple) had fled, some of the women attended Him as far as Golgotha (John xix. 25) and even as far as the grave, where they were also the first witnesses of His resurrection (cf. xxiii. 49, 55, xxiv. 1–10).

What a challenge and inspiration it must be for every woman to consider that, while nowhere in the four Gospels is mention made of any women who were hostile to Jesus, there are numerous references to ministration and marks of honour which they accorded Him. With much affection and faithful devotion they ministered to Him with their possessions (verse 3)—to Christ Jesus who became poor so that we might be made rich. What an example of service to be followed by every woman who believes in Him!

---

[1] Plummer rightly observes: " The incidental way in which the severity of Christ's labours is mentioned is remarkable " (in loc.).

[2] κηρύσσων = proclaiming openly and with authority. The content of what He thus preached is expressed by εὐαγγελιζόμενος τὴν βασιλείαν τοῦ θεοῦ. The " preaching " and the " proclaiming of the Gospel " are not two separate things. The latter gives the content of the former. " Whenever He proclaimed the evangel, He was preaching. Whenever He preached, He was proclaiming the evangel " (G. Morgan, in loc.).

[3] She is not to be identified with the sinful woman of vii. 37 (cf. Klostermann, in loc.). " We nowhere read that being possessed by evil spirits had any connection with marked sinfulness " (Greydanus, in loc.).

[4] Klostermann rightly observes that δαιμόνια ἑπτά " does not refer to the number seven of the Babylonian demons " as alleged by Clemen. But when he says: " but either to an attack with relapses (xi. 26) or to a specially severe attack (viii. 30) " (in loc.), we can only accept the second alternative as aplicable here.

[5] She is only mentioned again in xxiv. 10 in the New Testament. Godet (in loc.) conjectures that she was the wife of the nobleman of John iv. 46–53, who together with his whole house believed in Christ after the healing of his son. Zahn also feels inclined to accept this and

suggests that through Manaen (Acts xiii. 1), who stood in very close relation to Herod Antipas, Luke obtained particulars concerning other persons, such as Joanna and Chuza who also stood in close relation to Herod. Nothing can, however, here be said with certainty, although such a possibility exists.

[6] She is mentioned nowhere else in the New Testament.

PARABLE OF THE SOWER

(Cf. Matt. xiii. 1–23; Mark iv. 1–20)

viii. 4–15

4 And when a great multitude came together, and they of
5 every city resorted unto him, he spake by a parable:[1] The
sower went forth to sow his seed:[2] and as he sowed, some fell
by the way side; and it was trodden under foot, and the
6 birds of the heaven devoured it. And other fell on the rock;[3]
and as soon as it grew, it withered away, because it had no
7 moisture. And other fell amidst the thorns; and the thorns
8 grew with it, and choked[4] it. And other fell into the good
ground, and grew, and brought forth fruit a hundredfold.
As he said these things, he cried, He that hath ears to hear,
let him hear.[5]
9 And his disciples asked him[6] what this parable might be.
10 And he said, Unto you it is given to know the mysteries[7] of
the kingdom of God:[8] but to the rest in parables; that[9] seeing
they may not see, and hearing they may not understand.
11 Now the parable is this: The seed is the word of God.[10] And
12 those by the way side are they that have heard;[11] then
cometh the devil, and taketh away the word from their heart,
13 that they may not believe and be saved. And those on the
rock *are* they which, when they have heard, receive the word
with joy; and these have no root, which for a while believe,
14 and in time of temptation fall away. And that which fell
among the thorns, these are they that have heard, and as
they go on their way they are choked with cares and riches
and pleasures of *this* life, and bring no fruit to perfection.
15 And that in the good ground, these are such as in an honest
and good heart, having heard the word, hold it fast, and
bring forth fruit with patience.

The Saviour had previously spoken through parables, but from
this period in His public ministry until shortly before His crucifixion He made very frequent use of them. Also in Matthew and
Mark this fact comes clearly to light (cf. Matt. xiii. 10, 34; Mark
iv. 10, 12, 32, 33).

4 While the Lord went from city to city a great multitude
gathered around Him. His preaching and His miracles of healing

and raising the dead brought about a mighty popular movement in Galilee; the masses of people simply flocked to Him as far as He went.

During this period He commenced to teach more exclusively by means of parables. One of the most important and probably the first of the series of parables of that time, is the one that is reproduced by all three synoptic Gospels, the parable of the sower.

5–8 Here Jesus describes something that often occurred in the ordinary life of the peasants in Palestine and probably today still occurs there. He and many of His hearers had themselves seen this sort of thing. In Palestine there are often roads going through cultivated lands, so that the sower would unavoidably lose some of the seed on them. There are also many places where rocks crop out or are so near the surface that there is only a thin layer of soil. This shallow ground rapidly dries out after rain so that the small plants that have come up in it while it was wet soon wither away. In other places again there have been during the previous years thorn-bushes which have run to seed or been killed by frost down to the surface of the ground, and then again shoot up or sprout when the seed has been sown in the rainy season, with the result that the weak plants are killed by the tougher thorn-bushes.

The major portion of the land is, however, obviously free from the three dangers and obstacles mentioned, so that the seed germinates well there, grows satisfactorily and yields a rich harvest. But the good parts of the lands differ as regards fertility, so that one portion yields more fruit than others (cf. Matt. xiii. 8). The emphasis in Luke is, however, on the abundance of fruit which the right soil produces.

9, 10 In answer to what the disciples naturally asked Him when later on He was alone with them (cf. Mark iv. 10), Jesus first states in general why He now teaches mostly in parables. His answer, in part at least, amounts to this, that while God in His grace gave to His disciples the privilege of being initiated and instructed by Him in the mysteries, the deep truths concerning His kingdom, He now addresses the unbelieving multitudes in parables, so that they will no longer hear the deepest truths in explicit statements, but will only hear the outward form of the parables. While the followers of Christ receive an opened mind to understand the deeper truths taught in the parables, these truths remain concealed to the carnally minded multitudes who look only for outward things (by demanding for instance miraculous signs). When we take Jesus' answer, as reported in Luke, in conjunction with its fuller form in Matthew xiii. 10–17, we see why the Saviour adopted this course. For Matthew xiii. 13 states that Jesus excluded the multitudes from a deeper understanding of His teachings because they had up to that time wilfully continued deaf and blind to the real significance of His preaching and conduct. They had remained worldly-minded and had refused to learn from Him. Accordingly He now proceeds as a judgment upon their stubborn blindness to speak mostly in parables for the short period that He will still be among them before His crucifixion. Through their own unwillingness for so many months to open their minds to His spiritual teachings, they brought this judgment upon themselves. In future only those who truly seek His truth are given the privilege of learning to know the real meaning of His teachings. No longer can He continue to speak in explicit terms regarding the Kingdom of God inaugurated by His ministry to those who are unwilling to seek Him in sincerity. At the same time, however, His disciples and other faithful followers are to be more thoroughly instructed so as to be equipped as the future builders of His kingdom. Thus, while He has, as a result of the flocking together of the multitudes, to continue His preaching almost always in the hearing of the unsympathetic crowds, He does not " cast His pearls before swine ", but speaks in parables concerning the deepest mysteries of the kingdom. These parables are indeed so interesting and arresting that they grip the multitudes; but they do not discover what He really means thereby. To His true followers, however, He gives the necessary explanations at convenient times.

There were probably also other reasons why the Saviour at that time spoke so often by parables. The Saviour's conduct in this respect inevitably reminds us of the history of the Pharaoh of the Exodus. After Pharaoh had several times wilfully hardened himself in defiance of his word of honour, God hardened him —gave to his hardness of heart a fixed setting because he had so repeatedly hardened himself (cf. Exod. viii. 32 and ix. 12).

So also, since the carnally-minded Jewish multitudes wilfully persisted in spiritual ignorance, the Saviour allowed them to remain in that condition by speaking to them only in parables. However, the final purpose of this was also a purpose of love and grace. The greater the knowledge, the greater the responsibility, and the greater the opportunities that have been slighted, the greater the guilt. So, that their guilt might not accumulate, the Lord no longer addresses them directly in explicit teachings during the period immediately preceding His crucifixion, but in parables.

Many of them would, however, probably remember these striking word-pictures, and later on, when some of them were converted after Pentecost, the meaning of the once incomprehensible parables would become intelligible to them and contribute much to their spiritual moulding.

11-15 Here the Saviour Himself gives the explanation of the parable of the sower. The seed sown in the four different places, represents primarily Jesus Himself, the Word of God, and then the word of God preached by Jesus, and in the secondary sense also the message proclaimed by His followers, while the various types of places in which the seed fell, signify the various classes of hearers. The first kind are those who hear only with the outward ear without coming under deeper impressions, and even before the germination of the seed, before the preaching brings about a change of heart and life, the power of darkness has taken away all recollection and thoughts of it.

The second class, the seed falling upon the rock, are those who, when listening to the preaching, receive it with emotional excitement and superficial enthusiasm. These, however, do not allow the seed of the Word to penetrate deeply into their hearts and lives. Without being genuinely converted they are only temporarily taken up with the preaching of the Word; and when they go back to the practical struggle of life, the good influence exerted upon them disappears.

The third kind, where the thorns grow along with the seed, are those who do indeed allow the preaching to take root in heart and life. But their loyalty to Him is only one of many other and more powerful loyalties, so that it is eventually completely effaced. Wordly-mindedness and similar spiritual evils in their lives choke the spiritual life. Material want or material abundance and worldly pleasures so completely absorb the lives of these people, that the fruit borne in their lives by the preaching of the Word is ere long altogether destroyed.

But God be thanked, His Word never returns empty. Although some seed is sown in vain, much will fall on good soil and bear abundant fruit. There are always those hearers who accept the preaching in sincerity and who bear fruit of permanent character —some in a small measure, others in greater measure, and others in abundance (cf. Matt. xiii. 8). Our Lord stresses especially the fact that in the case of the faithful hearers the fruit will be very abundant (wheat ordinarily does not produce a hundredfold crop), above measure. The seed, the Word of God, has such vital power and is so pure and good, that wherever through faith in and obedience to Him, the right soil in human hearts is given to Him and His teachings, the harvest will be exceedingly great—far beyond human expectations.

Preachers of the Word are constantly being criticised by hearers. But here we have a parable of the perfect Preacher who subjects all *hearers* of the Word to the closest scrutiny, demanding from them hearts that are prepared for the word. " Take heed therefore how ye hear! " (verse 18).

---

¹ " Through word imagery one can represent something that is more difficult to explain by reasoning. The image addresses itself to the imagination and sets going the power of forming conceptions. By means of His parables the Lord has revealed the mysteries of God's kingdom more fully, more deeply and more gloriously to those who accept His Person and His message in faith. Those who did so among the multitudes and believed in Him, to the same extent experienced this more glorious revelation. Unbelief prevents one from seeing the real content and causes one to progress no further than the outward form " (Greydanus, *in loc.*).

² For the division by rabbis of their pupils into various groups cf. Major in *The Mission and Message of Jesus*, p. 68.

³ τὴν πέτραν here refers to rocky soil " with rock appearing at intervals and with no depth of ground " (Plummer, *in loc.*).

⁴ ἀποπνίγειν = to strangle, to throttle, to choke.

⁵ ὁ ἔχων ὦτα ἀκούειν ἀκουέτω. ἀκούειν ἀκουέτω probably reflects the emphatic Hebrew use of the absolute infinitive—" let him who has ears (i.e. who has the opportunity of hearing), by all means *listen*! "

⁶ According to Jülicher (*Gleichnisreden Jesu*, ii, p. 532) and many other critics and commentators (cf. Rawlinson, *St. Mark*, pp. 46 ff. and B.T.D. Smith on Matt. xiii), the parables as originally used by Jesus in His preaching were simple illustrations that were easily comprehensible. But later on in the church, they contend, after Jesus' departure, when the context in which He used the parables had been forgotten, they were more and more regarded as mysterious allegories which He explained only to His selected followers. According to these critics, the Gospels thus give a historically false representation by teaching that Jesus explained the parables to His disciples when He was alone with them. The explanation of the parables put into Jesus' mouth would then really be the explanation given to them by the Christian church during the years after His departure, and then, when the Gospels were written, Jesus Himself was represented as having given the explanations.

Jülicher and his followers can, however, adduce no conclusive proof to substantiate their supposition. It is a theory completely at variance with the unanimous testimony of all three synoptic Gospels, which teach clearly that Jesus did at a certain stage mostly speak in parables, and in such a manner that His disciples had to receive special enlightenment from Him in order to be able to understand their deepest meaning. (Cf. for an enlightening article on the correct understanding of the parables, Prof. Otto Piper, "The Understanding of the Synoptic parables", in *Evangelical Quarterly*, 1942, pp. 42–53.)

⁷ Originally μυστήριον (from μύω) meant a secret ceremony, revealed only to the initiated of a certain religious community. Afterwards it came to mean any kind of secret (cf. Luce, *in loc.*). In the New Testament it means "mysteries", i.e. "the secret riches and glories only to be known through divine revelation, which are not to remain secret but have been revealed, made known, however, only to those to whom such experience is granted by God" (Greydanus, *in loc.*). It is something entirely different from the "mysteries" of the pagan mystery-religions.

⁸ ἡ βασιλεία τοῦ θεοῦ here refers especially to the beneficent workings of the rule of God as already revealed in the present life, but to be finally revealed in full glory at the Consummation of the Age. Nevertheless the judicial effect of the Divine rule is not excluded here.

⁹ Where Matthew xiii has ὅτι instead of the ἵνα given here (as in Mark iv. 12), Matthew and Luke do not contradict each other but are mutually complementary (see our exposition at verse 10). In any case, ὅτι and ἵνα are both possible renderings of the Aramaic conjunction *di*. This is the conjunction used in the Aramaic paraphrase or Targum of the Old Testament passage (Isa. vi. 9 f.) which Jesus here quotes; and it is noteworthy that (as the account in Mark clearly shows) it was the Targumic version of the passage that Jesus quoted, and not the Massoretic or LXX text. (Cf. T. W. Manson, *The Teaching of Jesus*, pp. 75 ff.)

¹⁰ The similarity (which is stressed in this parable) between seed and the Word of God consists chiefly in the vital power in both.

¹¹ "Hearing is an urgent business. We assume that because initiative is with the speaker a message controls the hearer. But the parts may be reversed: the hearer may control the message. An appeal, even the appeal of Jesus, may be frustrated by unreceptiveness" (Buttrick, *The Parables of Jesus*, p. 51).

THE PARABLE OF THE LAMP

(Cf. Matt. iv. 21–25)

viii. 16–18

16 And no man, when he hath lighted a lamp, covereth it with
a vessel, or putteth it under a bed; but putteth it on a stand,
17 that they which enter in may see the light. For nothing is
hid,[1] that shall not be made manifest; nor *anything* secret,
18 that shall not be known and come to light. Take heed
therefore how ye hear: for whosoever hath, to him shall be
given; and whosoever hath not, from him shall be taken
away even that which he thinketh he hath.[2]

By His answer to their question and His explanation of the parable the Lord lit a light in the disciples. This light, He now teaches,
must not be hidden by them.

16, 17 Although He speaks in parables, it is nevertheless His
final purpose that the light of the Gospel should be spread in full
measure. He initiates His followers into the true knowledge of
the mysteries of the kingdom—not for them to hide such knowledge, but to make it known, without hindrance or reservation,
to all with whom they come in contact. Although He has been
compelled, owing to circumstances, as it were, to whisper the
truths in their ears, they will ere long have to enter the world and
to preach the Gospel openly—make known what was hidden and
bring to light what was concealed. The Lord here refers especially to the preaching of the glad tidings after His ascension
and after the pouring out of the Holy Ghost. So by these words
the Lord completely forbids the thought that He speaks in
parables in order that the Gospel message should remain hidden.
On the contrary, His final purpose even with this veiled form of
preaching is to let the light of the Gospel shine—for the illumination of His followers and thereafter through them also for that of
others.

18 Because it is so necessary for His followers to be light-
bearers, He commands them to see that they hear correctly, that
they listen carefully to His word with full attention and with a
steadfast conviction. The preaching of the Word must bear good
fruit in the heart and life of each and all of them—if not, the

247

results will be fatal. Those who do not pay heed to His word, will not go unpunished. While those who listen to Him with a believing, surrendered and obedient heart, will be given a deeper and more intensive insight into the spiritual life and into His Word, the indifferent and disobedient ones will lose even the little measure of spiritual knowledge and joy of life which they possess. Their hearts and lives will become darker and poorer.

Because we have been called to spread the light of His Gospel, we must see to it that we listen to Him with the right attitude and faith. Only when our own lives are brightly illuminated, shall we be able to let our light shine upon others. Every believer is called upon to "take heed how he hears" and to let His light shine in and through our life—in word and act.

[1] Note the beautiful poetical rhythm and parallelism in these verses.

[2] " Whoever gives a welcome to the word and appropriates it becomes worthy and capable of receiving more. But by not appropriating truth when we recognise it, we lose our hold of it, and have less power of recognizing it in the future " (Plummer, *in loc.*).

THE RELATIVES OF JESUS

(Cf. Matt. xii. 46–50; Mark iii. 31–5)

viii. 19–21

19 And there came to him his mother[1] and brethren,[2] and
20 they could not come at him for the crowd. And it was
    told him, Thy mother and thy brethren stand without,
21 desiring to see thee. But he answered and said unto them,
    My mother and my brethren[3] are these which hear the word
    of God, and do it.

Here again it is clear that Luke compiled his Gospel in a logical
and aesthetic sequence and not primarily in strict chronological
order. From Matthew and Mark it appears that this occurrence
was linked up with the Beelzebub address which Luke reports
later on in xi. 14–28. But because this occurrence (verses 19–21)
is a fitting conclusion to verses 1–18, he records it here.

19–21 On a certain day (Luke does not state when) Mary and
Jesus' younger brethren came to Him while He was surrounded
by a great multitude. From Matthew and Mark it appears that
they felt concerned concerning Him—they were afraid that He
was overtaxing Himself completely through His constant exertion
in word and deeds; so they desired to remove Him, practically by
force, to their home, away from the thronging multitudes. The
Saviour knew their thoughts and so, in His answer to the message
that His mother and brethren were waiting for Him outside, He
let them know clearly that He was not prepared to submit to the
mistaken judgment of even His mother and nearest blood-relations.
For, He said, He was in the deepest sense related not to those who,
humanly speaking, were the most closely related to Him, but to
those who believed and obeyed the word of God brought to them
by Him. So He would not allow the members of His home to
encroach upon the execution of His divine calling and discharge
of His duties. In His attitude towards His Father in heaven and in
the practice of His Messianic calling as Son of God, natural
kinship had to be relegated to a subordinate place. However
faithful and devoted He had been to His mother and home relatives through all the years, He frankly reprimands them when
they are actuated by defective human considerations to try to

249

limit and regulate His activities according to their limited and mistaken insights.

What a privilege it is to know that, if we really listen to Him and obey His word, we are still more closely related to Him than His mother and brethren were in a mere earthly sense. Through the habitation of His Spirit in us we are made one with Him.

[1] This story proves to us clearly that Mary was not the perfect saint as she is represented to have been by the Roman church. She was and is indeed the blessed one amongst women, because to her was given the privilege of being the mother of the Redeemer, but she was also a fallible mortal, beset with sin and weakness.

[2] Since in the New Testament Jesus' brothers and even sisters are frequently mentioned in a most natural manner as if they were His own brothers and sisters, born of Mary (Matt. xii. 46, xiii. 55; Mark iii. 32, vi. 3; John ii. 12), and since in Luke ii. 7 He is called the " first-born ", apart from various other considerations, there can be no doubt that the Lord really had blood-brothers and sisters. The Roman Catholic opinion that the " brethren and sisters " were step-brothers and step-sisters (children of Joseph by a former wife), or His " cousins ", is unfounded and would never have existed had it not been for Epiphanius, Jerome and later Roman leaders who embraced a false asceticism and regarded Mary as a woman who had remained a virgin throughout her life. Even Tertullian insisted on taking the " brethren and sisters " of Jesus as real children of Mary (*De Carne Christi*, vii).

Jesus' brothers were James and Judas (the two writers of the New Testament epistles that bear their names), and Joseph and Simon (Mark vi. 3). In addition He had at least two sisters (Mark vi. 3). He was, therefore, the eldest of a big family and, because Joseph probably died early, He had a large share in the maintenance of His mother and His younger brothers and sisters. For this reason also He worked for so many years as a carpenter in Nazareth until He began His public ministry.

[3] μήτηρ μου καὶ ἀδελφοί μου. No articles are used here primarily because these words form the complement of the sentence, but possibly also because Jesus does not mean " My *actual* mother and brothers" but " like my mother and brothers, and just as beloved ".

JESUS STILLS THE TEMPEST

(Cf. Matt. viii. 23-7; Mark iv. 35-41)

viii. 22-5

22 Now it came to pass on one of those days, that he entered into a boat, himself and his disciples; and he said unto them, Let us go over unto the other side of the lake: and
23 they launched forth. But as they sailed he fell asleep: and there came down a storm of wind on the lake;[1] and they
24 were filling *with water*, and were in jeopardy. And they came to him, and awoke[2] him, saying, Master, master, we perish. And he awoke, and rebuked the wind and the raging of the water: and they ceased, and there was a calm.[3]
25 And he said unto them, Where is your faith? And being afraid they marvelled, saying one to another, Who then is this, that he commandeth even the winds and the water,[4] and they obey him?[5]

While Luke has in the foregoing twenty-one verses held Jesus before us as the Great Preacher of the Gospel, he now shows Him to us as the Almighty Ruler even over the forces of nature.

22 From Mark iv. 35 ff. it appears that the Saviour towards the evening of the day when He had been so busy and told so many parables, said to His disciples: " Let us go over unto the other side of the lake." And because He was tired and exhausted, they took Him to the ship and launched forth.

23 When they were some distance away from the shore and Jesus had already in His weariness fallen asleep, there suddenly came down a storm of wind on the lake. It is a special characteristic of the sea of Galilee that, although it generally lies quite motionless, being practically surrounded by hills, storms sometimes arise there very unexpectedly. Especially from the eastern side, where there are high mountains, violent windstorms, often with extreme suddenness, come rushing down on the lake.

24 The disciples, who were experienced fishermen and had already had to brave many a storm, did everything in their power to steer the boat right and to prevent its being filled with water and sinking. But everything was in vain, and the danger of perishing seemed more and more threatening. Nevertheless the Saviour, who was utterly fatigued in body after the constant work of the

251

preceding day and days, continued to sleep on during the storm. But ultimately His disciples, in utter despair, awoke Him and said in terror: " Master, master, we perish! "

Undoubtedly the powers of evil, while the wearied Jesus was lying asleep, were trying to make the boat sink along with Him and His disciples through the violence of the storm. For by these means, as they thought, God's whole plan of salvation could then be frustrated.

Jesus knew that the evil one had a hand in the matter; therefore it is written that He " rebuked " the wind and the raging of the water. This was not because He regarded the wind and raging of the water as evil spirits. But because He saw in this particular storm the operation of the evil one, by rebuking the wind and waves, He actually rebuked the powers of Satan which at that moment were active in the elements. The earth " and the fulness thereof " belong to the Lord and He guides the courses of wind and weather. But, nevertheless, God sometimes permits the evil one to exercise power over the forces of nature within certain limits.

25 After the storm had subsided at Jesus' command and everything had calmed down, He asked His disciples: " Where is your faith? " How could they have feared that they would perish as long as He was in the ship? Even although He was asleep, He is the Almighty Lord who watches over the safety of His followers. How could they have feared that God would allow His Son, the promised Redeemer, and His disciples to perish?

Although the disciples had already previously learned much concerning His divine power, they were nevertheless amazed and even terror-stricken when they saw such a striking revelation of His omnipotence even over a raging tempest. We should observe that not only did He cause the storm to subside, but also immediately calmed down the lashing waves and brought them to rest. A moment before, the wind was roaring and the waves were raging furiously. But at His command everything was at once calm and the surface of the water was again motionless and unruffled. What a mighty revelation of the Omnipotence of Him through whom the Father created everything, including the earth and all forces of nature.

Just as it was impossible for that ship, with the Redeemer of the world on board, to founder, no matter how many storms broke over it, so it is equally impossible for the church of Christ, the body of which He Himself is the Head and Preserver, ever to be destroyed, notwithstanding all the forces of hell that continually assail it. To everyone who is full of fear and doubt as to the future of His kingdom, He puts the question: " Where is thy faith? " He is on board the ship of His church and therefore it can never perish, no matter how the storms may break and rage over it. Even so, it is with the vessel of every believer's life—it cannot perish, for Jesus, the Omnipotent Pilot, is on board.

[1] Plummer says of the hills around the lake: " These are furrowed with ravines like funnels, down which winds rush with great velocity " (*in loc.*).

[2] " That the Lord continued to sleep in spite of the raging tempest and lashing waves, revealed, apart from His inward restfulness and firm faith in God, also His great wearinesss " (Greydanus, *in loc.*).

[3] The sudden and complete calm which fell over the lake proved the reality of the miracle, especially in the eyes of the veteran fishermen who knew how impossible such a thing is in the natural course of events.

[4] As Creator and Maintainer of the whole of nature, the Son of God, who is One with the Father, can control the forces of nature by bringing higher laws into operation. He does not act in conflict with the God-given laws, but brings into operation laws which are still unknown to man, and by which the well-known natural laws are set aside in the accomplishment of His miracle. The Creator is present in His creation as the Maintainer of it, but as the Omnipotent One He is also exalted above it. Nevertheless He always continues, as Preserver of all things, to be the God of Law and order.

[5] For an interesting example of how a scholar who is unwilling to accept the facts as presented in the New Testament tries to give " reasonable " explanations of the supposed origin of such stories, we refer the reader to the exposition of Major in *The Mission and Message of Jesus*, p. 73. His representation strikes one as highly artificial and arbitrary. For Christians who believe in God as the Almighty Creator and Preserver of all things and in the divinity of our Lord, there is no difficulty in accepting the fact of His omnipotent power over nature.

THE POSSESSED MAN OF GADARA

(Cf. Matt. viii. 28–34; Mark iv. 35–41)

viii. 26–39

26 And they arrived at the country of the Gerasenes,[1] which is
27 over against Galilee. And when he was come forth upon
the land, there met him a certain man[2] out of the city,[3]
who had devils; and for a long time he had worn no clothes,
28 and abode not in *any* house, but in the tombs.[4] And when he
saw Jesus, he cried out, and fell down before him, and with
a loud voice said, What have I to do with thee, Jesus thou
29 Son of the Most High God? I beseech thee, torment me not.
For he commanded the unclean spirit to come out from the
man. For oftentimes it had seized him: and he was kept
under guard, and bound with chains and fetters; and breaking the bands asunder, he was driven of the devil into the
30 deserts. And Jesus asked him, What is thy name? And he
said, Legion;[5] for many devils were entered into him.
31 And they intreated him[6] that he would not command them
32 to depart into the abyss.[7] Now there was there a herd of
many swine feeding on the mountain: and they intreated
him[8] that he would give them leave to enter into them. And
33 he gave them leave. And the devils came out from the man,
and entered into the swine: and the herd rushed down the
34 steep into the lake, and were choked.[9] And when they that
fed them saw what had come to pass, they fled, and told it
35 in the city and in the country. And they went out to see
what had come to pass; and they came to Jesus, and found
the man, from whom the devils were gone out, sitting, clothed
and in his right mind, at the feet of Jesus:[10] and they were
36 afraid. And they that saw it told them how he that was
possessed with devils was made whole. And all the people
37 of the country of the Gerasenes round about asked him to
depart from them; for they were holden with great fear: and
38 he entered into a boat, and returned. But the man from
whom the devils were gone out prayed him that he might
39 be with him: but he sent him away, saying, Return to thy
house, and declare how great things God hath done for
thee.[11] And he went his way, publishing throughout the
whole city how great things Jesus had done for him.

Once more we see in this story how Jesus, who during the previous night had revealed His divine power over the forces of

nature, when He stilled the tempest, is the Omnipotent Victor over the forces of the devil. Where He commands, they have to obey Him—no choice is left them.

26 From Capernaum in Galilee our Lord and his disciples sailed to the south-east shore of the lake where there was a little town called Gergesa (to-day the name is Kersa).

27 Near the ruins of Kersa numerous tombs are still to be seen. Among the tombs of the town at that time the unhappy victim who was possessed of demons wandered about naked and attacked passers-by. When Jesus walked ashore, the possessed man came to meet Him, probably in order also to molest Him and His disciples.

28, 29 But as soon as the demoniac came to Him Jesus commanded the evil spirits to leave him. So the possessed man fell down before Him and the demons, who immediately recognised the Redeemer, cried out through their victim: " What have we to do with thee, Jesus, thou Son of God most high? " (see explanation at iv. 34), and the possessed man pleaded: " I beseech thee, torment me not."

Before the Son of God the evil spirits, who have so ill-treated their victim and brought him down to the level of a brute, were powerless and terror-stricken. They realise that they are conquered and beseech Him piteously not to take action against them.

30 In order to make the possessed man realise that he has a personality apart from the evil spirits that have entered into him Jesus asks his name. His answer shows that he cannot yet break loose from the state in which he has identified himself with the evil spirits in him. He calls himself " Legion ", by which he intimates that he is possessed of a large number of evil spirits.

31-3 The spirits are afraid of returning to the " deep "—the " abyss ", the present abode of the demons—their diabolical craving is to enter into human beings or animals in order to be able to exert their unholy influences. So they beseech the Son of God to allow them to enter into a herd of swine feeding nearby, and He suffers them to do this. But because all evil spirits are forces which, in accordance with their whole nature, work for destruction, the herd of swine, being under their influence, rush violently down the steep places into the lake. So the whole herd of swine were drowned and the demons probably had to return to the " abyss ", for after Christ had caused them to come out of the possessed man He would not have permitted them again to enter into other persons.

255

From various quarters objections have been raised against this occurrence. We have already dealt with the historical fact of demon-possession, and we have pointed out that everything indicates that with the incarnation of the Word, the Son of God, the forces of the devil also, in order to oppose Him as Man and in His work of redemption, endeavoured to incarnate themselves in human beings. The Evil One, as it were, also wanted to become man. It is for this reason that demon-possession was such a characteristic phenomenon of the time when Jesus was upon the earth.

But now objections are raised against the ethical implication of Jesus' behaviour with regard to the herd of swine. For the question is asked: what right did Jesus have to cause other people's animals to perish thus? There should, however, be no such question, for it was not Jesus that caused the swine to drown, but the evil spirits. Then someone may object that this at any rate happened with His permission. This may be so; but it would be wrong to conclude that He acted unjustly. For Christ is One with God, and the Sovereign God, who is the Creator and Maintainer of all things, has the absolute right over everything created by Him. Whatever He does is well-done. Even where He permits the devil to do certain things He still continues to act in full accordance with His love, wisdom and justice. It is only because we do not possess adequate knowledge that it sometimes appears to us, as in this case, that He has acted unjustly. The fault never lies with Him, but invariably with our obscured intellects and imperfect knowledge. Whatever the reason was why the Saviour allowed the evil spirits to enter into the swine, with the result that the animals were all drowned, we know that He acted in perfect wisdom and righteousness, and that He had the divine right to act as He did.

34-7 The inhabitants of the region and city, instead of believing in Jesus through the miraculous healing of the possessed man, and being grateful to Him, only recoil with fear from the visible revelation of His supernatural power and probably also because they were afraid that further disasters might befall them. From this it is evident that they had guilty consciences, otherwise they would not have been overcome by such an unhealthy fear. In addition, it is clear that they attached far more value to their earthly possessions than to the salvation of the possessed man and their own salvation as well. So they turned Jesus away, by asking Him to depart from them.

38, 39 When Jesus again wanted to sail back with His disciples (probably to Capernaum), the healed man besought Him

256

that he might henceforth be His follower. The Lord, however, had a different purpose for him, and so He commanded him to return home and tell his relations and acquaintances what a mighty work of redemption God had accomplished in his life. Christ had acted as plenipotentiary of God the Father, who had worked the healing through Him. The man knows spontaneously that Jesus, who has healed him and won his heart's allegiance, is also the divine Lord, and so he proclaims what He has done to him. Because that region was so secluded from the Jewish masses in Galilee, and since there existed no danger from inflamed Messianic passions, Jesus commanded him to make known what had been done to him. The man obeyed the Saviour and related what Jesus had done to him, not only among the people of his family, but throughout the whole surrounding territory.

While we know that we have to wrestle not against flesh and blood but against the principalities, against the powers, against the rulers of the darkness of this world, against wicked spirits in high places (Eph. vi. 12), it is heartening to be brought by this story to a fresh realisation that Christ Jesus is the Conqueror of all evil spirits. In the light of His holiness and might they are unable to proceed with their devilish works. And where God still permits them to make assaults upon the faithful, this is only to test and refine us, and He never gives them free play. Ere long an end will be put for ever to their activities, when He comes in power and glory to establish His everlasting and heavenly kingdom upon the new earth.

---

[1] For the difficult question of the true reading here—Γεργεσηνῶν, Γερασηνῶν or Γαδαρηνῶν—we may refer to Creed (in loc.) and Zahn (in loc.). Probably "Gergesenes" is the original reading of Luke (being supported by ℵ L X Θ Ξ, fam. 1, 33 157 251 700, syr. pal., boh., arm., eth.); as "Gadarenes" is of Matthew and "Gerasenes" of Mark. According to Gressmann, "the story does not suit the topography at all; it originated elsewhere and its localisation at the Sea of Gennesareth is only secondary" (cf. Klostermann, in loc.) But such a statement is quite inexplicable; for the surroundings of Kersa as identified by Sanday, Plummer, Thomson and others with the country of the Gergesenes, are in perfect agreement with the type of region in which the event was enacted (cf. Plummer at verse 33). It is well-known that along the shore of the Sea of Galilee opposite Capernaum there are in certain places steep rocky slopes where the swine could have tumbled down, and even to-day, near the ruins of Kersa, there are many tombs to be seen in the rocks (cf. Plummer at verse 27).

² Matthew viii. 28 mentions *two* demon-possessed men on this occasion. The one mentioned by Mark and Luke may have been the more prominent and loquacious of the two; or else Matthew, after his fashion, conflates two incidents here.

³ " T. H. Huxley, in his *Essays Upon Some Controverted Questions* (1892), made merry over the escapade of the Gadarene swine, running the seven miles between Gadara and the Lake of Galilee, crossing the deep river Yarmuk *en route*. The best-known Gerasa was a Greek city nearly forty miles south-east of the lake (modern Jerash in Trans-jordan); but the name of Mark's Gerasa survives in the modern village of Khersa, on the east shore of the lake. Luke's reading ' Gergesenes ' may represent even more accurately the ancient name of this place, as Origen knew of a Gergesa on the Lake of Galilee. But the city of Gadara owned some property round about Khersa, so that the district and the pigs could properly also be called Gadarene " (F. F. Bruce, *Are the New Testament Documents Reliable?* p. 52 n.). Cf. also Major, *op. cit.*, p. 75. The predominantly Greek character of the area (Deca-polis) explains how the inhabitants kept swine.

⁴ " Near the ruins of Khersa there are many tombs hewn in the rocks " (Plummer, *in loc.*). Schlatter justly observes: " The healthy man has a horror of a decaying corpse and avoids defilement; it is only deranged people who have any desire for death and decay " (at Matt. viii).

⁵ A Roman legion usually consisted of six thousand men. Here the word is merely used to indicate that there were *many* evil spirits in him. The idea, however, that the man was suffering from a " trauma " con-tracted in childhood through witnessing the violence of a *legion* of soldiers is unconvincing.

⁶ Thereby they recognise His absolute power over them.

⁷ ἄβυσσος. Cf. Revelation ix 1 ff., xi. 7 ff., xx. 1, 3. The word goes back to Sumerian *apsu* (" sea "); the old translation " bottomless pit " is based on a false etymology. " By this word the abode of the devils during this earthly dispensation is indicated.. After the day of judgment they will be cast into the lake of fire, Revelation xix. 20, xx. 10, 14, xxi. 8 " (Greydanus, *in loc.*).

⁸ " Demons are ever seeking some material or physical contact. Why? It is the restlessness of evil purpose; seeking some material or physical contact. Demons can only blight the work of God, in the creation and in this world, as they find vantage ground in the physical in man; and if not in man, then with some lower form of life " (Morgan, *in loc.*). The misery of such spirits so long as they are deprived of some corporeal or material form in which to embody themselves is generally recognised by heathen people (perhaps because of their more frequent commerce with demons). A Chinese driver explained the whirling sand spouts of the Gobi Desert as due to the possession of sand " bodies " by demons: " What they want is a body, and for lack of a better one they pick up a shroud of sand " (M. Cable and F. French, *Something Happened*, p. 191).

In answer to the question how spiritual beings can enter into brute animals and influence them Plummer writes that in such cases " our ignorance is so great that we do not even know whether there is a difficulty. Who can explain how mind acts upon matter or matter upon mind? Yet the fact is as certain as that mind acts upon mind or that matter acts upon matter. There is nothing in experience to forbid us from believing that evil spirits could act upon brute beasts; and science admits that it has no *a priori* objection to offer to such an hypothesis. . . . The influence may have been analogous to that of mesmerism or hypnotism " (*in loc.*).

[9] For the fullest summary of various explanations of this occurrence we refer to Plummer (at verses 26–39).

[10] καθήμενον τὸν ἄνθρωπον ἀφ' οὗ τὰ δαιμόνια ἐξῆλθεν ἱματισμένον καὶ σωφρονοῦντα παρὰ τοὺς πόδας τοῦ Ἰησοῦ. Note here the five-fold change that has taken place in the man: (*a*) he has been freed from the evil spirits; (*b*) he is no longer restless, but is sitting at the feet of Jesus; (*c*) he is no longer naked, but clothed (one of those present probably gave him his upper garment or went to fetch clothing); (*d*) he is in his senses again; and (*e*) he is sociable again, sitting at the feet of Jesus instead of avoiding or molesting people.

[11] This is by no means at variance with Jesus' conduct elsewhere where He commands the healed person not to tell anything. In those cases there was the danger that a false Messianic movement might be set on foot, while here, in a largely Gentile environment, there was no such danger.

THE DAUGHTER OF JAIRUS AND THE WOMAN
WHO SUFFERED FROM AN ISSUE OF BLOOD

viii. 40–56

40 And as Jesus returned, the multitude welcomed him; for
41 they were all waiting for him. And behold, there came a man
named Jaïrus,[1] and he was a ruler of the synagogue[2] and he
fell down at Jesus' feet, and besought him to come into his
42 house; for he had an only daughter, about twelve years of
age, and she lay a dying. But as he went the multitudes
thronged him.

43 And a woman having an issue of blood twelve years,
which had spent all her living upon physicians, and could
44 not be healed of any, came behind him, and touched the
border of his garment:[3] and immediately the issue of her
45 blood stanched.[4] And Jesus said, Who is it that touched
me? And when all denied, Peter said, and they that were
with him, Master, the multitudes press thee and crush *thee*.
46 But Jesus said, Some one did touch me: for I perceived that
47 power had gone forth from me.[5] And when the woman saw
that she was not hid, she came trembling, and falling down
before him declared in the presence of all the people for
what cause she touched him, and how she was healed im-
48 mediately. And he said unto her, Daughter, thy faith hath
made thee whole;[6] go in peace.

49 While he yet spake, there cometh one from the ruler of the
synagogue's *house*, saying, Thy daughter is dead; trouble
50 not the Master. But Jesus hearing it, answered him, Fear
51 not: only believe,[7] and she shall be made whole. And when
he came to the house, he suffered not any man to enter
in with him, save Peter, and John, and James, and the
52 father of the maiden and her mother. And all were weeping,
and bewailing her: but he said, Weep not; for she is not dead
53 but sleepeth. And they laughed him to scorn, knowing
54 that she was dead. But he, taking her by the hand, called,
55 saying, Maiden, arise. And her spirit returned, and she rose
up immediately: and he commanded that *something* be
56 given her to eat. And her parents were amazed: but he
charged them to tell no man what had been done.[8]

Once more Luke shows us the Saviour in His divine revelation
of power—He heals a woman who had for years suffered from a

humanly incurable disease, and He raises a maiden from the dead. He is the Lord of life and death, as has already been shown in the story of the young man of Nain.

40–2 From among the vast multitude that awaited Him on the shore near Capernaum there came a ruler of the synagogue, called Jairus, to beseech Jesus to go to his house where his daughter, aged twelve years, was at the point of death.

43, 44 But before Our Lord could accede to his request, and while He was still among the thronging multitude, a woman who had been suffering from a haemorrhage for twelve years without the physicians being able to heal her forced her way through the multitude up to the Lord, believing that if she touched His garment she would be healed. But although this might be classed as superstition, she nevertheless had a fervent faith in the Redeemer, and thus she was immediately healed.

45–8 The Saviour knew that she had come to Him and had touched His garment. He also knew who she was and that she believed and was healed. For her sake, however, He asks: " Who touched me? " According to the Jewish ideas of that time the woman was an utter outcast on account of her disease—she was not allowed to take part in any religious proceedings, could not come into the temple, could not touch other persons and had to be separated from her husband. Her disease came within the scope of the regulations of Leviticus xv. So she was not only impoverished through having had to give all her possessions to physicians in the hope that they might heal her—she was a despised and solitary woman. If her cure had taken place without the Saviour making it known publicly, she would have had the utmost difficulty in removing from the inhabitants of the town the prejudice and scorn that she had met with for years. For this reason the Saviour, who knew her in all her need and sorrows, and understood her circumstances, makes her appear before the whole multitude to testify publicly that she has been healed.

The Lord then confirms before everyone the fact of her being indeed healed. In addition, by stating, " thy faith hath made thee whole ", He brings her to a better realisation that it is not her contact with the border of His garment that has healed her (in a magical way), but her faith. Because she trusted in Him, in spite of her faith being mingled with superstition, she was healed by Him. And so He commands her in the presence of all to go " in peace " —being in the fullest sense saved by her faith in Him.

49, 50 Jairus had to endure some tense moments while the Saviour was held up by the healing of the woman; but, on the other hand, her miraculous cure proved to Jairus yet again how mighty the Lord was. Thus it would have been easier for him to believe that He would also heal his daughter. But alas, before they can get to her, someone comes to inform him that his daughter is already dead. The Saviour, on hearing this, immediately reassures the father by declaring: "Fear not: only believe, and she shall be made whole."

51-3 On arriving at Jairus's house, the Saviour commanded those who were bewailing her not to weep, because she was only asleep—meaning thereby not that she was, humanly speaking, not dead, but that her death was not permanent and that she would again be awakened from it through His miraculous power. Because the raising of the deceased maiden was such a tender, intimately homely matter, He did not allow anyone to enter her room except His three most intimate followers and the parents of the maiden. He does not desire to make a theatrical, spectacular business of the raising of the dead, and therefore He acts in so peremptory a manner towards the unbelieving mourners and others who were present by forbidding them to enter the room.

54-6 When He had shut out all intruders, He called back the spirit of the deceased maiden from the invisible realm, and restored her, alive and well, to her parents. As a proof that she was really resuscitated and would again have to follow the normal course of life, and also out of tender solicitude, the Saviour commands that food be given to her. And because He did not want them to lose the deep spiritual significance that the occurrence would bear for them (as they would do if they should at that moment go and discuss it with the multitude), He commanded them to tell no one what had taken place—they were to remain quietly with their restored daughter and worship God in the peaceful home circle and thank Him for the miracle. The three disciples would naturally testify to the fact that the maiden was again alive. And so those who were lamenting were informed that no funeral would take place.

What a privilege to know that Christ Jesus, who one thousand nine hundred years ago revealed Himself thus as the divine Physician and Lord of life, is to-day still just as mighty and perfect in love! He still heals either with or without human means, where believers pray to Him in faith for healing and where it is His will to heal. Although He no longer raises physically dead people from the grave, He nevertheless continually accomplishes the spiritual resuscitation of those who are spiritually dead, in sin and misery, through the regenerative working of His Spirit. And one day at

His coming He will cause all the faithful who have died to be physically raised as well, with glorified, heavenly bodies.

¹ The name means " he will give light " (=Old Testament " Jair ").

² " The chief function of the ruler of the synagogue was the conducting of divine service; he determined the persons who were to take part in public prayer or reading of the Scripture; he invited those with suitable capacity for the preaching of the sermon; he saw to it that everything was carried on in an orderly and decent manner " (Strack-Billerbeck, *op. cit.*, iv, p. 145).

³ " Her great faith in the Lord she showed in this, that she thought it sufficient for her cure if she could but only touch His garment unnoticed. And in this she was not put to shame. But the deficiency of her faith, on the other hand, again appeared in this, that she thought she could touch the Lord's garment without His noticing it, and also that she thought contact with His garment necessary " (Greydanus, *in loc.*).

⁴ ἱστάναι (" raise up ") was the common medical word in such cases (cf. Plummer, *in loc.*).

⁵ By this the Saviour does not mean that when someone touches Him with the desire of being healed virtue will spontaneously flow from Him. He knew that the woman touched His garment and believed in Him, and therefore He caused His healing power to accomplish a cure in her case. It was a fully conscious act and not a kind of magical emission of power. The reason why He did not address the woman directly was that she might be brought to testify voluntarily to her healing.

⁶ In Acts xix. 11, 12 we also have a case of superstition mingled with real faith. " Their faith expressed itself superstitiously. But they were healed. So with this woman, all of which is very revealing. If there be faith, even though the faith of Jairus is not the faith of the centurion, even though faith acts superstitiously, the superstition is ignored, the faith is honoured " (Morgan, *in loc.*).

⁷ " In his performing of miracles the Lord was not dependent upon the faith of man. Nevertheless He often accomplished it in connection with faith " (Greydanus, *in loc.*). It is here that some modern " faith healers " err, because, while professing to continue the healing ministry of the Saviour, they demand from the sick that they should first be " purified " and believe before they can be healed. The Saviour nowhere made it essential for anyone first to reform his life before He could heal him. Although He often healed people only after they had first believed in Him, there are nevertheless also numerous instances in the Gospels where there is no question of faith on the part of those healed by Him. As an act of love and divine power He healed them without expecting on their part as a prerequisite a consecrated life or faith. In many cases, however, this would have followed *after* the cures.

⁸ He did this " to keep them from letting the effect of this great blessing evaporate in vainglorious gossip. To thank God for it at home would be far more profitable than talking about it abroad " (Plummer, *in loc.*).

JESUS SENDS OUT THE TWELVE APOSTLES

(Cf. Matt. x. 5–42; Mark vi. 7 ff.)

ix. 1–6

1 And he called the twelve together,[1] and gave them power[2]
2 and authority[3] over all devils, and to cure diseases. And he
  sent them forth[4] to preach[5] the kingdom of God,[6] and to
3 heal the sick. And he said unto them, Take nothing for
  your journey,[7] neither staff,[8] nor wallet,[9] nor bread, nor
4 money; neither have two coats. And into whatsoever house
5 ye enter, there abide, and thence depart. And as many as
  receive you not, when ye depart from that city, shake off the
6 dust from your feet for a testimony against them.[10] And they
  departed, and went throughout the villages, preaching
  the gospel, and healing everywhere.

As the calling of the twelve apostles and the change in His
method of instruction through the frequent use of parables were
definite turning-points in His public Messianic ministry, so it
reaches a culminating point in the sending out of the apostles.

1 Because He is the divine Leader, He is not only able to
perform powerful miracles Himself, but also to give to His apostles
the power and authority to go and do in wider circles what He has
done and is still doing. An ordinary human leader, no matter how
wonderful he may be, cannot communicate to his followers
physical or spiritual powers to do what he is doing. But Christ
Jesus does it, and thereby we see yet again His divine greatness
and also his compassionate love—because through His apostles
He causes His work of mercy to be continued.

2 He sends out His twelve disciples with a twofold purpose: in
the first place they have to preach to the inhabitants of the
country the gospel of the dominion and kingship of God. They
must summon the lost to a realisation that God is indeed King,
that He rules over all, that He is going to establish His kingship
in the world through His power in the Messiah, and will one day,
at the consummation of the age, destroy all opposition and bring
the kingdom in full power and glory. In addition, they will have
to summon the people to true repentance, so that they will have
a full share of the dominion of God and be safeguarded against

the judgment to be brought upon the wicked by the coming of His kingdom.

They are, however, not only to preach the spiritual message but also to heal the sick—to care for the physical well-being of the people. The performance of the miracles is of secondary importance and must serve to reveal the reality of the divine rule that works salvation and to promote its acceptance by faith. The preaching of the kingdom is to remain the main purpose.

3 The task assigned to them is so important and urgent that they have to lose no time by first making all kinds of preparation for the journey—they have to go just as they are and trust to God that He will provide whatever is needful while they are engaged in accomplishing their task.

4 They should also waste no time by going from one house to another to look for better lodgings—when they have found in a city a place to stay in one of the houses they must remain there until they have completed their work in that city.

5 In order to make the hearers realise the earnestness of their preaching and work, they must, where they are not received, shake the very dust from their feet as a testimony against them—by this action they will indicate that they break all ties with them, and show in this decisive and irrevocable manner that they do not wish to have even a dust-speck from their streets upon them. This grave action will then serve as a last and urgent call to repentance.

6 Luke here mentions in only a few words the fact that the apostles carried out the instructions of Christ. Through this he shows that the equipment and power which He gave them were sufficient for the task upon which He sent them out. Thus we see His divine power and authority by which He enables His followers to do what He Himself has done.

In this pericope we have a description of the very first time that Jesus sent out some of His followers to represent Him in word and deed. The instructions given to them still continue binding, in a sense adapted to our circumstances, on all His followers. We must go into the world and (1) preach the kingdom of God—summon mankind to the realisation that His divine and saving sovereignty has been fully manifested in the advent, passion, and triumph of Christ, and that they must repent so that they may, to His honour, share in the wealth of His mercy as He even now imparts it to every member of His kingdom and as He will impart it fully at the end of the age; (2) we must continue His works of mercy by working also for the deliverance of mankind from their physical need—through poor-relief work, care for orphanages, hospital services (especially in the mission field), institutions for the blind, prayers for the sick, work among prisoners and other undertakings in the service of suffering humanity.

¹ Wellhausen (on Mark vi) declares that the sending out of the twelve disciples was no historical actuality but a later fabrication in order to justify the earliest mission work of the church. Bultmann, too, follows him in this supposition. But Creed admits that " there seems to be no conclusive reason why we should assume that Jesus did not at some period associate the twelve with Him in his work of preaching the advent of the kingdom " (*in loc.*) (cf. our notes at vi. 13 and p. 206, n. 2).

² δύναμις = might, power, ability to do something.

³ ἐξουσία = right, authority (here the authority to use the δύναμις —cf. our notes at iv. 32).

⁴ ἀποστέλλω = to send out with instructions to teach and act in the name of the Sender, on His authority (cf. p. 206, n. 2).

⁵ κηρύσσειν = to proclaim as a herald on the authority of a king or other person in authority.

⁶ τὴν βασιλείαν τοῦ θεοῦ. Here the reference is especially to the blessed working of the divine rule.

⁷ This means " no extra goods, aids . . . to make provision for the future " (Greydanus, *in loc.*).

⁸ Taken together with Mark vi. 8, the meaning here might be " no additional staff ". The common explanation, however, is that Mark's εἰ μή (" save ") and Luke's μήτε (" neither ") represent two very similar Aramaic words—אלּא (*'ellā*) and ולא (*wĕlā*) respectively— which might have been confused with each other; though scholars differ as to which was more probably mistaken for the other.

⁹ πήρα. According to an inscription analysed by Deissmann (*Light from the Ancient East*, p. 109) the Saviour probably meant a beggar's pouch. The meaning would then be that He forbids His disciples to beg—as pagan priests were at that time accustomed to do.

¹⁰ " One day, when the great day comes, it will appear that the Gospel was brought them but they rejected it definitely, completely and consciously. Therefore they cannot say that they have not heard or known about it. The shaking off of the dust is an undeniable act which confutes and convicts them. But even now it is a testimony against them, telling them what is to come, and thus still calling them to repentance " (Greydanus, *in loc.*). Thus in this command of the Saviour: " His sense of the vital, tremendous majesty and dignity of the mission emerges " (Morgan, *in loc.*).

266

HEROD THE TETRARCH AND JOHN THE BAPTIST

(Cf. Matt. xiv. 1–12; Mark vi. 14–29)

ix. 7–9

7 Now Herod[1] the tetrarch heard[2] of all that was done: and
he was much perplexed, because that it was said by some,
8 that John was risen from the dead; and by some, that Elijah
had appeared; and by others, that one[3] of the old prophets
9 was risen again. And Herod said, John I beheaded: but who
is this, about whom I hear such things? And he sought to
see him.

The final result of the mission of the twelve and of the Saviour's
own conduct is that even Herod Antipas becomes anxious about
the miraculous works of the Lord.

7–9 The fame of Jesus' miracles had already spread far and
wide in Galilee (where Herod Antipas ruled). But when the
twelve disciples went through the whole land from village to
village and from city to city, and as His representatives performed
such a powerful work of preaching and healing, this caused so
great a sensation that all kinds of conjectures arose concerning
Him. Some think that He is John the Baptist, beheaded by Herod
but again risen from the dead. Others regard Him as Elijah who
was to come, according to their interpretation of Malachi iv. 5.
Jesus, however, taught that Malachi iv. 5 refers to John the
Baptist who came like an Elijah, in the spirit and power of an
Elijah (Matt. xi. 14; xvii. 10–13, cf. Luke i. 17). Others again
thought that He was some great prophet or other. Herod also
was anxious on account of all the rumours concerning Him and
the conjectures as to His identity. In the other Gospels it appears
that Herod was sometimes driven by his guilty conscience to fear
that He was John the Baptist risen from the dead after he had been
beheaded by his orders. For this reason he wanted very much to
see Him to ascertain whether He was really John or not. In
xiii. 31 it appears that he afterwards decided to kill Jesus.

The result of the activity of the twelve disciples was that the
attention of the masses and even that of the ruler of the land was

directed towards Jesus. This has always been and is still the most important requisite for all preaching and work of mercy—the final result must be that everyone shall be pointed to Him. The preachers and labourers in His service—yes, even His church—should be in the background and He in the foreground. Everything must conduce to His reputation and honour.

[1] Luke had splendid opportunities of acquiring firsthand information concerning Herod Antipas (cf. notes on viii. 3, and see Acts xiii. 1).

[2] Although Matthew mentions the call of the twelve in another connection, his chronological intimations there are so vague that we cannot take him to mean that it did not take place at the time indicated in Mark and Luke. The chronological setting of the mission of the twelve in Mark and Luke is natural and logical.

[3] In Deuteronomy xviii. 15, 18 Moses promised that a great Prophet would be raised up by God. Some Jews in the time of Jesus wrongly distinguished the promised Prophet from the promised Messiah, who is Prophet, Priest and King (cf. Strack-Billerbeck, *op. cit.*, iv, pp. 764 ff.).

FIRST INCREASE OF THE LOAVES

(Matt. xiv. 13–21; Mark vi. 30 ff.; John vi. 1 ff.)

ix. 10–17

10 And the apostles, when they were returned, declared
unto him what things they had done. And he took them,
11 and withdrew apart to a city called Bethsaida.[1] But the
multitudes perceiving it followed him: and he welcomed
them, and spake to them of the kingdom of God, and them
12 that had need of healing he healed. And the day began to
wear away;[2] and the twelve came, and said unto him, Send
the multitude away, that they may go into the villages and
country round about, and lodge, and get victuals: for we are
13 here in a desert place.[3] But he said unto them, Give ye them
to eat. And they said, We have no more than five loaves
and two fishes;[4] except we should go and buy food for all this
14 people. For they were about five thousand men. And he
said unto his disciples, Make them sit down in companies,
15 about fifty each. And they did so, and made them all sit
16 down.[5] And he took the five loaves and the two fishes, and
looking up to heaven, he blessed[6] them, and brake; and
17 gave to the disciples to set before the multitude. And they
did eat, and were all filled: and there was taken up that
which remained over to them of broken pieces,[7] twelve
baskets.[8] [9]

In all four Gospels this miracle is described and in all four it
is presented as a great climax in the Lord's public ministry. From
now on attention is more and more drawn to the Saviour's approaching act of atonement—His death on Golgotha. In the
description of this first increase of the loaves the various Gospels
supplement one another in a most interesting fashion. For example
it is stated only in John that the Saviour, the day after, gave a
spiritual explanation of the miracle and reprimanded the multitudes for paying attention to its material rather than to its spiritual
aspect (John vi. 27 ff.). This is a valuable supplement to the
reports of the other Gospels.

10 After the return of the twelve (probably to Capernaum),
and after they had given an account of their work, the Saviour

269

took them away from the multitudes to a desert place on the mountains near Bethsaida (a small place situated a mile to the north-east of the Sea of Galilee). Mark mentions as one of the reasons for His taking them there that He wanted to let His disciples rest (Mark vi. 31).

11 The multitudes, with whom the Saviour was now amazingly popular, discovered that He had gone to the neighbourhood of Bethsaida and followed Him thither. We know from Mark vi. 34 that when the Lord saw the multitude He was moved with compassion towards them. They seemed to Him like sheep without a shepherd. He was well aware of their spiritual and physical needs. So He immediately resumed the preaching of the glad tidings of the kingly rule of God to them and the healing of the sick.

12-15 When the day began to wear away, i.e. shortly after midday, the disciples, probably from fear that the weaker persons in the multitude might collapse through hunger and fatigue if they had to spend the afternoon and the night in the open without provisions, asked Him to send the people to the surrounding towns and villages to find lodging and provisions. Jesus, however, answers that they must give the necessary food to the multitude. They point out to Him that they have only five loaves and two fishes (from John vi. 9 we know that they obtained these from a young boy), and therefore had far from enough for the multitude unless they were to go and buy supplies (which would have entailed an enormous expense—much more than they possessed). The Saviour, however, commands them to make the multitude (five thousand men and also many women and children) sit down in groups of fifty.

16 He then took the five loaves and the two fishes, blessed the food in prayer, and broke it into pieces for the disciples to set before the multitude.

17 In His divine omnipotence He caused the bread and the fishes to increase in such a manner that He continued to break off pieces until all had received enough. The food had increased to such an extent that twelve baskets of fragments (unused pieces broken off by Jesus) were picked up in addition, after all had been satisfied.

It is vain for us to attempt by ourselves to give real food to needy mankind with our five little loaves and two fishes—the insignificant gifts and powers possessed by us. But when we place at His disposal, in faith and obedience, everything we have received from Him, He will, in spite of our own insignificance and poverty, use us nevertheless to feed souls with the bread of eternal life. He sanctifies, blesses and increases our talents and powers, everything consecrated by us to His service.

[1] " This was plainly Bethsaida Julias, situated north of the Lake, and east of the Jordan. John describes the locality as the mountain, i.e. the high land on the other side of the Lake from Capernaum " (Major, *op. cit., in loc.*). Also cf. Dalman, *Sacred Sites and Ways*, pp. 161 ff.

[2] " This wearing away of the day commenced immediately after twelve noon " (Greydanus, *in loc.*). So we can understand how the disciples could expect Jesus still to let the multitude go to towns and villages to look for food and accommodation.

[3] Bethsaida Julias, situated close by, was a small place and there would have been altogether insufficient food to be bought for so large a multitude. ἔρημος τόπος " does not necessarily mean a desert, but a deserted place " (Luce, *in loc.*).

[4] " The statement expresses perplexity (Weiss), not sarcasm " (Plummer, *in loc.*).

[5] Mark relates that it was on the green grass. " The grass is green in Palestine only in the spring and Mark's statement about the grass agrees with that of John that the feeding of the five thousand took place shortly before the Feast of the Passover which falls in March–April " (Major, *op. cit., in loc.*).

[6] Mark has εὐλόγησεν without an object and thus refers mainly to the thanks returned by Him to God. (He may have used the ancient Jewish form of thanksgiving: " Blessed art Thou, O Lord our God, King of the universe, who bringest forth bread from the earth.") This, however, does not exclude the fact that after the usual grace before the meal He also " blessed " the loaves and fishes, so that through His divine power they were increased to such an extent that they more than sufficed for the great multitude. Mark lays more emphasis on the one aspect and Luke on the other, by adding to εὐλόγησεν the object αὐτούς, referring to the loaves and fishes.

[7] Here the reference is not to the fragments left over and thrown about by the multitude. The Saviour would not have distributed so much that there would be a waste. Luce, therefore, rightly remarks: " It is surely more natural, in view of the use of κατέκλασεν above, to take the word as intended to mean pieces broken up for distribution by Jesus and not used. The idea is that of divine liberality which provides more than enough for all " (*in loc.*). What was collected in the baskets was therefore still useful for subsequent meals.

[8] κόφινος refers to the type of basket which a Jew took with him on a journey so that he need not buy bread from the pagans. The baskets mentioned in connection with the feeding of the *four* thousand (Matt. xv. 37; Mark viii. 8) were σπυρίδες (" creels ").

[9] For all kinds of attempts to give rationalistic explanations of the

miracle of the increase of the loaves we refer to Wellhausen (at Mark vi); Luce (at Luke ix. 17); Major (*in loc.*). As B. Weiss has well said: " The criticism which is afraid of miracles finds itself in no small difficulty in the presence of this narrative. It is guaranteed by all our sources which rest upon eyewitnesses; and these show the independence of their tradition " (cf. Plummer, *in loc.*).

THE CONFESSION OF PETER

(Cf. Matt. xvi. 13–23; Mark viii. 27–33; John vi. 66–9)

ix. 18–22

18 And it came to pass, as he was praying alone,[1] the disciples
were with him: and he asked them, saying, Who do the
19 multitudes say that I am? And they answering said, John
the Baptist; but others *say*, Elijah; and others, that one of
20 the old prophets is risen again. And he said unto them,
But who say ye that I am? And Peter answering said, The
21 Christ of God. But he charged them, and commanded *them*
22 to tell this to no man; saying, The Son of man must[2] suffer
many things, and be rejected[3] of the elders and chief priests
and scribes, and be killed, and the third day be raised up.

It is remarkable that Luke, directly after his description of the
increase of the loaves, relates the story of the confession of Peter
and thus leaves unmentioned the events described in Mark vi. 45–
viii. 26 (cf. Matt. xiv. 22–xvi. 12). There are various possible
explanations of this. We notice throughout that he by no means
professes to give a full biography of the Lord. Out of many items
of information he reproduces only those which, under the
guidance of the Spirit of God, he regards as the most important in
composing his Gospel. We should remember that Luke could not
make his writing unlimited in length—among other things he had
to consider the question of not exceeding the limits of a normal
papyrus roll. As it is, his Gospel is the longest book in the New
Testament. So he used his space economically and recorded only
the parts which were most necessary for his purpose. If we check
the contents of Mark vi. 45–viii. 26, we see that no events are
there described which would be of special value for the progress of
the Gospel-narrative from the point of view of Luke's method and
purpose. And that purpose includes Acts as well as the Gospel
in its scope. In the previous chapters he was still engaged throughout in calling attention to the progressive self-revelation of Jesus.
In the mission and equipment of the twelve, as well as in the
mighty revelation of His divine mercy and power in the increase
of the loaves, such a climax had now been reached, that the whole-
hearted confession of Peter (as mouthpiece of the apostles) that

Jesus was the Christ of God, follows it very fittingly. So he chose
rather to relate that event immediately.

18 Chronologically this portion does not immediately follow
verse 17, for from Mark vii. 45–viii. 26 and Matthew xiv. 22–
xvi. 12 it is clear that a considerable period intervened. So Luke
here merely gives a vague time-indication by commencing with
the words: " And as he was alone praying " (without stating when
this was).

It is characteristic of Luke that he frequently refers to the fact
that Jesus prayed. He does so in seven places where the other
Gospels make no mention of it (namely before His baptism; when
His fame increased; before He chose the twelve; in this place before
He asked the disciples whom they thought Him to be; before the
transfiguration on the mount; before He taught His disciples how
to pray; and finally in Gethsemane before His arrest).

After He had prayed alone separately (with the disciples, nevertheless, near Him), He asks them: " Who do the people say that I
am? " He does not put the question because He does not Himself
know the answer to it, but in order to prepare the disciples for the
question in verse 20.

19 They then give the answers described in verses 7, 8. From
this it appears that the masses were thoroughly conscious that
He was an exceptional, supernatural Person; but because they had
always pictured the Messiah as an earthly ruler, they were unable
to see the true Christ in Him.

20 In order to bring the disciples to a definite confession, He
asks the question: " But who do *you* say that I am? " The Saviour
knew that the time was ripe for them to answer the question, and
for this reason He asked it so explicitly. Their answer to it would
then contribute towards making their faith in Him more definite and explicit. On behalf of the twelve Peter, their acknowledged and impulsive leader, answers frankly that Jesus is the
Christ, the Messiah of God, the promised Redeemer. Thus
Jesus' preparatory work and instruction bore good fruit and His
prayer was heard—His disciples learned through the working of
God's Spirit to see Him as the Christ, the Son of God, and to avow
Him openly as such (cf. Matt. xvi. 16, 17).

21 The Messianic opinions of the multitudes are, however, too
earthly (cf. John vi. 15) and mistaken, and there are also other
unfavourable circumstances, so He commands the disciples (who
themselves have not yet a *perfect* understanding of the nature of
His Messiahship) for the present to tell nobody that He is the
Messiah.

22   And now that the disciples have frankly avowed Him to be the Christ, Jesus immediately begins to prepare them for the violent shock awaiting them—He, the Messiah of God, will have to suffer, be rejected and even be done to death, and that through the agency of the spiritual and other leaders of the chosen people. But, God be thanked, He would arise again on the third day. From now on He frequently refers to His suffering, but also to His resurrection.

The final result of our preaching and work should always be that people are brought to the personal confession that Jesus is the Christ of God—the Messiah who is our Prophet, Priest and King, our Saviour and Teacher, who has procured redemption for us and who now intercedes for us and rules our lives. All this is included in the fact that He is the Christ, the Lord's Anointed.

¹ κάτα μόνας = " apart ", away from the multitude, and not in conjunction with the disciples, who indeed were also there.   In an actual sense Jesus always prayed alone, for prayer in His case was in this respect quite different from prayer in the case of others, in that with Him it was direct exercise of fellowship with His Father, but with His people it is offered through a Mediator, on the strength of His grace.

² δεῖ here expresses a divine necessity—it is essential to the fulfilment of His plan of salvation and is clearly prophesied in the Old Testament.

³ ἀποδοκιμασθῆναι—" The δοκιμασία was the scrutiny which an elected magistrate had to undergo at Athens, to see whether he was legally qualified to hold office. The hierarchy held such a scrutiny respecting the claims of Jesus to be the Christ, and rejected Him " (Plummer, in loc.).

TO TAKE UP THE CROSS

(Cf. Matt. xvi. 24-8; Mark. viii. 36-8)

23   And he said[1] unto all, If any man would come after me, let him deny[2] himself, and take up his cross[3] daily, and follow
24 me. For whosoever would save his life[4] shall lose it; but whosoever shall lose his life for my sake, the same shall save it.
25 For what is a man profited, if he gain the whole world, and
26 lose or forfeit[5] his own self? For whosoever shall be ashamed of me and of my words, of him shall the Son of man[6] be ashamed, when he cometh in his own glory, and *the glory* of
27 the Father, and of the holy angels. But I tell you of a truth,[7] There be some of them that stand here, which shall in no wise taste of death, till they see the kingdom of God.[8]

With reference to His prophecy of the *via dolorosa* awaiting Him, the Saviour here speaks of the way of the cross which His followers will have to follow if they really wish to be His disciples.

23 He who desires to become His disciple and servant will every day have to be willing to put his own interests and wishes into the background and to accept voluntarily and wholeheartedly (and not fatalistically) the sacrifice and suffering that will have to be endured in His service. The " cross " is not the ordinary, human troubles and sorrows such as disappointments, disease, death, poverty and the like, but the things which have to be suffered, endured and lost in the service of Christ—vituperation, persecution, self-sacrifice, suffering, even unto death, as a result of true faith in and obedience to Him.

24 Everyone who tries selfishly to secure for himself pleasure and happiness in life will in fact doom his life to failure—he will never find real joy or full life. He commits spiritual suicide. But he who lays his life upon the altar in the service of Christ, who strives for His honour and for the extension of His kingdom, while keeping self in the background, will spontaneously find true joy and life—here and hereafter.

25 It is absolutely necessary for everyone to lose his life for Christ's sake so that he may find true salvation and life, for what does it avail a man, if he gains even all possible earthly possessions, but causes injury to his soul, to his inner, spiritual life and his deepest being, and if the highest purpose of his life and his highest happiness should miscarry? Yes, what does it avail a man if he becomes a ruler and possessor of the world, but lacks fellowship with God, so that he incurs eternal destruction?

26 Even though Jesus is to enter upon the way of suffering and death, as recently predicted by Him, He proclaims just as clearly that He will eventually be revealed in glory with the Father and the holy heavenly beings as final Conqueror, and will appear as the divine Judge of the World (cf. Dan. vii. 13 and Matt. xxvi. 64). Then He, the Glorified One, will decide the eternal destiny of all; and those who have rejected Him through love of the world or of their own honour, their own convenience or anything else, will receive eternal condemnation as their self-chosen portion. From Jesus they can expect nothing but the sorrowful words: " I never knew you."

27 The Saviour declares with emphasis that some of those who are listening to Him at that moment, will yet see a mighty revelation of the kingly rule of God before they die. Note that the Lord says there will only be " some ". So this means that most of His hearers will already be dead before that special revelation of the divine rule in action. From this it follows that the Saviour does not mean His resurrection or ascension, or the outpouring of the Holy Ghost, for all this took place within a few months. Nor yet did He mean His coming and the Final Judgment, for the words " of a truth . . . shall in no wise taste of death *till* . . ." might imply that the few who will see the revelation of the divine dominion, will nevertheless still die, and this cannot happen any more after His coming. So the Lord referred to a special event which would take place during a period when the generation then living was at the point of passing away. And there was precisely such an event—the destruction of Jerusalem and the downfall of the Jewish national existence in Palestine in A.D. 70 (about forty years after Jesus' words were uttered). In an unparalleled manner God revealed His kingly dominion over the unbelieving Jewish nation in that execution of judgment. By these means He showed once and for all that the Old Dispensation had passed away and that the New Dispensation had indeed begun, that the ceremonial temple-religion had completed its preparatory task and that the old chosen people had to make room for the new people, the true Israel, the members (Jewish and Gentile) of the church of Christ. That event revealed the kingdom of God and His dominion in the history of man in an incomparable manner. Indeed, the execution of this judgment upon the Jewish people was so terrible that the Saviour, who had foreseen all this only too clearly, saw in it a foreshadowing of the Final Judgment at His coming (cf. the prophetic address in Matthew xxiv, Mark xiii, Luke xxi).

Every person is confronted with the choice either of denying himself together with his own reputation, his own desires and his own comfort, or of living for himself and the world and so denying Christ. On this choice there depends not only the deepest inward happiness of man in this life, but also the divine verdict on each of us in the day when everyone will be judged by Christ. Just as surely as Jesus' words in connection with the judgment of the Jewish people were fulfilled, so surely will His words with regard to the Final Judgment at His second coming be fulfilled.

[1] " The breaking off of the speech with ἔλεγεν in itself presumes that Jesus spoke the words thus introduced, if not on another occasion, at any rate not in immediate connection with what has gone before " (Zahn, *in loc.*). Luke has thus also in this place, between verses 22 and 23, made no mention of the episode recorded in Mark viii. 32–3.

[2] ἀρνησάσθω—" A strong word. Almost ' forget that he exists '; ' cease to consider his own interests in the slightest degree ' " (Luce, *in loc.*).

[3] ἀράτω τὸν σταυρὸν αὐτοῦ. The associations of the cross were such that this declaration must have been startling. The Jews, especially in Galilee, knew well what the cross meant. Hundreds of the followers of Judas and Simon had been crucified (Josephus, *Antiquities*, xvii, 10, 10). " It represents, therefore, not so much a burden as an instrument of death, and it was mentioned because of its familiar associations " (Plummer, *in loc.*).

[4] ἡ ψυχὴ αὐτοῦ denotes not merely man's " incorporeal part in distinction from his corporeal part. Here also it is not merely the life of man, but indicates that in which man has his life and happiness, without which his existence and life are to him no joy but bitter sorrow " (Greydanus, *in loc.*).

[5] ζημιοῦσθαι = to suffer loss as at a shipwreck.

[6] ὁ υἱὸς τοῦ ἀνθρώπου. See our Special Note on this self-designation of our Lord, p. 352.

[7] An account of various explanations of this saying of Jesus will be found in Plummer (*in loc.*). As an alternative to the view expressed in our exposition above, the comment of N. B. Stonehouse on the parallel passage in Matthew xvi. 28 may be reproduced: " Since . . . Matthew clearly regarded the exaltation of the Son of Man through the resurrection as inaugurating a new era, which was to be momentous both for Christ and for those who were his disciples, it is altogether

congruous to regard the expression 'the Son of man coming in his king-dom ' in Matthew xvi. 28 as referring to the supernatural activity of the risen Lord in establishing his church " (*The Witness of Matthew and Mark to Christ*, 1944, p. 240).

[8] τὴν βασιλείαν τοῦ θεοῦ here means the kingly dominion or rule of God. See our Special Note on p. 179.

THE TRANSFIGURATION
(Cf. Matt. xvii. 1–13; Mark ix. 2–13)

ix. 28–36

28 And it came to pass about eight[1] days after these sayings, he took with him Peter and John and James, and went up
29 into the mountain[2] to pray. And as he was praying,[3] the fashion of his countenance was altered, and his raiment
30 *became* white *and* dazzling. And behold, there talked with
31 him two men, which were Moses and Elijah; who appeared in glory, and spake of his decease[4] which he was about to
32 accomplish at Jerusalem. Now Peter and they that were with him were heavy with sleep: but when they were fully awake, they saw his glory, and the two men that stood with
33 him. And it came to pass, as they were parting from him, Peter said unto Jesus, Master, it is good for us to be here: and let us make three tabernacles; one for thee, and one for
34 Moses, and one for Elijah: not knowing what he said. And while he said these things, there came a cloud, and overshadowed them: and they feared as they entered into the
35 cloud. And a voice came out of the cloud,[5] saying, This is
36 my Son, my chosen: hear ye him. And when the voice came, Jesus was found alone. And they held their peace, and told no man in those days any of the things which they had seen.[6]

The Saviour's self-revelation had already progressed so far that the disciples had confessed explicitly that He was the Messiah of God (verse 20). Thereafter He began to allude to the path of suffering awaiting Him, but also to the final glorification. And now, before He sets His face with a fixed purpose (verse 51) towards Jerusalem where He is to be arrested, tortured and crucified, it is given to His three most intimate followers to see Him for a few moments in His divine glory. Through this His self-revelation attains to a glorious climax before He finally enters upon the way of suffering.

28 About a week (Matthew and Mark give the exact time—six days) after Peter's confession, the Saviour took His three most intimate followers, Peter, John and James, with him and went up into a mountain to pray (we do not know for certain which mountain it was, though Hermon is a reasonable suggestion),

According to verse 37 (compared with verse 32) it was probably during the night that He prayed and underwent the heavenly transfiguration.

Because He was again confronted with an important turning-point in His ministry upon earth, He withdrew Himself thus with a fixed purpose for prayer. He was beginning to approach the moment when He would finally accept the way of suffering. He was free to choose or not to choose that way. " This suffering was to Him no unavoidable necessity, no matter of force, but of voluntary and likewise willing obedience; cf. John x. 18; Hebrews v. 8 " (Greydanus, *in loc.*).

Because He knew how terrible the suffering would be, and because the choice to undergo it voluntarily as man demanded such boundless self-denial, He seeks communion with His Father in prayer. And the transfiguration which He passes through is the answer of His Father. By this it is unambiguously revealed that when Jesus chooses the way of suffering for the redemption of sinful mankind He does so quite voluntarily, as this event shows, for He is the beloved Son of God, who is without sin and is under no obligation to suffer or to die. In addition, the transfiguration is an assurance given by God of His approval of the Saviour's choice.

29-31 While He was praying, His divine majesty shone so gloriously through His human nature that even His raiment glistened in a white glow. Moses and Elijah appear in heavenly glory, to speak to Him in connection with His death and all that He must suffer and endure in Jerusalem. Jesus came to fulfil the Law and the Prophets, and so God specially sends Moses, through whom He had given the Law, and Elijah, the typical represent-ative of the prophets through whom God had spoken and prepared the way for the coming of Christ.

32, 33 The disciples, who had for some time been sleeping because it was night and they were fatigued, later on, probably owing to the glow of the heavenly vision, awoke and saw the Saviour with the two celestial messengers while His divine glory radiated from Him. To contemplate this heavenly sight a special gift was granted to the three disciples and, in addition, the faculty was given to them of recognising the two heavenly beings as Moses and Elijah. So when they realised that they really had the privilege of moving in this heavenly company, Peter, ever im-pulsive, said, without exactly comprehending the implication of his words: " Master, it is good for us to be here: and let us make three tabernacles; one for thee, and one for Moses, and one for Elijah ". To him it is so wonderful to contemplate the heavenly glory that he wants it to continue thus—he and his fellow-disciples will make three tabernacles so that the Saviour and Moses and Elijah may stay there always and he and James and John may serve them. From now on he wishes to remain for ever in the heavenly company. Indirectly his proposal is again an attempt to influence the Saviour not to choose the way of suffering, but to continue to live in divine glory.

34 The Lord, however, had finally accepted the way of suffering and death in order to carry out the divine plan of salvation, so the heavenly messengers again depart, and He returns to His state of humiliation. While the heavenly messengers enter into the cloud (cf. Acts i. 9), the disciples become afraid at the sight of this heavenly vision.

35 When the Saviour at His baptism accepted the work of redemption God spoke with a voice from heaven to assure Him of His divine pleasure in Him. And now that Jesus had voluntarily chosen the way of suffering anew, by remaining upon earth, and had again laid down His divine glory in order to suffer and to die in the form of a servant (Phil. ii. 7), God once more spoke with a voice from the heavenly cloud in order to express His pleasure in Christ and to proclaim to the world that He must be listened to—with attention, faith and obedience; for He is His beloved Son.

36 The disciples, when they began to hear the voice, fell down in worship, and only when everything was quiet again did they raise their eyes (Matt. xvii. 6, 7). Then they saw that Jesus was now alone with them, without the radiation of His divine glory and without the heavenly visitors and the cloud. Without relating, as Matthew does, that the Saviour commanded the three disciples to tell no one of the occurrence before His resurrection, Luke merely states that they told no one of it at that time.

The experience of the disciples, when they contemplated the heavenly glory on the mount of transfiguration, was of short duration. But although the heavenly vision soon disappeared, Jesus remained with them. In the spiritual life of a believer the most wonderful spiritual experiences are the exception and of short duration. But, God be thanked, our Redeemer and Lord is and always remains with and close to us.

---

[1] Luke says " about " eight days, probably taking into account the day when Jesus uttered the words of verses 23–7 as well as the day on which the transfiguration took place, so that there is no conflict between his dating and that of Matthew and Mark.

² Although even Plummer suggests that it was the mount of Hermon, it can nevertheless not be stated with certainty what mountain is meant. (Cf. Dalman, *Sacred Sites and Ways*, pp. 188 f., 202 f., where neither Hermon nor the traditional Tabor is accepted as the mount in question.)

³ Greydanus (*in loc.*) rightly observes that the transfiguration is related to the prayer, and adds: " God now, as it were, gave Him a free hand, the free choice of continuing to choose suffering or of giving it up and rejecting it. There was no need for Him to bear it as a burden of compulsion. So God lifted His chastening hand that was, as it were, pressing down upon the Lord in humiliation, and thus the radiation of the Lord's divine glory returned and shone forth in His whole appearance. . . . But not for one moment did the Lord hesitate. However severe and terrible His suffering is represented to Him by Moses and Elijah, He continues to choose it. And so God's chastening hand visited Him anew and took back His glory, and He was again in humiliation and suffering as before."

⁴ τὴν ἔξοδον αὐτοῦ. Greydanus, Luce, and others assume that this merely refers to His suffering and death. But Plummer, Morgan and others are of the opinion that His resurrection and ascension are also included. Probably the reference *is* only to His suffering and death.

⁵ By " the cloud " the " Shechinah ", symbolising the heavenly glory of God, is probably meant. And the " overshadowing " of the cloud then symbolises the divine presence (cf. Exod. xl. 34, 35).

⁶ Luce states: " The story as we have it is the materialised record of a subjective experience rather than the narrative of an objective supernatural demonstration " (*in loc.*). Wellhausen's and Bultmann's theory is that the story is originally a " resurrection story ". Harnack and E. Meyer, however, defend the view that the story is based upon an actual experience of the disciples during Jesus' life on earth. And E. Meyer rightly attributes the theories of Wellhausen and others to rationalistic prejudice (cf. Creed, *in loc.*). Creed suggests that there is a mythical element in the narrative but that the apostles did experience some sort of vision. Balmforth tries to explain it as a mystical experience perhaps only of Peter (*in loc.*). Those who refuse to accept the reality of this and other supernatural narratives in the Gospels or who try to tone it down (like Balmforth) to something different from what the Gospels teach, do so rather because they are unwilling to accept it than because they have any conclusive grounds for their theories. For this reason almost every one of these critics has a different theory in order to explain away or tone down the supernatural and divine element. As B. Weiss wrote long ago: " We are not here concerned with a vision produced by natural causes, but with one sent directly by God. . . . Our narrative presents no stumblingblock for those who believe in divine revelation " (*in loc.*).

The narrative in every respect bears the stamp of authenticity.

HEALING OF THE LUNATIC CHILD

(Cf. Matt. xvii. 14–21; Mark ix. 14–29)

ix. 37–45

37 And it came to pass, on the next day,[1] when they were come down from the mountain, a great multitude met him.
38 And behold, a man from the multitude cried, saying, Master, I beseech thee to look upon my son; for he is mine only child:
39 and behold, a spirit[2] taketh him, and he suddenly crieth out; and it teareth him that he foameth, and it hardly departeth
40 from him, bruising him sorely. And I besought thy disciples
41 to cast it out; and they could not. And Jesus answered and said, O faithless[3] and perverse[4] generation, how long shall I
42 be with you,[5] and bear with you? bring hither thy son. And as he was yet a coming, the devil dashed him down, and tare *him* grievously. But Jesus rebuked the unclean spirit, and
43 healed the boy,[6] and gave him back to his father. And they were all astonished at the majesty of God.

But while all were marvelling at all the things which he
44 did, he said unto his disciples, Let these words sink into your ears: for the Son of man shall be delivered up into the hands
45 of men. But they understood not this saying, and it was concealed from them, that they should not perceive it: and they were afraid to ask him about this saying.

The last painting by the famous Raphael is a representation on one huge canvas of the transfiguration on the mount and of the futile attempts of the disciples at its foot to heal the lunatic child. The contrast between the rest and glory on the mountain and the struggle and defeat below is indeed intense and gripping. After the transfiguration the Son of God humiliated Himself anew to walk this earth as Man. He returns to the yearning, struggling, and unbelieving world of men, to fulfil His work there as the divine Bringer of Salvation and finally to be sacrificed as the Lamb of God.

37–40 Luke omits the question of the disciples concerning Elijah (Mark ix. 9–13), because it is not exactly of importance to his Gentile readers, and goes straight on to the story of Jesus' descent from the mountain, the meeting with the multitude that once more came to seek Him, and the man beseeching help for his

284

lunatic son. How it must have grieved the Saviour that His disciples had not sufficient faith to heal the boy!

41 So He expresses His sorrow in words which point out the reprehensibility of their unbelief. Thereupon He commands the man to bring his son to Him.

42 Because the demon knew that he would be exorcised, he determined for the last time to do his evil work in his unhappy victim with such cruel violence that he might kill him. Through this he wished to frustrate the work of the Saviour and to bring Him into disfavour with the multitude. But Jesus rebuked the unclean spirit in time and made him depart from the boy, whom He then delivered to his father, healed.

43-5 Although the multitude are filled with admiration for the Saviour on account of the mighty miracle of healing performed by God through Him, He still continues to see the way of suffering clearly before Him. He knows that He will ere long lose His temporary popularity among men, and that He will be despised and put to death. So He calls urgently upon His disciples to remember carefully His prediction that He will be delivered into the hands of men to be crucified. But especially after His divine revelation of power in healing the child and in view of His present popularity among the masses, it seems to them impossible that He will have to suffer and to die. The words of the Saviour are, in consequence, still quite incomprehensible to them, and because they would as yet not be able to bear this truth in its full reality, He does not give them the insight to grasp its significance at this stage. But precisely because it is such a startling and incomprehensible declaration to them, they will remember it, and later on, when the right time has arrived (after His death and resurrection and especially after Pentecost), they will acknowledge and understand its rich significance. Because of the mysterious character of His words and conduct, they do not have the courage to ask Him for an explanation. The utter incomprehensibility of the idea that He, the Christ of God, will have to suffer and die casts them, as it were, into dumbstricken awe.

The condition of the lunatic child was extremely critical and, humanly speaking, his was a lost case. Even the disciples of Christ were unable to bring him salvation. But when Christ appeared on the scene the battle was immediately won. At His command even the most obstinate evil spirit is exorcised. Today, too, wherever His presence and redeeming power are called in through humble faith, no problem-case is too difficult—no matter in what field of life. He is the mighty Victor over all forces of evil.

[1] The natural conclusion from this is that the transfiguration took place during the night.

[2] Cf. the Special Note on " demon-possession " after iv. 37.

[3] ἄπιστος indicates unbelief as well as faithlessness.

[4] διεστραμμένη refers to utter perverseness, and here indicates the state of all who were present there. Not one of them laid hold on His power in such a manner that he could in childlike faith cause the might of the evil one to be broken.

[5] M. Dibelius regards these words as words of a divine being who appeared for a short time in human shape and soon returns to heaven. Creed (in loc.) is inclined to support this. By doing so they reject the words as unhistorical. But their whole opinion is quite arbitrary. As the story is described in the Gospels, the words fit in exceedingly well with the actual circumstances.

[6] After the evil spirit had left him, the boy needed physical healing, too, and so the Saviour accomplished the twofold miracle.

THE GREATEST IN THE KINGDOM OF HEAVEN

(Cf. Matt. xviii. 1–14; Mark ix. 33–7)

ix. 46–8

46 And there arose a reasoning[1] among them, which of them
47 should be greatest. But when Jesus saw the reasoning of their
48 heart, he took[2] a little child, and set him by his side, and said
unto them, Whosoever shall receive this little child in my
name receiveth me:[3] and whosoever shall receive me receiveth him that sent me: for he that is least among you all,
the same is great.

While the thoughts of the Saviour were increasingly fixed upon
the way of suffering awaiting Him, and while He had repeatedly
taught the disciples that this way of grief and death was awaiting
Him, their spirit was still in sharpest contrast with His self-
humiliation.

46–8 Although the disputation of the disciples was not held in
the presence of the Saviour, He nevertheless discerned the
reasoning of their hearts. What a depth of sorrow was caused to
Him through the fact that the minds of His disciples were still so
self-centred! From Matthew xviii. 18 it appears that after their
disputation the disciples came to the Saviour with the apparently
innocent question: " Who is the greatest in the kingdom of
heaven? " The Lord, however, knew that in the heart of every
one of them there was the parallel question: " Am *I* not the
greatest? "

At first the Saviour utters no word in answer to it, but He makes
a little child stand by Him and then teaches them in a graphic
manner that he who desires to be great must first learn to be
truly small. This humility must be revealed in this, that even to
the least ones (the child is typical of what is " smallest ") service
and aid shall be rendered in His name—for His sake and for love
of Him, because those that are the " insignificant, little ones " also
belong to Him. " To accept, and thus serve and help for the
Lord's sake that which is insignificant but in reality great with
God, this is what God in His mercy values highly, and this is what
makes us great. Everyone may strive after this type of greatness in
God's kingdom. And in this there can hardly be any question of
comparison with others " (Greydanus, *in loc.*).

287

The most difficult but one of the most indispensable lessons to be learned by every follower of Christ is to be truly humble and to be small in one's own eyes and faithful in service even to the most insignificant ones whom we are called upon to help.

[1] " The question of precedence seems to have occupied the minds of the disciples more than once. It reveals the ideas of the kingdom which made it difficult for them to understand the cross " (H. G. Wood, in *Peake's Commentary*, Mark ix.)

[2] ἐπιλαβόμενος παιδίον. " The action indicates that the child belongs to Him, is one of His: it represents the humblest among His followers " (Plummer, *in loc.*).

[3] " The service of love, in which true greatness consists, is tested by its operation towards the most insignificant " (Creed, *in loc.*).

"HE WHO IS NOT AGAINST US IS FOR US"

(Cf. Mark ix. 38–41)

ix. 49–50

49 And John answered and said, Master, we saw one casting
out devils in thy name;[1] and we forbade him, because he
50 followeth not with us. But Jesus said unto him, Forbid *him*
not: for he that is not against you is for you.

This pericope is closely linked with the lesson on humility that
preceded it, for it treats of tolerance, a natural result of humility.

49 John relates that he and the other disciples forbade someone to cast out demons, because, although he was exorcising in the
name of Jesus, he stood outside the circle of His disciples.
50 The Saviour declares that the disciples had acted wrongly,
" for he that is not against us is for us " (this may be the true
reading, as it is supported by Mark ix. 40). This pronouncement
is the direct opposite of what Jesus uttered on another occasion:
" He that is not with me is against me " (xi. 23). And yet both are
true. In this latter instance the Saviour is speaking of the conflict
with the Evil One. And in that conflict there is no room for
neutrality. But in verse 50 it is a question of someone who believed
in Jesus to such an extent that he cast out demons in His name and
who revealed such a humble attitude that he allowed the disciples to forbid him to continue the work. And so, although his
faith and attachment to Christ were not perfect, he nevertheless
acted in honour of Christ. The zeal of the disciples for the honour
of their Master in forbidding him to cast out demons in His name
was, therefore, a wrongful zeal—probably stimulated by pride
and selfishness. So the Saviour teaches them to be more magnanimous and more tolerant.

In the attitude adopted by people towards Christ in their
hearts and lives there is no room for sitting on the fence. Every
person is either for or against Him, whether he realises and
acknowledges it or not. Everyone must in his own mind make
sure before God which side he chooses. On the other hand,
believers must be magnanimous and tolerant towards persons
who, although they do not think or act exactly as themselves,

nevertheless work in His name. " He that is not against us is for us " is the test by which we should judge others; " he that is not for me is against me " the test by which we should judge ourselves.

[1] Creed states: " It is most unlikely that exorcism in the name of Jesus would be practised in his lifetime on earth " (*in loc.*), and then suggests that this incident is a later fabrication of the church to teach the faithful how to act towards persons who, strictly speaking, are not members of the church and nevertheless act in Christ's name. Loisy (*in loc.*) even declares that the story was framed in order to try and justify the work of Paul! But Luce rightly rejects this view and writes: " If Jesus performed works of healing as widely as the Gospels suggest, the use of His name in exorcism, even during His own lifetime, is not unnatural " (*in loc.*).

THE SAMARITANS TURN JESUS AWAY

ix. 51-6

51 And it came to pass,[1] when the days[2] were well-nigh come
that he should be received up, he steadfastly set his face[3] to go
52 to Jerusalem, and sent messengers before his face: and they
went, and entered into a village of the Samaritans,[4] to make
53 ready for him. And they did not receive him, because his
54 face was *as though he were* going to Jerusalem. And when his
disciples James and John saw *this*, they said, Lord, wilt thou
that we bid fire to come down from heaven, and consume
55 them?[5] But he turned, and rebuked them.[6] And they went
56 to another village.[7]

From iv. 14 to ix. 50 Luke was mainly engaged in describing
Jesus' ministry in Galilee and we were able to contemplate Him
in His progressive Messianic self-revelation. At verse 51 Luke
begins a new division of the Gospel and we may regard the whole
portion from ix. 51 to xix. 44 as a separate section in which the
Saviour's conduct and preaching on His way to Jerusalem is
described (cf. ix. 53, xiii. 22, 23, xvii. 11, xviii. 31). This is in
many respects the most important part of the third Gospel because
the major portion of its contents does not occur in the three other
Gospels. In addition, we find in these chapters many of the most
beautiful parables of the Saviour—e.g. that of the good Samaritan,
the prodigal son, the lost sheep, the lost coin, and so on. If these
priceless parables of the Saviour had not been recorded in Luke,
they would have been lost to us forever, for the majority of them
are not recorded in the other Gospels.

51 The self-revelation of the Saviour had already reached the
climax on the mount of transfiguration a week after the disciples
had confessed that He was the Christ of God (verse 20). He had
chosen finally to enter upon the path of humiliation, suffering and
death in order to accomplish the divine plan of salvation, and He
had already repeatedly indicated to His disciples what was lying
ahead—His condemnation as well as His victory. Now the time is
approaching when, after His suffering, death and resurrection,
He will again be taken up, reinstated in His former glory with the
Father and invested with the new glory He had won as Man.

291

Fully aware of what is awaiting Him on the path of suffering, He now of set purpose chooses the road to Jerusalem.

52, 53 In order to obtain lodgings and to prepare food for Him and His followers who accompanied Him the Lord sends out messengers ahead on the way through Samaria to Judaea. However, the inhabitants of the Samaritan village refuse to receive Him because He is on His way to Jerusalem. The Samaritans, who had their own place of worship on Mount Gerizim, were particularly hostile to Jews who were on their way to worship in the temple of Jerusalem. Through this wrong attitude they now even reject the Son of God who wanted to journey through their country in order to give to them also the opportunity of learning to know and honour Him as their Messiah.

54 James and John, the " sons of thunder ", as the Saviour called them (Mark iii. 17), full of fiery zeal for the honour of their Master, are vehemently indignant at the Samaritans' rejection of the Lord. Bearing in mind the course adopted by Elijah, as described in 2 Kings i. 9–11, they ask whether they should not also make fire descend from heaven to consume the hostile Samaritans!

55, 56 Once more, however, the Saviour urges them to be tolerant. Just as they have to act with magnanimity (verse 50) towards persons acting in His name but not following Him precisely as they did, so also they most act tolerantly towards persons who are hostile to Him and His followers. With His followers there must never be anything like revenge or violence against enemies. Jesus came not to destroy men through His divine power but to save them. After the Saviour had rebuked His disciples for their earthly and revengeful spirit, they departed to another village.

In our loyalty to Christ, however zealous it may be, we must be constantly on our guard that we do not act with a spirit out of harmony with His, or follow methods of which He would not approve.

---

[1] It is clear that from ix. 51 to xviii. 14 Luke made no use at all of Mark. There are indeed quite a number of passages in these chapters that are found also in Matthew, and the current view among New Testament critical scholars is that Matthew and Luke used a common source (" Q "), from which these passages are derived. (Cf. particularly Streeter, *The Four Gospels*, pp. 203 ff.) In our opinion it has by no means been *conclusively* proved that such a written source as " Q " really existed. Its existence has been argued against in recent years by

J. H. Ropes, *The Synoptic Gospels* (1934), pp. 92 ff., J. Chapman, *Matthew, Mark and Luke* (1937), pp. 95 ff., and M. S. Enslin, *Christian Beginnings* (1938). These writers maintain that Luke was directly dependent on the first gospel for his " Q " material. See our Introduction, pp. 26 ff., both for an account of the hypothetical "Q" document and also for a discussion of the " Proto-Luke " theory propounded by B. H. Streeter and V. Taylor. (Creed's critique of the " Proto-Luke " theory in *The Gospel According to St. Luke*, Intr., ch. iii, is superficial and inadequate.)

Although Luke, in ix. 51–xix. 44, often refers to Jesus as being on His way to Jerusalem, he does not follow here a strictly chronological order any more than he does elsewhere, but an aesthetic and logical order. It is, therefore, uncertain whether he is writing about one and the same journey to Jerusalem all the time. From John vii. 10, x. 22, xi. 6, xii. 1, etc., it would seem possible that Luke describes incidents belonging to different journeys of the Saviour between Galilee and Jerusalem, mostly during the last six months before His crucifixion. This consideration would of itself suffice to dispose of the view (cf. Luce, *in loc.*) that Luke is at variance with Matthew and Mark where they teach that Jesus followed the road east of Jordan on His final journey to Jerusalem; but see also note 7 below. What Luke emphasises in ix. 51–xix. 44 is the fact that our Lord had deliberately chosen the way to Jerusalem and the cross.

[2] The use of the plural (" days ") in the expression τὰς ἡμέρας τῆς ἀναλήμψεως αὐτοῦ shows that the reference is not only to the ascension of Jesus but also to His suffering, death and resurrection that preceded it and were closely connected with it.

[3] τὸ πρόσωπον ἐστήρισεν. A Hebraism: " it implies fixedness of purpose, especially in the prospect of difficulty or danger " (Plummer, *in loc.*).

[4] Luce sums up the facts concerning the Jewish-Samaritan antagonism thus: " The feud between the Jews and the Samaritans dates from the time of the rebuilding of Jerusalem under Ezra and Nehemiah, when the Samaritans were not allowed to join the Jews in building and consequently did their best to hinder the work (Ezra iv. 3; Neh. ii. 20). Soon a rival temple and priesthood were established on Mt. Gerizim and the breach became irreparable. At Jesus' time the feud was extremely bitter " (*in loc.*). The ultimate causes of the antagonism actually go much farther back than the post-exilic period—to the time of the judges and early monarchy. The Samaritans' Messianic hope was centred round the " Prophet " of Deuteronomy xviii. 15 ff., whom they called the *Taheb* or " Restorer ". To-day only a small group of Samaritans survive in Palestine who remain true to their ancestral religion.

[5] The words " as Elijah did " (ὡς καὶ ᾿Ηλίας ἐποίησεν), inserted here in the " Received Text ", are omitted from pap. 45, ℵ B L Θ Ξ 71 157 700 and from the Latin, Old Syriac, Coptic and Armenian versions, and must be regarded as a later interpolation.

293

[6] A further insertion appears here in the " Received Text ": " And He said, Ye know not what manner of spirit ye are of. For the Son of Man came not to destroy men's lives but to save " (καὶ εἶπεν Οὐκ οἴδατε οἷον πνεύματός ἐστε · ὁ γὰρ υἱὸς τοῦ ἀνθρώπου οὐκ ἦλθεν ψυχὰς ἀνθρώπων ἀπολέσαι ἀλλὰ σῶσαι), but here, too, the leading textual authorities lack them (pap. 45, ℵ A B C L W 28, etc.), and they are regarded by most scholars nowadays as an interpolation—Zahn and Blass being outstanding exceptions. However, the words fit the context very well and may represent an authentic oral tradition which later found its way into the text. That " the Son of Man came not to destroy men's lives but to save " is, in any case, true of our Lord's ministry.

[7] " In reality, Luke reports that Jesus wanted to journey through Samaria, but encountered resistance in a village near the Galilean border. Of necessity he then turned away and took the familiar alternative road to Jerusalem through the wady Galud. . . . Thus he journeyed literally ' between Samaria and Galilee ', went past Beth-Shan, crossed the Jordan, and reached Jericho via Perea " (R. Otto, *The Kingdom of God and the Son of Man*, Eng. tran., p. 18). See further note on Luke xvii. 11.

HOW JESUS IS TO BE FOLLOWED

(Cf. Matt. viii. 18–23)

57 And as they went in the way,[1] a certain man[2] said unto
58 him, I will follow thee whithersoever thou goest. And Jesus
said unto him, The foxes have holes, and the birds of the
heaven *have* nests;[3] but the Son of man hath not where to lay
59 his head. And he said unto another, Follow me. But he said,
60 Lord, suffer me first to go and bury my father.[4] But he said
unto him, Leave the dead to bury their own dead; but go
61 thou and publish abroad the kingdom of God.[5] And another
also said,[6] I will follow thee, Lord; but first suffer me to bid
62 farewell to them that are at my house. But Jesus said unto
him, No man, having put his hand to the plough, and looking
back, is fit for the kingdom of God.

Jesus' way was a way that led to the cross, and therefore those
who desire to follow Him will have to pay the highest price. So it
is particularly fitting that Luke here, after describing our Lord's
determination to follow the way to the Cross (ix. 51), relates the
story of three prospective followers of Jesus.

57, 58 On the journey someone tells the Saviour that he will
follow Him whithersoever He may go. He spoke with so much
self-confidence because he had no inkling of the way of sorrows and
death which the Lord would yet follow and also because he did
not realise his own weakness and instability. In answer to his
declaration of loyalty to the Master, the Saviour calls his attention
to the naked reality of His life of extreme privation. For Him
there is no rest such as is to be found even for the foxes and the
birds of heaven, for He has continually to proceed from one town
to another because He is repeatedly rejected or because there are
again and again new cases of need where He has to bring salvation,
or because the multitude is constantly pursuing Him so that He
gets no opportunity of resting from His labour or from the endless
conflict with the powers of evil. The Saviour draws attention to
this, not in order to moan or to complain about it. On the
contrary, with His whole heart He willingly performs and undergoes all this, however much is demanded from His strength. No,
He calls attention to it so as to make the prospective follower

realise the implications of his swearing allegiance, so that he may be able to decide with open eyes whether he will indeed follow Him.

59, 60 This time it is the Saviour who calls upon someone to follow him. The man answers, however, that He must first allow him to go and bury his father. This, of course, does not mean that his father was already dead, for then he would certainly have been at his parents' home to help with the preparations for the funeral. He probably means that his father is already old or ill and that he does not wish to desert him in that state. Only when he is dead and buried will he follow the Lord constantly. Jesus, however, answers that to follow Him is such an urgent matter that even the most intimate family ties must be laid aside when the call comes to follow Him. It is also not so absolutely necessary for the man to wait until his father is buried, for there are many other spiritually dead persons who in any case do not follow Him and who will be able to look after the funeral of those who die. So he must follow Him immediately and must help to preach the truths in connection with the kingdom of God.

61, 62 Yet a third person also desired to follow Jesus, but first wanted to bid farewell to the members of his family. The Saviour replies (without definitely saying " Follow me! " or " Return to your home! ") that He cannot accept any half-hearted service (Rev. iii. 16). Just as one who ploughs must look before him and devote his full attention to his work so as not to plough a crooked and bad furrow, so also he who desires to be a member of Christ's kingdom should never allow other matters to distract his attention from his holy calling. Complete devotion to His service and unconditional faithfulness to the task to which He calls are the indispensable requisites for true following of Jesus.

In none of the three cases does Luke relate what became of the prospective followers. The Saviour rejected none of them, but only drew their attention repeatedly to the demands made on those who wished to follow Him. We must not forget that the Saviour Himself fully complied with every one of those demands which He enjoins upon His followers. He followed the way of utter self-denial and privation to the bitter end. He even set aside the most intimate family ties with His mother, brothers and sisters where this was necessary for faithfully accomplishing His life's vocation; and without any division of attention or half-heartedness He set His hand to the plough with a fixed purpose and completed His task at the highest cost to Himself.

The privilege and the seriousness of following Christ are of such tremendous magnitude that there is no room for excuse, for compromise with the world, or for half-heartedness. What a challenge and inspiration to know that He who calls us to complete devotion and loyalty, Himself followed whole-heartedly the road of self-denial—yea, even to the death of the cross!

[1] From Matthew viii. 18 it appears that it was a journey from Capernaum across the Sea of Galilee. Luke also merely says " as they went in the way ", without indicating precisely what journey it was. So in ix. 51–xix. 44 he does not deal exclusively with data from the last six months before the crucifixion.

[2] A scribe (Matt. viii. 19).

[3] Foxes and birds of the air are mentioned, not as representatives of the whole of the animal world, but because they are species of animals not cared for by men. Even these wild animals have their resting-places, but Jesus has none.

[4] Greydanus, Plummer and others are of opinion that the man's father was already dead, but see our exposition at this verse.

[5] Cf. verse 2.

[6] Levi had done (v. 29) what this man wished to do, but with a different purpose and in a different spirit. He gave a farewell entertainment for his old associates, but he did this in order to introduce them to Christ. The banquet was given to *Him* (v. 29). This man, however, wants to leave Christ in order to take leave of his friends.

THE MISSION OF THE SEVENTY DISCIPLES

1 Now after these things[1] the Lord appointed seventy[2] others, and sent them two and two[3] before his face into every city
2 and place, whither he himself was about to come. And he said unto them, The harvest[4] is plenteous,[5] but the labourers are few: pray ye therefore the Lord of the harvest, that he
3 send forth[6] labourers into his harvest. Go your ways: behold,
4 I send you forth as lambs in the midst of wolves. Carry[7] no purse, no wallet, no shoes: and salute no man on the way.[8]
5 And into whatsoever house ye shall enter, first say, Peace *be*
6 to this house. And if a son of peace[9] be there, your peace shall rest upon him: but if not, it shall turn to you again.[10]
7 And in that same house remain, eating and drinking such things as they give: for the labourer is worthy of his hire.[11]
8 Go not from house to house. And into whatsoever city ye enter, and they receive you, eat such things as are set before
9 you:[12] and heal the sick that are therein, and say unto
10 them, The kingdom of God is come nigh unto you. But into whatsoever city ye shall enter, and they receive you not,
11 go out into the streets thereof and say,[13] Even the dust from your city, that cleaveth to our feet, we do wipe off against you: howbeit know this, that the kingdom of God is
12 come nigh. I say unto you, It shall be more tolerable in
13 that day for Sodom, than for that city. Woe unto thee,[14] Chorazin![15] woe unto thee, Bethsaida! for if the mighty works had been done in Tyre and Sidon, which were done in you, they would have repented long ago, sitting in sack-
14 cloth[16] and ashes. Howbeit it shall be more tolerable for
15 Tyre and Sidon in the judgement, than for you. And thou,[17] Capernaum, shalt thou be exalted[18] unto heaven? thou shalt
16 be brought down unto Hades.[19, 20] He that heareth you heareth me; and he that rejecteth you rejecteth me; and he that rejecteth me rejecteth him that sent me.
17 And the seventy returned with joy, saying, Lord, even the
18 devils are subject unto us[21] in thy name. And he said unto them, I beheld[22] Satan[23] fallen[24] as lightning from heaven.[25]
19 Behold, I have given[26] you authority to tread upon serpents and scorpions,[27] and over all the power of the enemy: and
20 nothing shall in any wise hurt you. Howbeit in this rejoice not,[28] that the spirits are subject unto you; but rejoice that your names are written in heaven.[29]

The Saviour's public ministry before His crucifixion was beginning to pass by quickly and there were still many Jewish towns and villages that had not yet been visited. So the Lord appoints seventy disciples to go in pairs before Him to the places which He still wanted to visit. Probably these places were all situated in Trans-Jordan. Luke has already related how the Saviour completed His ministry to the Galilean and Samaritan towns and villages, and how He had with a fixed purpose set His face towards Jerusalem (ix. 51) and journeyed, as John informs us, back and fore to Jerusalem through Trans-Jordan. Thus on His journeys He especially ministered to this territory during the six months or so before His crucifixion. The inhabitants of Trans-Jordan were at that time treated with much indifference by the Jewish religious leaders and were therefore much neglected spiritually. For this reason, probably, the Saviour sent out such a large number of disciples in order that they might in the short time still left minister to the towns and villages in that neglected region as intensively as possible.

1 The Lord had on a previous occasion (ix. 2) sent out the twelve apostles to preach the Gospel and to heal the sick, and in Samaria He had sent out a few messengers before Him to make arrangements for His visits to various places. But He now sends out a much larger number of disciples, two by two, to bring spiritual ministration and prepare His way in the towns and villages that He still wishes to visit during the few months before His crucifixion. This intensive spiritual ministration to those places undoubtedly demanded very great output of strength from the Saviour—there was almost no time for Him to rest, as He had continually to set out from one place to another.

2 Before sending them out, He first points out to them that while the spiritual need (especially in Trans-Jordan in its neglected state) is great, the labourers are few. Thus far only the Saviour Himself and the twelve apostles had attended to the spiritual ministration. Because the labourers are now too few for the ministration, Jesus commands His followers to pray that the Lord may send out more labourers on this task.

3 Realising the existing spiritual need, and with prayerful hearts, the disciples have to set out to accomplish their task. However, many dangers will threaten them there, so the Saviour warns them to be careful—they must know that they will be like defenceless lambs among wolves. God alone will be able to protect them.

4 To the seventy are given practically the same instructions

299

as had been given to the twelve (ix. 3). They are not to take all kinds of provisions for their journey, for the time is too limited and the work too urgent for any delay. They have to go just as they are, and God will provide for their needs. They are also not to waste their time along the road through long-winded salutations as is customary in the East. They must make haste to the places to which they have been sent and must see that nothing hinders the faithful and immediate accomplishment of their task.

5, 6 When they enter a house, they must salute its inhabitants with the customary oriental salutation: " Peace be to you ". But, coupled with the preaching of the Gospel of the kingdom which they bring there (verse 9), the salutation will bear a far deeper significance. In it there will be offered to the people the peace and salvation which Jesus, the Messiah and Prince of Peace, is bringing. He who accepts this in faith will receive and enjoy this peace and salvation for himself—the salutation of peace will rest upon him and bear rich fruit in his life. But when the recipients of this salutation do not accept it in faith, it will be of no use to them and will bear them no blessing.

7 Whenever they had taken up their abode with a family, they were not to regard themselves as intruders, but had to live together with the household as full members of it, for the food and maintenance received by them are not charitable doles but the just reward of their labour—they are fully entitled to it because they have been sent by Him to carry out that work. They were also not to regard themselves as a burden to the family and then go from house to house, thus wasting time and strength. The household where they were originally taken in must remain their abode and centre throughout their stay in the town visited by them. From there they must minister to the town.

8 In Trans-Jordan there were many Gentiles, and the Jews were not so punctilious as regards ceremonial purity. So it might be that some of the food put before the disciples is unclean. Therefore Jesus commands them, for the sake of the unimpeded continuance of their work, not to waste their time and strength by ascertaining before meals whether some of the food is not perhaps ceremonially unclean. The Old Dispensation of outward ceremonies was passing away and there was no longer time or room for fastidiousness in connection with such matters. Without any conscientious scruples they must eat whatever is set before them.

9 When the Saviour commenced His public ministry, He announced that the kingdom of God was at hand (Matt. iv. 17). Now that the end of His public ministry is approaching He sends out the seventy to heal the sick and to proclaim once more that the kingdom of God is at hand. The wonder-working healings will serve as an indication and proof of the fact that the royal sovereignty of God is exercised in and through Christ and His disciples. Thus the inhabitants of the towns and villages that are to be visited will have the opportunity of recognising and accepting the kingly sovereignty of God and will thus be able to experience its beneficial working in their own hearts and lives.

10, 11 But where the ambassadors of Christ are not received, they must, by publicly wiping off the dust from their feet, bring the people to realise that by this act they break off all bonds of communion with them. But whatever their attitude is, they must know that the kingdom of God has come near them—so that they have no excuse for not becoming partakers of it.

12 Because the inhabitants of such a city have wilfully rejected the splendid opportunities of becoming citizens of the kingdom of God, their judgment will be severer than that of the inhabitants of Sodom who never had such opportunities. The greater the privileges, the greater the responsibility.

13, 14 In Galilee the inhabitants of towns like Chorazin and Bethsaida had already shown that they rejected Jesus, the Messiah of God—notwithstanding the unparalleled opportunities they had had of believing in Him. Therefore a great judgment will come upon them. For the inhabitants of the pagan cities of Tyre and Sidon it will, however, be more tolerable on the day of judgment because they did not have so many opportunities for repentance.

15 For the people of Capernaum, too, who had had abundant opportunity (Matt. iv. 18–22, ix. 1; John ii. 12) of seeing and accepting the kingly dominion of God in Jesus, an inexorable execution of judgment is awaiting. In the Roman-Jewish war this prophecy was partially fulfilled. But the final fulfilment waits until the last judgment.

16 The disciples go as envoys and representatives of Christ, while Jesus is the envoy and representative of the Father. So those who reject the disciples reject Jesus, and those who reject Him, in the highest instance also reject the Father who sent Him to the world as the divine Worker of salvation. Therefore those who do not listen to Jesus' disciples are rejecting the redemption which God desires to give to man.

17 The Saviour probably arranged with the seventy that after a certain time they should again meet Him at a fixed spot. So they came back joyfully to Him and gave Him their report. Their labour in the neglected district of Trans-Jordan had been so wonderfully blessed that even the evil spirits had perforce to submit to Jesus' envoys because they acted in His name.

18 Here Jesus explains the reason why the demons submitted to the disciples: the might of Satan, the prince of all diabolical powers, is already broken. When Jesus utterly rejected the temptations of the devil (iv. 1–13), the victory over his power had already been won. Throughout the Saviour's public ministry this victory was revealed in the liberation of those possessed of the devil and in other manifestations of His power. And especially in the grand offensive by the seventy against the might of Satan it could plainly be seen how Satan had already lost his exalted position of power. Satan is a conquered enemy, and where action is taken in the name of Jesus, the Conqueror, victory is gloriously assured.

19 Because Christ has conquered Satan, He gives to His envoys the authority to triumph even over the most dangerous forces of evil. He Himself protects them against all danger. The danger referred to is that which arises from spiritual enemies.

20 From the original it appears that by this verse Jesus meant that the disciples must not seek their *permanent* ground for joy in the fact that the demons are subject to them, but in the fact that through the grace of God their names are written in the heavenly registers—they have been enrolled among God's elect. The fact of their redemption is the all-surpassing boon conferred upon them.

Christ has once and for all hurled Satan from his position of power, so that he is a conquered enemy. Where the faithful proceed in the name of the Conqueror, as His envoys and by His power, the result is a continuous experience that Satan has to withdraw his forces, in fact that he has already had to do so. But alas, where men attempt to take action without faith in Jesus they ever stand powerless in their own strength in the conflict against evil. At the consummation of the age, however, the victory already gained by Christ over Satan will be finally established and he will be unable to exert any further influence.

---

¹ Easton, Klostermann, Creed, Luce, with many other modern critics, reject in part or totally the historicity of the mission of the seventy disciples. So they regard it as a duplication of the mission of the twelve, or as a deliberate invention on Luke's part to try and justify his Pauline ideas. Such and similar opinions are mere subjective conjectures and altogether at variance with the available data as well as with Luke's express purpose to relate only actual facts (i. 1–4). No

conclusive evidence can be adduced to prove as unhistorical Luke's description of the mission of the seventy.

It is quite inadmissible to adduce the fact that the other Gospels make no mention of the mission as a proof that no such mission took place. With regard to Luke's description in ix. 51–xviii. 14 of events from the last months of Jesus' public ministry, Matthew and Mark make hardly any mention of events from that period. John does, indeed, describe a few episodes of that time, but not one of those described by Luke. Each writer had the right to select what he wished to describe, and to omit what he thought to be of less importance or relevance for the general scheme and purpose of his Gospel.

With regard to the measure of agreement between the instructions given to the twelve and those given to the seventy, it may be remarked that the work of the seventy was to such an extent the same as that of the twelve that they naturally had to receive the same kind of instructions. On the other hand, Luke also shows clearly that there was a real difference between the two missions. Thus, e.g., the twelve were sent out to go and work and preach independently, while the seventy were expressly commanded to go to definite towns and villages in order to carry out a preparatory ministry to the inhabitants before Jesus should Himself arrive there.

While the instructions to the twelve were of a more permanent character, those given to the seventy were temporary. "All the instructions are in keeping with a brief *pioneering* mission" (Jamieson, Fausset and Brown, *in loc.*). As has been shown in our commentary on this portion, it is historically easy to perceive why the Saviour sent out such a large number of disciples at that moment. (For a discussion of the whole question of the mission of the seventy cf. Zahn, Greydanus, and Plummer, *in loc.*)

That this mission was mainly to towns in Trans-Jordan follows *inter alia* from the impression conveyed to us by Luke that the ministry to Samaria and Galilee had already been completed. This is also accepted by Zahn, Greydanus, Plummer and others.

[2] It seems to be impossible to decide whether the correct reading should here be 70 or 72 (cf. Easton, *in loc.* and also Luce, *in loc.*). The symbolical meaning of this number probably refers to the fact (Num. xi) that Moses (the representative of the Old Covenant) appointed 70 or 72 (if Eldad and Medad are counted in) elders to help him. The further suggestion that, while the mission of the twelve was to the twelve tribes of Israel, that of the seventy was to Gentiles (the Gentile nations being traditionally seventy in number) receives some colour from the largely Gentile character of Trans-Jordan at that time. (For other views in connection with the symbolical meaning of the number cf. the list given by Plummer.)

[3] ἀνὰ δύο, two by two, in order to help one another and also because "in the mouth of two witnesses every word is established" (Matt. xviii. 16).

[4] On two other occasions (Matt. ix. 37 and John iv. 35) Jesus also

spoke of the white or plenteous harvest. This, however, by no means implies that He would not again mention this when sending out the seventy. On the contrary, the circumstances in all three instances were of such a nature that Jesus' words fitted in extremely well.

⁵ Because the people had been so neglected, there was so much to do.

⁶ ἐκβάλῃ. " The verb expresses either pressing need or the directness with which they are sent to their destination " (Plummer, in loc.).

⁷ βαστάζειν = " carry as a burden ", thus " carry in the hands". The Saviour therefore means that they are not to take extra shoes, but does not forbid the wearing of shoes on the feet. They are to take nothing with them that may hamper them in accomplishing their task swiftly. (For the phrase βαστάζειν ὑποδήματα cf. Matt. iii. 11.)

⁸ In the East salutations along the road are of extremely long duration. Complete devotion in the execution of their vocation is demanded of the disciples.

⁹ υἱὸς εἰρήνης—a Hebraism. It points to the fact that this person is completely dominated by this peace—the peace revealed by God in Christ—and is destined for it and manifests it in practical life.

¹⁰ Like the pronouncement of the blessing in public worship by the minister, this salutation of peace is not merely an utterance of words " but also a power that goes forth in fact and that causes its content to be received and enjoyed when it is accepted in faith. It does not work ex opere operato merely by its being spoken. To receive and to enjoy it, faith is demanded " (Greydanus, in loc.).

¹¹ Cf. 1 Corinthians ix. 7; 1 Timothy v. 18.

¹² Cf. 1 Corinthians x. 27; Matthew xv. 10–20.

¹³ Cf. with ix. 5.

¹⁴ Οὐαί σοι—" Woe unto thee ": " the phrase is not so much a curse as an expression of pity " (Luce, in loc.). " Alas for thee " gives the sense adequately.

¹⁵ Chorazin is nowhere else mentioned in the New Testament, Old Testament, or Josephus (only in Matt. xi. 21 the parallel text). This shows how much is left unmentioned in the Gospels in connection with Jesus' actions, for from His words here it is evident that He preached the Gospel intensively to the inhabitants of Chorazin, resulting in their great responsibility. The place is identified with the modern Kerazeh, about two miles north-east of the ruins of Capernaum (cf. Dalman, Sacred Sites and Ways, p. 153). Bethsaida is mentioned several times in the New Testament (Mark vi. 45, viii. 22; Luke ix. 10 ff.; John i. 45). See Dalman, op. cit., pp. 161 ff.

¹⁶ The sackcloth was made of coarse, hairy material, and to be clothed in such sackcloth and to sit in ashes served as an image of utter dejection and contrition through grief and remorse. The whole subject is dealt with exhaustively in Strack-Billerbeck, op. cit., iv., pp. 77–114.

¹⁷ The καὶ σύ makes us feel how these words came from the grief-stricken heart of the Saviour. For in Capernaum He had made His home, He had often appeared there, and yet the city as a whole had

rejected Him and so incurred a terrible judgment on its unbelieving inhabitants.

¹⁸ The reading ἤ . . . ὑψωθεῖσα, which underlies A.V. " which art exalted ", must give place to the better attested μὴ . . ὑψωθήσῃ, which underlies R.V. " shalt thou be exalted? "

¹⁹ ᾅδου—In the New Testament Hades does not mean the abode of all the dead (the good and the wicked) but " a place of punishment and condemnation, which was ordained exclusively for the ungodly " (Strack-Billerbeck, op. cit., iv., p. 1022).

²⁰ Plummer (in loc.) rightly remarks on these verses: " The desolation of the whole neighbourhood, and the difficulty of identifying even the sites of these flourishing towns, is part of the fulfilment of this prophecy. See Jos. B.J. iii, 10, 9."

²¹ ἡμῖν—is not emphasised here. The disciples do not put themselves into the foreground, but the mighty works accomplished in His name, through His power.

²² ἐθεώρουν. The force of the imperfect tense here is a much disputed question, but it probably means that during this mission and as a result of it Jesus was watching Satan fall from heaven.

²³ " Satan " in Hebrew means " adversary "; it is represented in Greek by διάβολος, " calumniator ". The devil is the age-long opponent of God and the accuser of His people. According to Strack-Billerbeck (in loc.), the decisive fall of Satan and his followers was expected at the end of the present age.

²⁴ πεσόντα. The aorist here refers to a fact that has been settled. " The point at issue here is the concept of having fallen, not the act of falling while it is taking place, nor its result, namely lying down. Satan had been cast out, thrown down from his exalted position of power. For this reason those who returned had been able to cast out demons. That was the proof of the Lord's complete victory over Satan. They could, therefore, also in future rely on full victory in His name " (Greydanus, in loc.). Moffatt brings out the idea well in his paraphrase: " Yes, I watched Satan fall from heaven like a flash of lightning."

²⁵ For Satan's fall from heaven cf. Revelation xii. 9, 12.

²⁶ δέδωκα (perfect) is the correct reading and means: " I have given to you, so that you now possess it."

²⁷ Serpents and scorpions are used in the Bible as symbols of cunning and dangerous enemies. Here the reference is to spiritual enemies.

²⁸ μὴ χαίρετε, present imperative: " Do not go on rejoicing (permanently or continually) ". They may indeed rejoice in the subjugation of the demons. But their lasting joy is to be sought in the fact of their eternal redemption by God's mercy.

²⁹ The inscribing of the names of children at birth in the official registers is used as a symbol for the established fact of the redemption of the faithful (cf. Exod. xxxiii. 32, 33; Phil. iv. 3; Heb. xii. 43; Rev. iii. 5, xxii. 19).

JESUS REJOICES IN SPIRIT

(Cf. Matt. xi. 25–30)

21 In that same hour[1] he rejoiced[2] in the Holy[3] Spirit, and said, I thank thee, O Father,[4] Lord of heaven and earth,[5] that thou didst hide[6] these things[7] from the wise[8] and understanding,[9] and didst reveal them unto babes: yea, Father; for
22 so it was well-pleasing[10] in thy sight. All things[11] have been delivered unto me of my Father: and no one knoweth[12] who the Son is, save the Father; and who the Father is, save the Son, and he to whomsoever the Son willeth to reveal
23 *him*. And turning to the disciples, he said privately, Blessed
24 *are* the eyes which see the things that ye see: for I say unto you, that many prophets and kings[13] desired to see the things which ye see, and saw them not; and to hear the things which ye hear, and heard them not.

This pericope is of the very greatest significance because of the insight it affords us into the intimate relationship existing between Jesus and His Heavenly Father.

21 While Matthew xi. 25 indicates but vaguely the time when Jesus uttered these words, Luke here shows us that they are very closely connected with the return of the seventy. Nowhere else in the New Testament is it said that Jesus rejoiced, but that He did so on more occasions cannot be doubted (cf., e.g., His words where He speaks of His joy in John xvii. 13). The Saviour, after His disciples returned with joy (verse 17) to render an account of their mission, rejoiced in spirit, and His joy was so great that He expressed it aloud to His Father. From these words it appears that the Saviour rejoiced in the fact that God in His wisdom, omnipotence and love has so arranged matters that insight is given into the redeeming truths of the kingdom not to those who are self-exalted and wise in their own esteem (as so many Pharisees and scribes were at that time), but to those (like His faithful disciples) who in childlike simplicity and humility feel their utter dependence on the Lord and accept without intellectual arrogance the truths revealed by God through Him. The contrast pointed by the Saviour is not that between " educated " and " uneducated " but

between those who imagine themselves to be wise and sensible and
want to test the Gospel truths by their own intellects and to
pronounce judgment according to their self-formed ideas and
those who live under the profound impression that by their own
insight and their own reasonings they are utterly powerless to
understand the truths of God and to accept them. Often " un-
learned " persons are in the highest degree self-opinionated as
regards spiritual matters, and on the other hand some of the most
learned are humble and childlike and accept the truths of the
Gospel unreservedly. So Jesus makes the contrast not between
educated and uneducated but between people with the wrong and
self-sufficient attitude and those with the right and childlike
attitude.

22 Here we have the classical verse (paralleled in Matthew
xi. 27) in which we see that between the first three Gospels and
the Gospel of John there is no essential difference in their representation of Christ. We see in this verse that Jesus, as is shown
more fully by John (who supplements the other Gospels), did
indeed bear unambiguous testimony to His unity with the
Father. The Father has given *everything* over to Him; He alone
knows the Father (in an absolute sense); and only through
Him can anyone come to know the Father. Not only does
the Son know the Father, but He is also able to reveal Him
to others, so that it follows that He is absolutely one with the
Father.

23, 24 After He had uttered in the hearing of the greater
multitude that had probably gathered around Him after the
return of the disciples the eulogy in honour of God and the
statement in verse 22 (and also the invitation to those that labour
and are heavy laden, Matt. xi. 28 ff.), He turned round to His
disciples and addressed the words of verses 23 and 24 especially
to them. There He calls their attention to the glorious privilege
they are enjoying—a privilege earnestly longed for by the prophets
and kings of old, who knew about the coming Messiah—the
privilege of seeing Him, the promised Redeemer and Revealer of
the Father, and of listening to His words. In this declaration
we again hear the divine self-testimony of Jesus—clearly and
unambiguously He points to Himself as the long-expected
Messiah.

However great the privilege of those disciples was, we who
possess in the New Testament the completed revelation of God in
Christ have a still greater privilege. They indeed saw Him in
the flesh, but we see Him in the New Testament not merely as the

307

Incarnate Son of God but also as the Crucified One, and as the Risen Redeemer and the glorified King of His church. And because our privilege is so great, a great responsibility likewise rests upon us. The people of that time who rejected the revelation of God in Christ did not escape the divine judgment. So much the more will those who reject the completed revelation of God in His Word also bring judgment upon themselves!

¹ *'Εν αὐτῇ τῇ ὥρᾳ* makes the connection between the return of the seventy and the words of our Lord in verses 21 ff. " close and express " (Plummer, *in loc.*).

² *ἠγαλλιάσατο*, a strong word, referring to exceptional rejoicing and exultation.

³ ℵ B C D and other MSS. have *τῷ ἁγίῳ* after *πνεύματι*, and this longer reading must, on the strength of the textual witnesses, be accepted as original. " The omission of these two words will be connected with the circumstance that it was thought that there was here a reference to the Lord's own human spirit " (Greydanus, *in loc.*). Jesus' rejoicing was, therefore, a holy joy, accomplished by the Holy Ghost.

⁴ *ἐξομολογοῦμαί σοι, πάτερ*. These words imply the acknowledging of God with eulogy, and honouring Him in what is here mentioned of Him.

⁵ This phrase refers to God's sovereignty and omnipotence, and His exclusive right to dispose matters as He ordains.

⁶ *ἀπέκρυψας*, means, first, " removed " and then " hid ". The revelation had also been given to those with the wrong attitude, but when they persistently rejected it it was taken away from them and they were permanently confirmed in their spiritual blindness.

⁷ The truth in connection with the kingdom of God preached by the disciples and taught and revealed by Jesus.

⁸ *σοφός* denotes practical and intuitive insight into matters.

⁹ *συνετός* = " clever ", " intelligent".

¹⁰ *εὐδοκία* refers to the sovereign and saving nature of the divine decree.

¹¹ Because this verse so clearly points to the fact that Jesus did indeed speak about Himself so " metaphysically " as recorded by John in his Gospel, repeated attempts have been made to shelve this as a later interpolation. All such attempts have, however, been unsuccessful, and Plummer's words remain true: " It is impossible upon any principles of criticism to question its genuineness, or its right to be regarded as among the earliest materials used by the evangelists, and it contains the whole of the Christology of the fourth Gospel " (*in loc.*). As regards the theory of a later interpolation, even Creed writes: " It is precarious to desert the evidence of the MSS." (*in loc.*). It is only because there are persons who refuse to recognise the divinity of Jesus, or at any rate to

believe that He proclaimed it so explicitly, that they try to get rid of this verse. They have, however, not the slightest real basis of proof for their *a priori* views.

[12] γινώσκει, present tense, refers to continuous, steady, " ever present action " (Greydanus, *in loc.*).

[13] e.g. Moses, Isaiah, Jeremiah, Daniel; David, Solomon, Hezekiah.

PARABLE OF THE GOOD SAMARITAN

x. 25–37

25 And behold, a certain lawyer[1] stood up and tempted[2]
him, saying, Master, what shall I do[3] to inherit eternal life?
26 And he said unto him, What is written in the law?
27 how readest thou? And he answering said, Thou shalt
love the Lord thy God with all thy heart, and with all thy
soul, and with all thy strength, and with all thy mind; and
28 thy neighbour as thyself. And he said unto him, Thou hast
29 answered right: this do,[4] and thou shalt live. But he, desiring
to justify himself, said unto Jesus, And who is my neigh-
30 bour?[5] Jesus made answer and said,[6] A certain man was
going down from Jerusalem to Jericho;[7] and he fell among
robbers, which both stripped him and beat him, and
31 departed, leaving him half dead. And by chance a certain
priest[8] was going down that way: and when he saw him, he
32 passed by on the other side. And in like manner a Levite also,
when he came to the place, and saw him, passed by on the
33 other side. But a certain Samaritan, as he journeyed, came
where he was: and when he saw him, he was moved with
34 compassion, and came to him, and bound up his wounds,
pouring on *them* oil and wine;[9] and he set him on his own
beast, and brought him to an inn, and took care of him.
35 And on the morrow he took out two pence, and gave them
to the host, and said, Take care of him; and whatsoever
thou spendest more, I, when I come back again, will repay
36 thee. Which of these three, thinkest thou, proved neighbour
37 unto him that fell among the robbers? And he said, He that
shewed mercy on him.[10] And Jesus said unto him, Go, and
do[11] thou likewise.

Here we have one of the most precious parables of the Saviour.
And if Luke had not recorded it, we should never have learned to
know it, as he was the only one who reported it in a document of
the New Testament.

25 The question as to how man can inherit eternal life—the
most important question that can be asked—was naturally put to
Jesus on more than one occasion. Indeed, it was a question that
just at that time was brewing in the hearts of many (cf. Matt.
xix. 16–22, xxii. 35–40; Mark xii. 28–34; Luke xviii. 18–23).

26-8 In reply to Jesus' counter-question the lawyer declares that according to the Law the requirements for inheriting eternal life are perfect love towards God and perfect love towards one's neighbour. Jesus thereupon replies that he has answered correctly and that if he observes these requirements faithfully, he will live —in the fullest sense of the word, for time and eternity alike.

29 The lawyer, who had probably asked Jesus the question from motives which were not unmixed, knows but too well that he does not possess eternal life and that he does not love all men perfectly. Jesus' answer cornered him, and he now tries to find a way out in order to still the voice of his conscience. He is looking for an excuse for not having treated all people alike with love. So he asks who his neighbour is, hoping to be able to prove that not all people (especially the kind that he does not like) are his neighbours, and that the law, therefore, does not demand love towards all men. In this manner he tries to suppress and hide his feeling of guilt.

30-5 In answer to his question Jesus tells the parable of the good Samaritan. Possibly it is not an ordinary parable, but an account of an actual occurrence. The rocky, tortuous road from Jerusalem to Jericho has through all the centuries been notorious as a place where robbers all too often attack travellers.

36, 37 In complete accordance with the Saviour's usual way of dealing with people who try to trip Him up with puzzling questions, He does not reply to the question of the lawyer as the latter would have it, but in reality He answers another question, because this is the question of greatest importance in view of the spiritual state of His questioner. Thus the lawyer asked Jesus the merely academic question: " Who is my neighbour? " But the Saviour, by means of a parable, gives an answer to the practical question: " Whose neighbour am I? " or, stated differently: " Do I behave myself as a neighbour to those who have need of my love and help? " According to the ideas of Jewish religious leaders at that time the commandment of love for one's neighbours related only to persons belonging to one's own blood (pure Jews and therefore not to Gentiles or Samaritans). In the parable of the good Samaritan Jesus, however, teaches explicitly that love for one's neighbour knows no bounds of nationality or of anything else, no matter what. Notwithstanding the fact that Samaritans and Jews were at that time arch-enemies, the Saviour depicts the Samaritan who helps the robbed and wounded Jew so whole-heartedly as the person who really reveals the disposition of love for his neighbour.

The man asked: " Whom should I love? " And Jesus answers

by means of the parable: If you are really well-disposed, and if you really love God, you will also love your fellow-man and you will show neighbourly love to everyone in need of your help, no matter who or what that person may be. Then you will not theorise as to who is your neighbour or who is not, but you will see your neighbour in everyone with whom you may come into contact.

Jesus' answer was so clear and challenging that the lawyer was compelled to acknowledge the deep truth conveyed by it. No doubt it inclined him to a deep conviction of guilt. Whether he reacted to this conviction in the right way we are not told. Luke as usual leaves out such details so that the incident itself and the words of Jesus may with full power speak personally to every reader. He describes such episodes not in order to satisfy the curiosity of his readers but to let us hear the authoritative word of Christ in our own hearts. Thus the words addressed by Jesus to the lawyer: " Go, and do thou likewise ", are also addressed to every reader.

The irrevocable word of God still remains valid, that he who observes the law perfectly will live. He who always loves God and his fellow-man will inherit eternal life. But alas, no man has ever been able to observe this law perfectly, nor can anyone do so. And because no imperfect observance of the law, however excellent it may be, can be accepted; and because the judgment of God that the soul that sins (even if only on a single occasion) shall die, is just as irrevocable, we know that no man can ever inherit eternal life on the grounds of his own merit. But God be praised that Christ Jesus as Man lived a life of complete love towards God and men and, as the entirely Innocent One, endured death for us on the cross, forsaken by God, so that by faith we are absolved from the death we deserve, and inherit eternal life. This, however, does not remove the obligation to obey Jesus' words: " Go, and do thou likewise." But the difference is as follows: the Law has said: "Do this and thou shalt live ", while Christ says: " I have given you eternal life through grace, and this new life in you will enable you to have real love towards God and your fellow-men and to carry it out in practice; so go forth and live a life of true love to God and to your fellow-men, through the power I give you."

[1] Creed, Klostermann, Loisy, Montefiore, Luce and many other critics regard this episode in connection with the lawyer as a duplication of the story described in Matthew xxii. 35-40 and Mark xii.

28–32, or as an artificial creation by Luke to provide an introduction to the parable. Godet, Zahn, Greydanus and others, however, point out that we are here concerned with two altogether different cases. All the circumstances, the time, place, results, etc., are different. So there remains " no further similarity . . . other than that here, as there, the two commands of love to God and love to one's neighbour are adduced " (Zahn, *in loc.*). The reason why Luke does not also include in his Gospel the episode described by Matthew and Mark is to be explained by the fact that after he had described this similar episode he did not consider it necessary to mention that. He had to be sparing in his choice of material and to see that his Gospel did not become too long. With regard to the similarity between the questions that were put, Godet rightly asks why there should not have been more than one lawyer or scribe having an interview with Jesus on this all-important question, which was asked by many in those days of spiritual yearning.

[2] We cannot state definitely whether the lawyer questioned Jesus with evil intent or whether he did this in order honestly to test His ability as a teacher. Nevertheless the compound word ἐκπειράζειν has usually an unfavourable meaning in the Bible (Matt. iv. 7; Luke iv. 12; 1 Cor. x. 9). In any case it is clear that the lawyer did not ask his question exclusively as a result of a deep spiritual need, otherwise he would not have " tempted " or " tested " Jesus by it. But even so, there seems to have been at least some yearning in him to know how to be saved.

[3] τί ποιήσας—aorist participle. " The tense implies that by the performance of some one thing eternal life can be secured. What heroic act must be performed, or what great sacrifice made? " (Plummer, *in loc.*). Thus he cherishes the false opinion that eternal life is to be acquired by one's own merit. This was the typical attitude of the Jewish religious leaders of that time (cf. Strack-Billerbeck, *in loc.*).

[4] τοῦτο ποίει, present imperative: " do so continually ", " keep on doing so ". The Saviour does not imply that this is possible. He meets the lawyer on his own platform, as it were, so as to make him realise his guilt and his impotence.

[5] It is alleged from the Jewish side that the Jews already at that time used the concept of " neighbourly love " in the wider sense of " love towards all fellow-men ". This is, however, contradicted by Strack-Billerbeck, *in loc.* All available data indicate that the Jewish religious leaders regarded only their own fellow-countrymen as their neighbours. " According to the *Halakhah* an Israelite's neighbour is any member of his nation, but not one who is not an Israelite " (Strack-Billerbeck, *in loc.*; cf. Strack-Billerbeck also at Matt. v. 43).

[6] Many critics dispute the genuineness of this story because Jesus in the parable failed to give a direct reply to the question of the lawyer. " This is quite true," even Luce declares, " but only a critic who, like Loisy, will never allow an evangelist to tell the truth, could on that ground reject a story such as this . . . it may be justly argued that not only does the parable, as it stands now, present a strikingly effective

answer to the question of the scribe, but that the method of its answer is entirely characteristic of Jesus. For to ask: ' Who is my neighbour? ' is not a worthy way to approach the duty of love to one's fellow-men, as if a man were to draw up a list of those who might be supposed to have some claim upon his kindness and be best pleased if he found the list a short one. There is to be no limit, Jesus says, to Love's field of action. Who needs me is my neighbour. The same method of reply, by emphasising the fundamental principle upon which all particular cases depend, can be seen in Jesus' answers to the questions put to Him about divorce, the tribute, and the afterlife " (in loc.).

⁷ Jericho was at that time pre-eminently a city of priests, so that priests were continually moving to and fro between Jericho and Jerusalem (cf. Strack-Billerbeck, in loc.). Many Levites also lived there.

⁸ The priests and Levites, although regarded as belonging to the higher class, were at that time in general much degenerated both spiritually and morally (cf. Matt. xxi. 13; John xviii. 13).

⁹ Oil and wine are " attested as a common remedy both among Greeks (Theophr., Hist. Plant., ix, 11, 1) and Jews " (Creed, in loc.). And Klostermann states that there are many proofs " for the use of oil and wine, either mixed or separately, as a means of healing " (in loc.).

¹⁰ The lawyer uses a periphrasis, " he that showed mercy on him ", rather than utter the hateful word " Samaritan ".

¹¹ ποίει, present tense, " do constantly ", in the sense of lifelong action (cf. note 4, above).

MARTHA AND MARY

38   Now as they went on their way,[1] he entered into a certain
village: and a certain woman named Martha[2] received him
39 into her house. And she had a sister called Mary,[3] which
40 also[4] sat at the Lord's feet, and heard his word. But Martha
was cumbered[5] about much serving; and she came up to
him, and said, Lord, dost thou not care that my sister did
leave me to serve alone? bid her therefore that she help me.
41 But the Lord answered and said unto her, Martha, Martha,[6]
42 thou art anxious[7] and troubled[8] about many things: but one
thing[9] is needful: for Mary hath chosen the good part, which
shall not be taken away from her.

Here we have another of the precious jewels which only Luke
has preserved for us. In John xi another story is related in which
Martha and Mary figure. And although they there appear under
quite different circumstances (in connection with the death and
raising of Lazarus), the portrayal of the two sisters' characters on
that occasion agrees exactly with what we find here in Luke. This
makes us realise once more the precision and vital genuineness of
the Gospels.

38   According to John x. 22 and other statements in John the
Saviour journeyed to Jerusalem on several occasions during the last
six months before His crucifixion. On this occasion (verse 38) He
was probably again on His way to or from Jerusalem, for it is clear
from John xi that Martha and Mary lived at Bethany near
Jerusalem and this little place was situated along the main road
from Jerusalem to Trans-Jordan. Luke does not mention the name
of the village, neither does he state whether Lazarus or the
disciples were also there. This is because He wishes to concentrate
full attention upon the occurrence itself and upon Jesus' words on
that occasion.

39, 40   While Mary made full use of the opportunity during
Jesus' visit at their home to be instructed by Him, Martha
(probably the elder sister, who bore the responsibility of house-
keeping, verse 38) was restlessly and agitatedly busy preparing for
the Master the best possible meal. Martha certainly meant well,
but alas, her too great zeal to entertain the Saviour well, caused

her to become sulky towards her sister who sat and listened, and also towards the Lord Himself because He did not tell Mary to go and help with the serving. She is so dissatisfied that she wants to instruct the Saviour as to what He should do, namely to command Mary to help her. In this way she disturbed the harmony between herself and her sister and between herself and the Lord through her unbalanced zeal to entertain Jesus as lavishly as possible.

41, 42 Our Lord, who has perfect knowledge of the human heart, saw through Martha's attitude and also knew that it was with a proper motive that Mary had withdrawn herself on this occasion from the ordinary household duties in order to hear the words of everlasting life from His mouth. So the Lord, although Martha's request that Mary should help her, was apparently reasonable, addresses her seriously, but at the same time sympathetically, with a repetition of her name. He points out to her that she is inwardly anxious and over-zealous and outwardly restless amid all her preparations for entertaining Him. But the most important task of all is not to try and serve Him by this kind of action, but through the spiritual exercise of fellowship as practised by Mary. Material things and the honouring of Him through outward means are evanescent matters, but the soul's communion with the Lord can never be removed, not even by death. Therefore the highest form of service consists in this. We must note that our Lord does not say that Martha had no share in Him (cf. also John xi. 5). Nor does He disapprove of Martha's activities as such, for they were also the outcome of love for Him and were meant to serve Him. It is her wrong attitude as revealed in her condemnation of Mary and her dissatisfaction with Himself that had to be set right and rebuked. And she had to be shown things in their true perspective and relative value.

This story should not be taken to mean that the Saviour taught that a life of quiet worship and contemplation is the right form of religion and that an active Christian life is to be disapproved of. There is here no question of such a contrast. What we do learn here is that in our life's active service we must not be anxious and agitated, sulky and dissatisfied with our fellow-Christians or with our Master, and that we should not busy ourselves to such an extent with outward things that we neglect the quiet worship of the Lord. The most important part of our religion is the spiritual exercise of communion with our Redeemer. When things are right in this respect, we shall also in our practical life be actively busy in His honour. It is certainly one of the most difficult lessons to learn, to maintain the right balance between the life of quiet worship in spirit and in truth and the practising of our religion in active service. And, indeed, it is only in the Word of God that this comprehensive form of religion is taught. Extra-Biblical religions lapse into either excessive contemplative forms of religion, or into dry outward formal religion. But Jesus calls us to a life of worship as well as practical service.

[1] A few critics, like Loisy and Bultmann, regard this story as a symbolical invention. However, there is not a single indication of this in the story. On the contrary, every part of it speaks of the fact that it has been drawn from real life.

[2] " Martha ", the feminine of Aramaic Mar, means " mistress ".

[3] " Mary " (Hebrew *Mariam* or *Miriam*) of uncertain derivation. The suggested etymology, " star of the sea ", is improbable.

[4] ἣ καί. Zahn (*in loc.*) regards the καί as a strengthening of the idea that she was so eager to hear Jesus' words that she went and sat down at His feet. C. Morgan takes it as follows: " Martha goes on and on until she is distracted; but Mary *also* sat at His feet. This is a most vital distinction. Some people seem to imagine that all she did was to sit herself down, to have a good time. If she had done that, Christ would never have commended her. Mary knew the one deep secret that love cannot finally express itself in service. It must take the place of devotion, of discipleship " (*in loc.*). But, as so frequently in Greek, καί here probably does little more than emphasise the relative pronoun.

[5] περιεσπᾶτο. " The verb means ' allowed her attention to wander ', which strictly implies that Martha had tried to listen but found she could not listen and think about the preparations for the meal at the same time " (Luce, *in loc.*).

[6] Μάρθα, Μάρθα. " The repetition of the name conveys an expression of affection and concern " (Plummer, *in loc.*).

[7] μεριμνᾷς refers to the agitated state of her mind.

[8] θορυβάζῃ indicates the outward noise caused by her in her excitement. The reading τυρβάζῃ of the " Received Text " is a later alteration. " Martha was not wrong in her dedication of herself to practical service, but in the method of her discharging it " (Major, *op. cit.*, p. 280).

[9] From the context it is clear that it is not " one course " or " one kind of food " that is meant (as several modern critics take it), for it appears from the next phrase that " the one thing " is the spiritual exercise of communion with Jesus.

THE LORD'S PRAYER

1 And it came to pass,[1] as he was praying in a certain place,
that when he ceased, one of his disciples said unto him, Lord,
teach us to pray, even as John also taught his disciples.[2]
2 And he said unto them, When ye pray, say,[3] Father,[4] Hal-
3 lowed be thy name.[5] Thy kingdom[6] come. Give us day by
4 day our[7] daily[8] bread. And forgive us our sins;[9] for[10] we
ourselves also forgive[11] every one that is indebted to us. And
bring us not into temptation.[12]

The " Lord's Prayer " also occurs in Matthew vi. 9-13, but not
exactly in the same words. In Matthew it occurs as part of the
sermon on the mount. There the Saviour uttered it of His own
accord, unasked, while He was engaged in teaching a large
number of His disciples *how* to pray (e.g. that they should not
pray a vain repetition of words). But here in Luke the Saviour
gives the prayer under totally different circumstances. It is very
natural that He should repeat the prayer on two or more different
occasions for the instruction of His disciples. It is also very
natural that He should give it substantially, but not exactly, in
the same wording, for His view of prayer was that it should not be
mechanical—He constantly warned against formalism and
verbalism. In addition, it is possible that Luke does not report
the prayer in full, although on the other hand we may take
Matthew's longer version as that which proved preferable for
liturgical use. (The requirements of the liturgy certainly explain
the well-known doxology at the end of the prayer: " For thine is
the kingdom, and the power, and the glory, for ever: Amen ",
which found its way into the text of Matthew, although it was not
there originally.)

1 Although Luke does not say where or at what period of the
ministry of Jesus this happened, he nevertheless describes precisely
the circumstances under which one of the disciples addressed this
request to the Master. Undoubtedly the disciple, whilst Jesus was
busy praying, was impressed by the reality and significance of our
Lord's communion with His Father in prayer. This aroused in
him a hunger and a longing to be able likewise to learn the secret
of real prayer. So, when the Master had concluded His prayer,

he made his request: " Lord, teach us to pray ", referring to the
fact that John the Baptist taught *his* disciples to pray. This
disciple was so conscious of his own and his fellow-disciples'
inability to pray in the manner of their Master that he longed that
He might teach them a model prayer.

2   The Saviour accedes to the disciple's request and gives this
model prayer. In Matthew vi. 9 Jesus said: " *After this manner
therefore pray ye . . .*", paying more attention to the question
" *How* or *in what way* shall we pray? " But here He says: " When
ye pray, *say* . . .", indicating the " Lord's Prayer " as the model
prayer which should constantly be used, and not merely as a
prayer from which we learn the principles of true prayer. But,
even so, it was not His intention that it should be repeated
mechanically or with slavish verbalism, otherwise the prayer would
not have been repeated in Matthew vi and Luke xi in somewhat
different wording. Nevertheless, His words here make it clear that
His followers should regularly use the " Lord's Prayer " as nearly
as possible in the form in which He taught it, and that they should
repeat it in the spirit of true prayer.

The opening word " Father " indicates the attitude in which
prayer should be offered to God—with faith in Him and love
towards Him as our Father—the One who is near us in mercy and
love and at the same time is high exalted above us (" Our Father,
which art in heaven ", Matt. vi. 9), the Almighty, divine Father.
So in prayer we must approach Him both in earnest faith and with
holy reverence, and also with the consciousness that in Him we
are at one with other believers. God is the Father of all believers,
hence when they pray together they say " *Our* Father " (as in
Matt. vi. 9). The Lukan version, however, seems to be the form
intended for individual petition. The single word " Father " in
Luke represents Aramaic *Abba*, the word which Jesus used Himself
(cf. Mark xiv. 36) and which from His example passed into the
vocabulary of the early church (cf. Rom. viii. 15; Gal. iv. 6).
The Jews in addressing God used the slightly formal *Abi* (" my
Father ") or *Abinu* (" our Father "), but Jesus used the ordinary
intimate form which children used (and in Hebrew-speaking
families still use) in addressing their father, *Abba*.

After the worshipper's heart has been rightly attuned to the
spirit of true prayer, the first objects of our petition should be
those which concern the glory of our heavenly Father. " Hallowed
be thy name." The name of God in the Bible is the expression of
His Being, especially in so far as He has revealed Himself to man.
So the first supplication is that God should be sanctified not only
in the one praying, but in all creation. The petition is that God

should so work inwardly upon the one who prays, and upon all others, that they shall recognise Him in His Self-revelation and serve Him as the Holy One—that they should render to Him, the divine Father, all honour and adoration and should love and obey Him with their whole heart. In fact, the petitions " Hallowed be thy name ", " Thy kingdom come ", and the Matthaean " Thy will be done, as in heaven, so on earth ", are in essence one petition expressed in a threefold way. " Thy kingdom come." This might be better rendered: " Let thy divine rule come." The prayer is that the Father's divine sovereignty should more and more fully attain its rightful place in the heart and life of fallen mankind, who otherwise are bound under the sway of the powers of darkness; that instead of living in sin and rebellion against God men should be brought to live their whole life more and more under the control of God's sovereign rule. So this supplication refers to the extension of the divine dominion in the life of mankind in this age. But in the highest instance it is a supplication that the kingly dominion of God which came with power into the life of mankind in the first coming of Jesus shall come in full glory and perfection through Christ's second coming. " Thy will be done, as in heaven, so on earth." This supplication, absent from the authentic text of Luke but present in Matthew, is practically a closer description of the preceding supplication. In heaven God's will is obeyed by all, spontaneously, with the deepest joy and in a perfect manner without a shadow of unfaithfulness. And the believer must pray that such a condition should also prevail on earth. Already in this age this supplication is being heard, but only when the " new earth " appears and the powers of evil have been destroyed, the will of God will be obeyed by all in fullness and perfection.

3, 4 After the supplication in connection with the glorification of God, prayer is now offered for providing for the needs of man. In reality this is already included in the previous supplication, for where the kingly dominion of God is perfect, all real wants of man are at the same time supplied. But because in this world, as a result of the sin of mankind, the kingly dominion of God is not accorded its full right, there are constantly prevailing or threatening conditions of material and spiritual need. Consequently one should pray expressly for divine aid and blessing in all fields of human life, not only for himself but for his fellows (" give *us* ").

" Give us day by day our daily bread." " Bread " here stands for everything that man really needs for his earthly existence—so that he can live and work in agreement with the will of God for each individual's life. Here the prayer is offered not on the grounds of one's own merit but in reliance on the grace of God for a constant providing for our needs—every moment we are utterly dependent on the blessing and gifts of our heavenly Father, even as regards our life on earth.

" And forgive us our sins; for we ourselves also forgive every one that is indebted to us." By praying for forgiveness, man at the same time confesses that he is sinful and guilty. The forgiveness is not asked *on the ground* of the fact that those who pray also forgive their enemies, but on the ground of the grace of God. But in order to utter this supplication in all sincerity, there should be no unwillingness on the part of a man to forgive his fellow-men—for then he would be playing the hypocrite. In order to receive the forgiveness of sin which God desires to grant by His grace alone, a man must also forgive those who have done him harm. In a true prayer for forgiveness a man should, therefore, be able to state honestly that in his own life there does not exist the stumbling-block of unwillingness to forgive. Only then will he be permitted to ask for forgiveness—forgiveness *through grace and grace only*.

" And bring us not into temptation." He who sincerely seeks and entreats forgiveness of sins, longs to be able to sin no more. So he prays, conscious of his own weakness, that God may guide his life away from circumstances in which he is exposed to evil temptations. God Himself does not tempt (John i. 13), but nevertheless He allows the faithful to be tempted in order to test and to purify us. According to James i. 2, when, under the guiding hand of God, a man finds himself in circumstances where temptations assail him, he should regard it as a cause for rejoicing, since he knows that Christ gives the victory and that everything of this kind contributes to the steadfast believer's purification and spiritual uplift. But nevertheless it is also necessary, and it is indeed the Lord's commandment, that we should pray that we may as far as possible be spared these temptations, for there is always the danger that we shall not live sufficiently in His power and that we shall accordingly be liable to be overcome by temptations. Therefore we must pray that we be led as seldom as possible into circumstances fraught with temptation. But when God nevertheless allows us to be led into such circumstances, we must rejoice in the Lord who gives us the victory and causes everything to contribute towards the good of those that love Him (Rom. viii. 28).

Matthew adds as a corollary to this petition the words: " But deliver us from evil." Here we pray that God may deliver us from

all influence of the power of darkness, from all sin and consequences of sin and from the workings of the evil powers. This
supplication also, like all those preceding, points ultimately to
the second coming of Christ when a full and decisive.end will be
put to all that is wrong, and when His perfect kingdom on the new
earth will become an accomplished and glorious fact.

In the " Lord's Prayer " our Saviour gave us not merely an
inexhaustible source of enlightenment in prayer, but also a perfect
prayer which we must often address to God. On the one hand we
should be on our guard not to let the use of this prayer degenerate
into a mechanical, ceremonial formality. On the other hand, we
should in our inner room as well as in our public worship guard
against neglect and heedlessness with regard to the use of the
" Lord's Prayer " as the model prayer given by the Saviour to His
Church and as the prayer that has already been repeated in the
past nineteen hundred years by millions of believers in hundreds
of languages and in an endless variety of circumstances. In this
prayer the whole Christian world of all the centuries has a glorious
common bond of unity and of mutual fellowship.

¹ In Matthew vi. 9–13 the " Lord's Prayer " forms such a real part
of the sermon on the mount that it was probably indeed uttered on that
occasion. In addition, Luke states so expressly on what occasion it
was uttered in the form in which he records it, that we cannot agree
with most of the liberal critics in their view (even supported by Zahn)
that the Saviour uttered the " Lord's Prayer " on only one occasion.
² " It was customary for a famous rabbi to compose a special prayer "
(Montefiore).
³ Greydanus remarks (*in loc.*) that " in the form here communicated
by Luke the Lord puts into the mouths of the disciples what they have
to pray, i.e. the content of prayer and not merely the manner of
praying ".
For a comparison between Jewish prayers of that time and the
" Lord's Prayer " cf. Strack-Billerbeck (at Matt. vi. 9–13) and also
Abrahams (*Studies*, second series, No. 12). Plummer rightly observes:
" We must notice how entirely free from Jewish elements the prayer
is. It is not addressed to the ' Lord God of Israel ' nor does it ask for
blessings upon Israel " (*in loc.*).
⁴ This is a prayer intended for believers—those who, through the
Beloved One, have become children of God (John i. 12).
God is not only the gracious and loving Father, but also the exalted,
holy and omnipotent Father. Thus He does not only listen sympathetically to prayers, but is also able to answer every true prayer in His
way and at His time.

⁵ " The name, according to the usage of Biblical speech, is an indication of the character; the name of God is the essence of the divine character, as He has revealed Himself to men " (cf. Keil at Matt. vi. 9–13).

⁶ Practically all recognised expositors of recent times (beginning with Plummer) translate βασιλεία by " kingly power " or " royal sovereignty " and not by " kingdom " (in a spatial sense). Cf. our note on Luke iv. 43. There is a little evidence for an early variant to ἐλθάτω ἡ βασιλεία σου, namely: ἐλθάτω τὸ πνεῦμά σου τὸ ἅγιον ἐφ᾽ ἡμᾶς καὶ καθαρισάτω ἡμᾶς (" let thy holy spirit come upon us and cleanse us "), probably originating with Marcion.

⁷ ἡμῶν. In our prayers, even with regard to providing for earthly needs, we must not forget the bond of communion with other believers.

⁸ ἐπιούσιον. No finality has thus far been reached as to the correct etymological derivation or precise meaning of this word (cf. the discussion in Kittel's *Theologisches Wörterbuch*). Whatever may be the exact derivation of this word (which is not known outside Matthew vi and Luke xi), in any case " it conveys the notion of what is needful and adequate for the requirements and satisfying of our material existence " (Greydanus, *in loc.*).

⁹ ἁμαρτίας. In LXX ἁμαρτία is used especially as the equivalent of the Hebrew חַטָּאת (*ḥaṭṭā'th*). The primary meaning of both the Greek and the Hebrew word is " missing the mark ", and hence " acting wrongly " and " breaking the law of God ".

¹⁰ The conjunction γάρ (" for ") indicates here, not the ground upon which God grants forgiveness, but the condition with which we ourselves must comply if we are to enjoy the forgiveness of our sins by God.

¹¹ ἀφίομεν, present indicative, expressing our present practice, and not what has been done in the past or will be done in the future.

¹² καὶ μὴ εἰσενέγκῃς ἡμᾶς εἰς πειρασμόν—" a situation which involves especially grave temptation to sin " (Creed). A similar petition is found in the Jewish morning service.

PARABLE OF THE IMPORTUNATE FRIEND

xi. 5–13

5 And he said unto them,[1] Which of you shall have a friend, and shall go unto him at midnight, and say to him, Friend,
6 lend me three loaves; for a friend of mine is come to me
7 from a journey,[2] and I have nothing to set before him; and he from within shall answer and say,[3] Trouble me not: the door is now shut, and my children are with me in bed;
8 I cannot rise and give thee? I say unto you, Though he will not rise and give him,[4] because he is his friend, yet because of his importunity[5] he will arise and give him as many as he
9 needeth. And I say unto you, Ask,[6] and it shall be given you; seek,[7] and ye shall find; knock,[8] and it shall be opened unto
10 you. For every one that asketh receiveth; and he that seeketh findeth; and to him that knocketh it shall be opened.
11 And of which of you that is a father shall his son ask a loaf, and he give him a stone? or a fish, and he for a fish give him
12 a serpent? Or *if* he shall ask an egg, will he give him a
13 scorpion? If ye then, being evil,[9] know how to give good gifts unto your children, how much more shall *your* heavenly Father give the Holy Spirit[10] to them that ask him?

The Saviour did not merely give a model prayer to His followers, but taught in a striking manner the certainty of answer to prayer.

5–8 In the foregoing verses the Saviour acceded to the request of the disciple when he asked: " Lord, teach us to pray." Now the Saviour goes further and teaches the disciples that when they pray they should pray with a firm faith that their prayer will be answered. In order to emphasise the certainty of prayer being answered, the Saviour first tells a parable. If even an imperfect human being, notwithstanding the inconvenience to which he is put, will arise at midnight to give a friend what he needs if he comes and asks him for help, how much more will God, the heavenly Friend, who is perfect in love, listen to the sincere prayers and supplications of His children who are really in need! It is important that we should remember that in the parable there is a friendship existing between the one who asks and the one who rises and gives, and that the request arises out of necessity and not out of selfishness. The answer to prayer is, therefore, only certain

324

in cases where the one who prays stands in a relation of friendship towards God, and loves and serves Him, and, further, only in cases where such a believer prays from real need and not from false motives.

9 Far more certainly than that this man should rise and give his friend what he needs will God, the perfect Friend, answer our prayers. For this reason, the Saviour says, His disciples must pray constantly and God will answer. They must *seek*, that is, they must do everything in their power, to receive what they ask in prayer, and they will receive it. They must *knock*, that is, they must pray urgently to God, and He will open the door to them to obtain what they have been praying for.

10 To strengthen what has been taught in the foregoing verse the Saviour adds these words. Where He thus points out the absolute certainty of answer to prayer, as here, we should not forget to read this in its true context. The principles hold good throughout, as laid down in verses 5–8, namely that only believers, those who live in the right relationship towards God, may depend on answer to prayer and this only when they pray to God in their real need.

11–13 While the Saviour in verses 5–8 referred to God as the heavenly, perfect Friend, He makes the likeness still more intimate here by referring to Him as the heavenly Father. If, says Jesus, even an earthly father, one with sins and shortcomings, will not give to his son useless (a stone for bread) and dangerous things (a serpent for a fish or a scorpion for an egg) instead of the necessary things for which the son asks him, how much more will God, the perfect heavenly Father, give to His children who pray to Him the things they need—and above all the Holy Ghost, the most important and indispensable Gift, in which all other good gifts are included!

No regenerate child of God should ever doubt that when he prays to God out of real need his prayer will be answered. He who doubts this does Him the greatest dishonour, for by not believing that He will give what we really need we in fact appear to regard Him as less sympathetic and less faithful than an ordinary earthly father or even an ordinary earthly friend. Therefore unbelief in relation to the answering of prayer is not only a weakness, but a serious sin and utter folly.

---

[1] " No grounds exist for the opinion that the Lord uttered these words on another occasion and that they were only added here by Luke " (Greydanus, *in loc.*).

² In the East people often travel at night to avoid the heat.

³ The Saviour does not state that the friend will say anything of this kind, but (according to verse 8) wants expressly to point out how impossible it is for a normal person to adopt such an unfriendly attitude. Many Bible expositors go astray here by saying that the person by these words refused to accede to his friend's request, and only later on, in order to get rid of the importunate friend, granted what he needed. The Lord does not here refer by any means to hesitation or to any unwillingness on the part of the friend. On the contrary, He expressly desires to make us realise how impossible it is even for a normal human being to refuse anything needful to his friend. How much more may we rest assured that God, the heavenly Friend, will never refuse anything needful for which sincere prayer is offered?

⁴ By these words the Lord does not suggest any doubt that the loaves are supplied to the friend, but merely refers to the motive according to which the man may act. It is so certain, Jesus says, that the man will give the loaves, that even if the bonds of friendship should not decide he would nevertheless arise and give his friend what he requires because his need is so great that he does not even hesitate to come and ask for help at such an inconvenient hour.

⁵ ἀναίδεια—" importunity ", " over-boldness ", " shamelessness ". This does not mean that the man keeps on asking and knocking from outside and thereby reveals an importunate disposition (as Jülicher, *Gleichnisreden Jesu*, ii, p. 275; Buttrick, *The Parables of Jesus*, p. 168; and many others think), the truth that Jesus emphasises is precisely this, that the friend will surely rise and accede to the man's request. His coming at such an inconvenient time is the ἀναίδεια. " In this he revealed how much he dared to ask and expect from the friendship, how strong he regarded it, so that he was entitled to ask this from it. And this high value attached to his friendship, together with such a bold reliance on it, would cause the person to whom the request was made to grant it, even though otherwise he would not have done so for the sake of the friendship alone " (Greydanus, *in loc.*).

⁶ αἰτεῖν refers to the act of praying where the will is earnestly fixed on the answering of the prayer. So the desire is not merely a vague or half-hearted one.

⁷ ζητεῖν—" seek with the object of finding or obtaining ". So this includes faithful prayer and all other exertion directed towards the purpose of obtaining the things for which the prayer is offered. While confidently awaiting God's answer, the one who prays must also from his side do everything that is necessary.

⁸ κρούειν, " to knock ", refers to the urgent sincerity exercised in praying and seeking. The present imperative in all three verbs refers to the continuous, uninterrupted act.

⁹ ὑπάρχοντες, " being already ", is much stronger than ὄντες and here refers to the inward character and nature of man.

¹⁰ Matthew vii. 11 has instead of πνεῦμα ἅγιον the generalised ἀγαθά (" good things "). In this Luke and Matthew by no means

contradict each other, for the Holy Ghost is the good Gift *par excellence* —the Gift which is indispensable and which brings about all true life and true happiness in the believer and is the Source of all good things.

Those who style Luke Ebionitic regard the fact that Luke has instead of ἀγαθά (as Matthew has it) πνεῦμα ἅγιον as one of the strongest proofs that he is under Ebionitic influence. But in this connection Plummer has justly remarked: " This may well be correct: in which case the total amount of evidence is not strong " (*in loc.*).

BLASPHEMY OF THE PHARISEES

(Cf. Matt. xii. 22–32; Mark iii. 20–30)

xi. 14–28

14 And he was casting out a devil[1] *which was* dumb.[2] And it came to pass, when the devil was gone out, the dumb man
15 spake; and the multitudes marvelled. But some of them[3] said, By Beelzebub[4] the prince of the devils casteth he out
16 devils. And others, tempting[5] *him*, sought of him a sign from
17 heaven. But he, knowing their thoughts,[6] said unto them, Every kingdom divided against itself is brought to deso-
18 lation; and a house *divided* against a house falleth.[7] And if Satan also is divided against himself, how shall his kingdom stand? because ye say that I cast out devils by Beelzebub.
19 And if I by Beelzebub cast out devils, by whom do your sons
20 cast them out? therefore shall they be your judges. But if I by the finger[8] of God cast out devils, then is the kingdom
21 of God[9] come[10] upon you. When the strong *man*[11] fully armed guardeth his own court, his goods are in peace:
22 but when a stronger[12] than he shall come upon him, and overcome him, he taketh from him his whole armour
23 wherein he trusted, and divideth his spoils.[13] He that is not with me is against me;[14] and he that gathereth not with
24 me scattereth. The unclean spirit when he is gone out of the man, passeth through waterless places, seeking rest; and finding none, he saith, I will turn back unto my house
25 whence I came out. And when he is come, he findeth it
26 swept and garnished. Then goeth he, and taketh *to him* seven other spirits more evil than himself; and they enter in and dwell there: and the last state of that man becometh worse than the first.[15]
27 And it came to pass, as he said these things, a certain woman[16] out of the multitude lifted up her voice, and said unto him, Blessed is the womb that bare thee, and
28 the breasts which thou didst suck. But he said, Yea rather, blessed are they that hear the word of God, and keep it.

Thus far Luke has shown us the Saviour mostly in His progressive self-revelation as the mighty, divine Messiah. However, in ix. 51 he has already announced that Jesus chose the road to Jerusalem, where suffering and death awaited Him. In this portion (verses 14–28) we notice how the hate of the Jews becomes more violent and things begin to move more and more plainly towards His final rejection by the nation at Jerusalem. From henceforth we shall see increasingly how He enters upon the way of suffering.

14, 15 Once again the Saviour revealed His divine power by casting out a devil from a possessed person. It was a kind of evil spirit that made his victim dumb as long as he prevailed over him. But after Jesus had exorcised the evil spirit by His authoritative utterance, the man could immediately talk again. What had happened was such an evident miracle that the onlookers were amazed at it. Some were even inclined to see in it a proof that the Nazarene was really the Messiah (cf. Matt. xii. 23). But others, because they would under no circumstances acknowledge Him as the Christ but could nevertheless not deny His having performed a mighty miracle, declared blasphemously that He performed the miracle through the power of Satan.

16 Others, who did not go so far as to suggest that He acted through the power of Satan, would nevertheless not see and acknowledge in His power over the evil spirits and in all His other words and deeds evidence that He was the Messiah. Without showing any signs of true desire for salvation, they demand that, if He were to be acknowledged as Messiah, He should cause an indisputable, divine miracle to take place which might prove openly the fact of His Messiahship. Otherwise, they reasoned in their unbelief and pride, they could not be sure whether the accusation of His acting through the power of Satan was not perhaps true.

17, 18 The Saviour, who discerned their hearts, however, laid bare the hollowness and falseness of his enemies' accusation. Satan performs his evil work by means of the demons who are his subordinates. It is, therefore, unthinkable that he will take steps against them and will deliver their human victims from their accursed domination, for then it would mean that he has resolved to work against himself and to destroy his own work which he performs through his underlings.

19 After exposing the absurdity of the accusation of His enemies, the Lord now reveals their wilful falseness by showing that they measure by two standards. It was at that time the general idea among the Jews that when a rabbi or other Jew delivered anyone from possession of the devil, it was a sign that God worked through him. But now that they see that Jesus (indeed in a far more signal manner) releases unhappy possessed people from demoniacal powers, they ascribe this in the wickedness of their hearts to the powerful workings of Satan. Thereby they declare, as it were, that their fellow-Jews also who in God's power freed people from demon-possession, did so through Satan. So they will be judged by their fellow-countrymen.

20 Instead of there being any truth in the accusation of His enemies, exactly the opposite is true. It is through the power of God that Jesus exorcises demons, and through the potent revelation of His power over Satan and his satellites it has been incontrovertibly shown that the kingdom of God, His royal dominion, has come upon earth and is active in the person of Christ.

21, 22 By means of the simile in these verses the Lord points out that He exorcises the demons because He has already (especially during the time of temptation in the wilderness) deprived Satan of all his power. Therefore He is able to undo Satan's evil work in people and to cast out demons by His mighty word. Satan has already been bound by Him, the Mighty One, the Son of God.

23 In the conflict against the powers of darkness there is no room for neutrality. He does not believe in Christ and follow Him, who does not along with Him oppose the powers of Satan; he is against Him and therefore a collaborator with Satan. Those who are not co-operating with Jesus to gather people into the kingdom of God are engaged in scattering souls and thus letting them become the prey of the Evil One. And how frightfully did the rejection of Jesus by the Jewish leaders bring about the fulfilment of these words with regard to the Jewish people! Within one generation from their final rejection of the Saviour the Jews of Palestine were completely overwhelmed by the Roman forces, and ever since then, until our own generation, the Jews have continued to be scattered over the world without their own national home, and through all these centuries the vast majority of them have constantly been the prey of the powers of darkness.

24-6 Here the Lord uses the simile of a person from whom the demon has been cast out but who has not let the Spirit of God take possession of his vacated heart—in other words, one who desires to remain neutral. Such neutrality is, however, impossible—the human heart is inhabited either by Christ or by Satan, and cannot remain empty. The result is that, when the man does not set his life open to the Spirit of God, he practically invites the exorcised spirit to come back. Now he is more helpless under the sway of the Evil One, so that the unclean spirit goes to fetch seven other demons as well, more wicked than himself, to dwell in their victim. And thus the state of that foolish person is worse than ever before.

330

From the context it is clear that the Saviour by means of this figure gives an earnest warning to the Jewish people. Through being preached to under the Old Covenant, and also especially under John the Baptist's baptism of repentance and through Jesus' purifying influence during the time that He spent among them, many members of the Jewish nation had been practically freed from the presence of demoniacal powers. Now, while He is still with them, they stand before the inescapable choice of believing in Him and letting Him enter completely into their national life, in order permanently to free them from evil, or of becoming the prey of the entry of Satan, thus to become more subject to his domination than ever before. We know, alas, the wretched choice that the majority of the people made, and how bad, in the sequel, their " last state " truly was.

This simile also refers to all other persons or nations who receive the opportunity of accepting Him in faith and who, instead of availing themselves of the opportunity, try to remain neutral and thus fall into the power of the Evil One.

27, 28 Struck by the power and earnestness of Jesus' word, a woman from among the multitude cries out in a typically oriental manner to give expression to her admiration of Him. In her eyes He is so wonderful that she beatifies His mother. The Lord does not criticise her beatification, but in His answer points out that there is something far more important than to be His mother— something within the reach of all, to be instructed by Him and to be obedient to the word of God preached by Him. Spiritual relationship to Him is of much greater importance than natural relationship.

This portion emphasises the impossibility of remaining neutral in the conflict of the centuries—the conflict between Christ's divine kingdom of light and love and the Satanic kingdom of darkness and death. Every person is fighting either on the one or on the other side. No one is merely an onlooker. He who is not definitely on the side of Christ is on the side of Satan—however beautiful or good the outward appearance of such a person's life may be. Every person is inhabited or controlled either by the Spirit of God or by the powers of darkness. God be thanked that Jesus has broken the powers of Satan, so that those who look to Him in faith are liberated from the influences of darkness.

[1] In these verses with their parallels in Matthew xii. 22–32 and Mark iii. 20–30 we have an interesting example of how the evangelists

supplement and explain one another. The sequence of events is, however, not the same in all three. None of them, of course, professes to report all the stories in exact chronological sequence, but each chose and arranged his material to fit his specific scheme and viewpoint.

[2] Styled thus, because he makes his victim dumb.

[3] Matthew xii. 24 says they were Pharisees.

[4] *Βεελζεβούλ* is used in the New Testament as a name for Satan. In Mishnaic Hebrew *Ba'al Zĕbūl* would have the meaning " Lord of the house " (*zĕbūl* meaning generally " residence " and more specifically the earthly or heavenly temple). This etymology thus throws light on the following references to the divided house (verse 17) and to the strong man armed guarding his " court " (verse 21), and also on the words of Matthew x. 25, " If they have called the master of the house Beelzebul . . ." The original sense of *Ba'al Zĕbūl*, however, is " Lord of the high place "; it is found in this sense as the name of a Canaanite deity in the Ras Shamra tablets (c. 1400 B.C.); this deity appears in 2 Kings i. 2 ff., where, however, his name is transformed by an ironical word-play into *Ba'al Zĕbūb*, " Lord of flies ". (Cf., further, Strack-Billerbeck and Zahn at Matt. x. 25.)

[5] They want to test Jesus, and also to tempt Him to use His divine power, not for the salvation of people in need or as a form of self-revelation in accordance with the will of the Father, but for outward show and self-exaltation. " The demand for a mere wonder to compel conviction was a renewal of the third temptation " (Plummer, *in loc.*).

[6] So they did not venture to utter their accusations openly before Him. Greydanus (*in loc.*), however, is of the opinion that Jesus did hear their words, and so by *τὰ διανοήματα* the " intentions " behind the words are referred to.

[7] The correct reading here is *καὶ οἶκος ἐπὶ οἶκον πίπτει* (" and house falls upon house "). When a kingdom is internally divided and thus comes to a fall, the separate houses (families and households), too, come into conflict with one another in the mutual struggle, and so go to ruin. The simile here refers to the kingdom of Satan, which, as it were, consists of different groupings of demons together constituting one kingdom.

[8] The corresponding passage in Matthew (xii. 28) has the synonymous phrase *ἐν πνεύματι θεοῦ*, which explains the metaphor " finger of God ". The expression " finger of God " in the Old Testament (Exod. viii. 19; Ps. viii. 3) denotes His power. Jesus cast out demons by the power of God; in other words, by His Spirit.

[9] *ἡ βασιλεία τοῦ θεοῦ*—cf. notes at iv. 43, vi. 20, ix. 2, etc. In Jesus Himself the kingly dominion of God came. " The presence of the Christ is the presence of the rule of heaven " (Schlatter, *in loc.*).

[10] *ἔφθασεν*. " In late Greek, *φθάνω*, followed by a preposition, commonly loses all notion of priority or surprise, and simply means ' arrive at ', ' attain to ' " (Plummer, *in loc.*). The wording here " expresses in the most vivid and forcible way the fact that the kingdom of God has actually arrived ", says C. H. Dodd, adding that Professor

Millar Burrows of Yale has pointed out that the words here used sound like an echo of Daniel vii. 22 in Theodotion's Greek translation (" the appointed time came and the saints received the kingdom "), where φθάνω also is used (*Parables of the Kingdom* [1935], p. 43).

[11] Satan is meant. With the fall of man, Satan, who has no actual right to rule mankind, had the world of human beings under his power to such a fearful extent, under the permissive will of God.

[12] Jesus here means Himself.

[13] τὰ σκῦλα does not refer merely to Satan's armour, but to all his possessions—i.e. also to his influence and sway over human souls. Only at the second coming of Christ will the deprivation of all his possessions be finally settled. However, in principle he has already been defeated.

[14] In ix. 50 the same truth, only viewed from the other side, is conveyed. Cf. our notes there.

[15] Even purely psychological considerations render it imperative that, when a person has passed through a crisis which has contributed to his renunciation of former sins and evil practices in his life, he must immediately in place thereof let his life be filled with what is beautiful and noble, otherwise the old sins and evils will return in renewed virulence. One's inner life cannot remain " vacant ". There cannot be a vacuum in man's soul.

[16] There is no reason to agree with several other expositors in presenting the woman in an unfavourable light. " Such beatification was common among the Jews at that time " (Greydanus, *in loc.*).

THE SIGN OF JONAH
(Cf. Matt. xii. 38–42)

xi. 29–32

29 And when the multitudes were gathering together unto him, he began to say, This generation is an evil generation: it seeketh after a sign; and there shall no sign be given[1] to it
30 but the sign of Jonah.[2] For even as Jonah became a sign unto the Ninevites, so shall also the Son of man be to this
31 generation. The queen of the south shall rise up in the judgement with the men of this generation, and shall condemn[3] them: for she came from the ends of the earth to hear the wisdom of Solomon; and behold, a greater than Solomon
32 is here. The men of Nineveh shall stand up in the judgement with this generation, and shall condemn it: for they repented at the preaching of Jonah; and behold, a greater than Jonah is here.

In verses 17–26 the Saviour replied to the accusation reported in verse 15. He now replies to the request of verse 16.

29, 30 After the healing of the possessed person (verse 14) and during the subsequent discussions (verses 15–28) the multitudes continued to gather in order to see the healed person and to listen to the conversations. In the hearing of the assembled multitude Jesus declares frankly that the Jewish generation of that time was spiritually corrupt and that for this reason (notwithstanding the clear and glorious revelations of Himself in His Messianic power and divinity) they still demanded an extraordinary, heavenly sign by which He is, as it were, to prove conclusively that He is indeed the Messiah. The Saviour replies that no sign will be given them such as they are seeking in their unbelief but " the sign of Jonah ", i.e. " a sign like that of Jonah ". This sign *will* be given, says the Lord. This, therefore, refers to the fact of His resurrection, as Matthew xii. 40 makes explicit. Jonah was a sign to the Ninevites, because he appeared there as one sent by God after having been miraculously saved from the great fish (as it were raised from the dead) as a proof that he was really sent by God. So also Jesus will by His resurrection prove conclusively that He has been sent by God as the Christ, the promised Redeemer.

334

31 The queen of the south (1 Kings x) came from the uttermost ends of the world as known at that time, and spared no trouble or expense in order to listen to the wisdom of Solomon given to him by God, and she believed the report she had heard of him. But most of the Jews who saw Jesus, who is immeasurably greater than Solomon, in spite of all their privileges did not listen to Him with the desire for salvation, but rejected Him in their unbelief. So the queen of the south will on the day of judgment justly condemn them as people who neglected and abused such incomparable opportunities.

32 So also those Ninevites who turned to God through the preaching of an ordinary person like Jonah will condemn the Jews who had the opportunity of being saved by the divine Envoy and Messiah, Christ Himself, but hardened themselves in unbelief.

We also have, through God's word, the glorious opportunity of seeing and hearing Him who is greater than Solomon and Jonah, and of truly turning to God. So there rests also upon us the great responsibility of making the right and full use of the privilege. Otherwise we also shall be justly condemned on the day of judgment by the believing queen of the south and by the repentant Ninevites.

---

[1] δοθήσεται, future tense: the sign will yet be given. The reference is, therefore, not to Jesus' preaching, but only to His resurrection.

[2] τὸ σημεῖον 'Ιωνᾶ. " The Lord does not state here that Jonah's preaching was a sign and that His own preaching will be a sign, but Jonah himself and his experiences were the sign " (Greydanus, *in loc.*).

For the various and divergent critical opinions in connection with the " sign of Jonah " cf. Creed (*in loc.*).

Plummer is right in stating: " Some have interpreted σημεῖον οὐ δοθήσεται as meaning either that Jesus wrought no miracles or that He refused to use them as credentials of His divine mission. It is sufficient to point to verse 20, where Jesus appeals to His healing of a dumb and blind demoniac as proof that He is bringing the kingdom of God to them. The demand for a sign and the refusal to give it are no evidence as to Christ's working miracles and employing them as credentials " (*in loc.*). The Jews held themselves blind to the deep meaning of the Saviour's divine, miracle-working action, and demanded from hypocritical motives that He should give a direct heavenly sign (such as a voice from heaven or a pillar of fire) so as to prove incontrovertibly that He is the Messiah. It goes without saying that the Saviour refused to accede to their request. But, the Lord declares, there will, nevertheless, be given them an indisputable sign— His death and resurrection.

[3] κατακρίνω means " by one's good example to render another's wickedness the more evident and censurable " (Grimm-Thayer, *Greek Lexicon of the New Testament*).

THE LIGHT OF THE BODY

(Cf. Matt. v. 15, vi. 22; Luke viii. 16)

xi. 33-6

33 No man, when he hath lighted a lamp, putteth it in a
cellar, neither under the bushel, but on the stand, that they
34 which enter in may see the light.[1] The lamp of thy body is
thine eye: when thine eye is single, thy whole body also is
full of light; but when it is evil, thy body also is full of dark-
35 ness. Look therefore whether the light that is in thee be not
36 darkness.[2] If therefore thy whole body be full of light,[3] having
no part dark, it shall be wholly full of light, as when the lamp
with its bright shining doth give thee light.

Through the similes of candle and light which the Saviour used
on several occasions in His preaching He here teaches that the
fundamental reason why the Jews demand a sign is that their
spiritual vision is so obscured through their unbelief and obduracy
that they do not see the clear, bright light shed abroad by Him in
and through His self-revelation.

33 Just as no normal person will light a lamp and then cover
it up so that it can shed no light, just so Jesus' refusal to give the
Jews the sign asked for does not mean that He wishes to hide the
light of His self-revelation, the light of the Gospel. On the contrary, He causes the light to be spread in full glory through His
words and works, and especially with His resurrection and
transfiguration the light will radiate strongly. The reason why the
hostile, unbelieving Jews still live in darkness and do not see and
accept Him as the Messiah is not to be attributed to a concealment
of the light of His revelation of salvation, but is (as is taught in
the subsequent verses) to be imputed to the wickedness of their
own hearts.

34, 35 The light of the body is the eye—the eye is the organ by
means of which the light is caught for the service of the body. A
lamp is not itself the light, but merely the instrument through
which the light is spread. So when there is anything wrong with
the lamp (e.g. a broken wick or a dirty and sooty chimney), it
cannot serve as a suitable instrument to provide light. So it is
also with the human eye which is the lamp of the body. When the

eye is sound and right and light is shining, the eye enables you to make full use of the light—you can see where you are, how to walk and how to do your work. But when there is something wrong with your eye you cannot make use of the light even when you are irradiated by the brightest light. Your whole body is then, as it were, wrapped in darkness, for you cannot see where to put your feet in order to walk, where to take hold with your hands to perform your work, and so forth. So, for all practical purposes, when your eyes are " wrong " you are in utter darkness.

In this simile the Saviour refers to the life of man. When a man's inner attitude or disposition is pure and right towards God, then the light of the Gospel of Christ, of the salvation revealed through Jesus, shines brightly in his heart and life—he is then walking in the light and sees Christ as his Lord and Redeemer. The light of Christ is constantly shining, but whether people are going to experience its blessed influence and workings of salvation or not all depends on their inner disposition and their attitude towards Jesus. Therefore the Lord utters a warning in verse 35 that everyone must take heed that the light in him be not darkness, i.e. each one must make sure that his inward attitude is not wrong, for in that case it hinders the light of Christ from shining into his life with beneficial results, and the light of the Gospel, in consequence, brings greater darkness into his heart. For he who refuses to accept in faith the revelation of God's salvation in Christ becomes more and more hardened and darkened spiritually. No one can, without injury to his own soul, attempt to withhold the light of the Gospel from his heart. Greydanus gives the meaning of this warning of Jesus in the following striking words: " See whether your inner nature is such that the light of the Gospel that shines upon you, also at the same time really sanctifies and renews you inwardly, kindles true love in you towards God and His Christ and His word and service and people, or whether in spite of all, there is still spiritual darkness with you, and sin and wrongdoing still prevail in your case. In the latter instance your eye is evidently wicked, the light in you is darkness, and an inward change must come to you—repentance, sanctification, renewal—so that the light of the Gospel may be shed in your heart for purification and salvation " (in loc.).

36 By means of this simile the Lord teaches that when a man takes heed that his whole person—desires, intellect, feeling and will—is illuminated and controlled by Him, he will indeed be spiritually illuminated and able to see. Then he will be just like a person with sound eyes in a room lighted by a good lamp so that he can see everything and know how and where to go, for he will

338

be able to see spiritual things in their proper relations and will know how to act and how to direct his life. If the Jews, to whom the Lord addressed these words, had seen to it that they were thus spiritually enlightened, they would not still have asked for a heavenly sign, but would have recognised Him to be indeed the Christ, and so would have believed in Him and known how to act and live.

If there is darkness in our spiritual life, this is never the fault of the light of the Gospel—for this light shines in full glory and power. It is man's wrong inner nature—unbelief, worldly-mindedness and other sins—that prevents the light of Christ from irradiating and renewing his life. What a tragedy that so many are struggling in darkness while the Gospel light is there all the time to make everything in their life bright and beautiful! As soon as man opens his life to Christ in faith His glorious light streams in.

[1] The simile here used by Jesus also occurs in Matthew v. 15 and Luke viii. 16. But there it refers to the responsibility of the disciples to spread the light of the Gospel in the world. Here, however, it refers to the fact that He Himself does not hide this light, but causes it to radiate to the full.

The view of many critics, that this simile, because it also occurs in other places, is a proof that Matthew or Luke or both are mistaken, is devoid of all foundation. Why could not the Lord have used the same figure more than once, especially in different connections? " Anyone who is not a captive to the unfounded idea that Jesus, in contrast to other great teachers, expressed Himself in proverbial sayings (whether He found them already in existence or coined them Himself) on one occasion only and not ten or twenty times, does not find himself confronted with the question whether Luke has given the proverbial saying its true historical setting here or at viii. 16. It is as appropriate here as in the earlier setting, and the variation of the expression in the passage lying before us is to be explained from what has gone before in this place only " (Zahn, in loc.).

[2] " The Lord says here: Take care now lest your faculty of perception has become so dark that you have no power to recognise the truth revealed in Christ " (C. F. Keil, quoted by Greydanus, in loc.).

[3] " Complete illumination is illumination indeed, and those who possess it have no need of a sign from heaven in order to recognise the truth " (Plummer, in loc.).

JESUS REBUKES THE SCRIBES AND THE PHARISEES

(Cf. Matt. xxiii. 1–39)

xi. 37–54

37 Now as he spake,[1] a Pharisee asketh him to dine[2] with
38 him: and he went in, and sat down to meat. And when the
Pharisee saw it, he marvelled[3] that he had not first washed[4]
39 before dinner. And the Lord said unto him, Now do ye
Pharisees cleanse the outside of the cup and of the platter;
but your inward part[5] is full of extortion and wickedness.
40 Ye foolish ones,[6] did not he that made the outside make the
41 inside also? Howbeit give for alms[7] those things which are
within; and behold, all things are clean unto you.

42 But woe unto you[8] Pharisees! for ye tithe mint and rue and
every herb, and pass over judgement[9] and the love of God:
but these ought ye to have done, and not to leave the other
43 undone.[10] Woe unto you Pharisees! for ye love the chief
seats[11] in the synagogues, and the salutations in the market-
44 places. Woe unto you! for ye are as the tombs[12] which
appear not, and the men that walk over *them* know it not.

45 And one of the lawyers answering saith unto him, Master,
46 in saying this thou reproachest us also. And he said, Woe
unto you lawyers also! for ye lade men with burdens
grievous to be borne, and ye yourselves touch not the
47 burdens with one of your fingers. Woe unto you! for ye build
the tombs of the prophets, and your fathers[13] killed them.
48 So ye are witnesses and consent[14] unto the works of your
49 fathers: for they killed them, and ye build *their tombs*. Therefore also said the wisdom of God,[15] I will send unto them
prophets and apostles;[16] and *some* of them they shall kill and
50 persecute; that the blood of all the prophets, which was
shed from the foundation of the world, may be required of
51 this generation; from the blood of Abel unto the blood of
Zachariah,[17] who perished between the altar and the sanctuary: yea, I say unto you, it shall be required of this
52 generation.[18] Woe unto you lawyers! for ye took away the
key of knowledge: ye entered not in yourselves, and them that
were entering in ye hindered.

53 And when he was come out from thence, the scribes and
the Pharisees began to press upon *him* vehemently,[19] and to
54 provoke him to speak of many things; laying wait for him,
to catch something out of his mouth.

340

In verses 14–28 we saw how the Pharisees simply would not believe in Christ and how in the wickedness of their hearts they uttered even the most blasphemous accusations against Him. Notwithstanding the unambiguous manner in which the Saviour had revealed Himself as the promised Messiah in His words and deeds, they hardened themselves in their unbelief. The clash between Jesus and the Pharisees begins to grow more and more violent.

37, 38 After the Saviour had spoken about the sign of Jonah and the light of the body, a Pharisee, one who was probably not yet openly hostile towards Jesus, invited Him to dine with him. Possibly he desired to become better acquainted with the Master and did not deliberately try to lead Him into a trap, for it is here stated that he *marvelled* when he saw that Jesus did not first perform the ceremonial ablutions before the meal.

39 The Saviour, who knew the inner disposition of his host and also that he, like the vast majority of his fellow-Pharisees, paid too much attention to conventional outward formalities, on purpose omitted to perform the ceremonial purifications on this occasion. Thus the opportunity was created to point out clearly to the Pharisees (his host and others who were also there) the folly of letting religion degenerate into a dead formalism. They are so punctilious in the performance of their ceremonial ablutions (many of which were prescribed by the tradition of scribes and other Jewish religious leaders and had not been commanded by God) that they even clean the outside of their cups and platters (" to clean " in these verses does not mean " to wash for the sake of cleanliness " but " to clean in a ceremonial sense "). In contrast therewith, however, their inner life is foul and tainted with all kinds of sin.

40 God is not satisfied with outward forms of religion. He has not only ordered man's material existence but has also created his inner life and soul. He is therefore the rightful Lord of man's spiritual life, and for this reason man must serve Him in an inward and spiritual manner through purity of heart, devotion, love and holiness.

41 Instead of concentrating all attention upon the outward ceremonial cleansing of cups and platters and other articles of use, they should rather exercise true love, and share their possessions with other people who need them. The simile in the first place refers to the distribution of the contents of cups or plates, but also means that all possessions of a person should be placed at the disposal of God in true charitable service for our fellow-men.

COMMENTARY ON THE GOSPEL OF LUKE

When a man's inner life is so purified that he acts in this manner, he will be " clean ", together with everything he possesses—he will stand in the right relationship to God without all kinds of ceremonial purifications.

42 With deep earnestness, so that they may be impressed and repent, the Lord calls attention to another example of how the Pharisees have fallen into a degenerate form of religion. While they are amazingly particular in the giving of their tithes, they neglect the observance of true justice and righteousness towards their fellow-men and of true love towards God. Their religion has become merely a matter of outward ceremony instead of a matter of the heart and of practical application of genuine love towards God and their fellow-men. Since Jesus' work of redemption was at that time not yet completed and the rigid demands of the Old Covenant were still in force, they were right to be faithful in the giving of tithes (as expressly commanded in the Old Testament, unlike subsequent man-made laws like the cleaning of plates and cups), but they must not let their religion become a matter of rigidly orthodox conduct through neglect of inner piety.

43 Their life is further to be condemned because their motives are not upright—too often they are zealous as religious leaders, not for the sake of God's honour but for the sake of their own.

44 According to Numbers xix. 16 everyone who touches a grave in the open is for seven days ceremonially unclean. For this reason the Jews as far as possible tried to mark all graves clearly by whitewashing them. Now Jesus says that the Pharisees are like graves not clearly marked; and just as people unconsciously walk over such graves and thus become ceremonially unclean, the Jews without realising it become unclean in their imitation of the Pharisees through the pernicious influence of those members of the party who in their hypocrisy profess to be the pious ones in Israel while in reality they are spiritually unclean.

45 One of the doctors of the law, who probably considered the Pharisees culpable in certain respects, feels that Jesus' words that were addressed to the Pharisees in reality also refer to him and his fellow-lawyers, and so he objects to this.

46 His objection induces the Lord also to draw attention in holy earnestness to sins of which the lawyers are specially guilty. Through all their additions (on the ground of human traditions) to the original Law of God, they made the religious life of the Jews unbearably difficult, even when (as in the case of some of their interpretations of the Sabbath law) their intention was to adapt the law to changing conditions. The lawyers themselves, however,

" probably knew all manner of theories and handy methods of escaping from the fulfilment of the commandments while keeping up the appearance of executing them. The Lord, who knew the Jewish manner of living, including the practice of the scribes, reproaches them with this without their apparently being able to answer the charge " (Greydanus, *in loc.*).

47, 48 With a good deal of outward homage they build and maintain the graves of the prophets murdered by their fathers. In reality, however, they are typical children of their fathers, filled with the same hate against the envoys of God and even against Christ—the One concerning whom the prophets had prophesied. In their real nature they are, therefore, murderers of prophets just like their fathers; and for that reason, although they pay outward homage, the building of the prophets' monuments simply serves to draw attention to the fact that they are children (in every sense of the word) of the forefathers who murdered the envoys of God. In reality they approve of the murder of the prophets and continue to proceed with the same conduct in their attitude towards Christ.

49-51 Because the Jewish people and its leaders are always thus disposed, says Jesus, God in His wisdom decided, after they had once more rejected His envoys (John the Baptist, the Saviour, and later on the apostles and the first Christians) and had killed some of them, to execute the final judgment on the generation responsible for the final rejection of these messengers. The Jews of former times who were responsible for the murder of prophets and men of God were verily guilty and paid dearly for their misdeeds (through exile, national disasters, etc.). But the Jewish generation that lived in the time of Jesus and of the establishment of the Christian church were guilty in an absolute sense because they rejected even the Son of God and caused Him to be crucified and afterwards persecuted His followers to the utmost during the years preceding the Jewish-Roman war. In this war, which began within a generation from the time of Jesus' crucifixion (A.D. 66–70) the words of the Saviour were fulfilled in an appalling manner. Never before did the judgment of God visit a nation as it did the Jews of Palestine—and particularly of Jerusalem—during those years. Every possible calamity—fratricide, plague, famine, the Roman sword—came upon them. The erstwhile chosen people were displaced because they refused to believe in Christ, and they paid a heavy penalty for their murder of apostles and prophets, but especially for the murder of the Messiah.

52 The lawyers removed the key that unlocks the way to acquiring true knowledge of the divine plan of salvation. They did so by wrong exegesis and by adding a host of rigid provisions by which the Word of God had been rendered powerless. In their spiritual degeneracy they not only themselves remained blind to the fact that the Old Testament prophecies of the coming Redeemer were fulfilled in Jesus, but as a result of their corrupt influence on the masses they also prevented the vast majority of the Jews from arriving at a true knowledge of the divine salvation revealed in Jesus. They, the lawyers and scribes, were the proper persons to show the people that Christ was truly the One indicated by the Old Testament Scriptures as the Redeemer. But alas, in their unbelief they kept their hearts and intellects shut and also deterred the rest from seeing the promised Redeemer in Jesus.

53, 54 Enraged at the direct words of the Saviour, the scribes and Pharisees put all kinds of ensnaring questions to Him, thereby trying to entice words from His mouth to use as evidence against Him, for they were now determined to accomplish His downfall.

The Pharisees and scribes were the acknowledged religious leaders of the Jewish people when the Saviour was on earth. On them rested the greatest responsibility of leading the people to Christ, the promised Redeemer. But alas, they were the ones who hardened themselves and remained spiritually dead, and consequently misled the masses and prevented them from finding redemption in Jesus. What a serious warning to all spiritual leaders of to-day is to be found in the history of those Jewish spiritual leaders and in the Master's rebuke addressed to them!

---

[1] ἐν δὲ τῷ λαλῆσαι, aorist infinitive: the action is completed: " when He had finished speaking ".

[2] The ἄριστον was the second meal of the day (about noon). The chief meal (the δεῖπνον) was held at about 4 p.m.

[3] " This man's wonder is evidence that his invitation was not a plot to obtain evidence against Jesus: he was not expecting any transgression " (Plummer, *in loc.*).

[4] Here the reference is to the ceremonial purifications, i.e. to manmade institutions (Matt. xv. 2).

[5] The *contents* are meant here (cf. Strack-Billerbeck, *in loc.*).

[6] Klostermann (*in loc.*) and a few others wrongly take this verse as a statement and not as a question.

[7] " Jesus estimates alms as an outward indication of a complete inward change of mind; in so far as they show that, instead of the former covetousness and malice, mercy and goodness have entered, the inference can be drawn from them: See, you are wholly clean! "

344

(cf. Strack-Billerbeck at Matt. xxiii. 26). Plummer remarks on this verse: " We are told that this is a peculiarly Ebionitic touch. But it is very good Christianity! " (*in loc.*).

Wellhausen, comparing the difficult Greek here (τὰ ἐνόντα δότε ἐλεημοσύνην) with καθάρισον πρῶτον τὸ ἐντός in Matthew xxiii. 26, suggested that καθάρισον represents Aramaic imperative singular *dakki*, but that Luke, finding in his source the imperative plural *dakkau* (" cleanse ye "), misread it as *zakkau* (" give alms ") (*Einleitung in die drei ersten Evangelien* [1905], p. 36). C. F. Burney, however, has shown that in Aramaic and Mishnaic Hebrew *zakke* means not only " to give alms " but also " to cleanse ", although the normal verb for the latter is *dakke* (*Aramaic Origin of the Fourth Gospel* [1922], p. 9).

[8] οὐαί " is an expression not merely of anger but of pity. . . . Its usual translation as a mere curse has led to misunderstanding of Jesus' attitude towards the Pharisees. His criticism of them was never merely destructive; if He denounced and ridiculed them, it was because He longed to rouse them to see their faults " (Luce, *in loc.*). Translate: " Alas for you Pharisees! "

[9] τὴν κρίσιν—Hebraistic, not passing of judgment or administration of justice, but " righteous action, dealing justly with all and especially with needy ones ".

[10] These words should not be taken as though they laid down a legal obligation also for Christian believers. When Jesus uttered these words the New Covenant had not yet been initiated by His sacrificial death. With the advent of the New Covenant the old rigid and ceremonial forms of religion also fall away. It is the vocation of the Christian not to give his tithes as a matter of rigid requirement but to consecrate himself and all his possessions to the service of his Lord. In most cases the result should be that believers should give at least one-tenth of their income for the definite service of the Lord. If the pious men and women of old under the Old Covenant, before they had learned to know the riches of God's love in Jesus as we have had the opportunity of knowing them, gladly gave their tithes, how can we give less seeing that we enjoy so many more spiritual privileges?

[11] " This was a semicircular bench round the ark, and facing the congregation " (Plummer, *in loc.*).

[12] " While they allow their people to admire them as living patterns of piety, they are inwardly full of mouldering remains of a piety which was formerly living in Israel, and therefore they should rather be avoided than honoured by their fellow-countrymen, for whom every contact with a corpse or a grave ranks as more or less defiling " (Zahn, *in loc.*).

[13] " ' Father ' according to Semitic use may mean either ' ancestor ' or ' pattern ', and this saying plays on the double meaning with savage irony " (Easton, *in loc.*).

[14] The Saviour does not condemn the building of the graves, but Zahn rightly points out that when " the building of costly monuments over the graves of the murdered prophets is carried out by people who

disregard or persecute the prophets whom God Himself has sent to them, and when that is regarded as a way of compounding for their failure to take to heart the word of God brought to them by the prophets of olden time and of their own present age, that is no honouring but a mockery of the prophets, for it is an active expression of the same ungodly attitude which brought the prophets to their death" (*in loc.*).

¹⁵ A few scholars, like Bultmann, regard these words, which occur nowhere in the Old Testament, as a quotation from an apocryphal writing. But, as Creed agrees, " this does not seem likely " (*in loc.*). " Jesus here speaks with confident knowledge of the divine counsels " (Plummer, *in loc.*). Comparison with the parallel passage in Matthew (xxiii. 34), which runs, " Therefore, behold, *I* send unto you prophets . . .", suggests that Jesus is here speaking as the very Wisdom of God. So Tatian in his *Diatessaron* or Gospel Harmony (c. A.D. 170) represents Jesus as saying (in a conflation of the two passages): " Behold! I, the Wisdom of God, send unto you . . ." (See J. R. Harris, *Origin of Prologue to St. John's Gospel* [1917], pp. 3 f., 57 ff.)

¹⁶ " Prophets and Apostles ". " Taken together, these words signify: speakers of God's word sent by Him. Thus both words may indicate the same persons, taken in different respects: as bringing God's word, and as sent for that purpose. In this manner these two words may indicate the New Testament divine messengers of that time: the apostles and prophets, as well as John the Baptist and the Lord Jesus Himself " (Greydanus, *in loc.*).

¹⁷ In the Jewish canon of the Old Testament the books of Chronicles came last. As the death of the prophet Zechariah is described in 2 Chronicles xxiv. 21 and no other murder of prophets is afterwards described in 2 Chronicles, Jesus therefore means all cases of murder of prophets described in the Old Testament. Cf. Creed (*in loc.*) for a refutation of the view of Wellhausen and others that another Zachariah is meant.

¹⁸ ἀπὸ τῆς γενεᾶς ταύτης. Apart from the reason mentioned in the running commentary why that generation in particular should pay the debt accumulated through the national history, we have to remember in addition that with the appearance of Jesus the preparatory significance of the Jewish people has been brought to a close. " With it the Jewish people had lost the reason for its existence, and need no longer be spared for the sake of the coming of Christ and for the completion of His work of expiation. The Christ of God had come. Presently He would be done to death, but then also again glorified. And thus the final reckoning of the blood-guiltiness made by the Jewish people could not touch God's prophets and messengers " (Greydanus, *in loc.*).

¹⁹ The original reading here is κἀκεῖθεν ἐξελθόντος αὐτοῦ ἤρξαντο οἱ γραμματεῖς καὶ οἱ Φαρισαῖοι δεινῶς ἐνέχειν, "and when He departed from there [i.e., the house of the Pharisee], the scribes and the Pharisees began to press sore upon Him [*or* to provoke Him sorely]."

This intransitive use of ἐνέχω is found also in Mark vi. 19 (where possibly we should understand χόλον, " grudge ", as the object of ἐνεῖχεν) and in the LXX at Genesis xlix. 23 (" The archers pressed sore upon him ").

The γραμματεῖς (scribes) are practically the same as the νομικοί (lawyers)—people who study and explain the Old Testament and especially the Law (cf. digression on " scribes " after xv. 17–26).

THE LEAVEN OF THE PHARISEES AND WHO IS TO BE FEARED

xii. 1-12

1 In the mean time,[1] when the many thousands of the multitude[2] were gathered together, insomuch that they trode one upon another, he began[3] to say unto his disciples first[4]
2 of all,[5] Beware ye of the leaven of the Pharisees, which is hypocrisy. But there is nothing covered up, that shall not
3 be revealed: and hid, that shall not be known. Wherefore whatsoever ye have said in the darkness shall be heard in the light; and what ye have spoken in the ear in the inner
4 chambers shall be proclaimed upon the housetops. And I say unto you my friends, Be not afraid of them which kill the
5 body, and after that have no more that they can do. But I will warn you whom ye shall fear: Fear him, which after he hath killed hath power to cast into hell;[6] yea, I say unto
6 you, Fear Him. Are not five sparrows sold for two farthings?
7 and not one of them is forgotten in the sight of God.[7] But the very hairs of your head are all numbered.[8] Fear not: ye
8 are of more value than many sparrows. And I say unto you, Every one who shall confess[9] me before men, him shall
9 the Son of man also confess before the angels of God: but he that denieth me in the presence of men shall be denied in the
10 presence of the angels of God. And every one who shall speak[10] a word against the Son of man,[11] it shall be forgiven him: but unto him that blasphemeth against the Holy
11 Spirit[12] it shall not be forgiven.[13] And when they bring you before the synagogues, and the rulers, and the authorities, be not anxious how or what ye shall answer, or what ye shall
12 say: for the Holy Spirit shall teach you in that very hour what ye ought to say.

While the Pharisees and scribes were busy outside the house of the Pharisee (xi. 37) asking Jesus all kinds of catch-questions, an exceptionally great multitude gathered there in much excitement. A spirit of hostility to Jesus probably prevailed among the major portion of the multitude owing to the influence of the enraged Pharisees and scribes. As a result, the Saviour in the long connected oration of verses 1-59 addresses Himself mostly to His disciples, although in the hearing of the multitude.

348

1 The Pharisees and scribes, on account of the tremendous thronging of the multitude, possibly ceased to put catch-questions to the Saviour. Now the Lord begins to speak and addresses His disciples. Before the whole multitude (Pharisees and scribes included) He warns His followers against the corrupt spirit of the Pharisees—the spirit of dissimulation and hypocrisy.

2, 3 Hypocrisy, especially in the field of religion, is not only an objectionable sin, but is, in addition, a vain attempt to hide the truth. Truth will always come to light (partly in this life, but completely at the Last Judgment). So it does not pay to play the hypocrite.

4, 5 The disciples should not, from fear of men, yield to the temptation of dissembling, for men can only kill their bodies (probably all the apostles except John afterwards died a martyr's death). But to God, who possesses all power for time and eternity and who will punish the evildoers, all real honour and reverence is due.

6, 7 The fear of the Lord should, however, not be a slavish fear, but should be combined with love for and faith in the heavenly Father who cares so faithfully for even the least of His creatures and especially for believers, and takes an interest in them even with regard to the most insignificant matters. Without fear of man, but with true and believing reverence for God as the All-preserver, the believer should reject all inclinations to hypocrisy.

8, 9 They must be specially on their guard against the hypocrisy of denying Jesus in word or deed, because those who deny Him, by refusing to acknowledge that He is the Messiah and that they are His followers, will at the Final Judgment also be denied by Him, through His disowning of any bond of true communion between them and Him. Those who proclaim Him as the Messiah and avow openly that they are His followers will, however, be openly acknowledged by Him as His followers before the Father and all the heavenly beings.

10 The disciples have to take courage to avow Him without fear of men, in the certainty that those who against their own conviction deliberately blaspheme against the Holy Ghost and persecute the faithful cannot escape the divine judgment.

Sins against Jesus in His state of humiliation will be forgiven, because the revelation of His divine glory whilst He is thus entering on the way of suffering as the lowly Son of Man is, as it were, held in abeyance. But after His ascension, when He will reveal the truth clearly through the Holy Ghost (in the Pentecostal miracle, in the preaching of His church, etc.), it will not be

349

forgiven to a man if he deliberately blasphemes against the Holy Ghost in the full light of His activity, e.g. by characterising His operations as the work of the devil.

11, 12 Again, disciples should not become unfaithful to Him and deny that they are His followers through fear of the persecutions which they may expect from hostile Jewish authorities. The Holy Ghost will enable them to defend themselves in the right way before their earthly judges and persecutors, and even if they should be unjustly condemned and killed they know that they are safe under God's protection (verses 4–7) and that Jesus will take action for their eternal welfare (verse 8).

Nothing is so injurious to a man's spiritual life as hypocrisy. And why should we play the hypocrite seeing that it does not profit us in any way to do so? But, above all, how could we dissemble whilst knowing that we are thereby being disloyal to our Master? There is no reason for dissembling, for in our heavenly Father who cares for us (verses 6, 7), in Jesus who intercedes for us (verse 8), and in the Spirit who instructs us (verse 12), we have everything we need to lead a sincere and fearless life in His service.

<hr/>

¹ ἐν οἷς, "under which circumstances". It indicates a close connection with the preceding occurrences.

² τῶν μυριάδων τοῦ ὄχλου, "the tens of thousands (or myriads) of the multitude": a hyperbolical description.

³ ἤρξατο "gives a solemn emphasis to what follows" (Plummer, *in loc.*).

⁴ "First" should probably be taken as the first word of Jesus' oration and not together with λέγειν. His words here will then read: "In the first place, above all, take heed. . . ." Sincerity in religion is a basic requirement, so the Saviour gives this urgent warning against hypocrisy.

⁵ Without any argument Creed states with regard to Jesus' words in this chapter: "We have here a group of discourses loosely put together, in a framework which may be ascribed to the Evangelist" (*in loc.*). Such a pronouncement is superficial. In the exposition of this chapter we particularly notice how closely the various parts of the oration are connected together—how logically the one pronouncement follows upon the other and how excellently it fits in with the historical circumstances described by Luke. Various portions of the oration do indeed also occur elsewhere in the Gospel narratives (e.g. in Matt. x. 26–33, xii. 32; Mark iii. 28 ff.), but, as Greydanus says (*in loc.*): "From this it does not follow that Luke joined together and linked up into one address words of the Lord spoken on different occasions. From Luke xii we receive no other impression but that the Lord spoke all these words on the same occasion." Obviously the Saviour used the same

or similar words on more than one occasion when addressing different groups of hearers. It is quite gratuitous to assume that He made certain pronouncements only once. It is commonly acknowledged that He practised pre-eminently the art of giving effective instruction; and surely one of the essential requirements of successful teaching is that truths should be repeated again and again—sometimes in the same form and sometimes illustrated from a different angle.

[6] γέεννav (" hell "), Graecised accusative from Ge-Hinnom (Valley of Hinnom) near Jerusalem where in former times children were sacrificed as burnt-offerings to the Canaanite god Molech. After Josiah (2 Kings xxiii. 10) had put an end to this pagan practice, all kinds of refuse and the corpses of criminals were thrown into this valley to be burned by a fire which presumably was constantly kept burning there, with the result that Gehenna was the symbolical name for the everlasting place of punishment of the lost (for ancient Jewish ideas about Gehenna cf. Strack-Billerbeck, vol. iv, 2, digression 31).

[7] God is the Great and the Omnipotent One, but also the One who cares for even the most insignificant ones. Nothing, however small, can exist without the maintaining power of the Creator, and even the most insignificant law of nature does not function without God's will to let it do so. God is transcendent and exalted above His creation; but at the same time immanent in the whole creation and in every particle of it. Only in the Bible is the exact balance maintained between the truth of God's transcendence and that of His immanence. All non-Christian religions overdo one or the other of these truths.

[8] Greydanus is right in stating: " There is indeed no hyperbole here, but pure reality, although God is at this point spoken of in a human manner, which should be understood θεοπρεπῶς, in a manner worthy of God. God pays an active attention even to what is most insignificant and His care takes notice of the smallest details " (in loc.).

[9] ὁμολογήσει ἐν ἐμοί—" they will make a confession in His case, and He will make a confession in theirs; their confession being that He is the Messiah, and His that they are His loyal disciples " (Plummer, in loc.). But ἐν is simply a literal rendering of the Aramaic idiom.

[10] ἐρεῖ λόγον, similarly εἴπῃ λόγον in Matthew xii. 32. But the parallel passage in Mark iii. 28 f. has the verb βλασφημεῖν. The underlying Aramaic may have been the phrase אֲמַר שְׁלָה ('ămar shēlāh), which occurs in Daniel iii. 29 and is rendered by βλασφημεῖν in LXX and εἰπεῖν βλασφημίαν by Theodotion's Greek version. (See T. W. Manson, Teaching of Jesus, p. 216.)

[11] Cf. our digression on " The Son of Man ", pp. 352 ff.

[12] The Holy Ghost does not appear in a visible form, as did the Son of God, who became man and " took the form of a slave ". No such visible form, which could conceivably serve as an excuse for disparagement in case of blasphemy, exists in the case of the Holy Ghost. Blasphemy against the Holy Ghost reveals hostility to what is unmistakably

divine and holy, and is therefore unpardonable. βλασφημήσαντι is the aorist participle, and thus does not denote a continuous action or a permanent attitude, but indicates that after this deed has once been done it is already finally decided. With regard to the *blasphemy against the Holy Ghost*, Dr. Impeta rightly states: " The sin here referred to by Jesus must consist in a conscious, wilful, intentional blasphemy of the clearly recognised revelation of God's grace in Christ through the Holy Ghost, a revelation which nevertheless out of hate and hostility is ascribed to the devil " (*Christ. Encycl.*, under " Heilige Geest "). Professor Bavinck has aptly described this as " a sin against the Gospel in its clearest revelation ", which consists " not in doubting or simply denying the truth, but in *a denial which goes against the conviction of the intellect, against the enlightenment of conscience, against the dictates of the heart; in a conscious, wilful and intentional imputation to the influence and working of Satan of that which is clearly recognised as God's work, i.e. in a definite blasphemy of the Holy Ghost* [our italics], in a wilful declaration that the Holy Ghost is the Spirit from the abyss, that truth is a lie, and that Christ is Satan himself. . . . For this reason the sin is unforgivable: although God's grace is not too small and too powerless for it, yet in the kingdom of sin there are laws and ordinances placed there by God and maintained by Him. And this law in the case of this particular sin is of such a nature that it excludes all repentance, cauterises the conscience, odurates and hardens the sinner once and for all, and in this way makes his sin unpardonable " (*Gereformeerde Dogmatiek*, 2nd ed., iii, p. 157). Using Platonic terminology, we may call it " the lie in the soul ".

[13] In Matthew xii. 31, 32 and Mark iii. 28 ff. we also read that Jesus spoke of the unpardonable sin. Accordingly He spoke of this serious matter on more than one occasion (as might have been expected). In Matthew xii. and Mark iii. an episode is related in which Jesus warns His enemies about blasphemy against the Holy Ghost. Here, however, in Luke xii the Saviour addresses His disciples, chiefly for their encouragement, by assuring them that the opponents who wilfully gainsay the workings of the Holy Ghost and blaspheme against Him will not go unpunished. So they must not allow themselves to be intimidated by hardened and wicked opponents of this type, for these already fall under God's judgment.

SPECIAL NOTE

THE SON OF MAN

In the Old Testament the expression " son of man " (Hebrew בֶּן אָדָם, *ben 'ādām*) usually denotes the insignificance and frailty of man in contrast with the greatness and omnipotence of God (e.g. in Job vii. 17, xxv. 6; Ps. viii. 5, cxliv. 3). The use of the phrase by Jesus to indicate Himself thus emphasises His real humanity, especially as

He used it particularly when referring to His sufferings and death (cf. Matt. viii. 20; Luke ix. 22, xviii. 31). In some contexts the phrase on His lips seems to be practically a periphrasis for the pronoun " I " (e.g. in Luke vii. 34).

But no adequate account of His use of the title can fail to emphasise its vital connection with Daniel vii. 13, where " one like unto a son of man " (Aramaic בַּר אֱנָשׁ *bar 'ĕnāsh*), coming with the clouds of heaven, approaches the Ancient of Days and receives universal and everlasting dominion. The crucial instance of our Lord's use of the title is the occasion when, before the Sanhedrin, He replied to the high priest's adjuration, " Art thou the Christ, the Son of the Blessed? " by saying, " I am: and ye shall see the Son of man sitting at the right hand of The Power [a reverent periphrasis for the Divine Name] and coming with the clouds of heaven " (Mark xiv. 61 f.). The reference here to Daniel vii. 13 is obvious, as also is the reference to the admittedly Messianic Psalm cx. His Messianic claim could not have been more uncompromisingly made; and it is plain that for Him the title " The Son of Man " was primarily one which denoted His Messianic dignity—one, moreover, which He habitually preferred to " Messiah " because of the political connotation which the latter bore in the popular mind of His day. " In three passages an appearance of the Son of Man which is still future to Mark and his readers is described (Mark viii. 38, xiii. 26, xiv. 62), but the ten other references to the Son of Man [in Mark] clearly imply that in his historical appearance Jesus was already the Son of Man. Moreover, the meaning which this title bears is not narrowly eschatological; it points to the heavenly, transcendent character of his person. His avowals of his right to forgive sins ' upon the earth ' and to exercise lordship over the sabbath spring from his consciousness of being the Son of Man (Mark ii. 10, 28). And the whole of the record of the final journey to Jerusalem is pervaded by the teaching, not that he was to become the Son of Man by his appearance on the clouds after an interlude of suffering, but that the necessity of his suffering was found in the conviction that he, the Son of Man, had come for this very purpose " (N.B. Stonehouse, *The Witness of Matthew and Mark to Christ* [1944], pp. 111 f.).

For further discussion of the subject, in addition to Dr. Stonehouse's able treatment in the above-mentioned book (pp. 110 ff., 237 ff.), see A. E. J. Rawlinson, *The New Testament Doctrine of the Christ*; R. Otto, *The Kingdom of God and the Son of Man*; T. W. Manson, *The Teaching of Jesus*; C. J. Cadoux, *The Historic Mission of Jesus*; and an important article on " The Background of the Term ' Son of Man ' " by J. Bowman in *The Expository Times*, 59 (1948), pp. 283 ff.

PARABLE OF THE RICH FOOL

13 And one out of the multitude said unto him, Master, bid
14 my brother divide the inheritance with me. But he said unto
15 him, Man,[1] who made me a judge or a divider over you? And
he said unto them, Take heed, and keep yourselves from all[2]
covetousness: for[3] a man's life[4] consisteth not in the abund-
16 ance of the things which he possesseth. And he spake a
parable unto them, saying, The ground of a certain rich
17 man brought forth plentifully:[5] and he reasoned within
himself, saying, What shall I do, because I have not where
18 to bestow my fruits? And he said, This will I do: I will pull
down my barns, and build greater; and there will I bestow
19 all my corn and my goods. And I will say to my soul, Soul,
thou hast much goods laid up for many years; take thine ease,
20 eat, drink, be merry. But God said unto him, Thou foolish
one, this night is thy soul[6] required of thee; and the things
21 which thou hast prepared,[7] whose shall they be? So is he that
layeth up treasure for himself, and is not rich toward God.

The Saviour had just been discussing the deepest and holiest
matters and was perhaps still in the act of doing so (verses 1–12)
when someone from among the multitude, without giving any
sign that he had paid any attention to Jesus' words, asked Him to
deal with a purely earthly affair. As a result of the question of
this materialistically-minded man, the Lord told the striking
parable of the rich fool.

13 Although the man had paid no attention to the deeply
spiritual words of Jesus and although he was selfish and worldly-
minded, he nevertheless acknowledges the Saviour as one with
authority and asks Him, not to investigate the matter, but to speak
to his brother (who was probably also present) to divide the
inheritance with him.

14 Because this man, on account of his own selfish, worldly
desires thrust himself forward while Jesus was busy with serious
matters, and because he (consciously or unconsciously) wanted to
tempt Him to enter a sphere that fell outside His calling, the
Saviour addresses him sharply and refuses his request. It is His

354

vocation to bring the revelation of God's salvation and not to act as judge between people in connection with merely worldly things.

15 The attitude and request of the man showed his character clearly. So the Saviour warns him and his brother (both being covetous—the one through refusing to divide the inheritance and the other through his feverish and selfish eagerness to have it divided), and also the whole multitude, against covetousness. For, as He points out, covetousness is folly—no man enjoys any happiness, rest for his soul, or peace, nor finds true life in the possession of even an abundance of earthly things. Man cannot live by bread alone.

16–20 In order to present a clear picture of the fatal folly of covetousness, the Saviour relates the parable of the rich fool who thought that he would find real happiness in earthly abundance, but who, on reaching the climax of his acquisition of wealth, was unexpectedly snatched away by death. He thought that he had collected a sufficient quantity of possessions and that he would henceforth enjoy life quietly by eating, drinking and being merry—i.e. by revelling in worldly and material pleasures. He considered that he had the full command over his life and over all his possessions and thus spoke about " *my* barns, *my* fruits, *my* goods, and *my* soul " (verses 18, 19). He did not regard his possessions as things *lent* to him by God's grace and to be used by him in the service of the Lord (for instance, in helping the needy). On the contrary, he considered that everything belonged exclusively to *him*, and that he had the full monopoly of it to use it for his own pleasure and enjoyments. But alas, when he had reached the zenith of self-satisfaction and absorption in material affairs God appeared and required his soul by means of death. And so it was suddenly proved that, notwithstanding all his wealth and self-satisfaction, he had no real say over his life and possessions— all his plans in connection with the enjoyment of his wealth collapsed at once, and his soul entered eternity without his being able to take with him even one particle of his riches. Poorer than the poorest beggar he had to leave this world.

21 Such is the fatal end of everyone who is spiritually dead while gathering earthly treasures and who does not primarily and above all (verse 37) take heed that he is rich in God, spiritually rich through living in close communion with Him and faithfully serving Him.

In this parable and these pronouncements the Saviour does not condemn the possession of worldly goods as such, but what He disapproves of is the covetous and carnal attitude with regard to earthly wealth, the trust in worldly things instead of in God, and

355

the fault of not regarding one's possessions gratefully as God's gracious gifts and using them in His service and according to His will to the glory of His name.

It is not only a terrible sin to make earthly riches and worldly pleasures the main purpose in life, but also a fatal act of folly, a deadly error.

¹ ἄνθρωπε. In the context here it is: " a severe form of address " (Plummer, *in loc.*), and it reminds the man of his insignificance and audacity.

² πάσης πλεονεξίας—all covetousness, covetousness in any form.

³ ὅτι οὐκ ἐν τῷ περισσεύειν τινί—" For not in being abundant to anyone ", i.e. " not in the fact that one possesses abundance of wealth "—ἡ ζωὴ αὐτοῦ ἐστιν ἐκ τῶν ὑπαρχόντων αὐτῷ—" is his life out of his goods." The meaning of this pronouncement is, therefore, that a man cannot secure or maintain his life by means of worldly possessions and abundant wealth—however rich a man may be, worldly possessions can never serve as a security for his life and can never make him the master of his own life. God retains the exclusive right over one's life and may require it whenever He so desires. Therefore this pronouncement refutes the delusion that specially wealthy possessions, striving after which is the essence of πλεονεξία guarantee to a man that he will preserve his life by means of those things which he calls his own " (Zahn, *in loc.*).

⁴ ζωή—" life " in the sense of *vita qua vivimus*, principle of life, the life by which we live. Thus Jesus teaches that " even mere existence cannot be secured by wealth " (Plummer, *in loc.*).

⁵ His wealth was not gathered by dishonest methods.

⁶ " The soul, life, man with everything that he is or possesses, are God's property which He may take back at any moment " (Greydanus, *in loc.*).

⁷ The Lord does not condemn progressiveness and thrift, but disapproves of the wrong use of earthly possessions.

THE CARES OF LIFE

(Cf. Matt. vi. 25–34)

xii. 22–34

22   And he said unto his disciples, Therefore[1] I say unto you,[2]
Be not anxious for *your* life, what ye shall eat; nor yet for
23 your body, what ye shall put on. For the life is more than
24 the food,[3] and the body than the raiment. Consider the
ravens,[4] that they sow not, neither reap; which have no
store-chamber nor barn; and God feedeth them: of how
25 much more value are ye than the birds! And which of you
26 by being anxious can add a cubit unto his stature?[5] If then
ye are not able to do even that which is least, why are ye
27 anxious concerning the rest? Consider the lilies, how they
grow: they toil not, neither do they spin; yet I say unto you,
Even Solomon in all his glory was not arrayed like one of
28 these. But if God doth so clothe the grass in the field, which
to-day is, and to-morrow is cast into the oven;[6] how much
29 more *shall he clothe* you, O ye of little faith? And seek not[7]
ye what ye shall eat, and what ye shall drink, neither be ye
30 of doubtful mind.[8] For all these things do the nations of the
world seek after:[9] but your Father[10] knoweth that ye have
31 need[11] of these things. Howbeit seek ye his kingdom, and
32 these things shall be added unto you. Fear not, little flock;
for it is your Father's good pleasure to give you the kingdom.
33 Sell that ye have,[12] and give[13] alms; make for yourselves
purses which wax not old, a treasure in the heavens that
faileth not, where no thief draweth near, neither moth
34 destroyeth. For where your treasure is, there will your
heart[14] be also.

After addressing the general multitude as a result of the question
of one of their number, Jesus now again turns to His disciples.
Nevertheless His warnings here, namely, that they should be free
from vexation about worldly things, are closely linked with His
previous warning against covetousness, because the best way to
combat covetousness and a feverish clinging to worldly goods is
the development of true faith in the fatherly care of God.

22 Man's life does not depend on the possession of earthly
goods, so the Saviour says that the disciples must not be anxious
and troubled as regards food and clothing.

23 God, who is the Creator and the Giver of man's life and body, will assuredly also care for the more insignificant things—food and clothing.

24 By what He provides in nature, God cares even for wild birds like ravens that receive no care from man and that are not themselves able to take precautions for the supply of food. How much more will God therefore provide for the disciples who are worth much more than the birds and who are gifted with intelligence and all manner of other gifts that enable them to take such precautions?

25, 26 To worry is utterly useless, for no man can accomplish even the slightest addition to his height or prolongation of his span of life by worrying; how much less can he then accomplish *great* things by this means? Therefore it is foolish to be troubled.

27, 28 Lilies do not toil, neither do they spin, but man can both toil and spin; the grass of the field has a brief existence, but man possesses an immortal soul. If God makes the very plants grow so wonderfully and endows them with such beauty, how much more will He care for the disciples, people to whom He has granted reason and intelligence and so many other gifts? Because God thus cares in His wisdom and omnipotence for the most insignificant things, He will most certainly also provide for His followers who trust in Him and give them what is best for them. And just as the flowers and grass of the field require days of sunshine as well as days of stormy weather to grow and develop, so His followers for whom He cares will be guided through darkness as well as sunshine, but everything will co-operate for the good of those who love Him.

29, 30 They should not make their chief aim or the passion of their lives the hoarding of material things. By this the Saviour does not in any way mean that they must be lazy and neglect their ordinary work and duties, but that they must not allow their hearts to become so attached to material things that their inner lives are controlled by these, and they are not to be vexed and anxious about these things. Everyone must perform his daily task, which God gives him, whole-heartedly and to the best of his ability, but the inner life of the believer must not be caught in the clutches of materialism and of anxiety with regard to worldly things.

People in general do make these things the main purpose of their lives, but He had already taught the disciples that the life of man in the deepest sense does not depend upon material things, therefore they must not follow the foolish example of the unbelievers. In addition, they have a glorious reason why they should not be vexed about worldly matters, in the fact that God, who is their Father, knows that they have need of food and clothing and other earthly things.

31 With regard to the material needs of the faithful, too, God will give them what they require—in the way that is most beneficial to them. But then they must love Him, or trust in Him and obey Him—it must be the main object and passion of their lives to seek, above all, the kingdom of heaven, to endeavour to serve God and to be guided and ruled by Him so that they may share in the benefits of His kingdom, in the blessings accomplished by His kingly sovereignty.

32 Although the faithful, especially as compared with the great nations of the world, are few in number and, as regards their own power, like a small flock of defenceless sheep, they should nevertheless have no fear, for their heavenly Father, because it is His good pleasure so to do, has given the kingdom to those who seek it. In principle they already possess it and share in its blessings; but at the end of the age they will receive it in fullness. The faithful who in this life are despised and persecuted by the world, will after the Second Coming live together with Him and rule to all eternity (Rev. v. 10, xxii. 5).

33 Because true life is not to be found in the selfish hoarding of earthly treasures and the real wealth of the faithful is in God they must inwardly be quite free from their worldly possessions and must regard and use these as gifts of God's love to them, to be consecrated by them to His service by bestowing them on the needy and on the promotion of the work of the Lord in general. When a man acts in this manner, and in the right spirit, his spiritual life grows and he accumulates indestructible treasures in heaven.

34 It is essential to be rich in the field of the spiritual and eternal, and to have treasures in heaven, because man's heart (his thoughts, ideals, inclinations and deeds) is attracted by the things that are his treasures. If one's wealth therefore consists in the first instance of earthly treasures (small or great), one's heart will be worldly-minded. But if one's real wealth is in God and in the eternal things, one will be heavenly-minded (no matter whether one is rich or poor in material possessions). It is not the possession of material things that makes one worldly-minded, but the attitude adopted towards them; nor does the lack of earthly things make one heavenly-minded, but the inward freedom from selfishness and covetousness, and consecration to the Lord.

It is not only wrong, but also foolish, unnecessary and useless to be vexed and anxious—especially on account of material things.

We are not, in the highest sense, dependent on earthly possessions, and God as our perfect heavenly Father knows, and is able and willing to give to us (on the strength of Jesus' merit), what we really need and what is really best for us.

¹ διὰ τοῦτο makes what Jesus says here refer back to the preceding warning against covetousness, in which He taught that true life is not to be found in material possessions.

² The Saviour's words used here also occur in Matthew vi. 25-33 in nearly the same form. " From this, however, it need not follow that Matthew and Luke drew from a common written source what they here relate of the Lord's words, nor even that in this connection they record the same oration of the Lord " (Greydanus, *in loc.*). Cf. our remarks at verse 1. Also Plummer declares: " It does not follow, because this lesson was given immediately after the parable of the Rich Fool, that therefore it was not part of the sermon on the mount; any more than that because it was delivered there it cannot have been repeated here " (*in loc.*).

³ " The fundamental thought of the whole series of proverbs is revealed in the fact that Jesus sees the gifts of God in the soul and body, and therefore also in food and clothing" (Schlatter, at Matt. vi. 25-32).

⁴ Creed writes concerning verses 24-32: " The freshness and originality of these words cannot be mistaken. For a just interpretation it is necessary to remember that Jesus and His disciples did not belong to ' the leisured classes ', and, in their application, that Jesus endorsed the popular judgment that the *labourer* is worthy of his hire " (verses 10 ff.) (*in loc.*).

⁵ ἡλικία. J. H. Moulton, in agreement with R.V. margin, argues for the meaning " length of life ", " span or duration of life " (as in John ix. 21, 23), and not bodily stature, as in the A.V. and R.V. text. But the secondary sense of " stature ", which suits the sense better here, as in Luke xix. 3, is found in classical and Hellenistic Greek alike. The use of the space-measure πῆχυς seems decisive here. " When J. H. Moulton expresses amazement that anyone should call the addition of eighteen inches to one's stature ' that which is least ', he must have been in an ultra-prosaic mood. Field remarks that a specific reason attaches to this scale of measurement, because τρίπηχυς was the current Greek equivalent for a short, and τετράπηχυς for a tall, man. The affirmation, then, is that nobody can modify his height even to the extent of a third of the average quantum of stature " (E. K. Simpson, *Words Worth Weighing in the Greek New Testament* [1944], p. 24).

⁶ " Wood being scarce in Palestine, grass is commonly used as fuel " (Plummer, *in loc.*).

⁷ μὴ ζητεῖτε = " seek not", in the sense of making it life's chief aim.

[8] μὴ μετεωρίζεσθε = " do not make yourselves anxious ". " This meaning is attested both for literary and colloquial Greek" (Creed, *in loc.*). It is derived from the simile of ships flung about by tempestuous waves and then means " waver not anxiously, be not tossed about with cares " (Plummer, *in loc.*).

[9] The nations of the world live only for worldly things because they have no eyes for the eternal things. So the disciples, who *have* received opened eyes, must not commit the same folly as the generality of mankind.

[10] ὁ πατήρ—the real Father, He who alone is Father in the perfect sense.

[11] χρῄζετε. " Here the Lord refers to having need of things, not coveting or having abundance " (Greydanus, *in loc.*).

[12] " Heaven is not to be bought with money; but, by almsgiving, what would be a hindrance is made a help " (Plummer, *in loc.*). There is here no condemnation of earthly possessions, but the command to put first things first and to regard and use all possessions as gifts lent to us by God to be devoted to His service.

[13] δότε, aorist imperative, " give " again and again (and not continuously without ceasing), every time that God brings you into touch with cases of need.

[14] καρδία heart, used here as elsewhere in the Bible as the centre and starting-point and the motive power of the whole man in every part of his life—feeling, thinking, desires, endeavour, will, and actions.

PARABLE OF THE WATCHFUL SERVANT

(Cf. Matt. xxiv. 45-51)

xii. 35-48

35 Let[1] your loins be girded about,[2] and your lamps burning;
36 and be ye yourselves like unto men looking for their lord,[3] when he shall return from the marriage feast; that, when he cometh and knocketh, they may straightway open unto him.
37 Blessed are those servants, whom the lord when he cometh shall find watching: verily I say unto you, that he shall gird himself, and make them sit down to meat, and shall come
38 and serve them. And if he shall come in the second watch, and if in the third, and find *them* so, blessed are those *servants*.
39 But know this,[4] that if the master of the house had known in what hour the thief was coming, he would have watched, and
40 not have left his house to be broken through. Be ye also ready: for in an hour that ye think not the Son of man cometh.
41 And Peter said, Lord, speakest thou this parable unto us,
42 or even unto all? And the Lord said,[5] Who then is the faithful and wise steward, whom his lord shall set over his household, to give them their portion of food in due season?
43 Blessed is that servant, whom his lord when he cometh shall
44 find so doing. Of a truth I say unto you, that he will set him
45 over all that he hath. But if that servant shall say in his heart, My lord delayeth his coming; and shall begin to beat the menservants and the maidservants, and to eat and drink,
46 and to be drunken; the lord of that servant shall come in a day when he expecteth not, and in an hour when he knoweth not, and shall cut him asunder, and appoint his portion with
47 the unfaithful. And that servant, which knew his lord's will, and made not ready, nor did according to his will, shall be
48 beaten with many *stripes*; but he that knew not, and did things worthy of stripes, shall be beaten with few *stripes*. And to whomsoever much is given, of him shall much be required: and to whom they commit much, of him will they ask the more.[6]

These words of the Saviour are very closely linked up with the previous warnings not to be worldly-minded but heavenly-minded. His disciples must inwardly be so bound to Him and so loyal to Him that the greatest passion of their lives will be to look

362

forward to His Advent, faithful in the performance of their daily vocation. Thereby it must be evident that their treasure is really in heaven and that, as a result, they are heavenly-minded.

35, 36 Like slaves who, since they are every moment expecting the return of their master from a wedding, with their long Oriental garments girded around their loins so that they may move quickly and with burning lamps to provide the necessary light, are ready to open the door for him as soon as He arrives, so the faithful must, during the time between Jesus' ascension and His second coming, be ready to receive Him back and to welcome Him.

37 He who remains thus in readiness to receive Him will be richly blessed by the Lord Himself.

38 The time of the second coming is uncertain (in the second or third night-watch); but he who, notwithstanding the uncertainty as to the time and notwithstanding the fact that it is long in coming, nevertheless continues to wait faithfully in full readiness, will be gloriously blessed.

39, 40 The Lord will come like a thief in the night, and therefore probably at an unexpected moment, and consequently the faithful must *always* be ready. Just as the master of the house who is not constantly on the watch is surprised and robbed by the thief, so also those who *are not ready* for His second coming (who neither believe in Him nor obey Him) will suffer irrevocable loss—His coming will bring with it their everlasting destruction. Therefore everyone must make sure that he is ready.

41 Because the Saviour has represented His second coming as something like the coming of a thief during the night, an occurrence which causes loss to those who are not prepared for it, Peter wants to know whether the words refer only to the disciples (for how, he probably felt, can the second coming of the Messiah be detrimental to His disciples?), or also to all (so that the possibility of suffering loss refers to the unbelievers among the hearers).

42 The Saviour does not give a direct reply to Peter's question, but through a counter-question and a parable He gives an answer which amounts to this, that He particularly means those whom He has appointed or will yet appoint as leaders over others to care for them (the disciples in the first place and after them all other spiritual leaders in His church). But although the words of the Saviour are especially addressed to all office-bearers, they are nevertheless also to be applied to every believer—each one is appointed to bear responsibility in the spiritual care of others.

43, 44 The office-bearers in His church who will duly and faithfully give what is needful to everyone over whom they have been placed will be richly rewarded. The words refer particularly to the communication of the glad tidings concerning the divine way of salvation. The fact of the impending second coming should therefore not cause the believers, and especially the leaders, to be content with a passive waiting for His coming, but should rather inspire and challenge them to be active in imparting what is necessary to those people for whose spiritual well-being they are responsible.

45, 46 That leader who, if Jesus does not come soon, begins to reason that He will not come at all, and who consequently lives as if he had no need to give an account to his Lord and acts tyrannically towards those over whom he has been put, will bring a fatal punishment upon himself.

47, 48 Especially those who have enjoyed particular privileges and who have known His will will have to bear the full responsibility for their misdeeds because they have sinned against the light. Those, however, who have enjoyed fewer privileges will bear some degree of punishment in so far as they disregarded the admonitions of conscience, but not to the same extent as the others who have been more privileged.

For those servants of Christ who labour faithfully and devotedly in His service every moment expecting the coming of their Lord and joyfully looking forward to it, the second coming of Jesus will be a matter of the greatest joy and of the most glorious gain. But for those who doubt His promises and who live in selfishness, imperiousness and worldly-mindedness, the second coming will be fraught with terror and irrevocable loss.

---

[1] " The expectation of the Lord's return does not paralyse energy. The imperatives call up a fine picture of preparedness " (Creed, in loc.).

[2] " The long garments of the East are a fatal hindrance to activity " (Plummer, in loc.). Therefore the command to be girded about refers to the fact that the believers must be ready to serve—ready for unhindered action in His service.

[3] The intention of the metaphor in verses 35 and 36 is, as Greydanus puts it: " the Lord's disciples and faithful ones are working in the Lord's house, they may be in His special service and may have the closest communion with Him, although He is here represented as absent for a time. This refers to the time between His ascension and His second coming. This saying is in a special sense intended for the Lord's disciples in a narrower sense and for the ministers of the Word " (in loc.).

[4] " There is nothing strange in the sudden change of metaphor, especially in Oriental language " (Plummer, *in loc.*).

[5] " Christ answers one question by another, which does not tell the questioner exactly what he wishes to know, but what it concerns him to know " (*loc. cit.*).

[6] In these last verses it is clearly taught that those who are eternally lost will undergo different grades of punishment, justly apportioned by Him who knows precisely how great the privileges were and thus also how great each one's responsibility was.

JESUS BRINGS FIRE AND DIVISION
ON EARTH
xii. 49–53

49 I came to cast fire[1] upon the earth; and what will I, if it is
50 already kindled? But I have a baptism to be baptized with;
51 and how am I straitened till it be accomplished![2] Think ye
that I am come to give peace in the earth? I tell you, Nay;
52 but rather division: for there shall be from henceforth five in
one house divided, three against two, and two against three.
53 They shall be divided, father against son, and son against
father; mother against daughter, and daughter against her
mother; mother in law against her daughter in law, and
daughter in law against her mother in law.[3]

Still surrounded by a great multitude, consisting of enraged
leaders, excited and curious crowds of people from among the
ordinary masses and His little group of disciples, the Saviour
utters these striking words.

49 Fire has a twofold effect—it destroys what is combustible
and purifies and refines non-combustible objects. The Saviour
here utters His deep longing that His work of salvation shall be
completed, so that His beneficial works may through the power
of the Holy Ghost enter into the lives of mankind in full measure—
to the undoing and destruction of evil and to the purification and
refining of the faithful. He indeed began to kindle this fire on
earth right at the commencement of His activities. But only after
His death of redemption, His resurrection and exaltation, and
after the pouring out of the Holy Ghost, was this fire fully
kindled.

50 Before this fire can in full measure be sent upon the earth—
for destruction and for purification—Jesus must first be plunged
into the flood of pain and suffering while He is accomplishing reconciliation. The Saviour, while He is the eternal Son of God, is
by virtue of His incarnation also truly man; and therefore the
thought of His approaching suffering and sacrificial death fills Him
with anguish—although He endures it willingly, He is fully
conscious of the terrible suffering awaiting Him.

51–3 The prevailing Jewish opinion of that time was that when
the Messiah came the Jewish nation would immediately be led to

366

victory over all their enemies and that after this they would enter into an untroubled Elysian life. Jesus does not wish His disciples to live under false impressions and points out to them frankly that He is not now bringing a state of peace on earth but rather one of dissension. For many He will be a stumbling-block. While some will choose His side, others again will choose against Him; and those who choose Him will be hated and persecuted by the others, even in the most intimate home circles. Jesus came to destroy Satan and sin. Through the fall all mankind is in the power of Satan and of sin. Therefore those who do not accept Him as their personal Redeemer and thus become liberated from Satan and sin will live in hostility towards Him and His followers—a fact which during the past nineteen centuries has been patent every day and continues to be so.

Christ is indeed the Prince of Peace (Isa. ix. 5) who came not only to bring peace into the heart of every believer but also to bring peace to its fullest extent among the whole of mankind. This will, however, only become a full reality after His second coming; that is to say, on the new earth. Until then the strife between good and evil will continue without a pause.

¹ " Fire " here is not merely the symbol of holiness (Plummer), or of faith (Zahn), or of dissension (Creed), or of judgment (Klostermann), but more generally of the spiritual power exercised by the Lord through His Word and Spirit on the strength of His completed work of redemption—to the undoing of those who reject Him and to the refining of those who believe in Him.

² " The prospect of His sufferings was a perpetual Gethsemane: cf. John xii. 27. While He longed to accomplish His Father's will, possibly His human will craved a shortening of the waiting" (Plummer, *in loc.*).

³ The " mother " and the " mother-in-law " in verse 53 is the same person, and therefore only five persons are referred to—father, mother, son, daughter, and daughter-in-law.

THE SIGNS OF THE TIMES

xii. 54-9

54 And he said to the multitudes also,[1] When ye see a cloud
rising in the west,[2] straightway ye say, There cometh a
55 shower; and so it cometh to pass. And when *ye see* a south[3]
wind blowing, ye say, There will be a scorching heat; and it
56 cometh to pass. Ye hypocrites, ye know how to interpret the
face of the earth and the heaven; but how is it that ye know
57 not how to interpret this time? And why even of yourselves
58 judge ye not what is right? For as thou art going with thine
adversary before the magistrate,[4] on the way give diligence
to be quit of him; lest haply he hale thee unto the judge, and
the judge shall deliver thee to the officer, and the officer shall
59 cast thee into prison. I say unto thee, Thou shalt by no means
come out thence, till thou have paid[5] the very last mite.

Jesus came to cast fire upon the earth; therefore it is necessary
that everyone should realise the seriousness of the time and take
heed to put things in order in his life while he still has the opportunity.

54-6 The Lord again addresses the multitude and calls attention to the fact that they are intelligent enough to notice the
special signs in nature foretelling rain or dry heat. Therefore it is
hypocrisy if they pretend that they do not notice the " signs of
this time ", the unambiguous proofs that He is the Christ. It is
not because they cannot see the signs that they persist in their unbelief, but because they are unwilling to discern the signs. So
Jesus addresses them as " Hypocrites! " On account of their unbelief and spiritual blindness they do not see the cloud of grace
and blessings which appears with Him to all who believe in Him,
nor do they observe the glowing heat of the judgment which He
brings for those who are disobedient.

57-9 The times are serious; therefore everyone, knowing that
he goes to meet the judgment of God, must discern and fulfil the
demands of righteousness and justice in his own life. All persons
are fellow-travellers on the way to God, the eternal Judge, and
everyone must see to it that his attitude towards his fellow-men is
put right while the opportunity is still there. But, above all, everyone

368

should see that his attitude towards *Christ* is put right while the time of grace is still present (i.e. before death or the end of the age). He who is not reconciled to Him in time, and is not bound to Him in faith, will meet with irrevocable sufferings—he will never be able to pay off his debt of sin.

The majority of the Jewish people of the time when Jesus was on earth failed to discern the signs of the times and did not recognise and accept Him as the Messiah. The result was that indescribable calamities visited them—calamities which reached a gruesome culminating-point in the total destruction of Jerusalem and the temple in A.D. 70. To-day also there are for us all many signs pointing to the seriousness of life and to the necessity of right living. Especially those who have the opportunity of reading the Bible and listening to the preaching of the Gospel have the fullest opportunities of discerning the signs of the times and of knowing that Jesus is the Redeemer. He who is blind to this and who does not take heed, while the period of grace continues, to have peace with God through the Saviour, must await a dark future.

---

[1] " Luke puts these words here, but nevertheless gives no indication that they were uttered by the Lord on another occasion. There is thus no sound reason to accept the latter view " (Greydanus, *in loc.*).

[2] The direction where the Mediterranean Sea is.

[3] The direction of the Arabian desert.

[4] ἄρχων, without the article, refers to the idea of authority and thus God is ultimately meant as the supreme Bearer of real Authority.

[5] ἀποδῷς, the aorist subjunctive used in the sense of the future-perfect: " will have paid ". And that moment never arrives. The full repayment or liquidation of debt is no longer possible for the guilty one. The condemnation then lasts for ever.

THE MURDER OF THE GALILEANS

xiii. 1–5

1 Now there were some[1] present at that very season[2] which
told[3] him of the Galilæans,[4] whose blood Pilate had mingled
2 with their sacrifices. And he answered and said unto them,
Think ye that these Galilæans were sinners above all the
3 Galilæans, because they have suffered these things?[5] I tell
you, Nay: but, except ye repent, ye shall all in like manner
4 perish.[6] Or those eighteen, upon whom the tower in Siloam[7]
fell, and killed them, think ye that they were offenders above
5 all the men that dwell in Jerusalem? I tell you, Nay: but,
except ye repent, ye shall all likewise perish.

Just as in xii. 54–9, so here and also in xiii. 6–9 the Saviour
points out the urgent necessity of timely repentance

1 Certain Jews brought to Jesus the news that Pilate, notorious
for his hard-hearted acts, caused a group of Galileans, while they
were busy sacrificing in the temple, to be attacked and slain by his
soldiers, thus, as it were, mingling their blood with their sacrifices.
Probably the Galileans (who were particularly rebellious by
nature) had contravened some Roman law or other and had thus
given to Pilate the opportunity of venting his bloodthirstiness on
them.

2, 3 At that time it was a generally accepted notion that whenever calamities visited people this was a proof that they were
exceptionally sinful and that for this reason God allowed them to
be overtaken by such disasters. Here, as elsewhere, Jesus rejects
this false idea and warns the Jews who brought the tidings that,
unless they repented in time, similar disasters awaited them too.
They are not to regard the murdered Galileans as more guilty
than themselves.

4, 5 In order to emphasise the seriousness of the matter still
further, the Lord refers to another instance where people were
overtaken by an extraordinary calamity, and declares that this
occurrence, too, is no proof that these people were more guilty
than the masses not visited by the calamity. All are guilty, and
those who do not repent in time are heading for a disastrous
future.

370

The Gospel is glad tidings, but only for those who leave the way that leads to destruction and come to true repentance. Those who remain unconverted are heading for inexorable destruction.

[1] παρῆσαν δέ τινες—" not ' they were present ' but ' they came ' or ' they had come ', as in Acts x. 21, xii. 20, etc., and in classical Greek " (Klostermann, in loc.). Also cf. Creed, Plummer, and others. So the translation " there were some present " should be altered to " some people came ".

[2] " Time and place are indefinite; but the connexion with what precedes is expressly stated, and the scene must have been away from Jerusalem " (Plummer, in loc.).

[3] What their motive was cannot be determined with certainty. From Jesus' words it appears in any case that they regarded themselves as less guilty than those Galileans.

[4] " The Galilean zealots were notoriously turbulent, and Pilate was ruthlessly cruel. Many massacres marked his administration " (Major, *The Mission and Message of Jesus*, p. 281). Here the occurrence referred to evidently took place quite recently and not many years before. The fact that Josephus makes no mention of this particular instance of Pilate's cruelty is of no importance. He leaves many incidents unmentioned. In any case he mentions a sufficient number of Pilate's actions to make us realise that this Roman ruler was an utter brute who on more than one occasion acted as in this case.

[5] Through these words the Saviour teaches that " physical disasters like physical advantages are no indication that those who experience them are either worse or better than their fellow-men " (Major, *op. cit.*, p. 281). Major rightly remarks in this connection: " In this respect, as in many others, the teaching of Jesus is in harmony with the conclusions of modern thought, but it conflicted acutely with the convictions of the ancient world " (*loc. cit.*).

[6] " The fate of these people is a reminder not of their sins—they were neither better nor worse than many others but of the urgency of the Gospel. Had they only known what was astir, been warned that Pilate was in a black mood or that the building was dangerous, they might have saved their lives. But there was nobody to warn them, and they perished. So this generation, says Jesus in effect, is walking politically and religiously—straight for disaster. But the warning has been given, first by John the Baptist and now by Jesus. It is a warning to change direction before it is too late " (T. W. Manson, *op. cit.*, pp. 565 ff.).

[7] The pool of Siloam was near the angle where the southern and eastern walls of Jerusalem came together. The tower of Siloam which fell was probably part of the ancient system of defence on the walls in the vicinity of the pool of Siloam. T. W. Manson is right in remarking: " The accident described in this verse is not mentioned elsewhere, which is not surprising, since it was an accident and not an ' incident '. It had no significance for the secular historian " (*op. cit.*, p. 566).

371

THE PARABLE OF THE FRUITLESS FIG TREE

xiii. 6–9

6   And he spake this parable; A certain man had a fig[1] tree planted in his vineyard;[2] and he came seeking fruit thereon,
7 and found none. And he said unto the vinedresser, Behold, these three[3] years I come seeking fruit on this fig tree, and find none: cut it down; why doth it also cumber the ground?
8 And he answering saith unto him, Lord, let it alone this year
9 also, till I shall dig about it, and dung it: and if it bear fruit thenceforth,[4] *well*;[5] but if not, thou shalt cut it down.

This parable fits in exceptionally well with what is described in verses 1–5, for through this parable Jesus once more calls attention to the urgent necessity of true repentance—a repentance which will bring forth fruit.

6–9   It was and still is the custom in Palestine to plant fig trees and other trees in a vineyard. Jesus here tells a parable about a fig tree which was thus planted in a vineyard—but which had throughout the probationary period of three years remained without fruit. Because it not only takes up room but also exhausts the soil in which it grows, the owner wants it to be cut down. The dresser, however, pleads that the tree should be spared for another year, and if, after being specially cared for, it still does not bear any fruit, it must then be cut down. The parable here evidently refers to Israel, to whom God gave full opportunity to bear fruit but who remain unfruitful, as appears from their rejection of Him, the promised Christ. But nevertheless God will give them a last chance, and if they should then still persist in unbelief and sin they will be irrevocably cut down from their privileged and protected position as the chosen people of God. After Jesus' crucifixion the Lord through His resurrection and ascension, through the Pentecostal miracle and afterwards through the preaching of the apostles and the growth of His church, once more ministered to the spiritual needs of the Jewish people to call them to repentance. The majority, however, refused to repent and thus they drew upon themselves the disasters which accompanied the Roman-Jewish war (A.D. 66–70), when their national existence in the Holy Land was irrevocably cut down.

God's patience is infinite and His mercy boundless towards the penitent; but those who persist in sin will in the end have to suffer. Although God through His grace postpones for such a long time the punishment of the impenitent, in order to give them the opportunity of repentance, the day will nevertheless finally dawn when the time of grace expires. This holds good for the life of every individual, of every nation and of all mankind—those who remain unrepentant, will finally be punished without mercy. He who does not desire to be saved in time brings inevitable judgment upon himself.

[1] The fig tree is frequently used as symbolical of the Jewish people (cf. Hos. ix. 10; Joel i. 7). " The position of the parable after the preceding narrative points to an interpretation of the fig tree as symbolical of the Jewish people, which is to be allowed yet a short period for repentance " (Creed, *in loc.*). In a secondary sense, however, the fig tree symbolises also every individual who remains unrepentant. Zahn (*in loc.*) wrongly regards the fig tree as the symbol of Jerusalem and not of the whole Jewish people. In verses 1–5 attention is called also to the guilt of the Galileans and not only to that of Jerusalem.

[2] " It was the custom in Palestine to plant fruit trees of all kinds in vineyards " (T. W. Manson, *op. cit.*, p. 566).

[3] " A fig tree is said to attain maturity in three years, and a tree that remained fruitless for so long would not be likely to bear afterwards " (Plummer, *in loc.*). The three years, therefore, refer to the sufficient opportunity given to Israel to come to true repentance (throughout the centuries before the coming of Jesus and especially the time of His public appearance among the people).

[4] $εἰς τὸ μέλλον$ = " thereafter " (Grimm-Thayer).

[5] In the original the " apodosis [is] suppressed by an idiom, common in Semitic and well recognised in Greek " (Creed, *in loc.*).

HEALING OF A CROOKED WOMAN

xiii. 10–17

10 And he was teaching in one of the synagogues on the sab-
11 bath day. And behold, a woman which had a spirit of
infirmity[1] eighteen years; and she was bowed together, and
12 could in no wise lift herself up. And when Jesus saw her, he
called her, and said to her, Woman, thou art loosed from
13 thine infirmity. And he laid his hands upon her: and immediately[2] she was made straight, and glorified God. And
14 the ruler of the synagogue, being moved with indignation
because Jesus had healed on the sabbath, answered and said
to the multitude, There are six days in which men ought to
work: in them therefore come and be healed, and not on the
15 day of the sabbath. But the Lord answered him, and said,
Ye hypocrites,[3] doth not each one of you on the sabbath
loose his ox or his ass from the stall, and lead him away to
16 watering? And ought not[4] this woman, being a daughter of
Abraham,[5] whom Satan had bound,[6] lo, *these* eighteen years,
to have been loosed from this bond on the day of the sabbath?
17 And as he said these things, all his adversaries were put to
shame: and all the multitude rejoiced for all the glorious
things that were done by him.[7]

This is the last instance in Luke where Jesus appears teaching in
a synagogue. The hostility of the Jewish authorities increased to
such an extent towards the end of the Saviour's activities that He
would afterwards no longer be allowed to appear in the synagogues.

10–13 While Jesus was busy teaching in the synagogue, there
was a woman who for eighteen years had been bowed together
through the influence of an evil spirit of infirmity. The Saviour,
who always noticed those among the multitudes that were in
exceptional need, observed her, called her to Him and healed
her.

14 The ruler of the synagogue, probably the head of the
council of ten Jewish men of the vicinity controlling the local
synagogue, was very much upset that Jesus should have performed
the healing on the Sabbath. He does not, however, venture to

374

rebuke Jesus personally. But through his rebuke of the multitude he nevertheless makes a covert attack on the Saviour.

15, 16 Jesus points out to him, and to the others present who agreed with him, their hypocrisy—while they do not hesitate to care for their animals on the Sabbath, they condemn the healing of a respectable woman (" a daughter of Abraham ") who has already for so many years been in the most extreme need.

17 The Saviour's action and words so mercilessly exposed the false attitude of His opponents that they were perforce put to shame while the multitude rejoiced because of the glorious works performed by Him.

When anyone is in need to an unusual degree, Christ takes a special interest in him or her. And although the condition of such a person may be hopeless, humanly speaking, He is able to bring salvation.

---

¹ πνεῦμα ἀσθενείας—a spirit causing infirmity. (Cf. our digression on demon-possession after iv. 33–7.) The particular infirmity was apparently *spondylitis deformans*: " the bones of her spine were fused into a rigid mass " (A. Rendle Short, *Modern Discovery and the Bible*, p. 91).

² " A characteristic of the healing work of Jesus was that it was immediate, it was complete. There was no wondering whether the person was healed when He healed. There was no hysterical delay. People may (these days) fling their crutches away, and have to pick them up again. They never picked them up when He healed " (C. Morgan, *in loc.*). The claims of modern " faith healers ", namely, that their work is the continuation of Jesus' work of healing, are therefore evidently false. No comparison is possible between His miracles and their doings.

³ The correct reading is ὑποκριταί, plural, not singular (as in A.V.). So the Lord is addressing the ruler and all those who agree with him.

⁴ Major rightly declares: " Though some have criticised the logic of the retort of Jesus, its cogency is irrefutable, which asserts that if the Sabbath rest may be broken to minister to the needs of beasts, how much more may this be done in order to minister to the needs of men " (*op. cit.*, p. 282).

⁵ " There is no suggestion in this story that there was anything of immorality in this woman's life. She was the victim of demon activity. . . . There is no hint of this mastery having produced an immoral effect in her life. As a matter of fact, here she was in the synagogue. She had found her way to the place of worship, and when Jesus presently called her a daughter of Abraham, He did not merely mean that

she was a Jewess: that was patent. He was using the term in its full spiritual significance as revealing her faith in God. Here, then, was a case of physical suffering, that was directly produced by the power of Satan. I am not attempting to explain this. . . . There are other things we have not fathomed yet in life, concerning the mystery of suffering, and the power of evil. We take the facts as revealed . . . " (C. Morgan, *in loc.*).

[6] The fact that Jesus could in any case heal the woman, proves His absolute omnipotence also to destroy the works of Satan.

[7] Plummer remarks in connection with Luke's description of this episode: " The details are manifest tokens of historical truth. The pharisaic pomposity of the ruler of the synagogue, with his hard and fast rules about propriety; Christ's triumphant refutation of his objections; and the delight of the people, who sympathise with the dictates of human nature against senseless restrictions—all this is plainly drawn from life " (*in loc.*).

PARABLES OF THE GRAIN OF MUSTARD SEED AND THE LEAVEN

(Cf. Matt. xiii. 31–3; Mark iv. 30–2)

xiii. 18–21

18 He said therefore,[1] Unto what is the kingdom of God like?
19 and whereunto shall I liken it? It is like unto a grain of
mustard[2] seed, which a man took, and cast into his own
garden; and it grew, and became a tree;[3] and the birds of
20 the heaven lodged[4] in the branches thereof. And again he
21 said, Whereunto shall I liken the kingdom of God? It is like
unto leaven,[5] which a woman took and hid in three measures
of meal, till it was all leavened.[6]

The blessed effect of His action as the promised Messiah that
was already noticeable (e.g. in verses 11–17) is only a slight
foreshadowing of the much more glorious growth of the kingdom
of God that is awaiting.

18 By commencing with this oratorical question, the Master
whets the attention of the hearers for what follows.

19 The grain of mustard seed is the smallest kind of seed that
was sown by farmers in Palestine and yet it grew (in a marvellously
short time) to be the biggest of all kinds of plants which they grew
from seeds. In the same way the beginning of the kingdom of God
with Jesus' appearance in the humiliated " form of a servant " is
infinitely insignificant from a human point of view; but just as
surely it will grow quickly and irresistibly to a vast movement in
which members of various nations will find protection and rest (as
the birds of heaven build their nests in the mustard tree).

This growth of the kingdom refers to the speedy development of
the church of Christ from Pentecost when already three thousand
souls were brought in. Within thirty years afterwards thousands
of souls from almost all known countries at that time had already
found a spiritual home within His church, and even in Rome, the
capital of the mighty Roman Empire, there was a flourishing
congregation. The final fulfilment of what Jesus taught in this
parable will, however, only set in at the grand Consummation,
when His kingdom will be revealed in perfection.

377

20, 21 The kingdom of God will, however, not grow merely to outward greatness but, like the leaven which leavens the whole loaf, it will one day transform the whole life of every believer and of the whole of saved mankind to perfect holiness. Through these two parables Jesus teaches that the kingdom of God, of which He is the Founder and Representative, will outwardly as well as inwardly come to perfect development notwithstanding its insignificant beginning and the opposition that will be offered it. Nothing will be able to stop its growth and full development. The Lord does not here state how and when this will take place. In the light of other pronouncements of His it is clear that the final fulfilment of it will set in only with His second advent.

Because Christ Himself is, through His Spirit, the life of His church, it is so vigorous that nothing in the world, not even the cruellest persecutions or the most cunning attacks of the evil one, will ever be able to destroy it or to arrest its full development when He comes in glory.

---

[1] The conjunction οὖν refers back to verses 11–17.

[2] " It is the smallness of the seed in comparison with the largeness of the growth that is the point " (Plummer, *in loc.*). There is here no question of *gradual* growth. The mustard tree is actually a plant that grows quickly. However, the points of comparison that come into prominence, are the *smallness* of the seed, the *irresistible vitality* of the germinating seed, and the *large size* of the plant.

[3] " In Palestine the mustard plant attains a height of eight or twelve feet " (T. W. Manson, *op. cit.*, p. 415). It is a plant growing to a great height, with strong stems in which the birds take shelter.

[4] Plummer here writes: " This was a recognised metaphor for a great empire giving protection to the nations " (*in loc.*). T. W. Manson agrees with this: " Both in apocalyptic and Rabbinical literature ' the birds of heaven ' stand for the Gentile nations " (*loc. cit.*).

[5] " Once the leaven has been put into the dough the leavening process goes on inevitably till the whole is leavened. And this although there is no comparison between the mass of dough and the small quantity of leaven " (T. W. Manson, *loc. cit.*). Here, also, the attention is called not to a gradual leavening, but to the irresistible development and to the perfection of the final result in contrast with the insignificant beginning. See O. T. Allis, " The Parable of the Leaven ", in *The Evangelical Quarterly*, 19 (1947), 254 ff.

[6] " There is a quality of originality in this teaching of Jesus about the kingdom which marks it as His. It is above the level of His contemporaries and His reporters " (Major, *op. cit.*, p. 72).

THE STRAIT GATE

22 And he went on his way through cities and villages,
23 teaching, and journeying on unto Jerusalem. And one said
24 unto him, Lord, are they few that be saved? And he said
   unto them,[1] Strive[2] to enter in by the narrow door: for many,
   I say unto you, shall seek to enter in,[3] and shall not be able.
25 When once[4] the master of the house is risen up, and hath shut
   to the door, and ye begin to stand without, and to knock at the
   door, saying, Lord, open to us; and he shall answer and say
26 to you, I know[5] you not whence ye are; then shall ye begin
   to say, We did eat and drink in thy presence,[6] and thou
27 didst teach in our streets; and he shall say, I tell you, I know
   not whence ye are; depart from me, all ye workers of iniquity.
28 There shall be the weeping and gnashing of teeth, when ye
   shall see Abraham, and Isaac, and Jacob, and all the prophets, in the kingdom of God, and yourselves cast forth with-
29 out. And they shall come from the east and west, and from
   the north and south, and shall sit down in the kingdom of
30 God. And behold, there are last which shall be first, and
   there are first which shall be last.[7]

No matter how perfect the growth of the kingdom of God may
be, there is a great danger that even those who have seen and
heard Him often will be shut out.

22 Although during the last period of His activities Jesus was
not always directly on His way to Jerusalem, His eyes were,
nevertheless, constantly turned towards the city where He was to
suffer, ever since the moment referred to in ix. 51. In the meantime, however, He still continued to teach and to work (probably
mostly in the Trans-Jordanian regions). (Cf. Schlatter at verses
31–3.)

23 During that period somebody asked Him the question
whether those that be saved are but few in number. Possibly he
observed how many people were opposed to Jesus and how few
followed Him faithfully.

24, 25 As very often happened, the Saviour does not give a
direct reply to the *speculative* question, but points out to those

379

present the *practical* side of the matter: they are not to waste their time and strength in arguments as to how many will be saved, but everyone must strive hard and make sure that he himself is saved, for whether the saved are to be many or few one thing is certain—the gate leading to life is strait, and only those who strive with might and main, and whole-heartedly to enter, will be saved. When once the gate is shut and the time of grace has expired, many will attempt to enter, but then they will not be able to do so, for it will then be for ever too late. The owner of the house (i.e. the Lord) will then already have locked the door, and it will be in vain for those to try to enter who did not do so when the door was still open.

26, 27 Although they may plead to be admitted on the strength of the fact that they have seen and heard Him and knew Him outwardly, He will reject them inexorably because they never came into intimate personal communion with Him and continued to live in unrighteousness, although they had the fullest opportunity to learn to know Him as their Redeemer.

28 They (that is, the majority of that generation of the Jewish people) will through their unbelief and the fact that they let the time of grace slip past endure inexpressible afflictions and pangs of conscience when at the end of the age, while they themselves are rejected, they see how their pious ancestors inherit the rich blessings of the kingdom of God.

29, 30 Their remorse will be so much the worse because while they, as members of the chosen people, are excluded, even Gentiles from all parts of the world will enter the kingdom of God. It will be the exact opposite of their own ideas, which were that the Gentiles would be excluded and that they, as members of the chosen people, would be the blessed and privileged ones. Thus the first shall be last and the last first.

Although it is true that we are saved only through grace, and never through our own strength, this does not relieve us from the urgent necessity of striving on our side with might and main to enter in at the strait gate. Moreover, there is no time for postponement, for ere long, when the time of grace has expired, entrance will no longer be possible.

---

[1] A typical example of how an over-subtle apportioning of sources in the Gospel records may degenerate into absurdity may be seen in Streeter's assertion (*The Four Gospels*, p. 284) that the author of Matthew in Matthew vii. 13 " conflated " two sources together, and that the

" gate " comes from " Q ", while the " way " comes from " M "
(Matthew's special source). In opposition to this excessively artificial
representation of how the Gospel writer framed his document, Creed
points out that " it is somewhat against this theory that the ' gate '
is not attested by Luke, and that the ' gate ' and the ' road ' harmonise
well in one picture " (*in loc.*).

There is no reason for assuming that Matthew vii. 13 and Luke
xiii. 24 are variants of the same pronouncement (cf. also Plummer,
in loc.).

[2] *Ἀγωνίζεσθε* refers to the "exerting of concentrated strength"
(Schlatter, *in loc.*). " The word signifies to ' contend ' as for the
mastery, to ' struggle ', expressive of the *difficulty* of being saved, as if
one would have to *force his way in* " (Jamieson, Fausset and Brown,
in loc.).

[3] Plummer's words here are of special importance: " Jesus does not
say that there *are* many who *strive* in vain to enter, but that there will
be many who *will seek* in vain to enter, *after the time of salvation is past.*
Those who continue to strive now, succeed " (*in loc.*).

[4] *ἀφ' οὗ ἄν* links up this verse closely with the preceding; it gives
the explanation why many will not be able to enter.

[5] *οἶδα* is here, as also elsewhere in the New Testament, used for
" to know ", with the secondary meaning of " to recognise " and " to
treat with good will " (cf. 1 Thess. v. 12).

[6] " A man's salvation does not result from familiarity [with Jesus].
It must be based on personal relationship " (Morgan, *in loc.*).

[7] The Lord used this expression on more than one occasion (cf.
Matt. xx. 16, xix. 30).

JESUS IS WARNED AGAINST HEROD

xiii. 31–5

31 In that very hour[1] there came certain Pharisees, saying
to him, Get thee out, and go hence: for Herod would fain
32 kill thee.[2] And he said unto them, Go and say to that fox,[3]
Behold, I cast out devils and perform cures to-day and to-
33 morrow, and the third[4] *day* I am perfected.[5] Howbeit I
must go on my way[6] to-day and to-morrow and the *day* following: for it cannot be that a prophet perish out of Jerusa-
34 lem. O Jerusalem,[7] Jerusalem, which killeth the prophets,
and stoneth them that are sent unto her! how often[8] would
I have gathered thy children together, even as a hen *gathereth*
35 her own brood under her wings, and ye would not! Behold,
your house[9] is left unto you[10] *desolate*: and I say unto you,[11]
Ye shall not see me, until ye shall say,[12] Blessed *is* he that
cometh in the name of the Lord.

The Pharisees' warning may have been perfectly sincere and
prompted by a concern for Jesus' safety; on the other hand, some
expositors have inferred that, enraged by His words recorded in
the foregoing verses, they wished to persuade him to leave Herod's
domain and go where he would be likely to fall into the hands of
the Jewish rulers.

31 In Trans-Jordan, where Jesus most probably was at this
time, the Jewish authorities did not have much power. The
northern part was ruled by Philip and the southern part by Herod
Antipas. If, therefore, the Pharisees' warning was insincere, it may
have been calculated to make Jesus flee to Judaea, where He would
be more exposed to the power of the Sanhedrin. In the absence of
clear evidence to the contrary, however, we should take it that
these Pharisees had received intelligence which led them to believe
(whether rightly or wrongly) that Jesus' life was in danger if He
remained in Herod's territory.

32 However, they do not succeed in terrifying Him. On the
contrary, He bids them tell Herod—" that fox " (a cunning but
weak ruler)—that He intends to defy his threats and stay there to

save people from spiritual and physical need until His task in those parts is perfected.

33 But although He is not going to flee through fear of Herod, His activity in the territory of this ruler is speedily approaching its end, and He is, in fact, already steadily advancing further on the road to Jerusalem. It is in the " Holy City " and not in the territory of Herod that He is going to die, for history has taught that it is precisely the " Holy City " that kills the divine messengers. Also on this occasion Jerusalem is not to be robbed of her " privilege "! " There is . . . a bitter irony in the words. Herod must not be greedy: for Jerusalem has first claim on the blood of God's messengers " (T. W. Manson, *op. cit.*, p. 569).

34 The Saviour is very deeply moved by the hardness of heart of the inhabitants of Jerusalem who through the centuries have again and again misjudged and killed God's messengers and also rejected all the persevering attempts of Jesus Himself to call them to true repentance. As a hen gathers her brood under her wings to protect them against threatening danger, so He desired to protect them against the impending judgments. With the utmost devotion and self-sacrifice He tried to lead them to spiritual and temporal safety, but they persistently opposed Him.

35 So they can meet with no other end but destruction and the devastation of their temple, the centre of their degenerate religion. While the temple was formerly called the house of God, it could no longer be called so after the Jews had rejected Christ. The temple and the people have become forsaken by God, and because His protection has been withdrawn complete destruction will ensue. And so the Jewish people will no longer have their Messiah, Jesus, as a blessing in their midst, until (by the repentance of individual Jews from time to time, and on a wholesale scale at the end of the age) they see and recognise Him as the true Messiah. Read in this connection, Jesus by these words signifies that those who did not accept His salvation while He was with them would, together with all other people (the saved and the unredeemed) at His second coming, acknowledge Him with pangs of conscience as the Christ of God. But then it will be too late.

Christ longs earnestly for the salvation of those who are lost; but when man is determined in his refusal to believe in Him, He ultimately leaves him to final destruction.

---

[1] " In the same hour " indicates that what follows here is closely linked up with what precedes.

[2] Herod was ruler over Galilee *and* Perea (Trans-Jordan), and consequently Major has no ground for his statement where he alleges that Luke has misplaced the incident (*op. cit.*, p. 282).

[3] " ' Fox ' in Jewish use has a double sense. It typifies low cunning as opposed to straightforward dealing, and it is used in contrast to ' lion ' to describe an insignificant third-rate person as opposed to a person of real power and greatness. To call Herod ' that fox ' is as much as to say he is neither a great man nor a straight man; he has neither majesty nor honour " (T. W. Manson, *op. cit.*, p. 568).

Morgan's words in connection with Jesus' behaviour towards Herod, in this and in other episodes related in the Gospels, are striking: " It is an appalling picture. Jesus evaded Herod, sent him a message of contempt, and when face to face with him (at His trial before Herod) had nothing to say to him. It is a solemnising story. A man may get into such a condition when he yields to the base, that even Christ has nothing to say to him " (*in loc.*).

[4] " Third day " is poetical for the moment when something is finished, completed, and perfected. " The course of the Messiah is determined, and will not be abbreviated or changed because of the threats of a Herod " (Plummer, *in loc.*).

[5] τελειοῦμαι " would be better translated by ' I am finished ', which has the same ambiguity as the original " (T. W. Manson, *op. cit.*, p. 568). It may then refer to Jesus' completion of His work in that territory at the appointed time, or to His death, the completion of His work of redemption.

[6] " Jesus will work His way towards Judaea and not flee thither " (T. W. Manson, *loc. cit.*). " Jesus is not afraid of a fox " (Schlatter, *in loc.*).

[7] For a refutation of the allegation of Harnack and others that these words are a quotation from an unknown Jewish document cf. T. W. Manson, *Mission and Message of Jesus*, pp. 393 f., 418. (Cf. our note at xi. 49–51.) Morgan says of these words of Jesus: " There is a heart-break in them, the heart-break of God. There is in them the threnody of eternal pity " (*in loc.*).

[8] Is there no reference in this to the fact that (as expressly stated by John) Jesus, especially during the last period of His public appearance, visited Jerusalem on more than one occasion? There is a tendency nowadays, even among the more liberal critics, to admit that the fourth Gospel was, after all, correct with regard to this matter—and others (cf. T. W. Manson, *op. cit.*, p. 419).

[9] " By the ' house ' which all Israelites can call theirs we are to understand nothing other than the temple in Jerusalem " (Zahn, *in loc.*).

[10] In the original the reading is simply ἀφίεται ὑμῖν. This means, therefore, " your temple is left to you to possess and to protect on your own, for God is going to forsake it in Christ and therefore it will be desolate ".

[11] The lament over Jerusalem was a rhetorical apostrophe (Zahn, *in loc.*), but the Saviour now again addresses the Jews who are present as representatives of the Jewish nation.

12 Probably the time of His second coming (when all, believers and unbelievers alike, will know that He is the divine Messiah) is meant here. And " the preceding passages suggest that the meaning is: ' The time will come when you will be ready to say to Me, " Blessed is He that cometh in the Name of the Lord! " but then it will be too late ' " (T. W. Manson, *op. cit.*, p. 420).

JESUS HEALS A MAN WHO HAS THE DROPSY

xiv. 1-6

1 And it came to pass, when he went into the house of one of
the rulers of the Pharisees on a sabbath to eat bread,[1] that
2 they were watching him. And behold,[2] there was before him
3 a certain man which had the dropsy. And Jesus answering[3]
spake unto the lawyers and Pharisees, saying, Is it lawful to
4 heal on the sabbath, or not? But they held their peace. And
5 he took him, and healed him, and let him go. And he said
unto them, Which of you[4] shall have an ass[5] or an ox fallen
into a well,[6] and will not straightway draw him up on a
6 sabbath day?[7] And they could not answer again unto these
things.

At verse 1 the second section of Luke's so-called "journeys to
Jerusalem" (ix. 51–xix. 28) begins. It extends from xiv. 1 to
xvii. 10 and practically contains only material which Luke alone
reports. He probably obtained his information from a person or
a source (or persons or sources) particularly well-informed concerning the activities of the Saviour during the last period before
His final arrival in Jerusalem.

1 Because the possibility still remained of influencing the
Pharisees for their own good, Jesus does not avoid them in
spite of the repeated revelation of their hostility towards Him.
He even accepts the invitation to go and eat on a Sabbath with one
of the leading Pharisees.

2 Probably immediately after His entrance into the house of
the Pharisee the Lord observes a sick person there—someone who
is suffering from dropsy. From the context it appears as if the
Pharisees, who were now watching Jesus continually with growing
hate, intentionally arranged matters in such a way that the
dropsical man was in the dining-room, so that they might see
whether He would not again contravene the Sabbath laws by
healing the sick man on the Sabbath day in order to be able to
lodge a complaint against Him with the Jewish council.

3 The Saviour immediately sees through their whole attitude,
and, instead of allowing the presence of the dropsical man to
embarrass Him, He at once asks them the explicit question whether

386

it is lawful to heal the sick on the Sabbath day or not. As a result, they were so confused that they did not venture to answer a single word. Jesus' question showed that He knew that they wanted to trip Him up, and in addition the question placed them in a difficult position—for if they answered that it was lawful to heal on the Sabbath day this would give Him the right to continue His Sabbath healings. On the other hand, they could not venture to declare that it was unlawful to heal on the Sabbath day, especially in view of the distress of the sick man, visible to all of them.

4 After He had in this manner disarmed His critics, He healed the dropsical man and sent him away, completely cured.

5 He next put a question to those present (probably mostly Pharisees) to make them feel how inconsistent they were in their opposition to the healing of the sick on the Sabbath. Should one of their animals fall into an open pit on the Sabbath, they would certainly not hesitate to go and save it. From this it is evident that they also recognised the principle that cases of real emergency pushed the ceremonial Sabbath laws aside. So they are hypocritical if they censure Him for healing on Sabbath days the sick who are in physical or spiritual distress. Although in most cases there is no immediate peril of their lives, their suffering and the distressing condition in which they find themselves (a condition also affecting the families of the sick people as well as the whole community) are such that love demands their being healed without delay. In addition, the healing work performed by Jesus is a wholly unselfish service of love in contrast with His critics' saving of their animals on the Sabbath, which is often performed not so much out of love for these animals as out of fear of the loss to be sustained should the animals perish.

6 The questions of the Saviour exposed the hypocrisy of His enemies so plainly and fully that not one of them could utter a word in reply.

There is still the constant danger that we may have dead and rigid views of the day of rest and that we may in our selfishness think only of our own interests instead of putting ourselves at God's disposal every Sunday (as on every other day) to be helpful to those who are in spiritual and physical distress.

[1] While Jews at this time took only two meals on week days, they had three meals on the Sabbath. " The chief meal took place after the close of morning service—that is, more or less in the neighbourhood of

noon. The participation of guests in the Sabbath meal was a general custom " (Strack-Billerbeck, *in loc.*).

² Zahn argues from καὶ ἰδού following upon παρατηρούμενοι that the presence of the sick man was unexpected by Jesus and that it was arranged by the Pharisees as an intentional trap for Him.

³ He " answers " their critical thoughts.

⁴ ὑμῶν bears the emphasis here.

⁵ The original reading may be υἱός (" son "), as in R.V. margin, and not ὄνος (" ass "). Jesus then asks " the son of which of you, *or even only* his ox . . . ." It is not necessary to suppose that the υἱός is a corruption of ὗς (" pig "—according to Rendel Harris) or of ὄϊς (" sheep "). υἱός fits in very well here, and in the light of present-day textual knowledge may be regarded as the best attested reading.

⁶ " Palestine abounds in unprotected cisterns, wells and pits " (Plummer, *in loc.*).

⁷ Montefiore's allegation that, while the lives of the son and the ox are in danger, the sick man would not have suffered by waiting for his cure until after the Sabbath, is technically correct but misses the point —the sick man's condition of suffering and distress demands that there should be no delay.

PARABLE OF THOSE THAT WERE BIDDEN
AND THE HIGHEST SEATS

xiv. 7–14

7 And he spake a parable unto those which were bidden,
when he marked how they chose out the chief seats;[1] saying
8 unto them, When thou art bidden of any man to a marriage
feast, sit not down in the chief seat; lest haply a more honour-
9 able man than thou be bidden of him, and he that bade thee
and him shall come and say to thee, Give this man place;
and then thou shalt begin[2] with shame to take the lowest
10 place.[3] But when thou art bidden, go and sit down in the
lowest place;[4] that when he that hath bidden thee cometh,
he may say to thee, Friend, go up higher: then shalt thou
have glory in the presence of all that sit at meat with thee.
11 For every one that exalteth himself shall be humbled; and he
that humbleth himself shall be exalted.[5]
12 And he said to him also that had bidden him, When thou
makest a dinner[6] or a supper,[7] call not[8] thy friends,[9] nor thy
brethren, nor thy kinsmen, nor rich neighbours; lest haply
they also bid thee again, and a recompense be made thee.[10]
13 But when thou makest a feast, bid the poor, the maimed, the
14 lame, the blind: and thou shalt be blessed; because they
have not *wherewith* to recompense thee: for thou shalt be
recompensed[11] in the resurrection of the just.[12]

The healing of the dropsical man took place before the guests
sat down to the meal. The Pharisees and the scribes who were
present were so silenced by Jesus' telling questions that there was
the necessary quietness for the Lord to teach them some other
things that they needed to know.

7–10 When the Saviour noticed how some of the guests were
ambitiously trying to secure the most important seats He told them
a parable in the form of everyday precepts (verse 7). Thus what
He said was not intended by Him as mere precepts of etiquette,
but as a lesson on eternal truths. The Lord does not here recom-
mend the practice of false humility, but calls attention to the fact
that, just as at a wedding-feast the occupying of seats of honour
does not depend on a person's self-assertive attitude but on the

discretion of the host, so also a place of honour in the kingdom of heaven does not depend on self-assertiveness or on a man's opinion of himself but on the righteous judgment of God.

11 He who exalts himself in this life will be brought to shame when the Lord, who knows the human heart and life perfectly, shows everyone his rightful place. He, however, who walks humbly in sincerity will be richly blessed.

12-14 After the Saviour had addressed the guests (verses 7–11), He now turns to the host and says that he must not invite only his friends, family and rich neighbours to meals with him, for then he does not yet practise any true love and does not render unselfish service. No, if he desires to receive a real blessing he must learn to invite regularly those who are needy and who are not able to recompense him for what he does for them. This is true hospitality and unselfish readiness to serve, which cannot but be a blessing to the host; and at the end of the age he will receive his recompense, when God raises and rewards the righteous.

It was not only the Pharisees of old who were inclined to exalt themselves above others and to be selfish in their motives. We also must constantly be on our guard against the cancers of the soul.

---

[1] " In the mixture of Jewish, Roman, Greek and Persian customs which prevailed in Palestine at this time, we cannot be sure which were the most honourable places at table " (Plummer, *in loc.*).

[2] ἀρξῃ " marks the contrast between the brief self-assumed promotion and the permanent merited humiliation " (Plummer, *in loc.*).

[3] For the other seats have in the meantime been occupied.

[4] " We are not to conclude that Jesus advocated false humility as a road to advancement; He speaks of consequence rather than purpose " (Grieve, *Peake's Commentary, in loc.*).

[5] This verse and the statement in verse 7 that He put forth a parable prove that His words do not only refer to good table manners as some expositors hold.

[6] τὸ ἄριστον " denotes lunch, the *prandium* of the Romans. In general, two meals were taken in the course of a day among the Jews; the Sabbath alone was distinguished by three obligatory meals (see on verse 1). The chief times for eating were the forenoon hours and the later afternoon hours: during the former they took breakfast (not lunch), פַּת שַׁחֲרִית [*path shachărīth*], the *ientaculum* of the Romans; during the latter they took the principal meal, סְעוּדָה [*sĕʿūdāh*], *cena*, δεῖπνον " (Strack-Billerbeck at verse 12).

[7] τὸ δεῖπνον, the chief meal, held during the week late in the afternoons, but on the Sabbath after the religious services of the fore-

noon shortly before midday (see note at verse 1). It was the custom to invite guests to the meal (*loc. cit.*).

8 μὴ φώνει, present imperative: " Do not habitually call " (Plummer); " Do not make a practice of inviting " (Grieve). One must not invite such persons *exclusively*.

9 The Saviour, as was His custom, puts the matter so clearly that it must draw the attention of the hearers. It is, of course, obvious that by these words He did not intend that one must neglect one's friends, family and rich neighbours.

10 " It is pleasant to entertain one's friends, seemly to entertain one's relations, advantageous to entertain rich neighbours. But these are not high motives for hospitality; *and we must not let our hospitality end there* " (Plummer, *in loc.*).

11 " The promise of reward for this kind of life is there as fact. You do not live in this way for the sake of the reward. If you do, you are not living in this way but in the old selfish way. Yet it is impossible to achieve, even for a moment, a pure unselfish kindness without knowing a blessedness that comes in no other way, a foretaste of something to be made perfect at the resurrection of the just " (T. W. Manson, *op. cit.*, p. 572).

For a discussion of Jesus' teaching in connection with future reward and punishment and its relation to ethical values cf. Storr, *Christianity and Immortality* (chapter ii); Rashdall, *Conscience and Christ* (appendix ii), and Geesink, *Gereformeerde Ethiek*.

12 " By the expression ἐν τῇ ἀναστάσει τῶν δικαίων, preserved here only in an utterance of Jesus, He certainly did not intend to teach in this connection that there is not also a resurrection of the ungodly, or that, if there is such a resurrection, it is not to be thought of as simultaneous with that of the righteous; for both of these cases would be a matter of indifference for the promise of a recompense on the other side for truly good action. Jesus might take it as obvious that a reward from God could only come to those who had been received into the future world and had shared in the resurrection to eternal life necessary for that " (Zahn, *in loc.*).

PARABLE OF THE GREAT SUPPER

(Cf. Matt. xxii. 1-14)

xiv. 15-24

15 And[1] when one of them that sat at meat with him heard
these things, he said unto him, Blessed is he that shall eat
16 bread[2] in the kingdom of God. But[3] he said unto him, A cer-
17 tain man[4] made a great supper;[5] and he bade many: and he
sent forth his servant at supper time[6] to say to them that were
18 bidden, Come; for *all* things are now ready. And they all
with one *consent* began to make excuse.[7] The first said unto
him, I have bought a field, and I must needs go out and see
19 it: I pray thee have me excused. And another said, I have
bought five yoke of oxen, and I go to prove them: I pray thee
20 have me excused. And another said, I have married a wife,
21 and therefore I cannot come.[8] And the servant came, and
told his lord these things. Then the master of the house being
angry said to his servant, Go out quickly into the streets and
lanes[9] of the city, and bring in hither the poor and maimed
22 and blind and lame. And the servant said, Lord, what thou
23 didst command is done, and yet there is room. And the lord
said unto the servant, Go out into the highways and hedges,[10]
and constrain[11] *them* to come in, that my house may be filled.[12]
24 For I say unto you,[13] that none of those men which were bidden shall taste of my supper.[14]

The Saviour's attitude and words before and at the commencement of the supper with the Pharisee not only silenced His critics
(verses 4, 6), but also made a deep impression on at least some of
those present, as appears from the exclamation recorded in verse 15.

15 In His words to the host the Saviour declared that if he
exercised true unselfish hospitality, he would be rewarded at
" the resurrection of the just " (verse 14). The words cause one
of those present to exclaim: " Blessed is he that shall eat bread in
the kingdom of God ", for, according to a prevailing Jewish idea,
a great and long-continued feast will be held when the Messianic
kingdom is established on earth after the resurrection. The person
who called out the words, like most of his Jewish contemporaries
(especially the Pharisees), regarded it as obvious that he and all

"respectable" Jews would have part in the Messianic celebrations, and so he took delight in the prospect. In the parable which Jesus tells in answer to his exclamation, He warns him and the others present that there is a danger that they will miss the blessings of the kingdom of God, for only those who accept the invitation of God will have a share therein.

16, 17 The Saviour sees through the self-satisfaction of the man who regards it as so obvious that he will share in the Messianic celebrations, and exposes the danger of such an attitude in the parable of those " invited to a great supper ".

As is customary in oriental countries, a certain man invited in good time a large number of rich persons to a banquet which he intended to give some time afterwards. And when the hour of the supper approached, he sent a servant, who, according to the usual Eastern custom, had to remind the persons who had accepted his first invitation that the supper was now ready and that they must come without delay. The " certain man " is God and " the supper " is the kingdom of God, regarded as a great and rich blessing which the Lord is ready to impart. The first invitation refers to the promises of the Old Testament and the messenger who takes round the final invitations is especially Jesus Himself.

Through the messengers of the Old Testament God invited the people of Israel to share in the blessings of the coming Messianic kingdom. Now the kingdom was close at hand in Christ, and John the Baptist and Jesus Himself proclaimed this plainly. This was the final invitation extended to the Jews.

18-20 When those who had been invited heard that the supper was ready, they all nevertheless asked to be excused. Three typical examples of the kind of excuses that were made are mentioned, and from this it is clear that they were merely " pretexts ". They do not adduce any real *reasons* why they are unable to go. Their excuses are false and valueless—for one does not first buy a piece of ground and only afterwards goes to see what it looks like; and if one has already bought a yoke of oxen it is useless to go only then to try them (for the sale is completed); the fact that one has got married is certainly not a sound reason why he should not go to the supper to which he has been invited. In the same way the Pharisees and most of the other Jews also make all kinds of excuses for not accepting Jesus' invitation to become true members of His kingdom. They are too much attached to worldly and visible things, and therefore they reject Him. Through the cares of this world and the temptation of riches (Matt. xiii. 22) and the pleasures of life (Luke viii. 14), they are deaf to the invitation of God which He brings.

21 The master of the house is justly angry at the attitude of those invited, because they have treated him with so much indifference, contempt and deceitfulness, and now he orders the poor, the maimed, the halt and the blind who loiter, neglected, in the streets and lanes, to be invited to his supper.

Most of the " respectable " Jews (the Pharisees and scribes) rejected Jesus although they had had the best opportunity, through their knowledge of the Old Testament, to see in Him the Fulfiller of the promises of God. And now He turns to the despised ones among Israel—the " publicans " and sinners.

22, 23 After the servant had told the master of the house that the poor folks of the town and other needy ones are already sitting at the feast, but that there is still room, the master of the house causes the people outside the city, who are to be found unsheltered in the hedges and lanes, to be invited to the feast. Because such persons consider themselves unworthy and unprepared to go to the feast, they must be " compelled " to go—not by outward violence but by the instant urgency of the invitation. The master of the house demands that every place at the feast shall be filled.

In this portion of the parable Jesus refers prophetically to the fact that, although the Gospel had to be brought first to the members of the old chosen people (Rom. i. 16), after the Jews as a nation have rejected the invitation of God the glad tidings will be carried to the Gentiles.

24 Although the people who had originally been invited, who stayed away by making all kinds of excuses, will nevertheless attempt later to gain admission to the feast, it will be refused to them—for by their foolish action they have finally excluded themselves.

When those people who have rejected the invitation of God, extended to them by Him in Christ, try to seek admission to His kingdom at the end-time when it will be revealed in full glory, it will be utterly refused to them—because they have allowed the time of grace to pass by, they have themselves to blame for their exclusion. In this verse Jesus Himself acts as the speaker and refers to His own Messianic " banquet ".

The Gospel message every day proclaims to every seeking soul the glorious invitation: " Come, for everything is ready—ready through the perfect work of redemption of God accomplished through Christ Jesus." He who refuses to accept the invitation, will through his own fault have no share in the rich blessings in the everlasting kingdom of God. But although many people may reject His invitation, others will accept it so that His " house " will be full. " Come, for everything is ready."

---

[1] The way in which Jesus' words about the resurrection (verse 14) make one of his fellow-guests think about the Messianic banquet is described as follows by Schlatter: " The whole piety of the Pharisees had its goal in the resurrection of the righteous. In order to participate in the community set free from need and death, brought to eternal life, they gladly and diligently endured the burden of the Law and made it their business not to err against any commandment. For this reason, too, they built the artificial hedge round the Law, so that by this means they might avert the possibility of coming in any situation to a serious infraction of what the Scripture commanded. If obedience was not easy and could be accomplished only through strenuous renunciation, then the pious man strengthened himself by looking at the glorious issue and refreshed himself by the contemplation of the blessedness with which God would one day recompense the toil of his service of God. How good will it be one day for those who are invited to the feast which God prepares for the righteous on the day when He shall manifest His sovereignty! " And then he continues appropriately: " The Pharisee could expect that Jesus would unconditionally agree with what he had said. Did not His beatitude declare, ' Theirs is the kingdom of God '? But it was just their hope that separated the Pharisees from Him. For by this hope, which he cherishes while he confidently expects to participate in the kingdom of God and yet rejects Christ, he means in fact that he is proceeding towards the kingdom of God and turning from it. He praises participation in the feast of God and disdains it " (in loc.).

[2] For the comparison of salvation to a joyful banquet as represented at that time by the Jews, cf. Strack-Billerbeck at Matthew viii. 11. T. W. Manson (op. cit., p. 421) notes that this remark " makes an excellent introduction to what follows, probably too good to be invented. The exclamation is apt to the circumstances of its utterance a d impeccable in its sentiment ".

[3] δέ may indicate that Jesus in His answer condemns a wrong attitude (of self-satisfaction) in the case of the speaker.

[4] Although there are certain similarities between this parable and that of Matthew xxii. 1-10, they are by no means identical and there exists no reason to assume that they are variants of one and the same original parable. Plummer is right in stating with regard to the two parables that " the context, as well as the points of difference, justifies a distinction " (in loc.).

[5] ἐποίει δεῖπνον μέγα—" Was about to make a great supper " (Plummer, in loc.).

[6] The omission of sending this second invitation would (according to oriental ideas) be regarded as " a grievous breach of etiquette, equivalent to cancelling the previous more general notification. To

refuse the second summons would be an insult, which is equivalent among the Arab tribes to a declaration of war " (cf. Plummer, *in loc.*).

7 " By three examples (verses 18–20) these excuses are illustrated according to the diversity of their arguments and the similarity of their intention " (Zahn, *in loc.*).

8 At first blush, one would think that the Pharisees could not be represented as persons who, through being too closely attached to worldly possessions and pleasures, reject the invitation of God; and yet it is true, as Schlatter writes: " The Pharisee falls through what he has in common with the other Jews, for even he, in spite of his longing for the kingdom of God, is dominated by natural desire and driven into opposition to Jesus " (*in loc.*). It is especially in their Messianic expectations their worldly-mindedness and spiritual bankruptcy are clearly to be seen.

9 " The two words combined stand for the public places of the town, in which those who have no comfortable homes are likely to be found " (Plummer, *in loc.*).

10 " This is doubtless meant to suggest a mission beyond the borders of Israel to the Gentiles " (T. W. Manson, *op. cit.*, p. 422).

11 ἀνάγκασον—here, of course, " not in the sense of external compulsion, but as in Matthew xiv. 22, Mark vi. 45, and also in classical Greek, of moral and logical constraint " (Zahn, *in loc.*). The single servant could not use physical violence, and those who refused were not compelled to go by outward force.

12 " Nec natura nec gratia patitur vacuum " (both nature and grace abhor a vacuum) (Bengel).

13 " The plural ὑμῖν shows that the speaker is no longer the host in conversation with his servant. . . . The speaker is now Jesus (cf. xi. 8, xv. 7, 10) " (Creed, *in loc.*). From this it appears, therefore, " that Jesus wishes this feast to be regarded as His feast, the table at which the guests are to recline as His table, and the coming kingdom of God as His kingdom: cf. xxii. 30 " (Zahn, *in loc.*).

Thus in unambiguous words the Saviour declares that He is not merely the prophetic preacher of the kingdom of God but the King, the Messiah of it.

14 The parable and these concluding words teach that only those persons who rejected the invitation were excluded. " Jesus does not here teach either a mechanically operating predestination, which determines from all eternity who shall or shall not be brought into the kingdom. Neither does He proclaim that man's entry into the kingdom is purely his own affair. The two essential points in His teaching are that no man can enter the kingdom without the invitation of God, and that no man can remain outside it but by his own deliberate choice. Man cannot save himself; but he can damn himself. And it is this latter fact that makes the preaching of Jesus so urgent. For He sees the deepest tragedy of human life, not in the many wrong and foolish things that men do, or the many good and wise things that they fail to accomplish, but in their rejection of God's greatest gift " (T. W. Manson, *op. cit.*, p. 422).

PARABLE ON FORETHOUGHT

25 Now there went with him great multitudes:[1] and he
26 turned, and said unto them, If any man cometh unto me, and
hateth not his own father, and mother, and wife, and children, and brethren, and sisters, yea, and his own life also, he
27 cannot be my disciple. Whosoever doth not bear his own
28 cross,[2] and come after me, cannot be my disciple. For which
of you, desiring to build a tower, doth not first sit down and
count the cost, whether he have *wherewith* to complete it?
29 Lest haply, when he hath laid a foundation, and is not able
30 to finish, all that behold begin to mock him, saying, This man
31 began to build, and was not able to finish. Or what king, as
he goeth to encounter another king in war, will not sit
down first and take counsel whether he is able with ten
thousand to meet him that cometh against him with twenty
32 thousand? Or else, while the other is yet a great way off, he
sendeth an ambassage, and asketh conditions of peace.
33 So therefore whosoever he be of you that renounceth not all
34 that he hath, he cannot be my disciple.[3] Salt therefore is
good: but if even the salt have lost its savour, wherewith
35 shall it be seasoned? It is fit neither for the land[4] nor for
the dunghill: *men* cast it out. He that hath ears to hear,
let him hear.

Ordinary human leaders take a delight in having the masses to
follow them. Jesus, however, does not accept a superficial
following of Him on the part of the masses, but subjects those
who desire to follow Him to the most severe sifting process through
the tremendous demands made by Him.

25 The Saviour's activities and words in Trans-Jordan had
made Him amazingly popular with the masses, and great multitudes who had begun to look upon Him as the possible Messiah
followed Him while He was on His way to Jerusalem. However,
He desires to check this light-hearted manner of following Him,
and so He turns to the multitudes and in a determined tone lays
down His absolute demands for everyone who wishes to be His
disciple and His true follower.

26 He who wishes to follow Him must choose Him so unconditionally as Lord and Guide that he makes all other loyalties and ties absolutely subordinate to his loyalty and devotion to Him. The Saviour, of course, does not mean that he who desires to follow Him must hate his parents and other loved ones as such, but certainly that if loyalty to Him clashes with loyalty to them he is to treat his loved ones in this connection *as though* they are persons whom he hates. But even when he acts thus towards them for the sake of his absolute loyalty to Christ, he must continue to love them and all other people, in accordance with Christ's law of love. Here Jesus, as He often did, utters the principle in a startling, categorical manner, and leaves it to His hearers to find out in the light of His other pronouncements what the qualifications are to which His utterance is subordinated.

27 Indeed, he who is not willing to die the most hideous death, by crucifixion, for the sake of his love and loyalty to Christ, cannot be His disciple. The general idea that these words of Jesus about " bearing the cross " refer to passive submission to all kinds of afflictions, like disappointments, pain, sickness and grief that come upon man in this life, is totally wrong. The people to whom Jesus spoke those words fully realised that He meant thereby that whosoever desires to follow Him must be willing to hate his own life (verse 26) and even to be crucified by the Roman authorities for the sake of his fidelity to Him. So in a wider sense this pronouncement of Jesus means that only that person who for the sake of His service surrenders all self-seeking and abandons all striving after his own interests can be His disciple.

28–32 He points out to all prospective disciples these tremendous demands, because it is essential that they should not just recklessly resolve to follow Him before they have first realised the seriousness of the matter and known what it is going to cost them. This lesson the Saviour emphasises by means of the two parables in these verses. These parables, like all the others, are not to be taken as allegories—we should not try to assign a symbolical meaning to each detail in them. Only the main points in a parable are of importance for its explanation. In these two instances the main point is this, that before anyone undertakes something important he should first of all make sure whether he will be able to finish the undertaking. Through this Jesus teaches that whosoever desires to follow Him should first make sure whether he is prepared to pay the full price, that is, the willing denial of himself to the utmost for His sake.

33 Here the Saviour declares expressly what the indispensable requirement is for anyone who wishes to become a real disciple of

His. He must relinquish *all* his possessions—not merely money and material things, but also his dear ones and everything that his heart clings to, yea, even his own life, his own desires, plans, ideals and interests. This does not mean that he must sell all his possessions or give away all his money or desert his dear ones and become a hermit or beggar or wanderer, but it means that he must give Christ full control over his whole life with everything that he is and all that he possesses, and that under His guidance and in His service he should deal with his possessions in the manner that is best. In some cases it has meant, or will mean, that a man will have to take leave of his worldly possessions and to go into distant lands to work for Christ. In most cases, however, it means that man in his ordinary life places his all at Christ's disposal to such an extent that, while still remaining in possession of his goods, he honours and serves Him thereby. The important thing is that whosoever desires to follow Him must be inwardly free from worldly-mindedness, covetousness and selfishness and wholly devoted to Him.

34, 35 Salt is valuable only when it possesses its special quality of saltness. So a follower of Jesus is of use and a blessing only when he possesses the particular character natural to a true disciple, and from the foregoing it is clear that the characteristic attribute of true followers of Jesus is absolute unselfishness and self-sacrificing loyalty towards Him. He who does not renounce everything and is not willing to sacrifice everything for His sake is, as a disciple, just as valueless as salt that has gone stale and is consequently thrown away as useless. The Saviour has spoken words of tremendous moment here. So He concludes with the impressive exclamation: " He who has ears to hear, let him hear! " Everyone who has listened to His words and has thus had the opportunity of learning these truths, must earnestly attend to what He has said, for the welfare of their immortal souls depends on it.

A great deal is entailed in being a disciple of Jesus. But the enrichment of one's whole life and the eternal welfare resulting from it, is still much greater and more glorious. In addition we must remember: not to be a disciple of Jesus means to be a disciple of the powers of darkness. And to be a servant of the world and of sin costs incalculably more than to be a disciple of Jesus— the price of it is the loss of the highest happiness in this life and darkness and affliction of soul throughout eternity. How insignificant is the price of self-renunciation in His service in comparison with the price to be paid for rejecting Him!

¹ Zahn argues from the great multitudes which followed Jesus at times and their desire to be His disciples that we are dealing here with a situation belonging to Peraea not long before the Passion.

² About A.D. 6 the Romans crucified hundreds of followers of the rebel, Judas the Gaulonite; and for the inhabitants of Palestine crucifixion was a common spectacle both before and after that date. So the words of the Lord probably made the hearers feel that He demanded that whosoever wished to follow Him had to deny himself to such an extent that he would even be prepared " to suffer the most cruel and ignominious death in the course of following Jesus " (Zahn, *in loc.*). " The taking up of the cross is the voluntary acceptance of martyrdom . . ." (T. W. Manson, *op. cit.*, p. 423). In a figurative sense it thus also means the acceptance of all sacrifice, suffering, persecution, etc., *experienced in the wholehearted following of Jesus*, and not just ordinary suffering.

³ " Discipleship of Jesus is not a mass movement " (Zahn, *in loc.*).

⁴ " The use of salt for manure is a well-attested practice for Egypt and Palestine, both in ancient and in modern times " (Creed, *in loc.*). οὔτε εἰς γῆν οὔτε εἰς κοπρίαν probably means " it is useless to put it on the land forthwith or to keep it on the manure-heap for future use " (*loc. cit.*).

PARABLES OF THE LOST SHEEP AND THE LOST PIECE OF SILVER

XV. 1–10

1 Now all the publicans and sinners[1] were drawing near
2 unto him for to hear him. And both the Pharisees and the
scribes[2] murmured, saying, This man receiveth sinners,
and eateth with them.
3, 4 And he spake unto them this parable, saying, What man
of you, having a hundred sheep, and having lost one of them,
doth not leave the ninety and nine in the wilderness,[3] and go
5 after that which is lost,[4] until he find it? And when he hath
6 found it, he layeth it on his shoulders, rejoicing.[5] And when
he cometh home, he calleth together his friends and his
neighbours, saying unto them, Rejoice with me, for I have
7 found my sheep which was lost. I say unto you, that even so
there shall be joy in heaven over one sinner that repenteth,
more than over ninety and nine righteous persons, which need
no repentance.
8 Or what woman having ten pieces[6] of silver, if she lose
one piece, doth not light a lamp, and sweep the house, and
9 seek diligently until she find it? And when she hath found
it, she calleth together her friends and neighbours, saying,
Rejoice with me, for I have found the piece which I had
10 lost. Even so, I say unto you,[7] there is joy in the presence of
the angels of God over one sinner that repenteth.

We have here the first two of the three parables on the seeking
grace of God which are preserved for us in chapter 15.

1 The " publicans " and sinners, people who were regarded
and treated as outcasts from the Jewish religious and national life,
found in Jesus One who did not despise and reject them, like the
Pharisees and scribes with their religion that was generally cold
and hard towards such people, but One who took a real interest
in them and pointed out to them the road to salvation and real
life. So they went to listen to Him regularly—something that they
would very seldom venture to do in the case of the ordinary Jewish
rabbis. The Pharisees and scribes were unwilling to have any
contact with such religious and social outcasts—through fear that

they might be polluted by them. Jesus, being spotlessly pure Himself, cherished no such fear.

2 The Saviour could come in close contact with those who had fallen low, and did so, without ever being polluted. No one else, not even the strict Pharisees, would have been able to approach the fallen in this manner without the risk of being themselves corrupted. As a result, they followed the safe road and separated themselves completely from " publicans " and sinners. And because they viewed things only in the light of their own condition and attitude, they regarded the Lord's intercourse with the outcasts in an evil light. Instead of rejoicing that at last One had come who called the lost ones in Israel to true repentance, they took it amiss that He preached to them.

3, 4 In order to point out to the Pharisees the perversity of their criticism, He relates the three parables. In this one He calls attention in the first place to the fact that the shepherd considers no trouble, sacrifice and suffering too great to find the lost sheep and bring it back. In spite of all hardships during the long search among forests, cliffs and gorges, the shepherd continues to seek until he has found the lost sheep.

Seeing that the Saviour's suffering—that was to be a suffering unto death on the cross—was so close at hand, would He not, when He put forth this parable, have in mind His own atoning death and thus also the love of God that through Him continues to look for the lost person until He recovers Him?

In the work of redemption on the cross Jesus revealed the seeking grace of God to the utmost.

5, 6 The second matter here emphasised by the Saviour is the joy of the shepherd at the recovery of the lost sheep and his action in calling his friends and neighbours together to join him in his rejoicing. Here Jesus earnestly calls upon His critics to rejoice with Him that some of the lost ones are saved instead of criticising Him because of His preaching to them.

7 It is far more necessary and becoming that they should rejoice at the bringing back of the outcasts, seeing that there is so much rejoicing in heaven over the salvation of sinners.

8 While in the preceding parable the fact is emphasised that the shepherd in spite of everything continues to seek until he has found the lost sheep, the emphasis in the parable of the lost coin is placed more on the thoroughness with which the search is carried out.

So the ancient church fathers were probably right in observing in this more especially a reference to the enlightening and penetrating working of the Holy Ghost through whom God brings the sinner to Himself.

9, 10 Once again the parable calls upon the Pharisees and scribes to rejoice over the fact that lost ones are saved.

Thus the Saviour in these two parables strikingly showed how right, natural and necessary it was that He should turn even to the outcasts of Jewish society and how wrong the attitude of His critics was.

In no other religion in the whole world does one come to know God as the One who in His love seeks the lost person to save him through His grace. In the writings of other religions we see how man seeks and yearns for God, but in the Bible we see how God in Christ seeks man to save him for time and eternity. Because the Saviour has paid with His precious blood for the redemption of man, every soul has an infinite value in God's sight and the way to the throne of grace lies open to everyone who desires to enter.

[1] " What drew those sinners to Jesus was their finding in Him not that righteousness, full of pride and contempt, with which the Pharisees assailed them, but a holiness which was associated with the tenderest love " (Godet, *in loc.*). And T. W. Manson is right in remarking: " The attitude of Jesus to publicans and sinners is not a mere humanitarian enthusiasm on His part: it is the manifestation of the will and purpose of God " (*op. cit.*, p. 574).

[2] It is indeed true that the Pharisees welcomed back repentant sinners. But with them there was not at all the *searching* love which was so perfect in Jesus. Sinners might indeed, *after* their conversion, come to them, but they did not first go to them to use their influence with them spiritually. The Saviour's attitude and conduct in this matter are quite original.

The seeking love of the Lord towards the fallen ones " has its foundation on the one hand in pity for those who have sunk most deeply, on the other hand in the worth which each individual human soul has in its eyes " (Zahn, *in loc.*).

[3] " The ' wilderness ' is not the sandy desert but open uncultivated pasture land where flocks and herds may be taken to graze " (T. W. Manson, *op. cit.*, p. 575).

[4] " Since the parables in Luke present that which Jesus does, it is strongly emphasised that the shepherd spares no pains to recover the sheep for this reason, that it is his own property. . . . His love is bestowed upon all that belongs to him and abandons none of it. The possession of the ninety and nine is no substitute for the loss of the one " (Schlatter, *in loc.*). " It is not that the shepherd does not value the ninety-nine, but the recovery of the lost one excites in him a peculiar emotion " (Luce, *in loc.*).

[5] The shepherd does not reproach or punish the lost one and does not complain of the trouble and self-sacrifice that the expedition of discovery has cost him. Although the joy of the shepherd is emphasised, it is true that " the characteristic feature of these two parables is not so much the joy over the repentant sinner as the divine love that goes out to seek the sinner before he repents " (T. W. Manson, *op. cit.*, p. 576).

[6] δραχμή—a silver coin with about as much silver as a shilling (cf. Plummer, *in loc.*).

[7] Note the tone of certainty in Jesus' pronouncements on what happens in heaven.

PARABLE OF THE PRODIGAL SON

xv. 11–32

11, 12   And he said,[1] A certain man had two sons: and the younger
of them said to his father, Father, give me the portion of *thy*
13 substance that falleth to me.[2] And he divided unto them his
living. And not many days after the younger son gathered
all together, and took his journey into a far country; and
14 there he wasted his substance with riotous living.[3] And
when he had spent all,[4] there arose a mighty famine in that
15 country; and he began to be in want. And he went and
joined himself to one of the citizens of that country; and he
16 sent him into his fields to feed swine.[5] And he would fain
have been filled with the husks[6] that the swine did eat: and
17 no man gave unto him. But when he came to himself he
said, How many hired servants of my father's have bread
18 enough and to spare, and I perish here with hunger! I will
arise and go to my father, and will say unto him, Father, I
19 have sinned against heaven,[7] and in thy sight: I am no more
worthy to be called thy son: make me as one of thy hired
20 servants. And he arose, and came to his father. But while
he was yet afar off,[8] his father saw him, and was moved with
compassion, and ran, and fell on his neck, and kissed him.
21 And the son said unto him, Father, I have sinned against
heaven, and in thy sight: I am no more worthy to be called
22 thy son. But the father said to his servants, Bring forth
quickly the best robe, and put it on him; and put a ring on
23 his hand, and shoes on his feet,[9] and bring the fatted calf,
24 *and* kill it, and let us eat, and make merry:[10] for this my son
was dead, and is alive again; he was lost, and is found.
25 And they began to be merry. Now[11] his elder son was in
the field: and as he came and drew nigh to the house, he
26 heard music and dancing. And he called to him one of the
27 servants, and inquired what these things might be. And he
said unto him, Thy brother is come; and thy father hath
killed the fatted calf, because he hath received him safe and
28 sound. But he was angry, and would not go in:[12] and his
29 father came out, and intreated him. But he answered and
said to his father,[13] Lo, these many years do I serve thee,[14]
and I never transgressed a commandment of thine: and *yet*
thou never gavest me a kid, that I might make merry with
30 my friends: but when this thy son came, which hath devoured

thy living with harlots, thou killedst for him the fatted calf.
31 And he said unto him, Son, thou art ever with me, and all
32 that is mine is thine. But it was meet to make merry[15] and be
glad: for this thy brother was dead, and is alive *again*; and
was lost, and is found.[16]

This parable deserves to be called the " Gospel within the
Gospel " because in it so many Gospel truths are proclaimed in
such a beautiful and graphic manner. This parable is closely
linked with the two preceding ones, but while the chief emphasis
in them falls on the seeking love of God and thus on the divine side
of repentance, the Saviour in this parable sheds a clear light also
on the human side.

11, 12 At that time the custom prevailed among the Jews that
a father could either bequeath his possessions to his heirs by
drawing up a testament or could even during his lifetime assign
them to his heirs in the form of presents. As a rule, however, as
in the case of the elder son in the parable, the father, although he
had allotted to each son his share, still retained the usufruct of it
until his death. In some instances, however, as in that of the
younger son in the parable, the father actually handed over the
allotted portion before his death.

13 So the younger son collected all his possessions that he had
received as a present from his father and lost no time in going and
enjoying his newly found freedom and goods in selfish indulgence.
He tears himself away from the parental home and goes to a distant
land in order to be as far away as possible from the watchful eye
of his father so that he may be able to live as he likes without
restraint. The result was that he soon wasted his substance in
riotous living with others. He had fled in order to be outside the
sphere of influence of his father and to be free and independent,
but in the distant country he had come under influences that
caused him to fall into the worst form of bondage—the fetters of
sin had bound him in their deadly toils. He had exchanged the
real freedom which consisted in obedience to his father's loving
will for the servitude of sinful profligacy, and together with the
precious treasures which he had received as a gift from his father
he lost his character too.

Thus a life of sin and error, our Lord teaches in this parable, is
in its deepest and innermost nature the rebellious breaking away
of man's life from God. Under a deceptive yearning for so-called
freedom such a person enters the distant country of sin, there to
waste in selfishness and dissipation the precious gifts which he has

received from God. All those things which a man wastes and destroys when he lives in sin he has received from God as gifts wherewith to glorify God and to experience real happiness in life; for who but the Creator gives to man his physical, intellectual and spiritual capacity and power; and who else is the Maker of everything in nature that is intended to redound to man's highest well-being?

14 After his substance had been wasted and irretrievably lost, there came, in addition, a great famine upon the " far country ", and not one of his so-called friends who had helped to waste his life and possessions could or would help him. The result was that he began to be in want.

When a man has sacrificed his life on the idolatrous altars of pleasure and selfishness in the far country, he is cruelly disillusioned by realising that this distant land has nothing to offer in lieu of the precious treasures he has wasted there—in his innermost being he is left impoverished and starved.

15, 16 At his wits' end and impelled by hunger, he accepts the most humiliating and repulsive form of servile labour—he herds the swine of one of the citizens of the distant country. But even this was not yet the lowest depth of his misery. He is treated worse than the swine that he has to feed—although he is suffering utter starvation he cannot even get a sufficient quantity of the swine's food to eat. In the far country of sin where the erring mortal desires to go and enjoy real happiness and freedom, he sooner or later falls into the cruellest and most hateful forms of servile bondage and spiritual famine. He is put to shame and suffers fatal injury.

17 Finally disillusioned by the unpleasant experiences in the " far " country, he realises how foolishly he acted in tearing himself away from his father. Mindful of conditions existing in his father's house, he now sees his own state of misery in all its naked reality.

The first step towards true repentance is that a man should become conscious of the misery into which he has fallen in the far country of sin—that he should see himself as he is in his intrinsic penury and shameful defilement.

18, 19 Now, however, he does not fall into despondency and self-pity, but decides to bid farewell to the " far country " and to return to his father. With his remorse for his sin there is also joined his faith that his father will not reject him at his house-door. At the same time, however, we must note that, from what he has decided to say to his father, it is clear that he has come to true repentance and a realisation of his guilt. He does not merely bewail his distress that forms such a glaring contrast even with the condition of his father's casual labourers; we must also observe that he does not decide to go back to his father merely in order to be freed from his distress. No, above all he bewails his deep guilt and desires to utter no other words but those of unconditional confession of guilt—the admission that he has sinned against God and against his father—and the entreaty to be received, not as his father's son, but simply as a hireling. For he feels that he is not worthy to be called his father's son. Whereas formerly he demanded his portion in self-sufficient pride, he is now quite willing, in his humility, to take the very lowest place and to obey his father's commands. Thus real remorse and the unconditional confession of sin are the indispensable requirements for true repentance. The lost one must first realise that he has no right to claim that he should be accepted as a child of God on his own merit. Whosoever desires to go to God, trusting in his own dignity or making excuses instead of confessing his sins openly, is in no condition to receive the forgiveness of God.

It is indispensable that there should be a sincere confession of sin and of utter unworthiness.

20 His resolutions are immediately transmuted into action— he arose and went to his father. And he could never have dreamed what a surprising reception was awaiting him on the part of his father. The heart of the father had continued to remain true in love for his prodigal son. Great and profound was his grief for his son in the " far country ". But he had never ceased to watch and to wait for his return and that was the reason why he saw him so soon when he arrived, and, driven by loving compassion for him, immediately ran to meet him, embraced and kissed him heartily. So inexplicably wonderful is the love of God that He not merely forgives the repentant sinner, but actually goes half-way to meet him and embraces him in His love and grace. Indeed, as the two preceding parables taught, He seeks and attracts the sinner through the redeeming work of Jesus and through the silent influence of the Holy Ghost, even long before the sinner shows remorse for his sins. He does all this without abandoning His holy righteousness, for Christ Jesus sacrificed Himself as an everlasting ransom, and whosoever comes to God in His name as a repentant sinner is welcomed by Him in perfect love, without reproaches, into the Fatherly home. The sinner may forget God, but He remains unalterably faithful in His seeking love and grace.

21 Profoundly touched by his father's inconceivable magnanimity and love, the prodigal son's realisation of sin is deeper than ever before and he confesses: " Father, I have sinned against heaven and in thy sight: I am no more worthy to be called thy son."

There is nothing that makes one realise so clearly the sinfulness of one's sin and one's utter unworthiness as the personal experience of the love with which the Heavenly Father welcomes the repentant sinner.

22-4 In his complete forgivingness the father does not even allow his son to voice his entreaty to be accepted as one of his hired servants. After his son's whole-hearted confession of sin the father immediately commands his servants to bring the robe of honour and to put it on him, and to give him a ring for his hands and shoes for his feet—everything as a sign that he accepts his lost son fully as a son and re-establishes him in a position of honour. In addition, they are to kill the fatted calf which is meant only for a special occasion, so that a worthy and joyful feast may be celebrated to rejoice that the son, who in the " far country " had been practically dead and lost to his father and his home, has come back to life. So the celebrations began immediately.

When the sinner returns to the Heavenly Father, He does not reproach and punish him, neither does He humiliate him to the position of a hired servant or a slave, but He accepts him in Christ as His beloved child—and gives to him the full status and all the privileges of real childship. And when a sinner has come to repentance, there is joy not only in his own heart but also in heaven with the Father.

25-8 Thus far the Saviour pointed in the parable to the bitter fruits of a life without God in the " far country " of sin, to the remorse and return of the erring one, to the welcoming love of the Father and His joy at the repentance of a sinner. And now, in describing the attitude of the elder brother, Jesus presents a clear picture of the folly of the Pharisees and scribes who are dissatisfied with Him for receiving publicans and sinners. Just as the elder brother, instead of rejoicing with his father at the return of his lost brother, was extremely annoyed at the joyful celebrations and at the honour shown to the returned one, so also the Jewish religious leaders reveal a spirit out of harmony with the Heavenly Father in His welcoming the " publicans " and sinners through Jesus.

It is noteworthy that the father also goes out to the elder brother to invite him to come in (second half of verse 28). He is not biased, but treats both his sons with the same tenderness and affection. He has perfect love for the elder brother as well as for the younger. So the Lord not only longs for the " publicans " and sinners to repent, but also that the Pharisees and scribes (those who outwardly still remained with the Father but were inwardly estranged from Him) should come to Him and share His love for the lost.

29, 30 From these words it is abundantly clear how the elder son had inwardly strayed from his father. " I have not at any time transgressed thy commandment," he declares, thereby saying in effect that he regarded his relation to his father as one of slavish bondage instead of the free and spontaneous relationship of a child. In addition his words reveal the fact that in his self-conceit he regards himself as the perfect son and in his bitter censoriousness looks upon his brother as exactly the opposite. In his own eyes he himself deserves all honour and veneration while his brother has no longer any right to what belongs to his father. So he regards his father's action as extreme partiality in favour of the prodigal whom he no longer recognises even as his brother (for he speaks of him as " thy son " and not as " my brother ").

In this way the Saviour effectively depicts the whole attitude of the Pharisees—for they also are inwardly estranged from God and have allowed their religion to degenerate into slavish bondage and self-righteousness. While they themselves remain spiritually cold and far removed from God, they despise and avoid persons like the " publicans " and sinners who in their eyes are no longer worthy to be members of the real people of Israel.

31 The father answers in deep sympathy that the accusation that he has not given him his due is devoid of truth. All his riches were and are constantly at his elder son's disposal. If he has not received any real enjoyment of them, he is the only one to blame for it—because he has become inwardly estranged from his father, he has been living as one of his servants and not as his child. He has left unused the riches allotted to him by his father.

By this the Saviour teaches explicitly that God has always been longing to give the religious people in Israel the first opportunity of entering His kingdom and of receiving and enjoying the fullness of life. So it is only their own inward estrangement of heart from His grace that renders them spiritually poor and unhappy.

32 The other accusation of the elder brother that the prodigal son is loaded with honours is also refuted by the father. He declares that it is impossible for a family not to rejoice when a prodigal son (however miserable his life has been) has returned home. The hearty welcome extended to the younger brother has, therefore, nothing to do with a reward according to deserts, but is wholly a matter for rejoicing and gratitude that one of the family has come back in the fullest sense of the word.

In this Jesus reveals the root of the error of the Pharisees and scribes by making them feel that God's attitude towards men is not paid for through so-called meritorious works like slavish observance of the Law and faithful compliance with outward forms, but through His love and grace towards everyone who truly turns to God and thus comes into real inward communion with Him.

The important question for each of us is: are we still in the "far country" of sin where final ruin awaits us, or have we already returned with true repentance, thus to receive through grace the joy of full sonship as our portion for time and eternity? Or are we like the elder son, outwardly pious and respectable but inwardly still empty and estranged from God?

¹ The words εἶπεν δέ denote this parable's independence of the foregoing ones, but nevertheless the Saviour probably related it in close relation to what goes before, and indeed possibly on the same occasion (cf. Zahn, in loc.).

² " A father could carry out the sharing of his goods among his children either by a testamentary bequeathal or in the form of gifts. In the former case he was bound by the prescriptions of the Torah; in the latter he had a freer hand " (Strack-Billerbeck, in loc., and cf. Gal. iii. 15). See also T. W. Manson, op. cit., pp. 578-9.

³ ἀσώτως—" unites in itself the senses of a life of unrestrained sensuality and spendthrift extravagance " (Zahn, in loc.).

⁴ " Sin consists in this, that a man monopolises the things with which God endows him in nature and makes them serve his own selfish desires. From this arises the godlessness of his thought and will; he is absorbed in the natural order. From this arises, further, his impoverishment and inward starvation. When a man has become godless, nature no longer supplies him with what he needs. He becomes wretched, lonely, helpless, hopeless; and human society affords no defence against this, for it founders on human self-seeking " (Schlatter, in loc.).

⁵ To the Jew especially the feeding of swine was a most repulsive occupation.

⁶ τὰ κεράτια does not mean " husks " but the fruit of the so-called " St. John's bread " or carob tree (ceratonia siliqua). " To be compelled to eat St. John's bread was synonymous with the bitterest poverty and need " (Strack-Billerbeck, in loc.).

⁷ For the Jewish custom of using the name of God as seldom as possible and substituting for it such a circumlocution as " heaven " cf. Dalman, Words of Jesus, pp. 204 ff.

⁸ We must remember that in a parable not all particulars should be explained allegorically (cf. our exposition at xiv. 28-32). Still less may we assume that all sides of a particular matter are illustrated in one

parable. Thus we may not regard the parable of the prodigal son as one in which all aspects of the truth of the forgiving love of God are elucidated. " This one parable does not offer, and was not meant by Jesus to offer, a complete compendium of theology " (T. W. Manson, *op. cit.*, p. 578). Where, e.g., no mention is here made of the sacrificial death of Jesus on the strength of which God forgives the sinner, we may not conclude (as Creed, Luce, and others are inclined to do) that the Saviour did not originally teach that His atoning death was necessary for the forgiveness of man's sins and that it is Paul and the later church that created the doctrine of expiation in conflict with Jesus' teaching. No, for the Saviour here illustrates only a few main facts in connection with forgiveness of sins and we must supplement these from what He taught on other occasions.

" The measure of the Gospel is constituted not by any one parable or word but by the sum total of the aspects under which Jesus is revealed, and if these elsewhere include the sense of a redeeming or expiatory purpose to be effected by the sufferings and death of the Messiah, the parable of the lost son, perfect illustration as it is of the joy of God over a sinner's repentance, is not to be pressed to the exclusion of that conception " (W. Manson, *in loc.*).

In his allegation that " Luke appears nowhere to associate the remission of sins directly with Christ's death " Creed (*in loc.*) is altogether at fault. Luke's whole Gospel is framed and arranged in such a manner that it creates the impression that it has been written to illustrate the Pauline text: " God commandeth his own love toward us, in that, while we were yet sinners, Christ died for us " (Rom. v. 8).

[9] " None of the three things ordered are necessary. The father is not merely supplying the wants of his son, who has returned in miserable and scanty clothing. He is doing him honour " (Plummer, *in loc.*).

[10] The parable teaches that forgiveness of sins also brings about true renewal of communion between God and man. " Therefore it is not only the exemption that remits the punishment, not only the quieting of our apprehension of God's wrath and judgment, but the receiving of perfect joy, in which the heavenly beings share. Therefore, too, it is not only the toleration of the wicked, but his overcoming, because it is the bringing into a status of sonship and it gives the guilty person life in fellowship with the Father " (Schlatter, *in loc.*).

How different from the ideas of the Pharisees is the preaching of the Saviour in this connection! While they regarded themselves as the just who needed no conversion, they regarded the converted sinners as a lower group. " That would be a mutilated love, which only half attains its goal " (*loc. cit.*). In contrast with this the Saviour proclaims the creating omnipotence of the divine love that makes everything new in the heart and life of the penitent one.

[11] The view of Wellhausen and others that the second part of the parable is a later addition and not derived from Jesus is altogether devoid of any good reason. Even Creed rejects this view (*in loc.*). The parable forms a solid unit and fits into the historical circumstances.

¹² To His critics (verse 2) the Saviour here puts " within the parable itself, in the form of the elder son, their frightfully repulsive reflection before their eyes " (Zahn, *in loc.*). And yet, however destructive the judgment is that overtakes them in this parable, the final scenes of the affectionate and friendly attitude of the father towards the elder son serve as a tender but urgent call to them also to return to true communion with God.

¹³ " When the Pharisee forbids Jesus to forgive, he reveals his own incapacity to forgive. Therefore he becomes an accuser of the brother who deprives him of his honour. But he can only do this by finding fault with the father, too " (Schlatter, *in loc.*). For the glorious truth is already proclaimed in the Old Testament that God takes no pleasure in the sinner's death, but longs that he should repent, receive forgiveness, and live (cf. Ps. ciii. 3–14; Ezek. xviii. 23, 31, 32).

¹⁴ The religion of most of the Pharisees and scribes was essentially one of rigid lack of freedom. It was a severe burden on them and made their lives cheerless, for their obedience to the law of God was constrained and not founded upon sincere love and gratitude towards God.

¹⁵ εὐφρανθῆναι is the outward celebration and χαρῆναι the inward experience of joy and gladness.

¹⁶ Plummer is right in stating: " Not the least skilful touch in this exquisite parable is that it ends here. We are not told whether the elder brother at last went in and rejoiced with the rest. And we are not told how the younger one behaved afterwards. Both those events were still in the future, and both agents were left free " (*in loc.*). With pent-up force this conclusion calls upon those who are to be identified with the elder brother to enter and to establish a living communion with the Father, thus sharing in the heavenly joy. And on the other hand it forcibly points to the glorious welcome awaiting every penitent sinner with God.

PARABLE OF THE UNJUST STEWARD

xvi. 1–13

1   And he said also[1] unto the disciples,[2] There was a certain rich man, which had a steward; and the same was accused[3]
2 unto him that he was wasting[4] his goods. And he called him, and said unto him, What is this that I hear of thee? render the account of thy stewardship; for thou canst be
3 no longer steward.[5] And the steward said within himself, What shall I do, seeing that my lord taketh away the stewardship from me? I have not strength to dig; to beg I
4 am ashamed. I am resolved[6] what to do, that, when I am put out of the stewardship, they may receive me into their
5, 6 houses. And calling to him each one of his lord's debtors, he said to the first, How much owest thou unto my lord? And he said, A hundred measures[7] of oil. And he said unto him,
7 Take thy bond, and sit down quickly and write fifty.[8] Then said he to another, And how much owest thou? And he said, A hundred measures[9] of wheat. He saith unto him,
8 Take thy bond, and write fourscore. And his lord[10] commended[11] the unrighteous steward because he had done wisely: for the sons[12] of this world[13] are for their own genera-
9 tion[14] wiser than the sons of the light. And I say unto you, Make to yourselves friends by means of the mammon[15] of unrighteousness; that, when it shall fail,[16] they[17] may
10 receive you into the eternal tabernacles. He that is faithful[18] in a very little[19] is faithful also in much: and he that is
11 unrighteous in a very little is unrighteous also in much. If therefore ye have not been faithful in the unrighteous mam-
12 mon, who will commit to your trust the true *riches*? And if ye have not been faithful in that which is another's,[20] who
13 will give you that which is your own? No servant can serve[21] two masters: for either he will hate the one, and love the other; or else he will hold to one, and despise the other. Ye cannot serve God and mammon.[22]

Opponents of Christianity have often tried to draw upon this parable for arguments denying our Saviour's integrity of character, but such arguments rest, without exception, upon unsound foundations.

1, 2 A certain steward, so the parable runs, did what the prodigal son (xv. 13) had done with the possessions his father had

414

given him—he wasted his master's goods. When the rich owner was informed of this, he commanded his steward to give an account of his stewardship, i.e. he had to give an exact statement of the actual condition of the property with the management of which he was entrusted. The object of this command was to expose clearly the extent of the wastefulness and disorder into which the steward had brought the business, so that it would be possible for his successor to take up his work. The owner apparently did not suspect the steward of conscious dishonesty, but thought that he had merely been irresponsible and extravagant in his management. So he did not have him forthwith arrested and punished for deceit or theft, but only informed him that he could no longer be his steward.

3, 4 The waster, who had been spoiled by a life of plenty and ease, saw no chance of accepting a strenuous or humiliating work to make a living. However, he had enough cunning and adroitness to devise a plan to look after his own interests in an easy (although a dishonest and underhand) manner.

5-7 So he sent for those persons who had formerly, when he was steward, raised loans or bought goods on credit in the business of his master. He spoke to them one by one separately, let them destroy their written acknowledgments of debt and draw up and sign new ones in which the amounts owed by them were considerably diminished. He thereby robbed his master deliberately and disgracefully, but gained the favour of the debtors whose load of debt had been lightened by him.

8 The owner came to know how the dishonest steward had set about providing for his own future by treating the debtors in such a manner that they would after his dismissal receive and maintain him in their homes. Because the shrewd steward had spoken to the debtors one by one and separately and had destroyed the old acknowledgments of debt, the master had not the necessary proofs or witnesses that could enable him to take legal steps against him. All that he could do, therefore, was to acknowledge that he had acted very cleverly. He did not praise his unjust and fraudulent act as such, but the " worldly wisdom " with which he had acted towards the debtors. The Saviour did not continue the parable so as to relate what happened next. It was His object (as appears from the last words of verse 8) to use the parable to call attention to the " wise " and diplomatic manner in which worldlings generally act towards their fellow-men in order to achieve their own selfish aims. In contrast with the diplomatic, clever conduct of such people, those who are members of the kingdom of light too often act unwisely and undiplomatically towards others. Instead of behaving in such a manner that they bind others to themselves, they act so that people are unnecessarily repulsed—like the Pharisees who by their attitude of self-righteousness and self-exaltation repel the " publicans " and sinners instead of attracting them and making them willing to receive their teachings. The Saviour Himself in verse 8 calls the dishonest steward " unjust ", and as He unconditionally condemned throughout, in word and act, every suggestion of fraud, there was no danger that His hearers would interpret His words as though He was recommending dishonest methods. Thus it is totally unjustifiable to launch attacks (as certain persons do) against the Saviour's ethical standards and against the New Testament on the basis of this parable.

9 In the parable there was a reference to material possessions (not merely to money), and as a result the Saviour adds these words as an express command in connection with the right use of material things (summarised under the metaphor of " the mammon of unrighteousness "). He calls worldly possessions *the mammon of unrighteousness*, because injustice is so often involved in the accumulation and use of earthly possessions. But the Saviour nowhere teaches that material possessions as such are sinful and unclean. It is man's sinful attitude and conduct in connection with worldly goods (money in particular) that make these things a curse. While in general in the world earthly possessions are rightly designated as the "mammon of unrighteousness", it must be quite different in the case of His followers. They must be so free from the low, selfish and covetous motives that dominated the unjust steward of the parable that they will use the worldly goods entrusted to them by the Father in a manner that will bring blessing to others and be conducive to their own eternal welfare. Especially does it mean that they should be so free from avarice and so inspired by real unselfish love that, as God leads them, they will whole-heartedly share their material possessions with persons who need them. In this way they will gain for themselves an imperishable treasure in heaven. In the Hereafter those who were helped by them in life by the right use they made of their worldly goods will, as it were, welcome them and testify in their favour. A sharp contrast is formed between this future welcoming of the faithful in the *eternal* dwellings where they will be with God, and the fate of the unjust steward who (suffering under the weight of a guilty conscience) would be received in the homes of fellow-sinners, and this only for a short time—as long as his " benefactors " remain well-disposed towards him and he remains alive.

416

10, 11 Because a man's character does not depend on the quantity of goods entrusted to him but on the real disposition of his heart, it proves, whenever he is unfaithful or unjust in the small things of life, that he is essentially false and therefore also unfaithful in the great things of life. Consequently, if one is unfaithful in the acquisition and use of worldly goods (which in the light of reality are " the least " things and of the smallest *intrinsic* value), how can a responsible task in connection with the eternal and " true riches " (the things of highest value) be entrusted to him? Whosoever is unfaithful and false in ordinary life, although he may pose as extremely pious, is also false and unfaithful spiritually, and so no spiritual gifts and blessings can be entrusted to him.

12 Everything that man possesses on earth (talents, privileges, money, etc.) belongs primarily to the Creator, who lends it so liberally in order that it may be a blessing to man himself and to his fellow-men and that it should be used to the honour of God. Accordingly, if anyone is unfaithful in connection with these " borrowed goods " how can he expect to receive God's eternal riches, the spiritual gifts given for time and eternity to the redeemed as their own?

13 In order to be able to serve and love God truly, man must be free from the servility accompanying avarice and attachment to material possessions. For although worldlings may labour under the delusion that they are free and independent, everyone who makes the accumulation and enjoyment of earthly goods the main object of his life is under the dominating power thereof and is every day performing servile labour for Mammon.

Do we use our worldly possessions in such a manner that there will be persons in Eternity who will be glad to receive us? Or will there be numbers who will point accusing fingers at us because we neglected or injured them through our unfaithful conduct in connection with the earthly goods entrusted to us?

---

[1] The καί before πρός indicates that the parable now introduced " followed the telling of the three parables of chapter xv without change of scene " (Zahn, *in loc.*).

[2] T. W. Manson rightly remarks in connection with this parable: " This parable has always presented difficulties for the interpreter, and like most of such difficulties they arise from trying to press the details of the story instead of seeking for the main point " (*The Mission and Message of Jesus*, p. 583). For we must remember that " every parable

contains details which are not intended to convey any lesson, although necessary to complete the picture, or to impress it upon the memory " (Plummer, *in loc.*). In this parable there are several subordinate details which should not be explained allegorically. Thus the rich man has no special significance as though he represents the Lord or Mammon or someone else.

³ διαβάλλειν—only here in New Testament. Although it is often used outside the New Testament with the meaning " to defame " or " accuse falsely ", it is also used with the general meaning " accuse ". That the accusations were well-founded in this case is evident from the course of events.

⁴ Here the same word (διασκορπίζειν) is used as in the parable of the prodigal son (xv. 13). It refers to the steward's wastefulness, carelessness, neglect of duty, and other faults through which his master's goods were squandered (cf. Zahn, *in loc.*).

⁵ This sentence proves that it is already a foregone conclusion with the owner that the steward is guilty of wastefulness and will have to relinquish his office.

⁶ ἔγνων—" The asyndeton and the aorist express the suddenness of the idea " (Plummer, *in loc.*). The usage is sometimes called the dramatic aorist (Easton, *in loc.*).

⁷ A hundred " baths " (βάτους) = 868 gallons (T. W. Manson, *op. cit.*, p. 583).

⁸ The meaning is obviously that he has to destroy the old bill and write out a new one.

⁹ A hundred " cors " (κόρους) = 1,083 bushels (T. W. Manson, *in loc.*).

¹⁰ With Zahn and others we must assume that by ὁ κύριος the rich man is indicated here and not Jesus, for otherwise the whole context would be disturbed. In verse 1 it is stated: " And he said also unto his disciples . . ." and in verse 9 we read: " And I say unto you . . ."; how then, can we regard verse 8 as words in which Luke describes what the Saviour said about the steward? Verses 1–8a is a continuous narrative, followed in verses 8b–13 by concluding remarks by Jesus on the moral of the story. There is no statement by the evangelist throughout. Thus ὁ κύριος in verse 8a can only mean the rich man, who is also called ὁ κύριος in verse 3.

¹¹ The owner praises the steward " not of course because of his unrighteousness but because he acted intelligently, with a view to the desired end, one might say with the wisdom of serpents (Matt. x. 16) " (Zahn, *in loc.*).

¹² " The Hebrew idiom ' sons of ' means ' those who share the characteristics of ' " (Luce, *in loc.*).

¹³ ὁ αἰὼν οὗτος in a great measure agrees with the Jewish הָעוֹלָם הַזֶּה, *hā-'ōlām hazzeh* (" this age "), the time before the dominion of the Messiah is present (in contrast with the הָעוֹלָם הַבָּא, *hā-'ōlām habbā*, the age that is coming after the advent of the Messiah). In the

New Testament, however, the expression " this age " or " this world " is used also, because Jesus as Messiah has already come, in reference to the present world in so far as it is still outside Christ and under the power of sin and Satan. So " children of this world " refers to the unbelieving worldlings.

14 εἰς τὴν γενεὰν τὴν ἑαυτῶν = towards their own generation, i.e. worldlings in their mutual intercourse are often more discerning and diplomatic than the faithful generally are. " The steward's cleverness is not an isolated phenomenon: it is part of the way of the world. The worldlings show far more *savoir faire* than the religious in dealing with their contemporaries. For even their roguery is often designed to procure them friends, while the pious too often estrange those who might be friendly to them " (T. W. Manson, *The Mission and Message of Jesus*, p. 584).

15 " Mammon " is derived from the Aramaic word מָמוֹנָא (*māmōnā*). The derivation of this Aramaic word is disputed, " but its meaning certain: it is wealth of every kind " (T. W. Manson, *op. cit.*, p. 425).

16 ἐκλίπῃ must be taken as the original reading. Thus verse 8b reads: " when it (your worldly property) disappears ". This takes place finally when one dies (cf. Zahn, *in loc.*).

17 The indefinite " they " in this context is really a substitute for " God ". " By the indefinite subject ' they ' (= ' one ') God is meant; this construction, avoiding the mention of the name of God, is very common in Rabbinic language " (Strack-Billerbeck, *in loc.*).

18 " To prevent a possible misunderstanding owing to the commendation of a dishonest servant, Christ here insists upon the necessity of fidelity in dealing with worldly possessions " (Plummer, *in loc.*).

19 Money and earthly possessions are also a gift of God, but then only the most insignificant of His gifts. By calling worldly goods " the least ", the Lord warns us against overrating their value.

20 ἐν τῷ ἀλλοτρίῳ. " Earthly wealth is not only trivial and unreal; it does not belong to us. It is ours only as a loan and a trust, which may be withdrawn at any moment. Heavenly possessions are immense, real, and eternally secure " (Plummer, *in loc.*).

21 δουλεύειν = to serve as a slave.

22 " The man who sets his heart on the money that is in his hand (Ps. lxii. 10) and therefore finds gifts to the needy annoying (Prov. iii. 27) may delude himself that he is maintaining himself in his position as master over his money and in his independence of other men; but in actual fact he is a slave of Mammon " (Zahn, *in loc.*).

THE AUTHORITY OF THE LAW

xvi. 14–18

14   And the Pharisees, who were lovers of money,[1] heard all
15 these things; and they scoffed at him.[2] And he said unto
them, Ye are they that justify yourselves in the sight of men;[3]
but God knoweth your hearts:[4] for that which is exalted
16 among men is an abomination in the sight of God. The law
and the prophets *were* until John:[5] from that time the gospel
of the kingdom of God is preached, and every man entereth
17 violently into it.[6] But it is easier for heaven and earth to
18 pass away,[7] than for one tittle[8] of the law to fall.[9] Every one
that putteth away his wife, and marrieth another, committeth
adultery:[10] and he that marrieth one that is put away from
a husband committeth adultery.[11]

In the foregoing portion the Saviour addressed His disciples
(cf. verse 1) in particular, although the Pharisees and other Jews
were also present. He now turns to the Pharisees.

14 Because the Pharisees were fond of money and regarded
riches as the rightful reward for their faithful observance of the
Law, they derided Jesus (who in contrast with most of them was
poor and was followed by a small group of poor disciples)—does
not His poverty and that of His disciples prove that they are not
honoured by God in the same degree as they themselves are
honoured?

15 The Saviour, however, calls attention to their error. By
distributing alms with public display and by pointing to their
riches as a proof that they are regarded by God as worthy
observers of the Law, they pose as just. But He knows their hearts
and knows what motives are hidden behind their public practice
of charity. The great question is not whether they are honoured
by men on account of their wealth and outward piety, but whether
God esteems them.

16 The appearance of John formed the transition from the
dispensation of the Old Testament to the dispensation of the New
Testament. He had begun and Jesus and His disciples had continued to proclaim that the kingly rule of God had come in
Christ, and everyone who listens to Him in faith (like many

" publicans " and sinners) presses with the greatest earnestness, self-denial and determination, as though with spiritual violence, into the kingdom—the sphere within which the kingly dominion of God is revealed. They strive hard to enter by the strait gate. But meanwhile most of the Pharisees refuse to believe in Him, and they deride Him. Thus they exclude themselves from the kingdom.

17 But although it is a fact that with His advent a new order, a new dispensation, is entered upon, this does not mean that the revelation of God under the Old Covenant is set aside or rejected. Although it is of a preparatory nature, it remains (naturally in a moral and spiritual sense and in the full light of the divine revelation in and through Jesus) absolutely authoritative.

18 The moral laws, e.g., may not be violated—adultery continues to be adultery, even although the time of preparation is superseded by the time of fulfilment.

People to-day are still disposed to regard those who have become rich and are known to give alms as people of the highest standing. God be thanked that there are many such wealthy people who are sincere and are a rich blessing to others, and live for the honour of God. Nevertheless, the Pharisaical types are, alas, still often to be found. Which of us is not to a greater or lesser degree infected by the same forms of spiritual blindness that in those days made the religion and life of so many Pharisees useless and dangerous?

---

[1] Although some writers like Montefiore, Easton and Luce, contradict the statement that the Pharisees were avaricious, the available data, nevertheless, show that it was indeed the case with many of them (cf. Strack-Billerbeck, in loc.), and, as Wellhausen wrote: " Moneymaking generally agrees well with religious separation, both among Jews and Christians " (cf. Creed, in loc.). " The covetousness of the Pharisees is independently attested, and they regarded their wealth as a special blessing for their carefulness in observing the Law. Hence their contempt for teaching which declared that there is danger in wealth and that as a rule it promotes unrighteousness " (Plummer, in loc.).
In the light of this, T. W. Manson's view (*The Mission and Message of Jesus*, pp. 587 f.) that Luke was wrong in here speaking of Pharisees (instead of Sadducees) appears both unnecessary and unfounded.

[2] " In their love of money they felt themselves hit by this last speech of Jesus, and in view of the disciples, possessed of little or nothing, to whom it was addressed, it seemed ridiculous to them " (Zahn, in loc.).

[3] This description fits the Pharisees admirably, but not the Sadducees, as T. W. Manson tries to prove (*ibid.*).

⁴ " We may perhaps supply an unexpressed concession: you do indeed give alms, but you only do so to justify yourselves before men " (Creed, *in loc.*). " Before men you can play your part as just men as you give yourselves out to be such (cf. verse 18a), and possibly indeed wish your riches to be regarded as a divine reward for that " (Klostermann, *in loc.*).

⁵ There exists no cogent reason why these words should be identified with those of Matthew xii. 12, 13. Why could not the Saviour on two occasions or still more often have made statements about John as a transitional person and about the " violent " pressing into the kingdom?

⁶ Rudolf Otto gives a good rendering of one aspect of the meaning of this sentence as follows: " The kingdom of heaven is stormed, is taken by force. . . . Hitherto is was only prophesied, only prepared; hitherto one could only hope for it, wait, prepare oneself and others for it, but now it is grasped, possessed, held fast as that which has come. . . . The Law and the Prophets could only prophesy it, John only prepare the way for it, but now one could seize it, gain it, come to participate in it " (*The Kingdom of God and the Son of Man* [Eng. ed., 1943], pp. 110-11). Although the kingdom has not yet come in final completeness, it nevertheless came into the world as a mighty actuality, already in and with Jesus' public appearance on earth. βιάζεται is here middle voice (cf. Klostermann, *in loc.*) and not passive.

⁷ " The authenticity of this saying should never have been called in question. Christ was hostile to the scribal tradition, but His attitude towards the Old Testament itself was one of unquestioning acceptance; to Him this was God's word, without qualification. The words of the Law, if rightly understood, were the sure guide to salvation " (Easton, *in loc.*).

⁸ It is generally accepted that the κεϱέα (a little horn) indicates a little stroke to distinguish certain Hebrew letters from others. However, Strack-Billerbeck, Cadbury, and others are of the opinion that it refers to the ornamental strokes drawn above certain letters on rolls of the Law. " These were no part of the Law itself, but an addition to it. . . . The saying thus comes to mean: it is easier for heaven and earth to pass away than for the scribes to give up the smallest bit of that tradition by which they make the Law of none effect " (T. W. Manson, *The Mission and Message of Jesus*, p. 427). But however attractive this theory might be, we cannot accept it, for if Jesus had intended this He would surely have indicated it by saying " one of their traditions ", or something to this effect, instead of " one tittle of the law ". How can the κεϱέαι of the Law, even although they were " scribal ornaments " subsequently added (T. W. Manson, *in loc.*), be taken as referring to the human traditions of the Pharisees? There is no reason why recourse should be had to such a far-fetched explanation. The Saviour's words here are a very natural way of emphasising the absolute authority of the Old Testament (at that time often referred to simply as " the Law ").

[9] " ' To fall to the ground ' as devoid of authority " (Plummer, *in loc.*).

[10] " The difficulty which we experience in determining what our Lord actually taught on this matter [divorce] impressively illustrates the absolute impossibility of basing detailed rules for the guidance of modern life upon isolated sayings of Christ. That the ideal is permanent monogamous marriage is undoubtedly the principle which Jesus taught; and that ideal still appeals to all the higher ethical feeling of our time. By what detailed enactments the ideal may best be promoted, which is the less of two evils when the ideal has been violated and made impossible, is a question which must be settled by the moral consciousness, the experience, the practical judgment of the present " (Rashdall, *Conscience and Christ*, p. 106).

[11] These words are especially directed against those Pharisees who allowed divorce to the husbands on various kinds of trifling matters, but violated the right of the wife in such a manner that no right of divorce was granted her if she was unjustly or cruelly treated by her husband. " She was bound to her husband, and it was only to the husband that the rabbis preserved the right to dismiss his wife at pleasure " (Schlatter, at xviii. 15–17). It was the milder rabbinical school of Hillel that allowed this easy divorce. It is remarkable that Jesus, whose teaching in general has more in common with the school of Hillel, should in this one respect have agreed rather with the stricter school of Shammai.

PARABLE OF THE RICH MAN AND LAZARUS

xvi. 19–31

19 Now there was a certain rich man,[1] and he was clothed in
20 purple and fine linen, faring sumptuously every day: and a
21 certain beggar named Lazarus[2] was laid[3] at his gate,[4] full of
sores, and desiring to be fed with the *crumbs* that fell from
the rich man's table; yea, even the dogs came and licked his
22 sores. And it came to pass, that the beggar died,[5] and that he
was carried away by the angels into Abraham's[6] bosom:[7] and
23 the rich man also died, and was buried.[8] And in Hades[9] he
lifted up his eyes, being in torments, and seeth Abraham afar
24 off, and Lazarus in his bosom. And he cried and said,[10]
Father Abraham, have mercy on me, and send Lazarus,[11]
that he may dip the tip of his finger in water, and cool my
25 tongue; for I am in anguish in this flame.[12] But Abraham
said, Son, remember that thou in thy lifetime receivedst[13]
thy good things, and Lazarus in like manner evil things:[14]
26 but now here he is comforted, and thou art in anguish. And
beside all this,[15] between us and you there is a great gulf
fixed, that they which would pass from hence to you may not
27 be able, and that none may cross over from thence to us. And
he said, I pray thee therefore, father, that thou wouldest send
28 him to my father's house; for I have five brethren; that he
may testify unto them, lest they also come into this place of
29 torment. But Abraham saith, They have Moses and the
30 prophets; let them hear them.[16] And he said, Nay, father
Abraham: but if one go to them from the dead, they will
31 repent. And he said unto him, If they hear not Moses and the
prophets, neither will they be persuaded, if one rise from the
dead.

In this parable the Saviour impressively illustrates the truth
uttered by Him in verse 15b: "that which is exalted among men
is an abomination in the sight of God." During his life on earth the
rich man was a splendid example of one who was highly esteemed
among men. But after his death his condition was a striking proof
that, notwithstanding the high esteem in which he was held by
men, he was, on account of his selfish and heartless life, an
abomination in the sight of God, the Judge of the human
heart, and the Judge who judges righteously.

19 The rich man was royally clothed and constantly gave splendid banquets, which he celebrated with outward splendour and pomp and exuberant joviality. He strove after no higher purpose in life than to use his riches in selfishness and ostentation for worldly pleasure.

20, 21 That the rich man had no open eye and sympathetic heart for the needs and sufferings of others, but had fallen completely into selfish pleasure-seeking, is evident from the fact that he had left the sick beggar uncared-for as he lay at his gate in his misery. In vain did the starving Lazarus long to still the cravings of hunger even if it could only be done with the crumbs that fell from the rich man's table. Through the scanty help which he received from others, he nevertheless lived for some time and lay daily at the gate of the rich man in the hope that he might eventually take pity on him and save him from his wretched state. But alas, the rich man with cruel heartlessness left him there hungry and unaided. Only the dogs took an interest in him and licked his sores.

22 Finally the beggar died of hunger and privation endured by him at the rich man's gate. But because the beggar trusted in God, and had even amidst his terrible suffering not become embittered, he was taken to the abodes of everlasting blessedness when he died.

23 The rich man, like the sick beggar, also died—neither his multitude of possessions nor his influence among men could protect him against the inevitability of death. In the hereafter his condition, owing to his sinful life of selfishness and heartlessness, is the exact opposite of what it had been on earth. While Lazarus enjoys full blessedness with Father Abraham, he who during his life had despised and neglected the beggar at his gate endured the utmost torment.

24 The rich man who, while on earth, had regarded himself as totally independent and had, on account of his wealth, never needed to ask for anything from anybody else, now experiences such misery that he begs for help, even if it is only a single drop of water for his thirsty tongue, at the hand of the formerly despised beggar. Now he, in his turn, is the beggar who yearns for relief from the inexpressible tortures endured by him in the flame of remorse and eternal despair.

25 Abraham, however, answers that things cannot be different from what they now are—he (the heartless and wealthy man) had chosen worldly riches and worldly pleasure and luxury as his highest good, he had revelled in it completely without accumulating treasures for eternity, and so it is his own fault that he has now become the beggar steeped in suffering. During his life he had regarded his worldly possessions as his own—as things to be used by him only for the sake of his own honour, ease and pleasure, and had not regarded them as gifts entrusted to him by God for the purpose of using them for the welfare of others (especially the needy ones) and to the honour of God. So he had chosen as his portion the earthly, evanescent things, and therefore he has only himself to blame that he is now in this pitiable state. He has not the least right to expect that his sufferings will be relieved. It is as a result of his own choice that he has been plunged into these awful sufferings. He had not made friends by means of the " mammon of unrighteousness " of which he had received so plentiful a supply, and so, when it failed, there was no one to welcome him into eternal habitations, as there would have been had he seized the opportunity to make Lazarus his friend. On the other hand, Lazarus, when he was on earth, had, without uttering a single word of hate or bitterness against the rich man or against God, accepted the painful trials that had come upon him. He had not allowed suffering to drive him away from God, but had remained a true child of Abraham—a God-fearing sufferer such as Job had been. Thus he had gathered for himself treasures in heaven, and therefore it is just and right that he should now live in blessedness. His choice in life was, above all, to receive true life from God, and now he has been given that which he had chosen.

26 During the life on earth the rich man and the beggar had the opportunity of choosing, and on that choice their fate in the hereafter absolutely depended. After death the time of grace is past—their fate has been sealed finally and forever, and no communication is possible between those who are lost and those who are saved.

27, 28 The rich man now realises that through his worldly, selfish and heartless life he has plunged himself irrevocably into everlasting pain, but entreats Abraham to send Lazarus to his brothers to warn them that they must repent of their evil life in time so that they should not also after death enter into the abode of torment.

29 Abraham, however, answers that they have no excuse if they remain unrepentant. They have the Law and the Prophets to teach them the way to salvation. If they listen to these—and they have full opportunity for it—they will be saved. Abraham's reply serves at the same time as a clear reminder to the rich man that he has no excuse for having lost his chance to be saved, for he, too, had the Law and Prophets to show him the way if he had been willing to follow the divine guidance.

30 The rich man reveals the typical attitude of the Jews who repeatedly ask for signs—signs so astounding as to *compel* them to believe in Jesus. He says that if Lazarus were to go back to them from the dead his brothers will be converted.

31 Abraham, however, answers that, if they are so full of unbelief and worldly-mindedness that they do not listen to the Word of God (the Old Testament at that time), they will persist in their unbelief even if someone were to arise from the dead.

These last words of the parable were undoubtedly uttered by the Saviour with a view to His own resurrection. The sign for which the Jews had so often asked would be given by His resurrection, but He knew that even this would not move the worldly-minded to a saving faith in Him. And this was abundantly proved by the actual course of events.

The Saviour related this parable not in order to satisfy our curiosity about life after death but to emphasise vividly the tremendous seriousness of life on this side of the grave—on the choice made here by us depends our eternal weal or woe. And however rich and honoured a man may outwardly be and however much his life may be filled with worldly pleasure, this will not in eternity be able to effect the slightest change in his condition if he has departed this life without the salvation of God. On the other hand, even if a man was a sick beggar on earth, but is really a child of God at heart and does not try to hide behind his poverty and misery in a life of embitterment and unbelief, he will inherit the richest blessedness. The parable, however, does not teach that the possession of worldly goods as such will cause a man to land in everlasting perdition, and that a life of poverty and want will of itself bring to a man eternal bliss. Everything depends on the attitude which a person reveals towards his wealth or towards his poverty—whether he believes in God with a repentant heart and serves Him, whatever his external circumstances may be, or whether he rejects Him—a thing which may be done in poverty as well as in wealth.

[1] There is no reason why, since the description of the rich man resembles the Sadducees rather than the Pharisees, it should be assumed (with T. W. Manson, *The Mission and Message of Jesus*, pp. 588 ff.) that this parable was particularly addressed to the Sadducees. The description of the man's richness and luxury is only meant as background for what follows. The chief point about the rich man is that he was so sunk in selfishness and worldly-mindedness that he let the opportunity slip by unused when he could have shown love to the

beggar, and remained unrepentant until his death, thus incurring eternal loss. Such an attitude was in those times to be found in Pharisees as well as Sadducees and others.

² Although Luke does not expressly state that this is a parable, and although the Saviour has given the beggar a name, it is by no means necessary to assume that we have here the story of something that really happened and not a parable (cf. Zahn, *in loc.*, for a detailed exposition). The name Lazarus is a Greek form of אֶלְעָזָר (*El-ʿāzar*), " God has helped ". The sick beggar was in the highest sense one who, being totally neglected by his privileged fellow-men, was yet helped by God (with the gift of eternal salvation). For this reason the Saviour called him by this name in the parable. The name also points to the fact that the beggar, amid his misery, looked to God for aid.

Creed's suggestion (*in loc.*) that the story of Lazarus's resurrection influenced Luke to construct this parable out of a simpler parable is altogether arbitrary and unnecessary. The name Lazarus was one that occurred frequently, and because it was such an appropriate name for the type of sick beggar our Lord wanted to depict in the parable, He called him by this name.

³ In late Greek βάλλειν often loses the notion of throwing with violence, and means simply " lay, place ". ἐβέβλητο, therefore means that the beggar was placed where he is now lying. βάλλειν is, however, also used in connection with " persons or animals prostrated by wounds of sickness " (T. W. Manson, *ibid.*), and it might have this sense here.

⁴ πυλῶνα—a high ornamented gate, indicating the luxury of the rich man's dwelling.

⁵ We must remember that we have here to do with a parable and not with a real occurrence and that " *it is no purpose of the parable to give information about the unseen world.* The general principle is maintained that bliss and misery after death was determined by conduct before death, but the details of the picture are taken from Jewish beliefs as to the condition of souls in Sheol, and must not be understood as confirming those beliefs. The properties of bodies are attributed to souls in order to enable us to realise the picture " (Plummer, *in loc.*).

⁶ These words prove that we should not regard the parable as a literal historical occurrence, for Abraham had died like other people and only his spirit is in the abode of bliss—not until after the resurrection at the second coming will his spirit and glorified body be united. So we cannot take in a literal sense the description given here of " carried by the angels into Abraham's bosom ".

⁷ εἰς τὸν κόλπον ᾿Αβραάμ must obviously be taken figuratively and " neither here nor in John i. 18 does it give the idea of reclining at table at Abraham's side (cf. John xiii. 23), but that of rest from the toil and neediness of earthly life in intimate fellowship with the father of the race, who is still alive and blessed in death " (Zahn, *in loc.*). To the same effect Strack-Billerbeck say: " Lying or sitting in Abraham's

bosom (חֵיק [hêq], Aram. חֵיקָא [hêqâ]) is . . . a pictorial expression to indicate the loving fellowship which exists in the beyond between Abraham and his pious descendants, derived from the love of a mother, who cherishes and protects her child in her lap " (*in loc.*).

8 The fact that mention is made of the rich man's funeral, whereas the beggar's funeral is left unmentioned, does not mean that we must understand that Lazarus was taken bodily to the abode of bliss, but rather reflects the fact " that the funeral of a rich man is the splendid conclusion of his brilliant life, whereas no fuss is made about the burial of a poor man " (Zahn, *in loc.*).

9 Ἅιδης (Hades) among the Greeks originally signified the deity of the underworld. Later on it became the name of the realm of the dead itself. In the Septuagint (Greek translation of the Old Testament) the word occurs sixty-one times as translation of the Hebrew word *Sheol* (which generally means the realm of the dead). In the New Testament Ἅιδης occurs eleven times (Matt. xi. 23, xvi. 18; Luke x. 15, xvi. 23; Acts ii. 27, 31; 1 Cor. xv. 55; Rev. i. 18, vi. 8, xx. 13, 14). The difference between γέεννα (hell) and Ἅιδης (realm of the dead) in the New Testament is expounded in J. Jeremias's articles on the two words in Kittel's *Theologisches Wörterbuch zum Neuen Testament*. It is nowhere taught in the New Testament that the faithful at their death first go to the realm of the dead (Ἅιδης). This was indeed the case in Old Testament days before the coming of Christ and His completed work of redemption. When a believer dies, he is immediately with Christ and in His presence (Acts vii. 59; 2 Cor. v. 8; Phil. i. 23; cf. Luke xxiii. 43). Spiritually he forthwith receives blessedness. But only at the second coming, when the spirits of the faithful are united with their glorified bodies in resurrection and the new earth appears, will full blessedness be the portion of the faithful. Unbelievers, however, go to the realm of the dead (Ἅιδης) when they die, where (already plunged into affliction) they are to await the final judgment (Rev. xx. 13, 14). For a comprehensive and reliable discussion of this subject cf. Salmond's classical work *The Christian Doctrine of Immortality*.

10 We must again remind our readers that we are here dealing with a parable and not with a real occurrence from which various questions in connection with the hereafter may be answered. Zahn is therefore right in saying: " What Jesus relates further about his conversation with Abraham does not in any case serve the end of unveiling the secrets of the beyond to the Pharisees, whom He addresses, or indeed to His disciples, who were present, but (as in His other parables) presents in intuitive forms which were familiar to His hearers an imaginary narrative in order to make them see and realise vividly what awaits them, if they combine with pride in being Abraham's sons and the appearance of conscientious attachment to Law and Prophets the rich man's sentiments and standards of life " (*in loc.*).

11 " The silence of Lazarus throughout the parable is very impressive. He never murmurs against God's distribution of wealth, nor against the rich man's abuse of it, in this world " (Plummer, *in loc.*).

[12] That the " flame " should not be taken literally but in a symbolical sense, appears from the fact that in the Bible mention is often made in connection with the unsaved (in the realm of the dead as well as in Gehenna) of the darkness and utter gloom which encompasses them. Flaming fire and darkness, of course, exclude each other. Thus in such Biblical expressions we have the symbolical description of the hapless plight of the lost. Schilder, however, was right in declaring: " Let nobody say: it is *only* symbolical *and therefore* not so terrible. By mere inversion one could say: if the symbol, the mere picture, is already awe-inspiring, how horrible must the original (the actual) be! " (translated from *Wat is de hel?*, 2nd ed., p. 40).

[13] ἀπέλαβες has the force of " thou receivedst *fully* ". He had striven exclusively after worldly things and amassed nothing for heaven. So he has received all he strove after, all that he chose.

[14] Here, as is evident from the whole context, the teaching is not (as Montefiore and a few other commentators declare) that the rich man suffers in eternity because on earth he was rich and cheerful and that the beggar is blessed because he suffered on earth. See our exposition.

[15] For various representations of the realm and state of the dead, etc., cf. Strack-Billerbeck, *in loc.*, and elsewhere, and cf. 10).

[16] From these words it follows that the rich man was lost because he did not listen to the Law and the Prophets, and not because he was rich. " The Old Testament forbids neither being rich nor the mere enjoyment of earthly goods; but next to the love of God it demands above everything else practical love to one's neighbour, in which this rich man had completely failed as regards the poor man at his door, who was indeed his neighbour (cf. x. 29) " (Zahn, *in loc.*).

And as Stanton states: " Surely the selfish absorption of the rich man in his own pleasure, and his indifference to misery that lay so near at hand, could not be more vividly portrayed; and what sins could be more heinous? For these he is condemned . . ." (*The Gospels as Historical Documents*, ii, p. 235). So Plummer is right in saying: " There is no taint of ' Ebionitic heresy ' in the parable. It emphasises the dangers of wealth, but it nowhere implies the unlawfulness of wealth " (*in loc.*). Nowhere in the parable does Abraham say that it was wrong for the man to be wealthy. Indeed, Abraham himself was a rich man when he was on earth, and nowhere is he blamed for it. It is the abuse of riches and the neglect of the needy neighbour that is here condemned so unconditionally. The fate in the hereafter of the heartless rich man of the parable is intended as a deterrent example of what awaits those who display the same attitude.

CONCERNING OFFENCES

1 And he said unto his disciples,[1] It is impossible but that occasions of stumbling should come: but woe[2] unto him,
2 through whom they come! It were well for him if a millstone were hanged about his neck, and he were thrown into the sea, rather than that he should cause one of these little ones[3] to
3 stumble. Take heed to yourselves: if thy brother sin, rebuke
4 him; and if he repent, forgive him. And if he sin against thee seven times[4] in the day, and seven times turn again to thee, saying, I repent; thou shalt forgive him.
5 And the apostles said unto the Lord, Increase our faith.[5] And the Lord said, If ye have faith as a grain of mustard seed,
6 ye would say unto this sycamine tree,[6] Be thou rooted up, and be thou planted in the sea; and it would have obeyed you.
7 But who is there of you, having a servant plowing or keeping sheep, that will say unto him, when he is come in from the
8 field, Come straightway and sit down to meat; and will not rather say unto him, Make ready wherewith I may sup, and gird thyself, and serve me, till I have eaten and drunken; and
9 afterward thou shalt eat and drink?[7] Doth he thank the ser-
10 vant because he did the things that were commanded? Even so ye also, when ye shall have done all the things that are commanded you, say, We are unprofitable servants;[8] we have done that which it was our duty to do.

Most exegetes regard this portion as a number of loose sayings of the Saviour, recorded here by Luke with no connection between them. Nevertheless it appears to us that there is a unity between the various pronouncements and that (although Luke does not expressly say so) they were uttered on one and the same occasion.

1, 2 The Saviour here addresses His disciples expressly and warns them (cf. verse 3a: " Take heed to yourselves ") against the danger that their example, their words, their attitude or neglect of duty may do spiritual harm to others (especially the weaker ones in the circle of disciples—e.g. former " publicans " and outcast sinners who had turned to Him). So terrible will be the punishment to be undergone by one who causes offence to another that it would be better for him if, *before he can offend anyone,* he could die

431

a violent death. For thereby he will escape the heinous sin and also the punishment that will follow—a much more severe punishment than to be cast into the depths of the sea and to be drowned. By pointing out so clearly the criminality of causing anyone to fall into sin through one's life and attitude, the Saviour does not mean that those who have allowed themselves to be so influenced do not also bear their own measure of responsibility for falling into sin. Here He deals only with the responsibility resting upon all to live in such a manner that they do not lead others into sin.

3, 4 Just as it is necessary for His disciples not to put obstructions in the way of others, so it is necessary for them to be forgiving towards those who offend them or sin against them. But their forgivingness is not to be weakness; by no means, for they must first rebuke the guilty one, call his attention to his wrong behaviour (and not slander him behind his back!) After that, if he shows signs of repentance, he must be forgiven. Disciples of Christ should, of course, always be without inward rancour or lovelessness, and should be forgiving. But when anyone has sinned against a believer he should not give him the assurance of forgiveness before he has shown that he truly repents. True love is strong for the sake of the guilty one who is to be moved to repentance.

There should be no limits to forgivingness towards those who are repentant.

5 The foregoing pronouncements impressed the disciples profoundly with the severe demands made upon them, and they feel spontaneously that they will require supernatural grace and divine strength in order so to live that they may avoid offending others and always be prepared to forgive the repentant. So they ask the Saviour to give them greater faith—the faith that will make them spiritually stronger, and enable them to act as He has just commanded them to do.

6 The Saviour replied that they have no need of more faith, but of the right kind of faith—a vigorous, living faith. The grain of mustard seed is exceedingly small, but it contains the germ of life which, when it germinates, shoots up irresistibly into a tree. If the disciples had had faith of the same quality of life and vigour, no problem or task would have been too difficult for them. (After being filled with the Holy Ghost at Pentecost, they possessed in a rich measure this kind of faith which enabled them to perform so many mighty deeds for the extension of His church.)

7-9 When believers have received the gift of a living faith and as a result are able to perform glorious things in His service, there is great danger that they may become self-satisfied and may think themselves entitled to special marks of honour. Such an attitude, however, is quite wrong and sinful. In ordinary life it is unthinkable that, after a servant has completed his daily task, his master will invite him to sit by his side at table and will attend upon him and praise him as though he deserved special rewards and honours for the mere execution of his duties. How much less has a man the right to demand, even if he has done everything he ought to do (and no one is capable of this), that he should be honoured and rewarded by God in a special manner as if he were such a meritorious and indispensable person in His service!

10 For this reason also, when believers have been enabled to carry out their charges loyally, they must continue to be humble under the profound realisation that all their love, strength, time and faithful service rightly belong to the Lord and that they may lay no claim to honour or reward. What God does indeed give in the way of " rewards " He gives purely out of grace and not because man could ever deserve it. Where it is His command that we must be so humble, even if we have done everything we ought to have done, how much more necessary is it for us (who have all left much undone and have done many things wrongly) to live in true meekness—grateful and happy on account of the *privilege* of being *allowed* to serve Him.

Do we as individuals and as a church live in such a manner that we keep others back from Jesus and make it difficult for them to walk in the right road, so that they fall into sin? Do we act with so much wisdom, love and patience towards the weak and erring ones that they are helped on life's way, or do we, in our indifference, want of love, neglect of duty and insincerity, put obstacles in their way, so that their fall will also be debited to our account? What an important question this is, especially to parents and teachers with regard to their children, and to ministers and office-bearers in the church with regard to their congregations!

---

¹ Probably only a wide circle of disciples (the twelve and other followers of Jesus) were present, for it is not likely that the Saviour would have discussed such intimately personal matters with His disciples in the hearing of hostile Pharisees and others.

² The " woe " does not refer to being " cast into the sea ", but to a much more severe punishment which is to be avoided thereby.

³ The insignificant and weaker members of the group of disciples are meant here. " As nothing has hitherto been said about little ones, τούτων must refer to people present, and these can only be called

μιϰϱοί in comparison with other members of the same circle" (Zahn, *in loc.*). This pronouncement need not necessarily be identified with Matthew xviii. 6. Why could not the Saviour have made a similar pronouncement on more than one occasion?

[4] This is the customary way to indicate an unlimited repetition.

[5] A similar request also occurs in Matthew xvii. 19, 20 and Mark ix. 23.

[6] The roots of the sycamine tree were regarded as extraordinarily strong; " it was supposed that the tree could stand in the earth for six hundred years " (Strack-Billerbeck, *in loc.*). Thus the symbolical expression of Jesus refers to " something which is humanly impossible ". " At the present time both the white and the black mulberry are common in Palestine; and in Greece the latter is still called συϰαμινέα" (Plummer, *in loc.*).

[7] These words "reflect the general custom " (Strack-Billerbeck, *in loc.*).

[8] Cf. Paul's words 1 Corinthians ix. 16. T. W. Manson rightly remarks: " Unprofitable here is much the same as ' having nothing to glory of' or ' not claiming merit ' " (*The Mission and Message of Jesus,* p. 595).

HEALING OF THE LEPERS

xvii. 11–19

11   And it came to pass, as they were on the way to Jerusalem, that he was passing[1] through the midst of Samaria and
12 Galilee. And as he entered into a certain village, there met
13 him[2] ten men that were lepers,[3] which stood afar off: and they lifted up their voices, saying, Jesus, Master, have mercy
14 on us. And when he saw them, he said unto them, Go and shew yourselves unto the priests. And it came to pass, as they
15 went, they were cleansed. And one of them, when he saw that he was healed, turned back, with a loud voice glorifying
16 God;[4] and he fell upon his face at his feet, giving him thanks:
17 and he was a Samaritan.[5] And Jesus answering said, Were
18 not the ten cleansed? but where are the nine? Were there none found that returned to give glory to God, save this
19 stranger? And he said unto him, Arise, and go thy way: thy faith[6] hath made thee whole.

Here commences the third and last part of the so-called " Journeys on the road to Jerusalem " portion of the Gospel of Luke ix. 51 xix. 48)—a portion which for the most part contains material given only by Luke.

11–13   As in ix. 51, 52 and xiii 22, so here Luke tells us that Jesus was on His way to Jerusalem. When the Samaritans barred His way through their territory He turned east and made His way *between* Samaria and Galilee (as R.V. margin rightly renders the words in this verse), going past Beth-shan and crossing the Jordan, to continue His journey to Jerusalem through Trans-Jordan (recrossing the Jordan at Jericho). It was while He was making His way between Galilee and Samaria that these ten leprous men came to meet Him. No doubt they had already heard a great deal about Him, how in Galilee and elsewhere He had healed large numbers of sick and performed other mighty deeds. So they seek His aid with the urgent call that He should take pity on them. Obedient to the laws regulating the behaviour of lepers, they do not venture to come near Him, but call to Him from a distance.

435

14 In v. 12–16 an instance is related where Jesus did not shrink from touching a leper while He uttered the authoritative word of healing. In this case, however, He does not touch any one of the ten, but merely commands them to go and show themselves to the priests who supervise the observance of the purification laws in the various villages or towns whence they come. Whenever a leper receives such a command, it means that he must assume that he is healed and that he must now go to be pronounced clean by the priest so that he may again be allowed to enter ordinary society. The Saviour's command to them is at the same time also His authoritative utterance through which they are cured. This time He causes the healing to take place while they, in obedience to His command and trusting in His power, are on their way to the various priests under whose authority they are.

15, 16 Only one of the ten, a Samaritan, as soon as he noticed that he was healed (and before he went to the priest), immediately turned back and glorified God, praising Him for the marvellous cure. He also fell down at Jesus' feet and thanked Him.

17, 18 The Saviour is grieved at the revelation of gross ingratitude on the part of the other nine lepers, who do not glorify and thank God, but are so selfishly taken up by their cure that they (probably all Jews) do not even take the trouble of turning back to Him out of gratitude, as the Samaritan did.

19 He thereupon commands the cleansed Samaritan to arise and assures him that his faith has saved him—not merely cured him of his bodily sickness, but saved him in the fullest sense of the word, because he really believes in Him and has entered into a personal relation with Him. Although the other nine had also received their healing, they had no further connection with Him, owing to the superficiality of their faith (which was merely a belief in " miracles ") and their ingratitude.

He who has received only blessings from His hand and does not come close to Him in humble but heartfelt gratitude will always forgo what is the highest and most glorious in life. But he who, on receiving gifts out of His hand, turns to the Giver Himself in real gratitude, will partake of fullness of life and happiness. There is nothing that can bind one more closely to Him than sincere gratitude—" we love him because he first loved us ".

---

[1] There is little doubt that διὰ μέσον (‫א‬ B L, etc.) is the earlier reading, and preferable to διὰ μέσου (A and most MSS.). See

Luce, *in loc*. Apart from the textual evidence, διὰ μέσου ("through the midst") cannot be right, because "this sequence [Samaria before Galilee] would be at best permissible for a journey starting at Jerusalem; but 'between ', 'on the border of' [is the true sense], i.e. in the direction of Peraea and, finally, Jerusalem" (Klostermann, *in loc*.). Thus the translation "through the midst of Samaria and Galilee" (A.V., R.V. text) is incorrect and should be replaced by "between S. and G." (R.V. margin). "It means 'through what lies between ', i.e. along the fronter, or simply 'between' (Plummer, *in loc*.). Similarly Zahn says that διὰ μέσου means "that Jesus journeyed between Samaria and Galilee, i.e. He took a road which ran for a long time on the frontier of the two regions" (*in loc*.). "The geographical indication explains how Jews and Samaritans happened to be together" (Easton, *in loc*.). For further evidence on the true sense of the words cf. Otto, *Kingdom of God and Son of Man*, Eng. tran., p. 18.

[2] It is quite arbitrary to allege (as Wernle does) that this description is a variant account of the narrative in v. 12–16 and Mark i. 40 ff.

[3] "On the frontier He would be likely to meet with a mixed company of lepers, their dreadful malady having broken down the barrier between Jew and Samaritan" (Plummer, *in loc*.). Major (*The Mission and Message of Jesus*, p. 283) also agrees with this.

[4] "The turn of expression means: to give God the honour which acknowledges Him or the acknowledgment which honours Him. That can happen in various ways according to circumstances: through praise . . . through thanksgiving . . through the recognition of His truth . . . through the acknowledgment of God's majesty and will . . . through repentance and turning to God . . . through believing trust in God's promise" (Strack-Billerbeck, *in loc*.).

[5] After the carrying off of the kingdom of the Ten Tribes, a large number of Israelites still remained behind in Samaria and the surrounding country. They had become interbred with the pagan immigrants who had been sent into the country by the Assyrians, and thus a new race, the Samaritans, gradually originated. Nevertheless they had in many respects still remained Jewish in their religion, although they accepted only the first five books of the Old Testament and established their own sanctuary on Mount Gerizim near Shechem and did not go and worship in Jerusalem. Even after the destruction of their temple on Gerizim by the Jewish Hasmonean ruler John Hyrcanus, they retained their own form of worship (cf. John iv. 20 ff.). Until recently there were about a hundred Samaritans at Nablus in Palestine (the ancient Shechem) remaining faithful to their views and customs. These have now crossed into the territory of the state of Israel and settled there. In New Testament times (and long before) there prevailed a violent enmity between Jews and Samaritans. In the hour of common affliction, however, such differences are often wiped out, as in the case of this group of Jewish lepers amongst whom there was at least one Samaritan.

[6] "The faith of which Jesus speaks is not merely that which brought

437

him back. By this return he has sealed forever the previous transitory connection which his cure had formed between Jesus and him; he recognises His word as the instrument of the miracle, he unites himself closely to the entire person of Him whose power only he had sought at the first. And thereby his physical cure is transformed into a moral cure, into salvation " (Godet, *in loc.*).

ON THE SUDDEN COMING OF THE
KINGDOM OF GOD

xvii. 20–37

20 And being asked by the Pharisees,[1] when the kingdom of
God cometh, he answered them and said, The kingdom of
21 God cometh not with observation:[2] neither shall they say,
Lo, here! or, There! for lo, the kingdom of God is within
you.[3]
22 And he said unto the disciples, The days will come, when
ye shall desire to see one of the days of the Son of man,[4] and
23 ye shall not see it.[5] And they shall say to you, Lo, there! Lo,
24 here! go not away, nor follow after *them*: for as the lightning,[6]
when it lighteneth out of the one part under the heaven,
shineth unto the other part under heaven; so shall the Son of
25 man be in his day. But first must he suffer many things and
26 be rejected of this generation.[7] And as it came to pass in the
days of Noah,[8] even so shall it be also in the days of the Son
27 of man. They ate,[9] they drank, they married, they were
given in marriage, until the day that Noah entered into the
28 ark, and the flood came, and destroyed them all. Likewise
even as it came to pass in the days of Lot; they ate, they
drank, they bought, they sold, they planted, they builded;
29 but in the day that Lot went out from Sodom it rained fire
30 and brimstone from heaven, and destroyed them all: after
the same manner shall it be in the day that the Son of man
31 is revealed.[10] In that day, he which shall be on the housetop,
and his goods in the house, let him not go down[11] to take
them away: and let him that is in the field likewise not return
32, 33 back. Remember Lot's wife. Whosoever shall seek to gain
his life shall lose it: but whosoever shall lose *his life* shall pre-
34 serve it. I say unto you, In that night there shall be two men
on one bed; the one shall be taken,[13] and the other shall be
35 left. There shall be two women grinding together; the one
37 shall be taken, and the other shall be left.[14] And they answering say unto him, Where, Lord? And he said unto them,
Where the body *is*, thither will the eagles also be gathered
together.[15]

Probably the great majority of religious Jewry, as a result of the
numerous prophecies in the Old Testament and the statements in
the inter-testamental apocalyptic writings concerning the coming

439

Messiah, looked forward at this time to the speedy advent of the day when the Messiah would come to establish His kingdom on earth.

20, 21 There was no more burning question, especially to the Pharisees, than that concerning the time when the kingdom of God would be called into being by the Messiah. It is, therefore, quite natural that Pharisees, on a day when they were possibly under the impression that Jesus possessed prophetic gifts, should ask Him when, in His opinion, the Messiah would come to establish the kingdom. The Saviour, however, replies that the sovereign dominion of God does not come in such a manner that one will be able to determine, through accurate observation of signs, the exact time of its coming. People will not be able to say: "See, here is the Messiah!" or "Look, there He is coming!" There is a twofold reason for this; in the first place the sovereign dominion of God *has already come* on earth in the person of Jesus as a saving and judging force in the life of the Jewish people— saving in the cases where He is recognised and obeyed as the Messiah, but judging in the lives of those who reject Him. In the second place (as is taught by verses 22–37) the final coming of the kingdom will take place so suddenly and unexpectedly that no one will be able to prophesy with any degree of accuracy when the day of His second coming will arrive.

22 Here the Saviour turns to His disciples and prophesies that days will come (especially when they have to pass through dark times) when they will yearn for His immediate coming so that they may be able to view the glory of the Messianic kingdom and thus rejoice in the victory over the powers of darkness.

23, 24 When the faithful, through the distress of the times and for other reasons, long earnestly for the final coming of the kingdom, seducers will try to mislead them by all kinds of false statements about the exact time or place of His appearing, or by pointing out some human figure or other as the Messiah who has arrived. They must, however, by no means let themselves be deceived by such persons, for the coming of the Son of Man will be (verse 24) so sudden and universally visible that there will be no room or time for all kinds of exact prophecies or descriptions of it. In the twinkling of an eye He will appear in the sight of all.

25 The disciples, however, must not labour under the delusion that His appearance in glory will take place soon and will demand no preceding sacrifices. By no means, for He Himself will first have to endure much suffering and even be rejected by the present generation of the Jewish people—the chosen people who should have accepted Him as their Messiah.

26, 27 As in the time before the Deluge, the great masses of people will, even up to the moment of His advent, be completely engrossed in earthly, material and evanescent affairs and will not take heed to be prepared for His coming. Owing to their foolish attachment to worldly things, the judgment will overtake them suddenly and unexpectedly, and there will no longer be any time for deliverance. The time of grace will be forever past and the judgment will overtake them.

28–30 The people of Sodom at the time of Lot lived in such utter worldly-mindedness as to render themselves incapable of repentance, and as a result they all perished when they were visited by God's judgments after Lot's departure from the city. Just so assuredly will the judgments of God visit impenitent mankind at the second coming, for this event, too, will take place without any preceding or definite indications of its day or hour. From other pronouncements of the Lord (cf. Matt. xxiv) it is clear that He indeed taught that certain perceptible signs would precede His coming. Those signs, however, will indicate only in a general way the fact of the approaching end—but with regard to the actual year, day or hour of the second advent it will be impossible to prophesy. The advent will take place suddenly and unexpectedly, and those who have not prepared themselves in time for His coming in His glory will be irretrievably lost. After being invisible to the eyes of the world since His ascension, He will suddenly be revealed at His second coming—visible to all, to believers and unbelievers alike.

31 In these figurative terms the Saviour warns against sinful, selfish attachment to worldly things. For those who seek their highest happiness in material things and fix their thoughts thereon above all else, the coming of the Son of Man will be fraught with fatal consequences. Therefore everyone should take care to be free at heart from earthly things and should give to the kingdom of God the first place in his heart and life.

32 Lot's wife, although she had tried to flee from Sodom, nevertheless remained attached in heart to the doomed city and consequently came to a fatal end. But history should ever warn the faithful against such worldly-mindedness.

33 Everyone who selfishly tries to seek fullness of life and happiness in earthly things and consequently lives estranged from God and denies Christ will never find true life or happiness. He, however, who leads a life of unselfishness and self-sacrifice, yea, who does not even shrink from dying for the sake of Christ's honour and service, will receive and enjoy true life in the fullest and most glorious sense of the word—even though

441

it may seem in the eyes of the world that he is throwing his life away.

34, 35 When the Son of Man appears in His glory, a complete and final separation will be brought about between the faithful and the unbelievers, and even the most intimate bonds between people will not prevent their being separated from one another, the faithful being taken up to meet Him and the unbelievers being left to undergo the judgment.

37 In reply to the inquisitive question as to where the unredeemed will be left, the Saviour gives no direct answer, but in what was probably a well-known Palestinian proverb points out that where there is spiritual decay judgment will follow relentlessly and assuredly—this refers to what happens through all ages, but especially to the time of the end, when the judgments of God will visit the unregenerate, after the faithful have been finally united to their glorified Lord and Redeemer.

However different the lives of people may be in many respects, they will all be identical in one respect—everyone will have to meet the Lord Jesus face to face at His second advent, when He comes in divine power and glory. So the urgent question for each one is: am I prepared for His coming?

---

[1] There is no reason for assuming that the Pharisees in this instance put the question with evil intent (cf. Zahn, *in loc.*, and also Klostermann, *in loc.*).

[2] παρατηρήσεως. The noun παρατήρησις, found here only in Biblical Greek, is not known in classical writers, but occurs in the Hellenistic authors and survives in Modern Greek. It is not quoted as occurring in the papyri. The verb παρατηρεῖν is frequent in the New Testament, LXX (where it refers mostly to hostile observation) and in medical writings (in the sense of diagnosis, accurate observation of symptoms). Here it means " the observing of signs in the sky, perhaps also the apocalyptic reckoning of the fixed time when it is to come " (Klostermann, *in loc.*). Strack-Billerbeck also say that μετὰ παρατηρήσεως means "in such a way that it can be outwardly observed or perceived " (*in loc.*). " There will be no such signs as would enable a watcher to date the arrival " (Plummer). " The kingdom of God does not come in such a way that one can observe its coming as a bystander (recognise it by outward signs)" (Zahn, *in loc.*). In our opinion, the meaning we ought to attach to these words (verse 20b) depends on the meaning of verse 21b. Just as we take verse 21b (which is connected with what precedes it by " for ") to refer to the coming of the kingdom of God as it came in the beginning with Jesus' public appearance among the Jewish people, so also

448

verses 20b and 21a must be taken in the same sense. So the Saviour in the first place points out that the initial coming of the kingdom is not attended with external signs such as the Jews thought in their earthly coloured Messianic expectation. Probably, however, the Lord, by this saying, pointed in a secondary sense also to the fact that no man will be able to prophesy the day and hour of the final coming of His kingdom through a human diagnosis of the signs of the times. This pronouncement, however, is by no means at variance with His other pronouncements, where, in a broad sense, He points to signs that will precede His coming. In general the spiritually alert will probably discern when the time of the second advent is approaching, but, nevertheless, the actual moment of the advent will arrive suddenly and unexpectedly.

[3] ἐντὸς ὑμῶν should, according to the ordinary and natural use of ἐντός, be translated by "within you" (cf. Liddell and Scott's Lexicon). Nevertheless there are instances in the Classics (Xen. *Anab.*, 1, 10, 3; *Hellen*, ii, 3, 19), where it means "among you" (cf. Creed, *in loc.*, and also Plummer, *in loc.*). Zahn, Creed, Plummer, T. W. Manson, J. Weiss, and others accept this latter meaning. So the Saviour declares that the kingdom has already arrived and is among the Jews in Him as the representative thereof. If, however, we accept the usual meaning ("within you"), the Saviour declares that the kingdom of God, through its efficacy and power brought by Him on earth, is already within the circle of Jewry—for the salvation of the faithful and the judgment of those who reject Him. "The kingdom of God is not coming only on some future day but is already present within the circle of those who are still asking when it is coming and who meant that if only it would come they would recognise it with certainty: it is there and they do not see it. That disproves their desire which they display for the kingdom of God. If they really longed for it, they would perceive that it is with them. . . . But because the Pharisee thought only of what the people already possessed, Jesus' answer remained a riddle for him. Where then in the midst of the Israel then present and in the midst of the Pharisaic community did he see the kingdom of God? How are His almighty grace and all-ordering righteousness now becoming active? Jesus' answer was: the Christ is present, and in the emergence of faith the almighty grace of God reveals itself, in the emergence of unbelief His all-powerful judgment reveals itself, even in the Pharisaic circle" (Schlatter, *in loc.*). Some critics take verse 21b in an exclusively eschatological sense, and it should then be taken as meaning "One moment the world is just its normal self: then lo! the kingdom of God is among you" (T. W. Manson, *The Mission and Message of Jesus*, p. 596). Cf. also Scott's *The Kingdom and the Messiah* (pp. 108 ff.). We are, however, in doubt as to whether verse 21b should indeed be understood thus.

However, the contention of some critics that the Saviour by these words taught that the kingdom of God is merely an inner, spiritual condition in the human heart, must very definitely be rejected. "An inner condition of the soul may qualify for admission to the kingdom,

443

but it is not itself the kingdom " (Creed, *in loc.*). Similarly: " The kingdom of God is not here under discussion as a state of mind or a disposition in men. It is a fact of history, not of psychology. Moreover, Jesus speaks elsewhere of men entering the kingdom, not of the kingdom entering men. The kingdom is a state of affairs, not a state of mind " (T. W. Manson, *The Mission and Message of Jesus*, p. 596). We may sum up Jesus' preaching about the kingdom by saying that He teaches that the kingdom of God is already a present reality in Him but that its final consummation lies in the future when He comes in divine majesty.

⁴ " ' The days of the Messiah ' is the usual expression for the Messianic period in rabbinic literature " (Strack-Billerbeck, *in loc.*). " The understanding of μίαν as a Semitism for πρώτην [' first '] (Plummer) would indicate especially the breaking in of the Messianic age " (Klostermann, *in loc.*).

⁵ Because the time will not yet have arrived. This saying is a strong refutation of the contention that Jesus meant that His second advent would follow quickly upon His crucifixion.

⁶ " Just as suddenly and as visibly everywhere on earth will Jesus appear from heaven in kingly glory, coming forth out of the invisible world " (Zahn, *in loc.*).

⁷ With regard to the contention that this sentence is an interpolation, T. W. Manson rightly says: " ' Suffer many things and be rejected ' is very vague, if it is an *ex post facto* reference to the crucifixion. An interpolator would surely have given something more precise, something which left the reader in no doubt that it was His own death on the cross that Jesus was predicting " (*The Mission and Message of Jesus*, p. 434).

⁸ " Noah in the Old Testament story is no paragon of the virtues, much less Lot. But both realised that the catastrophe must come, and both took means to save themselves. The Christian message is not for those who think that they deserve a better fate than their neighbours, but for those who, in the midst of universal indifference and complacency, realise that desperateness of their situation, and ask, ' What must I do to be saved? ' The things that happened in the remote past have a real bearing on the present. The most dangerous of all theological errors is that which says, ' He's a good fellow, and 'twill all be well ', rashly assuming that our indifference and carelessness have their counterparts in heaven and that God's holy purpose must inevitably come to terms with our shallow optimism " (T. W. Manson, *ibid.*, p. 436).

⁹ " The imperfects and the asyndeton are very vivid: ' They were eating, they were drinking, etc.' The point is not merely that they were living their ordinary lives, but that they were wholly given up to external things " (Plummer, *in loc.*).

¹⁰ ἀποκαλύπτεται—" a technical expression for the παρουσία " (Klostermann, *in loc.*). Cf. 1 Corinthians i. 7; 2 Thessalonians i. 7.

¹¹ These commands " demand decisive readiness to let everything

go which binds one to the course of this world as a valuable possession or an object of affection, which meets its end at the return of Jesus. The fulfilment of this demand attains its peak only in the surrender of the soul to physical death, in order to rescue it for eternity " (Zahn, *in loc.*).

[12] Here the Saviour used the words in a figurative sense to point out the necessity of not being attached to worldly things. In Matthew xxiv. 15 ff., however, He made similar pronouncements with a literal meaning in connection with the flight of the Christians before the destruction of Jerusalem. There is nothing improbable in His having sometimes said certain things literally and on other occasions figuratively. " As in this place there can be no idea of actual flight [for no one can flee from His second coming], we are to take the words here only in an allegorical sense: you must make up your mind to give up every earthly thing on that day, life itself included " (Klostermann, *in loc.*).

[13] " That those who believe on Him go to meet their returning Lord in order to welcome Him finds repeated expression as something which is a matter of course. And that the day of the Son of Man has to do with His reunion with the body of His disciples who have been left on earth is so frequently and variously attested by Jesus that we are to understand by this what is meant by παραλαμβάνεσθαι, ['to be taken'] and its opposite ἀφίεσθαι ['to be left'] " (Zahn, *in loc.*). Cf. Matthew xxiv. 31; 1 Thessalonians iv. 17.

[14] At this point the later MSS. insert from Matthew xxiv. 40 the words which appear as verse 36 in the A.V. text: " Two men shall be in the field, the one shall be taken and the other left ".

[15] Sometimes all kinds of fantastic explanations were given of this pericope (verse 37b) by the ancient church fathers and also by later exegetes. If, however, we take it in the context in which it occurs, after the question in connection with the place where the lost ones will be left, it is clear that verse 37b means: " where the spiritually dead people are, there the judgment will be executed ". " Where that which is ripe for judgment is present, there also will the judgment take place " (Zahn, *in loc.*). " Where that is, which needs dealing with, there the coming will be " (Morgan, *in loc.*). " ' As birds of prey scent out the carrion, so wherever is found a mass of incurable moral and spiritual corruption there will be seen alighting the ministers of divine judgement,' a proverbial saying terrifically verified at the destruction of Jerusalem, and many times since, though its most tremendous illustration will be at the world's final day " (Jamieson, Fausset and Brown, *in loc.*). σῶμα, used as the term for a dead body, is quite classical, and is always so used in Homer, a living body being called δέμας (cf. Plummer, *in loc.*). The parallel passage, Matthew xxiv. 28, has πτῶμα, " carcase ". Then verse 37b means " Upon all who are dead to the claims of the kingdom ruin will fall " (*loc. cit.*).

445

PARABLE OF THE UNJUST JUDGE

xviii. 1–8

1 And he spake[1] a parable unto them[2] to the end[3] that they
2 ought always[4] to pray, and not to faint; saying, There was in
   a city a judge, which feared not God, and regarded not
3 man: and there was a widow in that city; and she came[5] oft
4 unto him, saying, Avenge me of mine adversary. And he
   would[6] not for a while: but afterward he said within himself,
5 Though I fear not God, nor regard man; yet because this
   widow troubleth me, I will avenge her, lest she wear me out[7]
6 by her continual coming. And the Lord said, Hear what the
7 unrighteous judge saith. And shall not God avenge his elect,
   which cry to him day and night, and he is long suffering over
8 them?[8] I say unto you, that he will avenge them speedily.[9]
   Howbeit when the Son of man cometh,[10] shall he find faith[11]
   on the earth?

Here we have again, as in xi. 5–13, a " parable of contrast ",
i.e. in the parable certain features are portrayed which are in
sharp contrast with other features, so that by this means the main
truth is powerfully delineated.

1 In xvii. 20–37 the Saviour emphasised the fact that no one
will be able to determine in advance the time of His second coming.
He now teaches in this parable that when His coming is apparently
slow in taking place believers are not to become discouraged, but
should persist in prayer, knowing that He will indeed come at the
right time and will answer their supplication by destroying the
powers of evil and by causing His chosen ones to triumph. The
parable has, however, also a more general meaning, namely, that
the faithful should persevere in prayer with regard to all other
matters when the answer is not immediately granted.

2 The unjust judge stands in the sharpest contrast to the Lord.
The judge has no reverence for the commands of God and does not
pay any heed to the opinion or interests of his fellow-men. The
Heavenly Father, however, is perfectly holy and just in everything,
and aims at the highest well-being of those that call to Him in
prayer.

446

3 The widow who continually goes to plead with the unjust judge that he, as the appropriate official, should see that the injustice done to her by a certain person should be rectified also stands in sharp contrast to the elect of God who call upon Him in prayer. In the eye of the unjust judge she is an unknown, troublesome person in whom he takes no interest and about whose fate he does not worry. But the chosen ones of God are well known to Him and loved by Him, and He takes the keenest interest in them.

4, 5 Although the judge was so heartless and unjust, and although the widow was in his eyes a troublesome stranger, he nevertheless finally decides to vindicate her cause; not because his attitude has been changed towards her, but because he is afraid that she will continue to trouble him and by her persistence deprive him of all peace and comfort.

6, 7 If even the unjust judge grants the request of the troublesome widow, how much more will the heavenly Judge, who is perfect in love and righteousness, cause justice to be done to His chosen ones whom He loves and towards whom He shows the highest long-suffering—forgiving their sins and answering their prayers notwithstanding their own unworthiness?

8 When the fullness of time has arrived, God will suddenly and without delay put an end to the distress into which His chosen ones will be plunged by a hostile and evil world. There is no doubt about the certainty that Jesus will come again and that God will then make the righteous cause of the faithful triumph completely and forever. But the serious question is whether, according to His promises, the faithful are going to persevere in faith, so that when Jesus, the Son of Man, will come in glory He will find on earth real faith in Him and in His promises. This question by no means implies that at Christ's coming the Christian church will no longer exist—for He says expressly (verse 7) that God's own elect will still continually be praying to Him that justice should be done to them. No: His question (verse 8b) is intended as a warning that believers should take heed not to let their faith waver, notwithstanding His apparent delay in coming. So He concludes the parable with a powerful summons to His followers to maintain true belief in Him, through whom the Father will give final victory.

---

[1] As in xxi. 36, this exhortation to persistent prayer follows upon sayings of the Lord in which He pointed to the uncertainty of the time of His advent.

² αὐτοῖς here indicates that it is still the same persons as those addressed in xvii. 23-37, who are the hearers at this stage.

³ The contention (cf. T. W. Manson, *op. cit.*, p. 597) that the introductory words do not fit in with the parable is unfounded—the truth taught by the parable that God will certainly answer the prayers of His own elect, gives the express reason why one should continue in prayer without being discouraged, even if the answer is not immediately visible.

⁴ "This admonition did not correspond to the Jewish viewpoint and custom" (Strack-Billerbeck, *in loc.*). It was the Jewish custom to pray only three times a day (*in loc.*).

⁵ ἤρχετο, imperfect tense, indicates the continuance of the action.

⁶ ἤθελεν, again imperfect tense.

⁷ ὑπωπιάζῃ may mean "hit in the face" or "beat black and blue", or merely "cause much trouble". We should probably (with Plummer, Creed and others) accept the last meaning here.

⁸ Opinions differ very widely as to the meaning of this phrase. J. Weiss, Bengel and others take it together with βοώντων: "the elect cry to God, and God listens to them in His long-suffering". Jülicher-Fascher regards it as a gloss. T. W. Manson (*op. cit.*, pp. 599 ff.) thinks that it is a mistranslation of the Aramaic original, which meant that God delays executing His wrath on the persecutors of the elect in order to give them time to repent. Zahn explains: "What Jesus says here about God is that He makes His long-suffering rule over His elect" (*in loc.*). Plummer also translates: "and He is long-suffering over them" (*in loc.*). The original Greek would seem to allow some justification for the rendering of the 1946 Revised Standard Version ("will he delay long over them?") but not for that of the 1901 American Standard Version ("and yet he . . ."). The English R.V. (1881), "and he is . . .", seems still to be the most correct rendering. Taken thus, it helps to bring out still more sharply the contrast between the unjust judge who has no sympathy with the widow, and God, who is full of compassion towards His elect and is long-suffering in dealing with their weaknesses.

⁹ "We must always remind ourselves that ταχύς, ταχέως, ἐν τάχει do not mean 'after a short time', but . . . 'quick', 'fast', 'sudden', from which, with a varying starting-point from which to reckon according to the circumstances, the meaning 'soon', 'in a short time', arises. According to the context the teaching here is that the final events will be very long in coming (cf. verse 4, ἐπὶ χρόνον; verse 7, μακροθυμεῖ; cf. also xii. 45, χρονίζει). Therefore ἐν τάχει ['speedily'] cannot here denote a short time until the Parousia, to be measured from the standpoint of the speaker or even only from the beginning of waiting for the Parousia, but the untarrying intervention of God after the end of His μακροθυμεῖν ['long-suffering'] over His church (verse 7b), the ripeness of their faith (verse 8b) and the ardour of their prayer (verse 7a) are attained" (Zahn, *in loc.*).

¹⁰ No doubt is here expressed or implied as to the coming of the

Son of Man, but only as to what He will find at His coming. " There is therefore no reason for conjecturing that the parable received its present form at a time when belief in the second advent was waning " (Plummer, *in loc.*).

[11] τὴν πίστιν clearly refers to the faith that is here being discussed—faith in Jesus as the Christ, the Messianic Son of Man, through whom God will vindicate the cause of the elect. The Saviour had Himself already answered this question in xvii. 26–37. From this it appears that at His second advent the vast majority of people will live in unbelief, but that there is nevertheless also going to be a faithful remnant that will persevere to the end. These words, therefore, contain an exhortation that the disciples should take heed " that they themselves, and those whose guidance is enjoined upon them, should maintain this faith to the end " (Zahn, *in loc.*).

PARABLE OF THE PHARISEE AND THE PUBLICAN

xviii. 9-14

9 And he spake also this parable unto[1] certain which trusted
in themselves that[2] they were righteous, and set all others at
10 naught: Two men went up[3] into the temple to pray; the one
11 a Pharisee, and the other a publican. The Pharisee[4] stood[5]
and prayed thus with himself,[6] God,[7] I thank thee, that I
am not as the rest of men, extortioners, unjust, adulterers, or
12 even as this publican. I fast[8] twice in the week; I give tithes[9]
13 of all that I get.[10] But the publican, standing afar off,[11]
would not lift up so much as his eyes unto heaven, but smote
14 his breast,[12] saying, God, be merciful to me a sinner.[13] I say
unto you, This man went down to his house justified[14] rather
than the other: for every one that exalteth himself shall be
humbled; but he that humbleth himself shall be exalted.[15]

While the preceding parable referred mainly to continuous
prayer in connection with Jesus' second advent (where it also has
a wider application in a secondary sense), this parable indicates
the right attitude with which individual believers should pray
their daily prayers.

9 Luke does not say when this parable was related, but he does
state to whom it was particularly addressed, namely, to certain
persons (probably Pharisees) who regarded themselves as righteous and looked down scornfully upon other people—whom they
regarded as unclean sinners.

10 At one of the fixed times for prayer, or perhaps at an exceptional time when there were no others praying in the temple,
a Pharisee and also a " publican " went to the temple to pray.

11, 12 The Pharisee was a typical example of those people
who look upon themselves as righteous and exalt themselves above
others. Indeed, he does not even hesitate to thank God in his
prayer in the temple that he is better than other people. He
bases this delusion on two real facts: firstly, he is not a wicked
person outwardly, for he is not a robber, or unjust in his actions,
or an adulterer, or such a contemptible sinner as the " publican "
who is also in the temple; in the second place, he performs certain

exceptional acts of piety: he fasts regularly twice a week (much more frequently than is demanded by the Old Testament laws) and gives tithes of *all* his income (while the Law requires this of only certain kinds of income).

13 The " publican ", again, is a typical example of the kind of persons who were despised by the Pharisaic " righteous ones " on account of their sinful life. He is, however, deeply conscious of the real sinfulness of his life. However earnestly he may yearn for forgiveness, he is so deeply under the impression of his utter unworthiness before God that he remains standing far from the holier parts of the temple and does not even venture to raise his eyes. And as an unconditional avowal of his guilt before the Holy God, he beats upon his breast and beseeches Him to be merciful to him, a sinner—confessing thus that he has no claim to the goodness of God but deserves rather to be cast out and sentenced. He has come to true repentance and casts himself with unreserved confession of sin before the Throne of Mercy.

14 The Saviour declares that the Pharisee, who, when viewed outwardly, is the righteous one of the two, is not regarded as such by God (his religion being mostly of a formal nature and infected with self-conceit and uncharitable contempt of others), but that the " publican ", who in his soul's need and humble consciousness of guilt has fled to God and humbly begged for mercy, is granted forgiveness so that he departs as the one who in God's eyes is accounted righteous. The " publican " did not deserve forgiveness on account of his submissive prayer, but through his self-despising confession of guilt was in a condition to receive the forgiveness granted by God to the penitent. For the Pharisee and the " publican " the general rule held good that he who (in self-conceit) exalts himself will be abased by God, but he who really humbles himself (with sincere confession of guilt) will be exalted.

In everyone of us there is a " Pharisee "—all of us are but too prone to regard ourselves as good and others as wicked. Therefore we must take heed, especially in our prayers, that we do not become self-exalted. How great is the need that we should continually pray to be kept truly humble!

---

[1] πρός may here mean " concerning " or " with regard to ". But in accordance with the ordinary use of the word in Luke, we should rather translate it by " unto " or " to " (cf. T. W. Manson, *op. cit.*, p. 601).

[2] ὅτι should here be taken in the sense of " that " and not " because " (cf. Creed, *in loc.*).

³ ἀνέβησαν, " went up " from the low-lying part of the city to the temple-mount.

⁴ For an account of the pride of many Pharisees, cf. Strack-Billerbeck's excursus, " Pharisäer u. Sadd., No. 2 " (op. cit.). " That spiritual pride was a real and ever-present danger in Pharisaism is sufficiently obvious " (T. W. Manson, in loc.).

⁵ " It held good as a general rule that a man prayed standing, עוֹמֵד ['ōmēd], מְעוּמָד? [mĕ'ūmād]; however, it was not forbidden to pray sitting, walking, or lying down " (Strack-Billerbeck, in loc.).

⁶ πρὸς ἑαυτόν after ταῦτα is most probably the correct reading. " The character of his prayer shows why he would not utter it so that others could hear " (Plummer, in loc.). He would not have displayed such gross audacity as to say his prayer loudly so as to be heard by the " publican " and others. Creed, T. W. Manson and others have not sufficient grounds for their choice of the reading of " D ": " the Pharisee stood by himself and prayed thus ".

⁷ " He glances at God, but contemplates himself " (ibid.).

⁸ " A public fast for all took place on the Day of Atonement, on the 9th of Ab (the day of the destruction of the temple) and in general cases of national need (drought, failure of crops, plague, war) " (Strack-Billerbeck, in loc.). Thus it was an exceptional act to fast twice a week. (That those Jews who did so fasted on Monday and Thursday may be inferred from the Didaché, 8, 1.)

⁹ Cf. Strack-Billerbeck, in loc., in connection with the giving of tithes among the Jews.

¹⁰ For other self-exalting prayers among Pharisees at that time cf. Edersheim: Life and Times of Jesus the Messiah, ii, pp. 289-91.

¹¹ The " publican " probably remained standing in the outer court while the Pharisee " chose his stance in the inner court " (Strack-Billerbeck, in loc.).

¹² " In order to say that everything (sin and guilt) flows from there " (Strack-Billerbeck, in loc.). He thus confesses his own deep sinfulness and guilt.

¹³ " The publican is overwhelmed by the sense of his own unworthiness, and rightly so. It is a great mistake to regard the publican as a decent sort of fellow, who knew his own limitations and did not pretend to be better than he was. It is one of the marks of our time that the Pharisee and the publican have changed places; and it is the modern equivalent of the publican who may be heard thanking God that he is not like those canting humbugs, hypocrites and kill-joys, whose chief offence is that they take their religion seriously. This publican was a rotter; and he knew it. He asked for God's mercy because mercy was the only thing he dared ask for " (T. W. Manson, op. cit., p. 604).

¹⁴ δεδικαιωμένος perfect participle passive. The passive points to the fact that he is justified by an act of God, and the perfect tense teaches that the act is already accomplished so that the " publican " is now in a permanent state of being justified. From the then current usage of the word it appears " that by the ' righteous ' we are to under-

stand one whose sin was forgiven. If the Jewish scribes had been asked, they would have raised the sharpest objections against this judgment of Jesus on the tax-collector " (Strack-Billerbeck, *in loc.*). This parable teaches, among other things, " that the decisive thing is not the past record, whether good or bad, but the present attitude towards God. Every moment before God is an opportunity to have life determined by the future rather than by the past " (T. W. Manson, *op. cit.*, p. 604).

[15] With regard to the statement by some that, since this saying also occurs elsewhere (xiv. 11), Luke inserts it here himself without Jesus having really uttered it here, we cannot help repeating Plummer's question: " Why is it assumed that Jesus did not repeat His sayings? " (*in loc.*).

JESUS AND THE INFANTS

15 And[1] they brought unto him also their babes,[2] that he
should touch them:[3] but when the disciples saw it, they
16 rebuked them. But Jesus called them unto him, saying,[4]
Suffer the little children to come unto me, and forbid them
17 not: for of such[5] is the kingdom of God.[6] Verily I say unto
you, Whosoever shall not receive the kingdom of God as a
little child,[7] he shall in no wise enter therein.

The narrative of Luke, which from ix. 51 has covered a field
mostly not covered by the other Gospels, here again links up with
Matthew and Mark.

15 On a certain day some of the ordinary Jews, who as a result
of their faith in His power were constantly bringing the sick to
the Saviour to be healed by Him, also brought some of their
infants to Him to be touched by Him in blessing. The disciples,
however, regarded this as an unnecessary waste of the Lord's
time and strength, and severely reprimanded the parents not to
come to Him with their children.

16 Jesus, however, being animated by the tenderest love
towards little children, immediately called the parents with their
children to Him and warned those present to take heed that they
are not the cause of preventing any little ones from coming to Him.
For, the Lord declared, of such is the kingdom of heaven; it
belongs to those who are as receptive and trustful as little children
with their natural humility and whole-hearted faith.

17 A little child who is brought up naturally receives artlessly
what is given to him, without doubting the good intentions of the
givers—he believes whole-heartedly that what is given to him is
good for him and accepts it without thinking conceitedly that he
deserves it. So, also, only those who do not doubt the love of God
and who do not rely on their own supposed merits may partake
of the redemption and blessings offered in the sovereign dominion
of God and may in reality enter the kingdom of heaven.

Notwithstanding the unambiguous manner in which Jesus
commands that the little children should be brought to Him and

that no obstacles should be placed in their way on coming to Him, it still continues to be the great weakness of most Protestant churches that spiritual ministration to children is taken in hand far too superficially. Jesus said: " Suffer little children to come unto me ", but in the life of the church too often nearly ninety-nine per cent of its time, money and strength is devoted to ministration to adults, whereas to the children is devoted only a fatally insignificant portion. Only those congregations which, by means of thorough training of Sunday-school teachers, regular and effective services for children, Sunday-school libraries, etc., take heed that the command of the Saviour is obeyed can hope to be flourishing congregations in the future.

[1] Up to the commencement of the narrative of our Lord's Passion Luke relates in the section starting at verse 18 mostly the same material as Mark, with a few omissions (Mark x. 35-45, xi. 12-14, 20-5, xiv.3-9), and a few additions (Luke xix. 1-29, xxi. 20-6, xxii. 14-38).

[2] τὰ βρέφη = babes, infants. Mark has παιδία (the more general term for children). Possibly most of the children were about a year old, so that (although they could still be called infants) they were already able to accept what was offered them and to show their attachment to Jesus (the Representative and Bringer of the kingdom of heaven).

[3] " That a benedictory laying-on of the hands is meant—cf. also verse 16—is certainly not saying too much in the circle of Jewish people, who knew from the history of the patriarchs how they blessed their sons " (Van Leeuwen, at Mark x. 13).

[4] " To judge by certain precepts in the Wisdom literature, the attitude of the Jews to children was disciplinary and severe. That of Jesus was tender and sympathetic. He was undoubtedly interested in children and fond of them. His reference to their playing at marriages and funerals in the market-place; His refusal to order them to be silent when they sang Hosanna in His honour in the temple; His citation of the words of the psalmist: ' Out of the mouths of babes and sucklings hast thou perfected praise '; His selection of a little child as an example to His apostles; and also the incident related here support the view that Jesus may be justly acclaimed as the lover of little children " (Major, *The Mission and Message of Jesus*, p. 128).

[5] Jerome pointed out long ago that " It is not these children, but those who are childlike in character, especially in humility and trustfulness, who are best fitted for the kingdom " (Plummer, *in loc.*).

[6] Cf. note at iv. 43.

[7] " There is in children a twofold receptivity, negative and positive, humility and confidence " (Godet, *in loc.*). Schlatter (*in loc.*), has fittingly remarked: " It is not any general willingness to accept gifts that makes the child specially fitted to set forth the way in which

entrance into the kingdom of God is attained, but it is his attitude towards the kingdom of God that makes him apt for this purpose. The child accepts it without opposing his own theories and desires to it. He has none of these things, but he stands before the divine grace willing and completely ready to receive it. The statement would have no meaning if there were no event in which the kingdom of God is shown to the child. This event, however, is provided through the presence of Jesus. The child's attitude to Jesus is his attitude to the kingdom of God, and thus he shows to all how the kingdom of God is received." Klausner (*Jesus of Nazareth*, p. 306) compares with these words of Jesus two rabbinical pronouncements: " ' Touch not my anointed ones '— the children at school " (T. B., *Shabbath*, 119b), and " Children receive the presence of the Shekinah " (Tractate, *Kallah Rabbati*, 2). Compare also the Roman poet Juvenal: *maxima debetur pueris reverentia* (" the greatest reverence is due to children ").

THE RICH YOUTH

(Cf. Matt. xix. 16–22; Mark x. 17–22)

18 And a certain ruler asked him, saying, Good Master,
19 what shall I do[1] to inherit eternal life? And Jesus said unto
   him,[2] Why callest thou me good?[3] none is good, save one,
20 *even* God. Thou knowest the commandments, Do not
   commit adultery, Do not kill, Do not steal, Do not bear false
21 witness, Honour thy father and mother. And he said,[4] All
22 these things have I observed from my youth up.[5] And when
   Jesus heard it, he said unto him, One thing thou lackest yet:
   sell all that thou hast, and distribute unto the poor, and
   thou shalt have treasure in heaven: and come, follow me.
23 But when he heard these things, he became exceeding
24 sorrowful;[6] for he was very rich. And Jesus seeing him
   said, How hardly shall they that have riches enter into the
25 kingdom of God! For it is easier for a camel[7] to enter in
   through a needle's eye, than for a rich man to enter into the
26 kingdom of God. And they that heard it said,[8] Then who can
27 be saved? But he said, The things which are impossible with
28 men are possible with God.[9] And Peter said, Lo, we have
29 left our own, and followed thee. And he said unto them,
   Verily I say unto you, There is no man that hath left house,
   or wife, or brethren, or parents, or children, for the kingdom
30 of God's sake, who shall not receive manifold more[10] in
   this time, and in the world to come[11] eternal life.

From the details given in Mark it appears that Jesus was in a
house when the little children were brought to Him (cf. Van
Leeuwen, at Mark x. 17). He had probably gone into the house
along the road to rest a while. He had blessed the children and
was just coming out again to continue His journey (Mark x. 17),
when a rich young man rushed to meet Him.

18 Luke makes mention of the fact, not mentioned by
Matthew or Mark, that the rich youth was a leading personality
among the Jews. Earnestly and with inward uncertainty he asks
the Saviour what he must do to inherit eternal life. Although he

457

does not yet by any means regard Jesus as the Messiah, he nevertheless feels drawn to Him and esteems Him to such a degree that he addresses Him in an unusual way as " Good Master ".

19 Jesus does not here mean, as many critics have inferred, that He is not entitled to be addressed as " Good Master ". He merely asks: " Why callest thou me good? " and points out to the young man that only One is good in an absolute sense, namely, God. By this He wishes to teach the young man that only if he regards Him as the Son of God, who is one with God, may he call Him " good ". The young man, however, as Jesus knew, had no inkling of His real nature, and thus, as he regarded Him as merely human and not as the Son of God, he ought not to address Him as " Good Master ". The words of the Saviour may, therefore, by no means be regarded as a denial of the fact of His sinlessness and divinity. On the contrary, as the whole context shows, Jesus here teaches indeed that He is one with God and thus claims absolute authority over the life of man (" follow Me ", verse 22). Thus he who knows Him as the Son of God may address Him as " Good Master ", but from one who regards Him merely as human (as the rich young man does) He has no desire for such a superficial and flattering form of address.

20 The young man asked what he had to *do*, i.e. how he might inherit eternal life through his own exertion. So Jesus refers him to the Ten Commandments, for the Word of God still holds good that " Whosoever does these things perfectly, shall live ". If a man throughout his whole life observes the commandments of God without any failure or deviation, he will inherit eternal life. No one, however, except Jesus, has ever been able, or will ever be able in this life, to be so perfect. And because God's Word teaches that everyone, even if he should transgress only one commandment, is guilty in the sight of God, the only way to redemption is the way of grace. But whosoever is unwilling to admit his own guilt and to plead the grace of God has only one way open to him—he will be judged according to his acts (measured by the standard of the divine Law). So if the young man desires to know what he must *do* he can only be referred to the Ten Commandments.

21 In his inadequate understanding of what true fulfilment of the Law invo lves, the young man answers with all sincerity that he has kept all the commandments from his youth up. Thus it is a great disappo intment to him that the Master refers him only to the Ten Commandments which he himself knows so well and has observed so faithfully (according to his own view), for his

experience has taught him that in this kind of observance of the
Law to which he has been accustomed from his youth up he
could, nevertheless, receive no real rest for his soul and no real
peace—for this reason he had come to Jesus to learn whether there
was not perhaps something special, something great and heroic,
which he must do that it may give him this inward rest and
assurance of redemption.

22 The Saviour does not express His opinion on the truth of
the young man's claim to have observed the whole Law so faithfully. However, as the perfect discerner of the human heart, He
has observed that in the path of this earnest seeker after eternal
life there is one great obstacle—he has become so attached to his
earthly possessions that a barrier has arisen between him and God
—he has never yet set his inner life free from worldly riches and
chosen to serve the Lord alone; he is still engaged all the time in
trying to serve God along with Mammon. If, therefore, he really
desires to inherit eternal life, this great stumbling-block must be
removed from his life. So in his particular case it is necessary for
him to prove the sincerity and wholeheartedness of his yearning
after eternal life by giving up all his possessions—selling them and
distributing the proceeds among the poor. And when he thus
gives the first place in his life unconditionally to eternal things,
he must come and follow the Saviour, for then the obstacles that
have kept him away from Jesus will have been removed.

23 That in his case his attachment to worldly riches is the
great stumbling-block is proved by the fact that he became very
sorrowful when he heard the Master's words. An inward struggle
arose in his soul—his whole being yearned for real life, his heart
was starved and without rest and he longed to inherit eternal life;
but on the other hand he was so attached to his earthly wealth
and had sold his soul to it to such a degree that he was unwilling
to obey Jesus' command—and thus he departed thence with a
heavy heart.

24, 25 From Mark x. 17–31 it appears that Jesus became very
fond of the young man and earnestly longed that he should be
saved from the clutches of his worldly-mindedness. Thus it was
with deep sympathy and grief that when the young man departed
in sorrow He pointed out to His disciples how hard and humanly
impossible it is for a rich man to be saved—because one who is
rich is so easily dominated by his wealth and held prisoner by a
blind attachment to worldly possessions. Just as it is impossible
for a camel to go through a needle's eye, so it is impossible,
humanly speaking, for a rich man to be saved. No one is able, in
his own strength, to overcome the temptation of earthly wealth

459

—whosoever tries in his own strength to wrest himself free from the satanic hold of love for worldly riches, will always fail.

26 Because it was the general view among the Jews at that time that wealth was a sign of God's special favour towards the owner of it, and that poverty was a punishment for the sins of the poor, the hearers ask in amazement who can then be saved—if even the rich ones have no chance, how much less ordinary people and the poor?

27 Jesus, however, replies that the things which are impossible with men are nevertheless possible with God. Humanly speaking, it *is* impossible for a rich man (or anyone else) to be saved, but through the grace and might of God the rich as well as the poor may be saved.

28 Peter, always impulsive, acted as mouthpiece of the disciples, as he frequently did, and pointed out to the Saviour that he and the other disciples had in fact left all and were following Him. After Jesus' severe pronouncement of the impossibility of salvation for anyone apart from the power and grace of God, the disciples probably felt anxious as to whether they themselves might not perhaps also be excluded from the kingdom of God. This, then, was the reason why Peter spoke thus.

29, 30 The Lord does not give a direct reply to the question in their minds, but declares (note the absolute authority with which He is speaking) that everyone who has made a sacrifice *for the kingdom of God's sake* will assuredly inherit life everlasting and will in addition receive rich blessings in this life (not indeed always or often materially, but in a spiritual sense—inward riches, spiritual friendships, true happiness). Jesus does not here declare that every believer must leave his family and possessions, nor does He state that if one becomes a hermit he will be blessed. By no means! But he says that whosoever (not for personal honour or in pursuance of his own ideas, but for the kingdom of God's sake, in His service and under His guidance) leaves loved ones and possessions will be richly blessed. But if anyone desires to follow Him for his own profit, like Judas, for him this promise does not hold good, neither does it avail for world-escaping hermits who selfishly seek only peace of mind for themselves.

Whosoever desires to inherit life everlasting must be inwardly free from the power of all possessions as well as from all faith in his own deserts, and must willingly obey the command of Jesus. If He commands us to give up certain things because they hamper our spiritual life, we must do so unhesitatingly. In each case He acts according to the special needs and circumstances of the person concerned—He does not call upon everyone to sell his belongings or to leave his family, but He calls upon all to surrender to Him unconditionally the first place in their hearts and lives.

[1] The version in Matthew xix. 16 is: " Master, what good thing shall I do . . . ? " Taken together with Luke xviii. 18, the complete question may have been: " Good Master, what good thing . . . ? " And Jesus may have replied: " Why callest thou me good and askest me about good things? " Thus the Gospels supplement one another. It is unwarranted in such cases to speak of a contradiction between them.

[2] " There is no instance in the whole Talmud of a rabbi being addressed as ' Good Master ' " (Plummer, in loc.). Only God was called " good " by them (cf. Strack-Billerbeck at Mark x. 17).

[3] Here no thought is expressed, even in the slightest degree, that He regarded Himself as sinful. It is quite arbitrary to say that something of this nature is meant here, as Montefiore, Luce and others do (see our exposition).

[4] " The reply exhibits great ignorance of self and of duty, but is perfectly sincere " (Plummer, in loc.). By his answer the rich man proves " that hitherto he has taken a very light view even of the commandments of God which are well known to him, and in this he has not proved substantially different from the worst Pharisees (cf. xvii. 11). But he shows that he is different from those self-righteous people in this respect, that he has found no contentment in such observance of the Law, as he himself can testify, and has derived from it no assurance of the good pleasure of God with what he does and refrains from, and no certain hope of eternal life. That is why he went to Jesus for better instruction " (Zahn, in loc.).

[5] " That it was possible to keep the whole Law is an idea which is frequent in the Talmud " (Plummer, in loc.). Cf. the testimony of Paul in Philippians iii. 6.

[6] " The deep grief reflected on his face bears witness to the struggle which preceded his defeat " (Zahn, in loc.).

[7] Some expositors attempt to make this pronouncement sound less drastic by translating $\varkappa\alpha\mu\eta\lambda o\nu$ by " cable " or " rope ", or by changing $\tau\varrho\eta\mu\alpha\tau o\varsigma\ \beta\varepsilon\lambda\acute o\nu\eta\varsigma$ into " a narrow passage for pedestrians ". They have, however, no ground for this and, in addition, it is unnecessary to try to alter the pronouncement. Jesus intended to say something drastic and to make His hearers realise how humanly impossible it really is.

[8] " The Jews of this period viewed the possession of wealth as a mark of the divine favour. ' The blessing of the Lord maketh rich, and He addeth no sorrow to it,' was a saying of the wise. On the other hand, it was the families of evil men who were supposed to fall into poverty in

Israel " (Major, *op. cit.*, p. 131). "Just as Jesus had shocked contemporary Jewish morality by teaching the indissolubility of marriage, so He shocked it again by His statement that it was easier for a poor man to enter the kingdom than for a rich man " (*ibid*).

⁹ " It is a miracle of grace when those who have wealth do not put their trust in it. . . . Man cannot, but God can, break the spell which wealth exercises over the wealthy " (Plummer, *in loc.*).

¹⁰ By this it is not meant that the life of the believer will always be easy and without suffering. On the contrary, the Saviour declared expressly (Mark x. 30) that, together with the spiritual and other blessings, they will also receive persecution.

¹¹ ἐν τῷ αἰῶνι τῷ ἐρχομένῳ—" In the age which is in process of being realised " (Plummer, *in loc.*). In Jesus the future age was then, and is now, already becoming an actual reality. But only at His second coming will it be fully established.

JESUS PREDICTS HIS SUFFERING

(Cf. Matt. xx. 17-19; Mark x. 32-4)

xviii. 31-4

31 And he took unto him the twelve, and said unto them, Behold, we go up to Jerusalem,[1] and all the things that are written[2] by the prophets[3] shall be accomplished unto the Son
32 of man.[4] For he shall be delivered up unto the Gentiles,[5] and shall be mocked, and shamefully entreated, and spit
33 upon: and they shall scourge and kill him: and the third
34 day he shall rise again. And they understood none of these things;[6] and this saying was hid from them, and they perceived not the things that were said.

For the fourth time now the Saviour announces that He will be delivered to suffer and to die (ix. 22, 44, xiii. 33). In xviii. 31-xxi. 38 we have the description of Jesus' last journey to Jerusalem and His last teachings in the city. From now on everything is under the dark shadow of the cross, until at the empty grave the full light of the victory again beams forth.

31-3 Owing to the solemnity of the announcement, the Saviour takes His disciples aside and again informs them that as they are now finally on their way to Jerusalem everything foretold by the prophets concerning Him will be fulfilled. While the Saviour in ix. 22, 44 and xiii. 33 announces only the fact that He must suffer and be killed, He here not only gives further particulars of how He is to be ill-treated and put to death, but points out by His words: " Behold, we go up to Jerusalem, and . . ." that the suffering and death, as foretold, are now at last actually coming. Thus we see how the Saviour by degrees gave His disciples more and more information concerning His impending suffering and death. In addition, however, He again (cf. ix. 22) expressly declares that He will not remain in death, but will arise as victor on the third day.

34 The announcement of His suffering and death as well as of His resurrection is so tremendous and so utterly different from what the disciples pictured to themselves that they could by no means understand what Jesus meant by it. Notwithstanding all

463

the teachings of the Saviour, they had still in a great measure been clinging to materialistic Messianic expectations and could not comprehend how Jesus, in whom they saw the Messiah, could speak of suffering and death that awaited Him—for according to their ideas He was forthwith to triumph over all foes as the mighty Conqueror and to establish the Messianic kingdom on earth. They could not grasp it that the Saviour's prophecy concerning His suffering had to be taken literally. But precisely because it was so incomprehensible to them, the pronouncements remained fixed in their minds, so that after His resurrection they could recollect everything clearly. It was, however, necessary for the Saviour to warn them, so that after His crucifixion and resurrection they could understand things better and could realise that He was not unexpectedly overwhelmed by suffering and death but that He was fully aware of what was awaiting Him and voluntarily paid the full price for the sake of the redemption of man.

The suffering and death of the Saviour were no fortuitous occurrence, or merely the unavoidable result of the combination of certain circumstances. By no means, for from eternity this had been the predetermined centre of the plan of salvation of the Triune God. The Father gave His Son as the outcome of His everlasting love to be sacrificed; Jesus, the Only-begotten Son of God, gave Himself voluntarily to the utmost for the expiation of sin and through the Eternal Spirit offered the all-sufficient sacrifice for the redemption of immortal souls. The divine plan of salvation was already announced in the Old Testament—always more and more clearly and to a fuller extent (cf. Isa. xlix, l, liii, etc.). And in accordance with the divine prophecies uttered through the Old Testament messengers, Jesus followed the path of suffering to its utmost depths of darkness and death until He finally triumphed as Conqueror.

---

[1] From ix. 31 onwards, where Jesus' impending suffering in Jerusalem is referred to, Jerusalem is again and again indicated as the place in the direction of which the Saviour definitely set His face and the place where His work of redemption would be accomplished (cf. ix. 51, xiii. 22, xvii. 11, xviii. 31).

[2] " According as Jerusalem comes nearer, and the crisis assumes a clearer picture to His consciousness, the forms of the conflict and of the destruction come out more sharply " (Van Leeuwen, at Mark x. 32–34).

[3] $\delta\iota\grave{\alpha}$ $\tau\tilde{\omega}\nu$ $\pi\varrho o\varphi\eta\tau\tilde{\omega}\nu$. " This is the regular expression for the utterance of prophecy: they are spoken *by means* of the prophets. The prophet is not an originating agent, but an instrument " (Plummer, *in loc.*).

[4] Cf. Special Note on " The Son of Man ", pp. 352 ff.

[5] In Luke the emphasis is placed mostly on the fact that the Saviour was delivered to the Gentiles and sentenced by Pilate. In Mark, on the other hand, more emphasis falls on the share of the Jewish authorities in the condemnation of Jesus. In this there is no contradiction; the one supplements the other—the Jews as well as the Gentile rulers were guilty of the Redeemer's condemnation and crucifixion.

[6] " This cannot refer to the words of Jesus, to which no mystery was attached, but it will signify that they rejected what Jesus said as utterly impossible and incredible " (Schlatter, *in loc.*). The idea that the Messiah would have to suffer and die was completely foreign to their minds. No Jewish teachers or believers of those times seem to have understood the Old Testament prophecies of the Suffering Servant in a Messianic sense. Only at a somewhat later time, no doubt under the influence of Christian teaching, do the Jewish rabbis appear to have taught that there would be a suffering Messiah ("Messiah ben Joseph ") as well as a triumphant Messiah (" Messiah ben Judah ").

THE BLIND MAN OF JERICHO

(Cf. Matt. xx. 29–34; Mark x. 46–52)

xviii. 35–43

35 And it came to pass, as he drew nigh unto Jericho,[1] a
36 certain blind man sat by the way side begging: and hearing
37 a multitude going by, he inquired what this meant. And
38 they told him, that Jesus of Nazareth passeth by. And he
cried, saying, Jesus, thou son of David,[2] have mercy on me.
39 And they that went before rebuked him, that he should hold
his peace: but he cried out the more a great deal, Thou son
40 of David, have mercy on me. And Jesus stood, and commanded him to be brought unto him: and when he was
41 come near, he asked him, What wilt thou that I should do
unto thee? And he said, Lord, that I may receive my sight.
42 And Jesus said unto him, Receive thy sight: thy faith hath
43 made thee whole. And immediately he received his sight,
and followed him, glorifying God: and all the people, when
they saw it, gave praise unto God.

The Saviour was now for the last time on His way to Jerusalem
and had to pass through Jericho.

35, 36 Like so many other blind beggars in Palestine, a certain
blind man sat by the wayside begging and heard the multitude
that were accompanying Jesus pass by.

37 In reply to his question he is told that Jesus of Nazareth is
passing by.

38 The blind beggar had already previously been informed of
the Man who had healed so many sick and crippled, and who was
regarded by many of the masses as the possible Messiah. After
what he had heard about Him he was already beginning to believe
in Him as the Christ. And now that the glad tidings are at last
brought that this Jesus is at hand, he immediately cries out to Him
as the Son of David, the Messiah, to have mercy on him and to
save him from his misery.

39 Others try to make him hold his peace, but nevertheless his
faith in the Passer-by is so great and his yearning to be delivered
from his condition of blindness and beggary is so strong that he
cries all the more to Jesus to deliver him.

40 The Saviour, who always has an open eye and ear for needy people in the crowds, heard his supplication, stood still and commanded him to be brought nearer to Him.

41 In order to give the blind man the opportunity of giving utterance to the real need of his life, Jesus asks him what he desires Him to do to him. The blind beggar is deeply conscious of his blindness and of all the misery emanating from it (to himself as well as to others), and he longs so passionately to be delivered from it that he replies without hesitation: " Lord, that I may receive my sight."

42, 43 Through Jesus' authoritative utterance the blind beggar, who believed in Him, was immediately healed of his blindness. From that moment he followed Him and glorified God by giving Him the honour, praise and thanks for healing him through His Messiah. The vast multitude that were present and at that time cherished great expectations with regard to Jesus were constrained, when they observed this marvellous cure of the blind beggar, to acknowledge with praise the glorious and mighty works accomplished by God through the Nazarene.

Whosoever, like the blind beggar, in consciousness of his own misery, and believing in Jesus, cries to Him whole-heartedly will just as assuredly be healed of spiritual blindness through His word of power.

---

[1] If we take the accounts of Mark and Luke together, we may present to ourselves the following picture of the correct sequence of events: " When the entry into Jericho takes place, Bartimaeus is sitting by the wayside; his cries are drowned by the noise of the multitude and are not heard by Jesus; then follows the meeting with Zacchaeus and the delay in his house; the blind man, who hopes to be healed by Jesus, has changed his place and is now awaiting Jesus where He is to pass out of Jericho. The evangelist Luke has divided the two occurrences: the healing of the blind man and the meeting with Zacchaeus, and has related each one separately as a complete whole. The evangelists do not write as reporters and do not mention every particular from minute to minute. In their writings are preserved the things that really matter, in this instance the power of the word of the Messiah, a word that takes effect wherever He meets with faith " (Van Leeuwen, at Mark x. 50–3). A simpler suggestion, however, is that Bartimaeus was cured of his blindness at some point after Jesus had passed through old Jericho (the site of the Canaanite city), that He then passed through New Jericho (the recently built Herodian city), where He had His interview with Zacchaeus. In any case, the chronological order of the incidents

of Bartimaeus and Zacchaeus is unimportant and is not stressed in the narrative.

From Matthew xx. 29–30 it appears that together with Bartimaeus there was another blind beggar. Probably he was not so well known to the later Christian community as Bartimaeus, with the result that Mark and Luke make no mention of him; or Matthew may be conflating two separate incidents.

2 " Son of David " was a Messianic title: about the middle of the first century B.C. it is so used in the " Psalms of Solomon " (xvii. 23).

ZACCHAEUS

1, 2 And he entered and was passing through Jericho.[1] And
behold, a man called by name Zacchaeus;[2] and he was a
3 chief[3] publican,[4] and he was rich. And he sought to see
Jesus who he was; and could not for the crowd, because he
4 was little of stature. And he ran on before, and climbed up
into a sycamore[5] tree to see him: for he was to pass that
5 way. And when Jesus came to the place, he looked up, and
said unto him, Zacchaeus, make haste, and come down; for
6 to-day I must abide at thy house. And he made haste, and
7 came down, and received him joyfully. And when they saw
it, they all murmured, saying, He is gone in to lodge with a
8 man that is a sinner. And Zacchaeus stood, and said unto
the Lord, Behold,[6] Lord, the half of my goods I give to the
poor;[7] and if I have wrongfully exacted[8] aught of any man,
9 I restore fourfold.[9] And Jesus said unto him, To-day is salvation[10] come to this house,[11] forasmuch as he also is a son
10 of Abraham. For the Son of man came to seek and to save
that which was lost.

Here, a few days before the crucifixion, we have a beautiful
example of the triumph of the forgiving grace of God in the action
of Jesus. And so we can read the Passion history that follows in
the light of the Saviour's words to the redeemed " publican":
" The Son of Man is come to seek and to save that which was
lost " (verse 10).

1 On the way to Jerusalem, where the cross is awaiting Him,
Jesus passes through Jericho.

2 Because Jericho was situated on the main road from
Trans-Jordan to Jerusalem, there were many " publicans " who
had to collect the customs. Amongst them there was a certain
Zacchaeus, who occupied the position of chief " publican " and
who had already enriched himself (probably by lawful and unlawful methods alike).

3, 4 Undoubtedly he had already previously heard of this
exceptional Man who had performed so many miracles and did
not scruple to have intercourse with and to minister spiritually to

469

persons like himself who were so despised, especially by the Jewish religious leaders. He was no doubt moved by curiosity, but probably also by a deep yearning to see for himself this Jesus who had acted so sympathetically towards so many of his fellow-" publicans ". So, when he could not see Him because of the vast multitudes surrounding Him and on account of his short stature, he ran on in advance and climbed into a wild fig-tree along the road where our Lord had to pass. He was so eager to see Him that, although he was a wealthy leader among the " publicans ", he did not even shrink from doing something that would make him look ridiculous in the eyes of those present.

5 When Jesus came to the tree, He looked up to him, called him by his name and commanded him to come down, for He wanted, so He told him, to abide at his house that day.

6 Whatever Zacchaeus's attitude had previously been, it was now, after he had at last seen the Master and addressed Him, one of the greatest respect and love for Him. The result was that he came down without any delay and received and entertained Jesus.

7 Among the Jews it was an unheard-of thing for a rabbi or any other religious leader to lower himself (in their eyes " pollute " himself) by staying at the house of a " publican ". So they were greatly offended at His allowing Himself to be entertained in the house of Zacchaeus, a prominent member of this despised class.

8 A mighty revolution had taken place in Zacchaeus's life through his becoming personally acquainted with Jesus. As a result, probably when they again left his house and the Lord was about to rejoin the multitude to go to Jerusalem, he declares openly that he has decided (as a spontaneous act of repentance, love and gratitude) to give the half of his goods to the poor and in every case to restore fourfold whatever he had taken in the past by heartless extortions (when collecting the customs). The Saviour's influence on his life made him realise his selfish attitude towards his possessions and his sinful uncharitableness towards persons from whom he had exacted more than the lawful amount in customs. So fixed is his determination, as the outcome of his change of heart, to give the half of his goods to the needy and to redress any wrongs committed, that he declares: " I give." He does not here say what he has been accustomed to do in the past, but confesses by implication that he has been guilty in the past but wishes to change everything immediately, now that Jesus has come into his life. Probably he immediately began handing out money to those that needed it.

9 By these words the Saviour clearly teaches that Zacchaeus had indeed been a guilty and sinful man, that he had been lost in actual fact, but that (as appeared from the revolution that has come about in his life) salvation had come to him and to his whole house that day. He who, although a " publican ", was yet a descendant of Abraham, has now also in a spiritual sense become a true son of Abraham through his faith in Jesus, and therefore he and his house are saved.

10 It was possible for such a miracle of grace to take place, because Jesus had come precisely for the purpose (as the shepherd seeks the lost sheep, xv. 4) of seeking and saving that which was lost (in sin and unbelief). And, as the ensuing chapters describe, He entered, in His seeking love, upon the path of utmost suffering—even to His death on the cross.

Whosoever accepts Jesus whole-heartedly in his life and becomes personally acquainted with Him receives real salvation, a salvation which brings about an effective and practical revolution in his life, inwardly and outwardly. When Jesus comes into a person's life, and gains authority there, selfishness and dishonesty are irresistibly eradicated.

[1] Major rightly observes in connection with this story: " The whole scene is extraordinarily vivid and is full of grace, not without a touch of humour " (*op. cit.*, p. 281). There is no foundation for declaring, like Klostermann, that this story in Luke " does not appear to be a unitary composition " (*in loc.*), and regarding it as a variant of the call to Levi (v. 29–32). The slight resemblances between the story of Levi and that of Zacchaeus are completely outweighed by the differences. The resemblances arise from the fact that both Levi and Zacchaeus were " publicans " and were thus related to each other as regards circumstances and needs. It is, however, quite arbitrary to see in this any evidence that the Zacchaeus-story is a variant of that of Levi. Luke xix. 1–10 throughout bears the mark of historical reliability and vital genuineness.

[2] " Zacchaeus ", according to Strack-Billerbeck (*in loc.*), is derived from זַכַּי *Zakkai* (Ezra ii. 9, Neh. vii. 14) = " the righteous one ". According to Clement of Alexandria (Hom., iii, 63), Zacchaeus was afterwards bishop of Caesarea (cf. Zahn, *in loc.*).

[3] " Zacchaeus was probably the general tax-farmer of Jericho " (Strack-Billerbeck, *in loc.*).

[4] " Jericho would naturally be an important customs station from its position at the passage of the Jordan from Judaea to the lands east of Jordan " (Creed, *in loc.*).

⁵ συκομορέαν, " a fig-mulberry tree ", "recalls the English oak, and its shade is most pleasing. It is, consequently, a favourite wayside tree. . . . It is very easy to climb, with its short trunk, and its wide lateral branches forking out in all directions " (Tristram, *Natural History of the Bible*, pp. 398. ff).

⁶ ἰδού " indicates a sudden resolution, rather than one which had been slowly reached " (Plummer, *in loc.*). " By ἰδού with the present this is suitably expressed, because the declaration made at this moment before many witnesses and forthwith to be translated into action is the real bestowal " (Zahn, *in loc.*).

⁷ That he is not referring to what he was accustomed to do appears from the considerations (*a*) that he would then be justifying himself (like the Pharisee in the temple) and Jesus would not have stated that he was saved; and (*b*) no one will extort anything from anyone if he knows that he will afterwards have to compensate him fourfold.

⁸ εἴ τινός τι ἐσυκοφάντησα practically means " from whomsoever I have wrongfully exacted anything "—amounting to an admission that this had sometimes happened (cf. Plummer *in loc.*).

⁹ Cf. Exodus xxii. 8 and 2 Samuel xii. 6. Zacchaeus thus confesses that the extortion is theft.

¹⁰ " The σωτηρία is imparted to him with the reception that he gave to Jesus. With this the passion narrative begins, and at its opening the joy of forgiveness is placed. Jerusalem falls, but the individual, the guilty one, is won, and therewith the mission of Jesus finds its fulfilment " (Schlatter, *in loc.*).

¹¹ It is important to note that " the salvation which Jesus comes to bring is imparted not only to the individual man whom Jesus has in view in the first instance (verse 5), but to his house. It is not just in the story of the apostles' missionary activity, but as early as the days of Jesus' ministry, that we find evidence of the bonds of the family and of common membership of a household as means and ways of the expansion of the faith that saves " (Zahn, *in loc.*). For other instances where the saving grace of God embraces whole households cf. Luke x. 5; John iv. 53; Acts x. 1–48, xviii. 8, etc.

PARABLE OF THE POUNDS

11 And as they heard these things,[1] he added and spake a
parable,[2] because he was nigh to Jerusalem,[3] and *because*
they supposed[4] that the kingdom of God was immediately to
12 appear.[5] He said therefore,[6] A certain nobleman[7] went
into a far country, to receive for himself a kingdom, and to
13 return. And he called ten servants of his, and gave them ten
pounds,[8] and said unto them, Trade ye *herewith* till I come.
14 But his citizens hated him,[9] and sent an ambassage after
15 him, saying, We will not that this man reign over us. And
it came to pass, when he was come back again, having
received the kingdom, that he commanded these servants,
unto whom he had given the money, to be called to him, that
16 he might know what they had gained by trading. And the
first came before him, saying, Lord, thy pound hath made
17 ten pounds more. And he said unto him, Well done, thou
good servant: because thou wast found faithful in a very
18 little,[10] have thou authority over ten cities. And the second
came, saying, Thy pound, Lord, hath made five pounds.
19 And he said unto him also,[11] Be thou also over five cities.
20 And another[12] came, saying, Lord, behold, *here is* thy pound,
21 which I kept laid up in a napkin: for I feared thee, because
thou art an austere[13] man: thou takest up that thou layedst
22 not down,[14] and reapest that thou didst not sow. He saith
unto him, Out of thine own mouth will I judge thee, thou
wicked servant. Thou knewest that I am an austere man,
taking up that I laid not down and reaping that I did not
23 sow; then wherefore gavest thou not my money into the
bank, and I at my coming should have required it with
24 interest? And he said unto them that stood by, Take away
from him the pound, and give it unto him that hath the ten
25 pounds. And they said unto him,[15] Lord, he hath ten
26 pounds. I say unto you, that unto every one that hath shall
be given; but from him that hath not, even that which he
27 hath shall be taken away from him.[16] Howbeit these mine
enemies, which would not that I should reign over them,
bring hither, and slay them before me.[17]
28 And when he had thus spoken, he went on before, going
up to Jerusalem.

473

Only a few days are still to elapse before the crucifixion. The Saviour is already prepared to begin the last journey along the winding and steep road of seventeen miles from Jericho up to Jerusalem. Before commencing this last journey to the city He teaches His followers an important truth and addresses an urgent warning to those who hate Him.

11 Just after Jesus' statement that salvation is come to Zacchaeus and his house because He has come to seek and to save the lost ones (verses 9, 10), while the multitude is still pondering this word (still listening, as it were, to its echo in their own hearts), He relates to them yet another parable. He does so in view of the fact that, since He and the crowd of disciples and other Passover pilgrims are already approaching Jerusalem, there is probably among many of the multitude an expectation that the sovereign dominion of God will now, through Him as the Messiah, be speedily and miraculously revealed. Notwithstanding all Jesus' teachings, even His most intimate followers persisted (even until after His resurrection, Acts i. 6) in their earth-bound Messianic expectations—they believed that the Saviour would appear suddenly in outward power and glory, would create a Jewish-Messianic kingdom on earth, and would lead the Jewish people to victory over all their enemies. So the Saviour related the following parable in order to teach them: (1) that the final revelation of the sovereign dominion of God will not take place immediately, (2) that a great responsibility rests on each one of His followers to work faithfully until He comes, (3) that the full coming of the kingdom of God is not going to bring along with it a Jewish political triumph, but the Final Judgement, when the faithful will be rewarded and the unfaithful and hostile punished.

12 This parable should be regarded allegorically, though not in every particular. The man who journeys *to a far country* (this points to the fact that his return will not take place soon) to receive a kingdom (from the hand of the lord of the country to which he is going), represents Jesus who goes to the Father to be reinstated in His position of honour and glory after He has completed the path of humiliation, suffering and death, and who will again come back after a long (but indefinite) time.

13 To each of His followers the Saviour has given the glad tidings of redemption through Him, so that each one may, as it were, make it bear interest—may cause its beneficent operation to spread through the whole world. Every believer must be faithfully employed in this work for the extension of His sovereign dominion on earth until He comes back.

474

14 The Jewish leaders and the majority of the people rejected Jesus, thus telling God, as it were, that they refuse to have Him for their King.

15 The Jews' hate and rejection of the Saviour, however, did not affect His reinstallation in power and glory or His reception of the divine kingship. By His ascension He has already been exalted to the right hand of the majesty on high, and at the final Consummation He will return in full glory. Then the faithful will have to render an account of the execution of their vocation as labourers in His vineyard, preachers (by word and act) of the Gospel message, extenders of his kingdom on earth.

16, 17 Whosoever has faithfully and diligently made the most of the opportunities given by Him to serve His cause will be richly rewarded in the everlasting and heavenly kingdom by the praise which the Lord will bestow upon him and by the commission to fulfil a far more glorious and important calling (the good servant in the parable does not receive the ten cities as his possession, but obtains dominion over them in order to administer their affairs on behalf of his master).

18, 19 Whosoever has been faithful and diligent to a lesser degree will also be rewarded, but in a smaller measure.

20-5 The believer who, through a wrong attitude towards the Lord, proves unfruitful in His service will at His advent be rebuked and will have no part in the privilege of reigning in the heavenly kingdom and sharing the authority of the eternal King. Although no believer can perish, the unfaithful and those who forsake their vocation will meet with disgrace and loss.

26 Whosoever makes full and faithful use of the opportunities of fruitfulness in His service will always receive further opportunities of working for Him, and will thus be more richly blessed in Eternity. But whosoever neglects his opportunities and is unfaithful in the Lord's service will become spiritually impoverished, will receive still fewer opportunities for service and will appear poor and naked before His throne at his second advent.

27 A fatal end awaits everyone who refuses to acknowledge and to obey Jesus as King and Lord. In the disasters that befell the Jewish people (especially during the Roman-Jewish war of A.D. 66-70 when Jerusalem was completely destroyed and hundreds of thousands of Jews were killed), these words have already found fulfilment. At the second advent of Jesus, however, they will be completely and finally fulfilled when all who have rejected Him will reap the retribution of everlasting loss.

28 The Saviour in the preceding parable taught His disciples how necessary it was for them to persevere faithfully and diligently

475

to the end in His service, and warned the Jewish people of the bitter consequences of refusal to accept Him as the divine King. Thereby He again prepared His followers for what was coming, and He once more called the unbelieving Jews to repentance, and now He finally and of set purpose entered upon the way to Jerusalem.

Not only ministers and other spiritual leaders, but all believers, have received the opportunity (as a gift from the Lord) of working for Him (by word and deed, in prayer and offerings, and in many other ways). Whosoever avails himself of every opportunity which the Lord gives him will become inwardly richer and will always have more and better opportunities of working for Him and of thus laying up a rich treasure in heaven. But he who, through estrangement of heart towards Him, neglects the precious opportunities of working for Him commits spiritual suicide.

---

[1] We may render this sentence as follows: " After Jesus had said this and while these words still echoed in the ears and hearts of those present, Jesus added the following parable " (Zahn, *in loc.*).

[2] προσθεὶς εἶπεν παραβολῆ—Hebraistic וַיֹּסֶף וַיְדַבֵּר (*wayyôseph wayĕdabbēr*). We can translate it: " He went on to speak a parable " (Creed, *in loc.*).

[3] Jerusalem is situated about seventeen miles from Jericho.

[4] Cf. Mark x. 35–45, xi. 9 ff.; Acts i. 6 ff.

[5] ἀναφαίνεσθαι " describes an intensive and positive appearance. They were expecting something climacteric, a crisis of manifestation. All of which simply means that they expected that now He would assert Himself as Messiah, as they understood Messiahship " (Morgan, *in loc.*).

[6] For a long time now it has been held by most critics except those of the conservative school that this parable in Luke is a variant version of the parable of the talents in Matthew xxv. 14–30, or that both Matthew and Luke give touched-up renderings of an originally simpler parable. This view is held by Jülicher-Fascher, Weiss, H. Holzmann, Bultmann and Klostermann. But Strauss, Ewald, Harnack, Wellhausen and T. W. Manson hold that Luke has fused two different parables into one.

However, there is no conclusive reason for accepting either of these views. Moreover, it is noteworthy how the aforementioned critics differ on the question. Together with Zahn, Plummer, Schlatter, and others, we are convinced that verses 11–28 as well as Matthew xxv. 14–30 are true accounts of two parables uttered by Jesus on different occasions (as related by Matthew and Luke). The few resemblances between the two parables in Matthew and Luke (of the approximately

476

three hundred words in verses 11–28 only about sixty words or parts of words are the same in Matthew and Luke) are of such a nature (being mostly proverbial expressions, cf. Zahn, *in loc.*) that we are by no means constrained to accept the view that Matthew and Luke reproduce the same parable of Jesus. Besides, the differences in time, circumstances, contents, etc., are so great that we cannot but agree that "An estimate of the probabilities on each side seems to be favourable to the view that we have accurate reports of two different parables and not two reports of the same parable, one of which, if not both, must be very inaccurate " (Plummer, *in loc.*).

We must remember that " Jesus did not belong to those inept teachers or inartistic spirits who, according to Schleiermacher, avoid all repetition " (Zahn, *in loc.*). The parable in Luke xix fits in excellently with the circumstances in which the Lord uttered it, and so also the parable in Matthew xxv, as part of the prophetic oration, fits in beautifully with the circumstances described in Matthew.

The most important differences between the parable in Matthew and the one in Luke are well summarised in Plummer and in Zahn. Cf. also Schlatter, *in loc.* T. W. Manson is undoubtedly correct in stating: " It must be confessed that the resemblances are far outweighed by the differences " (*op. cit.*, p. 605).

⁷ The Saviour probably derived the details of this parable from the actual history of Archelaus, the son of Herod, who after his father's death went to Rome to receive the sovereignty over part of his father's kingdom in accordance with the intentions of his father's testament. Its confirmation by the Roman emperor was necessary, because Herod's empire in reality formed part of the Roman Empire. A Jewish deputation at that time also went to Rome to dispute Archelaus's claim to kingship, but the emperor nevertheless appointed him as ruler (though not as a fully sovereign king) over half of his father's kingdom (cf. Josephus, *The Jewish War*, ii, 6; and *Antiquities*, xvii, 8, 11).

⁸ μνᾶ, Hebrew מָנֶה *maneh*; Aramaic מְנָא *měnē*; Latin *mina*, was about £5 or 16 dollars in value. In the parable of the talents (Matt. xxv. 14–30) the servants receive great sums of money (but each a different amount). Here, however, each one receives only a small sum *as a test* of his faithfulness.

⁹ Fr. Hauch (*in loc.*) regards verses 14 and 27 as a separate allegory incorporated by Luke into the parable of the pounds. There is, however, no proof for his contention. Why could our Lord not have told the parable in this form with some allegorical portions in it? Surely He was not bound by the ideas of modern scholars as to the nature of His parables. He did not follow stereotyped forms of discourse but made the different forms of speech subservient to His purpose. No wonder that His parables are so unique and matchless and so unfathomable for our minds!

¹⁰ The vocation of the believer on earth, however glorious and great it may be, is, by comparison with that which awaits every faithful

477

follower of Jesus in His eternal kingdom, of extremely little significance (" the least ")—so great and glorious is the task to be assigned to the faithful ones after the consummation of the age.

11 Note that this servant is not merely going to receive a more insignificant charge, but in addition is not praised by his lord as the first one.

12 ὁ ἕτερος (the other one). Because an account is here demanded of only three servants, T. W. Manson (*op. cit.*, p. 607) and others regard this as a proof that Luke has fused two different parables into one (the one parable that mentions ten servants and the other that deals with three). This argument is, however, unconvincing. As in xiv. 18–20, the Saviour mentions " by way of example " (Klostermann, *in loc.*) only three out of the greater number—these three are examples of the various types (the faithful, the less faithful, and the unfaithful ones). The reason why Jesus says *the* other one (and not merely *another* one) is rightly stated as follows: " The two first classes having been described, the representative of the remaining class may be spoken of as ὁ ἕτερος, especially as he is of quite a different kind. They both belong to the profitable division, he to the unprofitable " (Plummer, *in loc.*).

13 αὐστηρός occurs only here in the New Testament, and means " strict ", " exacting ", " a man who expects to get blood out of a stone " (Moulton and Milligan, *Vocabulary of the Greek Testament*, i, p. 93a).

Jülicher-Fascher declares that if the parable had originally been intended to refer to Jesus the man would not have been described as " an austere man . . .". To this the right answer has been given by Creed: " The Lord is a harsh taskmaster to the idle servant alone, and that because the idle servant has not their Lord's business in his heart. Those who make their Lord's interest their own find that their duty becomes a joyful service " (*in loc.*).

14 αἴρεις ὃ οὐκ ἔθηκας—" Proverbial for unjust appropriation of another's labour " (Creed, *in loc.*).

15 Whether the words should be taken as an interjection from the hearers of Jesus or as that of the servants of the King (in the parable), " in any case the remonstrance serves to give point to the declaration which follows " (Plummer, *in loc.*).

16 " He alone possesses, who uses and enjoys his possessions " (*loc. cit.*). For this reason he may be spoken of as one " that hath not ". Applied to the congregation of Christ, it teaches that " their circle must grow. They must give thought not to their own salvation alone, for thus they would lose it. What they have received they must give to all who are open to receive their word " (Schlatter, *in loc.*).

17 " We may be horrified by the fierceness of the conclusion; but beneath the grim imagery is an equally grim fact, the fact that the coming of Jesus to the world puts every man to the test, compels every man to a decision. And that decision is no light matter. It is a matter of life and death " (T. W. Manson, *op. cit.* p. 609).

THE ENTRY OF JESUS INTO JERUSALEM

(Cf. Matt. xxi. 1–11; Mark xi. 1–11.)

xix. 29–44

29 And it came to pass, when he drew nigh unto Bethphage[1] and Bethany,[2] at the mount that is called *the mount* of Olives,[3]
30 he sent two of the disciples, saying, Go your way into the village over against *you*; in the which as ye enter ye shall find a colt tied,[4] whereon no man ever yet sat: loose him, and
31 bring him. And if any one ask you, Why do ye loose him?
32 thus shall ye say, The Lord hath need of him. And they that were
33 sent went away, and found even as he said unto them. And as they were loosing the colt,[5] the owners thereof said unto
34 them, Why loose ye the colt? And they said, The Lord hath
35 need of him.[6] And they brought him to Jesus: and they threw their garments upon the colt, and set Jesus thereon.
36 And as he went, they spread their garments in the way.[7]
37 And as he was now drawing nigh, *even* at the descent of the mount of Olives, the whole multitude of the disciples began to rejoice and praise God with a loud voice for all the mighty
38 works which they had seen; saying, Blessed *is* the King that cometh in the name of the Lord:[8] peace in heaven,[9] and
39 glory in the highest. And some of the Pharisees from. the multitude[10] said unto him, Master, rebuke thy disciples.
40 And he answered and said, I tell you that, if these shall hold their peace, the stones will cry out.[11]
41 And when he drew nigh,[12] he saw the city and wept over
42 it,[13] saying, If thou hadst known in this day, even thou, the things which belong unto peace![14] but now they are hid
43 from thine eyes.[15] For the days shall come upon thee,[16] when thine enemies shall cast up a bank about thee, and
44 compass thee round, and keep thee in on every side,[17] and shall dash thee to the ground,[18] and thy children[19] within thee; and they shall not leave in thee one stone upon another[20] because thou knewest not the time of thy visitation.[21]

The prophet Zechariah had foretold a few centuries earlier that the Messiah-King would enter Jerusalem not as a triumphant military conqueror, but as a lowly Prince of Peace (Zech. ix. 9). And here we see how Jesus, when He came to Jerusalem, by finally offering Himself to the Jewish people as the Messiah-King, fulfils this prophecy literally.

29-34 At last Jerusalem, the temple city in which the greatest and holiest drama on earth will be staged the following week, is in the immediate vicinity—Bethany being only two miles from the city and Bethphage still nearer. Formerly, during His public ministry, Jesus had as a rule refused to be openly honoured as Messiah. Now, however, the moment has arrived when He is going to announce Himself as the promised King in the centre of the Holy Land so that the people can finally take sides for or against Him. Nevertheless He is not going to appear with outward power, but will enter the holy city as Prince of Peace. So He sends two of His disciples to go and fetch a colt. He informs them that they will find the colt tied and that if the owner should ask them why they are loosing the colt they must tell him: " The Lord hath need of him." From this it appears that the Saviour had probably often passed through Bethphage, so that the owner of the colt already knew him as " Lord " and honoured Him to such an extent that he and his household would allow the colt to be taken to Jesus without any opposition.

35, 36 Our Lord probably waited in Bethany, at the southeastern foot of the Mount of Olives, until the two disciples brought Him the colt. From there He now rides forward on the colt along the road leading to Jerusalem across the Mount of Olives. The tension among the great multitude of disciples (in the widest sense of the word) who follow Him becomes greater and greater—notwithstanding Jesus' teachings to the contrary, they nevertheless expect that He will now reveal Himself in full power and glory as the Messiah-King. To such a degree do they honour Him that they even spread out some of their clothes in the way for Him to ride over.

37 At last the procession reaches the highest part of the road on the Mount of Olives and they at once see their holy city (which the Messiah would now, according to their expectations, enter triumphantly). It lies spread out before them, with the beautiful buildings of the temple standing out majestically on the temple-mount. Spontaneously and irresistibly they now give vent to their excitement and greatest expectations by praising God exultantly for the mighty deeds which He has done through Jesus in Galilee and elsewhere, but especially when He raised Lazarus from the dead (xi. 45) and healed blind Bartimaeus, events still fresh in their minds—events which have revealed Him as Messiah in the eyes of His followers.

38 In addition, they call upon Jesus Himself as the blessed King that comes in the name of the Lord, as His representative and deputy: in other words, as the Messiah, through whose coming peace has been established between God and His people so that the All-Highest is now truly glorified. From Matthew xxi and Mark xi it appears that the excited multitude gave vent also to various other exclamations and panegyrics. The atmosphere was in the highest sense laden with Messianic expectations, and the enthusiasm of the multitude knew no bounds.

39 Apart from the great multitude of disciples now accompanying Jesus, there are naturally also many other Jews, among whom are some of the Pharisees. The latter are exceedingly annoyed at the Messianic reverence shown to the Nazarene against whom most of them have long ago taken sides. In addition, they are afraid that the public applause given to the Saviour will cause the severe Roman governor, Pilate, to take action against the people by force of arms. However, they do not venture to try and impose silence on the exultant multitude itself. The only alternative is, therefore, that they must ask Jesus to silence His disciples (who naturally were playing a prominent part in the applause and reverence shown to Him here).

40 On this occasion, however, Jesus wants to enter the city openly as Messiah, and so He unhesitatingly rejects the request of the Pharisees, declaring that it is an absolute impossibility for Him not to be applauded as the Messiah on this occasion. Even though His human followers should now hold their peace, He will nevertheless be exultantly greeted on this occasion of His entry into the temple city, even if it must be inanimate objects of nature that are to cry out in His honour (for He comes as the Representative and Messiah of God).

41 In glaring contrast with the rejoicing of the excited multitude, Jesus weeps over Jerusalem now that the city is actually here in front of Him and now that the request of the Pharisees (verse 39) proves to Him anew how the Jewish leaders (and through them the Jewish people) persist in their rejection of Him.

42 Weeping in His passionate pity for the people that will have to pay such a heavy penalty, the Saviour cries out: " If thou hadst known, even thou, at least in this thy day, the things which belong unto thy peace! " In these words Jesus gives utterance to His sincere longing that even now at the eleventh hour the Jewish people should yet accept in time the redemption offered by God through Him. But, alas! He realises only too well that it is already too late; their persistence in their wicked unbelief has blinded them to the opportunities for redemption still remaining;

through their own fault the way to salvation is hidden from their sight.

43, 44 Because the people as a whole are thus going to persist in unbelief and hardness of heart, terrible judgments will come upon them. For by their refusal for three years to believe in Him, notwithstanding all His words and deeds, it has been proved over and over again that they will never believe in Him. In the providence of God a mighty enemy (naturally the Romans—the only world-power that would at that time be able to play such a part) will soon come to besiege Jerusalem and destroy the whole city with its inhabitants amid fearful havoc. All this will happen (and actually did happen within forty years from Jesus' prophecy) because they did not avail themselves of the time of Grace, when God visited them in their Messiah, in order to offer them (first among all the nations) redemption and everlasting salvation.

In Jesus God has proved once and for all that He is indeed the God of love. He is, however, also the God of holy righteousness, the Almighty who is not mocked. Every nation or person who rejects the opportunity offered by Him to be saved through Christ, will be inexorably visited by His judgment.

---

[1] It cannot yet be definitely determined whether Bethphage was only a small suburb of Jerusalem or a separate village. Most expositors, however, assume that it was a small suburb just outside the south-eastern walls of Jerusalem.

[2] " The name (Bethany) applied not only to the village but to the whole of the south-east slope of Olivet. The village lies about two miles from Jerusalem, almost at the foot of the mount, hidden amongst groves of olive, fig and almond trees, at the very edge of the desert hills, that reach without sign of human habitation to Jericho " (Stirling, *An Atlas of the Life of Christ*, p. 24). At present the place is called El-Azaryeh (after Lazarus, who lived there).

[3] The Mount of Olives is, as briefly summarised by Stirling, " the central eminence of a ridge of three rounded summits, directly opposite the temple area. There is little evidence to-day of the trees from which it originally derived its name, but its green slopes remain the most pleasing feature in the neighbourhood of Jerusalem. From the summit of the mount the holy city lies below spread out map-like, and every object of the plateau can be clearly distinguished " (*in loc.*).

[4] " That the whole had been previously arranged by Jesus is *possible*, for He gives no intimation that it was not so. But the impression produced by the narratives is that the knowledge is supernatural, which on so momentous an occasion would be in harmony with His purpose " (Plummer, *in loc.*).

⁵ Matthew's statement that the foal's mother was brought to Jesus as well as the foal does not necessarily contradict Mark and Luke. Matthew's account is probably intended to emphasise that Zechariah's prophecy was literally fulfilled.

⁶ " If, in accordance with Jesus' forecast, the bare statement ὁ κύριος αὐτοῦ χρείαν ἔχει made the owner of the beast willing to let the disciples take it, it follows that this man belonged from an earlier occasion to the circle in which Jesus was the acknowledged and unique Lord and was so called " (Zahn, in loc.).

⁷ See Special Note on the Triumphal Entry (pp. 486 ff.).

⁸ ἐν ὀνόματι κυρίου " expresses the difference which marks this King off from all other kings; He is King by God's commission, as the One sent by God so that God's kingly work is done through Him " (Schlatter, in loc.).

⁹ Zahn gives a clear and powerful account of the acclamations: " With the coming of the promised King the period of God's wrath over Jerusalem seemed to have reached its end and the time of peace seemed to have come. But even the enthusiastic crowds could not imagine that the Messiah's reign of peace would take shape on earth without a struggle. It is still in heaven, in the counsel and gracious will of God; it will only appear on earth in the Gospel of peace proclaimed through Jesus and in the hearts of those who have believed in it. That is why the disciples cried ἐν οὐρανῷ εἰρήνη. But because they believed in it, they also perceived the determination with which Jesus set about His entry into Jerusalem, the decisive beginning of the coming into effect of God's will for man's salvation, and therefore they could add δόξα ἐν ὑψίστοις " (in loc.). Cf. also Schlatter, in loc.

¹⁰ Wellhausen objects to this detail; but, as Creed points out, " it is appropriate that the enthusiasm of the multitude should call forth an answering complaint from the standing enemies of Jesus " (in loc.).

¹¹ " Hitherto the Lord had discouraged all demonstrations in His favour; latterly He had begun an opposite course . . . if not offered by the vast multitude, the acclamation would have been wrung out of the stones rather than be withheld (Hab. ii. 11) " (Jamieson, Fausset and Brown, in loc.). This is the primary meaning of the words, but probably Jesus also alluded to the destruction of Jerusalem: " The disciples will be silent one day, when the opposition of Jewry makes every confession of Jesus impossible; and then the stones of destroyed Jerusalem will proclaim that Christ came to it and was cast out by it. If we understand it in this way, the lament of Jesus over the downfall of Jerusalem —the downfall which comes upon it precisely because it rejects Him— gives a meaning to the enigmatic utterance " (Schlatter, in loc.).

¹² Wellhausen and Easton declare that it would have been impossible for Jesus, after He had so jubilantly been acclaimed by the multitude, to weep over Jerusalem. This is a very superficial view of the matter. Creed rightly states: " The lament of Jesus over the city while He is surrounded by the shouting multitude makes a fine dramatic contrast " (in loc.). So also T. W. Manson writes: " The lamentation over

Jerusalem comes with tremendous dramatic effect in the midst of the jubilant enthusiasm of the crowd " (*The Mission and Message of Jesus*, p. 611). See our exposition for the reasons why it was natural, and indeed inevitable, that our Lord, who had such a penetrating insight into the actual state of affairs and into the impending fate of the city and the nation, wept over Jerusalem at that point.

[13] ἔκλαυσεν—stronger than ἐδάκρυσεν (John xi. 35). The word " does not mean merely that tears forced themselves up and fell down His face. It suggests rather the heaving of the bosom, and the sob and the cry of a soul in agony. We could have no stronger word than the word that is used there.

> ' The Son of God in tears,
> The wondering angels see.
> Be thou astonished, O my soul,
> He shed those tears for thee.'

For while He wept over the city, the city was merely the crystallised centre of human attitude towards Him, and of human sin; and in the presence of it He wept " (Morgan, *in loc.*).

[14] εἰ ἔγνως ἐν τῇ ἡμέρᾳ ταύτῃ καὶ σὺ τὰ πρὸς εἰρήνην. " The aposiopesis is impressive. In the expression of strong emotion sentences are often broken " (Plummer, *in loc.*). These words of Jesus assume that the city has already had several opportunities of receiving salvation, and that this is now a final opportunity. From the Gospel of John we know, moreover, that the Saviour often appeared in Jerusalem and was again and again opposed and persecuted by the Jewish leaders.

[15] These words " certainly do not point to a divine judgment of blindness as the cause of the fruitlessness of the offer of salvation (cf. viii. 10), nor yet to a framing of the announcement of salvation that brings it about that some recognise it while the others fail to do so (cf. x. 21). . . . The words νῦν δὲ ἐκρύβη κτλ, by the very form of the sentence, cannot serve as the ground of Jerusalem's lack of contrition. Rather do they set over against Jesus' desire, that Jerusalem if possible might turn even yet, the fact which is the exact opposite of saving recognition " (Zahn, *in loc.*). Jesus had already declared (ix. 22, xiii. 33 ff.) that the Jewish authorities had finally taken sides against Him. Because they persisted in rejecting Him, they are now hopelessly blind to the fact that He has come as Messiah and Redeemer.

[16] It has become a tradition with critics of a certain school to declare that these words were not uttered by Jesus, but are a *vaticinium post eventum*. But as Vincent Taylor rightly asks: " Was it difficult for anyone familiar with the social and political situation as it existed in our Lord's day to foresee the peril of the city? " (*op. cit.*, p. 123). Even ordinary prophets like Isaiah and Jeremiah had in their days predicted the rejection of the Jewish people and the destruction of Jerusalem. How much more would Jesus, even if it were solely through His clear grasp of prevailing trends, have been able to predict the downfall of

the city? Thus even Luce (who will not be accused of ultra-orthodoxy) admits that " granting the use of the Old Testament, such a passage as the present, of which the details are more or less characteristic of all sieges, might well have been produced *before* the event " (*in loc.*). And T. W. Manson rightly says: " To describe these verses as a Christian composition after the event is the kind of extravagance that brings sober criticism into disrepute " (*op. cit.*, p. 612). As a result of the unanimous testimony of the Gospels in this respect, there is no doubt that just as surely and unambiguously as Jesus foretold His suffering and death He also announced the divine judgments on the Jewish people. And the gruesome history of the Roman-Jewish war (A.D. 66–70), including the destruction of Jerusalem in A.D. 70, proves how correct His predictions were.

[17] The Romans did this so thoroughly that during the closing months of the siege of Jerusalem (in A.D. 70) there was no possibility for the Jews of getting reinforcements from outside, with the result that thousands died of hunger before the final overwhelming of the city (cf. Josephus, *The Jewish War*, v and vi).

[18] ἐδαφιοῦσιν may mean " will shatter against the ground " or " will level to the ground ". The first meaning is probably the correct one here (cf., however, T. W. Manson, *op. cit.*, pp. 612–13: " what the verse says is that the city will be sacked and destroyed with its inhabitants in it ").

[19] τέκνα includes children as well as adults: all the inhabitants of the city.

[20] What the Saviour here prophesies hyperbolically was literally fulfilled as regards the temple and also to an amazing degree as regards the whole city. When the Romans after a bitter struggle of five months finally overwhelmed the fanatical Jewish defenders, the furious soldiers mercilessly slew every Jew they met (except the most handsome and the strongest young men and leaders whom they captured to make them meet their death afterwards at the victory celebrations in gladiatorial fights and the like), and sacked the whole city and ruined it completely (except part of a wall—to-day the famous wailing wall—and a few tower fortifications). For a full description of the terrible manner in which the predictions of Jesus were fulfilled, we refer to our Christian historical novel in Afrikaans, *Ween oor julleself* (" Weep for yourselves "), in which the whole history of the downfall of the Jewish people in the Roman-Jewish war is described.

[21] ἐπισκοπῆς. Here and in 1 Peter ii. 12 the reference is to a " visit of God " for the purpose of bringing salvation and blessing. In Jesus, during His public ministry in the midst of the Jewish people, God visited them for the purpose of saving and blessing them unto eternity, but they were obdurate in their unbelief and hostility towards Christ, His Son, and thus blinded themselves to the salvation which He offered them. We must not, of course, suppose that the disaster which befell Jerusalem in A.D. 70 was an *arbitrary* penalty imposed by God upon the city because of its treatment of Jesus. In accordance

with the eternal principles of God's righteous government of the universe, the destruction of the city, and especially of the temple and its ritual, was the *inevitable* sequel to the rejection of Jesus, with His message of salvation and His teaching of love, and to the deliberate choice of a very different way from His.

SPECIAL NOTE

THE TRIUMPHAL ENTRY

Many critics reject the historicity of the statement in the Gospels that Jesus openly and of fixed purpose entered Jerusalem as Messiah on this occasion. While a conservative expositor like Plummer writes that the Saviour through the manner in which He arranged the entry " publicly claims to be the Messiah " (*in loc.*), Luce contends (*in loc.*) that " the entry is not mentioned as evidence against Jesus at His trial ", and therefore it could not really have been Messianic. This reasoning is, however, far-fetched—for the Lord was actually condemned for professing to be *the* Messiah, the King of the Jews, and who knows whether in the testimonies against Him no reference was made to His entry? Of the numerous charges made against Him during his trial, only a few are recorded in the Gospels, and those in few words. It goes without saying that many more accusations were brought up against Him than were recorded.

Dalman (*op. cit.*, pp. 221, 222) again contends that the whole of the Messianic tenor of the Gospel narratives of the entry is due to the misconception of the writers as to the meaning of the term " Hosanna! " However, he is at fault, for although it is true that " Hosanna! " was originally a cry for help, it was later on used as a " cry of rejoicing with which a sovereign was honoured " (Van Leeuwen, at Mark xi. 8-11). Major correctly explains as follows: " The cry Hosanna is the equivalent of our English ' God save the King '. . . . It could only be be used in saluting a sovereign or his vice-gerent " (*op. cit.*, p. 139).

Loisy, still more radical, declares that the whole story has been built up by the writers (or by the writers of their sources) from the various Old Testament prophecies, as e.g. Zechariah ix. 9. V. Taylor again (*Behind the Third Gospel*, p. 236) declares that Jesus' entry bore no Messianic character, but that the first Christians gradually represented it thus.

For all these and other theories there are no grounds except the preconceived views of those who conceive them. The testimony of the Gospels is clear and unanimous that the entry was to Jesus and to those who accompanied Him indeed Messianic in character—of course not in the sense of earthly military power and the like, as the Jews represented it, but it was " a deliberate symbolic action of Jesus intended to proclaim publicly the real character of His Messiahship to the inhabitants of Jerusalem " (Major, *op. cit.*, p. 139). The latter fact thus explains why so many Jews who had formerly been sympathetic towards Him, subsequently joined in the clamour against Him—He entered the city humbly as Prince of Peace and not as a military Messiah. By the manner of His entry He proved clearly that His kingdom is not of this world and that He had not come to establish a Jewish-Messianic kingdom with outward violence, but to found the universal and spiritual kingdom of God. When He did not follow up the triumphal entry by such moves as a military conqueror might be expected to make, they began to lose faith in Him, and lost it altogether when they saw how unresistingly He allowed Himself to be arrested and led to execution.

PURIFICATION OF THE TEMPLE

(Cf. Matt. xxi. 12–17; Mark xi. 11–17)

xix. 45–8

45 And he entered into the temple,[1] and began to cast out[2]
46 them that sold,[3] saying unto them, It is written,[4] And my
house shall be a house of prayer: but ye have made it a den
of robbers.[5]

47 And he was teaching daily in the temple. But the chief
priests and the scribes and the principal men of the people
48 sought to destroy him: and they could not find what they
might do; for the people all hung upon him, listening.

" Behold, I send my messenger, and he shall prepare the way
before me: and the Lord, whom ye seek, shall suddenly come to
his temple, and the messenger of the covenant, whom ye delight
in; behold, he cometh, saith the Lord of hosts." So clearly and
unambiguously had the prophet (Mal. iii, 1) prophesied centuries
before concerning the coming of the divine Messiah to His
temple, the centre of the religious life of the Jewish people that
were chosen to serve as the channel through which the Redeemer
was to be given to the world. At the commencement of His
public ministry (some time after the beginning of the appearance
of John the Baptist, the promised forerunner) Jesus entered the
temple and cleansed it drastically (cf. John ii. 13–25). The
Jewish religious leaders, however, resisted Him, and soon all the
old malpractices again prevailed in full swing in the temple. So
it was a matter of course, that the Saviour, when He again went
to the temple shortly before His crucifixion, should manifest
Himself once more as the inexorable opponent of all unholy
practices in the temple. So the prophet rightly continued, after
the above-mentioned prophecy (Mal. iii. 1): " But who may
abide the day of his coming? and who shall stand when he
appeareth? for he is like a refiner's fire, and like fullers' soap "
(Mal. iii. 2).

45, 46 From Mark xi. 11 it appears that the Saviour after His
entry into Jerusalem entered the temple late that afternoon,
examined things there and then, without doing anything further,
because it was already late, went to Bethany for the night. The

following day He went to the temple with the fixed purpose of driving out all those who were engaged in secularising and desecrating it. Instead of using the temple as a place consecrated to God where He could be worshipped in spirit and in truth, the Jews, through all kinds of business transacted in the courts of the temple, were degrading it to a den of thieves—a place where people who were carrying on their businesses in a dishonest manner, and were robbing other people, could enjoy a safe refuge.

47, 48 Luke has given only a very succinct account of the purification of the temple and now tells us in summary form and in quite general terms that Jesus, during that last week before His crucifixion, was engaged every day in teaching the people who collected around Him in great numbers, in the temple which He had purified at least of the buyers and sellers. Although His drastic action in purifying the temple, His exposure of the hypocrisy of so many of the Jewish leaders and His claims to be the divine Messiah, greatly upset the Jewish authorities; and although for a long time now they were firmly resolved to do away with Him, they were nevertheless still powerless against Him—so great was the admiration with which the ordinary masses of the people regarded Him at this stage. The broad masses of the people undoubtedly noted with inward satisfaction how He exposed the errors of the Jewish religious leaders under whose heavy yoke they had to suffer much, and all the people were naturally talking about His mighty miracles. How many of them could testify that they themselves witnessed how He healed the sick, restored sight to the blind, cured the crippled and even raised people from the dead! Many still expected, to a greater or less degree, that He would yet come forward with power and glory as the promised Messiah. Among the multitudes there were, in addition, probably several hundreds of persons who were whole-hearted disciples of Jesus (at Pentecost a hundred and twenty were gathered together, Acts i. 15, and in Galilee Jesus appeared to five hundred of His followers on one single occasion after His resurrection, 1 Cor. xv. 6), and who at that time still had great influence among the masses through their enthusiastic and open reverence for their Lord (cf. Luke xix. 37). So it would have been fatal for the Jewish authorities to attempt openly at that stage to do away with Him. For this reason, until after His capture (through the treachery of Judas), they directed their attacks against Him in a roundabout way and tried only surreptitiously to plot His destruction.

489

Christ Jesus is and remains the divine Purifier. For He is perfect in love as well as in righteousness and holiness. He cannot tolerate any deceit or unrighteousness. According as fuller control is given to Him over the life of a believer, of a church or of a nation, He continues to bring about an ever mightier change by casting out everything that is false and unholy. And where He is refused admission, He sooner or later—and at His second advent with finality—takes action as the Almighty Purifier by pronouncing the divine judgment upon those who persist in opposing Him in unbelief and disobedience.

[1] There is no conclusive proof that Jesus did not purify the temple on two occasions. On the contrary, in our opinion it seems almost impossible that the Saviour would not on both these occasions—at the commencement of His public ministry (John ii. 13 ff.), and again towards its conclusion (Luke xix. 45 ff.)—give expression, by such powerful and unmistakable action, to His holy indignation at the desecration of the temple which ought to have been the hallowed centre of true divine worship. The fact that Matthew, Mark and Luke make no mention of the first purification of the temple by no means proves that John is incorrect in his placing of the occurrence. It is quite arbitrary to describe the first purification of the temple as a fiction, merely because the first three Gospels omit to mention it. It is also quite unwarranted to reject the synoptic dating of the purification of the temple towards the end of Jesus' ministry (as many modern critics do, now that they are beginning to attach greater value to John's historical data). The evidence of the four Gospels, and historical and psychological considerations, too, compel us to assume that Jesus purified the temple both at the commencement and also towards the end of His public activity.

[2] Loisy, Luce, and others declare that it is historically impossible that the temple authorities and other Jewish leaders would have tolerated Jesus' action in purifying the temple so drastically. Loisy consequently does not hesitate to declare that the whole story of the temple purification is pure fiction (built up out of Old Testament prophecies like Zechariah xiv. 21). Their reasoning, however, does not take actuality into account, for if Jesus' influence and authority among the masses were at that time (as Loisy, Luce, and others allege) indeed so insignificant that He could not successfully purify the temple of malpractices, it is inexplicable why the Jewish authorities, when Jesus exposed their frauds in the temple and made such tremendous claims, did not immediately have Him arrested and brought to trial. From the Gospel narrative it appears as clear as daylight that the Saviour during that week before the crucifixion did have a tremendous hold on the masses, so that the Jewish authorities were not able to prevent Him from purifying the temple, teaching people daily in its courts, and

exposing the hypocrisies of the Pharisees and other Jewish leaders. So great was Jesus' influence that they were compelled to have Him taken by an armed band only towards the end of the week (when the Passover had already commenced), and this with the assistance of Judas the traitor, during the night (when there was no danger of a riot on the part of the people), and then to try him hurriedly and have Him dragged before the Roman governor. Throughout one can feel how apprehensive the Jewish authorities were that the masses would take His part. However, when Jesus had already been arrested and stood before Pilate, it was no longer difficult for the Jewish leaders to arouse the masses against Him, although they had so recently hung on His lips. For then they saw very clearly that the Saviour was no triumphant earthly Messiah as they would have liked Him to be. And who does not realise how easily their superficial admiration for Him could change into savage bloodthirstiness? It is our firm conviction that if some critics would make a more determined effort to penetrate into the real historical circumstances, they would advance far fewer objections against the trustworthiness of the Gospel narrative.

[3] " Some have seen in the cleansing of the Court of the Gentiles a deep concern on the part of Jesus for the religion of the Gentile world, and have held that His action foreshadows the Call of the Gentiles and the extension of the true religion of the divine Father to all mankind. It is more probable that we have in the cleansing of the temple a deliberate symbolic action by Jesus, setting forth an aspect of His Messianic office: the purging of contemporary Jewish religion from commercialism and materialism " (Major, *op. cit.*, p. 142).

[4] Cf. Isaiah lvi. 7 and Jeremiah vii. 11.

[5] For a detailed description of the activities in the courts of the temple cf. Edersheim, *Life and Times of Jesus the Messiah*, pp. 364–74, and also Abrahams, *Studies in Pharisaism and the Gospels*, i, pp. 83 ff. " A market for the supply of sacrificial victims . . . and other materials for sacrifice (e.g. wine, oil, and salt) appears to have been carried on in the outermost court of the temple (the ' Court of the Gentiles ') under the sanction of the authorities. . . . At the *tables of the money-changers* Jews from abroad were provided at an expensive rate of exchange with the necessary half-shekel (cf. Exod. xxx. 12b.; Matt. xvii. 24) for the payment of the temple tax, which seems at this time to have been payable only in coins of the Phoenician standard, the Tyrian two-drachma piece being the best type of ' half-shekel ' available " (Rawlinson, *St. Mark, in loc.*).

Because the court of the temple was thus transformed into a busy Eastern mart, the position was that " instead of being impressed by the majesty of the place, and stirred by the realisation of the divine presence, the pilgrim found himself involved in a heated crowd, sellers intent only on getting the highest possible price, buyers protesting furiously against the sums demanded. The house of God, the precincts of which were meant to isolate it from the profanations of the world, had become the centre of an oriental bazaar " (M. J. Lagrange, at Mark xi. 11–17, Eng. tran. by Rawlinson, *in loc.*). Through the Saviour's unequivocal action against this kind of desecration of the temple, " it is immediately made clear what the presence of Christ means for Jerusalem. His presence brings for it the end of that ceremonial worship which afforded a shelter to wrongdoing " (Schlatter, *in loc.*).

THE BAPTISM OF JOHN

(Matt. xxi. 23–7; Mark xi. 27–33)

xx. 1–8

1 And it came to pass, on one of the days, as he was teaching
the people in the temple, and preaching the gospel, there
came upon him the chief priests and the scribes with the
2 elders;[1] and they spake, saying unto him,[2] Tell us: By what
authority doest thou these things? or who is he that gave thee
3 this authority? And he answered and said unto them, I also
4 will ask you a question; and tell me: The baptism of John,[3]
5 was it from heaven, or from men? And they reasoned with
themselves, saying, If we shall say, From heaven; he will say,
6 Why did ye not believe him? But if we shall say, From men;
all the people will stone us: for they be persuaded that John
7 was a prophet. And they answered, that they knew not
8 whence *it was*. And Jesus said unto them, Neither tell I you
by what authority I do these things.

The purification of the temple by Jesus was indeed a drastic
interference in the religious life of the Jewish people. Only a
person who was invested with the very highest authority in the
religious sphere among the Jews would have been able to venture
on bringing about even a slight measure of reform in matters
concerning the temple. So it was natural for the Jewish authorities
(although they could not venture to arrest the Saviour at that
moment because of His great influence over the masses, xix. 48)
to ask Him on whose authority He had acted. They, no doubt,
hoped that He would give a reply to their question in a manner
that would bring Him into disfavour with the multitude. They
had, however, grossly miscalculated.

1, 2 In these chapters on Jesus' last days in Jerusalem Luke
gives very few particulars about the days of the week on which the
various occurrences related by him took place. So he states here
in quite general terms that on one of those days (during Holy
Week) when the Saviour was busy teaching the people (who came
in great multitudes to listen to Him, xix. 48), and continued to
preach the glad tidings of God's kingly rule, a deputation from the
Jewish Council came to Him. They were very much upset on

493

account of Jesus' actions, especially His purification of the temple, and now wanted to know from Him by whose authority He had dared to act thus. They, the leaders of the Jewish people, holding the monopoly of regulating the religious affairs of the nation, had not given Him the right to act in that manner in the temple. The only person who would be at liberty to interfere in the temple business without their permission was the Messiah. And because they refused to accept Jesus' Messianic claims as genuine, they thought that by asking this question they would drive Him into such a corner that He would be exposed as an unlawful intruder into the life of the temple before the multitudes that at this time were still to a great extent His enthusiastic admirers.

3 Once more the Saviour is master of the situation, and He answers them with a counter-question—a question which places them, instead of Him, before an unescapable dilemma.

4 Was the baptism of John, the Lord asks them, a purely human affair which he carried out by his own authority, or was it in accordance with the will of God and thus undertaken by *His* authority?

5, 6 The Jewish authorities to whom Jesus put this question were intelligent enough to realise that they would have to be extremely careful about their answer. For if they should say that John acted as a messenger of God, the Nazarene would be entitled to ask them why they had not believed him and accepted his claim to be the promised forerunner of the Messiah, whom he had identified with Jesus. And, on the other hand, if they should reply that John had not acted as God's messenger, but merely on his own human authority, there was great risk that the masses might stone them, for (cf. Luke 3) they regarded and honoured John as a great prophet of God and had themselves been baptized by him in thousands (and because this had happened only a few years ago, the recollection of John's activity was still fresh in men's minds).

7 So effectively were they cornered by Jesus' question that the Jewish leaders, who had always pretended to be almost omniscient in religious matters, and despised ordinary people as ignorant, were compelled to admit to Him whom they hated so much, and that in front of the great multitude, that (even on such a weighty matter) they did not possess enough knowledge to answer His question.

8 From the whole attitude of the Jewish authorities towards Jesus, to whom John had so clearly referred as the Messiah (John i. 29), it was clear that they critically and haughtily denied the divine authority with which John had acted. Nevertheless they

494

had been too afraid of the people to acknowledge openly and honestly that they did not recognise him as a prophet, but had even gone in a hypocritical spirit to be baptized by him (cf. Matt. iii. 7, and Van Leeuwen at Mark xi. 31 ff.).

And because they refused to give an honest answer to Jesus' express question, our Lord also refused to reply to their question. So their attempt to lead Him into a trap failed and led to the exposure of their insincerity and also their incompetence to act any longer as spiritual leaders. Because on such a most important matter, in connection with which all the people urgently needed guidance, they stated: " We do not know ", they showed that they had forfeited their right to be regarded as teachers of the people, and consequently they no longer had the right to question Jesus about His own actions. Accordingly He definitely refused to answer their question. If you do not recognise authority when you see it, He said in effect, no amount of arguing will convince you of it. In this manner it was they and not Jesus who stood exposed as unlawful intruders in the regulation of the religious life of the people.

Jesus, in a manner equalled by no person before or after Him, had practised perfect and genuine love towards God and man. At the same time, in an equally unparalleled manner, He acted with absolute authority. And, when it was required for the sake of truth and righteousness, He never hesitated to assert this unwavering authority even against the highest earthly authorities— although it cost Him His life in the end. With Him there was no question of compromise, and never did He seek the favour of earthly potentates: without any hesitation He followed the straight path to the bitter end in obedience to His divine vocation.

---

1 The "elders" formed a separate group in the Jewish Sanhedrin alongside the chief priests and scribes. " Although the whole Sanhedrin is called τὸ πρεσβυτέριον (Luke xxii. 66; Acts xxii. 5), and the members as a body are πρεσβύτεροι (senators), this title comes to be given especially to those who, without belonging to the priestly aristocracy or to the rabbinical profession, yet had a seat and a voice in the Sanhedrin; they were the ' chief of the people ', distinguished and rich persons like Joseph of Arimathaea (Matt. xxvii. 57; Luke xxiv. 50), representatives, so to speak, of the ' secular' aristocracy. Josephus often calls them οἱ δυνατοί and οἱ γνώριμοι, ' the notables'" (Zahn, in loc.).

2 " It was fear of the people which kept His opponents from proceeding against Him; and therefore their first object was to discredit

Him with His protectors. Then they could adopt more summary measures " (Plummer, *in loc.*).

³ Because John's baptism and preaching were undertaken entirely in the light of the coming of the Redeemer, and formed the preparation and heralding of Jesus' Messianic actions, the Saviour asked this question. " As Jesus joins Himself with John, so also He shows the people of Jerusalem His oneness with the prophets. He renews their mission. Thus He grounds His work in that which gave Israel its existence, in its being chosen to be the sanctified people of God. Because He does what the prophets did, and treats Israel as the people chosen by God for God, for that very reason He bears the cross " (Schlatter, *in loc.*).

The Saviour asks the question in connection with John, not in order to evade the question of the Jewish authorities, but because the right answer to His question was also to be the answer to theirs.

PARABLE OF THE HUSBANDMEN

(Cf. Matt. xxi. 33–46; Mark xii. 1–12)

xx. 9–18

9 And he began to speak unto the people this parable:[1] A
man planted a vineyard,[2] and let it out to husbandmen,[3] and
10 went into another country for a long time. And at the season
he sent unto the husbandmen a servant, that they should give
him of the fruit of the vineyard: but the husbandmen beat
11 him, and sent him away empty. And he sent yet another
servant: and him also they beat, and handled him shame-
12 fully, and sent him away empty. And he sent yet a third: and
13 him also they wounded, and cast him forth. And the lord of
the vineyard said, What shall I do?[4] I will send my beloved
14 son: it may be they will reverence him. But when the husbandmen saw him, they reasoned one with another, saying,
This is the heir: let us kill him, that the inheritance may be
15 ours.[5] And they cast him forth out of the vineyard, and
killed him. What therefore will the lord of the vineyard do
16 unto them? He will come and destroy these husbandmen,
and will give the vineyard unto others. And when they heard
17 it, they said, God forbid. But he looked upon them, and said,
What then is this that is written,
The stone which the builders rejected,
The same was made the head of the corner?[6]
18 Every one that falleth on that stone shall be broken to pieces;[7]
but on whomsoever it shall fall, it will scatter him as dust.[8]

By the entry into Jerusalem and the purification of the Temple
the Saviour had already clearly and vigorously announced His
Messiahship. And now He once more announces it by means of
this parable, and at the same time He shows His enemies that He is
fully aware of their murderous plans against Him and warns them
that if they should carry out those plans an awful fate is awaiting
them. Moreover, the parable is also the answer to their previous
question—He is acting on the authority of the Father who sent
Him.

9 While His questioners (the Jewish leaders, verse 1) were still
there (cf. verse 19), Jesus relates to the multitude the parable of
the husbandmen. To a greater degree than most of the other

R   497

parables, this one should in many respects (though not in all respects) be interpreted allegorically. The vineyard thus symbolises, as it often does in the Old Testament (cf. Isa. v. 1-7; Jer. ii. 21, etc.), the chosen people, and the husbandmen the Jewish leaders to whom the care of the people has been entrusted.

10-12 The servants who were sent to fetch of the fruit of the vineyard represent the various prophets and other messengers of God in Old Testament days who from time to time were sent to the Jewish people and were but too often ill-treated and rejected by the Jewish leaders (cf. Jer. vii. 25, xxv. 4; Amos iii. 7; Zech. i. 6).

13 In this verse the Messianic consciousness of Jesus is expressed very clearly. In these words He declares plainly that, while He is a divine Messenger and One who acts on God's authority, He is quite different from all the other divine messengers, as, e.g., the prophets. He is altogether unique—the beloved Son of the Father. In addition, He is the very last One to come to the people, and indeed to the whole world. After His coming no higher revelation and no mightier manifestation of God's love is to be expected. Through His coming to the people they (and especially the leaders) have now their last chance.

14-16 During Jesus' public activity among the Jews it has already become quite clear that they will not stand in awe even of Him; in fact, the Jewish leaders were already hard at work making preparations to bring about His death. Just as the wicked husbandmen had lost sight of the fact that, even if they slew the son, the owner was still there to call them to account, so Jesus warns the Jews who are engaged in these murderous plans against Him that they will shortly have to do with God, the Almighty Owner and Lord of all—to their fatal undoing. The Jewish rulers (and along with them the unbelieving part of the people) will be visited by the judgments of God and will no longer have the privilege of acting as the spiritual leaders of God's people. Believers in Jesus (from whatever nation) will be the new, true Israel, God's vineyard, and other leaders will be the workers in His vineyard—namely, the apostles, and after them all who have been called to minister spiritually to His church on earth (this ultimately extends, therefore, to every ordinary believer).

17 The divine purpose, however, reaches farther than this parable could reveal. For while that beloved son is killed and the owner is left to administer to the evil-doers their utmost and well-deserved punishment, Jesus, the Beloved Son of the Father, will, notwithstanding His being done to death, triumph over death and the grave and all hostile forces, and will be exalted (reinstated in His former glory and invested with fresh glory) as Head and Lord (" the corner-stone ") of the real Israel, the eternal divine empire.

18 As a blind man who stumbles and falls over a stone and injures himself against it, so those who through their unbelief and falseness of heart are spiritually blind will find Jesus, as it were, a stumbling-block in their path and so in a spiritual sense they will fall and come to grief. Even in the ordinary course of life this will happen to those who do not believe in Jesus. But whosoever persists in the state of unbelief until the time of grace is expired will be completely crushed by the judgment of God, carried out by the Son—and be pulverised like one on whom a tremendous rock crashes down.

When the terrible judgments of God visited the Jewish leaders and the unbelieving section of the people in Palestine during the Roman-Jewish war, the words of Jesus in verses 17 and 18 came true. But only at His second advent will their final fulfilment take place—and that for everyone (from whatever race or station he may be) who has not rendered Him faith and obedience as the Son of God.

¹ Because the Saviour in this parable pointed so clearly and plainly to His unique relationship to the Father (" the beloved Son ") and warned the Jewish authorities so expressly, many critics have refused to accept it as genuine. According to them, Jesus would not have made such claims to Sonship and would also not have been able to point in advance to His death and to the judgment that would come upon those who were guilty of it. Luce (*in loc.*) gives a short summary of the usual arguments in this connection. Bultmann (*Die Geschichte der synoptischen Tradition*, p. 9) calls this parable a Palestinian *apophthegm* and suggests that it is a fictitious creation of the first Christians in Palestine. However, he adduces no real evidence for his hypothesis. We simply record our conviction that but for the prejudice against believing in Jesus' consciousness of His unique relationship with the Father there would never have been any objection raised against the genuineness of the parable. Cf. Albertz, *Die synoptischen Streitgespräche*, p. 234.

² Cf. Deuteronomy xxxii. 32, 33; Psalm lxxx. 8 ff.; Isaiah v. 1–7; Jeremiah ii. 21; Ezekiel xv. 1–6, xix. 10–14; Hosea x. 1; Joel i. 7; and other texts where God's own people are represented as the vineyard of God.

³ " By the lessees of the vineyard only the rulers in Israel for the time being could be understood, who derived additional personal advantages from their position over and above their official authority " (Zahn, *in loc.*).

Plummer (*in loc.*) feels that verses 15 and 16 prove that by the husbandmen the whole Jewish people and not only the leaders are understood, and by the vineyard not the people but the spiritual privileges of the people. We cannot, however, agree with this. The vineyard was throughout the Old Testament used as symbol of the people of Israel. So here also it will stand for the true Israel, the real people of God. Then it follows of its own accord that the husbandmen in the first instance refer to the leaders. In a secondary sense, however, it includes also that portion of the Jewish people that identifies itself with the conduct of their wicked leaders. It should be borne in mind that no parable symbolises every aspect of a truth—it only sheds a clear light on certain points which require special emphasis.

[4] These particulars should not be literally applied to God. " All this is the setting of the parable, and must not be pressed as referring to God. This man represents God, not by his perplexity, but by his longsuffering and mercy " (Plummer, *in loc.*).

[5] When this reasoning of the husbandmen is termed improbable and doubt is cast on the genuineness of the parable, it is due to a complete misapprehension—for it is precisely Jesus' intention to call attention to the folly of the Jewish leaders' attitude towards Him by using as an example the foolish reasonings of the husbandmen. " They imagine that they have but to settle accounts with Jesus, and that then their spiritual tyranny over the people will be permanently established " (Van Leeuwen, at Mark xii. 7). They pay attention only to the One that has been sent and not to the One who has sent Him.

[6] These words have been taken from Psalm cxviii. 22. The psalm, according to Prof. A. Noordtzij, was sung after the completion of the wall of Jerusalem in 444 B.C. The verse quoted referred to the chosen Israel that was despised by the pagan nations but afterwards (on their return from banishment and on being re-established in Palestine) again became exalted to the status of a nation. Israel, however, exists " only for and through the Messiah, who is the ground of Israel's choice and who was to come forth from among Israel. So what is sung about Zion in Psalm cxviii contains in itself a prophetic perspective and finds its actual content and its fulfilment only in the Messiah. Thus Christ Himself could be the first to recognise and bring to light the deep sense and the wide application of this word, inspired by the Holy Ghost. And the Church of Christ also correctly understood it of His rejection and exaltation and applied it to this " (Van Leeuwen, at Mark xii. 11).

[7] " Through His sojourn on earth, but still much more as the One brought to the cross through the Jewish ruling body, Jesus had become a stone of stumbling for the majority of His people (Luke ii. 34; Rom. ix. 32 f.; 1 Cor. i. 23; 1 Pet. ii. 6, 8). But when the judgment which He prophesied breaks in upon Jerusalem and the Temple (Luke xiii. 35, xix. 43 f., xxi. 20-4, xxiii. 28-31), and Jesus Himself returns, clothed in kingly glory, then those who would not admit Him

as their Redeemer and King will be carried away like chaff and stubble before the tempest " (Zahn, *in loc.*).

⁸ λιχμήσει. " Not only in classical authors, but also in LXX it means ' to winnow chaff from grain ', from λιχμός, ' a winnowing fan '. . . . Hence ' to blow away like chaff, sweep out of sight or out of existence ' " (Plummer, *in loc.*). These words of the Saviour point to the same event as had been predicted long before in Daniel ii. 34-5.

THE QUESTION OF GIVING TRIBUTE

(Cf. Matt. xxii. 15–22; Mark xii. 13–17)

xx. 19–26

19 And the scribes and the chief priests sought to lay hands on
him in that very hour; and they feared the people: for[1] they
20 perceived that he spake this parable against them. And they
watched him, and sent forth spies, which feigned themselves
to be righteous,[2] that they might take hold of his speech, so as
to deliver him up to the rule and to the authority of the
21 governor. And they asked him, saying, Master, we know
that thou sayest and teachest rightly, and acceptest not the
22 person[3] *of any*, but of a truth teachest the way of God: Is it
23 lawful[4] for us to give tribute[5] unto Caesar, or not? But he
24 perceived their craftiness,[6] and said unto them,[7] Shew me a
penny.[8] Whose image and superscription hath it?[9] And
25 they said, Caesar's.[10] And he said unto them,[11] Then render[12] unto Caesar the things that are Caesar's, and unto
26 God[13] the things that are God's.[14] And they were not able
to take hold of the saying before the people: and they marvelled at his answer, and held their peace.

The attempt made by the Jewish leaders to call Jesus to account
for the cleansing of the temple had failed, and in addition Jesus
had uttered a powerful warning to them through the parable of
the husbandmen. From Mark xii. 12 it appears that they went
away after this without having accomplished anything. However,
their defeat added only more fuel to their rage against Jesus.

19, 20 However much the Jewish leaders desired to take Jesus
without delay and to cause Him to be done to death, He still had
too great a hold on the multitude. In impotent rage, especially
after He had so clearly exposed their murderous intentions through
the parable of the husbandmen, they tried to devise all manner
of plans to bring him into disfavour with the multitude or into
conflict with the Roman authorities. After their previous defeats
they now evidently act with great caution and subtle cunning.
This appears from the fact that, instead of again sending official
members of the Sanhedrin to Him, they send a small group of
their disciples (Matt. xxii. 16) to try to entangle Jesus in His
speech. These younger men could more easily pretend to be

502

seriously seeking for an answer to the question which they had to put. The deadly nature of this new attack launched against Jesus becomes clear from the fact that, in order to carry it out, the Pharisees act in unison with the Herodians in an unholy alliance (Mark xii. 13), so that the two parties, as a rule bitterly hostile to each other, are temporarily united in the conspiracy to destroy their common foe (cf. also Mark iii. 6).

21 The young deputies commence their veiled attack by using the language of flattery. Probably they wanted in this way to create the impression that they were engaged in a dispute over the matter and could not find the necessary guidance from the ordinary Jewish leaders, and that they now desired to have the dispute settled by His authority, as a Teacher who would tell the whole truth without fear or favour. Everything said by them of Jesus in this hypocritical, flattering manner, was true. He *was* straightforward and fearless in His words and teachings and *did* utter the inviolate truth to all without seeking human favour. No one can ever say anything too good about Jesus; but it is, of course, possible to say the best things from the worst motives—and this was precisely what these men did.

22 After their flattery they asked Him this question: " Is it lawful to give tribute unto Caesar or no? " Because it was at that time an extremely topical question, it could easily appear as if they were in all earnestness seeking an answer to the question. In reality, however, they intend it to be a craftily devised catch-question and hope that Jesus will give an answer which will enable them to denounce Him to the Roman authorities as a rioter or a rejector of the Roman authority. They probably imagined that, after He had presented Himself as the Messiah at the entry, in the purification of the temple and in so many of His utterances (e.g. verse 13), He could not possibly reply that the tribute should be given, for then He would lose all hold on the masses (who above all regarded the Messiah as one who would break off the Roman yoke from the people). So the object of their question was (verse 20) to compel Him to give an answer that would enable them to accuse Him to the Romans of incitement to insurrection. That such was indeed their aim, also appears from the fact that at Jesus' trial they did not shrink from bringing this accusation against Him falsely before Pilate, that He " perverted the people and forbade them to give tribute to Caesar " (xxiii. 2), notwithstanding that He had taught the very opposite.

23 The questioners tried by their question to confront Jesus with an inescapable dilemma and in addition to compel Him to give a definite and unambiguous answer. They put the case as simply as possible and demand of Him a categorical " Yes! " or " No! "

24 Mark xii. 15 gives the further particular that the Saviour commands the questioners to go and fetch a penny ("Bring me a penny that I may see it "). This shows us clearly the masterliness of Jesus' conduct: the interval caused by sending for a coin created the necessary psychological atmosphere in which the answer of the Lord would speak with full force to each of those present. The coin which Jesus sent for was a Roman silver coin with Caesar's image on it. After the coin had been brought, the Master, instead of giving the expected " Yes " or " No " to the puzzling question, Himself asks them a counter-question as an introduction to the answer that He is going to give.

He asks them the simple question: " Whose image and superscription are on the coin? " After their acknowledgment that it is Caesar's, the following two facts are vividly brought to light through Jesus' masterly handling of the situation:

(1) Coins with Caesar's image and superscription are in use among the Jews;

(2) The coins are evidently the property of Caesar, otherwise they would not have borne his image and superscription.

From these two facts it thus follows that the Jews had accepted the imperial rule as a practical reality, for it was the generally current view that a ruler's power extended as far as his coins were in use.

25 After Jesus had thus, with such unsurpassed wisdom, made the necessary preparations for His reply, He now, in that tense moment, gives His vigorous answer to His assailants' catch-question, firstly: " Render unto Caesar the things which are Caesar's."

In this reply there is no evasion of the question put to Him but a clear and straightforward declaration that they must pay Caesar tribute and everything due to him as their ruler. Under God's providence the course of history has been so arranged that they have been brought under Roman domination, and through their free use of Caesar's coins they have shown that they acknowledge Caesar as their earthly ruler, and therefore they are under the obligation to pay to Caesar what is due to him as long as matters remain thus. Jesus does not here enumerate everything that is included in what is due to Caesar. Undoubtedly He was referring more especially to the tribute. From other pronouncements made by Him (e.g. John xix. 11), and especially from His whole attitude and action towards the Roman authority, it appears, however, that

Jesus also meant reverence, submission and obedience (in so far as these did not conflict with their highest loyalty, which was due to God).

To Jesus, however, the relationship of man towards God is of paramount importance. Therefore He immediately continues: " and unto God the things which are God's ". By this He means (as appears from His whole life and from all His utterances) nothing less than the unconditional surrender and consecration of the whole man to his Creator. From this it also follows that " rendering unto Caesar the things which are Caesar's " (although it is also a necessary requirement) is quite subordinate to " rendering unto God the things which are God's ". By this second part of the pronouncement Jesus not only laid down the limits for carrying out the command that to Caesar should be rendered what is Caesar's due, but at the same time also revealed the secret as to how this should be done. It is as though Jesus declares: " When you render unto Caesar the things which are Caesar's—and this you have to do—you must never forget that the final Throne to which you owe loyalty is the Throne of God." In the last analysis the " rendering unto Caesar the things which are Caesar's " is in reality only a subordinate part of the all-embracing obligation to " render unto God the things which are God's ". Because obedience to the secular authority (in so far as it is not in conflict with the law of the Lord) is a command of God, the observance of it is in reality also a part of the obedience due to Him, the King of all kings and the Lord of all lords. Above all persons and all causes is God, and to Him alone divine reverence and final loyalty are due—this was what Jesus proclaimed throughout by word and act.

26 So logical and convincing was Jesus' answer, uttered by Him with such resounding emphasis, that the craftily devised plan of the Jewish leaders to trap Him utterly failed. Amazed and completely silenced by His action and answer, the youthful questioners departed without having accomplished anything (Matt. xxii. 22). Nevertheless the Jewish authorities, in their murderous rage, did not hesitate later on to have Jesus accused before Pilate, in a false and unworthy manner, of " perverting the nation, and forbidding to give tribute to Caesar " (xxiii. 2).

Modern trends in the world indicate that (as is already the case in many countries) the fiercest and most dangerous attacks by the world against the church of Christ will henceforth be delivered on the political front—the state more and more demands the sole right over the life of its subjects, even with regard to the forming of their characters and their philosophy of life. As happened during the first centuries after the foundation of Christianity, believers will more and more be called upon to choose between absolute loyalty to Christ and loyalty to secular authorities who deny and reject the supreme right of God. The faithful, however, must never be disobedient to Jesus' command to " render unto Caesar " the things which are really due to him (in accordance with the law of God).

¹ γάρ (" for ") must be taken as explaining ἐφοβήθησαν (cf. Plummer, in loc.).

² " It was as though they would entreat Him, without fear or favour, confidentially to give them His private opinion; and as though they really wanted His opinion for their guidance in a moral question of practical importance and were quite sure that He alone could resolve their distressing uncertainty " (Farrar, *The Life of Christ*, p. 349).

³ οὐ λαμβάνεις πρόσωπον—a Hebraism " which originally meant 'raise the face', i.e. make the countenance rise by favourable address, rather than ' accept the face '. Hence it came to mean ' regard with favour ', but not necessarily with *undue* favour. . . . But the bad sense gradually prevailed; and both here and in Galatians ii. 6 partiality is implied " (Plummer, in loc.).

Dalman (*Words of Jesus*, p. 30) maintains that the expression is also Aramaic.

⁴ ἔξεστιν—representing rabbinical *muttār* (literally, " loosened "), a fixed expression for " does the Law permit it? " Not secular law, but the law of God is meant (cf. Kittel, " Das Urteil des Neuen Testament über den Staat " [" The Judgment of the New Testament on the State "], in *Zeitschrift fur systematische Theologie*, vol. 14, p. 659).

⁵ φόρον—a tax paid by a subject nation (Abbot-Smith, *Manual Greek Lexicon of New Testament*); here probably referring to a poll-tax imposed by the Roman government on every Jewish citizen. After A.D. 6, when Archelaus was deposed from his rule and Idumaea, Samaria and Judaea became Roman provinces under a *procurator Caesaris*, this tax was levied on the Jews (cf. Rawlinson, *St. Mark, in loc.*). The tax was extremely unpopular, and when it was levied the first time provoked the rebellion of Judas the Galilean (cf. Acts v. 37 and Josephus, *Antiquities*, xviii, 1, 1). The rebellion was suppressed, but the ideas for which Judas died continued to live, especially among the Zealots. These extremists (who had tremendous influence among the whole nation) regarded the payment of the tribute as a punishable national infidelity towards God and ascribed all the misery of their country and people to this. Their view was that the Roman yoke should be thrown off by force of arms. Among the masses, however, (probably through the influence of the Pharisees), the current view

was that God would Himself remove the foreign overlordship and would do so through the actions of the Messiah (cf. Friedrich Hauch, *in loc.*, and also Rengstorf and Büchsel, *in loc.*).

⁶ " Remembering the ever-watchful jealousy of Rome, the reckless tyranny of Pilate, and the low artifices of Herod, who was at the time in Jerusalem, we instinctively feel how even the slightest compromise on the part of Jesus in regard to the authority of Caesar would have been absolutely fatal " (Edersheim, *op. cit.*, p. 383). For this reason the Jewish leaders were so eager to lead Him into such a trap that He (as they vainly expected) would not be able to avoid inculpating Himself in this delicate matter.

⁷ The original text does not include the words " Why tempt ye me? " (found in A.V.). Evidently they crept into the text of Luke from the text of Mark xii. 15.

⁸ δηνάριον (" penny ") had the value of about ninepence (Rawlinson, at Mark xii. 15); " it represented the Roman monetary unit. Herod had never had the right to strike silver coins. The Romans reserved this privilege for themselves. For current use they struck bronze coins, and, to spare the scruples of the Jews at seeing human portraits which had for them an idolatrous savour, these little local coins had emblems imprinted on them from the world of nature, ears of corn, palms, vine-leaves, or other objects. But the denarii, Roman money ' par excellence ', bore the emperor's portrait " (cf. Luce, *in loc.*).

⁹ Coins still extant of Caesar Tiberius have been found on which there appears an image with the following superscription round the image: TI(BERIVS) CAESAR DIVI AVGVSTI F(ILIVS) AVGVSTVS (Tiberius Caesar Augustus, son of the divine Augustus). Cf. Deissmann, *Light from the Ancient East*, p. 252; and Madden, *Jewish Coinage*, p. 247.

¹⁰ This fact proved that they tacitly accepted Caesar's rule, for " it was regarded as a generally acknowledged principle that a king's domain extended as far as the limits within which his coins were valid " (Strack-Billerbeck, *Das Evangelium nach Matthäus*, p. 884). See also Fr. Hauch, *in loc.*, and cf. the words of the Jewish scholar Maimonides: " Wherever the coinage of any king is current, there the inhabitants acknowledge that king as their ruler " (cf. Godet, *in loc.*).

¹¹ Rawlinson (at Mark xii. 16) is completely at fault when he declares: " The Lord's answer is an evasion of the dilemma." The words of the Saviour, on the contrary, form a clear and unambiguous answer to their question.

¹² ἀπόδοτε imperative of ἀποδοῦναι, " to render back ", " to pay what is owing ". By the use of the compound verb ἀποδοῦναι here instead of the simple δοῦναι (" give ") which occurs in the question of the young men, it is pointed out that the payment of the tribute to Caesar is not only permissive but a moral duty. The Jews, by taking this kind of coin into use, showed that they acquiesced not merely in the pressure but also in the material advantages for daily life that

accompanied the ordered Roman rule, and consequently they had no moral right to " call the payment of tribute in question as a matter of religious scruple" (Zahn, *Evangelium des Matthäus*, p. 640). And Jesus teaches here that to render to Caesar the things that are Caesar's is " neither a matter of indifference to God nor one repugnant to Him, but one which is positively willed by Him " (Kittel, *op. cit.*, p. 663).

[13] " It was an age which paid divine honour to the Caesar; Jesus showed no disrespect towards him, but by distinguishing so sharply between Caesar and God He made a tacit protest against the worship of the emperor. That pregnant sentence does not present us with two equal magnitudes, Caesar and God: the second is clearly the superior of the first; the sense is ' Render unto Caesar the things that are Caesar's; and, *a fortiore*, unto God the things that are God's '. The portrait and legend (inscription) were an ocular demonstration of the right of the sovereign who coined the money to demand tribute from the provincials. The claims of God were in no sense affected, for they are as high as the heavens above this world's claims " (Deissmann, *op. cit.*, p. 252).

[14] The most important implication of these words to the Jewish hearers that day was that they had to accept Jesus' Messianic claims as valid. " Let there be agreement between their attitude with regard to the imperial regime and what God the Lord demands: that Jesus be recognised as Messiah " (Van Leeuwen, *Markus*, on Mark xii. 17).

Dr. Brouwer (*Jezus en de Sociale Vragen*, p. 244) sees in Jesus' reply also the following meaning: " The coin bears Caesar's image; man bears the image of God. So give the coin, the tribute, to Caesar and give yourself to God." Although Rawlinson declares with regard to this frequently repeated view that " this seems too subtle to be the immediate sense of the passage " (*op. cit.*, p. 166), it is nevertheless possible that the words of the Lord were indeed—although only incidentally—a reference to the fact that man was created as image-bearer of God and should therefore be wholly devoted to Him.

Decidedly untrue is the statement in the article on the State in *Die Religion in Geschichte und Gegenwart*, that the answer of Jesus means " in truth: Why do you bother me with such unimportant matters as questions of the law and the state? Jesus leaves the state alone and does not touch upon our duty with regard to it—not because He does not honour the state, but because it does not seem to Him worth His while to trouble about it ".

Jesus by no means adopted such a contemptuous and indifferent attitude towards the secular government and its authority and its own peculiar right, but laid it down clearly and emphatically that its due must be rendered to it.

This side of Jesus' answer should, however, not be emphasised without also clearly and unconditionally presenting in the same breath the other side of His answer—God's absolute and peculiar right in respect of every man individually and of all men collectively—an exclusive and paramount right possessed by God alone.

Thus in this pronouncement Jesus completely rejected the view of the Zealots (the politically radical group among the Jews of that time) that sovereignty over Israel was confined to God and His sacral, theocratic representatives from among the Jewish people, as He also rejected the State cult of the Romans in which Caesar was deified.

Other important passages of the New Testament in which this topic of " Government and Subject " is discussed are the following: John xix. 10–11; Romans xiii. 1–7; 1 Corinthians vi. 1–4; 1 Timothy ii. 1–4; Titus iii. 1; 1 Peter ii. 13–17; Revelation xiii. 1–18, xvii. 11–14.

Apart from the literature already mentioned and the commentaries in which the above-mentioned scriptures are dealt with, we may also mention an important article by Heinrich Schlier: " Die Beurteilung des Staates im Neuen Testament " (" The Judgment Regarding the State in the New Testament ") in *Zwischen den Zeiten*, vol. 10, 1932.

THE SADDUCEES AND THE RESURRECTION

(Cf. Matt. xxii. 23–33; Mark xii. 18–27)

xx. 27–40

27 And there came to him certain of the Sadducees,[1] they which say[2] that there is no resurrection;[3] and they asked
28 him, saying, Master, Moses wrote unto us,[4] that if a man's brother die, having a wife, and he be childless, his brother should take the wife,[5] and raise up seed unto his brother.
29 There were therefore seven brethren: and the first took a
30, 31 wife, and died childless; and the second; and the third took her; and likewise the seven also left no children, and died.
32, 33 Afterward the woman also died. In the resurrection therefore whose wife of them shall she be?[6] for the seven had her
34 to wife. And Jesus said unto them,[7] The sons of this world
35 marry, and are given in marriage: but they that are accounted worthy to attain to that world,[8] and the resurrection from the dead,[9] neither marry, nor are given in marriage:
36 for neither can they die any more: for they are equal unto the angels;[10] and are sons of God,[11] being sons of the resurrec-
37 tion.[12] But that the dead are raised, even Moses shewed, in *the place concerning* the Bush,[13] when he calleth the Lord the God of Abraham, and the God of Isaac, and the God of
38 Jacob. Now he is not the God of the dead, but of the living:
39 for all live unto him. And certain of the scribes answering
40 said, Master, thou hast well said. For they durst not any more ask him any question.

Some Sadducees were among the members of the Sanhedrin who asked Jesus by whose authority He acted, and were put to shame in consequence (verses 1–8, many high priests were Sadducees). Thus it is quite natural for some of them to attempt subsequently to bring the Saviour into confusion and thus into disfavour with the multitude, in order that in this way they may repair their reputation.

27–33 In Deuteronomy xxv. 5 ff. it is commanded that if brothers dwell together and one of them die, and have no child, one of his brothers shall marry his wife and the firstborn son of this marriage shall bear the name of the deceased. The Sadducees did not believe in the doctrine of the resurrection. They knew, however, from the trend of many of Jesus' statements that He did believe in it. So they now asked Him whose wife a woman seven times married will be if there is going to be a resurrection of the dead. Evidently their object in asking the question is to make the belief in the resurrection look ridiculous and in this manner also to make the Master, who believes in the resurrection, look ridiculous in the sight of the multitude.

34, 35 By His answer, however, the Lord makes their whole scheme collapse. He first points out that at the resurrection the ordinary kind of human existence is not continued. Moreover, not all (or all the Jews as was thought at the time) would have a share in the blessed life of the resurrection, but only those who will be considered worthy of it by God.

36 The reason why the life of the resurrection will not merely be a continuation of ordinary human life, and why there will be no such thing as marriage in it, is that all the redeemed who share in the life of the resurrection will be immortal (thereby the necessity for the marriage relationship disappears *inter alia* because it is then no longer necessary to maintain the race by begetting offspring). And the reason for their immortality is that at the resurrection the redeemed are invested with glorified, heavenly bodies and will thus, as children of God, have a real share in His divine nature.

Like the immortal celestial beings, the angels, they, too, will then be immortal and celestial. Thus the Sadducees had completely misrepresented the life of the resurrection in supposing that in it there would be a continuation of the ordinary earthly relationships and way of living. So, instead of the Sadducees making Jesus ridiculous, He revealed to the multitude their ignorance and blundering.

37, 38 After the Saviour had pointed out to them that their question was based on altogether wrong hypotheses, He next shows that even Moses (who, according to the Sadducees, did not believe in the resurrection) had already indicated the fact of immortality (and thus also of the resurrection—for the two are closely inter-related) by recording how the Lord revealed Himself many centuries after the decease of the patriarchs as " the God of Abraham and the God of Isaac and the God of Jacob " (cf. Exod. iii. 6). If these patriarchs were not immortal, God would never call Himself their God (such a thing would be unworthy of Him), for He is not a God of the dead, but of the living. His covenant relationship with these patriarchs is everlasting and also personal. From this it follows that after their death they are still living and will one day share in the life of the resurrection. Real life (in the Biblical sense) is life in soul and in body alike; therefore immortality (in the Biblical sense) includes resurrection (the union of the soul with the glorified, " spiritual " body). The most important reason why the faithful continue to live after their corporeal death and will one day arise in perfection is that the chief object of human existence is to live for God and to His honour—and how could this object be attained if the faithful die for ever after a brief span of human life?

39 So convincing and so original was the answer of the Saviour, that some of the scribes (probably adherents of the Pharisees, who did believe in the resurrection) could not but acknowledge that He had replied effectively to the question of the Sadducees.

40 After the Sadducean questioners were thus reproved by Him (through the exposure of their ignorant and erroneous ideas about the resurrection) they did not again venture to ask Him a question.

Jesus, the Only One who came from Eternity as Man upon earth, is the Only One who could with absolute authority enlighten man with regard to life after death, the hereafter. And, God be thanked, He has not left us in the dark. He has not indeed, in order to satisfy mere human curiosity, given us all kinds of details about the hereafter. But He clearly announced the main truths concerning the life beyond the grave, truths necessary for man's highest welfare, and He *proved* the truth of what He said by His own life, death, resurrection and ascension. In His answer to the Sadducees He declared that there is indeed a resurrection of the dead, but that the faithful will arise with celestially glorified bodies so that the ordinary earthly relationships will not be continued, and by His resurrection from the dead and His appearance to His disciples with a glorified, celestial body He proved the truth of these declarations. That the Saviour, when He declared that in the hereafter there will no longer be ordinary earthly relationships, did not mean thereby that the faithful would be so different that they will not be recognisable to one another, is clear (*inter alia*) from the fact that after His resurrection, although He then appeared with a glorified body, Jesus was nevertheless still recognisable to His followers, and at His ascension it was promised that He would return in like manner at the second advent (Acts i. 11). The faithful will recognise one another and share collectively in the joy of the Lord.

[1] The Sadducees were the priestly aristocracy among the Jews by whom the political life of the people was largely controlled from the time of Alexander the Great onwards. They tried to live in close contact with the Roman rulers after 63 B.C. so that they might as far as possible promote the secular interests of their people. Consequently they took little interest in religious matters and in many respects clashed with the Pharisees, especially as regards the Pharisees' attachment to the " traditions of the elders " which made Jewish religious life so intricate. Everything which, according to their views, was not taught by " the Law of Moses " (the first five books of the Old Testament) was rejected by the Sadducees as forbidden innovations. So, as the Jewish scholar Montefiore puts it: " They were in a sense conservative. The letter of the Law was enough for them; they did not want the developments of the rabbis. In doctrine, too, they were against innovation. . . . Many of these priests, and many of the nobles and ' rulers ', possessed, I should think, but a very formal and outward religion. We may compare them with many of the bishops, barons and rulers of the middle ages " (*Synoptic Gospels*, part i, p. 102).

At the time of Jesus the Sadducees were few in number and no longer had much influence, because the masses in their hatred of foreign domination had more sympathy with the nationalistic Pharisees.

[2] We know also from Josephus's writings that they did not believe in the resurrection (cf. Josephus, *The Jewish War*, ii, 8. 14; *Antiquities*, xviii, 1, 4). Cf. also Acts xxiii. 8.

[3] For a detailed discussion of Jewish views regarding the resurrection cf. Charles, *A Critical History of the Doctrine of a Future Life*.

[4] Deuteronomy xxv. 5 ff.

[5] This is called the levirate marriage (from Latin *levir*, " brother-in-law ", " husband's brother ").

[6] " The question is a plausible appeal to the rough common sense of the multitude, and is based upon the coarse materialistic views of the resurrection which then prevailed " (Plummer, *in loc.*).

[7] From Mark xii. 24 it appears that Jesus first rebuked the questioners in the words: " Is it not for this cause that ye err, that ye know not the scriptures, nor the power of God? "

[8] ὁ αἰὼν ἐκεῖνος, " that age " in distinction to " this age " (ὁ αἰὼν οὗτος), " means the age beyond the grave regarded as one of bliss and glory " (Plummer, *in loc.*).

[9] That not only the faithful but all mankind will arise at the End-time appears from Jesus' words in John v. 28, 29: " For the hour cometh, in which all that are in the tombs shall hear his voice, and shall come forth: they that have done good, unto the resurrection of life; and they that have done ill, unto the resurrection of judgment." The ἀνάστασις ἐκ νεκρῶν indicates the resurrection of the redeemed to life, as contrasted with the resurrection of the unsaved, which is practically no resurrection at all, as it is but the gateway to eternal death, the judgment which the lost receive in a state of bare existence, which is totally different from spiritual life, for they have no personal

intercourse with God. In distinction from the resurrection to judgment of the spiritually dead, the resurrection to life of the redeemed is thus rightly called " the resurrection *from* (ἐκ) the dead " (from among the dead ones).

¹⁰ The Lord does not say that they will be angels, but " equal unto the angels ", and from the context it appears that " it is the *immortality* of the angels, not their sexlessness or immateriality, that is the point of the argument " (Plummer, *in loc.*).

¹¹ υἱοί εἰσιν θεοῦ " in its context is not to be understood of the religious relationship of the man who has turned to God and been born again, but in the sense in which the angels are called ' sons of God ' (Ps. lxxxix. 7; Job ii. 1), of the natural condition which befits a son of God " (Zahn, *in loc.*).

¹² The resurrection to life, the only real resurrection, is meant.

¹³ " The Jewish Scriptures were at this time divided into sections, the most notable of which had distinctive titles. The chapters and verses of our Bibles belong to a much later date " (Major, *op. cit.*, p. 150). The words " the place concerning " in some translations of the Bible (including the R.V.) do not occur in the original. " The Bush " was the title of the history (described in Exod. iii) of Moses at the burning bush (cf. Strack-Billerbeck, at Mark xii. 26).

THE CHRIST, THE SON OF DAVID

(Cf. Matt. xxii. 41–6; Mark xii. 35–7)

xx. 41–4

41 And he said unto them, How say they that the Christ is
42 David's son?[1] For David himself saith in the book of
Psalms,[2]

> The Lord said unto my Lord,[3]
> Sit thou on my right hand,
43 > Till I make thine enemies the footstool of thy feet.

44 David therefore calleth him Lord, and how is he his son?[4]

Until the end the Saviour tried to bring to their senses the
Jewish leaders and people who did not believe in Him. In various
ways He called on them to reflect seriously and not persist blindly
in rejecting Him. Jesus was not cold and hard towards His
persecutors. With a weeping heart (xix. 41) for the hardness of
heart of the leaders and the people, His main purpose, even when
He reproves His enemies most severely, is constantly to call them
to repentance in time. He does not rejoice in the fact that His
persecutors will be visited by the judgments of God, but weeps for
their fate (xix. 41–4) and makes all possible attempts to save them
from their folly.

41 The greatest grudge that the Jewish spiritual leaders bore
Jesus was that He laid claim to divinity so unambiguously and
called Himself the beloved Son of God (verse 13). They did not
see into the Old Testament prophecies concerning the promised
Messiah clearly enough to realise that He would not merely be an
earthly King, but a divine Redeemer. The Saviour desires to
deliver them from this error and therefore asks why the Jewish
leaders (and also most of the people) think that the Christ (the
Messiah) will be merely a descendant of David and therefore
only a human ruler.

42–4 After He, the Teacher of all teachers, had by His question
reduced His hearers to silence and reflection, He showed how in
the Old Testament it is expressly taught that the Messiah is much
more than a son of David. For, the Saviour declares, David himself in one of his psalms (Ps. cx) called the Messiah his Lord.
Although, therefore, He is, according to the flesh, indeed a

515

descendant of David, as foretold in the Old Testament (e.g. 2 Sam. vii. 8–29; Isa. ix. 5–7; Mic. v. 2), and plainly stated in the New Testament (e.g. Matt. i. 1; Rom. i. 3), He is much more than a human ruler of Davidic descent. Jesus' claim that as Messiah He is also the Son of God is thus in perfect conformity with what was foretold in the Old Testament (cf. also Ps. ii. 7, 12).

The outstanding significance of the Old Testament lies in this, that from beginning to end (through express prophecies, through characters and ceremonies that are typical foreshadowings of Jesus and His work of redemption, through events with a symbolical meaning, and through the plain record of how, over a period of thousands of years, the world was prepared for His coming) it points to the promised Messiah. In the Saviour's coming to the world as Man this was already fulfilled in part, and with His second advent in glory the perfect fulfilment will be inaugurated—then all shall see and know that He is truly the divine Lord to whom God has said: " Sit thou at my right hand, until I make thine enemies thy footstool " (Ps. cx. i).

<hr />

¹ Together with several critics of the radical school, Middleton Murry states with reference to Jesus' words here: " Jesus by His own manifestly authentic saying shatters the legend of His birth in Bethlehem, from the line of David " (*Life of Jesus*, p. 258). Even Easton, however, rejects this view, for he declares: " Mark, Luke and Matthew all transmit this saying in evident unconsciousness that it is in any way inconsistent with a Davidic descent of Christ. This tells very strongly against its ever having borne any such meaning " (*in loc.*).

Creed similarly says: " The suggestion that Jesus was appealing to Psalm cx to rebut an objection that he was not of Davidic descent does not commend itself. The text gives no hint that such an objection was urged. Luke himself has already insisted on the fact, generally accepted in the early church (see Rom. i 3), that Jesus was son of David. See i. 32, iii. 23 f. We can hardly suppose that he understood this passage to deny the fact. He probably took it to mean that the Christ, the son of David, is entitled to an appellation more honourable than ' son of David ' " (*in loc.*).

² For an exposition of Psalm cx cf. W. O. E. Oesterley, *The Psalms* (1939), pp. 461 ff., and B. D. Eerdmans, *The Hebrew Book of Psalms* (1947), *in loc.* It has been fashionable for a long time to hold that Psalm cx was written in honour of Simon Maccabaeus (143–135 B.C.) as chief priest and secular ruler in one, and an attempt was made, with the help of some textual emendation, to find in the psalm an acrostic on his name. Oesterley rejects this view as " fantastic " and ascribes the psalm to the time of the monarchy at a " comparatively early date ".

Cf. E. R. Hardy in *Journal of Biblical Literature*, 64 (1945), pp. 385 ff., who argues that it celebrates an early Israelite ruler of Jerusalem who is proclaimed in it as true successor of Melchizedek, priest-king of that city in patriarchal days. We might go a step farther and suggest (in accordance with the oracle of Ps. cx. 4) that the psalm was written at the time when David captured Jerusalem and made it his capital in the eighth year of his reign.

[3] Strack-Billerbeck show in a detailed digression on Psalm cx (*op. cit.*, part iv, pp. 452–65) that during New Testament times Jewish scholars regarded Psalm cx as a Messianic psalm, but that subsequently, when the Christians used this psalm so generally to prove that the Old Testament had prophesied that the Messiah would be a divine Redeemer, they rejected its Messianic interpretation. So from about A.D. 100 to 250 they applied this psalm to Abraham! But afterwards they again accepted it as a Messianic psalm (for then the conflict with the Christians was no longer so violent, since the church then consisted mostly of non-Jewish members and the church and the Jewish community each went its own way).

[4] By this Jesus does not wish to contradict His descent from David according to the flesh, but wants to make His hearers realise that (as foretold by the Old Testament) He is far more than " Son of David " and an earthly ruler—He is the Lord. He had already declared (xi. 31) that He is more than a son of David like Solomon; by His entry into Jerusalem (xix. 37–40) He showed that He must be regarded as the Messiah, in xx. 9–18 He taught that He is no ordinary divine messenger but the Beloved Son, and now He indicates that He is the divine Lord. Thus He left no doubt as to the absoluteness of His claims (cf. Zahn, *in loc.*).

JESUS WARNS AGAINST THE SCRIBES

(Cf. Matt. xxiii. 1; Mark xii. 38-40)

xx. 45-7

45 And in the hearing of all the people he said unto his
46 disciples, Beware of the scribes,[1] which desire to walk in
long robes, and love salutations in the marketplaces, and
chief seats in the synagogues, and chief places at feasts;
47 which devour widows' houses, and for a pretence make long
prayers: these shall receive greater condemnation.

However much the Saviour's heart weeps over the state into
which the leaders of the people have fallen and over their impending punishment (xix. 41-5), He does not shrink from exposing
their insincerity and other sins. Although He knows but too well
that thereby He is stimulating their murderous rage against Him,
He comes out squarely for the truth and utters a fearless warning
against the sins of which so many of the Jewish leaders are guilty.

45-7 Not in secret, but openly, before all the people, the Lord
warns His followers against the Jewish scribes, by exposing them
fearlessly in their true character. While they, as Jesus declares,
seek, on the one hand, to be recognised and honoured among the
people and to be considered as particularly pious, they are, on the
other hand, so lacking in sympathy and love that they do not even
hesitate to deprive helpless people like widows of their possessions (by living on their kindheartedness and by constantly
insisting that they should give large temple gifts and contributions
for public worship—contributions which are too high for their
limited means). What makes their conduct so much the more
culpable is that they do all this under the semblance of earnest
piety, to the accompaniment of long prayers. Therefore, especially because as scribes they have so many opportunities of
practising true piety, they will receive a severer judgment than the
other Jews who do not lay any claim to special piety and do not
enjoy as many spiritual privileges as they do.

The history of the scribes of that time, with their outward
religiousness but so much inward insincerity, must be to us especially, who are called to be spiritual leaders in His church, a

constant challenge to examine ourselves and to trust in God to preserve us from hypocrisy and spiritual decay. Human nature is still liable to the same dangers as at that time.

[1] Jewish scholars like Montefiore and Abrahams raise objections against Jesus' censure of the scribes (the Jewish rabbis). They declare that His judgment of them is exaggerated. We readily agree (and the Saviour undoubtedly did the same) that there were noble exceptions. Nevertheless it remains an incontrovertible fact that the Jewish spiritual leaders, taken as a whole, in those times had fallen into the stranglehold of a dead formalism, piety according to the Law, self-satisfaction and hypocrisy. And we must not forget that, although there were so many outward signs of real piety among them, the Jewish religious leaders as a class were spiritually so blind and degenerate that they caused the Son of God, who manifested so much self-sacrificing love among the Jews, to be condemned and crucified, and afterwards persecuted the apostles and other believers in Christ.

THE POOR WIDOW'S MITE

(Cf. Mark xii. 41-4)

xxi. 1-4

1 And he looked up,[1] and saw the rich men that were
2 casting their gifts into the treasury.[2] And he saw a certain
3 poor widow casting in thither two mites.[3] And he said, Of
a truth I say unto you, This poor widow cast in more than
4 they all: for these did of their superfluity cast in unto the
gifts: but she of her want did cast in all the living that she had.

The Saviour's opponents were all silenced by His calm dignity
and by the finality of His words, and no one any longer ventured
to ask Him catch-questions (xx. 40). He had given His last
warning against the false religion of the Jewish spiritual leaders,
and now there was a moment of calm.

1 Probably from weariness after all the contentious discussions with His persecutors and from grief over the obduracy and
spiritual inanition of the Jewish leaders, the Master sat there with
downcast eyes in one of the temple courts. After a while He looked
up and saw some of the rich Jews casting their gifts into the
treasury of the temple.

2 While He is looking on, a poor widow also comes along and
casts two small coins of trifling value into the treasury.

3, 4 The contributions of the rich left Him unmoved, for He
knew that it cost them no sacrifice to give them—their possessions
are so abundant that the contributions made by them were,
comparatively speaking, trifling. But because the widow, in spite
of her extreme need, gave all that she had to live on, her gift
(however insignificant) is in His eyes greater than the gifts of all
the rest. It cost her a great deal to bring this offering, but because
it was the holy urge of her life to give to God as much as she
possibly could, she did not shrink from giving what she had in
hand. She no doubt went back, trusting in her God, to earn again
what was necessary for her and her household.

It is not the amount that one gives to the cause of God that
matters most, but the spirit in which the gift is bestowed. And
when this spirit is right a man will spontaneously give as much as

he possibly can, however much it may cost him. Whosoever, therefore, imagines that he is giving in the right spirit but only makes a small contribution from his abundance is deceiving himself. The widow in whole-hearted devotion contributed in her penury *everything* she had to live on.

[1] *'Αναβλέψας.* Mark mentions the detail that He was sitting. " The long discussions had wearied Him, and He had been sitting with downcast or closed eyes " (Plummer, *in loc.*).

[2] *γαζοφυλάκιον,* " treasury: also, apparently, the trumpet-shaped chests into which the people's temple-offerings were thrown" (Abbott-Smith). Compare Edersheim, *The Temple,* p. 26. According to John viii. 20, it could also be used in the sense of that portion of the temple where the treasury was, i.e. the " women's court ".

[3] *λεπτὰ δύο,* " little copper scale-like coins equivalent in value to a farthing " (Major, *op. cit.,* p. 155). According to the Jewish laws at that time it was not permissible to cast in less than two gifts (Plummer, *in loc.*).

THE PROPHETIC DISCOURSE. THE
DESTRUCTION OF JERUSALEM

(Cf. Matt. xxiv. 15–28; Mark xiii. 1 ff.)

xxi. 5–24

5 And as some spake[1] of the temple,[2] how it was adorned
6 with goodly stones and offerings, he said, As for these things
which ye behold, the days will come, in which there shall
not be left here one stone upon another,[3] that shall not be
7 thrown down.[4] And they asked him, saying, Master, when
therefore shall these things be? and what *shall be* the sign when
8 these things are about to come to pass? And he said,[5] Take
heed that ye be not led astray: for many shall come in my
name,[6] saying, I am *he*; and, The time is at hand: go ye not
9 after them. And when ye shall hear of wars and tumults,[7] be
not terrified: for these things must needs[8] come to pass first;
but the end is not immediately.

10 Then said he unto them,[9] Nation shall rise against nation,
11 and kingdom against kingdom: and there shall be great
earthquakes, and in divers places famines and pestilences;
and there shall be terrors and great signs from heaven.[10]
12 But before all these things,[11] they shall lay their hands on
you,[12] and shall persecute you, delivering you up to the
synagogues[13] and prisons, bringing you before kings and
13 governors for my name's sake. It shall turn unto you for a
14 testimony.[14] Settle it therefore in your hearts, not to medi-
15 tate beforehand[15] how to answer: for I will give you a
mouth and wisdom, [16] which all your adversaries shall not
16 be able to withstand or to gainsay. But ye shall be delivered
up even by parents, and brethren, and kinsfolk, and friends;
17 and *some* of you shall they cause to be put to death. And ye
18 shall be hated of all men for my name's sake. And not a
19 hair of your head shall perish.[17] In your patience ye shall
win your souls.[18]

20 But when ye see Jerusalem[19] compassed[20] with armies,
21 then know that her desolation is at hand. Then let them that
are in Judaea flee unto the mountains;[21] and let them that are
in the midst of her depart out; and let not them that are in
22 the country[22] enter therein.[23] For these are days of vengeance, that all things which are written may be fulfilled.[24]
23 Woe unto them that are with child and to them that give
suck in those days! for there shall be great distress upon the

24 land,[25] and wrath unto this people. And they shall fall by the edge of the sword, and shall be led captive into all the nations:[26] and Jerusalem shall be trodden down of the Gentiles, until the times of the Gentiles be fulfilled.[27]

After all the revelations of the determined hostility of the Jewish leaders towards Jesus, it was already clear as daylight that they (and also the majority of the people who followed their example) were not going to turn to God or to acknowledge and honour His Messiah and Son. The end of the people with their leaders, their city and their temple will, therefore, be utter destruction. So terrible, the Saviour warns them, will be the judgments soon to burst forth over the people of Jerusalem who so persistently rejected Him that the events accompanying those judgments upon the guilty city will be the foreshadowing of the Final Judgment at His second advent. For this reason, Jesus' prophecies in connection with the events of the End-time are so closely linked up with those concerning the destruction of Jerusalem and the temple that it is extremely difficult in studying the Prophetic Discourse (Matt. xxiv and xxv; Mark xiii; Luke xxi. 5–36) to distinguish between the portions of it that refer to the Jews and Jerusalem and those referring to the Final Judgments at His second advent in power and glory. This is especially the case with Matthew and Mark. In Luke the classification is much clearer. We must remember that the Gospel writers do not profess to give a full account of Jesus' words and discourses. Each one merely reproduces certain parts of what He said. From the nature of the case it was impossible to commit to writing everything that was spoken by Jesus, with the result that some of Jesus' discourses occur in one Gospel and others in another. In this instance Luke, although he does not give such a full report of the Prophetic Discourse as Matthew, was evidently the most successful in so relating it that we can see comparatively clearly which portions refer to the destruction of Jerusalem and preceding events, and which refer to the Final Judgment. And according to the principle that the more obscure portions of the Word should be understood in the light of the clearer portions, the exposition of the Prophetic Discourse as written down in Matthew and Mark should be given in the light of its clearer account in Luke. As will appear from the exposition, verses 5–24 deal practically throughout (except verses 8, 9) with predictions concerning the destruction of Jerusalem and the preceding events, although in a secondary sense even some of these predictions also refer to the Last Things. But in verses 25–8 Jesus looks beyond the fore-

523

shadowings of the Final Judgment to that Judgment itself and its attendant signs, in association with His second advent. In verses 29–33 He exhorts His hearers to watch for the former set of events, which are to be accomplished within " this generation ", while in verses 34–6 He warns them (and through them the whole Christian church) to watch faithfully for the latter set of events, which are to take place at a day and hour known to none save God the Father.

5, 6 At that time the temple of Jerusalem, owing to its massive size and grandeur, was regarded as one of the wonders of the world. For about a thousand years since Solomon built the first temple on the temple-mount (c. 965 B.C.), it was, except during the Babylonian captivity (586–537 B.C.) and the period of its desecration by Antiochus Epiphanes (168–165 B.C.), the centre of the religious life of the chosen people. Apart from the element of fraud that had in the course of centuries crept into the temple religion and often dominated it, there were also, nevertheless, year in and year out, people of true piety who sought and worshipped God there. And how gloriously God had frequently revealed Himself there to His faithful worshippers. This is borne out, e.g., by the story of Isaiah's call as a prophet (Isa. vi).

Already long before Jesus' coming upon earth God announced that He, the Messenger of the Covenant, the divine Messiah, would come to the temple (Mal. iii. 1) and that His coming would be for purging and judgment (Mal. iii. 2–5). Now Luke had already described how the Saviour had not merely come among the Jewish people, but had entered the temple as the Messiah, had purged it drastically of the evil practices which defiled it, had frequently taught the multitudes in its courts, had reproved the obdurate Jewish leaders and vigorously proclaimed His divine mission. His opponents, however, proved that they were persistently determined to reject Him, thereby sealing their own fate and that of the city and the temple. So when some of the disciples spoke about the elegance of the temple, Jesus expressly announced that ere long the beautiful building would be completely destroyed. Through His personal advent to the people and to the temple, the Old Dispensation in which God had to be worshipped by outward ceremonies and sacrifices in the temple, had come to an end. Six centuries before, in Jeremiah xxxi. 31, it was foretold that God would make a new Covenant by which religion would become an inward and spiritual matter (Jer. xxxi. 33). Because the Jewish leaders have rejected Him and the vast majority of the people do not believe in Him as Messiah but are merely " interested " in Him (and will ere long act together with their leaders in urging the Gentile judge to have Him crucified), it is evident that they have chosen to continue with the old form of outward temple religion. For this reason the temple will be destroyed as a judgment upon their spiritual blindness and as a proof that the Old Dispensation is gone once and for all and must make room for the New Dispensation. One greater than the temple has come, and because the people have rejected Him and desire to retain the temple as the centre of their own religion, there is no other alternative—the temple must be utterly destroyed and the unbelieving people visited with the doom which He had sought to avert from them.

7-9 The disciples immediately accept the Saviour's prediction as the truth. Perhaps with their earthly and nationalist Messianic expectations (cf. Acts i. 6) they thought that the temple was going to be destroyed to make room for a much more glorious Messianic temple. In any case, they desire to know when the events in which the temple is to be destroyed will take place and what sign there will be to indicate when this will happen. The disciples, when they asked this question, no doubt thought that the destruction of the temple would take place at the same time as His coming in glory (the full revelation of His Messianic power) and the end of the world, with the establishment of His Messianic kingdom (cf. Matt. xxiv. 3). Therefore Jesus warns them first in verses 8 and 9 not to expect His second advent and the end so soon. They must not allow themselves to be misled by people who profess to be the Christ and announce that the End-time is close at hand. And, also, when they hear of wars and insurrections among the nations, they must not be terrified and imagine that the end is already drawing near. All these events will take place, but the end will not come so soon.

10 After the Saviour has thus warned the disciples against being misled by people or events, He outlines in verses 10-19 all the things that will happen before the destruction of the city and temple takes place. First there will be, He declares, commotion and strife among the nations. Jesus here probably referred especially to the Jewish insurrection against the Romans, which was constantly brewing until in A.D. 66 it broke out fully and the sanguinary struggle between the Palestinian Jews and the Roman empire was launched and finally led to the total destruction of Jerusalem and the temple in A.D. 70.

11 Moreover (before the final downfall of the temple and the Jewish kingdom) there will be great earthquakes, famines, pestilences and terrifying signs—things which actually did occur during the years preceding the destruction of the temple (cf. our note on this verse).

12 Before these things happen, however, the disciples will have to endure a time of cruel persecution. This also took place just as Jesus had prophesied. The church of Christ had hardly been established when the first persecutions commenced—Peter and John were taken and summoned to appear before the Jewish Council (Acts iv), ere long all the apostles were arrested, imprisoned (Acts v. 17 ff.), and beaten (Acts v. 40); shortly afterwards Stephen was stoned (Acts vi. 8 ff.); Saul of Tarsus persecuted the faithful, delivered them into the hands of the Jewish leaders, and dragged them to prison and death; subsequently James, the brother of John, was done to death by King Herod (Acts xii. 1, 2); Paul, as well as other Christians, was dragged before pagan governors and judges, persecuted in synagogues and subjected to many other forms of ill-treatment. Thus all Jesus' predictions in this regard came true in the first years after His ascension, and before the Jewish-Roman war broke out.

13 But all these persecutions, the Saviour declares, will give the faithful the opportunity of bearing witness to the honour of their Redeemer, and to the redemption from God sent through Him, the promised Messiah. In the history of the apostles and other members of the first Christian churches these words of Jesus were also again and again fulfilled (cf., e.g., Acts v. 29–32).

14, 15 Believers, however, should not be anxious as to what they shall say in their defence when they are thus summoned to appear before the Jewish and pagan authorities. Jesus himself through His Spirit (cf. Mark xiii. 11) will give them the necessary words and wisdom which their opponents will be unable to refute. This also was fulfilled during the years after Jesus' ascension. Again and again it appeared that the persecutors of the faithful were not able to overthrow their testimony and defence. From this, however, it does not follow that they were always acquitted. On the contrary, their persecutors were generally filled with such blind hate towards them that, even though they could prove nothing against them, they nevertheless condemned them to be imprisoned and beaten and even in many instances to be put to death.

16, 17 So terrible will be the hate and rancour against the faithful because they believe in Jesus and serve Him that even some of their own relatives and friends who reject Christ will take them and deliver them to the hostile authorities. And thus many of them will die as martyrs. As far as can be ascertained, all the apostles (except John) died a violent death through the action of Jewish or pagan persecutors, and many other believers were killed by the Jewish authorities in Jerusalem and elsewhere, as persecution flared up from time to time (in some instances as a result of the action of their own blood-relations). About A.D. 64 many Christians in Rome were cruelly tortured to death under the Emperor Nero. Then also relatives and former friends acted as their accusers. The Jews looked upon them as blasphemers because they believed in the crucified Jesus as Messiah. And the pagans accused them of all kinds of atrocities because they separated themselves from the immoral and barbarous forms of social recreation and from the various public acts of pagan worship, in particular the cult of the emperor.

18 But although they are to suffer physical pain and death, they can never be plucked from the protecting hand of God— nothing will happen to them outside His will, and He will make all things work together for their highest welfare and their eternal salvation, and at His second advent they will arise with glorified, celestial bodies in which there will be no defect or injury.

19 The great essential, however, is that the faithful must persevere and not lose heart, even though they have to go through numerous periods of distress and persecutions. Through perseverance they must achieve true and full life, and be spiritually strong and triumphant in all circumstances.

20 In verses 8 and 9 Jesus warned the disciples, who were then still subject to so many misconceptions, that they must not be misled into expecting His second advent and the final Consummation too soon. In verses 10–19 He taught them what to expect during the coming years before the destruction of Jerusalem and how they must conduct themselves under the persecutions. And now at last Jesus tells them of the sign which is to indicate that the destruction of the city and the temple is close at hand. It will be something quite different from His second advent. Thus the destruction of Jerusalem will not be preceded by the revelation of His Messianic glory. By no means, for when the city begins to be threatened by earthly armies (see note on this verse), the faithful must know that its destruction at the hands of those armies is at hand.

21 The approach of the hostile armies must be to the faithful the signal to flee from the city without delay, and even from the whole environment and province of Judaea, as far as the mountains on the other side of the Jordan. History indeed records that the faithful in Jerusalem and its environs obeyed the warning of the Saviour. When the first signs appeared that Jerusalem was going to be surrounded by the Roman forces practically all the Christians fled from the city and its environs across the Jordan to the Trans-Jordanian town of Pella (the modern Kherbit-al-Fakil), where they remained until after the destruction of Jerusalem.

22 The faithful must flee from the city and its environs when the hostile armies approach, for the judgments of God will then visit its inhabitants. Because the city did not recognise the time of its visitation but rejected Jesus and the deliverance which He offered them, even after they had crucified Him and the glad tidings had constantly been preached among them by His followers (in verses 12–27 Jesus predicted that they would continue to reject Him and His envoys), therefore there was no averting of the doom of which He warned them and against which He so yearned to protect them. And thus all the warnings in the Old Testament, that the people would pay the penalty in full if they forsook righteousness and truth, would have their fulfilment.

23 So great will be the distress in the Jewish land in those days of retribution that, instead of motherhood being a joy and a blessing, it will be a curse and a source of affliction. Even a merely superficial acquaintance with Josephus's description of the overwhelming of the Jewish land and the siege and destruction of Jerusalem by the Romans makes one realise the truth of this prophecy of Jesus.

24 The defenders of the city will be either slain or scattered as prisoners of war among the nations of the world, and Jerusalem will fall into the hands of pagan nations and be dominated by them until the times of these nations are fulfilled, which probably means until the end of this present world-order, when Christ will come with divine majesty and power to establish His eternal kingdom on the new earth after the Final Judgment (cf. verses 25–33). The first part of the prophecy in this verse became literally true at the destruction of Jerusalem in A.D. 70. After a siege of about five months by a mighty Roman army under the command of Titus, the son of the Emperor Vespasian, the Romans eventually overwhelmed the whole city, completely destroyed and plundered the temple and slew tens of thousands of the Jews, men, women and children. And when they were satiated with the slaughter, they carried off the remainder (except the weak and the aged, whom they killed without exception) as prisoners of war, so that not a single Jew was left alive in the city. For many years after the destruction of the city no Jew was again allowed in the city or even in its surroundings. Only on the day on which the destruction of the temple was commemorated every year were they allowed to go and mourn from the hills in the vicinity of the destroyed city.

The first Jews who were again permitted to inhabit a part of the destroyed city were the Christians of Jewish descent who had fled to Pella and who had some time after the conclusion of the Roman-Jewish war received permission to inhabit a certain portion of the ruined city. For years this settlement of Christians, under the leadership of Simeon (probably a cousin of Jesus, and successor to James the Just as president of the Jerusalem church), formed the only inhabitants of Jerusalem apart from the soldiers of the famous Tenth Legion of the Romans (the " Fretensian " Legion) which guarded the city for many years. In A.D. 132 Jerusalem again became the centre of a Jewish insurrection, under the pseudo-Messiah Bar-Kokhba, and was again taken and destroyed by the Romans. The Emperor Hadrian then determined to make it a permanently pagan city; he refounded it as a Roman colony and renamed it Aelia Capitolina—a name which combined his own family name (Aelius) with the title of Jupiter Capitolinus, in whose honour a new shrine was built on the temple-mount. From the reign of Constantine the city passed under Christian domination, but in 637 it was taken by the Muslims under Omar. To this day a Muslim sanctuary, the Dome of the Rock, stands on the temple-mount. Jesus' prediction was terribly and completely fulfilled.

The history of the judgments that visited the Jewish people, the city and the temple after Christ was rejected by them is written large in poignant letters as a warning to all nations and individuals who rebel against God by refusing to believe in His Son.

---

[1] Luke makes a quite general statement that Jesus uttered the prophetic discourse in connection with remarks made by some of the disciples about the temple. Matthew and Mark give further particulars that supplement Luke's summarised statement (cf. Matt. xxiv. 1 ff. and Mark xiii. 1 ff.). There is no ground for seeing in this a contradiction between the Gospels.

[2] Cf. our note on the Temple, pp. 533 ff.

[3] Cf. Josephus, *Jewish War*, vi, for a description of the total destruction of the temple.

[4] While some liberal critics allege that Jesus did not predict that the temple would be destroyed and that this prophecy is thus a *vaticinium ex eventu*, even the Jewish commentator, Montefiore, writes: " It is in accordance with his prophetic character that Jesus should predict the destruction of the temple. . . . It is also a mark of His originality, and of His elevation above the religious level of his age. For though it is exaggerated to say that the Jews believed that God lived in the

temple and not elsewhere, or that the presence of God among His people was conditioned by the existence of the temple, the old ideas did still hang about men's minds, and the continuance of the religion apart from the temple, and all the better for its loss, was hard to conceive " (*Synoptic Gospels*, i, p. 296).

If even a Jewish scholar, who does not regard Jesus as the Christ and still less as the Son of God but only as a Great Prophet, could write thus, how much more is it not obvious to Christian believers that He whom we acknowledge as our Lord and Redeemer did utter this prophecy?

[5] E. Meyer declares (*Ursprung und Anfänge*, i, p. 129) that the whole of the prophetic discourse has nothing to do with the historical Jesus, but is the creation of the first Christian community.

Wellhausen and many other radical critics regard the discourse (as recorded in Mark) as a Jewish apocalyptic writing which circulated in Palestine in the years before the fall of Jerusalem and was " Christianised " by Christians and then represented as being actually spoken by Jesus. According to some (Klostermann, Major and others) Luke then took the " Christianised " so-called " Little Apocalypse " from Mark, and reproduced it in a revised form in his Gospel. Dr. Vincent Taylor (*Behind the Third Gospel*, chap. iv), J. Weiss and others, however, declare that Luke used quite another document than Mark's for framing the prophetic discourse in his Gospel. Thus there is no consensus of opinion among the liberal critics in their rejection of the authority of the prophetic discourse as the actual words of Jesus (cf. Klostermann, at Luke xxi. 5–36). The main argument against regarding the whole of this discourse as an authentic utterance of Jesus is that it seems to contradict the admittedly genuine passage in xvii. 20–37, where the coming of the Son of Man is said to be unheralded by signs. But we suggest in our exposition of verse 31 below that there is not really a discrepancy here, and in xvii. 37 a very real sign is indicated, though it is concisely and cryptically expressed (see pp. 442, 445 above).

We may ignore, of course, those arguments which are not based on the evidence of our texts but simply on the presumption that any prediction—ascribed to Jesus or anyone else—which corresponds with what actually happened must be a *vaticinium ex eventu*. The evidence that Jesus prophesied that the divine judgments would visit the Jewish people and that He would come back in glory is abundant: He did so not only in this prophetic discourse, but also on many other occasions. (Cf. ix. 49–51, xii. 40, xiii. 34, 35, xvii. 23, 27, xviii. 8, xix. 15, 43, xx. 16, and also Matt. vii. 22, x. 23, xix. 28, xxi. 44, xxvi. 64, etc.)

[6] Because, as far as can be ascertained, there were no persons who represented themselves as Christ during the years from Jesus' ascension until the time of Jerusalem's destruction in A.D. 70, this warning refers to the whole course of events until the End-time, and especially to the last days just before His second advent when many false " Christs " will appear.

⁷ This also refers to conditions through all the centuries and especially to the last days before the End-time. Jesus probably also had in mind the periods of civil war and insurrection which were to follow Nero's death in A.D. 68 during the Roman-Jewish war. Those were terrible times in the years before A.D. 70 and therefore Jesus forewarned His disciples not to become panic-stricken because of these events and not to expect that His second advent was close at hand.

⁸ δεῖ. These things must happen because they are part of the prophetic programme of the End-time in general, and so are divinely decreed; but they do not usher in the *immediate* end. The fall of Jerusalem and the events leading up to it were morally, though not chronologically, of an eschatological character.

⁹ τότε ἔλεγεν αὐτοῖς—" The formula marks a transition from the warnings of verses 8–9 to the definitely prophetic passage which follows " (Creed, *in loc.*).

¹⁰ Warschauer gives the following summary of a number of the historical events that took place as a fulfilment of Jesus' words before the destruction of the temple in A.D. 70: " In A.D. 61 there had been a severe earthquake in Phrygia, which had done vast damage . . . in 63 an eruption of Vesuvius had laid half Pompeii in ruins; there had been famines in the reigns both of Claudius and Nero, the Jewish rebellion against Rome, and the war which led to the capture and destruction of Jerusalem, had begun or was to begin in A.D. 66 " (*The Historical Life of Jesus*, p. 289).

Schlatter writes: " The agitation among the Jews in the years 66–70 did in fact bring forth ' terrifying apparitions in heaven ' (warring armies and the comet) and ' great signs ' (the opening of the temple gate, the audible departure of the celestial beings from the temple) " (*in loc.*).

For the original description of the terrifying events and signs before the fall of Jerusalem cf. Josephus, *The Jewish War*, vi, 31. Also the Roman historian Tacitus (born *c.* A.D. 53) recorded this in his works (*Historiae*, v, 13).

Amongst other things a comet (called by Josephus a " tailed star ") appeared over the city every night for a considerable time in the form of a sword. Read the whole of the moving description in Josephus (*loc. cit.*).

¹¹ πρὸ δὲ τούτων πάντων indicates that before the destruction of Jerusalem and the terrifying events which precede it the disciples will endure what is described in the following verses. These words indeed, in a secondary sense, refer to all times of the world's history until the Last Days (Zahn, *in loc.*), but only because they are the foreshadowing of the much worse things that will then happen. In the first instance, however, they refer to the events preceding A.D. 70 and were literally fulfilled, as has been shown.

¹² Jesus had also already previously warned His disciples that they would suffer (cf. vi. 22, ix. 23, xi. 49, xii. 4–12, 51–3, xiv. 26).

¹³ All these things fit in with the circumstances as they developed

after Jesus' ascension. They do not refer primarily to the Last Days before the second advent, but are nevertheless a foreshadowing of those times when the faithful will again be persecuted.

¹⁴ Not of their innocence (Zahn, *in loc.*), but for a testimony concerning Jesus. " The proceedings in the law-courts present the disciples with the opportunity and the obligation to be Jesus' witnesses " (Schlatter, *in loc.*).

¹⁵ προμελετᾶν—" the proper term for preparing a speech " (Creed, *in loc.*).

¹⁶ " By στόμα is meant the power of speech; by σοφία the choice of matter and form " (Plummer, *in loc.*).

¹⁷ " This proverbial expression of great security must here be understood spiritually; for it has just been declared (verse 16) that some *will* be put to death " (Plummer, *in loc.*). Zahn, however, is of the opinion (*in loc.*) that it also refers to the fact that with the resurrection at the second advent the faithful will receive bodily perfection —in a glorified, heavenly sense.

¹⁸ κτήσεσθε τὰς ψυχὰς ὑμῶν—" You will gain possession of your souls (or lives) ", i.e. achieve true salvation.

¹⁹ Luke is writing for Greek readers who would not understand what Jesus meant by the Jewish expression " the abomination of desolation " (cf. Mark xiii. 14 and Dan. ix. 27, xii. 11; 1 Macc. i. 54), he so paraphrases it. In his Gospel we find the same phenomenon throughout, namely, that he translates, paraphrases, or altogether omits typical Jewish names or expressions. That Jesus by this Jewish expression did indeed mean the threat to Judaea and Jerusalem by hostile armies, appears from the fact that also in Mark xiii. 14 we read that He said that the faithful were to flee from Judaea when they " shall see the abomination of desolation . . . standing where he ought not ". So the " abomination of desolation " is the symbol of the pagan, hostile forces that will invade the Holy Land and threaten the city. Therefore the faithful are warned to flee to the mountains in time. And because they are told to flee from Judaea, the mountains can only mean the mountainous country of Trans-Jordan—thither then the Christians accordingly fled towards the end of A.D. 66 or the beginning of 67, after the first Roman force under Cestius Gallus marched against Jerusalem. " In October (66) the army of Cestius Gallus was repulsed from the city, and routed near Beth-horon in its retreat. Here was the signal which the Lord had given . . . and the Christians fled to Pella beyond Jordan " (Gwatkin, *Early Church History*, i, 88). Although Jesus by " the abomination of desolation " (which is personal in Mark xiii. 14; cf. R.V.) probably referred in a secondary sense to the appearance of the Anti-Christ, it referred in a primary sense to the Roman force that would overwhelm Jerusalem, and therefore Luke's paraphrase of the Saviour's words in verse 20 for the sake of his Gentile readers is perfectly right.

In the opinion of Streeter (*The Four Gospels*, p. 540) and many other critics the fact that Luke, instead of the expression of Mark xiii. 14, expressly mentions the threat to Jerusalem in xxi. 20 as part of Jesus' discourse proves that he wrote his Gospel only after A.D. 70, and thus altered Mark's words in the light of the historical events. Vincent Taylor (*Behind the Third Gospel*, chap. iv) and Easton (*in loc.*), however, dispute this view and allege that Luke used as his primary source an apocalyptic document drawn up before A.D. 70. Even Luce admits, merely from historical considerations, concerning verse 20 that " it's form is vague enough not to demand a background of actual events " (*in loc.*) and H. G. Wood declares: " the prediction of Jerusalem's fall, the anticipation of disaster and tribulation for His own people . . . clearly come from Jesus Himself " (*Peake's Commentary*, at Mark xiii).

While it has generally been held that the Lukan version of these words of Christ is an interpretation of the original form which Mark has preserved, it should be noted that arguments in the opposite sense have been sustained. C. H. Dodd, in the *Journal of Roman Studies*, 37 (1947), pp. 47–54 (article: " The Fall of Jerusalem and the ' Abomination of Desolation ' "), concludes that the Lukan version, with the reference to Jerusalem being encompassed with armies, stands on its own feet, and is not coloured by the event of A.D. 66–70: " so far as any historical event has coloured the picture it is not Titus's capture of Jerusalem in A.D. 70, but Nebuchadnezzar's capture in 586 B.C. There is no single trait of the forecast which cannot be documented directly out of the Old Testament." Similarly C. C. Torrey, in *Documents of the Primitive Church* (1941), pp. 20 ff., believes that the Lukan form is original (the surrounding of Jerusalem with armies being in perfect accord with the Old Testament prophetic programme as outlined in Zech. xiv. 2, etc.). He thinks the reference to the abomination of desolation found its way into the discourse at the time of crisis in A.D. 40 caused the attempt of the Emperor Gaius to set up his image in the temple. However that may be, it is very likely that this discourse of Jesus was circulated by itself in written form (according to the Markan version) at the time of that crisis, and that echoes of its circulation at that time may be traced ten years later in 2 Thessalonians ii.

SPECIAL NOTE

THE TEMPLE

The original temple of Solomon was an exceptionally magnificent building, but was destroyed in 586 B.C. by the Chaldaeans. It was rebuilt by Zerubbabel and his companions after the return of the Jews from the Babylonian captivity. This rebuilt temple was comparatively small and simple. Herod the Great (who ruled over the Jewish people from 37 to 4 B.C.) was a great lover of architecture. And it is due to him that the temple, with its environs on the temple mount, was built up to such a massive and artistic building complex (nearly five hundred yards long and four hundred yards wide). Herod the Great drew up a grand architectural plan according to which the whole temple with all its surrounding buildings had to be rebuilt. He even caused a thousand priests to be trained as builders to do the work (so that the Jews could not accuse him of having the temple built by " unclean hands "). With this rebuilding a commencement was already made in 19 B.C., but it was only completed in A.D. 63 under Agrippa II and Albinus. This reminds us of what the Jews said to Jesus in reply to His figurative words about the breaking down and erection of the temple. They understood Him to speak of the temple building and then said: " Forty and six years was this temple in building, and wilt thou build it up in three days? " (John ii. 20). When they uttered these words (c. A.D. 28), the temple was therefore already forty-six years in rebuilding. It would take another thirty years and longer before it was to be completed. And it had been finished for hardly seven years when in A.D. 70 it was completely destroyed in fire and blood notwithstanding the fanaticism with which the Jews tried to defend it.

The group of buildings belonging to the temple as it was rebuilt by Herod occupied a much larger area than that of Solomon, and the whole of the temple-mount was surrounded by a high, strong wall with towers on the northern side. On the other sides there were no towers, because the steepness of those sides of the hill on which the temple was built and the height of the wall made it impregnable on those sides. On the temple square there were beautiful colonnades, stairs and gates by which the various temple buildings (collectively called the ἱερόν) were combined to form a whole. The actual temple (called the ναός) was built on an elevation of white marble blocks with golden ornaments. So it dominated all the buildings on the temple site. The Jewish historian Josephus (who was born in A.D. 37 or 38) in his book *The Jewish War* (written about A.D. 73) gives the following description of the temple: " The whole of the outer works of the temple was in the highest degree worthy of admiration; for it was completely covered with gold plates, which, when the sun was shining on them, glittered so dazzlingly that they blinded the eyes of the beholders not less than when one gazed at the sun's rays themselves. And on the other sides, where there was no gold, the blocks of marble were of such a pure white that to strangers who had never previously seen them (from a distance) they looked like a mountain of snow " (v, 14).

Although the temple was completed only in A.D. 63, it was already *substantially* completed about the time of the crucifixion. So the temple which Jesus visited was practically the same magnificent temple as was destroyed in A.D. 70. It was, therefore, not strange that the disciples on the occasion when they walked out of the temple with the Lord (Mark xiii. 1–3) should have spoken to Him about the beauty and grandeur of the temple buildings.

For a detailed account of the temple in those times read the description of Josephus (*The Jewish War*, v, 14), and of the Mishnaic tractate *Middoth*. Edersheim's *The Temple, Its Ministry and Service in the Time of*

Christ is still a valuable work on this subject. Olmstead in *Jesus in the Light of History* also gives a detailed account of the temple. Also cf. the various encyclopaedias.

[20] κυκλουμένην—" *Being* compassed: when the process was completed it would be too late " (Plummer, *in loc.*). Easton also gives the meaning as follows: " When a military investment of Jerusalem begins (note the present participle) " (*in loc.*). Thus Schlatter is wrong in saying that in these sentences Jesus does not warn the Christians of Jerusalem but only those outside Jerusalem, for when the city is already surrounded they will no longer be able to flee. The Saviour warns (as is indicated by the present participle) that when Jerusalem begins to be encircled or threatened the faithful must flee.

[21] Cf. the ancient church historian Eusebius's description (*Historia Ecclesiastica*, iii, 5, 3) of how the Christians fled in time to Pella, a town in Trans-Jordan to the south of the Sea of Galilee. Pella was one of the Greek towns of the Decapolis, and there the Christians remained free from Roman warfare and Jewish persecution until they were again permitted to return to the destroyed Jerusalem. According to Eusebius, another special revelation was given to the faithful (apart from the warning of Jesus in the prophetic discourse) that warned them to flee in time.

[22] χώραις, " *country*, opp. to town " (Abbott-Smith).

[23] αὐτήν, according to the context (see note 22), can mean nothing but Jerusalem.

[24] From the commencement of the history of the Jewish nation, God through His servants warned them clearly that if they behaved unfaithfully and wickedly they would reap disastrous retribution. Cf. especially the striking words in Deuteronomy xviii. 15–68. There is almost no form of calamity that visited the Jews during the Roman-Jewish war, not mentioned here in Deuteronomy. The words, of course, also referred to other judgments that visited the people when they sinned throughout the centuries. In their fullest sense, however, they were fulfilled in A.D. 66–70, and in such a form (as appears from the manner in which Jesus again and again makes the predictions concerning this event also point ahead to the Final Judgment—this is especially clear in Mark) that they always serve as a terrible foreshadowing of the Final Judgment. Cf. also texts like Leviticus xxvi. 31–3; Deuteronomy xxxii. 35; 1 Kings ix. 6 9; Daniel ix. 26; Micah iii. 12; Zechariah xi. 6.

[25] " By τῆς γῆς we cannot understand the whole earth, for what good would it do in that case to flee from Jerusalem? The Jew called the whole ' land of Israel ' . . . also ' the land ' *sans phrase* " (Zahn, *in loc.*). The territory of Judaea is chiefly meant here.

[26] According to Josephus (*The Jewish War*, vi, 9) 1,000,000 Jews perished at that time with the destruction of Jerusalem (through famine, pestilences, fratricide, and the Roman sword) and 97,000 prisoners were taken and carried off everywhere. Josephus probably exaggerates. But in any case it is certain that hundreds of thousands perished.

The Roman historian Tacitus states (*Historiae*, v, 13, 4) that the normal population of Jerusalem was 600,000 before A.D. 70. And if we bear in mind that before the investment of the city the Jews poured into Jerusalem in tens of thousands for the Passover and could not again return to their homes and thus remained in the city throughout the five months' siege, it may be understood that hundreds of thousands would perish in the over-populated city. In any case not a single one was left alive in the ruined city.

[27] καιροὶ ἐθνῶν was, according to A. J. Grieve (*Peake's Commentary*, *in loc.*), "an apocalyptic catchword; the period set for the Roman Empire". But he gives no evidence for this, and it seems arbitrary to restrict the scope of the expression to the Roman Empire. It refers rather to the whole period during which the Gentile world-powers are in command, until the time comes for the "saints of the Most High" to possess the kingdom (cf. Dan. vii. 27). "As the words ἔσται πατουμένη ὑπὸ ἐθνῶν express that this condition [the trampling underfoot of Jerusalem, referred to also in Rev. xi. 2] is to last a long time, so the words ἄχρι οὗ πληρωθῶσιν καιροὶ ἐθνῶν extend this time to the end of the course of the world" (Zahn, *in loc.*) Cf. also Schlatter, *in loc.* Christ nowhere implies that the "times of the Gentiles" will be followed by Jewish dominion over the nations. The kingdom of this world is to give place to "the kingdom of our Lord and of his Christ" (Rev. xi. 15)—not a glorified Jewish kingdom, as certain modern chiliasts hold, but the eternal reign of God (cf. verse 31).

THE PROPHETIC DISCOURSE. THE COMING OF THE SON OF MAN

(Cf. Matt. xxiv. 29–35; Mark xiii. 24–32)

xxi. 25–33

25 And there shall be signs in sun and moon and stars;[1] and upon the earth[2] distress of nations,[3] in perplexity for the
26 roaring of the sea and the billows;[4] men fainting for fear, and for expectation of the things which are coming on the
27 world:[5] for the powers of the heavens[6] shall be shaken.[7] And then[8] shall they see the Son of man[9] coming in a cloud with
28 power and great glory. But when these things[10] begin to come to pass, look up, and lift up your heads;[11] because your redemption draweth nigh.[12]
29 And he spake to them a parable:[13] Behold the fig tree,[14]
30 and all the trees: when they now shoot forth, ye see it and know of your own selves that the summer is now high.
31 Even so ye also, when ye see these things coming to pass,
32 know ye that the kingdom[15] of God is nigh. Verily I say unto you, This generation[16] shall not pass away, till all things be
33 accomplished. Heaven and earth shall pass away: but my words shall not pass away.

In the previous portion Jesus foretold the dreadful fate awaiting the people of Jerusalem in the destruction of their city and temple. It will be so terrible (and actually was so) that the Saviour held it up as a clear foreshadowing of the Last Days and the Final Judgment, as appears from Mark xiii, where the predictions concerning the fate of the city Jerusalem are constantly expanded into prophecies concerning the Last Days. In Luke's shorter report of the prophetic discourse the predictions are far more clearly marked off from each other. After referring in verse 24 to the period when the times of the nations will be fulfilled, i.e. to the end of the present age (see exposition and note, *in loc.*), there is in verse 25 an immediate transition to the predictions concerning the Last Things before and at Jesus' second advent.

25, 26 While before the fall of Jerusalem there were only a few miraculous signs (cf. verse 11 " in divers places "), before the end of the age all creation and the whole of the human world will be plunged into dreadful commotions—in the sun, the moon and the stars there will appear miraculous and alarming signs, the whole life of the nations on earth will be disrupted through the anxiety and terror that will overwhelm the people and render them desperate.

27 In the midst of these circumstances of utmost distress the Son of Man, the exalted Christ, will come in His divine power and majesty, and in such a manner that every eye will see Him.

28 While the onset of the great oppression of the Last Days, throwing the impenitent into terror and despair, will be the sign that the judgments of God are finally visiting the rejecters of His Son, it will be to believers the signal that their full redemption (in soul and body) is at hand. So Jesus commands His followers (He addresses the disciples as representing the faithful of all ages, including those of the Last Days), when they see the beginning of these predicted things, to be inspired with courage and faith in the knowledge that His second advent, and with it their redemption, are at hand. Although they do not know the precise day and hour of His coming, they will know that His coming is no longer far off.

29-31 Just as, when the trees in nature begin to bud, one knows that spring is near, so assuredly Christ's followers must know that when the prophesied events begin to occur His second advent and likewise the visible and full revelation of the sovereign dominion of God are close at hand. His coming will indeed be like a thief in the night (xii. 40) and no one will be able to determine beforehand when it will be, and unbelieving mankind will indeed be engaged in their ordinary secular activities in spite of all the portents of His coming (xvii. 26–30), but none the less the predicted events will be a sign to the faithful believers when His coming is at hand, so that they will not be taken unawares by that day (xxi. 34).

32 This verse has occasioned great difficulty. If Jesus said this in connection with the time of the End, then His words mean that the Jews will continue to exist until the end (the Greek word translated by " generation " is sometimes used for " a race " or " a people ", as well as for " a generation " in the sense of people living contemporaneously). Moreover, it is a noteworthy fact that, although there is no nation on earth that has ever been persecuted to such an extent as the Jewish people, or that has had to wander about in foreign parts so long without a country of its own, this nation still continues to exist as a nation and shows no signs of disappearing. If, as is more probable, the Saviour uttered these words in connection with the prophesied distress of the

Jewish people and the destruction of Jerusalem, His words mean that, before the generation then living should have died out, these things would occur. And this is what actually happened. Towards the end of A.D. 70 (i.e. some forty years after Jesus uttered these words) everything predicted by Him in verses 10–24 in connection with the events before and during the destruction of Jerusalem was already fulfilled—the temple was destroyed to the last stone, all Jerusalem was a ruin, the Jewish people were slain by hundreds of thousands (cf. notes on verses 20–4) and carried off into captivity.

33 After all these tremendous announcements, Jesus stresses absolute certainty of His prophecies—everything will be fulfilled. He does not say as the prophets and other men of God had done: " thus hath God spoken through me and therefore it will assuredly happen ". No: He speaks with His own absolute authority because He is Himself God and One with the Father. No one else has ever yet had the right to speak thus. " Heaven and earth shall pass away: but *My* words shall not pass away." He is not merely the foreteller of the course of history, but is Himself, in unity with the Father and the Spirit, the almighty Disposer thereof. He Himself, after His exaltation to the right hand of the Father, will take action to carry out the divine judgments upon the wicked and to save the faithful.

How glorious it is to know that the final purpose of the history of mankind is not the chaos and misery into which the world is plunged through the domination of sin and unrighteousness, but that it is the complete triumph of the divine sovereignty—a sovereignty of love and righteousness to be realised in practice through the exalted Christ at His second advent in glory. Thus will God Triune be fully glorified and the redeemed participate in the highest salvation.

---

¹ These words do not refer to the occurrences preceding the destruction of Jerusalem or to the course of events through the centuries (as C. Morgan, *in loc.*, alleges), but to the occurrences immediately preceding the second advent, for " these natural phenomena are distinguished from those mentioned in verse 11, firstly because of their world-embracing character: nations and mankind without distinction are reduced to a state of trepidation through them and filled with anxious expectation of what is to come further, and in contrast to $\varkappa a \tau \grave{a}\ \tau \acute{o} \pi o v \varsigma$ (verse 11) we read here that these events break in over the whole $o i \varkappa o v \mu \acute{e} v \eta$. Secondly, we have not to do here as there with natural phenomena such as take place ever and anon in the whole course

of the world's history, but with an overturning of the stability of the world " (Zahn, *in loc.*).

Before the destruction of Jerusalem there were various dreadful natural phenomena (cf. notes on verse 11), insurrections and wars, but these were not of a world-embracing, universal nature like the predicted events of verses 25, 26.

[2] τῆς γῆς is here used in the ordinary sense of the whole world (Abbott-Smith). This appears from the whole context (cf. note 1 above).

[3] Here mention is made of " nations " and not of " this people " as in verse 23. This is a further proof that the Last Days are here spoken of and not the events before the destruction of Jerusalem.

[4] The image of the roaring sea and waves is often used in the Scriptures to symbolise turbulent conditions in the life of nations. Here it is used in a universal sense.

[5] οἰκουμένη denotes here the whole of the inhabited world (Abbott-Smith). Also cf. Plummer, at iv. 5. " As distinct from the special judgment upon Jerusalem, this is to be a judgment upon the whole earth " (Creed, *in loc.*).

[6] αἱ δυνάμεις τοῦ οὐρανοῦ, not angelic beings (as some ancient church fathers alleged), or earthly authorities (as Morgan, *in loc.*, declares), but the heavenly bodies mentioned in verse 25—sun, moon and stars (cf. Plummer and Zahn, *in loc.*), " with which also other invisible parts and forces of the world-system, by which it is held in equilibrium, are to be included " (Zahn, *in loc.*).

[7] Not only uncommon natural phenomena (such as were observed e.g. in the so-called " meteoric shower " in the nineteenth century, or comets) are meant, but a complete disruption of all nature, " a tumult of the elements, by reason of which the most important parts of the universe lose their equilibrium, and their mechanism seems to become unhinged. That is the immediate introduction of the reappearance of the Son of Man " (Zahn, *in loc.*).

[8] καὶ τότε (" and then "), i.e. not at or immediately after the destruction of Jerusalem but much later (after the " times of the Gentiles be fulfilled ", verse 24, and after the world-embracing events of verses 25 and 26 have taken place). Cf. 1 Thessalonians iv. 16, 17; 2 Thessalonians i. 7, 8, ii. 8; Rev. xix. 11–16.

[9] Cf. Daniel vii. 13, 14; Rev. i. 7; and special Note on " Son of Man " (pp. 352 ff.). Cf. also Strack-Billerbeck, at Matthew xxiv. 30.

[10] Under τούτων naturally Jesus' second advent itself is not included, for this advent will be an instantaneous occurrence (xvii. 20–37) and will be accompanied by immediate salvation to the faithful. So the events preceding His coming are meant.

[11] " The disciples present are regarded as representatives of believers generally " (Plummer, *in loc.*). And the command obviously refers in the highest instance to the faithful who will be on earth when these signs will appear before His second coming.

[12] It is not permissible to apply these words to the events before the

destruction of Jerusalem (as Lightfoot and others do), and to make " redemption " refer to the deliverance of the disciples from the power of their Jewish persecutors. From the context here, as also in Mark xiii (cf. especially Mark xiii. 32, where the use of " that day " and " that hour " expressly refer to the second coming), it is evident that the words refer to the deliverance of the faithful from distress (through persecution and other misery on earth) at His second advent. Of course these words in verse 28 have, in a secondary sense, a meaning also for all other times of oppression that the faithful are called upon to pass through. History also has proved that Jesus did not here mean the downfall of the Jewish state and the deliverance of the disciples from the oppression of Jewish persecutions, for even before the fall of Jerusalem, e.g., at least two (Peter and James) of the four apostles (cf. Mark xiii. 3) had already died the death of martyrs. Also Andrew and all the other apostles (except John) first died as martyrs after the fall of Jerusalem. In addition, the church after the downfall of the Jewish state through the power of the Romans often endured terrible times of persecution (far worse than under the Jews before A.D. 70.

[13] " Here also, as in so many other parables, ' nature ' is to Christ a symbol for the things of the kingdom of His Father, because ' nature ' for Him does not exist by itself, and what takes place in it is not a ' natural process ' but because He sees and recognises in everything the omnipresent and omnipotent power of God " (Van Leeuwen, at Mark xiii. 28).

[14] It is quite impermissible to take the fig-tree here as symbol of the Jewish people and to teach that a revival of Jewish national life in Palestine is meant. For the words used here are not merely " Behold the fig-tree ", but also " and all the trees ". The parable simply means: Just as the appearance of leaves on the fig tree and other trees are a sign of the approach of summer, so these events described in the preceding verses are a sign of the approach of the kingdom of God.

[15] βασιλεία—the full and final revelation of God's sovereign dominion is meant (cf. note on Luke iv. 43).

[16] That these words may be taken in only one of the two senses mentioned by us in the exposition of this verse, and not as if Jesus meant that His second advent itself would take place in that generation, is clear from the following considerations. The Saviour (as we have seen in the exposition of this chapter) taught that even before the destruction of Jerusalem a considerable time would elapse (verse 12) and thereafter again a considerable time, when one after another (" nations ", plural) of the Gentiles will rule over Jerusalem (verse 24). And only when the " times of the Gentiles " are fulfilled (verse 24) (obviously a long period), will the signs of verses 25 ff. come, and only after that His second advent. All these things could certainly not be meant to take place during the lifetime of one generation. On other occasions, also, Jesus made it clear that His second coming must not be expected too soon (e.g. xii. 35–48; xix. 12. Cf. also Matt. xxii. 7 ff. with Matt. xxiv. 14; Mark xiii. 10).

No modern critic can know better what is meant by these words than Luke, who himself wrote them down in his Gospel. And obviously he did not regard the words as teaching that Jesus declared that His advent would take place still within that lifetime, for if it be true (as many of those critics allege who interpret the words thus) that Luke wrote his Gospel only after A.D. 80, the generation living at the time of Jesus' crucifixion had already passed, and yet His second advent had not taken place. So evidently Luke put a different construction upon these words and no one may interpret them in a sense con- flicting with the evangelist's own construction of them. From Acts i. 7, words also recorded by Luke, it appears that Jesus did not predict that His second coming would take place within a generation.

Thus we have to take the words of the Saviour in this verse in one of the two senses mentioned by us above. Zahn, Klostermann, Plummer and others are no doubt right in taking the meaning to be " this generation will not pass away before everything *in connection with the destruction of Jerusalem* (foretold by Jesus, verses 10–24, in reply to their question, verses 5–7) will have taken place ". J. A. C. van Leeuwen, Morgan and others, however, take them in the sense of " this (Jewish) race will not cease to exist before everything (*the prelude to the End and the second advent itself*) will have occurred ". This inter- pretation is improbable, for although γενεά may have the varied senses of " race, stock, family or generation " (Abbott-Smith), yet the emphasis here requires the meaning " generation ". The relevance of this emphatic assertion is clear from the Markan version of the dis- course. The division of this discourse has been set out admirably in an article by Edgar M. Wilson in the *Princeton Theological Review* for 1928, as follows: Mark xiii. 1–4 (cf. Matt. xxiv. 1–3; Luke xxi. 5–7) gives the occasion of the discourse; Mark xiii. 5–8 (cf. Matt. xxiv. 4–8; Luke xxi. 9–11) warns against being misled by false prophets or great calamities; Mark xiii. 9–13 (cf. Matt. xxiv. 9–14; Luke xxi. 12–19) foretells persecution and promises help; Mark xiii. 14–23 (cf. Matt. xxiv. 15–28; Luke xxi. 20–4) predicts the destruction of Jerusalem and dispersion of the Jews; Mark xiii. 24–7 (cf. Matt. xxiv. 29–31; Luke xxi. 25–8) predicts the coming of Christ; Mark xiii. 28–31 (cf. Matt. xxiv. 32–5; Luke xxi. 29–33) exhorts to watchfulness for the events leading up to the destruction of Jerusalem (" this generation shall not pass away, until all these things be accomplished "); Mark xiii. 32–7 (cf. Matt. xxiv. 36–41; Luke xxi. 34–6) exhorts to watchfulness for the coming of Christ (" but of *that* day or *that* hour "—in contrast to the events to take place within " this generation "—" knoweth us one . . . but the Father ").

THE PROPHETIC DISCOURSE. WATCHFULNESS

xxi. 34–6

34 But take heed to yourselves, lest haply your hearts be
overcharged with surfeiting,[1] and drunkenness, and cares of
35 this life, and that day come on you suddenly as a snare:[2] for
so shall it come upon all them that dwell on the face of all the
36 earth.[3] But watch ye at every season,[4] making supplication,
that ye may prevail[5] to escape[6] all these things that shall come
to pass, and to stand before the Son of man.[7]

On every occasion that the Saviour referred to His second
coming and to the events preceding it He impressed it upon the
minds of His disciples that they must so live in faithful vigilance
that they will be prepared for His coming. His predictions concerning the End are not intended to satisfy human curiosity about
the programme of the centuries or to give His disciples occasion
to rejoice in the final downfall of the wicked. By no means, for
He mainly emphasises the challenge of the coming events—a
challenge to true repentance and to faithful vigilance. What the
Saviour gives is not a systematic exposition of future events in the
smallest details but a message for practical life.

34 Thus the Saviour concludes His prophetic discourse by
earnestly warning His disciples (as representatives of all the faithful) to take heed that they do not, by a life given up to worldly
interests, become faint and burdened with earthly cares so that
His second advent will find them unprepared. Although these
words are primarily meant for those believers who will be alive
in the Last Days, they were and are meant for all the faithful.
" Each several generation, living at this or that time, occupies
for the period of its life the place of those who are to be alive at
the time of the Coming of the Lord " (Bengel). All are called
upon to be always prepared. In the final sense of the word, Christ
is coming only at His second advent. But in a special sense He
is also constantly " coming " in the life of every individual through
circumstances of tribulation, suffering and other critical and
decisive moments, and especially at the time of death. So all are
called upon to live continually like people who any moment
expect His coming and the Final Judgment.

543

35 The second advent will not affect merely certain people or a certain portion of the earth (as at the destruction of Jerusalem only the Jews of Palestine were affected), but will in its mighty universality embrace the whole world and finally and forever determine the eternal fate of every individual.

36 Therefore everyone must constantly watch against sin and straying in his own heart and life, and must pray that God will enable him to stand firm amidst all the temptations, struggle and distress that will accompany the prelude to the End, so that he may be able to stand before Christ as one of the redeemed and not shrink away from Him with shame into everlasting wretchedness. This command, too, refers chiefly to those who will be called upon in the Last Days to endure great tribulations; but it is also intended for all other believers.

When anyone's interest in the Scriptural announcements of the Last Things and the second advent degenerates into a subtle drawing up of precisely worked-out future events, then he has strayed a long way from the content and spirit of Jesus' prophetic utterances. As soon as attempts are made to draw up a programme of the future worked out in greater detail than is offered to us in God's Word it causes discord and sectarian dissensions. Clearly and gloriously the Scriptures present the main facts with regard to our Redeemer's second advent. What a mighty comfort lies in the prophesied facts, and, moreover, what a tremendously urgent call that we should be vigilant and prepared!

¹ κραιπάλη, "drunken nausea" (Abbott-Smith), "drunkard's intoxication", as a symbol of various forms of spiritual degeneration, inward disease and deadness.

² According to the majority and the best of MSS. and other textual evidence, ὡς παγίς belongs to the preceding verse and γὰρ should come after ἐπεισελεύσεται. Then verse 34b reads: "and lest that day come upon you unawares as a snare"—take you unprepared and unexpectedly, so that you will come to disgrace and everlasting injury instead of its being a day of rejoicing and eternal redemption to you. Verse 35 will then read: "For it (or 'he') shall come on all them that dwell on the face of the whole earth." Zahn's reasoning, that if this sentence be taken thus it is of no actual importance in the context, does not hold good. For in the context of the whole prophetic discourse, in which the Saviour also prophesied the destruction of Jerusalem, it was indeed of great importance to point out to the disciples that at His second advent not merely certain people or a certain nation would be implicated in it, but the whole world. Verse

35 (as rendered above according to the best textual evidence), then, has the special value that " the universality of the Final Judgment is emphasised, as compared with the previous judgment upon Jerusa lem " (Creed, *in loc.*). No one, therefore, may imagine that he will not be affected thereby (like those Christians who by their timely flight from Judaea placed themselves at a distance from the events accompanying the destruction of Jerusalem).

[3] πάσης τῆς γῆς—" here not ' the land ' but the whole ' earth ' which is affected by the Parousia " (Klostermann, *in loc.*).

[4] ἐν παντὶ καιρῷ " will belong not to δεόμενοι (like πάντοτε in xviii. 1) but to ἀγρυπνεῖτε as the principal predicate and the exact contrary of the temporary drunkenness and oversleeping of verse 34 " (Zahn, *in loc.*).

[5] It is uncertain whether καταξιωθῆτε (" be accounted worthy ") or κατισχύσητε (" be able ") is the correct reading. The textual evidence is very evenly divided, with a slight preponderance in favour of κατισχύσητε.

[6] Because in the previous verses it is clear that the faithful will be placed in the midst of the distress on earth and are commanded, when these things happen, to lift up their heads (verse 30), knowing that their redemption is at hand, " escape " does not mean that they will be snatched away *before* the tribulation; but just as verse 18 refers to spiritual security in the midst of terrible outward distress, so also " to escape all these things that shall come to pass " refers to the fact that the faithful will not meet with utter ruin by the terrifying events and the Final Judgment, but will remain safe in the highest sense of the word— will escape the everlasting destruction that will visit the wicked.

[7] Since all, including the redeemed, will have to appear before the Judgment Seat of Christ (Rom. xiv. 10), " to stand before the Son of Man " cannot here mean to be set before Him as judge, but " to pass the rest of judgment " (Zahn, *in loc.*). While the guilty ones will be rejected, the faithful will forever remain in His presence as the redeemed.

THE REWARD OF TREACHERY

(Cf. Matt. xxvi. 1–5, 14–16; Mark xiv. 1, 2, 10, 11)

xxi. 37, 38–xxii. 6

37 And every day he was teaching in the temple; and every
night he went out, and lodged in the mount that is called *the*
38 *mount* of Olives. And all the people came early in the morning to him in the temple, to hear him.[1]
1 Now the feast of unleavened bread drew nigh,[2] which is
2 called the Passover. And the chief priests and the scribes
sought how they might put him to death; for they feared
the people.[3]
3 And Satan[4] entered[5] into Judas who was called Iscariot,
4 being of the number of the twelve. And he went away, and
communed with the chief priests and captains,[6] how he might
5 deliver him unto them.[7] And they were glad,[8] and covenan-
6 ted to give him money. And he consented, and sought
opportunity to deliver him unto them in the absence of the
multitude.

In this account of Judas's arrangements to betray Jesus and in
the parts that follow from xxii. 7 to xxii. 38 we have the introduction to the Saviour's passion proper (xxii. 39–xxiii. 56).

37, 38 Luke has described only a few incidents belonging to
Jesus' last week in Jerusalem before His crucifixion, and concludes
this chapter by referring in very general terms to the fact that the
Lord was busy teaching the masses of the people in the temple
every day during that week. He still had such a hold on the
masses that they continued to come to the temple early in the
morning in thousands (" all the people ") to listen to Him. He
was so much reverenced and admired by the people, and regarded
by so many as the possible Messiah, that the Jewish authorities,
who had already long ago taken sides against Him, did not dare
to forbid His appearance in the temple or to have Him arrested.
In the evening, after the teachings of the day, Jesus spent the
night outside Jerusalem on the Mount of Olives.

xxii. 1, 2 The reason why the Saviour had come to Jerusalem
along with His disciples and so many other Jews was in order to

be there for the celebration of the Passover that was to be held towards the end of that week. One day after another passed, and the time for the commencement of the festival was drawing near. Although the Jewish authorities tried with so much subtle cunning and determination to bring Jesus into disfavour with the people and thus to open the way to have Him arrested, all their attempts were unsuccessful (xx. 1–40). The Jewish leaders, however, were fully determined on having the Lord done to death, and so they deliberated how they might carry out their plans concerning Him without causing an insurrection. From Mark xiv. 2 it appears that after deliberating they came to the decision to wait until after the conclusion of the festival before seizing Him, as they saw clearly that the masses (probably especially those from Galilee and Trans-Jordan who were attending the festival) would not tolerate any action being taken against Him. As soon as the multitudes had departed from the city and the danger of an insurrection was removed, then, they decided, they would in some way or other kill Him. But God's decree was different from what they had planned—it was His will that Jesus, " the lamb of God ", should die on the great festival day as the perfect expiatory offering. For this reason the decision of the Jewish authorities was of no avail.

3 Judas Iscariot, one of the twelve who had been chosen to be Jesus' most intimate followers, was not inwardly at one with the Saviour although he had been with Him for such a long time. For various reasons (in John xii. 6 his covetousness is mentioned) he decided to betray the Saviour, and as a result of his inward estrangement from the Lord he came completely under the sway of the evil one and was thus incited to commit such black treachery.

4–6 Surrendered to the power of Satan, Judas goes to the high priests and captains of the temple and informs them that he is prepared to deliver Jesus to them in such a manner that no insurrection will take place. What an unexpected and pleasant surprise for the persecutors of the Master that one of His own followers offers to bring their hated Enemy into their power! Elated because of this relief from the difficult problem of having Him arrested without the risk of a riot, they willingly agree to give him a sum of money for his help. From that moment Judas was finally determined to betray Jesus into the hands of His enemies, and he waited for the right opportunity when he would be able to do so without its becoming known to the multitudes attending the festival, who admired Him and might cause a riot. Thus on the part of His enemies and of the powers

547

everything was in readiness to send forth the innocent and holy Son of God upon the way of suffering, humiliation and death.

The history of Judas, who, although he occupied such a privileged position as one of Jesus' twelve apostles, nevertheless betrayed the Master, serves as a permanent and powerful warning to every member of the church of Christ—there is always the terrible possibility that even among us who apparently live in the closest connection with the Lord there may be those who are inwardly false and are busily engaged in betraying Him.

---

[1] The cursive MSS. known as the Ferrar group here continue with the *pericope de adultera* (John vii. 53–viii. 11), probably because John viii. 1, 2 corresponds so closely to Luke xxi. 37, 38.

[2] ἡ ἑορτὴ τῶν ἀζύμων ἡ λεγομένη πάσχα. The actual Passover was the festival celebrated towards the evening of the 14th Nisan, and the feast of the unleavened bread was the seven days' festival from the 15th to the 21st Nisan. In practice, however, these two festivals were regarded as one, and the whole feast was, in common parlance, merely called the Passover. So also Josephus writes in his *Antiquities*, xiv, 21, 1: κατὰ τὸν καιρὸν τῆς τῶν Ἀζύμων ἑορτῆς ἦν φάσκα λέγομεν (" at the season of the festival of unleavened bread which we call Passover "). The majority of modern critics (e.g. Montefiore, Luce, Easton, Strack-Billerbeck) agree that Luke is here correct in calling the whole festival the " Passover ".

[3] " At the time of the festival the city would be full of pilgrims from Galilee and elsewhere, and there would be many who knew and admired Jesus. Thus any attempt to arrest Him openly might be followed by a disturbance. This fact explains why Jesus was not arrested when He was teaching each day in the temple (Luce, *in loc.*).

[4] " The word σατανᾶς which according to predominant testimony is here anarthrous . . . is not to be taken as a proper name but as a generic name " (Zahn, *in loc.*).

[5] " But there is no hint that Judas is now like a demoniac, unable to control his own actions (Hahn). Judas opened the door to Satan. He did not resist him, and Satan did not flee from him. Jesus must suffer, but Judas need not become the traitor " (Plummer, *in loc.*).

[6] στρατηγοῖς—" The officers of the temple police, a numerous body composed chiefly of Levites. It was under the chief command of the στρατηγός, an important official (Acts iv. 1; v. 24 f.). As these functionaries were responsible for all arrests, it devolved on them to negotiate with Judas " (Easton, *in loc.*).

[7] It cannot be determined with certainty why Judas betrayed the Saviour. From Matthew xxvi. 14, xxvii. 4–10, and John xii. 4 ff. it appears that his covetousness was at least a secondary factor. Judas undoubtedly followed the Saviour from selfish motives. Possibly he

had expected that Jesus would take action as an earthly Messiah and that he, as one of His followers, would then receive a full share of the material advantages. When it became evident, towards the end of the Lord's ministry, that He was not going to act as a triumphant earthly Messiah, the ties that held Judas to Him were broken and he decided to betray Him and by so doing to secure, at any rate, some money for himself. The view expressed by Major (*in loc.*) and others that Judas betrayed the Saviour not from evil motives but owing to an urgent desire as it were to compel Jesus to reveal His Messiahship in a forceful manner, is not supported anywhere in the New Testament, and must be regarded as simply a conjecture.

8 Judas's unexpected action cancelled the decision of the Jewish leaders not to have Jesus arrested during the festival, for by Judas's treachery the way was opened to them to have Him taken at such a time and in such a manner that no disturbance would be caused. Because they wanted to run no risk of Jesus' escaping them, and because they naturally wanted to have Him in their power as soon as possible so that He might not be able during the feast to continue to influence the people against them by exposing the insincerity of their behaviour, the Jewish authorities, in this new situation which Judas's offer created, naturally rescinded their former decision and immediately seized the opportunity. Thus, viewed in true perspective, it is not, as some writers have alleged, the Gospel writers who err in relating on the one hand the decision of the Jewish authorities (Mark xiv. 2) and stating on the other hand that Jesus was nevertheless taken and killed during the festival. On the contrary, it is these critics who once more prove how unwilling they are to accept the trustworthiness of the Gospel narrative and to try to penetrate into the actual historical circumstances in which the events related by the Gospels were enacted. The history of the treachery of Judas and the action of the Jewish authorities is psychologically and historically unexceptionable.

THE LAST PASSOVER

7 And the day of unleavened bread[1] came, on which the
8 passover must be sacrificed.[2] And he sent Peter and John,
saying, Go and make ready for us the passover,[3] that we may
9 eat. And they said unto him, Where wilt thou that we
10 make ready? And he said unto them, Behold, when ye are
entered into the city, there shall meet you a man bearing a
pitcher[4] of water; follow him into the house[5] whereinto he
11 goeth. And ye shall say unto the goodman[6] of the house,
The Master[7] saith unto thee, Where is the guest-chamber,[8]
12 where I shall eat the passover with my disciples? And he will
shew you a large upper room[9] furnished:[10] there make
13 ready.[11] And they went, and found as he had said unto
them: and they made ready the passover.
14 And when the hour was come, he sat down, and the
15 apostles with him.[12] And he said unto them, With desire
I have desired[13] to eat this passover[14] with you before I
16 suffer: for I say unto you, I will not eat it,[15] until it be ful-
17 filled[16] in the kingdom of God.[17] And he received a cup,
and when he had given thanks, he said,[18] Take this,[19] and
18 divide it among yourselves: for I say unto you, I will not
drink from henceforth[20] of the fruit of the vine,[21] until the
19 kingdom of God shall come. And he took bread, and when
he had given thanks, he brake it, and gave to them, saying,
This is my body[22] which is given for you: this do in remem-
20 brance of me. And the cup in like manner after supper,
saying, This cup is the new covenant in my blood, *even* that
21 which is poured out for you. But behold,[23] the hand of him
22 that betrayeth me is with me on the table. For[24] the Son
of man indeed goeth, as it hath been determined: but woe
23 unto that man through whom he is betrayed! And they
began to question among themselves, which of them it was
that should do this thing.[25]

Ever since the prediction of the pious Simeon to Mary in the
temple when he took up the child Jesus in his arms (Luke ii. 24 ff.),
the shadow of the cross fell over the whole of the Gospel history.
The Saviour Himself frequently referred to His approaching
suffering and death (e.g. ix. 22, xviii. 31). All four Gospels show
us clearly that the death of Christ came to Him not as an unexpected or accidental occurrence—He was fully aware that the

way of suffering awaited Him and he chose voluntarily and of set purpose to lay down His life as a sacrifice, even unto death (ix. 51, xviii. 31–4). And so we find here in the Gospel narrative that on the eve of His crucifixion He makes definite preparation with a view to His death and departure—preparations necessary to the continuing life of His church on earth. One of these preparations is the institution of the Holy Communion.

7, 8 The Jewish custom at the time of Jesus (and to-day still) was that families on the night before the Passover, i.e. in the evening following the 13th Nisan (the month which usually commences during the second half of March), searched through their houses thoroughly and collected every bit of leaven or leavened cake to burn it on the following day. Towards noon on the following day (the 14th Nisan) there must be no more leaven in the houses and the unleavened loaves must be made ready for the passover. Therefore Luke rightly calls this day the " day of unleavened bread ". Between about 2.30 p.m. until about 6 p.m. on that day (14th Nisan) the paschal lambs had to be slaughtered and made ready for the Passover, which commenced a little after sunset (according to Jewish chronology it was thus, after sunset, the beginning of the 15th Nisan, the first day of the seven days' " festival of the unleavened bread ", sometimes also merely called " Passover ").

Thus it was on a Thursday (cf. xxiii. 54), the 14th Nisan (probably 5th April, A.D. 30), that the Saviour the day before His crucifixion sent Peter and John to make the necessary preparations so that He and His disciples might hold the paschal repast that evening.

9 Jesus and His disciples had no dwelling or even accommodation in the city, and spent the nights on the Mount of Olives or in Bethany (xxi. 37; Mark xi. 12). The Passover on the evening of the 14th Nisan (or, more accurately, the beginning of the 15th Nisan) had, however, to be held in Jerusalem. And now the disciples ask the Lord where they must go and prepare for the banquet.

10–12 Judas Iscariot had already, a few days before, agreed with the Jewish authorities to deliver Jesus to them for a sum of money, under circumstances which would ensure that no disturbance should be caused through His arrest. Such a convenient moment would be especially afforded on Passover Eve, when the hundreds of thousands attending the festival would all be indoors together in small groups engaged in the celebrations, and hardly a single Jew would be in the street. If Judas could find out in good time where the Saviour would hold the paschal repast, he could arrange with the Jewish authorities to arrest him unexpectedly that evening. Because of their violent hatred of Him and their fear of the masses, and also from fear that He might, during the celebrations of the seven days' feast following upon the paschal repast, gain still greater influence among the people, the Jewish authorities would not have shrunk from availing themselves of such a favourable opportunity even though it was Passover Eve. The Saviour was aware of Judas's diabolical plans and of His persecutors' murderous determination to have Him done to death. He had, however, still very much to say to His disciples during that Passover Eve, and in particular He desired first of all to celebrate for the last time with His disciples the Paschal Feast that pointed on to His perfect work of redemption, and then to institute the Holy Communion in its place. Therefore Judas must not succeed in delivering Him to His enemies until everything was completed. And because the Saviour never made use of miracles to defeat the wicked schemes of His enemies when He could do so by taking natural precautions, He kept the place where He was going to celebrate the Passover with His disciples a secret right up to the end. Probably the Saviour had made arrangements earlier in the week with one of His followers who owned a house in Jerusalem that he should keep one of the rooms in his house in readiness for Him and His disciples to celebrate the Passover there (verse 12). In addition, He had probably arranged with him that at a given time during the morning before the Passover he should be with a pitcher of water at a certain place near the portal where his disciples would enter the city, so that some of His disciples could meet him there and be taken by him to his house. Because it was the custom in Palestine that only women carried the pitchers of water, it would be easy for the disciples to notice this man with the pitcher and to follow him.

13 So Peter and John went and found everything as Jesus had told them and prepared everything for celebrating the Passover.

14 The Saviour would probably have gone towards evening, just before the hour for the celebration arrived, to the house where the preparations had to be made. So Judas had no previous opportunity of going to the Jewish authorities to inform them where the Lord would celebrate the Passover. And so it came about that the Saviour could still sit down undisturbed along with His disciples to this last paschal repast.

15 Luke does not give a detailed account of the institution of the Holy Communion. He knew that it was already well-known among Christians everywhere through the preaching of Paul and others (cf. 1 Cor. xi. 23 ff.). Ever since the beginning of the existence of the church of Christ the celebration of Holy Communion has occupied such a central place in the life of the faithful that the history of its institution by the Saviour that last evening before the crucifixion was undoubtedly one of the first things in which every new convert to Christianity had been thoroughly instructed. In the last chapters of Luke's Gospel we notice throughout how he relates the history of the events as briefly as possible. His Gospel was already of a length sufficient for being contained conveniently within the limits of a normal papyrus roll. So he confines himself in his descriptions to such matters as he deems essential to his account of the Gospel narrative. Thus we are not surprised to notice that he does not make any mention at all of several particulars which are mentioned in the last chapters of Mark. We see here, for instance, how he gives merely a brief account of the events of that last evening. Nevertheless he mentions quite a number of important particulars not related in the other Gospels. Thus, e.g., he mentions in this verse the fact that the Saviour during the evening (probably immediately the actual paschal repast was finished, after the eating of the lamb) told His disciples how intensely He had longed to celebrate that last Passover with them. This reminds us of the Saviour's words in xii. 49 where He said: " I am come to cast fire upon the earth; and what will I, if it is already kindled? " We shall never be able to sound the depths of these two sayings. Nevertheless we see how the Saviour in His perfect incarnation looked forward with intense anxiety to the moment when the climax of His ministry and self-surrender would be attained and His work of redemption (along the path of suffering and death) would be accomplished. And it was because the institution of the Holy Communion on the occasion of the celebration of that last paschal repast was as it were the sign that everything was now ready for the final accomplishment of His work of redemption and that the preparatory Old Dispensation had now to give place to the New Dispensation that the Saviour had so earnestly looked forward to celebrating that paschal repast together with His disciples.

16 On the eve of His crucifixion Jesus knows that the whole course of His life of self-sacrifice and humiliation on earth is now drawing to an end. But He also knows that the day will come when He as the Triumphant One will lead His followers to the beautiful heritage of complete redemption and blessedness. This full blessedness which will commence with the end of the age has often been represented by the symbol of the celebration of a Messianic banquet. For this reason the Saviour here refers to the

celebration of the feast on that coming day when the sovereign
dominion of God has come to full revelation and the redemption
wrought by the grace of God, as symbolised in the Passover
celebrations, has become a blessed and perfect reality.

17 In accordance with his policy of brevity here (see what has
been said at note 14 above) Luke does not give a full report of
what Jesus said at the distribution of the cup, but simply states
that He took a cup given to Him by one of His disciples, gave
thanks and then gave it to the disciples to divide among themselves.

18 Once more the Saviour refers to the fact that this is His
last paschal repast together with His disciples on earth and that
He will not again celebrate it with His followers until the kingdom
of God shall have come and until the grand Consummation has
arrived with the final victory over all the evil powers. The
Saviour naturally intends His words to be taken in a figurative
sense (cf. verse 16).

19, 20 In the accounts of the institution of the Holy Communion in Matthew xxvi, Mark xiv, and 1 Corinthians xi, first the
dispensing of the bread and then that of the wine is mentioned.
But it is possible (see notes on verses 19 and 20) that verse 19b
(from " which is given for you . . . ") and verse 20 did not belong
to the original text of Luke. Then verse 17 must be regarded as
the verse referring to the giving of the communion-cup, in which
case Luke, by first mentioning the wine and then the bread, gives
the sequence differently from Matthew, Mark, and 1 Corinthians
xi, but conformably to 1 Corinthians x. 16. Even if this be so,
there is no contradiction between the four renderings of the
institution, for it is noteworthy that neither Matthew, nor Mark,
nor Paul (1 Cor. xi) explicitly says that the Saviour *definitely*
distributed the wine *after* the bread. All that is taught in Matthew,
Mark, and 1 Corinthians xi in the original Greek is that on the
occasion of the Passover the Saviour instituted the Holy Communion by giving bread and also by giving wine. They do not
state in what definite sequence these were given. Under the
guidance of His Spirit, however, the Christian church at the
celebration of the Holy Communion mostly took the bread first
and the wine thereafter. It does not make any essential difference
to the significance of the Holy Communion in what sequence the
bread and wine follow each other, and so, in the divine overruling, the New Testament does not expressly state the sequence
in which Jesus instituted it.

If the supposition which is endorsed by the majority of expositors of the Bible (liberals as well as conservatives), namely,

that 19b and 20 are later interpolations, is right, then Luke in verse 19 merely mentioned the fact in quite general terms that the Lord also broke bread and distributed it and taught His disciples that the broken bread is the symbol of His body (which for their sake will be broken in His sacrificial death).

21   At a certain stage in the course of that evening (not one of the Gospels in their brief renderings of what occurred that last evening says exactly when, before or after the paschal repast, it took place), Jesus declared in express terms that one of the twelve disciples with Him at the Passover table was engaged in betraying Him.

22   In accordance with the divine plan of salvation He, the Son of Man, must be delivered up and killed (as an offering for the sins of lost mankind), but His betrayer is committing the treachery wholly on his own responsibility and is thus calling down a terrible judgment upon himself. Judas is acting against the voice of his own conscience, of set purpose and in accordance with his own free choice, and is therefore guilty of the betrayal of the Son of God.

23   Luke does not mention in detail by what means the Saviour pointed out Judas as the betrayer or what the disciples said and thought (cf. Matt. xxvi; Mark xiv; John xiii), but merely makes a general statement that the disciples were dismayed at the news and wondered which of them was the traitor.

The sacrificial death of the Saviour was not the outcome of a fortuitous combination of circumstances, but was in accordance with the divine plan of salvation which had already been foreshadowed in the Old Testament, especially in the sacrifice of the paschal lamb, centuries before. Moreover, the Saviour allowed Himself knowingly and voluntarily to be sacrificed as the perfect paschal lamb. For this reason His sacrificial death possesses an eternal, all-sufficient, divine value.

---

[1] " Luke calls precisely the 14th day, by the morning of which at the latest (*Pesachim* i. 3 f.) all leaven and all leavened bread must be removed from the houses and the unleavened bread must be prepared, ' the day of unleavened bread ' in contradistinction to ' the feast or festival of unleavened bread ' which began that day " (Zahn, *in loc.*).

[2] By these words it is expressly stated that on that day it was the 14th Nisan, and that therefore the Last Supper was really a paschal repast and not an " antedated paschal repast " as alleged by various expositors. In the Excursus " The Day and Date of the Crucifixion " at the end of this commentary we deal with this question in detail.

Suffice it to state here that we are convinced that there is no contradiction between the first three Gospels and the fourth Gospel.

Speaking generally in connection with the objections to the Gospel statements that Jesus was crucified on the day of the feast, we may here quote the following words of Major: the question is, he asks, " whether an unscrupulous and violent hierarchy, intent on judicial murder, might not, on the plea of necessity, override hampering ritual regulations. Modern minded persons would feel that a sacred day or religious festival was desecrated by a public execution; but more primitive peoples felt that an additional sacredness and solemnity was contributed by such an event " (*op. cit.*, p. 167).

³ This command of the Saviour further indicates that the real paschal repast is meant.

⁴ " In the East it is women who bear pitchers of water; men carry water-skins " (Major, *op. cit.*, p. 168).

⁵ It is most probably a trustworthy tradition that declares that this house belonged to Mark's parents and was therefore the same house as is mentioned in Acts xii. 12. In addition, many expositors assume that the young man mentioned in Mark xiv. 51 was Mark, who had secretly followed the Lord and His disciples to Gethsemane.

⁶ Possibly Mark's father was still living at the time, but died fairly soon afterwards, so that the house in Acts xii. 12 was called the house of Mary, the mother of Mark. Or else Mark himself already acted as master of the house for his widowed mother. When the Christians who had fled to Pella shortly before the destruction of Jerusalem (A.D. 70) were again allowed to inhabit the south-western portion of the city they rebuilt the ruins of this house into a *coenaculum*, a building in which they assembled for celebrating the Holy Communion and for other religious gatherings.

⁷ The owner, therefore, was not only acquainted with Jesus, but knew Him as " the Master ", i.e. " the Teacher" (Gk. ὁ διδάσκαλος, representing *hā-rāb*).

⁸ " It was a common thing for the inhabitants of Jerusalem to lend a room to pilgrims for the Passover, the usual payment being the skin of the paschal lamb and the vessels used at the meal " (Plummer, *in loc.*).

⁹ ἀνάγαιον—anything raised above the ground; here an upper chamber (Abbott-Smith).

¹⁰ ἐστρωμένον—"spread, furnished—with *what*, depends upon the context, which here suggests couches or cushions " (Plummer, *in loc.*).

¹¹ The preparation would normally include providing a paschal lamb (slaughtered at the temple); bitter herbs, unleavened bread, cups, wine, etc.

¹² καὶ οἱ ἀπόστολοι σὺν αὐτῷ. Similarly Mark: " he cometh with the twelve " (Mark xiv. 17). The Synoptists make it plain that none but the twelve apostles sat with the Lord at the Last Supper: this excludes the theory favoured by Streeter and others that the " beloved disciple " who was present (John xiii. 23) was a young friend of Jesus outside the ranks of the twelve.

[13] Brooke and Burkitt (*Journal of Theological Studies*, July 1908, pp. 569 ff.) have maintained (and others have often repeated it since) that these words indicate that the Saviour did *not* celebrate the Passover and only had a strong desire to do so. They admit, however, that it was Luke's opinion that Jesus did celebrate the real Passover and the words ἐπιθυμίᾳ ἐπεθύμησα (which he is supposed to have copied from some or other source) were wrongly regarded by him as indicating that Jesus was referring to the Passover which He had celebrated. Zahn has sufficiently replied to this: " If that had really been the meaning of Luke's documentary source, then Luke would not be to blame for misunderstanding it. For what Greek would have expressed himself in so clumsy and misleading a fashion! " (*in loc.*). There can be no real doubt that Jesus by these words expressed His relief that at last He could take part in the Passover to which He had so eagerly looked forward (partly for the reason mentioned in our exposition above). Thus Creed writes: " The meaning [of these words] is that Jesus had earnestly desired to eat this passover, and that his desire is fulfilled " (*in loc.*). Also Easton declares that these words express " profound relief " and not a disappointed expectation. When the Saviour uttered the words it was " the point of transition between two economies and their two great festivals, the one about to close forever, the other immediately to open and run its majestic career until from earth it be transferred to heaven " (Jamieson, Fausset and Brown, *in loc.*).

[14] τοῦτο τὸ πάσχα. In the context in which these words occur (e.g. the words of verses 7, 8, 13), they certainly cannot refer to a Passover which was not going to be held until the following day, but only to the Passover celebrated that same evening. If the Fourth Gospel had not been taken to imply that Jesus did not really celebrate the Passover, no one would ever have regarded these words as an expression of frustrated hope, as even V. Taylor, *Jesus and His Sacrifice*, p. 180, and Streeter, *op. cit.*, p. 243, regard them (see Excursus, pp. 649 ff.)

[15] οὐκέτι οὐ μὴ φάγω—"After this present occasion " (Plummer). Of exceptional importance are Zahn's words (*in loc.*): " The glance at the years which are to follow this year's Passover and the passion of Jesus, which οὐκέτι expresses, also calls forth the thought of the termination of these years, of the more distant future, in which God's perfect dominion will come or be made manifest (cf. ix. 27, xix. 11). Then the idea of the legal Passover will come to fulfilment, to full realisation. As this was a joyful celebration of grateful remembrance of the deliverance of Israel from Egypt (Exod. xii. 14, 24–7), so in the manifested kingdom of God the deliverance of the community of Jesus, which shall have attained its consummation in the revelation of the kingdom of God, will be celebrated in grateful remembrance. That is the fulfilment of the prophetic meaning of the legal Passover, and can therefore be treated as an eternal Passover feast."

[16] " The conception of the Passover as a type of the coming kingdom is common in Jewish literature, whether with or without specific

reference to the Messianic Banquet " (Easton, *in loc.*). In xii. 37, xiii. 25–9, xiv. 15, 24, xxii. 30, also, the blessedness of the redeemed is represented under the symbol of a banquet.

[17] Cf. Zahn, *in loc.*, quoted in note 15 above.

[18] Jesus' words in this place are not the same as those recorded in Matthew, Mark and 1 Corinthians xi. V. Taylor rightly states in this connection: " in narratives which are not reports, there is no reason to infer that the one excludes the other, since more was actually said at the Supper than any one narrative records " (*op. cit.*, p. 183). The Gospels, instead of contradicting, in reality supplement one another. Apart from the reasons mentioned in our running commentary on verse 14 as to why Luke refers only briefly to the institution of the Holy Communion, another possible explanation is " that the Evangelist regarded the narrative of institution as an *arcanum fidei*, to be reserved for believers but hidden from profane eyes " (V. Taylor, *op. cit.*, p. 178). This explanation is especially favoured by J. Jeremias (*Die Abendmahlsworte Jesu*, 1935, pp. 45 ff.). Dalman also declares that it is possible that " the words in connexion with the wine were suppressed, since they might be misunderstood, and lead to accusations against Christ's followers " (*Jesus-Jeshua*, p. 156). Taylor very aptly says: " If the Lukan account is regarded as a narrative of institution and a record of what was said and done, its omissions are serious indeed; but such an assumption is the delusion of an obsolete criticism, . . . such a narrative as Luke gives must be judged in connexion with the narratives which contain them " (*op. cit.*, p. 179).

[19] Expositors differ on the question whether the Gospels teach that Jesus Himself first drank from the cup or not. In our opinion, the question cannot be answered with any certainty.

[20] The A.V. here omits the words ἀπὸ τοῦ νῦν of the original text. The Saviour's words are here, according to the original: ' 'Henceforth I will by no means drink . . .' "

[21] γένημα τῆς ἀμπέλου " is a literal translation of פְּרִי הַגֶּפֶן (*pĕrī haggephen*) in the Passover ritual " (Zahn, *in loc.*)

[22] Although only D a e ff[2] omits verses 19b (from τὸ ὑπὲρ) and 20, and all other MSS. contain it, practically all expositors (conservative as well as liberal) agree that the Western text is the original. The reasons for this are briefly the following: (1) If the original text had indeed included verses 19b and 20, it is inexplicable why " D " and the others omitted them. (2) Would Luke twice have spoken of the giving of the wine, as is the case if verses 19b and 20 are original? (3) The words in verses 19b and 20 agree almost so precisely with Paul's words in 1 Corinthians xi. 25 that it seems as if this is an interpolation of these words in Luke's original text. (4) Verses 19b and 20 would not have been intelligible to Luke's Gentile or Gentile-Christian readers. " Paul could speak thus to a Christian church (1 Cor. xi. 26), after he had first related xi. 17–24 with reference to the Lord's Supper (cf. also 1 Cor. x. 16, 21); but not Luke to the Gentile

Theophilus, who had never attended a celebration of the Lord's Supper " (Zahn, *in loc.*).

Consideration (2) especially carries great weight, since it appears from Matthew xxvi and Mark xiv that Luke xxii. 17, 18 refers to the institution of the Holy Communion cup and not to the dispensing of another one of the four cups given at the paschal repast, for in Matthew xxvi. 29 and Mark xiv. 25 there is the same pronouncement as in Luke xxii. 18. For it is unthinkable that Luke, after already referring to the institution of the Holy Communion cup in xxii. 17, 18, would again describe it in a following verse.

In any case, we know from Matthew, Mark and I Corinthians xi that, even though Luke did not record those words in verses 19b and 20 (for the reasons already mentioned), he certainly, as an experienced Christian and intimate friend of Paul's, knew them well and also knew that Jesus had made those pronouncements. Zahn also is convinced that Luke renders the story of the institution so briefly because he intended " to limit the instruction about this innermost sanctity of Christianity to the members of the Church " (*in loc.*). So nothing is lost by admitting that everything points to the fact that these words are an interpolation of the words from I Corinthians xi in Luke's original text (cf. Hort, *Introd.*, Appendix, pp. 63 ff.).

For an exposition of verses 19b and 20 cf. commentaries on I Corinthians xi (e.g. that by R. St. J. Parry in *Cambridge Greek Testament*, and by A. Robertson and A. Plummer in the *International Critical Commentary*).

[23] Although Matthew and Mark relate the prediction concerning Judas's treachery before describing the story of the institution, they nowhere declare that this was the historical sequence, and so it cannot be alleged that they contradict Luke and John in this respect.

[24] Because the A.V. and other translations fail to translate the γάρ (" for ") of the original text (see R.V.), the close interrelation between 21 and 22 is to a certain extent lost. The " for " or " because " explains how such an amazing thing (21) has come to pass. But Jesus by the words of verse 22b immediately explains that, although the betrayal does not fall outside the overruling will of God, Judas nevertheless acts from his own choice and on his own responsibility and is not the puppet of blind fate.

[25] From verse 24 of this chapter Luke reproduces many particulars not occurring in Mark, and omits most of the details given in Mark. According to Streeter, Taylor and others, this is to be explained from the fact that Luke had already written a preliminary Gospel (" proto-Luke ") before he obtained a copy of Mark. After he had Mark at his disposal, so Streeter argues, he then inserted portions of Mark in sections in his earlier draft. From xxii. 14 until the end he would, on this supposition, have inserted only certain isolated verses from Mark (cf. Streeter, *op. cit.*, p. 216). Creed (*op. cit.*, p. 262) and others, however, contest this view. Such matters can probably never be ascertained with certainty. In any case we know that, under the guidance of the

Holy Ghost, Luke selected from the wealth of reliable information, obtained by him through his careful investigations, what was most important for the particular purpose and scheme which he had in mind when he wrote his Gospel. Each of the Gospel writers obviously had to make a selection from the mass of available particulars concerning Jesus, and as they often made different selections they supplement one another, and thus the four Gospels taken together give a perfect and adequate picture of the Gospel history, the glad tidings concerning Jesus, our Redeemer and Lord.

SPECIAL NOTE

THE USUAL PROCEEDINGS AT A PASCHAL REPAST

In the main the proceedings at a paschal repast in the time of Jesus were as follows. After the household or group of friends who celebrated the feast together were seated around the table on which everything was in readiness for the banquet, and after a blessing had been asked on the feast, the first cup of wine was emptied. After this the father, or another head of the group (generally in reply to the question of the eldest son, Exod. xii. 26 ff.), would relate the story of the Passover (Exod. xii). Next all would join in singing Psalms cxiii and cxiv (the " little hallel "); the second cup of wine was emptied; and then the actual paschal repast (with the sacrificed lamb as main constituent) was eaten. After the conclusion of the meal the third cup (probably the one used by Jesus in instituting the Holy Communion) was sent round after thanks had been returned for the paschal repast. After this another cup of wine was emptied and Psalms cxv–cxviii (the " great hallel ") were chanted to conclude the proceedings. During the proceedings unleavened bread and bitter herbs were eaten. (For a detailed exposition cf. Strack-Billerbeck at Matt. xxvi; Edersheim, *The Temple*, chaps. 11 and 12.)

THE GREATEST SHALL BE THE LEAST

xxii. 24–30

24 And there arose also[1] a contention among them,[2] which of
25 them is accounted to be greatest.[3] And he said unto them,
The kings of the Gentiles have lordship over them; and they
26 that have authority over them are called Benefactors.[4] But ye
shall not *be* so: but he that is the greater[5] among you, let
him become as the younger; and he that is chief, as he that
27 doth serve. For whether is greater, he that sitteth at meat, or
he that serveth? is not he that sitteth at meat? but I am in the
28 midst of you as he that serveth.[6] But ye are they which
29 have continued[7] with me in my temptations;[8] and I appoint[9]
30 unto you a kingdom,[10] even as my Father appointed unto me,
that ye may eat and drink at my table[11] in my kingdom;[12]
and ye shall sit on thrones judging[13] the twelve tribes of
Israel.[14]

Because the disciples were filled with ambition and were constantly viewing the Saviour's Messiahship in the light of their
materialistic expectations, they had frequent dissensions as to
which of them should be accounted the greatest (cf. Matt. xviii.
1–5, xx. 24–8; Mark ix. 33–7, x. 41–5; Luke ix. 46–8).

24 Even on the eve of the crucifixion and probably just before
or during the paschal repast (cf. John xiii. 2), the disciples again
began to quarrel among themselves as to which of them should
be regarded as the most important. The events of the previous
days, in conjunction with all the solemn sayings of Jesus, e.g. in
connection with the destruction of Jerusalem and His second
advent (xxi. 5–36), undoubtedly created an atmosphere of tense
expectation among the disciples. Although the Saviour had so
often taught them that His kingdom was a spiritual and heavenly
kingdom, they could not break away from their expectations that
He would ere long reveal Himself with divine power as Victor
and Ruler on earth and that they then would act under Him as
leaders and rulers over all the other people. They failed to realise
the actuality of His predictions concerning His condemnation and
death; and so they spoiled the sacred atmosphere even on that
evening—the eve of the crucifixion!

Most probably this dispute among the disciples was the immediate cause of the Lord's action in washing their feet, as described in John xiii. When He noticed—we may thus picture the course of events to ourselves—how full of self-seeking and personal ambition His disciples still were, even after all His previous teachings, He stood up without a word, girded Himself and washed their feet (John xiii). When He had finished this and all were again seated quietly round the table, He uttered the words recorded in Luke xxii. 25–30. How forcibly these words would have spoken to the disciples under those circumstances!

25, 26 The rulers and leading men of earthly kingdoms act with outward power and make their inferiors realise very thoroughly that they are their rulers. Obviously, under such circumstances there is a constant competition among the earthly rulers—whosoever acts with the most dominating force is regarded as the most important. In addition, earthly potentates are often so conceited that they claim the title of " benefactors "—they look for fame and honour which they even extort forcibly. Among His followers, however, such a state of affairs must not prevail, Jesus declares. Instead of exploiting their positions (as the eldest or as leaders) to rule over others, the eldest one among them (i.e. the one to whom special honour is due by reason of his more advanced years) must regard himself as the younger one (who does not expect this special reverence). Likewise the one who is called upon to act as leader must carry out his task like one who serves and not like one who has to be served. Leadership should not be regarded as a means of enjoying special privileges over others, but as a specially responsible form of service to be rendered in deep humility before God.

27 In the ordinary condition of affairs the person seated at table is regarded as the important personage and the one who attends upon such a person is looked upon as the inferior. Jesus, however, is the recognised leader among His disciples, and yet His whole life along with them was a life of service—once more proved in a striking manner by the washing of the feet (John xiii).

28–30 After the Saviour had expressed His disapproval of the disciples' ambitions, He points out to them (verse 28) that He appreciates the faithfulness which they had shown to Him during His public life throughout all the difficult circumstances (e.g. owing to the indifference of the people and the hostility of the Jewish authorities). Although He had given to some of them (e.g. Peter) special commissions to exercise leadership, yet their reward will not consist in the receiving of greater or lesser worldly honour and power (as is the case in earthly kingdoms) according to the leading or less leading parts which He assigns to them. On the contrary, their " reward " consists in this, namely, that He makes a covenant with them (just as the Father has allotted authority to Him), that they will at the consummation of the age be privileged to partake with Him of the joy of His kingdom (a joy which is represented by the symbolic words, " eat and drink at my table ") and of the responsibility of leadership in it (represented by the symbol of " sitting on thrones to judge the twelve tribes of Israel "). So the disciples are not to expect earthly glory and worldly power as a reward, but heavenly joy and a holy vocation in His eternal kingdom.

These last two verses show in a striking manner how Jesus, even on the eve of His crucifixion, was perfectly conscious of His divine Sonship. So He goes to meet His death in the firm conviction that the power of divine authority has been given to Him and that His kingdom will eventually be established in perfection, although He must first enter upon the Way of the Cross and persevere in it to the bitter end.

From the nature of the case there are always persons who are called by Christ to give the lead in His church. But those who are called to leadership must never abuse their positions to acquire for themselves fame and power. Leaders in the church of Jesus are called upon to lead through unselfish service for love of Christ and to the honour of God.

---

[1] Luke does not state when this took place, but because he puts it here between verses 23 and 31 and also because John xiii (especially verse 14) practically assumes that such a dispute arose among the disciples at the Last Supper, it is virtually certain that Luke refers to something that took place during the paschal feast.

The measure of agreement existing between Matthew xx. 25–8; Mark x. 42–5 and this section in Luke, is no proof that Luke describes the same occurrence as Matthew and Mark. It was quite natural that such disputes frequently occurred among the disciples, and why could not the Saviour have answered their arguments in words more or less similar to those He had previously uttered in cases of this nature? Although we have here a certain amount of agreement between Luke and Mark (and Matt.), there is also a considerable difference. Thus in Mark x. 42–5 (Matt. xx. 25–8) the question is " how a man *may become* great ". But in Luke xxii. 24–30 Jesus explains how one to whom leadership has been given should act (cf. Schlatter, *in loc.*).

[2] Plummer's suggestion (*in loc.*) that the dispute arose when the disciples seated themselves at the paschal repast, appears to be very convincing—each of the ambitious ones was eager to occupy a seat of

honour at the table. W. Manson (*in loc.*) refers with approval to Dalman's similar suggestion, that the dispute was about the order of precedence at that table.

³ " There is great dramatic, even tragic, power in the way the dispute is brought into the story of the last meal of Jesus and the disciples " (T. W. Manson, *The Mission of Message of Jesus*, p. 630). And then the story fits in excellently in the historical circumstances of that evening (cf. our running commentary on verse 24). In Matthew xx and Mark x the immediate cause was quite different. There James and John (through their mother) had asked the Saviour to assign to them at an early stage positions of the highest honour.

⁴ εὐεργέται καλοῦνται should here be taken as in the " middle voice ": " get themselves called benefactors ", Luce, *in loc.*; " claim the title ", Plummer, *in loc.*; *hunc titulum sibi vindicant*, Bengel, *in loc.* In the Hellenistic world it was a prevalent custom for Gentile rulers to adopt the title Euergetes (cf. Deissmann, *op. cit.*, pp. 253 ff.). " He [Jesus] mentioned the title not without contempt, and forbade His disciples to allow themselves to be so called: the name contradicted the idea of service in brotherhood " (*loc. cit.*). Ptolemy VII of Egypt, one of the Hellenistic rulers who claimed the name εὐεργέτης, was such a villain that his subjects gave him the sarcastic nickname of κακεργέτης (" evildoer ").

⁵ It is assumed that Peter was the eldest: he already possessed his own house and was married, iv. 38, when he joined Jesus as a disciple, and about A.D. 63 he described himself as an " elder " (1 Pet. v. 1). John was the youngest (this is taught by tradition and also follows from the fact that he long survived his fellow-disciples and died only about A.D. 100).

⁶ That Jesus suited His action to these words of His, and taught the disciples the lesson of service on this occasion by practice as well as by precept, is plain from the incident of the feet-washing narrated in John xiii. 4 ff.

⁷ διαμεμενηκότες—" The idea of *persistent loyalty* is enforced by the compound verb " (Plummer, *in loc.*).

⁸ " The things that could move them to forsake Jesus, those were His πειρασμοί. Thus the same formula is used to denote the end of Jesus that every pious Jew employed when he accepted from God's hand suffering imposed upon him. His suffering is a test, a confirmation of the reality and perfection of the faith offered to God and of the obedience accorded Him. So for Jesus too the unbelief of Israel and the rejection and execution which arose from it constitute the test by which He makes visible the truth of His divine Sonship and of His mission. But what served Jesus as a test and strengthening could separate the disciples from Him " (Schlatter, *in loc.*).

⁹ διατίθεμαι is the verb corresponding to the noun διαθήκη in its Biblical sense of " covenant " (Heb. בְּרִית *bĕrīth*), " through which God orders His relation to men according to His will. He orders

it now through that which the Christ is doing " (Schlatter, *in loc.*).
Cf. also Creed, *in loc.* In the covenant which He, their divine Redeemer, makes with them, He promises them the privilege of sharing
with Him in the joy and responsibilities in His kingdom.

¹⁰ βασιλείαν (without the article) should here be translated by
" authority " ("abstract *Herrschaft* ", Klostermann, *in loc.*) and not by
" a kingdom ". It would seem best to take it as the object only of
διέθετο. Then Jesus clearly gives the reason how it is that He, on
the eve of His death, has the right to promise His disciples the privilege
of one day eating and drinking with Him (symbol of " sharing in
joy ") and of sitting on thrones and judging (symbol of " bearing
responsibility ")—because His Father has conferred authority on
Him, He is able to confer these privileges on His faithful disciples.
Verses 29 and 30 should then be translated as follows: " I appoint
unto you, as my Father has assigned authority unto me, that you may
eat and drink at my table . . ." This translation agrees with the punc-
tuation of Westcott and Hort. Zahn, Plummer and Otto contest this
view, but Moffatt, Creed, T. W. Manson, W. Manson, Wellhausen,
Klostermann and Easton accept it. Thus Moffatt translates: " so even
as my Father has assigned me royal power, I assign you the right of
eating and drinking at my table in my Realm. . . ." V. Taylor
similarly says: " It is best to find the object of the verb (διατίθεμαι)
in the clause: ' that ye may eat and drink, . . .' and to reserve
βασιλείαν in the sense of ' lordship ' or ' kingly rule ' (as distinct from
τῇ βασιλείᾳ ' the kingdom ' in verse 30) as the object of διέθετο.
The idea is that, in virtue of the royal power which He has received
from His Father, Jesus can guarantee their participation in the joy of
the perfected rule of God " (*op. cit.*, pp. 188 ff.).

¹¹ That everlasting bliss was often described under the symbol of a
banquet, is evident from the illustrative material supplied by Strack-
Billerbeck, iv., pp. 1154 ff.

¹² τῇ βασιλείᾳ (with the article) should here from the nature of the
case be translated by " kingdom " (and not " authority ").

¹³ κρίνειν here does not mean " to judge " but " to rule " (Wellhausen,
Das Evangelium Lukas), and is thus the symbol for " having a share
in the responsibilities ".

¹⁴ The expression " the twelve tribes of Israel " is not intended
literally, but is " a conventional expression for the members of the
kingdom " (V. Taylor, *op. cit.*, p. 289).

PETER IS WARNED

(Cf. Matt. xxvi. 33-5; Mark xiv. 27-31; John xiii. 36-8)

xxii. 31-4

31   [1]Simon,[2] Simon,[3] behold, Satan asked[4] to have you, that
32 he might sift you[5] as wheat: but I made supplication for thee,
      that thy faith fail not: and do thou, when once thou hast
33 turned again,[6] stablish thy brethren. And he said unto
      him, Lord, with thee I am ready to go both to prison and to
34 death. And he said, I tell thee, Peter,[7] the cock shall not crow[8]
      this day, until thou shalt thrice deny that thou knowest me.[9]

Luke often does not state at what time precisely the Saviour
uttered certain words.

31   Thus all we can say of verses 31-4 is that they contain
words uttered during the evening before His crucifixion. From
Matthew xxvi. 33 and John xiii. 31, 36-8 it appears, however,
that the Lord warned Peter only after they had left the house in
which the paschal repast was held. By addressing Peter as
" Simon, Simon " (with the repetition), the Saviour calls upon
him to realise the seriousness of the matter which He is going to
discuss. And by calling him " Simon " instead of " Peter ",
Jesus reminds him of his human weakness—he is, as regards his
own powers, not " Peter ", " the rock ", but a mere helpless
human being. Satan, the powerful opponent of Him and His
followers, had—Jesus declares—asked for and obtained the right
of subjecting all the disciples to a severe test (hoping that their
loyalty towards Christ and their faith in Him might be proved
unreal and evanescent). Just as in Job's case, God allowed Satan
this liberty, but always within bounds—the Evil One has no free
and unlimited right to act against the faithful, but must always
submit to the overruling and permissive authority of the Lord.
    In the impending events (His arrest and crucifixion) Satan will
make a last desperate attempt to break up the circle of Jesus'
disciples and to cast out its members like chaff scattered by the
wind. Satan desires that in the sifting process " no wheat shall
remain ", but that all (like Judas) will be blown away like chaff.
    32   The Saviour, however, prayed for all His faithful disciples

566

(John xvii), and specially prayed for Peter, who played and still had to play such a leading part, that God should preserve him from utter shipwreck of his faith. While Satan thus acts as the cunning adversary, Jesus acts as the intercessor, the advocate of His disciples and especially of that particular one whom He had previously pointed out as the leader amongst them. So the Saviour assures Peter that, as a result of His intercession, his faith will not be completely destroyed, although he will stray and become unfaithful for a time. However, after being again brought back to his former faith and loyalty through the power of God, he must help the other disciples (who will also stumble and be temporarily overwhelmed through the severe test to which they are to be subjected) to become strong again in their faith and loyalty towards Christ.

33 Peter, however, is so sure of himself and of his own power and loyalty that he is unwilling to believe that he will become unfaithful and will have to undergo a " conversion ". Impulsive and impetuous as ever, he declares that he is prepared to go along with Jesus even into prison and death.

34 The Saviour, however, knows Peter's inward human weakness too well (cf. Peter's impetuosity in climbing out of the ship and going to Jesus on the water, and his terror when he began to sink), and warns him very expressly that he will not remain firm, but will deny Him, not once but repeatedly, and not in the distant future but during that very night, before daybreak.

In the story of Peter's fatal self-confidence and pitiable fall every believer has a permanent and powerful warning never to rely arrogantly on his own strength. A healthy confidence is indeed necessary to every Christian, but this must be in the sense of reliance on God—i.e. faith, not in our own resources, but in the power given to us by Him.

---

[1] $\varepsilon \tilde{\iota} \pi \varepsilon \nu$ $\delta \grave{\varepsilon}$ $\mathring{\sigma}$ $\varkappa \acute{\upsilon} \rho \iota o \varsigma$ (before the repeated $\Sigma \acute{\iota} \mu \omega \nu$) is evidently a later addition, since it would not have been omitted by the majority of MSS. if it had been original. It is, however, easily understandable that copyists would insert these words here, as each feels that a new conversation commences here.

[2] It is true that Luke first relates in verse 39 that Jesus went to the Mount of Olives, but he does not there state that He departed *after* He had pronounced the preceding words (verses 31–8), but merely $\varkappa a \acute{\iota}$ $\mathring{\varepsilon} \xi \varepsilon \lambda \theta \grave{\omega} \nu$ $\mathring{\varepsilon} \pi o \rho \varepsilon \acute{\upsilon} \theta \eta$ (" and having gone out, He went "). Luke, therefore, by no means professes here to give a chronological record of the events and words. He does indeed, as he himself declares in i. 1–4,

relate the Gospel narrative in an ordered form—logically, aesthetically and also chronologically (*in its salient features*), but nowhere pretends to give all his sub-divisions as well in strictly chronological order. Consequently it is unwarranted to say, as so many expositors do, that Luke here contradicts the three other Gospels (e.g. Mark xiv. 26–31).

[3] " The name Simon, which his father gave him . . . reminded him of his inborn nature, which made him susceptible to attacks of every sort " (Zahn, *in loc.*).

[4] ἐξητήσατο—" obtained you by asking " (so R.V. margin; cf. Plummer, *in loc.*, who goes on: " The aorist of the compound verb necessarily implies *success* in the petition "). Cf. Job i. 12, ii. 6.

[5] It was Satan's purpose to bring the disciples to utter ruin, but because Jesus prayed for them, these very temptations worked together for their good: " The sifting of wheat, through which alien matter is separated from it, is an indispensable and wholesome process. As Satan undertakes this ' sifting ', he destroys that which Jesus also hates: all untruthfulness, all play-acting, all ὑπόκρισις " (Schlatter, *in loc.*).

[6] ἐπιστρέψας should here be taken in an intransitive sense as in Acts iii. 19, " having turned (having been converted) ". It is an historical fact that Peter was the first of the disciples to whom Jesus appeared after His resurrection (1 Cor. xv. 5; cf. Luke xxiv. 34), and from then on (especially on the day of Pentecost) he acted as the leader and builder up of the first believers. Thus Jesus' prayer was answered and Peter obeyed the Saviour's command to strengthen his brothers.

[7] " Jesus' word ' Peter ' (' thou who art called Rock ') is pregnant with the contrast at this moment between his disciple's high calling and his downfall " (W. Manson, *in loc.*).

[8] In the New Testament the night, according to the Roman usage, is divided into four watches: 6–9 p.m., 9–12 p.m.; 12–3 a.m., 3–6 a.m. The third night watch has also been described as extending from midnight until the cock crows. It is indeed a fact that cocks crow practically regularly at about 3 a.m. Occasionally, however, it does happen that they crow at about midnight. The regular time for the cock-crow is, however, about 3 a.m. When, therefore, as in Matthew xxvi, Luke and John xiii, cock-crow in general is mentioned, the time of the night is meant which ends about 3 a.m. Mark, however, states that Jesus said: " before the cock has crowed *twice* ", and mentions in his account of Peter's denial that during that night a cock-crow was heard twice (one before and one just after Peter's third denial). We observe throughout how (as tradition also teaches) in Mark there are numerous indications that it was especially Peter's personal recollections that were recorded in that Gospel. It is, moreover, obvious that, especially in such a case as the prediction concerning this denial and the denial itself, Peter would have had an ineffaceable recollection of the smallest details of the Saviour's words and the succeeding events. So we are not surprised that in Mark the prophecy and course of the events are described in greater detail than in the other Gospels

Substantially, however, the accounts amount to much the same thing: Jesus prophesied that before the end of the third night-watch Peter would already have denied Him repeatedly. Matthew, Luke and John reproduce the main gist of the Lord's words and of the relevant events. Mark, however, as recorder of Peter's recollections, also mentions the smaller details; Mark " relates more definitely; the others more generally " (Irwin). Thus the Gospels supplement one another.

[9] It has been well said: " The inclusion of this prediction in the Gospel tradition and its subsequent fulfilment is a testimony to the historical truth of that tradition. It is impossible to imagine that such a story could have been circulated in the primitive church about its chief apostle unless the story were true " (Major, *op. cit.*, p. 174).

THE TWO SWORDS

35 And he said unto them,[1] When I sent you forth without
purse, and wallet, and shoes, lacked ye anything? And they
36 said, Nothing. And he said unto them, But now, he that
hath a purse, let him take it, and likewise a wallet: and he
37 that hath none, let him sell his cloke, and buy a sword.[2] For
I say unto you, that this which is written must be fulfilled in
me, And he was reckoned with transgressors: for[3] that which
38 concerneth me hath fulfilment. And they said,[4] Lord, behold,
here are two swords.[5] And he said unto them, It is enough.[6]

For many months, indeed for several years, the disciples
enjoyed the privilege of associating with the Master during the
time of His public ministry. The hour of parting is, however,
approaching, and a complete, drastic and far-reaching revolution
is impending.

35 During the time when the Saviour, because of His miracles
of healing and other charitable work among the needy multitudes,
did not yet experience much opposition and enmity, His disciples, when He sent them out (ix. 3; x. 4), were treated with
great respect by the people. Although the Lord at that time
commanded them to go without purse, scrip and shoes, they were
so hospitably received wherever they went, that they suffered
no want. Everything was made easy and prosperous for them,
and they returned with joy (x. 17).

36 But, says the Saviour, the hour has now struck when
everything is going to be different. From now on He will no
longer be with them in the same way as before and they will no
longer be honoured and entertained, as before, because they are
the disciples of an honoured and beloved Master. He has already
been rejected by the Jewish authorities and ere long He will be
killed and looked upon as a hated criminal by practically the
whole people. The immediate result will be that they, as the
followers of the Crucified One, will likewise be despised, pushed
out and persecuted. So they can no longer depend on any
generous provision for their needs on the part of the people.
Therefore they will henceforth, with all their strength and energy,
have to find their own way through a hostile world. They must,

the Saviour declares in a striking figure, as His followers in the struggle of life, be just as determined and whole-hearted as a fighting man who gives up everything, even his garment, as long as he only possesses a sword to continue the struggle with.

37 This state of affairs will arise because the predictions (Isa. liii) concerning Him, that He will be reckoned as a transgressor and killed as such, are now going to be fulfilled. And as things are going with Him, their Master, so it will henceforth go with them, too—therefore it is so necessary that for their spiritual warfare they must be thoroughly equipped and armed at whatever cost with an unbreakable courage and determination, so that they will not relinquish the struggle.

38 The disciples are still blind to the spiritual nature of the Lord's work and kingdom. They are still hoping that He will establish an earthly Messianic kingdom with physical force. So they take the Saviour's words regarding the buying of a sword in a literal sense and do not understand their real meaning. In the light of the Saviour's other teachings (e.g. in the sermon on the mount) and of His perfect example, the disciples should never have taken those words literally. He does not rebuke them because they still have such a false notion of things that they could expect Him to be commanding armed violence, but ends the discussion sorrowfully. Later on during the night He forbade His disciples to use the sword, and by healing the wounded servant (verse 51) He taught them plainly and visibly that the use of the sword is not lawful in the defence of His cause. Therefore His words in verse 36 should not be taken literally but in a figurative sense.

To be a whole-hearted follower of the Crucified One in a world which is in the power of sin and of the Evil One brings unavoidably for the believer scorn and hate on the part of those who reject God and His Christ. And the only way to remain firm in such a world is to be spiritually equipped with His power and armed with the sword of His Word. The use of material force in the vindication and extension of His church on earth, as has, alas, been advocated by some sections of Christendom, is quite foreign to the teaching of Jesus.

[1] V. Taylor rightly states of the whole of this pericope: " Every detail in the section is true to the situation in which Jesus found himself on the last night of His earthly life and can readily be understood in relation thereto " (*Jesus and His Sacrifice*, p. 192).

[2] Although a few, like J. Weiss and Goguel (*The Life of Jesus*, p. 454), declare that these words are intended literally, there is no doubt (in the light of Jesus' whole teaching and life) that the Lord intended them in a figurative sense. Most expositors are agreed on this point. Thus Dr. Luce declares: " Jesus' words are metaphorical and spoken with a sad irony " (*in loc.*). And Plummer: " Christ does not mean that they are to repel force by force; still less that they are to use force in spreading the Gospel. But in a figure likely to be remembered He warns them of the changed circumstances for which they must now be prepared ". V. Taylor, Lagrange, Easton, Zahn and others also take the words in a figurative sense. And T. W. Manson is right in stating: " The verse has nothing to say directly on the question whether armed resistance to injustice and evil is ever justifiable. It is simply a vivid pictorial way of describing the complete change which has come about in the temper and attitude of the Jewish people since the days of the disciples' mission. The disciples understood the saying literally and so missed the point; but that is no reason why we should follow their example " (*The Mission and Message of Jesus*, p. 633). Schlatter expresses it beautifully: " Because He was not thinking of their weapons, the disciples require that courage which regards a sword as more necessary than an upper garment and surrenders even its last possession, but cannot give up the struggle " (*in loc.*).

[3] καὶ γάρ. Plummer's view is the best here, where he declares that the words are " an extension of the argument . . . this fulfilment is not only necessary—it is reaching its conclusion. . . . The phrase τέλος ἔχειν is used of oracles and predictions being accomplished " (*in loc.*).

[4] " That Jesus should have been misunderstood by the twelve is part of the dramatic irony of a tense situation. The cry: ' Lord, behold, here are two swords,' reveals the fact that they have merely caught the surface meaning of His words " (V. Taylor, *op. cit.*, p. 193). In his notorious papal bull *Unam Sanctam*, Boniface VIII (A.D. 1302) built on this text his doctrine that the Pope has the right to exercise secular as well as spiritual autocratic rule over mankind—the two swords, he said, are the spiritual sword and the secular sword.

[5] It was very natural that at least the impetuous and impulsive Peter should, under the circumstances of extreme tension, have had a sword with him that evening, even though it was against the Jewish ordinances. There is, however, no proof that at the time of Christ it was forbidden to carry weapons on Easter Eve (Edersheim, *Life and Times*, ii, *in loc.*, and Strack-Billerbeck, at Matt. xxvi. 51). So this verse gives no indication, as is often maintained, that this was not Passover Eve.

[6] These words are " both a formula of dismissal (Deut. iii. 26 in LXX) and an utterance of the deepest sadness: ' It is enough ' " (V. Taylor, *loc. cit.*). With this expression " Jesus, disappointed at their obtuseness, lets the subject drop " (Luce, *in loc.*). Cf. also Plummer, Creed, T. W. Manson, W. Manson.

JESUS IN GETHSEMANE

(Cf. Matt. xxvi. 36–46; Mark xiv. 32–4)

xxii. 39–46

39 And he came out, and went, as his custom was,[1] unto the
40 mount of Olives;[2] and the disciples also followed him. And
   when he was at the place,[3] he said unto them, Pray[4] that ye
41 enter[5] not into temptation. And he was parted from them
   about a stone's cast;[6] and he kneeled down[7] and prayed,
42 saying, Father,[8] if thou be willing, remove this cup[9] from
43 me: nevertheless[10] not my will, but thine, be done.[11] And
   there appeared unto him an angel from heaven, strengthen-
44 ing him.[12] And being in an agony[13] he prayed more
   earnestly: and his sweat became as it were[14] great drops of
45 blood falling down upon the ground. And when he rose up
   from his prayer, he came unto the disciples, and found them
46 sleeping for sorrow,[15] and said unto them, Why sleep ye?
   rise and pray,[16] that ye enter not into temptation.

We now enter into the inner sanctuary of the Gospel history
and behold the awe-inspiring commencement of our Lord's
passion—a suffering which ended only after He had endured the
experience of being totally forsaken by God on the cross, and
entered into the obscure depths of death. Here, at the commencement of this passion, we see the final drama of His voluntary
and complete self-surrender to God.

39 The time had now arrived for Jesus to surrender Himself
as the Eternal Expiatory Sacrifice into the hands of His enemies
to be condemned and crucified. For this reason He does not try
to frustrate the plans of Judas, who earlier in the evening (we do
not know exactly when) had left the supper-room in order to go
and betray Him. He goes, accompanied by His eleven faithful
disciples, to the Mount of Olives where He had mostly spent the
nights during the week since His entry into Jerusalem—to the
place where Judas is expecting Him and whither he will lead the
band that is to arrest Him. At an earlier period of His ministry
the Saviour had on several occasions evaded His enemies by
supernatural power or by means of special precautions when they
desired to kill Him. His hour at that time had not yet come.

573

Now, when His public ministry was concluded and He had given the sign that the Old Dispensation was now passing away by instituting the Holy Communion to supersede the Old Testament Passover—now that everything has been completed, He knows that His hour has struck and He goes to the place where He knows that His enemies will soon come to arrest Him.

40 The Saviour all the time continues in His complete faithful devotion towards His disciples, and although His impending suffering is already looming so dreadfully in His mental vision (verse 37), He takes their interests so much to heart in His selfless love that He still makes time to urge on them the necessity of maintaining communion in prayer with God so that they may remain firm amidst the deluge of temptations soon to burst forth over them.

41 Luke gives only a brief summary of the events in Gethsemane, and in so doing he makes no mention, e.g., of the fact that Jesus at first made His three most intimate followers stay near Him (Matt. xxvi. 37), nor of the fact that the Lord came to these three disciples several times and then went back to wrestle in prayer.

42 In every normal person there exists the urge to continue to live, accompanied by an aversion from suffering and death. Obviously, therefore, Jesus, who was completely Man and not subject to any blunting of His emotions or to any form of inward hardening, is infinitely more sensitive in His feeling of repugnance to unnatural things. It is impossible for Him, in His perfect humanity, not to experience a feeling of opposition to the idea of impending humiliation, suffering and death. And all this is made the more intense through His knowledge that He is not only going to suffer and die, but that He will have to undergo this as the expiatory sacrifice for the sin of guilty mankind. The holy and just wrath of God against sin fall on Him in full measure, because He has put Himself unreservedly in the place of guilty mankind. The judgment pronounced on sin is death—spiritual as well as physical. And spiritual death means being utterly forsaken by God. How dreadful, then, must the idea have been to Christ, who had from eternity lived in the most intimate and unbroken communion with His Father, that He would have to endure all this! How terrible the knowledge that He, who Himself was without sin, would on the accursed tree, sentenced like a condemned criminal, be laden with the sin of all mankind as the willing and sacrificial Lamb of God! No man will ever be capable of sounding the depths of what the Saviour experienced in Gethsemane when the full reality of His suffering in soul and

574

body penetrated into His immaculate spirit. When we hear His words on the cross: " My God, My God, why hast thou forsaken Me? " the veil is lifted for a moment once more that we may see something of what He endured for the sake of a guilty world.

However much the Saviour's whole being recoiled from all that awaited Him, and however violently the power of evil in those moments made a last attempt with all possible subtlety to frighten Him away from the way of crucifixion, yet, notwithstanding all this, Jesus did not entertain even the least degree of sin or refusal to follow the road to the bitter end. It is natural and right that under the intense pressure of circumstances He should pray: " Father, if thou be willing, remove this cup from me! " But immediately He continues: " Nevertheless not my will, but thine, be done! " And thus He surrenders Himself again, voluntarily and unconditionally, to drain the cup of suffering and death to the last drop, in accordance with the will of God as revealed in the Old Testament prophecies and in the heart of the Saviour Himself ever since the commencement of His public ministry.

43 Jesus had finally chosen to be sacrificed as the Lamb of God. The dreadfulness of all the anguish that He endured in the garden when He had to make His final choice demanded so much from His strength in soul and body that an angel is sent from heaven to strengthen Him, so as to enable Him to complete the way of suffering and not to die before His task is accomplished.

44 In spite of His complete and willing surrender to bear the sin of the world in His sacrificial death, He feels its full dreadfulness so intensely as He prays that His body, too, is taxed to the utmost, so that His sweat was like drops of blood running from Him and falling down to the ground.

45 At last the wrestling in prayer is over and He returns to His disciples with inward composure and strength, willing and ready to enter upon the road to the cross and to follow it to the end. The experiences of the previous days, and especially of that final night, coupled with the words of warning uttered by Jesus, and His whole demeanour that evening, had overwhelmed the disciples and left them strengthless and sorrowful. For this reason, and also because it had been a busy day and night was now far advanced, they had fallen asleep.

46 The Saviour, knowing in what circumstances of extreme distress they are soon to find themselves, wakens them and urges them once more to watch and pray, for only by remaining in living communion with God will they be able to resist the temptations that will assail them in the terrible happenings of that night and the following days.

We shall never be able to understand or feel the full depth of the struggle and distress which Jesus as our Substitute experienced in Gethsemane, while remaining perfect in loyalty towards His Father. But this we know: it was there that He made His final choice to take our sins upon Him, and for the sake of our redemption to suffer and to die. Shall we then not choose to devote our all to His service as the least thank-offering we can pay to His honour?

¹ The expression κατὰ τὸ ἔθος " helps us to understand the happenings, because we are thus guarded against the supposition that Jesus went there to hinder or delay the arrest. He betook Himself to the place where Judas was looking for Him " (Schlatter, *in loc.*).

² It is untrue, as some object, that persons attending the paschal repast were forbidden to leave Jerusalem. The only rule in this connection at the time of Jesus was that those taking part in the paschal repast might not go farther than the surrounding spots, like Bethphage (cf. Strack-Billerbeck, ii, p. 883; and Dalman, *Sacred Sites and Ways*, pp. 250 ff., and *Jesus-Jeshua*, pp. 95 ff.).

³ Luke omits the Jewish name " Gethsemane " (oil-press), because it would not be intelligible to his Greek readers. By " the place " he means " the place at the Mount of Olives where Jesus was accustomed to spend the nights".

⁴ προσεύχεσθε—the word for prayer in general—worship, thanks, confession, supplication, the exercise of communion with God in prayer.

⁵ εἰσελθεῖν, " enter into ", signifying *to yield to* (Godet, *in loc.*).

⁶ The question is sometimes asked: how could the apostles have known how Jesus prayed and what He experienced in Gethsemane, since He had separated Himself from them and they were asleep? The answer is that, as Matthew and Mark inform us, Jesus was close to His three intimate disciples. Obviously He was engaged in prayer a long time and the disciples did not immediately fall asleep. They would undoubtedly have been awake for at least half an hour or so and would have seen and heard Him and themselves have prayed for some time before falling asleep. And—the youthful Mark was probably close at hand (cf. Mark xiv. 51-2).

⁷ The usual manner of prayer at that time was to pray in a standing position. That Jesus knelt down proves the violence of His struggle in Gethsemane (cf. Strack-Billerbeck, *in loc.*, for a description of attitudes of prayer at that time).

[8] Luke again omits the Aramaic word " Abba " (Father), preserved in Mark xiv. 36, because this word would be unknown to his Greek readers.

[9] The contention that the Saviour's struggle in Gethsemane proves that He did not know and foretell at an early time during His ministry that He would be killed, has no foundation in fact. " That Jesus should foretell his passion and yet shrink from the appalling form which it had now assumed before his mind, is explicable, when we do not discount altogether the human nature of Jesus " (W. Manson, *in loc.*). " His desire, according to His human nature, could not be otherwise than to live, and to wish that the judgment and His being forsaken by God might be averted; His perfect, normal manhood would probably have shuddered and shrunk from this. An *absence* of such an effect is abnormal, a fruit of sin which blunts sensation; and when the fear of death has been overcome, then it is only because of Him, who ' was heard in that he feared ', Hebrew. v. 7 " (Van Leeuwen at Mark xiv. 36).

[10] On the significance of the struggle in Gethsemane Godet writes: " The Lamb of God must be distinguished from typical victims by His free acceptance of death as the punishment of sin; and hence there required to be in His life a decisive moment, when, in the fullness of His consciousness and liberty, He *should accept* the punishment (for the guilty world) which He was to undergo. At Gethsemane Jesus did not drink the cup; He consented to drink it " (*in loc.*).

[11] " The weakness of the flesh, in which He as substitute undergoes the fear of death, was at no moment clearer than in the struggle in Gethsemane; but the boundary line between weakness and sin was not crossed: He submitted it to the Father's will" (Van Leeuwen, *loc. cit.*).

[12] There exists no conclusive proof that verses 43 and 44 do not belong to the original text of Luke. On the contrary, even Harnack, Streeter, Loisy, Creed and others defend their authenticity. Most probably the verses were omitted by later copyists because they had no clear idea of the Saviour's real humanity and could therefore not understand why an angel had to strengthen Him and why He had to experience such a conflict.

[13] C. Morgan says with regard to the Gethsemane story: " All I can say is that as I ponder it, through that darkened window there is a mystic light shining, showing me the terrors of the Cross more clearly than I see them even when I come to Calvary " (*in loc.*).

[14] " As Luke, by the use of ὡσεί, says plainly enough that he is using a simile, and is speaking neither of a change of the sweat into drops of blood nor of a mixture of sweat with blood, his meaning cannot be that in these words he is describing something physically miraculous " (Zahn, *in loc.*). Luke merely wishes to call attention to the fact that, as a result of the severe strain so much sweat was wrung from the Saviour that it trickled down and fell upon the ground in great drops. When the Saviour awakened the disciples, they could

easily have noticed how violently He had perspired and how fierce the latter part of His conflict must have been.

[15] Only Luke, the physician and the expert connoisseur of the human mind, mentions this fact as an explanation why the disciples could not remain awake throughout.

[16] Even the Jewish scholar, Montefiore, declares concerning the story of the events in Gethsemane: " One cannot but marvel at the wonderful grace and beauty, the exquisite tact and discretion, which the narrative displays. There is not a word too little; there is not a word too much " (at Mark xiv; Vol. i, p. 342).

JESUS IS ARRESTED

(Cf. Matt. xxvi. 47–56; Mark xiv. 43–50; John xviii. 2–11)

xxii. 47–53

47 While he yet spake, behold, a multitude, and he that was
called Judas,[1] one of the twelve, went before them; and he
48 drew near unto Jesus to kiss him.[2] But Jesus said unto him,
49 Judas, betrayest thou the Son of man[3] with a kiss? And when
they that were about him saw what would follow, they said,
50 Lord, shall we smite with the sword? And a certain one[4]
of them smote the servant of the high priest, and struck off
51 his right[5] ear. But Jesus answered and said, Suffer ye thus
52 far.[6] And he touched his ear, and healed him.[7] And Jesus
said unto the chief priests,[8] and captains of the temple, and
elders, which were come against him, Are ye come out, as
53 against a robber, with swords[9] and staves? When I was daily
with you in the temple, ye stretched not forth your hands
against me: but this is your hour,[10] and the power of darkness.[11]

In the silence and seclusion of Gethsemane where Jesus was
alone with His Father He had knelt down to Him in utter anguish
of spirit. But now, after His final and complete surrender of
Himself to be sacrificed and thus to bring to fulfilment God's
eternal plan of salvation, He acts with perfect calmness and fearlessness. Before His Father He had knelt down deeply in complete
self-surrender, but, just as in His former ministry, so now, in the
last stages of the way of humiliation, suffering and death He shows
not the least sign of weakness or fear of His persecutors and judges.
That He, in His perfect humanity, is master of the situation in the
presence of His enemies, even when outwardly it seems as though
He is their powerless prey, comes out forcibly in the story of His
arrest.

47, 48 The crisis concerning which Jesus had warned the
disciples was closer at hand than they ever could imagine. While
He is still talking to them, a multitude led by Judas appears on
the scene. Through fear of possible resistance on the part of
His disciples, a comparatively large group of temple guards and

579

members of the Sanhedrin came to arrest Him. The traitor had arranged with Jesus' persecutors that the one whom he would salute with a kiss would be the Nazarene whom they sought, so that, especially since it was night, there might be no risk of their capturing the wrong person and of Jesus' possible escape. When they came to the Saviour and His disciples, the traitor immediately stepped forward to salute the Lord with a kiss and thus to indicate Him as the one whom they had come for. From Mark xiv. 45 we know that the Saviour permitted him to do this, and only afterwards said to him: " Judas, betrayest thou the Son of man with a kiss? " In these last words of the Lord to one who had so often had the opportunity of learning from Him and of knowing and loving Him, but who loved the darkness more than the light, He for the last time tries to bring him to his senses and to a realisation of his terrible conduct, so that he may still come to true repentance in time.

49, 50 Even before the Saviour could reply to the question of the disciples (probably the two armed with " swords ") whether they must try to prevent His arrest by the power of the sword, the impetuous Peter had already grazed the head of Malchus, the servant of the high priest (John xviii. 10), and cut off his right ear.

51 Through Peter's thoughtless act the Saviour is placed in a difficult position. For now His enemies may easily accuse Him of being the leader of a group of violent men. The Lord therefore immediately forbids His disciples to offer any further resistance. And in order to remedy the injury already inflicted, He immediately heals the wounded servant. The Saviour *must* be killed as the Sacrificial Lamb of God. But there must not be the slightest cause for His enemies to accuse Him! So the Saviour repairs the mischief wrought by His impulsive disciple in his foolish short-sightedness, and thus He could subsequently declare before Pilate without fear of contradiction: " My kingdom is not of this world; if my kingdom were of this world, then would my servants fight, that I should not be delivered to the Jews: but now is my kingdom not from hence " (John xviii. 36).

52, 53 The Saviour acted with such evident calmness and fearlessness, yea, even with kingly majesty (John xviii. 6), towards His betrayer and persecutors, that they were still too much overawed to lay their hands on Him. During the silence that followed upon the healing of the servant, the Saviour addressed the Jewish leaders who had come along with the soldiers to be present at His arrest. By His question and subsequent words He rebukes them for the glaring insincerity and cowardice of their whole conduct:

although they know well enough that He is no thief or murderer against whom action must be taken by force of arms, they bring an armed force against Him as though He were a dangerous criminal. If He were really guilty, they could long ago have had Him taken in public when He was teaching in the temple. But because they themselves are in the wrong and He is innocent, they come under cover of night outside Jerusalem to carry out their wicked plans here where there are none of the people present. Thus Jesus' words reveal the fact that, instead of conducting themselves as the real upholders of right and justice, they are acting with underhand means and dark motives. They will succeed in carrying out their unholy plans, not merely because they are working under cover of natural darkness, but especially because in that hour the evil powers of darkness, Satan and his henchmen (men and spirits alike), are being permitted by God to bring the Son of the Highest down into the grip of humiliation, suffering and death—not because He is not mighty enough to prevent all this, but because He voluntarily delivers Himself to be sacrificed for the salvation of guilty mankind.

Judas had for a long time had the privilege of associating with the intimate circle of Jesus' disciples, and yet he had allowed the powers of evil to dominate his inner life to such an extent that he betrayed the Master. And to-day also there is always the dreadful possibility that even persons who are regarded as intimate followers of Christ may in small matters or in great commit treachery against their Master and Lord.

---

[1] The motive for Judas's conduct is not divulged. " The rule remains in force that the sinful course is not brought to light any further than it reveals itself " (Schlatter, *in loc.*). In any case it is clear from the Gospel records that Judas's action was base in the extreme. " Nothing I can say in denunciation of Judas would begin to approach the realm of words sufficient to denounce the dark and dastardly act. No brilliant essayist or clever novelist has ever been able to redeem Judas in the thinking of upright men from the evil of that betrayal " (Morgan, *in loc.*).

[2] From John xvii. 4 it appears that the action of Jesus who stepped forward fearlessly and of His own accord declared that He was the One they sought, rendered the sign given by Judas superfluous and even ridiculous.

[3] The Saviour here calls Himself " Son of Man " in order to make Judas realise that he is busy in betraying not merely a human being but the divine Messiah. Thus his guilt is all the more heinous.

⁴ When John wrote his Gospel long after Luke, there was no longer any danger that the Jewish authorities would take action against Peter who had conducted himself so aggressively towards the servant of the high priest, so he mentioned his name in John xviii. 10. Moreover, as a result of his acquaintance with the high-priestly household, he remembered the name of the servant.

⁵ Only Luke, the physician, mentions the particular that it was his right ear.

⁶ Ἐᾶτε ἕως τούτου—" It is better to refer τούτου to the arrest: ' Let events take their course—even to my arrest ' " (Creed, *in loc.*). " Let them alone even up to this point " (Luce, *in loc.*). " Suffer My assailants to proceed these lengths against Me " (Plummer, *in loc.*). It is far better and more natural to take it as the above expositors put it than to regard the words as a request to His enemies to excuse the conduct of His disciples.

⁷ Here Luke again mentions a fact in which he obviously takes more interest as physician than Matthew and Mark.

⁸ " There is nothing improbable in the presence of the ἀρχιερεῖς [' chief priests '] who are mentioned by Luke alone. Anxiety about the arrest, which might be frustrated by a miscalculation of time, or by the people or by a miracle, would induce them to be present " (Plummer, *in loc.*). Especially in the description of the last occurrences of the Gospel story, it is necessary to remember that very much more was done and said than is recorded in the separate Gospels or even in all four together.

⁹ There is no evidence that it was forbidden to carry weapons during the Passover at the time of Christ (cf. Strack-Billerbeck, ii. p. 828). In addition, extraordinary circumstances demand extraordinary action—when the Jewish authorities felt justified in causing anyone to be arrested on the day of the festival if they regarded him guilty of blasphemy, they would also have felt justified in sending an armed band to do so.

¹⁰ " This is your hour of success allowed by God; and it coincides with that allowed to the power of darkness " (Plummer, *in loc.*).

¹¹ It is true that, as Godet has put it, " darkness is favourable to crime; for man needs to be concealed not only from others, but from himself, in order to sin. For this reason, night is the time when Satan puts forth all his power over humanity; it is *his hour.* And hence, adds Jesus, it is also *yours,* for you are his instruments in the work which you are doing " (*in loc.*). The Saviour's words, however, include still more (see our exposition).

PETER DENIES JESUS

(Cf. Matt. xxvi. 69–75; Mark xiv. 66–72; John xviii. 15–27)

xxii. 54–62

54 And they seized him, and led him *away*, and brought him
55 into the high priest's house. But Peter followed afar off. And
when they had kindled a fire in the midst of the court, and had
56 sat down together, Peter sat in the midst of them. And a
certain maid seeing him as he sat in the light *of the fire*, and
looking stedfastly upon him, said, This man also was with
57 him. But he denied, saying, Woman, I know him not.
58 And after a little while another saw him, and said, Thou also
59 art *one* of them. But Peter said, Man, I am not. And after
the space of about one hour another confidently affirmed,
saying, Of a truth this man also was with him: for he is a
60 Galilæan. But Peter said, Man, I know not what thou
sayest. And immediately, while he yet spake, the cock crew.[1]
61 And the Lord turned, and looked upon Peter.[2] And Peter
remembered the word of the Lord, how that he said unto
him, Before the cock crow[3] this day, thou shalt deny me
62 thrice. And he went out, and wept bitterly.

Although the disciples that evening undoubtedly had presentiments of impending disaster, they nevertheless, in spite of
Jesus' warnings, could never think that matters would take their
course so quickly and fatally.

54 Just as a flock, when the shepherd is struck down, becomes
terrified and scattered in flight, so the circle of disciples dispersed
in confusion when Jesus was arrested. We do not know whither
the other disciples fled, but we do know that Peter followed his
captured Lord at a distance and that John, the beloved disciple,
was also present at the trial in the house of the high priest (John
xviii. 15).

55–7 In the inner court of the high-priestly dwelling Peter,
after being admitted through the intercession of John who was
well acquainted with the high priest (John xviii. 15), joined the
soldiers and others who were sitting there around a fire. The
portress, when Peter entered, already formed the suspicion that
he was a follower of Jesus (John xviii. 17), and when he took his

place amongst the group at the fire she looked at him earnestly and then openly declared that he was a follower of the Prisoner. Overcome with fear, Peter immediately denies that he knows Him. What a pathetic figure Peter is here! He is the man who had, only a few hours before, declared with so much self-confidence and impetuosity that he would never deny Jesus, but was ready even to enter into death along with Him! After he had denied the Saviour for the first time, he went to the outer court. It was about midnight, and when he reached the outer court he heard a cock crow (Mark xiv. 28). Afterwards he returned to the inner court. But this time he does not go and sit among the group as before (verse 55), for, as he was far from feeling himself at home, he went and *stood* with them (John xviii. 18).

58 The portress again noticed him there (Mark xiv. 69). She does not, however, again address the apostle himself, but tells those present that he belongs to the Prisoner's circle of disciples (Mark xiv. 69). Stimulated by her words, some of the group round the fire looked at Peter, and when one of them also recognised him as a follower of the Nazarene, he (on behalf of the others who were with him, John xviii. 25) put it to the apostle that he *was* a disciple of Jesus. And again Peter denies it.

59, 60 Some time afterwards another of the bystanders (as mouthpiece of the group in the inner court, Mark xiv. 70) declared that Peter was definitely a follower of the Nazarene because his speech proved that he was a Galilean, and it was well known that His followers were mostly Galileans (it was highly improbable that there would have been another Galilean that night among the soldiers and other Jerusalemites in the inner court of the house). But Peter denied most emphatically (Mark xiv. 71) that he had ever had anything to do with Jesus or that he even knew Him. While he was still busy denying Jesus with many imprecations, the cock crew again (probably about the time that cocks usually crew during the third watch, i.e. between 1 and 3 a.m.).

61, 62 At that moment the Saviour was in a place where Peter could see Him. When the guilty apostle looked up, Jesus looked at him, and who can sound the depths of what passed in those moments in the mind of the tortured Prisoner or that of His fallen apostle? In any case, we know that unfathomable love for and sympathy with His disillusioned disciple spoke from His eyes. And this, in conjunction with the crowing of the cock that reminded him of Jesus' warning, was enough—Peter was overwhelmed by remorse and fled outside, where he wept bitter tears.

Judas had, in his wickedness of heart, betrayed the Saviour, and when he realised the dreadfulness of his wicked act he fell into dark qualms of conscience and entered into the eternal night by way of suicide. Peter, however, had denied his Lord and Master through frailty, not because he did not love Him or did not believe in Him, but because he was spiritually too weak to resist the terrible temptation to deny Jesus that rushed upon him during that calamitous night. And when he came to realise how he had denied his Lord, he was overwhelmed by deep sorrow for his disloyalty, and through genuine repentance he qualified himself for complete reinstatement in his former leadership among the disciples.

[1] The contention that during the Passover there would not have been a cock (declared " unclean " in the Talmud) in the precincts of the high priest's palace carries no weight. And Plummer is right in stating: " Sadducees would have no scruples about what was not forbidden by the written Law. Certainly Romans would have no such scruples " (*in loc.*).

[2] Not one of the Gospels gives a detailed account of the events of that night, so that it is impossible to know exactly where the Saviour was when He looked at Peter. It is not the purpose of the Gospel narratives to give all the details of what took place, but to recount the principal facts regarding his passion.

[3] Cf. note on verse 34.

JESUS BEFORE THE SANHEDRIN

(Cf. Matt. xxvi. 57–68; Mark xiv. 53–65; John xviii. 12–27)

xxii. 63–71

63 And[1] the men that held *Jesus* mocked him, and beat him.
64 And they blindfolded him, and asked him, saying, Prophesy:
65 who is he that struck thee? And many other things spake
   they against him, reviling him.
66 And as soon as it was day, the assembly of the elders of the
   people[2] was gathered together, both chief priests and scribes;
   and they led him away into their council,[3] saying,[4] If thou
67 art the Christ, tell us.[5] But he said unto them, If I tell you,
68 ye will not believe: and if I ask *you*, ye will not answer.[6]
69 But from henceforth[7] shall the Son of man be seated at the
70 right hand of the power of God. And they all said, Art thou
   then the Son of God? And he said unto them, Ye say that
71 I am.[8] And they said, What further need have we of
   witness? for we ourselves have heard from his own mouth.

If we take the date of all four Gospels together we see that the
Saviour went through the following trials: (1) a preliminary trial
before Annas (the ex-high priest who still had great influence
among the Jews), John xviii. 19–23; (2) a preliminary trial before
Caiaphas and the members of the Jewish Council, Matthew
xxvi. 57–68 (probably in the night between 1 and 3 a.m.); (3)
a final trial before the whole Council after the arrival of daylight when a legal trial could take place, Luke xxii. 66–71; (4)
before Pilate; (5) before Herod.

If the different Gospels had each given a description of all
the trials, this would have taken up a comparatively large
portion of each. Each one of them therefore gives only a few
selections from the whole course of events. Luke especially gives
a condensed account of the trials before the Jewish authorities.
And yet in these few sentences he depicts in an impressive manner
the humiliation and suffering which our Saviour had to endure
as prisoner of the Jewish authorities.

63–5 His persecutors, having Him completely in their power,
try to do Him as much harm as possible in mind and body alike:

586

they mock, beat and slander Him. At a certain stage they blindfold Him and while He is blindfolded some of the bystanders hit Him in the face and then say that He must tell who has struck Him. In this way they mock at His claims that He is the messenger of God who possesses supernatural knowledge and prophetic power. Calm and dignified, without answering a single word to their questions and slanders, He bears all this outrageous humiliation and pain. These things probably took place during the intervals between the trials.

66 No session of the Jewish Council was regarded as valid if it were held during the night. Although the Jewish authorities held preliminary trials of the Saviour during the night, they must nevertheless assemble after daybreak and try Him again.

67, 68 Because the Jewish land is under the power of the Romans, the Jewish Council has no right of itself to execute the death sentence on anyone. So they have now to formulate a charge against Him which they may lay before Pilate as an adequate reason why he must sentence Him to death. In this instance the only possible thing to do is to tell Pilate that He professes to be the Messiah, the Jewish King, and that He is, therefore, a danger to the state and must be killed. If they can induce the Saviour Himself to declare before the whole Jewish Council that He is the Messiah it will make it easy for them to accuse Him before Pilate of trying to instigate rebellion against Caesar. It is for this reason that they ask Him the question whether He is the Christ, and not because they would really like to know whether He is or not. The Saviour knows their intention and does not answer their question, because, as He declares, they will not believe Him in any case, for they have already prejudged the issue and are not asking the question sincerely. And if He puts questions to them (e.g. as to the reason why they have asked Him this), Jesus continues, they will not answer Him. They will, among other things, not be prepared to discuss the Old Testament truths regarding the Messiah or to answer questions such as He had formerly asked with reference to John the Baptist (xx. 4)—questions that should lead up to the clear proof of the genuineness of His Messiahship.

69 But although they are thus prejudiced against Him and unwilling to accept the fact that He is the Messiah, He assures them that from now on He will, as the divine Son of Man (Dan. vii. 13) be associated with God in power and glory. And obviously He will then act as judge on those who turned their backs on Him.

70, 71 They knew but too well that in speaking of the " Son of Man " (the divine Being mentioned in Dan. vii. 13) Jesus meant Himself, and so they ask: " Art thou the Son of God? " They are eager that He should make such a claim expressly, for then He will, according to their ideas, commit blasphemy, and for this there is, according to their Law, only one punishment— death. In the later codification of Jewish law blasphemy was defined as involving the utterance of the Ineffable Name of God (*Yahweh*); but here it is evident that a claim to Messiahship was adjudged blasphemous (unless it were true—a consideration which was not taken into account) especially when it was couched in language denied from Daniel vii. 13 and Psalm cv. 1. The accusation that He is guilty of blasphemy will, indeed, carry no weight with Pilate as a pagan. But with the masses of the people, whom they must now at all costs incite against the Nazarene, this will be of tremendous force. So when Jesus, by using the expression " Ye say that I am ", expressly declares that He is the Son of God, they cry out enthusiastically. " What need we any further witness? for we ourselves have heard it from his own mouth." And thus His persecutors are armed to accuse Him before Pilate (on the charge of His professing to be the Messiah), and to make the people take sides against Him (by accusing Him of blasphemy).

Not merely during the days when Jesus was admired by the masses or even when He was alone with His disciples did He lay claim to full divine Sonship. But when He was alone amongst His enemies with perhaps only John, the beloved disciple, in the vicinity (John xviii. 16), and when He knew that such a pronouncement would give them the final ground for having Him cast out by the people and put to death, even then He declared unambiguously that He was the divine Messiah and nothing less than the Son of God. And this forms the very corner-stone of Christianity, by which it must stand or fall. Only those who believe unconditionally that He is really and truly the Beloved Son of God have the right to be called Christians.

---

[1] By the time Luke's Gospel reaches this stage, it had very nearly attained to the maximum manageable length for a writing on papyrus rolls, and thus he is compelled the more to be concise in his account of the events. " Apart from such single details which claim little space, it appears ever more clearly that Luke, limiting himself to the facts which held most significance for him, is hurrying to the end of his book " (Zahn, *in loc.*).

[2] Here, as the Greek wording makes plain, " the assembly of the elders of the people " (τὸ πρεσβυτέριον τοῦ λαοῦ) refers to the whole

Sanhedrin, while the following words, " both chief priests and scribes " (ἀρχιερεῖς τε καὶ γραμματεῖς), indicate its two main constituent groups. See also note on xx. 1.

³ The Sanhedrin, or Jewish Council at Jerusalem, consisted of seventy members plus the chairman (the high priest), and exercised the supreme authority over the ordinary as well as the religious life of the Jewish people (though at that time in subordination to the Roman authorities). With the destruction of Jerusalem in A.D. 70 the existence of the Sanhedrin in this form came to an end, though it was later reconstituted as a purely religious body by Johanan ben Zakkai at Jabneh.

⁴ It should be noted that the trial is here being led by the Council as a body and not by the high priest alone as in the preliminary examinations during the night (Matthew xxvi. 62–5).

⁵ With regard to the degree of agreement between this trial and that conducted during the night, Plummer correctly states: " That portions of what is recorded of one examination should resemble portions of what is recorded of another is natural. Before Annas, Caiaphas, and the Sanhedrin the same questions would be asked. At this last and only valid trial everything of importance would have to be repeated " (in loc.).

⁶ The words ἢ ἀπολύσητέ με (" nor let me go ", A.V.) are omitted by most important MSS., and, therefore, cannot be accepted as authentic. Their chief witnesses are A D N W, with the Latin, Syriac and Armenian versions.

⁷ " The term ' henceforth ', would seem to indicate, not some future, apocalyptic advent of Jesus, but a progressive, spiritual ascendancy, beginning with His crucifixion—the equivalent of the Johannine ' now is the Son of Man glorified ' (John xiii. 21) " (Major, op. cit., p. 181). Although there is an element of truth in these words of Major, Jesus' pronouncement here (especially if we note the context in which " Son of Man " occurs in Dan. vii. 13), has, however, the further purport that He is the divine Judge who at the grand Fulfilment will come in glory to establish His eternal and heavenly kingdom. " The vision of the Son of Man sitting on the Right Hand of the Power of God . . . began from the year of the crucifixion (cf. Acts ii. 33 f., vii. 55; Rom. viii. 34; Heb. i. 3 f.; 1 Pet. iii. 22; Rev. ii. 21, xii. 5; ' Mc.' xvi. 19), and is to be followed in due course by the vision which all must see of His return (Rev. i. 7). The Jewish leaders by their rejection of His Messiahship secured His exaltation (Phil. ii. 9) and their own ultimate confusion " (H. B. Swete on Mark xiv. 62).

⁸ The fact that the Jewish Council took these words of Jesus as an affirmative answer to their question is a conclusive proof that it was indeed a customary form of expression for an affirmative reply to a question. The parallel passage in Mark xiv 62 gives Jesus' reply as simply Ἐγώ εἰμι (" I am ").

JESUS BEFORE THE SECULAR JUDGES

(Cf. Matt. xxvii. 1–13; Mark xv. 1–20; John xviii. 28 xix. 16)

xxiii. 1–25

1 And the whole company of them rose up,[1] and brought
2 him before Pilate.[2] And they began to accuse him, saying,
We found this man perverting our nation, and forbidding to
give tribute to Caesar,[3] and saying that he himself is Christ
3 a king.[4] And Pilate asked him, saying,[5] Art thou the King
of the Jews? And he answered him and said, Thou sayest.[6]
4 And Pilate said unto the chief priests and the multitudes,[7]
5 I find no fault in this man.[8] But they were the more urgent,
saying, He stirreth up the people, teaching throughout all
6 Judaea, and beginning from Galilee even unto this place. But
when Pilate heard it, he asked whether the man were a
7 Galilaean. And when he knew that he was of Herod's[9]
jurisdiction, he sent him unto Herod, who himself also was
at Jerusalem in these days.[10]
8 Now when Herod saw Jesus,[11] he was exceeding glad: for he
was of a long time desirous to see him, because he had heard
concerning him; and he hoped to see some miracle done by
9 him. And he questioned him in many words; but he
10 answered him nothing. And the chief priests and scribes stood,
11 vehemently accusing him. And Herod with his soldiers[12]
set him at nought, and mocked him, and arraying him in
12 gorgeous[13] apparel sent him back to Pilate. And Herod and
Pilate became friends with each other that very day: for
before they were at enmity between themselves.
13 And Pilate called together the chief priests and the rulers
14 and the people,[14] and said unto them, Ye brought unto me
this man, as one that perverteth the people: and behold, I,
having examined him before you, found no fault in this man,
15 touching those things whereof ye accuse him: no, nor yet
Herod: for he sent him back unto us;[15] and behold, nothing
16 worthy of death hath been done by him.[16] I will therefore
17 chastise him,[17] and release him.[18] But they cried out all
18 together, saying,[19] Away with this man, and release unto us
19 Barabbas:[20] one who for a certain insurrection made in the
20 city, and for murder, was cast into prison. And Pilate spake
21 unto them, again, desiring to release Jesus; but they shouted,
22 saying, Crucify, crucify him. And he said unto them the third

time, Why, what evil hath this man done? I have found no
cause of death in him: I will therefore chastise him and
23 release him. But they were instant with loud voices, asking
24 that he might be crucified. And their voices prevailed. And
Pilate gave sentence that what they asked for should be
25 done. And he released him that for insurrection and murder
had been cast into prison, whom they asked for; but Jesus he
delivered up to their will.

Throughout the night, since His arrest, the Saviour was
slandered, mocked, and subjected to many other forms of mental
and physical ill-treatment by the Jewish authorities and their
underlings. Already the Jewish tribunal, the Sanhedrin, had
condemned Him to death on the charge of blasphemy (Mark
xiv. 64). The Jewish authorities, however, had themselves no
right to execute a death sentence without ratification by the
Roman government. So they make haste to have Him sentenced
to death as speedily as possible by the provincial governor,
Pilate.

1 Shortly after daybreak the Jewish leaders held an official
session of their great Council (xxii. 66) to give official confirmation to the sentence which had been delivered by them at the
preliminary examinations during the night, and to agree what they
should do in order to have Him sentenced to death by Pilate.
After they had prepared everything and had warned Pilate in
good time that they were bringing someone who had to be tried
urgently, they arose as a body and took Jesus to Pilate. The
Saviour's arrest and the proceedings of the night had been kept
so secret that there was as yet no flocking together of the common
people (in addition, it was still early in the morning before the
multitudes were in the streets). The Jewish leaders were so afraid
of the people (xx. 19) that they obviously did their best to prevent
the masses to discover as yet what was going on. This was the
reason why they arranged everything with such feverish haste
(Jesus was crucified as early as nine o'clock that morning according to Mark xv. 25). When they had carried matters so far that
the Lord was in the hands of the pagan authorities as an apparently helpless and unresisting prisoner, they had, however, also
practically won their case with the people, and they could easily
succeed in instigating the masses against Him whom they had so
recently still admired as the Messiah or at any rate as a great
prophet.

However, when they took Jesus to Pilate, only the Jewish
authorities and their henchmen were already present. What an

indication of the terrible vengefulness of the Jewish authorities, that the whole multitude of them—Sadducees, Pharisees, and other groups that hated one another with a deadly hatred—now acted in unison (and this even during the Passover) to have Him done to death!

2, 3 Luke gives a very brief summary of the trial before Pilate, but makes it quite clear what the charges were which they laid against Him, hoping that Pilate would confirm their illegal death sentence upon Him.

Before the Jewish Council He was found guilty of blasphemy because He called Himself the Son of God. Such an accusation, which related to the religious views of the Jews, would have carried no weight with Pilate. So His accusers now prefer totally different charges against Him. With subtle cunning and abominable deceitfulness they accuse Him before Pilate of being trebly guilty of high treason: (1) He perverts the people, stirring up disaffection and insurrection throughout the country; (2) He forbids the people to give tribute to Caesar; and (3) He professes to be the Messiah, a king—one who is ostensibly the rival and opponent of Caesar. If Pilate could be convinced that these charges were true, he would not have hesitated for a moment to condemn the Saviour to death. Most probably, however, he at once became suspicious that the Jewish accusations were false. For it was certainly a very strange thing that, if He really aimed at throwing off the Roman yoke, they should come and accuse Him to Pilate, the hated Roman ruler. What could so suddenly have actuated them to come forward as champions of Roman honour and Roman interests?

Pilate's distrust of the genuineness of the Jewish accusations had, after a conversation with Jesus in his palace (cf. John xviii. 33–8), grown into a firm conviction that the Saviour was innocent of any treason or rebellion against the Roman government. Jesus, indeed, did acknowledge, in answer to his question, that He was the King of the Jews. But He made Pilate understand so clearly and convincingly that His kingdom is a spiritual kingdom (John xviii. 36), that the Roman judge could see through the whole plot of the Jewish authorities—they had delivered Him to Pilate *out of envy* or *spite* (Matt. xxvii. 18; Mark xv. 10).

4 Fully convinced of the Saviour's innocence, Pilate gives the official verdict (openly, in the presence of the Jewish leaders and the multitude that had meanwhile flocked together) that Jesus is *Not Guilty*.

5 Thus far the examination before the Roman judge had taken an orderly and lawful course. The Prisoner was accused of high treason, the judge had investigated the matter and acquitted Him. But the Saviour's accusers, in their blind hatred of Him, are determined that He *must* be sentenced to death. Accordingly they do not resign themselves to the official, judicial verdict of Pilate, but begin to force the hand of the law according to their wishes. With determined insistence they now, even more violently than before, accuse the Saviour before the Roman judge. They declare that He is stirring up the whole nation, throughout the Jewish land, with His teaching, and that He has been doing this ever since His first appearance in Galilee.

6, 7 Pilate is placed in an extremely difficult position: he knows but too well that the Accused is not guilty. Nevertheless, from the fanatical attitude of the Jewish leaders he perceives quite clearly that they are determined to have the death sentence pronounced on Him. In addition, he knows very well what the fanatical Jewish priests and authorities are capable of, once they are determined upon a matter. Although he is notorious for his callousness and although he has already often forced his Jewish subjects by the sword to conform to his wishes, he does not feel inclined to have any trouble with them again if he can avoid it. Especially since Jesus has been accused of rebellion, he is afraid (although he knows that the charge is false) that the Jews may go and accuse him to Caesar of taking an insurgent under his protection. Tiberius Caesar, with his suspicious nature, would have been only too ready to believe such an imputation and would have taken action against Pilate. Consequently the Roman judge does not see his way clear to refuse the demand made by the Jews. For his own sake, therefore, he begins to set aside the requirements of right and justice, and he does not issue orders for Jesus to be released. On the other hand, it is obvious that the strong, pure personality of Jesus makes an inescapable impression on him. Yes, even a secret fear of Him had arisen in the heart of the usually callous Roman (John xix. 8). So he shrinks from sentencing Him to death.

Pilate therefore seizes the opportunity of sending the Accused to Herod, hoping that he will judge Him, as one of his Galilean subjects. Whatever Herod's verdict may be, it will exempt Pilate from responsibility in the matter.

8, 9 Herod, especially since he was the ruler over the districts where Jesus had mostly appeared in public, had often heard of His miracles and exceptional personality, and had already for some considerable time longed to see Him. At a certain stage, when the Saviour was very popular among the masses, Herod feared that He was John the Baptist, risen from the dead after he

(Herod) had caused him to be beheaded. Afterwards this fear had apparently disappeared, and he wanted to be able to see Him out of mere curiosity. He desired very much, for the sake of the sensation, to see how Jesus performed miracles. At an earlier period of his life Herod had shown signs of interest in the message of God (for he had already listened to John the Baptist), but in the course of years he had fallen into utter spiritual and moral degradation (iii. 20) and had even allowed the innocent John the Baptist to be beheaded. And because he had so completely surrendered himself to spiritual blindness and moral decay, and wanted to make His acquaintance merely out of curiosity, Jesus remained silent in his presence. Herod had made no use of the opportunity given him of repentance when John rebuked him for his sinful life (iii. 19), and he had by this time sunk so deeply into sin that even the Saviour had no longer a word for him.

10, 11 Although the chief priests and the scribes accuse Him so violently before Herod, the latter, knowing the innocence of His actions in Galilee, was well aware of the falseness of their charges. The degenerate monarch who had caused John to be beheaded in cold blood when his cruel wife demanded it through her daughter, declines this time to sentence the Accused to death—possibly from superstitious dread. Nevertheless he lacks the courage to declare Him innocent. He was offended at Jesus' unwillingness to perform miracles or to answer his questions (verse 9), so he takes his revenge, along with his soldiers, in treating Him with contempt and mocking Him. After this they arrayed Him in a shining garment, to be worn only by kings and other leaders. By so doing, they mock at His claims to Kingship. And thus Herod sends Him back to Pilate without making the slightest attempt to investigate His case judicially.

12 Although Pilate, in sending Jesus to Herod, had not succeeded in evading the responsibility of finally having to decide his fate, his gesture of paying homage to this potentate resulted in settling an enmity of long standing that had existed between them.

13-16 Pilate, who earlier that morning had so openly and expressly given judgment as to Jesus' innocence, had already shown his irresolution when, from fear of Jewish fanaticism, he sent Him to Herod to be tried by him. And now that Herod had sent Him back, he begins to waver more and more and to prostitute his judicial vocation. Instead of seeing to it that right and justice should be exercised towards the Innocent One at all costs, he descends to such a level that he, the Roman judge, begins to argue with Jesus' bloodthirsty and wily persecutors. He proposes that, although both he and Herod had found Him innocent, he will have Him chastised and then release Him. He hoped by this kind of compromise to satisfy the revengefulness of the Jewish authorities and to elicit the sympathy of the multitude for the One who was subjected to this torture.

17-19 The bloodthirsty multitude, however (not only the authorities but ordinary Jews as well who had by this time been incited against Jesus), noticed Pilate's wavering—he offered them an inch and they were bent on securing an ell. So they definitely refuse to be satisfied with a compromise. Even when they are confronted with a choice between Barabbas (a rebel and murderer) and Jesus, they demand the release of Barabbas and the death of the Saviour.

20, 21 Pilate was so convinced of the innocence of the accused and cherished such a secret fear of Him that he did not yet completely yield to his wavering inclination for the sake of his own convenience and safety to give way to the clamour to have Jesus crucified. Pagan as he was, and especially since he could not but observe the Saviour's nobility of character, His fearlessness and His spiritual and moral superiority over His accusers, Pilate felt perhaps that this Prisoner might possibly be a divine being who had come to the world and would sooner or later reveal His power. But whatever his motives might be, Pilate found himself placed in a situation the like of which he had never before experienced. Never before had he had to deal with a person like this Prisoner (and we must remember that Jesus was the most remarkable Man of all who ever have been or will be upon earth), and never before had any of his subjects clamoured for the death of an innocent man, as these fanatical Jews were shouting in their blind hatred against Jesus. Pilate tried in vain to persuade the seething masses to forgo their demand, and the "Holy" (!) city resounded with the bloodthirsty clamour of "Crucify, crucify Him!"

22 For the third time the Roman judge declares Jesus to be innocent; how can he then have Him done to death? He again proposes to have Him chastised and then released. And from John xix. 1 it appears that he actually did have Him chastised in an attempt to calm the hate of the Jews.

23, 24 But Jesus' persecutors and the incited multitude exploit the Roman governor's weakness. Even after he has had Him chastised, they clamour in their bloodthirstiness that He must be crucified. And in the end the tremendous coercion on the part of the Jews prevailed upon the unstable mind of Pilate to yield to their demand.

25 And thus did the Roman judge, who had allowed the voice of right and justice in his breast to be smothered by selfish considerations (for the sake of his own safety and interest, John xix.12), degrade himself to the level of a servant to the bloodthirsty persecutors of the innocent Son of God. He releases Barabbas, the insurgent and murderer, to please the Jews, but delivers Jesus to be crucified according to the wishes of His enemies.

The Jews rejected Jesus, the King of the eternal and spiritual kingdom, and chose Barabbas, the man of outward violence. Apart from the few thousand who after Pentecost accepted Him as Redeemer and Lord, the Jewish people as a whole persisted in rejecting Jesus during the years after His crucifixion, and to follow earthly, fanatical leaders. The result was that the nation, and the leaders as well, were plunged into irretrievable disaster in the Roman-Jewish war (A.D. 66–70).

To this day humanity as a whole, and each individual separately, is still faced with the choice: Barabbas or Jesus? And the temporal and eternal weal or woe of everyone depends upon who is chosen.

---

[1] " The Jewish Sanhedrin did not possess the *ius gladii* or power to inflict the death sentence upon an offender. This appertained exclusively to the Roman procurator " (W. Manson, *in loc.*). According to the Jerusalem Talmud, tractate *Sanhedrin*, i. 1, " Forty years before the destruction of the temple the right to try capital cases was taken away from them " (i.e. from the Jews by the Romans); cf. similar statements in the Babylonian Talmud, *Sanhedrin*, 41a, and *Abodah Zarah*, 8b.

[2] Cf. Special Note on Pilate, p. 600. Tacitus, the Roman historian (born between A.D. 52 and 54), also declares that Jesus was crucified under Pontius Pilate (*Annals*, xv, 44). So also Josephus in his *Antiquities*, xviii, 3—a passage which, while it has suffered from Christian interpolations, is in its main outline authentic.

[3] And this, after Jesus had so expressly commanded the opposite (xx. 25)!

[4] βασιλέα " explains the Jewish title " (Creed, *in loc.*). " They add βασιλέα that Pilate may know the political significance of Χριστός " (Plummer, *in loc.*). They accuse Jesus of trying to be an earthly Messiah, although the precise reason why the Jews had rejected Him was that He desired to be no earthly king but a spiritual King; whereas they wanted an earthly Messiah.

[5] " Here, again, Luke omits much of detail, and in a severely condensed form gives us the salient facts. Evidently he resolutely omitted certain things, in order that the great climacteric things might stand out clearly and sharply " (Morgan, *in loc.*). Obviously Pilate would, before pronouncing judgment, have first asked many more questions

and discussed matters with Jesus as well as with His accusers. Even the more detailed narrative in John xviii and xix relates the events and discussions only in outline. If, however, we take the data of the four Gospels together, we have an account of matters sufficient to make us feel how psychologically and historically convincing is the Gospel account of Jesus' trial and condemnation. Only superficiality and prejudice can blind anyone to this. Read the apocryphal writings that were written afterwards to get some idea of what the fictitious accounts of these events look like. The Gospels present the historical facts to us in a sober and unadulterated form, in contrast with the fantastic fabrications of the apocryphal writings.

⁶ *Σὺ λέγεις*, " Thou sayest it ". Although these words embrace an affirmative reply, Jesus, nevertheless, at the same time also gives Pilate to understand that He replies to his question affirmatively only with certain reservations. The Saviour " did not desire to be the king of the Jews in the sense that Pilate assigned to it, but the King of Israel, the Messiah " (Van Leeuwen, at Mark xv. 2). Cf. C. H. Dodd's paraphrase of John xviii. 37: " ' King ' is *your* word. As a matter of fact my mission in the world is to bear witness to the Truth. My subjects are those who are loyal to the Truth " (*How to Read the Gospels*, p. 24).

⁷ By this time the fact that Jesus was being tried before the Roman judge was obviously beginning to be common knowledge among the people, so that a multitude had already flocked together at the governor's palace (probably the castle of Antonia near the temple).

⁸ " It is important here that we should recognise that this was not an expression of a pious opinion. It was a legal finding, in the very terminology of the law court of the time; just as in an English court of justice the verdict would be ' not guilty '. To recognise this is to see the point at which Pilate's breakdown occurred " (Morgan, *in loc.*). According to Roman law, Pilate ought at once to have commanded Jesus' release. However, the agitation by the Jews causes him to waver and from now on " he was calculating between policy and justice " (*loc. cit.*) until he utterly trampled on the law and yielded to the will of the Jews.

⁹ Cf. Special Note on Herod, p. 600.

¹⁰ " Herod had come up to keep the feast, and probably occupied the palace of the Asmonaeans " (Plummer, *in loc.*). Like his father, Herod the Great, he celebrated the Jewish feasts in order to retain the favour of the people.

¹¹ Creed (following Dibelius and others) contends that the trial before Herod was pure fiction that arose under the influence of Psalm ii. 2 (" the rulers take counsel together, against the Lord, and against his anointed "). His arguments are as follows: (1) " If the story rested on early tradition, it is strange that it should not appear in Mark " (*in loc.*). This argument, however, does not carry the least weight, for what right have we to suppose that Mark recorded all events—even all important events? Each of the Gospels gives a selection from the wealth of available details. (2) " Moreover, it does not seem likely

that Pilate would send a political prisoner to be tried before Antipas within his own jurisdiction " (*in loc.*). Only one who does not try to enter into the actual circumstances of that day (with Pilate's inward conflict and his eagerness to evade the responsibility of a final and definite decision), can bring forward an argument of this nature. Even Warschauer admits: " If Herod was paying a visit to the capital he was certainly the competent authority for dealing with one of his subjects, and the acknowledgment of his jurisdiction by the Roman governor was at once a compliment which the tetrarch was likely to appreciate, and offered Pilate a way out of a situation he did not like " (*op. cit.*, p. 326). Cf. also Easton, *in loc.*

Another argument advanced by Creed is that the narrative contains contradictions. Thus, e.g., verse 10 implies that the Jewish leaders went to Herod together with the rest, while verse 15 would seem to indicate that they remained with Pilate. This, however, is an arbitrary way of explaining verse 15.

No valid argument can, in fact, be adduced against the historicity of the trial before Herod. If we think of Luke's intimate contacts with the house of Herod (cf. viii. 3; Acts xii. 20, xiii. 1), it immediately becomes clear why he described this trial. His information was obtained from first-hand sources.

¹² Obviously his bodyguard. This episode, therefore, has nothing to do with the action of the Roman soldiers to whom Pilate delivered Jesus to have Him crucified. So Major's (*op. cit.*, p. 187) argument against the historicity of this episode at Herod's palace falls to the ground.

¹³ ἐσθῆτα λαμπράν " denotes not a purple garment, but a white mantle, like that worn by Jewish kings and Roman grandees on high occasions " (Godet, *in loc.*). Cf. also Plummer, *in loc.*

¹⁴ " Pilate in taking the matter in hand again summons not only the hierarchy, whose bitterness against Jesus he knew, but the populace, whom he hoped to find more kindly disposed, and able to influence their rulers " (Plummer, *in loc.*).

¹⁵ The correct reading here (according to most expositors) is: ἀνέπεμψεν γὰρ αὐτὸν πρὸς ἡμᾶς (" for he [Herod] sent Him back to us "), and not ἀνέπεμψα γὰρ ὑμᾶς πρὸς αὐτόν (" for I sent you to him ", A.V.). Although Pilate here uses " us ", this gives us no right to allege (like Creed, *in loc.*) that the words mean that the Jewish authorities did not go to Herod (as stated in verse 10). Possibly, after it became clear to them that Herod was not going to pronounce the necessary sentence, they went back to Pilate so that, when Herod sent the Saviour back to him (after he and his soldiers had mocked Him), they were already again there. Consequently it is mere captiousness to see in verse 15 a contradiction of verse 10.

¹⁶ Major (*op. cit.*, p. 187) declares with regard to Pilate's wavering attitude: " It is scarcely credible historically that a Roman governor imbued with the principles of Roman justice could behave in this way in the presence of a subject population." He then tries to explain the

whole story of Pilate's irresolution and the Jews' agitation against Jesus by the desire of the Christians to lay the blame of the crucifixion on the Jews. But to us the Gospel narrative of the trial before Pilate does not bear the slightest mark of a fictitious account. On the contrary, we feel the pulsation of true history in every detail of it. In the trial of an ordinary prisoner Pilate could have acted as " an automaton of Roman administration of justice ". But in the trial of Jesus, who is not only the Innocent One but the Unique One among men, other powerful factors play their part—factors which made the hard-hearted, cruel Pilate recoil from sentencing Him to death, although in his own interest it appeared to be the only way out, because of the fanatical determination of the Jews. The consequent conflict in Pilate's mind caused him to act as described in the Gospel narrative: Major's reasoning therefore reveals a lack of appreciation of the real historical situation.

[17] Scourging always preceded the crucifixion of a condemned person. Pilate, however, wanted to try to appease the Jews by this " chastisement " so that he could release Him. Scourging was an " extremely cruel torture, carried out with a scourge plaited out of strips of leather, provided here and there with knots or bits of metal " (Van Leeuwen at Mark xv. 15). " Scourging was sometimes fatal " (Plummer, in loc.).

[18] Verse 17, ἀνάγκην δὲ εἶχεν ἀπολύειν αὐτοῖς κατὰ ἑορτὴν ἕνα ("for of necessity he must release one unto them at the feast " (A.V.), is omitted by R.V., following such authorities as A B L a sah; but its omission is by no means certain, as it is attested by ℵ W Δ Θ Ψ 28 and the majority of Latin and Syriac authorities, as well as by the bulk of later Greek MSS. Cf. John xviii. 39.

[19] Even Montefiore admits: " That the people are now against Jesus is not psychologically quite incredible. Jesus had disappointed them. . . . The hope he had aroused in them had been dashed to the ground by his arrest. . . . It is also possible that the priestly party had helped to this change of feeling " (op. cit., i, p. 375). We must remember, too, that while the crowds who acclaimed Jesus on Palm Sunday were in the main Galilean pilgrims, those who clamoured for His death on Good Friday would be in the main the city mob.

[20] " Barabbas was a representative of the same revolutionary spirit of which the Sanhedrin were accusing Jesus. To give up Jesus to the cross and to demand Barabbas was to do at the same moment two significant acts. It was to repudiate the spirit of submission and faith which had distinguished the whole work of Jesus, and which might have saved the people. It was at the same time to let loose the spirit of revolt which was to carry them to their destruction " (Godet, in loc.).

SPECIAL NOTES

PILATE

Pontius Pilate was the fifth Roman governor who after the deposition of Archelaus in A.D. 6 ruled over Judaea (A.D. 26–36). According to the description of Pilate by the Jewish-Hellenistic writer Philo (who died in A.D. 50), he was a man of unyielding character but nevertheless corruptible; he was notorious for his cruelty and unbearable coarseness; he often ill-treated and executed persons without a preceding judicial sentence. He was an arbitrary tyrant and respected no one's feelings, except when his own interests were imperilled. Josephus (*The Jewish War*, ii, 14) describes how Pilate at the commencement of his term of office one night made his soldiers march into Jerusalem with the Roman military standards (*aquilae*) which were regarded by the Jews as idolatrous objects and never allowed within Jerusalem. When the Jews made a violent protest against this, he threatened to have them murdered by his soldiers in great numbers. But when the Jews still would not yield, and fanatically showed their determination by continuing to demand the removal of the pagan military tokens from their city, he finally gave in to their demands (probably from fear of a sanguinary insurrection that would have brought him into disfavour with Caesar). So in this instance he had also shown irresolution and had yielded to the determination of his Jewish subjects.

Shortly afterwards (Josephus, *loc. cit.*), however, he again rudely stirred up the feelings of the Jews by threatening to take part of the consecrated temple funds to carry out certain improvements in the water supply of Jerusalem. When the Jews again protested against this, he unexpectedly caused the demonstrators to be attacked by his soldiers and in a sanguinary manner nipped the imminent insurrection in the bud.

Eventually his acts of cruelty exceeded all bounds to such an extent (when numbers of Samaritans were murdered) that he was dismissed from his post in A.D. 36. According to ancient but doubtful traditions, he ended his life by committing suicide.

HEROD

Herod Antipas was a son of Herod the Great and Malthake. After his father's death in 4 B.C. he became tetrarch of Galilee and of Peraea in Trans-Jordan. Like his father, he was a great lover of great and artistic architectural works, and thus, e.g., built the beautiful Tiberias as capital of his kingdom on the shore of the Sea of Galilee.

He was married to a daughter of Aretas, king of Arabia, but afterwards divorced her and took away from his half-brother, Herod Philip, his wife Herodias. Her influence over him subsequently led to his utter ruin. When her brother, Herod Agrippa, in A.D. 37 received the title of king (of the territory formerly governed by the tetrarchs Philip and Lysanias), she insisted, owing to her ungovernable ambition, that her husband should also go and ask this title from the Emperor Gaius Caligula. So Herod Antipas accompanied her to Italy, but instead of being honoured with the title of king, he was dismissed from his post and banished to Gaul, where he died a few years later in exile.

JESUS ON THE WAY TO GOLGOTHA

xxiii. 26-32

26 And when they led him away, they laid hold upon one Simon[1] of Cyrene,[2] coming from the country,[3] and laid on him the cross,[4] to bear it after Jesus.

27 And there followed him a great multitude of the people,
28 and of women[5] who bewailed and lamented him. But Jesus turning unto them said, Daughters of Jerusalem,[6] weep not
29 for me,[7] but weep for yourselves, and for your children. For behold, the days are coming, in which they shall say, Blessed are the barren, and the wombs that never bare, and the
30 breast that never gave suck. Then shall they begin to say
31 to the mountains, Fall on us;[8] and to the hills, Cover us. For if they do these things in the green tree, what shall be done in the dry?[9]

32 And there were also two others, malefactors, led with him to be put to death.

For about three years Jesus had, without intermission, ministered by word and act to the spiritual needs of the Jewish people, in order to bring them to believe in Him and thus to redemption and true life. In a manner equalled by none before Him, He had cured hundreds and even thousands of the inhabitants of the Holy Land physically and had delivered many of them spiritually from the powers of darkness. Like a bright light shining in a pitch-dark night, which dispels the darkness as far as its rays can reach, even so His activities among the people kindled a bright light in the life of the Jews. Some of the inhabitants of Palestine rejoiced in this light and allowed themselves to be illumined by it. But the people as a whole showed that they loved the darkness more than the light. And that was the reason why Jesus, notwithstanding the fact that He was the perfect Man who in utter self-surrender served others, was at the end of His public ministry led away outside the city to be crucified.

26 The Saviour had to carry His cross Himself from the palace of the Roman governor where He had been sentenced, scourged and mocked (John xix. 17). After His spiritual wrestlings in Gethsemane the previous evening, after all the spiritual and physical

suffering endured by Him during that night without a moment's sleep
or rest, and after everything that had happened at His trial and
condemnation that morning, His body was undoubtedly in an
utterly exhausted and bleeding state when He had to bear His
cross through the narrow streets of Jerusalem on the way to
Golgotha. And it was probably from fear that He would succumb
before reaching the hill that the soldiers compelled Simon of
Cyrene, whom they met just outside the city, to bear the cross
behind Jesus.

27 The news that the Saviour had been arrested and brought
before Pilate's judgment seat obviously soon reached every part
of Jerusalem, so that even before His final condemnation a large
multitude had flocked together at the governor's palace. This
multitude had probably increased, so that by the time Jesus had
to enter upon the *via dolorosa* to Golgotha a vast multitude followed
Him. Now that the Jewish leaders had obtained their wish and
He had been delivered over to be crucified, the fiendish shouting
of " Crucify, crucify Him " had spontaneously died away. And
a group of women of Jerusalem had such a degree of sympathy
with Him that they could not but follow Him as closely as
possible and mourn for Him in wailing and lamentation.

28–30 The weeping of the women of Jerusalem over Him
again arouses Jesus' deepest pity for the people of the city who
were busy invoking upon themselves the judgments of God by
their rejection of Him. So the Saviour stood still for a moment,
turned round to the wailing women, and instead of thanking
them for their friendly sympathy with Him, urges them not to
weep for Him, but for themselves and their children. The Lord
does not in any way disapprove of their mourning for Him as
though this were in itself something wrong. Undoubtedly He
appreciated their sympathy. But because He knows what terrible
judgments will ere long visit Jerusalem, He expresses in these
words His unfathomable pity for the doomed people. It is
beautiful and good that they should manifest such tenderness
and sympathy with Him on His way to the cross. But they are
unable to see things in their right perspective and do not realise
what is awaiting them and their people if they should persist in
their unbelief. It is far more urgent that they should weep for
themselves and their children: even at this late hour such tears
may lead to repentance and avert the approaching doom. He
impresses on them the appalling peril in which they stand. When
once the doom bursts upon them, it will be of long duration and
will involve not only the destruction of the national existence but
also the eternal woe of every member of the nation who persists

in unbelief. So dreadful will be the judgments that are to visit the city and the people, says our Lord, that barrenness and childlessness, which were always regarded as a curse among the Jews, will be really a blessing because the childless ones, however much they themselves will have to endure, will nevertheless not be called upon to watch the sufferings of their children as well. Anyone who follows the history of the Roman-Jewish war that led to the total destruction of Jerusalem and the downfall of Jewish national existence in Palestine comes to realise how these words of Jesus depicted the actual truth.

31 Just as it is unnatural for succulent, green wood to be burned, so contrary to nature is it for Jesus, the Innocent and Perfect Man, the Son of God, to undergo suffering and death. And where even He, who is guiltless of any sin against God or man, is to suffer and be crucified, how much worse will be the fate of the guilty nation which, like dry wood ready to be burned, is ripe for the impending judgments.

In the light of full reality it is, therefore, far more necessary for the women of Jerusalem to weep for themselves and for their children. Thus Jesus' words to the women of Jerusalem, when He was worn out by ill-treatment and on the way to His death upon the cross, conveyed a last exhortation to repentance, addressed to the Jewish people.

What a moving revelation we have in this episode of the Saviour's total freedom from self-pity, and of His unshakable conviction that the attitude adopted towards Him would decide the weal or woe of the people. He does not merely give utterance to His sympathy for the doomed people, but warns them frankly that unparalleled misery is awaiting those who have rejected Him.

32 Jerusalem and the people were warned for the last time, and now Jesus is led away along with two other condemned persons, two criminals, to be crucified.

Christ does not merely desire to be regarded with emotional sympathy as the great Sufferer. He needs no one's sympathy, for His suffering is forever past. He has, once and for all, entered upon the *via dolorosa* and drained the cup of suffering to the dregs, and was at His resurrection and ascension exalted to God's right hand in His perfect, divine glory. We have indeed to think with contrite and grateful hearts of the suffering which He endured for our sakes. But sympathy for Him is now out of place, because He is the glorified Lord and King who is coming in divine majesty to judge the quick and the dead. The form of condescending interest (if we may so term it) and sympathy for Jesus as the perfect Sufferer, which is found in many modern thinkers and others who by no means believe in Him as divine Lord and Redeemer, is forcibly disclaimed by Jesus' words to the women of Jerusalem. It is not sympathy but sincere faith in Him and genuine repentance that Jesus expects from us. And whosoever rejects Him in unbelief should much rather weep for his unforgiven debt of sin and for the judgment which will visit all rejecters of the Son of God just as surely as it visited Jerusalem 1,900 years ago.

¹ From Mark xv. 21 it appears that at least two sons of this Simon were afterwards believers. Possibly also Paul in Romans xvi. 13 refers to a son of Simon and to Simon's mother. If this is so, it is very probable that Simon himself was also a believer, but died comparatively soon after the crucifixion.

² "That Cyrene was the chief city of the district, which is the Tripoli, is shown by the name Cyrenaica and by Acts xi. 10 " (Plummer, *in loc.*).

³ This particular is often adduced as a proof that Jesus was not crucified on the first day of the Feast, but with no justification, for it is not stated that Simon had come from a long distance, and the law for a feast day was that one must not go further than a " Sabbath day's journey ". Besides it is not stated that Simon came from work or something else that was forbidden on a feast day. At that time it was customary for thousands of feastgoers who came to Jerusalem from elsewhere to stop in villages or hamlets or even in the open country around the city. Thus it is most probable that Simon came from such a " lodging " outside Jerusalem on his way to the temple. In any case, this detail affords not the slightest proof that Jesus was not crucified on the 15th Nisan.

⁴ Probably only the cross-bar is meant.

⁵ Here the reference is not to the women-followers of Jesus (for their grief and dejection would have been too great to bewail Jesus so openly and loudly in the presence of the multitude), but ordinary inhabitants of Jerusalem who had perhaps seen and heard the Saviour and regarded Him as a benefactor and prophet, and now saw Him a prey to the ruthless authorities. It is not suggested that they believed in Him as the Christ.

⁶ The women, therefore, were not the Galilean women who had followed Jesus on His journeys (viii. 1–3, xxiii. 49).

⁷ " In the last analysis, Jesus is never an object of pity on the part of sinful, condemned humanity " (Morgan, *in loc.*).

⁸ " The wish is that the mountains may fall on them and *kill* them, not hide and protect them " (Plummer, *in loc.*).

⁹ Godet's view on these words still appears to us to be the best: " The more contrary to nature it is that Jesus should die as a rebel,

the more is it in keeping with the nature of things that Israel should perish for rebellion. Thus Jesus makes the people aware of the falsehood which ruled His condemnation, and the way in which God will take vengeance " (*in loc.*). " If the innocent Jesus meets such a fate, what will be the fate of the guilty Jerusalem? " (Creed, *in loc.*).

THE CRUCIFIXION

(Cf. Matt. xxvii. 33-56; Mark xv. 21-41; John xx. 1-18)

xxiii. 33-49

33 And when they came unto the place which is called The
skull,[1] there they crucified him, and the malefactors, one
34 on the right hand and the other on the left. And Jesus
said,[2] Father, forgive[3] them;[4] for they know not[5] what they
do. And parting his garments among them, they cast lots.
35 And the people stood beholding. And the rulers also scoffed
at him, saying, He saved others; let him save himself, if this
36 is the Christ of God, his chosen. And the soldiers also
mocked him, coming to him, offering him vinegar,[6] and
37 saying, If thou art the King of the Jews, save thyself.
38 And there was also a superscription[7] over him,[8] THIS IS THE
KING OF THE JEWS.
39 And one of the malefactors which were hanged railed on
him, saying, Art not thou[9] the Christ? save thyself and us.
40 But the other[10] answered, and rebuking him said, Dost thou
not even fear God, seeing thou art in the same condem-
41 nation? And we indeed justly; for we receive the due
reward of our deeds: but this man hath done nothing amiss.
42 And he said, Jesus,[11] remember me when thou comest in
43 thy kingdom.[12] And he said unto him,[13] Verily I say unto
thee, To-day[14] shalt thou be with me[15] in Paradise.[16] [17]
44 And it was now about the sixth hour, and a darkness came
45 over the whole land[18] until the ninth hour, the sun's light
failing:[19] and the veil[20] of the temple was rent in the midst.[21]
46 And when Jesus had cried with a loud voice,[22] he said,
Father, into thy hands I commend my spirit;[23] and having
47 said this, he gave up the ghost. And when the centurion saw
what was done, he glorified God, [24] saying, Certainly this
48 was a righteous man. And all the multitudes that came
together to this sight, when they beheld the things that were
49 done, returned smiting their breasts. And all his acquaintance, and the women that followed with him from Galilee,
stood afar off, seeing these things.

When the Saviour was in Nazareth, first as a child and afterwards in full-grown Manhood, He was in every respect, spiritually and physically, perfect and attractive, so that He continued

to increase in favour with God and man (ii. 52). In Him God's ideal of Creation was realised in the highest measures. He was the perfect Man in soul and body. However, with His public ministry it became more and more evident that He would have to be sacrificed as the Lamb of God in pain, utter humiliation and death. And now finally on Golgotha the words were fulfilled that had been uttered by the prophet: " He is despised and rejected of men; a man of sorrows, and acquainted with grief: and we hid as it were our faces from him; he was despised, and we esteemed him not. . . . He was wounded for our transgressions, he was bruised for our iniquities: the chastisement of our peace was upon him; and with his stripes we are healed " (Isa. liii. 3–5).

33 Like the other evangelists, Luke does not dwell on the manner in which the Saviour was crucified. He merely mentions the terrible fact that Jesus, the Son of God, the Immaculately righteous One, was crucified—crucified between two criminals. And thus He, the Holy One, was " numbered with the transgressors ". Crucifixion was the most agonising and shameful form of execution ever devised (the Romans confined this form of punishment to slaves and criminals of the lowest type), and yet the physical agony which Jesus had to endure was but the faintest reflection of the spiritual suffering He had to undergo as the Bearer of the sin of lost mankind. For this reason the Gospels give practically no details of His physical suffering, so that the reader's attention should not be concentrated upon outward things and thus overlook the deepest essence of His suffering. What a pity that in so much Christian art His physical sufferings have been brought so greatly into prominence.

34 As in numerous other instances, each of the Gospels gives only a few details from the story of the crucifixion and of Jesus' suffering on the cross. Thus no Gospel gives all the words spoken by Him on the cross and we have to take the accounts of all the four Gospels together in order to get a sufficiently full picture. Luke was the only one to record the prayer of the Crucified One for His enemies. It is in perfect agreement with Luke's predilection throughout his Gospel to let the light fall as brightly as possible on Jesus' illimitable love for sinners and the forgiveness of God, that he particularly recorded these words.

And how this prayer of the Crucified Redeemer reveals not merely His wonderful self-forgetfulness, but also His magnanimity and His earnest longing that his persecutors should be given another chance to repent before the otherwise inevitable judgment is executed on their sins! Even as the gardener prayed to the owner of the vineyard to give the fig-tree a last chance, so Jesus in this prayer besought a last chance for the guilty people. And the Father, who is One with the Son in long-suffering and love, heard the prayer of the Saviour. After the people of Jerusalem had tempted heaven by casting out Jesus in this manner and causing Him to be crucified, the Father, who is also the God of history, gave them for another forty long years the opportunity, through the mighty signs of Pentecost and the ministry of the apostles and other believers, to repent in time and to be saved. Several thousands made use of this period of grace and were saved, but the majority were in their folly precipitated into the abyss.

Luke, after recording the Saviour's prayer for His enemies, mentions the fact that the soldiers parted His raiment and cast lots for it. And what a picture this gives us of the fact that He was now robbed of everything—of His honour, His followers, His life (for already He was, as it were, in the stranglehold of death), and even of the last remnant of His earthly possessions, His clothing. Thus He became absolutely poor for our sakes so that we might be made rich in Him.

35 While Jesus was suffering on the cross, the people in great numbers (during the festive period especially hundreds of thousands of Jews had assembled in and around Jerusalem) stood and looked on from a distance. And together with them the Jewish leaders mocked Him and said jeeringly: " He saved others; let him save himself, if he be Christ, the chosen of God." They admit that He saved others (by healing them and even by raising some of them from the dead), but look upon the fact that He does not make use of supernatural power to save Himself as conclusive evidence that He is not the Messiah. Through their spiritual blindness and earthly-mindedness they could cherish no other view of the Messiah except that He must be one who acts with power and violence, vindicates Himself by force, destroys all opposition and triumphs over His enemies. The idea of a suffering Messiah, One who sacrifices Himself in complete self-surrender for the sake of saving sinners, was totally unfamiliar to them (although they ought to have learned this in the Old Testament).

36, 37 The Roman soldiers, too, who were familiar with the way in which all emperors and other worldly rulers looked after their own interests and avenged themselves even though they had to act with the cruellest violence against their enemies, looked upon Jesus' demeanour as the height of folly, and therefore mocked at His claims to kingship while He was helpless in the hands of His enemies.

38 It was the custom, when a condemned man had to be crucified, to hang a notice-board round his neck with the description of the crime for which he was condemned, or else it had to be indicated in some other manner why he was going to be executed. In Jesus' case, where even Pilate had openly admitted that He was innocent, there was really nothing to be recorded to describe the nature of His offence. Nevertheless, in order to avenge himself on the Jewish fanatics who had practically compelled him against his wishes to have Jesus crucified, Pilate caused a superscription to be written over Him more or less to the following effect: " He is the King of the Jews." From John xix. 21 we know that the Jewish authorities sensed the Roman governor's venomous thrust at them in this superscription, and requested Pilate, in vain, to alter it. He had granted their wishes to have the Innocent One crucified, but now it is his turn to take revenge, for by means of this superscription over the Crucified One he proclaims aloud to all that the Jews are a subject people without king, and that whosoever dares to make himself king of the Jews will die in this fashion. Because we know that Pilate was thoroughly conscious of the fact that Jesus laid no claim to kingship (in an earthly sense), it is certain that by means of this superscription he revenged himself on the Jews and was not mocking Jesus. Unconsciously, however, Pilate told the truth in his superscription, for although Jesus is not " king of the Jews " in an earthly and political sense, He is nevertheless the Messiah-king of Israel—the Head of an everlasting kingdom.

39–41 Even one of the crucified criminals treated Jesus with contempt. But the other (who in the beginning probably also took part in mocking Him, Matt. xxvii. 44), began to change his attitude under the impression made on him by the Saviour's personality and demeanour even on the cross, and rebuked his fellow-criminal for his derisive language. He had seen and heard enough of Jesus that day to know that He was innocent of any crime, and in His presence he sensed his own sinfulness. So he admits that he and his fellow-criminal are receiving the due reward of their deeds, but that Jesus is suffering unjustly.

42, 43 In those moments, after the crucified robber had in His presence come to such a conviction of guilt and to repentance, he stretched out, still in time, the beseeching hand of faith to the Redeemer. Undoubtedly Jesus' prayer that the Father should forgive His enemies had made a tremendous impression on this man, and when he observed by Jesus' demeanour and personality that He was no ordinary man, but the Holy One, the faith was born in his heart that He was not only the Messiah but also *the*

One who could in His mercy save him. However defective his faith was still, in all probability, he nevertheless besought Him in sincere trustfulness to take pity on him. Because he still pictured to himself that Jesus was the Messiah who would one day come in Messianic glory, he prayed to the Saviour to remember him when He should come to establish His kingdom. In this primitive form of supplication there was, however, a believing expectation in his attitude towards Jesus, and therefore Jesus assures him that He will not only remember him one day at His second coming, but that he would, on that very day, be with Him in paradise and would partake with Him in the heavenly joy as a redeemed one.

44, 45 The most sacred and solemn hour of crisis in the history of mankind arrived when Jesus as the Lamb of God had to suffer and die on the cross, and above all to bear the wrath of the Holy and Almighty One against the sin of the world. Already by His incarnation the Saviour had proved His willingness to be sacrificed for the sake of fallen mankind. When He voluntarily underwent the baptism of John the Baptist, He confessed openly that He was identifying Himself with a sinful people. In Gethsemane He chose finally to bear the punishment for the sin of mankind. And because this punishment is everlasting death, Jesus had on the cross to experience absolute forsakenness of God, and the pangs of hell itself. It was a time of utter spiritual darkness that the Son of God had to pass through, as the Substitute for the guilty world. Therefore it was also inevitable that the world of nature, the creation of God through the Son (John i. 3), should on that day be radically affected. And so darkness came over the whole earth from twelve to three o'clock and an earthquake rent the rocks in the vicinity (Matt. xxvii. 51). At the same time the veil in the temple, which separated the " holy place " from the " holy of holies " (where under the Old Order God specially revealed Himself), was rent in the midst. This was the sign that through the perfect offering of the Lamb of God the way was opened for every repentant and believing sinner to enter into the most intimate communion with the Holy God without any further offerings for sin. In addition, it was the sign that the temple and the old form of ceremonial religion were no longer necessary— the Old Dispensation, which had been of merely preparatory significance, had finally made room for the New Dispensation founded upon the all-sufficient work of redemption of the Son of God.

46 From Matthew and Mark we know that Jesus, when the darkness ended, called out: " My God, my God, why hast thou forsaken me? " This was the utterance of the terrible sense of God-forsakenness experienced by Him during those hours as our Substitute. After this, being conscious that His suffering and sin-bearing according to the scriptures had been accomplished, He cried out: " It is finished! " (John xix. 30), and then entered into death after He had said: " Father, into thy hands I commend my spirit! " These words show us that in the Saviour's mind there was again a calm restfulness after the hours of darkness and dereliction were past and He was again conscious of the closest communion with God. In addition, it shows us that Jesus, after everything endured by Him spiritually and physically, then revealed that He was the Lord of life and death who died, not because He was forced to do so, but because He Himself of set purpose and volun-tarily laid down His life as the perfect Sacrifice. And so, having committed His spirit to God, He died.

47 The Roman centurion who supervised the crucifixion was so powerfully impressed by the extraordinary and holy personality of the Crucified One as revealed in His prayers, words and demeanour, and proved by the awe-inspiring natural phenomena which accompanied His suffering that he cried out spontaneously: " Truly this was a righeous man". (The Markan version has: " Truly this man was a son of God" Mark xv. 39, R.V., margin.)

In the events of that day and in Jesus he saw the hand of the living God, and acknowledged that the claims of Christ had after all been genuine. And thus he glorified God.

48 The multitude that had gone to see the spectacle of the crucifixion undoubtedly experienced great terror during the hours of darkness and during the earthquake. And, struck by the miraculous occurrence, they smote their breasts with a feeling of guilt and secret presentiments of approaching calamity, and went back to the city. Many of them no doubt knew deep down in their hearts that they were guilty before God because they had caused the Nazarene, who was certainly innocent, to be crucified. Obviously the experiences of that day prepared at least some of them also to become followers of the Crucified One after the Pentecostal miracle had occurred and the fact of Jesus' resurrection and ascension had been proclaimed. This was one of the reasons why on the Day of Pentecost so many thousands were converted. Moreover, the miraculous occurrences that accompanied the crucifixion of the Saviour help to explain why the Jewish author-ities did not immediately dare to take action against the disciples and the first Christians.

49 Because of their unutterable grief and inability to com-prehend what had occurred, most of Jesus' followers had watched the crucifixion only from a distance. Nevertheless His mother, several other women and John were at the cross before He died (John xix. 25 ff.).

The crucifixion of Jesus is the central point of God's whole plan of salvation. The whole of the revelation in the Old Testament had pointed to this fact. By describing the fall of man and by emphasising the holy righteousness of God the necessity for a Redeemer was pointed out, and already in Genesis iii. 15 God had promised that the Redeemer would undo the work of Satan by His suffering. By the institution of the offerings, by the history of Israel, and by numerous other means God had in the Old Testament Dispensation prepared everything for the expiatory death of His Son who had offered Himself from eternity as the Sacrifice for the sins of our fallen humanity. And because His expiatory death forms the basis of the New Dispensation, it is for the whole history of salvation the central point around which everything rotates. For this reason the motto of the Christian church must always be: " We preach Christ crucified " (1 Cor. i. 23).

---

[1] Luke, according to his custom, omits the Aramaic name Golgotha, because it will mean nothing to his Greek readers, and gives the Greek form of the name, κρανίον, a skull. (This is translated in the Latin version as *calvaria*, whence " Calvary " of the A.V.). This hill was so called not because the skulls of executed persons lay unburied there, for then it would be called the place of the skulls (plural). Moreover, the Jews would never have tolerated it that unburied skulls should lie so close to the city. " A rocky protrusion, resembling a skull in form, is no doubt the meaning. Thus Cyril of Jerusalem speaks of it as ' rising on high and showing itself to this day, and displaying even yet how because of Christ the rocks were then riven', *Catechetical Lectures*, xiii, 39" (Plummer, *in loc.*). There exists a great difference of opinion as to where Golgotha was exactly situated. The ancient view was that the so-called " church of the Holy Sepulchre " in Jerusalem was built on the hill, but others think that a hill outside the modern Jerusalem (on the north side) was the real Golgotha. Has not God ordered this uncertainty as to the exact locality of Golgotha, so that men's minds should not be excessively occupied with the external aspect of the crucifixion?

[2] Although this prayer of Jesus is omitted by a number of MSS. (א&a; B D* W θ, etc.), it nevertheless occurs in most of the important MSS. (א* A C D² L N, etc.), and there is no proof that it is not authentic. The reason why some copyists have omitted it must probably be sought in the fact that they looked upon the destruction of Jerusalem as a

proof that God had not forgiven the Jews, and they could not make it appear as if a prayer of Jesus had remained unanswered. Streeter (*op. cit.*, p. 138), Harnack, Schlatter, Zahn and many others accept the authenticity of this prayer. We agree with Major that "Luke's Gospel, undoubtedly, makes use of much original material drawn from feminine sources. It was women followers of Jesus who stood nearest to the cross, and doubtless Luke owes to them these words from the cross which are not recorded in the other Gospels" (*op. cit.*, p. 195).

³ "In the soul of Jesus there was no resentment, no anger, no lurking desire for punishment upon the men who were maltreating Him" (Morgan, *in loc.*). The Saviour's prayer was indeed heard. Those responsible for His death deserved to be immediately exterminated by God because of their murdering the Messiah. But through His intercession God forgave this deed and gave them another forty years to repent, and because the people nevertheless persisted in unbelief and sin the inescapable judgment overtook them. "The end of the Gospel gives this ἄφες its mighty ring; it ends with forgiveness and the invitation to repent and the promise of the coming kingdom. That is ἄφεσις, cancellation of the crime committed against Jesus, which undoes what Jerusalem has done, and renews the shattered communion. Jesus is afresh the bringer of grace for Jerusalem" (Schlatter, *in loc.*). After all the privileges already enjoyed by the chosen people and after their scandalous treatment of Jesus they were more than ripe for immediate destruction, and yet God gave them a last chance (cf. Isa. liii. 12).

⁴ That Jesus did not pray for the Roman soldiers but for the guilty Jewish people follows from the fact that such a prayer for the soldiers was unnecessary, for they only carried out orders and had no share in His condemnation. From the context (verse 33) it appears that Jesus' prayer refers to His crucifixion through the agency of the Jews.

⁵ Because of their spiritual blindness, the Jews did not realise what they were doing by causing the Son of God to be crucified.

⁶ Cf. John xix. 29 ff. The Saviour refused the soporific drink which they offered Him (Matt. xxvii. 34), because He desired to remain fully conscious and clear in mind during His suffering and death. But the pure vinegar that was given to alleviate for a moment the terrible thirst of the crucified was taken by Him after He had practically completed the suffering and forsakenness on the cross (John xix. 29).

⁷ The Gospels do not profess to give the superscription verbally and fully. Possibly the full superscription was: "This is Jesus, the Nazarene, the King of the Jews." Each of the Gospels, however, gives the main contents of the superscription. It is also possible that the superscription was not exactly the same in the different languages. Then Luke may render the Greek form, Matthew and John (more fully) the Hebrew and Mark the Latin version. In any case we must not look for any stenographic renderings of such details in the Gospels, which are intended to be proclamations of the glad tidings and not full biographies.

8 Probably the added detail, " in Greek and Roman and Hebrew letters ", crept into Luke's original text from John xix. 20 (cf. Plummer, *in loc.*). It is omitted by ℵ^{ca} B C* L, the Old Latin MS. " a ", the Old Syriac and Coptic versions.

9 *Οὐχὶ σὺ εἶ* (" Art thou not . . .? ") is the correct reading. " ' Art thou not ' is a more bitter taunt than ' if thou art ' " (Plummer, *in loc.*).

10 Obviously this robber would not have realised from the very commencement that Jesus was no ordinary man. And it was quite natural for him, as a hardened criminal, along with his companion, to insult the Saviour who was mocked by all for His claims to Messiahship (Mark xv. 32). But after further revelations of His holiness, he changed his attitude and rebuked the other malefactor. This explanation is certainly not the outcome of " harmonistic prejudice ", but the logical result of the actual circumstances.

11 *'Ιησοῦ*, and not *Κύριε* (" Lord ", A.V.), is the correct reading here (cf. Zahn, *in loc.*).

12 He recognises the Messiah in Jesus and knows that the Messiah will have a kingdom. *ἐν τῇ βασιλείᾳ σου* is the correct reading and not *εἰς τὴν βασιλείαν σου*, which is the reading of " B ", " L ", and the Latin version. It refers to " the return of the Messiah in glory " (Luce, *in loc.*).

13 Jesus knows that even in death, before His resurrection, He will be in communion with the living God, His Father, and will, free from all suffering and afflictions of the earthly life, enjoy heavenly bliss with God (represented under the image of " Paradise "). And He assures the repentant criminal that he will share with Him in this bliss, in the heavenly life in Paradise, on the very day, after they have entered death. Thus, in agreement with the rest of the New Testament, it is here clearly taught that the saved immediately after death associate spiritually with Jesus in heavenly bliss (cf. 2 Cor. v. 1, 8; Phil. 1. 23).

14 " In our Lord's answer, the word *today* stands foremost, because Jesus wishes to contrast the nearness of the promised happiness with the remote future to which the prayer of the thief refers. *Today*, before the setting of the sun which is shining on us " (Godet, *in loc.*). To take together with *I say*, as some interpreters do, is altogether unjustifiable, for then *today* has no force here (cf. Plummer, *in loc.*).

15 *μετ' ἐμοῦ*—" ' Not merely in My company (*σὺν ἐμοί*), but sharing with Me.' The promise implies the continuance of consciousness after death. If the dead are unconscious, the assurance to the robber that he will be with Christ after death would be an empty consolation " (Plummer, *in loc.*).

16 The image for the abode and condition of heavenly bliss with God after death. Perfect bliss, however, only comes after the resurrection when the saved will partake of the heavenly joy in soul *and* in body. In the meantime every deceased believer is in full spiritual happiness with the Lord. *παράδεισος* is " a short way of indicating the heavenly abode of the blessed " (Strack-Billerbeck, *in loc.*). The word

is derived from Old Iranian *pairi-daeza*, a " walled round " garden or park. This abode of bliss is, according to Revelation ii. 7 and 2 Corinthians xii. 2, 4, in heaven. The transition of meaning from the earthly Paradise to the heavenly abode has its ground in the fact that the bliss which was lost through the fall of man is restored to the faithful by Christ in the life everlasting.

17 By answering the robber's prayer, Jesus acts according to the rule of the divine grace proclaimed by Him so clearly in His teachings: To him who prays, shall be given; whosoever repents, shall be absolved, and whosoever comes to Him, even in a dying state, shall receive true life (cf. Schlatter, *in loc.*).

18 By ὅλην πὴν γῆν is most probably meant " the whole land " (according to Luther, Calvin, Plummer, Zahn).

19 The reading τοῦ ἡλίου ἐκλείποντος (B C*, etc.) or τοῦ ἡλίου ἐκλιπόντος (א L, etc.) can only mean " the sun being (or having been) eclipsed ". True, ἐκλείπω by itself means " cease, fail " (Abbott-Smith), but in conjunction with ἥλιος it can mean nothing but " eclipse ". An eclipse at the time of full moon is out of the question. This reading is very likely due to the corruption of a marginal note like τοῦ ʾΗλείου ἐλλείποντος (" the passage about Elias being omitted "), referring to Luke's omission of Mark xv. 34b–36. See E. C. Selwyn in *Expositor*, VIII, ix (1915), pp. 144–50; J. W. Burgon, *The Revision Revised* (1883), pp. 61 ff. The true reading here is no doubt καὶ ἐσκοτίσθη ὁ ἥλιος, " and the sun was darkened " (A C³ D W Θ, etc.). In some way or other, we do not know how, God in His omnipotence brought darkness over the earth and caused the earthquake to take place. In the apocryphal " Gospel of Peter " it is stated that it was so dark that numbers of people went about with lamps, thinking that it was night.

Origen (*Contra Cels.*, ii, 33) and Eusebius (*Chron.*) quote words from Phlegon (a Roman historian) in which he makes mention of an extraordinary solar eclipse as well as of an earthquake about the time of the crucifixion (cf. Zahn and Plummer, *in loc.*).

20 " Here the veil hanging before the holy of holies should be pictured " (Van Leeuwen at Mark xv. 38).

21 We do not know how God so ordered it that the veil was rent. In any case some of the priests were eye-witnesses of it and this fact became known amongst the Christians, most probably through the large number of priests who became believers after Pentecost (Acts vi. 7). The fact that the veil was rent in twain would obviously soon become known among all the priests, even had there been only a few of them in the " holy place " when it happened.

In the Jewish Talmud (the Gemara) it is stated that forty years before the destruction of Jerusalem (i.e. at the time of the crucifixion) the massive doors of the temple opened of their own accord (T. Bab., *Yoma*, 39b). Josephus (*The Jewish War*, vi, 5) also makes mention of various miraculous occurrences that took place and of voices heard in the temple during the time before the destruction of Jerusalem. And

Jerome (in his exposition of Matthew xxvii. 51) relates still other supernatural occurrences in the temple during the crucifixion.

[22] These words are not " the last sigh of a pining man, with which this life ends, but a cry of supplication, audible far and wide, bearing witness to a residue of physical strength and at the same time to the full consciousness of the one who was dying " (Zahn, *in loc.*).

[23] " The πνεῦμα is that which produces life; in death it is severed from the man. In handing it over to God, Jesus praises God as the One who has given Him life and as the One from whom He will receive newness of life " (Schlatter, *in loc.*).

[24] His action glorified God, for " whoso gives truth and righteousness their honour contributes to the glorifying of God " (Zahn, *in loc.*).

THE BURIAL

(Cf. Matt. xxvii. 57–66; Mark xv. 42–7; John xix. 38–42)

xxiii. 50–6

50 And behold, a man named Joseph, who was a councillor,
51 a good man and a righteous (he had not consented to their
counsel and deed), *a man* of Arimathaea,[1] a city of the Jews,
52 who was looking for the kingdom of God: this man went to
53 Pilate, and asked for the body of Jesus. And he took it down,
and wrapped it in a linen cloth, and laid him in a tomb that
54 was hewn in stone, where never man had yet lain. And it
was the day of the Preparation,[2] and the sabbath drew on.
55 And the women, which had come with him out of Galilee,
followed after, and beheld the tomb,[4] and how his body was
56 laid. And they returned, and prepared spices and ointments.[5]
And on the sabbath they rested according to the
commandment.[6]

The Gospel narrative of Jesus' passion ends on a note of
exceptional beauty in the description of His burial. For in it
we see how the dead body of the Saviour, from the time that it
was removed from the rough cross by hands of affection, was
cared for by no other hands than those of His faithful followers.
He had lived through the deepest humiliation, the pangs of hell
and death, and had thus already completed the full work of
expiation. Through His death He immediately joined His
Father in spirit in the celestial Paradise. (His words " To-day
shalt thou be with me in Paradise " and " Father, in thy hands I
commend my Spirit ", prove this conclusively.) So His way of
suffering, humiliation and death was past and ere long His
victory would be revealed by His resurrection. For this reason
the Father ordains that the funeral is attended to by His faithful
and beloved worshippers. And thus the prophecy was fulfilled
which declared that although a grave was allocated to Him
along with malefactors (because the death-sentence of a felon
was carried out on Him), yet He was with the rich man in His
death (Isa. liii. 9). Never again will He be the object of human
mockery, humiliation and violence. He had already finished all

618

(John xix. 30), and His honourable burial in the new rock-hewn tomb of the noble Joseph of Arimathaea, is the prologue to His exaltation and glorification.

50-3 Joseph of Arimathaea, one of the secret followers of the Saviour (Matt. xxvii. 57), was a wealthy and distinguished man and even a member of the Jewish Sanhedrin in Jerusalem. In addition, he was a good and righteous man and on the ground of Jesus' teachings expected the revelation of the sovereign dominion of God. Obviously, therefore, he did not agree with the actions and decisions of the Jewish Council which had compassed the condemnation and death of Jesus. Although to this disciple of the Lord it must have been a matter of great sorrow and disappointment that He had to die on the cross after being condemned, nevertheless his love for the Saviour was so ineradicable that he defied persecution on the part of the Jewish authorities and asked Pilate for permission to bury the body of Jesus. With the help of another Sanhedrist of note, Nicodemus, who was also a secret follower of Jesus (John xix. 39), he then took it down, embalmed it with an abundance of myrrh and aloes, wrapped it in fine linen and buried it in a tomb hewn out of rock in which no one had previously been buried.

54 The Saviour died at about three o'clock in the afternoon, so that, by the time that His body was buried, the evening hour (the commencement of the new Jewish day), and thus the beginning of the Sabbath, was at hand.

55, 56 Although the women who had followed Him from Galilee so faithfully (viii. 3), did not venture to go and help with the burial, they nevertheless followed Joseph and Nicodemus and looked carefully where they laid down His body. It was their intention later on, as a proof of their tender love for Him, to go and embalm His body further with spices and ointment. For this reason they quickly went to the city, and during the short period before the Sabbath dawned commenced to prepare the spices and ointment. They did not, however, have a sufficient supply, and after they had rested on the Sabbath, the last of the Old Dispensation (which passed finally with Jesus' resurrection), they went to buy and prepare what was still wanting at the commencement of the first day of the week (i.e. the evening of the following day, Mark xvi. 1), in order to take it with them to His tomb on the following morning.

In the hours of crisis it is often the Peters who have sworn loyalty to Jesus with big gestures and fullness of self-confidence, that disappoint, and it is the secret and quiet followers of the

Master (like Joseph, Nicodemus and the women) that do not hesitate to serve Him in love—at whatever cost.

[1] Arimathaea was Joseph's native town, but at that time he was an inhabitant of Jerusalem (otherwise he would not have been a member of the Sanhedrin and would probably also not have possessed a tomb near the city). Arimathaea is regarded by some as identical with Ramah (*Ramathaim-Zophim*), the birthplace of Samuel. This is, however, not certain.

[2] παρασκευῆς (' preparation ') was the technical name for Friday, (which in ecclesiastical Greek and Latin is still known as *Parascevē*). Even although this particular Friday was the first feast-day, could still be called simply παρασκευή, according to rabbinical writings of that time (Strack-Billerbeck, ii, pp. 828–32). This does away with the argument that, since Luke here calls the day on which Jesus was crucified παρασκευή, it proves that He was not crucified on the Feast Day. Cf. our Excursus on this subject, pp. 649 ff.

[3] ἐπέφωσκεν is here used figuratively and indicates the commencement of the Sabbath (which, according to the Jewish division of the day, commenced in the evening). " ' It was dawning ' easily comes to mean ' it was beginning ' " (Plummer, *in loc.*).

[4] " Matthew's remark that the women sat ' over against ' it, suggests that the sepulchre was situated on a hillside in a valley, on the other side of which (presumably the Jerusalem side) the women sat. This opinion that the sepulchre was hewn on a hillside is also supported by Mark's statement(xvi. 4) that the women on approaching it looked up. These points are small, but they do seem to indicate a definite primitive Christian tradition of a particular sepulchre " (Major, *op. cit.*, p. 198). To-day, however, there exists no certainty as to where this sepulchre was.

[5] If we render this verse as it is rendered in the A.V. (" And they returned, and prepared spices and ointments; and rested the Sabbath day according to the commandment "), the natural explanation of the apparent contradiction between Luke and Mark xvi. 1 is to be found in the account we have given above in our exposition of verse 56. If, however, we take the verse as it is given in the R.V. and in the most generally accepted Greek text (where καὶ τὸ μὲν σάββατον ἡσύχασαν commences a new paragraph and goes along with xxiv. 1), then Luke in verse 56a only in a very general way mentions the fact that they went to prepare spices and ointment, without explaining why they did so. And then 56b should be removed to chapter xxiv. Thus Moffatt translates: " On the Sabbath they rested in obedience to God's command, but on the first day of the week . . ." Only if Luke had in verse 56b written " thereafter ", would there have been question of a contradiction between Luke and Mark. As it is, it is hypercritical to see a contradiction here, whether we take verse 56b together with chapter xxiv or not.

[6] It was the law that on the Sabbath day a body might be embalmed, but it was forbidden to *buy* and *prepare* ointment and spices and other necessaries on the Sabbath (Strack-Billerbeck, at Mark xvi. 1). On other feast days, however, it was permitted to buy things, as long as the quantity and the price were not mentioned. Therefore Joseph could have bought the linen on the feast day (Strack-Billerbeck, ii, p. 823).

THE RESURRECTION

(Cf. Matt. xxviii. 1–16; Mark xvi. 1–8; John xx. 1–17)

xxiv. 1–12

1 But on the first day of the week, at early dawn,[1] they[2]
came unto the tomb, bringing the spices which they had
2 prepared. And they found the stone rolled away from the
3 tomb. And they entered in, and found not the body of the
4 Lord Jesus.[3] And it came to pass, while they were perplexed
thereabout, behold, two[4] men[5] stood by them in dazzling
5 apparel: and as they were affrighted, and bowed down their
faces to the earth, they said unto them, Why seek ye the
6 living among the dead? He is not here, but is risen: remem-
7 ber how he spake unto you when he was yet in Galilee,[6]
saying that the Son of man must be delivered up into the
hands of sinful men, and be crucified, and the third day rise
8, 9 again. And they remembered his words, and returned from
the tomb, and told all these things to the eleven, and to all
10 the rest. Now[7] they were Mary Magdalene, and Joanna,[8]
and Mary[9] the *mother* of James: and the other women with
11 them told these things unto the apostles. And these words
appeared in their sight as idle talk;[10] and they disbelieved
12 them. But Peter arose, and ran unto the tomb; and stooping
and looking in, he seeth the linen cloths by themselves; and
he departed to his home wondering at that which was come
to pass.[11]

The certainty of Jesus' resurrection permeates the whole of the
New Testament with its bright effulgence. In each of the Gospels
we receive the glad tidings that He, who as the Sacrificial Lamb
went down voluntarily and completely into death and hell to
expiate the sins of mankind, arose from the dead as Victor and
is now the exalted Head and Lord of His church. In Acts we see
how the little group of disciples, who at the crucifixion were
despondent and powerless, now carried into the world the glad
tidings of the resurrection with unwonted power and vigour—
empowered thereto by the risen and living Christ. In the epistles
of Paul and the other apostles we see what a central place,
alongside the sacrificial death of Jesus, His resurrection and
exaltation took up in the life of the church. And in Revelation

622

we see how the risen Christ is ready to return in the fullness of time in divine glory as the Victor over grave and death and hell, and as the Eternal King and Prince of Peace.

1-3 On the previous evening, as soon as the Sabbath was past, the women made all the necessary preparations (Mark xvi. 1) and on the following morning (Sunday morning) as soon as it was light enough, went to the sepulchre with the prepared spices and ointment. To their surprise they not only discovered that the stone had been rolled away from the opening to the sepulchre, but when they entered in they saw that the body of the Saviour was no longer there.

4-8 They stood there, surprised and perplexed, and unable to find an explanation of the circumstances. But as angels had proclaimed the glad tidings of Jesus' nativity, so now God again sent some of these celestial beings from the Invisible World to bring to the women the tidings that He had risen from the dead. As in every instance where human beings suddenly came face to face with celestial beings, so here too the women became exceedingly afraid when they beheld the two angels standing by them in shining garments. The angels by their question: " Why seek ye the living among the dead? " pointed out the folly of thinking that Jesus was still to be counted among the dead. He is the Living One, yes, even Life itself, so how can they seek Him among the dead? No bonds of grave or death could keep Him bound, and it is the spontaneous outcome of His whole being as perfect Man and Son of God, that, after He had accomplished full expiation through His suffering and sacrificial death, He arose from the dead in triumph. And thus the celestial messengers proclaim the most glorious tidings—Jesus is not here where His body was laid down in death, but He has arisen, and He lives. The angels gently rebuke the women for coming to seek the Saviour among the dead. They ought to have known that He, who is the Life, would never have remained imprisoned by the bonds of death, and in addition the angels remind them that Jesus Himself, when He was still with them in Galilee, had expressly warned them that He would be delivered over and would be crucified, but also that He would arise on the third day (cf. ix. 22; xviii. 31-3).

It stands to reason that, although the Saviour had so repeatedly warned His followers that He would be killed and had assured them that He would rise again, they nevertheless did not realise the actuality of His words. Their ideas about the manner in which the Messiah would triumph over His enemies were so different from what Jesus had prophesied and from what was accomplished, that His crucifixion left them completely bewildered and perplexed. And just as they were but little prepared for the violent removal of their Master, so little did they realise after His crucifixion that He would indeed rise again. His former words were unintelligible to them (xviii. 34). Perhaps some of them expected that He would again appear at the end of the age, but not one of them could imagine that He would so soon arise from the grave in a glorified body. This was such an unheard-of thing and seemed so impossible after they had seen their Master dying that cruel death on the cross, that His words in which He assured them that He would rise again on the third day never entered their minds during those days of sorrow and despondency. But when they found the sepulchre empty, and when the angels brought them the glad tidings of the resurrection and reminded them of Jesus' words, a light entered into their despondent hearts, and they could again clearly recall the words of the Saviour.

9, 10 Luke does not describe the various visits to the sepulchre mentioned in the other Gospels, but only states concisely that the women who were at the sepulchre saw the angels and heard the tidings, and then went to communicate this to the disciples. It is not Luke's object to give a complete account of the occurrences, but to proclaim the fact, the glorious certainty, of the resurrection. He does not wish to distract our attention from the main fact by various details of the actions and experiences of people. So he merely gives, in a summarised form, a general picture of the fact that the sepulchre was found empty and that the angels proclaimed the glad tidings of Jesus' resurrection.

11, 12 The words of the women concerning the empty sepulchre and the tidings of the angels, seemed to the perplexed group of disciples like senseless women's talk, and they would not believe them. But Peter, impulsive as ever (accompanied by John, John xx. 2), ran to the sepulchre excitedly and beheld with his own eyes the truth of the women's words. Surprised, and not yet capable of realising that Jesus had indeed arisen, he departed again.

When a Child was born in Bethlehem in the humblest circumstances, a new and unutterably glorious song was born in the heart of certain people. And during the years He spent as Man on earth, He brought joy into the hearts of many. But throughout that time, ever since the prediction of the pious Simeon that a sword would pass through Mary's soul (ii. 35), the joyful tidings of the angels at His birth were obscured by the dark shadow of the cross that fell over His life. This shadow became darker and darker, until, when Jesus had to endure the dereliction of God on the cross, nature itself was enveloped in darkness as a sign of the black night into which the Lamb of God was plunged for the salvation of sinners. But the Son of God, who is Life itself, was mightier than death and darkness, and arose triumphantly from the grave. Then the glad tidings that had been proclaimed at His birth and public appearance, resounded through heaven and earth with irresistible power. And ever since then the world has been filled with a bright light and a beautiful song which through every century have given true life and joy to millions, such as had never yet been experienced upon this earth. For Jesus has conquered, so that we also may be more than conquerors. As the risen Lord He raises us from spiritual death to true life, and at His second advent He will also cause us to arise from physical death, with celestial, glorified bodies, to everlasting bliss.

---

[1] ὄρθρου βαθέως, literally, as Easton puts it, " at deep earliness ", " at the first dawn ".

[2] Luke does not mention the names, because he merely gives a general portrayal of the incidents in a summarised and concise form.

[3] τοῦ κυρίου Ἰησοῦ is omitted by the Western text, and is possibly an early interpolation.

[4] When Mark xvi. 5 refers to the same event, the fact that he mentions only one man (angel) and Luke mentions two, may be explained from the fact that " where, out of two or more, only one is spokesman, he is necessarily remembered. The other or others may easily be ignored or forgotten. It is an exaggeration to call such differences absolute discrepancies " (Plummer, in loc.). Obviously only one of the angels would act as spokesman.

[5] In Acts i. 10 and x. 30 also angels are called ἄνδρες. By referring to Jesus' words in Galilee, the angels make the women realise that He had already warned them in good time.

[6] It is a far-fetched assertion that Luke of set purpose altered the angels' words of Mark xvi. 7 to fit in with his alleged view that Jesus appeared only in Jerusalem and not in Galilee. Luke in fact never states that Jesus did not also appear in Galilee. He gives an extremely summarised account of the appearances. That He was conscious of the fact that there were many more than he recorded, appears from his words in Acts i. 3. And as an intimate follower of Paul, and, in addition, as an active and accurate investigator of the story of Jesus (i. 1–4), he would surely have known of at least all the instances mentioned by Paul in 1 Corinthians xv. 1–7. The fact that he makes no mention of those other appearances, is in keeping with the scheme and purpose of his writing; and we must also remember that his space was

limited and that he could therefore record only the main facts and matters which he considered important with a view to his version of the Gospel history.

The reason why Luke did not record the words of the angel that the disciples had to go to Galilee, is that, since he had decided to mention only the appearances in Judaea, these words of the angels would be left hanging in air. The angels undoubtedly said more than is recorded in any of the Gospels. Each evangelist merely records those words that were necessary for his form and scheme of proclaiming the resurrection of Jesus.

⁷ The R.V. rendering of this verse, with the heavy stop after " James ", represents the best attested text, but its awkwardness makes one suspect that the relative pronoun αἱ (preserved by the Textus Receptus) has been accidentally lost after ᾿Ιακώβου and that the A.V. is therefore preferable: " It was Mary Magdalene, and Joanna, and Mary the mother of James, and other women that were with them, which told these things unto the apostles." Luke mentions a few women's names and indicates that there were others as well who went to tell the disciples that the sepulchre was empty. He does so in order to call attention to the definite certainty that the sepulchre was indeed empty. So many witnesses, including some well-known and noble women, saw it and therefore it is historically unassailable. In this verse Luke combines all the various visits of the women (see note on The Resurrection, below) and their reports to the disciples, and does not refer merely to the one visit related in veres 1–9.

⁸ Cf. viii. 3. Luke probably obtained from Joanna the particulars which he mentions here, and also those in xxiii. 8–12 (Plummer, *in loc.*).

⁹ Probably the same as Mary, the wife of Cleopas (John xix. 25).

¹⁰ λῆρος = " ' Nonsense '; the word is applied in medicinal language to the wild talk of the sick in delirium " (cf. Plummer, *in loc.*).

¹¹ It is practically certain that this verse (omitted by the Western texts), which is a kind of short summary of John xx. 3–10, is an early interpolation in Luke's original text (cf. Zahn, Plummer, Luce, and nearly all expositors).

SPECIAL NOTE

THE RESURRECTION OF JESUS

(a) The Sequence of the Events.

Because the Gospels are primarily accounts of the apostolic preaching about Jesus and not complete biographies, we are not entitled to look in them for a connected narrative of all the various events. When we are faced with assertions (sometimes of a very arbitrary character) that the Gospels contradict one another as regards the particulars of the resurrection-appearances, we should bear in mind that the Gospels give such a condensed and selective account of the resurrection that no one knows whether the episodes described in one Gospel are the same as those mentioned in one or more of the others. We are considerably handicapped in this matter by the fact that Mark's account does not carry us beyond xvi. 8 of his Gospel (whether by original design or later accident need not be discussed here). Mark xvi. 9–20 gives a later summary of resurrection-appearances. And because we know so little of the less important particulars of those events, we are unable to see how the various narratives fit into one another. In any case, all the Gospels proclaim the main facts and leave no doubt as to the certainty that Jesus did arise.

If, indeed, we should make an attempt to give some account of the approximate course of events from the data of all four Gospels, it is possible to suggest the following sequence.

Very early on the Sunday morning the resurrection took place, the earthquake followed, the angel descended and rolled away the stone) Matt. xxviii. 2–4), and the guards of soldiers fled (Matt. xxviii. 11). A little later Mary Magdalene, Mary the mother of James and Salome hastened to the sepulchre while another group of women followed with the spices. Mary Magdalene reaches the sepulchre first, sees that it is empty and immediately goes to inform Peter and John (John xx. 1 ff.). The other Mary and Salome approach and see the angel (Matt. xxviii. 5). Thereafter the other women with Joanna among them come along; they see the two angels and receive the message that Jesus has risen (Luke xxiv. 1 ff.). In the meantime Mary Magdalene reaches Peter and John, and they hasten to the sepulchre (John xx). Mary also follows them again and arrives at the sepulchre after the others have already departed.

She weeps at the sepulchre (John xx. ii ff.) and sees the two angels, who ask her why she is weeping. After this she sees Jesus Himself (John xx. 14). In the meantime the other women had gone to the other disciples and told them their experiences. But their words were regarded as idle tales (xxiv. 11) until Peter and John confirmed them. When the women were afterwards probably again on their way to the sepulchre, Jesus meets them (according to the true text of Matthew xxviii. 9, which simply reads: " And behold, Jesus met them and said . . ."). Later in the day the Saviour appeared to Peter alone (Luke xxiv. 34 and 1 Cor. xv. 5), towards evening to the men of Emmaus, and a little later to the whole group of disciples, with the exception of Thomas (Luke xxiv. 36–43; John xx. 19–24).

A week later He again appeared to the disciples, including Thomas, who was convinced of the certainty of the resurrection (John xxi. 1–23). And during the forty days before His ascension the Lord also appeared in Galilee to the seven disciples at the Sea (John xxi. 1–23) (obviously the Galilean disciples, especially after Jesus' command that they should go thither, left Jerusalem after a few weeks for Galilee). He also appeared to five hundred of His followers in Galilee (as a result of the command of Mark xvi. 7 they would probably, after the reports concerning Jesus' resurrection had been brought to them, have assembled spontaneously in expectation of His appearance). When Paul wrote 1 Corinthians xv. 6, most of the five hundred were still alive as living witnesses of the fact of the resurrection.

From Acts i. 3, 4, and from the whole history from the commencement of Christianity, it appears that during the forty days before His ascension Jesus often appeared to His followers and spoke to them about many things in order to prepare them as builders of His church. Towards the end of the forty days He no doubt commanded them to go to Jerusalem and to remain there until the promise of the Holy Ghost should be fulfilled. After their return to Judaea the Saviour also appeared to James (1 Cor. xv. 7) and to the apostles (Luke xxiv. 33–53; Acts i. 3–12); and after His ascension He appeared to Paul near Damascus (Acts ix. 3–6, 1 Cor. xv. 8) and again in the temple (Acts xxii. 17–21, xxiii. 11). Also Stephen, the first martyr, saw Jesus after His resurrection (Acts vii. 55). Last of all, the Saviour also appeared to John, the grey-haired exile on Patmos (Rev. i. 10–19).

Thus we have a mighty cloud of witnesses that Jesus has indeed arisen as the Conqueror over the grave, death and hell, and lives forever!

(b) The Fact of the Resurrection.

The unambiguous announcement of the New Testament that Jesus arose from the dead and was exalted as King and Lord is confirmed amongst other things by the following facts.

(1) The origin and continued existence of the Christian church. It is historically and psychologically impossible that the followers of Jesus, who at His crucifixion were so completely despondent and perplexed, would within a few weeks thereafter enter the world (as they did) with such unheard-of joy, power and devotion, if it had not been for the fact that He had risen from the dead, had appeared to them, and had proved that His claims to be the Son of God were genuine. Only the living, risen Christ could have changed His disciples, with all their disappointment, sorrow and fear, so radically that they laid upon the altar their all so joyfully as bearers of the glad tidings and that they even faced persecution and martyrdom in His service without flinching.

(2) If Jesus had not risen, the New Testament would never have been written. For who would have taken the trouble to write the biography of anyone who had laid tremendous claims to Messiahship and divinity, but whose career terminated in a shameful death? But (God be praised) Jesus did arise, and that is why the group of men who wrote the books of the New Testament took up their pens with such enthusiasm and holy conviction. And throughout their writings we perceive the clear note of their firm conviction that Christ Jesus, who had died, rose again from the dead and was invested with divine

power and glory, over and above that which He had with the Father " before the world was ".

Apart from the resurrection-narratives in the Gospels, we have the following important references to the resurrection in the New Testament: Romans i. 4, iv. 24 ff., vi. 4, vii. 4, viii. 11, 34, x. 7 ff., xiv. 9; 1 Corinthians vi. 14, xv. 1–58; 2 Corinthians iv. 14, v. 15, xiii. 4; Galatians i. 1; Ephesians i. 20, ii. 6; Philippians iii. 10; Colossians i. 18–iii. 1; Thessalonians i. 10, iv. 14; Hebrews xiii. 20; 1 Peter i. 3, iii. 21; Revelation i. 5, 18, ii. 8.

(3) The empty sepulchre is also a powerful indication of the fact of the resurrection. For from this it follows that, if Jesus had not arisen, His body must have been removed either by His enemies or by members of His circle of disciples, and both are impossible, for (apart from the fact that guards had been placed before the sepulchre and that it had been sealed), if any of His enemies had removed His body, they would, when the disciples announced that Jesus had risen, surely have produced it again, or would at any rate have declared that they had removed it, so that in this manner they might deal the death-blow to the belief in the resurrection. Now it is an historical fact that nothing was done and that no such statement was made. This clinches the fact that Jesus' body was not taken away by His enemies. And it is just as certain that His disciples would not have done it. For one thing, it is utterly unlikely that they would have got away with this fraud. And for another, it is impossible that they would have sacrificed their possessions and their blood in the service of Christ if their announcement of His resurrection had been based upon deceit. How could the ineradicable joy, certainty and power have come into their lives after His crucifixion if their whole faith were a gigantic lie? Everything points to the fact that there is only one explanation for the empty sepulchre: Jesus' claim to be the Son of God was true, and no bonds of death and darkness could keep Him confined to the grave. He did arise, and He lives.

(4) The fact that the Christian church from an early date (cf. Acts xx. 7; 1 Cor. xvi. 2; Rev. i. 10) had observed Sunday instead of Saturday as the day of rest, can only be explained from the fact of the resurrection of Jesus on the Sunday morning. The church observed Sunday as the day of worship not only from the time that Constantine the Great proclaimed it officially as the day of rest, but from the earliest times; cf. the express statements to this effect in the letter of Barnabas, written about A.D. 80, and see Major, op. cit., p. 213. And if we bear in mind that the first congregations consisted mainly of converted Jews (who were firmly attached to Saturday as the Sabbath) and that the leaders of the church were men like Paul who had had a strict training according to the Law, then only the fact that Jesus arose on a Sunday and exalted that day to be " the day of the Lord " can explain why the old Jewish custom was given up and the first day of the week was accepted as the day of rest—in honour of the risen Christ and as a symbol that the Old Testament dispensation of ceremonial religion

was past and was superseded by the New Dispensation of freedom and spontaneous inward worship of God in the name of Jesus.

(5) Another remarkable phenomenon in the early church points to the certainty of the resurrection. From the New Testament and from other ancient Christian writings (e.g. the letters of Ignatius) it appears that one of the most characteristic features of the early church was the celebration of Holy Communion, and that this celebration, although it was held in memory of Jesus' death, was characterised by a spirit of gratitude and joy. Major rightly states: " If the death of Jesus on the cross had not been followed by the belief in His resurrection, it would be impossible to account either for the existence of the Eucharistic rite or for its joyous character " (*op. cit.*, p. 214).

A detailed exposition and refutation of the various theories (which are constantly changing and cancelling one another) of those who do not accept the fact of Jesus' resurrection, belongs to a separate work on this subject.[1] Suffice it for us to declare that not a single attempt to adduce a conclusive proof against the genuineness of the New Testament account of the resurrection of the Saviour has been successful. All such attempts fall to the ground in face of the unambiguous testimony of the New Testament and the other facts that prove that Jesus did indeed conquer and that He lives.

(6) And through the centuries there are untold multitudes, the poor and the rich, the simple and the educated, the aged and the young, millions who day after day experience in their own hearts and lives the assurance that Jesus has indeed arisen and that He lives as Lord and King. In the testimony of the Holy Ghost in the heart of every reborn child of God no doubt exists, and together with the believers of all ages our hearts sing:

> He lives! He lives!
> Christ Jesus lives to-day!
> He walks with me, and talks with me
> Along life's narrow way.
> He lives! He lives!
> Salvation to impart:
> You ask me how I know He lives?
> He lives—within my heart!

[1] Reference may be made to one such work out of many: G. R. Beasley-Murray's *Christ is Alive!* (Lutterworth Press, 1947).

THE MEN OF EMMAUS

13 And[1] behold, two of them[2] were going that very day to a
village named Emmaus,[3] which was threescore furlongs[4]
14 from Jerusalem. And they communed with each other of
15 all these things which had happened. And it came to pass,
while they communed and questioned together, that Jesus
16 himself drew near, and went with them.[5] But their eyes were
17 holden that they should not know him. And he said unto
them, What communications are these that ye have one with
18 another, as ye walk? And they stood still, looking sad. And
one of them, named Cleopas,[6] answering said unto him,
Dost thou alone sojourn in Jerusalem and not know the
19 things which are come to pass there in these days? And he
said unto them, What things? And they said unto him,
The things concerning Jesus of Nazareth, which was a
prophet[7] mighty in deed and word before God and all the
20 people: and how the chief priests and our rulers delivered
21 him up to be condemned to death, and crucified him. But
we hoped that it was he which should redeem Israel. Yea
and beside all this, it is now the third day since these things
22 came to pass. Moreover[8] certain women of our company
23 amazed us, having been early at the tomb; and when they
found not his body, they came, saying, that they had also
24 seen a vision of angels, which said that he was alive.[9] And
certain of them that were with us went to the tomb, and
found it even so as the women had said: but him they saw
25 not. And he said unto them, O foolish men, and slow of heart[10]
26 to believe in all that the prophets have spoken! Behoved
it not the Christ to suffer these things,[11] and to enter into
27 his glory? And beginning from Moses and from[12] all the
prophets, he interpreted to them in all the scriptures
28 the things concerning himself. And they drew nigh unto the
village, whither they were going: and he made as though he
29 would go further.[13] And they constrained him, saying,
Abide with us: for it is toward evening, and the day is now
30 far spent. And he went in to abide with them. And it came
to pass, when he had sat down with them to meat, he took
the bread, and blessed it, and brake, and gave to them.[14]
31 and their eyes were opened, and they knew him; and he
32 vanished[15] out of their sight. And they said one to another,
Was not our heart burning within us, while he spake to us

33 in the way, while he opened to us the scriptures? And they
rose up that very hour, and returned to Jerusalem, and found
the eleven gathered together, and them that were with
34 them, saying, The Lord is risen indeed, and hath appeared
35 to Simon.[16] And they rehearsed the things *that happened* in
the way, and how he was known of them in the breaking of
the bread.

Instead of mentioning all the various occasions on which Jesus
appeared, Luke describes the appearance on the Emmaus road
comparatively fully, because in it there is so strikingly depicted
what was going on in the hearts of the Saviour's followers on that
day, and how Jesus, by word and act, as He appeared to them,
Himself removed all their pangs of despair.

13 Two members of the wider circle of Jesus' disciples were
on their way to the village of Emmaus, situated about seven miles
from Jerusalem. They had probably remained in the city for the
most important days of the " Feast of the Unleavened Bread ",
or had possibly tarried longer in Jerusalem than they intended, as
a result of the crucifixion of their Master. They were now on their
return journey to their home in Emmaus.

14-16 Like many other disciples of Jesus, they not only loved
Him affectionately as their Master and Leader, but they saw in
Him the promised Messiah and expected that He might assert His
Messiahship with power at the great Feast and establish the
Messianic kingdom. But then all the terrible events in connection with His arrest and crucifixion had taken place, and they
had also heard that the sepulchre where Jesus' body had been
laid, was empty and that the angels had appeared to the women
and to others. All this was to them quite inexplicable and full
of problems. Why was it necessary that He should die? And what
was the meaning of the strange occurrences on this first day of the
week? Harassed by these questions, they began to reason with
each other concerning them. And while they were thus talking
together on their way to Emmaus, the risen Christ joined them.
Because they had never expected this and did not realise that
He had really risen, and also because Jesus' resurrection body
was not so easily recognisable owing to its heavenly nature, the
two disciples did not recognise Him.

17-22 Just as before His crucifixion, He again uses the effective
method of asking questions and of persuading them to unburden
their inmost thoughts. One of them, Cleopas (see note 6 below),
answered by expressing his surprise that their Questioner did not

know what had happened in Jerusalem during the past days and why they were so upset and sorrowful. The two disciples would no doubt at first have felt offended at the obtrusiveness of the unknown Stranger, especially since they were talking so earnestly while they were walking and were so sorrowful and despondent. By asking them another question, Jesus, however, elicits the necessary confession from them. And now that they were persuaded to do this and saw that the Stranger's interest was genuine, they poured out their hearts in words that testified to their ardent love for the Crucified One and to their steadfast conviction that He was at least an exceptional divine messenger, " mighty in deed and word before God and all the people ". The blame for His crucifixion they attributed roundly to their chief priests and other rulers. It was they who had delivered Him over to the pagan judge and had caused Him to be condemned and done to death. They had hoped fervently that He, who had been so mighty in deed and word, who had performed such wonderful works of deliverance (healing the sick, and raising the dead), and who had taught with such authority, was not merely an ordinary prophet, but the promised Messiah. They had hoped that He would act with Messianic power and would deliver the people from all earthly and spiritual enemies, and would reveal His glory. But now He had actually been rejected and crucified by the leaders of the people, and moreover it was already the third day since His death—so that there seemed to be no longer any hope that He would suddenly appear miraculously in Messianic glory and take action as the promised Redeemer.

23, 24 On the other hand, they continued, there was a possibility that something extraordinary had indeed taken place that might perhaps still cause their hopes to be realised. For certain women-followers of Jesus had gone to the sepulchre early that morning and had brought the dismaying news that the sepulchre was empty and that they had seen angels who said that He was alive. Some of the disciples had also gone to the sepulchre and found that the women had told the truth. But after they had left the circle of disciples, not one of the disciples had yet seen Jesus.

In this confession of the men of Emmaus one clearly sees the violent struggle between hope and fear that raged in their hearts. And this gives us a clear picture of what went on that day in the hearts of all the other perplexed followers of the Crucified One.

25-7 After the Saviour had given the two disciples the opportunity of unburdening themselves, He began to chide them gently for being so obtuse and slow of heart in not believing *everything* that the prophets had spoken. If they had known the Scriptures and really believed in the living God they would have known that not only had the glory of victory been promised Him as Messiah in the Old Testament but that God had clearly proclaimed through the prophets that He was to suffer and to die and thus to attain to glory. In their spiritual deficiency they had seen and believed only one side of the Messianic prophecies. For this reason His crucifixion and death had caused them to despair, although in the light of the Old Testament prophecies this should have made them see that He was truly the Redeemer, and they should have known that He would again arise from the dead (cf. Gen. iii. 15; Ps. xxii; Isa. liii etc.).

And then the Saviour, who knows the Word of God perfectly, because of His intimate union with the Spirit who is its Primary Author, expounded to them in broad outline all the Scriptures that referred to Him, from the first books of the Old Testament and right through to the end. With burning hearts (verse 32), but still unaware that it was Jesus Himself who was teaching them, they listened to His incomparable exposition of the deepest contents of the Old Testament. And thus they learned that everything that had happened to the Saviour was in agreement with the prophetic Word and that He would still be revealed as Conqueror.

28, 29 Meanwhile they arrived at Emmaus, and when they saw that He made as though He would have gone further, and because they felt spontaneously and powerfully drawn to Him, they earnestly besought Him to abide with them, especially because it was already toward evening. No doubt it was the Saviour's wish that they should invite Him so that He could make Himself known to them after He had so thoroughly instructed them. He would, however, not have stayed with them uninvited. The words " He made as though He would have gone further " may not be taken as meaning that Jesus did so merely as a pretext and for the sake of appearance. If they had not invited Him He would have passed on, and they would have forfeited the inexpressible privilege of discovering that it was their risen Lord who had been with them and had instructed them.

30, 31 When the food was prepared and they sat down at the table, the Saviour took the leading place at the meal: He took the bread, gave thanks to God before the meal, broke the bread and gave it to the two men. As ordinary disciples they had not attended the institution of the Holy Communion; but probably the apostles had told them and the others how He had acted at the paschal repast on the evening before His

crucifixion. And apart from this, during the period that they
followed Jesus they would probably often have seen His procedure
in breaking and distributing the food at ordinary meals. Probably
there was something characteristic in His way of doing it, and no
doubt He said grace before the meal in a special and intimate
manner. And so the two men of Emmaus, as soon as He said
grace and broke the bread and distributed it, realised that their
fellow-traveller and guest was no other than Jesus Himself. By
these means the Saviour attained His purpose perfectly; for now
they knew that He had risen, and so again He vanishes from their
sight, for they have to learn that He will no longer be permanently
and physically visible to them as before His crucifixion. From now
on they are to have communion with Him as the risen Lord, and
ere long also as the One that has ascended to heaven in glory.

32-5 All of a sudden everything became clear to the two men
and they realised why they had been so moved by the manner in
which the Stranger had expounded the Scriptures to them on the
way. Although Jesus had departed so soon after they had
recognised Him, all doubt was now banished from their hearts.
They know now that He is risen and that He lives as the Messiah,
the promised Redeemer. And this certainty immediately brings
such a light and joy into their hearts, that they have an irresistible
urge to give others also a share in their joy. So without delay
they went back to Jerusalem the same evening. Sustained by the
extraordinary enthusiasm created in their souls, they went thither
quickly and probably arrived there about nine o'clock that
evening. And even before they could relate their sacred experiences, some of the others told them that Jesus had truly arisen,
for not only had the sepulchre been found empty and the angels
proclaimed His resurrection, but He had, in addition, already
appeared at least to Peter. Thereupon they also related their own
experience.

If the men of Emmaus had not invited Jesus into their home,
He would have passed on, and how poor would their lives have
been then! But because He had spoken to them thus on the way,
their hearts burned with love for Him and they invited Him in
and thus received the richest blessings, even the Lord Himself as
the Living King of their lives. How often does He address us
also on life's way. And He still desires to enter where He is invited.

[1] The various attempts to explain this story as a fiction are purely
subjective and are not founded upon any real arguments. The

635

Emmaus story in these verses bears throughout the stamp of genuineness, and every unprejudiced reader of it feels that it has been taken from actual life. And Plummer is right in stating: " Luke almost certainly obtained his information from one of the two disciples, and probably in writing. The account has all the effect of personal experience. If this is accepted, then Cleopas may be regarded as the narrator; for Luke would know and be like to name the person from whom he received the account " (*in loc.*).

² It is practically certain that Mark xvi. 12, 13 also refers to this occurrence, summarising it as part of the longer Markan appendix.

³ It cannot yet be definitely ascertained where this village was precisely situated or with what modern place it is to be identified. The traditional site at ' Amwas (Emmaus—Nicopolis), on the Jerusalem-Jaffa road, cannot be maintained in spite of the similarity of name, because it is twenty miles from Jerusalem. A most probable location is at Kubeibeh, seven miles north-west of Jerusalem on the Roman road, which was pointed out to the Crusaders as the site of Emmaus.

⁴ σταδίους ἑξήκοντα, " nearly seven miles " (Luce, *in loc.*).

⁵ Apart from the reasons already mentioned by us, why the disciples did not recognise Jesus, it is also possible that the Saviour by His divine power so arranged matters that He could first instruct them before they recognised Him.

⁶ It is not certain if he should be identified with Cleopas (cf. John xix. 25) who, according to Hegesippus, quoted by Eusebius, *Historia Ecclesiastica*, iii, 11, was a brother of Joseph (the foster-father of Jesus) and the father of that Simeon who was the leader of the Christian community that returned to Jerusalem after its destruction in A.D. 70. Schlatter (*in loc.*), Zahn (*in loc.*), Creed (*in loc.*), and others accept the genuineness of the tradition. There exists no ground for the idea that Luke himself was the other man of Emmaus. On the contrary, this is extremely improbable, as Luke was of Gentile descent, and from xxiv. 20 it follows that the two men were Jews.

⁷ ἀνὴρ προφήτης—" The ἀνὴρ is perhaps a mark of respect, as in addresses (Acts i. 16, ii. 29, 37, vii. 2) " (Plummer, *in loc.*). Zahn (*in loc.*) takes it to mean " a prophetic man ".

⁸ ἀλλὰ καί points to the contrast between what follows and the disappointing facts previously mentioned.

⁹ Wellhausen regards verses 22–4 as an interpolation. However, even Creed (*in loc.*) rejects his theory.

¹⁰ " Ἀνόητοι, ' fools ', refers to the understanding; βραδεῖς, ' slow ', to the heart " (Godet, *in loc.*).

¹¹ Although the New Testament taught this so plainly, the Jews at the time of Jesus seem only to have noticed the prophecies concerning the glory and victory of the Messiah. For a detailed and convincing statement of the evidence reference may be made to Strack-Billerbeck ii, pp. 273–99. It is true, of course, that the opinions recorded in the Talmud and Midrashim, from which Strack and Billerbeck draw their material, are mostly later than the Apostolic Age, and that the

rabbinical interpretation of the Messianic passages of the Old Testament (especially of those which the Church used most as "testimonies") is marked by a reaction to the Christian interpretation. This is evident, e.g., in the Targum of Pseudo-Jonathan on the Prophets, where the references to the Servant's glory in Isaiah lii. 13—liii. 12 are applied to Messiah, but the references to the Servant's suffering are applied to Israel. The Talmud and other Jewish writings preserve some trace of an earlier and more consistent interpretation; e.g. a Messianic interpretation of Isaiah liii. 4 is quoted in the Bab. Talmud, *Sanhedrin*, 98b, and it was from the word נָגוּעַ (*nāgūa'*) ("stricken") in this verse that some rabbis gave the Messiah the title "the leprous one".

But it is plain, none the less, that the idea of a suffering and dying Messiah was preposterous to our Lord's disciples, and indeed to the majority of His contemporaries. His question, "How is it written concerning the Son of man that he should suffer many things and be set at naught?" (Mark ix. 12), must have been a real enigma to His hearers. In the light of the glorious rôle ascribed to "one like unto a son of man" in Daniel vii. 13 f., and in the light of the development of this conception in the pseudepigraphic book of Enoch, which considerably influenced popular eschatological ideas in the time of Christ, we can realise, as Otto says, "how monstrous it must have seemed to those who believed in Jesus as the Son of Man, that any person who claimed to be the Son of Man should be brought into a synthesis with the despised, God-smitten man of suffering depicted in Isaiah liii." (*Kingdom of God and Son of Man*, p. 255). But the synthesis was made by Jesus Himself, who combined and fulfilled both these prophetic concepts in His own person.

Strack-Billerbeck (*loc. cit.*) quote numerous examples of the artificial and even ridiculous explanations given by the Jews of those times of Messianic prophecies in the Old Testament referring to Messiah's suffering and death. At all costs they reasoned away all prophecies of the expiatory death of the Messiah and defended their own earthly view of a triumphant Jewish Messiah. Among the ordinary pious Israelites there were, however, a few like Simeon, Anna, John the Baptist's parents and others who had a clearer understanding of the truth. For a complete list and discussion of Messianic prophecies in the Old Testament cf. Edersheim, *Prophecy and History in Relation to the Messiah*, and A. M. Hodgkin, *Christ in all the Scriptures*.

[12] The second ἀπό (not rendered in the A.V.) before πάντων indicates that Jesus drew His exposition from each individual prophetic book. As Plummer says: "There is nothing incredible in the supposition that He quoted from each one of the Prophets" (*in loc.*).

[13] "No unreal acting a part is implied. He began to take leave of them, and *would* have departed, had they not prayed Him to remain" (Plummer, *in loc.*).

[14] No celebration of Holy Communion is meant here, but an ordinary

meal (cf. Luce, *in loc.*, Zahn, *in loc.*, and especially Plummer, *in loc.*). " The blessing and breaking of the loaf recalls a characteristic action of Jesus in his lifetime, cf. ix. 16 " (Creed, *in loc.*).

[15] ἄφαστος—" Frequent in Greek literature of a supernatural disappearance " (Creed, *in loc.*). Godet writes: " The sudden disappearance of Jesus has a supernatural character. His body was already in course of glorification, and obeyed more freely than before the will of the spirit. Besides, it must be remembered that Jesus, strictly speaking, *was* already *no more with them* (verse 44,) and that the miracle consisted rather in His appearing than in His disappearing " (*in loc.*).

[16] The private appearance of our Lord to Peter is nowhere described in the New Testament. Some of those who think that Mark continued his gospel after Mark xvi. 8 suggest that he went on to relate this appearance; but of this there can in the nature of the case be no proof. (See B. H. Streeter *The Four Gospels*, pp. 343 ff.; C. H. Turner, *Catholic and Apostolic*, pp. 192 ff.) This appearance is, however, given pride of place by Paul among the resurrection appearances which he enumerates in 1 Corinthians xv. 5 ff.

JESUS APPEARS TO THE DISCIPLES

(cf. John xx. 19 ff.)

xxiv. 36–49

36 And as they spake these things,[1] he himself stood in the
37 midst of them, and saith unto them, Peace be unto you.[2] But
they were terrified and affrighted,[3] and supposed that they
38 beheld a spirit.[4] And he said unto them, Why are ye
troubled? and wherefore do reasonings arise in your heart?
39 See my hands and my feet, that it is I myself: handle me,
and see: for a spirit hath not flesh and bones,[5] as ye behold
40 me having. And when he had said this, he shewed them his
41 hands and his feet.[6] And while they still disbelieved for joy,[7]
and wondered, he said unto them, Have ye here anything to
42 eat? And they gave him a piece of a broiled fish.[8] And he
took it, and did eat before them.[9]
43, 44 And he said unto them,[10] These are my words which I
spake unto you, while I was yet with you,[11] how that all
things must needs be fulfilled, which are written in the law
of Moses, and the prophets, and the psalms, concerning me.
45 Then opened he their mind, that they might understand
46 the scriptures; and he said unto them, Thus it is written,[12]
that the Christ should suffer, and rise again from the dead
47 the third day; and that repentance and remission of sins
should be preached in his name[13] unto all the nations, begin-
48 ning from Jerusalem. Ye are witnesses of these things.
49 And behold, I send[14] forth the promise of my Father upon
you: but tarry ye in the city,[15] until ye be clothed with
power on high.[16]

From the Gospel account of the Resurrection it is as clear as
daylight that nothing and no one except the risen Jesus Himself
convinced His perplexed followers of the fact that He had indeed
arisen. Even the testimony of the angels, of the women, of Peter
and of the men of Emmaus was not sufficient to reassure the rest
completely. These testimonies did indeed cause hope to flare up
brightly in their hearts off and on (verse 34). But the final re-
assurance came only when Jesus Himself appeared to them and
banished all doubt. And He did this in such a way that even
the sceptical Thomas at length cried out spontaneously: " My
Lord and my God! " (John xx. 28).

36, 37 That same Sunday evening, while the disciples and other followers of Jesus were conversing indoors about everything that had happened during the day, and while the struggle between hope and despair was still raging in many a heart, the Saviour suddenly stood amongst them. Although the doors were shut (John xx. 19), He appeared by supernatural power within the closed apartment because He was already clothed in a glorified, celestial body that was not bound by limitations of an ordinary earthly body. Because it was all so wonderful and unexpected, the first reaction on the part of the disciples was one of terror and fear. Although they had already heard the testimonies of Peter and others concerning His resurrection, and had at times already begun to believe firmly that He had arisen, they did not yet realise the actuality of it and could form no picture of what His risen body was like. So it was quite natural that, when Jesus appeared so suddenly and supernaturally within the shut room, they were at first upset and thought that what they saw was an incorporeal spirit that had only the appearance of a person.

38–40 By His question, " Why are ye troubled? and why do thoughts arise in your hearts? " He calls upon them to look upon the actual circumstances in a sober manner. Then only did He reassure them that it was really He and no one else who was with them (" Behold my hands and my feet, *that it is I Myself*"). And then by the words, " Handle me, and see; for a spirit hath not flesh and bones, as ye see me have ", He makes them realise that it is not merely His spirit that has appeared before them but that it is He Himself—in spirit and in body. (His body of course, to this extent different from an ordinary body in that it was now a glorified, celestial body. Cf. 1 Cor. xv. 35–58, where Paul gives a clear explanation of this whole subject.)

41–3 After He had pointed out to them that it was really He who was speaking to them as the risen Lord, the disciples were exceedingly glad that they were finally able to see Him themselves (cf. John xx. 20). Indeed, their joy was so great that for a moment it was even an impediment to their faith. They were so glad that everything appeared to them too wonderful to be true. And for this reason Jesus, who always knew the human heart perfectly, in order to calm their feelings and to make them realise quietly that He had really been raised in body from the dead, asked them whether they had something to eat, and when they had brought Him food, He ate it in their presence. After this He again departed and after a week, again on a Sunday, He appeared to the disciples when Thomas was also present (John xx. 26–9).

44 It is about time for Luke to bring his Gospel to a conclusion, as it is now exceptionally long for a papyrus writing. In addition, he had already decided to write a sequel to his Gospel (the Book of Acts), in which he would give further particulars of the time between Jesus' resurrection and ascension. So in the concluding verses of his Gospel he gives only an extremely succinct account of what happened further. He does not even mention the other important appearances of Jesus to separate persons like James (1 Cor. xv. 7), or to the five hundred disciples in Galilee (1 Cor. xv. 6). But it was not his purpose to give a full account of all the events. However, through the episodes which he does describe and the words which he does record, he clearly and powerfully proclaims the glad tidings that Jesus, who had died, was raised from death and exalted in the glory which the Father bestowed on Him.

So concisely does he now relate the events, that in verse 44, without mentioning the place or the time, he records a number of important pronouncements made by the risen Lord to His disciples during the forty days before His ascension. Jesus here calls their attention to the fact that everything they saw happening recently (His humiliation, death and resurrection) is the fulfilment of what He has previously so repeatedly foretold them (cf., e.g., ix. 22, xviii. 31-3); namely, that everything that was prophesied of Him, the promised Redeemer, in the various parts of the Old Testament, must be fulfilled.

45-7 On that first day He had explained to the men of Emmaus the deepest meaning of the Old Testament (verses 27, 28), and now He also opened the minds of the whole group of disciples, and gave them the spiritual capacity to understand the real meaning of the Scriptures. To sum up, the main theme taught by the Scriptures is that the Messiah had to suffer, that He should rise again on the third day, and that the ultimate purpose of all this was that the glad tidings of repentance and forgiveness of sin should be proclaimed in His Name, on the ground of His work of redemption and through His saving power. And although this preaching must first take place in Jerusalem among the people of Israel, it must also be made known to all nations over the whole world. (In various Psalms, but especially in the second part of Isaiah, it is clearly prophesied that the ultimate purpose of the divine revelation was that the glad tidings of salvation must be brought to all peoples.)

48 And now the tremendous responsibility of preaching the glad tidings rests upon those who are witnesses of His death and resurrection. They and other believers after them will have to go out into the world as the messengers of God to preach what they have seen and heard and experienced.

49 In their own strength they will never be capable of performing this high and holy task, but Jesus Himself, as the risen King of His church, will (after His ascension) send to them the promise of His Father. By this the Saviour means the Holy Ghost, who is the greatest of all gifts, through whom all good gifts are given. Already in the Old Testament (cf. e.g. Ezek. xxxvi. 27; Joel ii. 28), God had promised to send His Spirit in the hearts of believers, and Jesus Himself also repeatedly made the same promise (cf. John xvi). The promise will, however, not be immediately fulfilled, and the disciples have to remain in Jerusalem until the Holy Ghost in His fullness comes to dwell in His church and in them individually and equips them with His divine strength for the great task to which they have been called as witnesses of His death and resurrection.

Only the living Christ Himself was able to conquer the fear, perplexity and doubt of His disciples and to prepare them to enter the world as preachers of the glad tidings. And in like manner to-day it is only the risen Saviour Himself who can banish all fear from our hearts, and give us the inward rest and peace to enable us to act as living witnesses of our living Redeemer. And all the spiritual equipment that we need, He gives us through the Spirit, already given to His church in His fullness on that first Pentecost and to every believer in the moment of regeneration. And now there rests on every regenerate man and woman the responsibility of being so completely surrendered to Him and of so looking up to Him in faith and obedience, that He will from moment to moment equip us with His divine strength for the task to which we have been called.

---

[1] John xx. 19 ff. nowhere states that only the apostles were present when Jesus appeared that Sunday night (cf. Zahn, *in loc.*). From Luke xxiv. 33–6 it appears that other disciples were also present.

[2] καὶ λέγει αὐτοῖς Εἰρήνη ὑμῖν does not occur in Western textual evidence and is most probably an interpolation from John xx. 19 (as nearly all expositors agree).

[3] The contention of Creed and others, that this fear and terror show that the disciples were not yet prepared for Jesus' appearance through the fact of the empty sepulchre and the events related in xxiv. 1–35, reveals a certain inability to think themselves back into the circumstances and occurrences of that day. Even Luce says in this connection: " Such criticism seems perverse. Even if the clearest

warning has been given, the surprise and alarm are natural in the presence of a visitant from another world " (in loc.).

⁴ πνεῦμα—here " an incorporeal being " (Abbott-Smith), and we may practically render the word by " spirit " or " ghost " (cf. Luce, in loc.).

⁵ " He says not ' flesh and blood ' for the blood is the life of the corruptible body (Gen. ix. 4), which ' cannot inherit the kingdom of God ' (1 Cor. xv. 50); but ' flesh and bones ', implying the identity, but with diversity of laws, of the resurrection-body " (Jamieson, Fausset and Brown, in loc.).

⁶ This verse (40) also is omitted by Western textual testimony, and probably rightly.

⁷ Concerning this remark by Luke, it has been rightly declared: " with many similar expressions we owe this remark to the most profound psychologist among the evangelists ".

⁸ καὶ ἀπὸ μελισσίου κηρίου (' and of a honeycomb ') is undoubtedly a later interpolation. Only a few of our important MSS. contain these words, although most of the later ones have them. It was probably " because honey played a part in the Eucharist and in the baptismal liturgy " that it was added here for the sake of its symbolical meaning (Klostermann, in loc.).

⁹ " The objection that, if Jesus took food in order to convince them that He was no mere spirit, when food was not necessary for the resurrection body, He was acting deceitfully, does not hold. The alternative—' either a ghost or an ordinary body needing food '—is false. There is a third possibility: a glorified body, capable of receiving food (but not needing it). Is there any deceit in taking food, which one does not want, in order to put others, who are needing it, at their ease? " (Plummer, in loc.).

¹⁰ " The connecting words εἶπεν δὲ πρὸς αὐτούς leave it indeterminate whether Jesus uttered the following words as the immediate sequel to the previously related incident, or after an interval filled out with other incidents and sayings, or on another occasion altogether " (Zahn, in loc.). All that appears from the context is that the succeeding words were addressed by the risen Christ to His followers during the time before His ascension. That Luke did not intend the words to be regarded as uttered on the same occasion as those in verses 36–43, follows from the fact that the contents of verse 44 do not at all fit in with those circumstances. The whole portion (verses 44–9), however, bears unmistakable signs of its having been pronounced as a farewell message in which there is a reference to all that is past. And from Acts i. 4 it appears that these words were indeed the Saviour's farewell words to His disciples before His ascension. This disposes of the arguments so frequently adduced to prove that Luke in the last chapter of the Gospel teaches expressly that Jesus' resurrection, appearances and ascension all took place on one and the same day. And as Schlatter rightly declares: " It is unthinkable that Luke should introduce a contradiction between the end of the Gospel

and the beginning of Acts, and that he intended the end of the Gospel to be displaced by the beginning of Acts " (*in loc.*).

There can be really no doubt that the condensed form in which Luke here records the history (verses 44–53) is so manifestly intended " to prepare for Acts that the latter work must have been begun as soon as the Gospel was finished, if, indeed, it was not already in preparation " (Easton, *in loc.*).

¹¹ " The expression: ' while I was yet with you ', is remarkable; for it proves that, in the mind of Jesus, His separation from them was now consummated. He was with them only exceptionally; His abode was elsewhere " (Godet, *in loc.*). Cf. also Plummer, *in loc.*

¹² καὶ οὕτως ἔδει (" and thus it behoved ") has only slight support and must be regarded as an interpolation (according to all well-known modern editions of the Greek text).

¹³ " On the basis of all that His name implies: it is His Messiahship which makes repentance effectual " (Plummer, *in loc.*).

¹⁴ ἐξαποστέλλω, present tense for what will be done speedily and certainly. Note the absolutely divine authority of Christ's utterances here.

¹⁵ It is quite impermissible to deduce from these words (as is done by Luce, Creed and others) that Luke teaches that the disciples never went to Galilee between the resurrection and the ascension and that he thus contradicts Matthew, Mark, John and 1 Corinthians 15. Luke indeed, as we have shown in note 10, does not represent verses 44–9 as having been uttered on the same occasion as verses 36–43. And in Acts i. 4, 9 he expressly states that the words were uttered only at the end of the forty days. In the meantime the disciples had been to Galilee and there the appearances had taken place which are referred to or described in Matthew, Mark, John and 1 Corinthians xv.

¹⁶ Ere long He will, as regards visible appearances, withdraw Himself from them, and therefore they must be endued with this special equipment. And it will be such that " the power of the apostolic message does not rest upon the visibility of Christ, but upon the presence of the Spirit " (Schlatter, *in loc.*).

THE ASCENSION

(Cf. Acts i. 9–11)

xxiv. 50–3

50   And he led them out[1] until *they were* over against[2] Bethany:
51   and he lifted up his hands,[3] and blessed them. And it came
to pass, while he blessed them, he parted from them, and was
52   carried up into heaven.[4] And they worshipped him,[5] and
53   returned to Jerusalem with great joy; and were continually
in the temple,[6] blessing God.

At the commencement of the story of Jesus as Man on earth,
the angels said to the amazed shepherds: " Fear not, for behold I
bring you good tidings of great joy, which shall be to all people,"
and a moment afterwards the heavenly host praised God and
said: " Glory to God in the highest, and on earth peace." This
message and panegyric of the heavenly beings, however, finds a
glorious and mighty actualisation in the last scenes of the Gospel
history described in these four verses.

50, 51 Everything was at last complete and ready. The
Saviour had lived perfectly through the life of man with all the
struggles, temptations, afflictions and death, and had in everything obeyed and honoured His Father; He had accomplished
the work of atonement; had conquered death and all the powers
of darkness, and had arisen; He had appeared to His followers on
numerous occasions; had banished from their hearts all doubt as
to His resurrection; had during the forty days (Acts i. 3, 4)
taught them everything that was necessary (especially the right
insight into the Holy Scriptures) with a view to the building-up
of His church; and had caused them to come back from Galilee
to Jerusalem, there to await the outpouring of the Holy Ghost
and to start from there to preach the glad tidings of redemption
in His name. On that Easter Sunday He had already arisen with
a glorified, celestial body. But now He is to be exalted in His
divine power and glory at the right hand of the Father. Accordingly He leads His disciples at the end of the forty days to a place
on the Mount of Olives near Bethany (Acts i. 12), and addresses
His parting words to them. Thereupon, like the high priest when
he came forth from the temple on great feast days, He lifts up

645

his hands and blesses His disciples as the eternal High Priest (cf. Ps. cx and Heb. vii–ix). And so, with outstretched hands, whilst the disciples look up to Him with receptive and worshipful hearts (Acts i. 9), He is parted from them and He, who had from all eternity been with the Father in divine glory, had again entered the Invisible World, and had returned to Him, but now with a human though glorified and heavenly body (cf. Acts i. 11). Through His Spirit, however, He is still and remains forever with all His people on earth (Matt. xxviii. 20).

52, 53   So grand and mighty was the revelation of His divine Sonship in His majestic ascension, that the disciples spontaneously worshipped Him as Lord and King. To His disciples His ascension in divine glory was the final proof that He was truly the Christ, the Son of God, and that He as the Almighty was able to fulfil His promises. In addition, the angel (Acts i. 11) once more gave the joyful assurance that (as Jesus Himself had so often prophesied, e.g., in His eschatological discourse) He would return in person, not in order to suffer once again, but to bring the sovereign dominion of God to complete and everlasting realisation, and to establish His heavenly kingdom in perfection. By reason of all this, the disciples, although they had to say farewell to Him as regards His visible presence, returned to Jerusalem with jubilant hearts. And there, while awaiting the fulfilment of the promise of the Holy Ghost, they continued together in prayer (Acts i. 13, 14) and went to the temple regularly, praising and thanking God that He had accomplished such a mighty work of redemption in Jesus and that in all this He had so wonderfully blessed and privileged them. And just as the Gospel history commenced in an atmosphere of worship, panegyric and joy, so it ends here in the last words of Luke on a note of unparalleled joy and fervour of divine worship.

Ineradicable joy, irresistible longing to glorify God, and deep gratitude—this was the characteristic of the lives of the first Christians (although they also had their human frailties). Therefore, only in so far as we also possess these characteristics in our hearts and lives, are we truly Christians. And God be praised, the way *is* also open to us to be partakers of this true spiritual life, for He who 1,900 years ago was taken up to heaven in glory, is ever the same in His love, wisdom and power, and through the mighty power of the Holy Ghost abides with and dwells in every child of God.

[1] Luke merely mentions the fact without in any way explaining or indicating in what relation this stands to what has gone before or when

it took place. There is here, therefore, no question of his pretending that the ascension took place on the same day as the resurrection. Here he merely gives a short sketch because in Acts he is going to give further particulars.

² ἕως πρός, the correct reading, here indicates " to the neighbourhood of " (cf. Luce, *in loc.*, and also Zahn, *in loc.*). In Acts i. 12 Luke gives further particulars concerning the place. Luke is fond of double prepositions, especially when ἕως is one of them.

³ Cf. Leviticus ix. 22.

⁴ The words καὶ ἀνεφέρετο εἰς τὸν οὐρανόν are bracketed by Westcott and Hort as a " Western non-interpolation "—to employ their ungainly terminology for indicating something omitted by the Western text and interpolated in the " Neutral " text, as they called it. In addition to the Western authorities, " ℵ* " also omits these words, but " ℵᶜ " adds them. Klostermann, J. Weiss, Wellhausen and others agree in regarding them as an interpolation; Zahn, Streeter, E. Meyer, Loisy, Luce and others defend their authenticity. Streeter (*Four Gospels*, p. 143) suggests that their omission in " ℵ* " " D ", the Old Latin, Old Syriac, and Augustine, " is an attempt to remove a contradiction between the Gospel and the Acts; it is the text which omits, not that which inserts, that has suffered harmonistic correction ". On the other hand, it may be that when the four Gospels were gathered together as one collection (*c.* A.D. 100) and the two parts of Luke's history were severed from each other, this clause was added here to round off the Gospel narrative with an explicit statement of the Ascension; if so, the verb ἀνελήμφθη (" was taken up "), which is also a non-Western reading, was accordingly added at the same time in Acts i. 2 where the scope of the " former treatise " is summarised.

⁵ The words προσκυνήσαντες αὐτόν are also bracketed by Westcott and Hort as a " Western non-interpolation " (" D ", the Old Latin, Old Syriac, and Augustine omit them). Zahn (*in loc.*) suggests that their omission was due to the fear that they might be thought to contradict Acts i. 11.

⁶ Obviously the meaning is not that they were there throughout, but that they made use of every opportunity (as during the seasons of prayer) to go and worship in the temple. Although the New Dispensation had already been inaugurated, it was only by gradual stages the Holy Spirit taught them the lesson of freedom from the old forms of temple worship and the like that had completed their preparatory task, because in Jesus the whole of the Old Testament revelation had been fulfilled, to the salvation of countless souls and to the glory of God.

EXCURSUS

THE DAY AND DATE OF THE CRUCIFIXION

There exists practically no difference of opinion on the fact which is unanimously taught by the Gospels that Jesus was crucified on a Friday.[1] But when we ask what the date (according to Jewish chronology of that time) of that Friday was, no unanimity is to be found among Bible expositors. The reason for this is that there is an *apparent* contradiction between the evidence for the dating of the crucifixion in the first three Gospels and that in the fourth Gospel.

In brief the following " solutions " of this problem are propounded:

(A) *Solutions which involve the rejection of either the Synoptist or the Johannine evidence.*

The following are the main schools:

(1) Those who allege that the first three Gospels render the correct facts (or partly so) and that John misrepresents matters.

In the nineteenth century especially the Tübingen school played an important part in this connection. Under the leadership of F. C. Baur they declared that the story of John's Gospel was a fiction and that the writer in his desire to represent Jesus as the Paschal Lamb and in order as far as possible to throw the Jewish Passover into the shade, falsely put the crucifixion on the day *before* the Feast. D. F. Strauss also favoured this view.

In the twentieth century it is especially *Gustaf Dalman*[2] who has advocated this trend, although he is by no means so radically critical towards the fourth Gospel. In a masterly manner he refutes the imputations against the trustworthiness of the data of the Synoptists and shows that Jesus did indeed celebrate the Passover in accordance with the Law on the evening before His crucifixion.

In most recent times also Walter Bauer[3] expressed himself in favour of this view. He declares that Dalman has refuted the objections against the synoptic data and alleges that John, in

---

[1] Westcott was an exception: he argued for a Thursday (*Introduction to the Study of the Gospels*, 7th ed., 1888, pp. 343 ff.).
[2] Cf. his works *Jesus–Jeshua*, pp. 86 ff.; *Sacred Sites and Ways*, pp. 315 ff.
[3] *Das Johannes-Evangelium*, p. 163.

649

his desire to represent Jesus as the perfect Paschal Lamb, ante-dated the crucifixion.[1]

In an amended form even Schlatter[2] favours this view. He accepts the accuracy of the data of the Synoptists and says in relation to John xix. 14: "Although Matthew's report un-mistakably lay near him, John did not regard it as necessary to say expressly that Jesus' execution did not take place on the first day of the Passover but on the day before; on the 14th, not on the 15th. This silence also shows that John did not attach high importance to chronological exactitude."

(2) A second main school on the critical side consists of those who champion John's evidence, as they understand it, and reject the synoptic representation as incorrect.

In most recent times the vast majority of liberal Bible ex-positors and several others are champions of this view. We mention a number of the most important ones: C. F. Nolloth,[2] M. Dibelius,[3] C. G. Montefiore,[4] Luce,[5] Macgregor,[6] Maurice Jones,[7] Burkitt,[8] A. E. Brooke,[9] W. F. Howard,[10] B. H. Streeter,[11] A. E. J. Rawlinson,[12] B. T. D. Smith,[13] Gloag,[14] Sanday,[15] W. Lock,[16] Vincent Taylor,[17] A. J. Grieve,[18] J. Moffatt,[19] A. S. Peake,[20] R. H. Strachan,[21] Sir Edwyn Hoskyns,[22] R. H. Kennett,[23] D. R. Fotheringham,[24] G. Ogg,[25] T. W. Manson,[26] C. J. Cadoux.[27]

According to this school the writer of the fourth Gospel had

---

[1] *Der Evangelist Johannes*, p. 346.
[2] *The Fourth Evangelist* (1925), p. 118.
[3] *A Fresh Approach to the New Testament and Early Christian Literature*, p. 49.
[4] His various commentaries, *in loc.*
[5] Cambridge Greek Testament, *St. Luke*, *in loc.*
[6] *The Gospel of John*, p. xiii.
[7] *The New Testament in the Twentieth Century*, p. 412.
[8] *The Last Supper and the Paschal Meal* (cf. Rawlinson, *St. Mark*, p. 262).
[9] *Peake's Commentary*, "St. John."
[10] *The Fourth Gospel in recent Criticism and Interpretation*, pp. 148 ff.
[11] *The Four Gospels*, p. 422.
[12] *St. Mark*, pp. 262 ff.
[13] *St. Matthew.*
[14] *Introduction to the Johannine Writings*, *in loc.*
[15] *The Criticism of the Fourth Gospel*, *in loc.*
[16] *A New Commentary on Holy Scripture* (ed. C. Gore), *in loc.*
[17] *Jesus and his Sacrifice*, p. 116.
[18] *Peake's Commentary*, p. 653.
[19] *Introduction to New Testament Literature*, *in loc.*
[20] *A Critical Introduction to the New Testament*, *in loc.*
[21] *The Fourth Gospel*, p. 265.
[22] *The Fourth Gospel*, *in loc.*
[23] *The Last Supper* (1921), pp. 33 ff.
[24] *The Date of Easter* (1928), pp. 29 ff.
[25] *Chronology of the Public Ministry of Jesus* (1940), p. 242.
[26] *Rylands Bulletin*, 28 (1944), p. 127.
[27] *Life of Jesus* (1948), pp. 176 ff.

access to the real facts in connection with the dating of the crucifixion and of set purpose contradicted the dating of the other three in John xiii. 1, xviii. 28, xix. 31, 42.

They maintain further that not only does John contradict the Synoptists, but that the data of the Synoptists are themselves often ambiguous and in certain places contradict themselves. Thus, e.g., the Synoptic representation of the crucifixion, of Jesus' funeral, etc., on the great Feast Day, they reject as historically impossible.

According to them, Jesus did not celebrate the lawful Passover with His disciples on the evening before the crucifixion, and He was crucified on the 14th Nisan and not on the Feast Day, the 15th Nisan (as the Synoptists declare).

Some of them then allege that the Last Supper, of which mention is made in John xiii. 2 and in the other Gospels, was an antedated[1] paschal repast (without, however, the paschal lamb). In most recent times, however, most liberal critics seem to accept the following view: The Last Supper was not at all a paschal repast, but the weekly " Qiddush "[2] (purification meal for the Sabbath). According to them, even the evidence of the Synoptists would prove that the Last Supper was not a paschal repast but the " Qiddush " meal.

Others again[3] represent it as not being the weekly " Qiddush " meal, but the so-called " Passover Qiddush " the meal (or ritual purification meal for the Passover). But, as Vincent Taylor rightly states in this connection, " unfortunately, in neither of these cases was the meal in question eaten on a Thursday, and it is still necessary to assume that it was anticipated by a day ".[4] Nothing is, therefore, attained by this and later on we shall see in our exegesis that the Last Supper according to the Gospel evidence was indeed the paschal repast (as Dalman, Strack-Billerbeck and others have again and again already indicated so clearly).

H. Lietzmann[5] and Rudolf Otto[6] also favour a view similar to the above. They allege that it was a " Habûrôth " meal (a

---

[1] Cf. Vincent Taylor, *Jesus and His Sacrifice*, p. 116.
[2] Cf. G. H. Box, "The Jewish Antecedents of the Eucharist," *Journal of Theological Studies*, iii (1902), pp. 357 ff.; F. C. Burkitt, *J. T. S.*, xvii (1916), pp. 291 ff., and A. J. Grieve in *Peake's Commentary*, p. 653. B. W. Bacon also favours this view (cf. Howard, *The Fourth Gospel*, p. 154).
[3] E.g. G. H. C. Macgregor, in *Eucharistic Origins*, pp. 37 ff., and W. O. E. Oesterley in *The Jewish Background of the Christian Liturgy*, pp. 156–193 (cf. Vincent Taylor, *Jesus and His Sacrifice*, p. 115).
[4] *Jesus and His Sacrifice*, p. 116.
[5] *Messe und Herrenmahl*, p. 210.
[6] *Reich Gottes und Menschensohn*, pp. 234–41.

kind of religious community meal) and not the lawful paschal repast.[1]

(3) The more radical school which rejects both representations (that of the synoptists and that of John) as untrustworthy.

Thus Maurice Goguel alleges that from the data of the four Gospels we can learn nothing in this connection beyond the bare fact that Jesus was crucified[2] approximately at the time of the Jewish Passover.

(B) *Solutions which accept both the Synoptists and the Johannine evidence, regarding the discrepancy between them as only apparent.*

(1) During the first centuries after Christ.

There is not the least indication in the writings of the ancient church fathers that during the first hundred and fifty years A.D. any problem (and still less a contradiction) was seen in the four Gospels in connection with the dating of the crucifixion.[3]

Only about A.D. 170 do we come across signs for the first time that indicate that confusion arose concerning the evidence of the four Gospels for the dating of the crucifixion. It was about at that time that a conflict arose in Asia Minor as to the day and date of the celebration of the Christian Passover.

Now some maintain that the history of the conflict proves that the church since the earliest days accepted[4] the so-called Johannine representation. This contention, however, is unfounded. What the conflict indeed teaches us is that towards the second half of the second century a difference of opinion arose on these matters.[5]

There is, however, no evidence to show that the view was accepted before that time that Jesus had been crucified on the 14th.[6]

---

[1] For a refutation of the above theories cf. Joseph Klausner, *Jesus of Nazareth*, pp. 326 ff., Zahn, and Dalman, *Jesus–Jeshua*, p. 86.

[2] *Life of Jesus* (Eng. tran.), pp. 434 ff.

[3] Cf. Holtzmann, *Einleitung in das Neue Testament*, pp. 461–3, and Zahn, *Introduction to the New Testament*, vol. iii, pp. 275 ff.

[4] e.g. A. J. Grieve in *Peake's Commentary*, p. 653; also Godet, Weitzel, Beyschlag, Weizeäcker, and others (cf. for full list, Holtzmann, *Einleitung in das Neue Testament*, p. 462).

[5] Cf. Gwatkin *Early Church History*, vol. i, pp. 263–6, and Zahn, *Introduction to the New Testament*, vol. iii, pp. 273–93.

[6] Holtzmann, *Einleitung in das Neue Testament*, pp. 461–3. It is nevertheless remarkable that it was precisely in Asia Minor (where the Apostle John spent so many years) that there were the Quartodecimans and that "most of them claimed St. John's authority for placing the crucifixion Nisan 15 " (Gwatkin, *Early Church History*, vol. i, p. 263). (They therefore celebrated the anniversary of the Last Supper on the previous day, i.e. 14th Nisan, and it is for that reason that they were called Quartodecimans, "Fourteenthers".) The Quartodecimans kept the Christian Passover as near the actual anniversary as possible, without regard to the day of the week; their opponents (led by the Roman church) kept Easter Day on the first day of a

So, taking into consideration all the evidence bearing on the views held by the church fathers until 160–170, we come to the conclusion that the church of the first hundred and fifty years (when the contact with the apostles was still fresh and at first hand) saw no problem in the date of the Gospels as to the dating of the crucifixion. As far as we have been able to ascertain, Tatian, in compiling his *Diatessaron* or Harmony of the Four Gospels (*c.* A.D. 170), was the first who began to realise the problem. However, he solved it as follows. He put back John xiii. 1–20 to a day before the Passover and thus made it a separate meal and adds Luke xxii. 7–16, John xiii. 21 ff. Most probably he rendered John xviii. 28 by " that they might not be defiled while celebrating the seven days' feast of the unleavened loaves."[1]

Eusebius tried to solve the problem by representing that the Jews were so busy with their persecution of Jesus that they postponed the eating of the paschal lamb for a day, and thus John might have been correct in writing as he did in John xviii. 28.[2]

Chrysostom again apparently held before his readers a number of possible solutions without taking sides, *inter alia*, that John by the Passover meant the whole of the seven days' feast, or that Jesus anticipated the paschal repast by a day.[3]

Jerome strongly defended the synoptic version and apparently harmonised John's data with it. Under his influence, and especially through the clear statements of the Synoptists, the Synoptic version gained more and more ground and eventually became the generally accepted view of the Christian church, and continued to remain so throughout all the centuries until the nineteenth century.[4]

(2) In modern times.

---

week. Thus it was possible that the Quartodecimans might be celebrating the resurrection on the day which to the others was Good Friday—a manifestly undesirable discrepancy. One party had to relinquish its practice in the interests of Christian fellowship, and it was the Quartodeciman party that did so.

[1] Cf. Zahn, *Introduction to the New Testament*, vol. iii, p. 293. In his *Forschungen zur Geschichte des Neuen Testament Kanons*, i (1882), p. 211, Zahn reconstructed Tatian's text here as follows: "And they took him and led him to the gate and gave him into Pilate's hands, and they themselves did not enter into the inner parts into the hall lest they should be defiled, so that they might first eat the lamb in holiness." These last words are reconstructed on the basis of a free quotation by Ephrem in his commentary on the Diatessaron, preserved in an Armenian translation (cf. also M. J. Lagrange, *Évangile selon St. Jean*, on John xviii. 28).

[2] Eusebius, *On the Paschal Festival* (a large extant fragment of which has been published in Mai's *Nova Patrum Bibliotheca*, vol. iv, pp. 209–16). A translation of the relevant passage (sections 8–12) will be found in J. Drummond, *Character and Authorship of the Fourth Gospel* (1903), pp. 491–3.

[3] Chrysostom, *Homily 83 on St. John's Gospel*. But in *Homily 84 on St. Matthew's Gospel* he agrees with the view of Eusebius.

[4] Cf. Godet, *St. John's Gospel*, part iii, p. 303.

(*a*) Godet, Westcott, Lindsay, Farrar and Plummer are on the side of the so-called Johannine representation, namely, that Jesus did not celebrate the ordinary Jewish Passover and that He was crucified during the morning before the Passover. Moreover, they maintain that the evidence of the Synoptists is not really at variance with this.

However, it is a hopeless task to defend their point of view, and hardly a single Bible expositor of note to-day agrees with their opinion.

(*b*) In 1892 D. Chwolson in his *Das Letzte Passmahl Christi und der Tag seines Todes* introduced a new view.

In more recent times Strack-Billerbeck, the expert authorities on the rabbinical writings from the earliest times, proposed[1] a modification of Chwolson's theory.

They suggest that the solution of our problem must be sought in the controversy concerning the correct interpretation of Leviticus xxiii. 9–11 between the Pharisees and the sons of Boethus (a Sadducee family that filled the office of the high priest between 24 B.C. and A.D. 65). The latter are said to have maintained that the offering of the firstlings had always to be brought to the Lord on the day after the Sabbath which falls in the feast of the unleavened loaves. The Pharisees, on the other hand, taught that the offering, apart from the day on which the Sabbath falls, had always to be brought on the second day of the feast, since the first day of the feast was regarded as a Sabbath in the religious sense.

Furthermore, according to Strack-Billerbeck, there is evidence that indicates that there was sometimes a controversy over the official fixing of the beginning of the month Nisan (which ushered in the Jewish ecclesiastical year). According to them, " the house of Boethus ", to support their view concerning the offering of the firstlings, would have caused the 15th Nisan to coincide with the Sabbath in the year of the crucifixion. Against this the Pharisees would then have raised objections and the result was a compromise, according to which the Pharisees were allowed to follow their own chronology in the matter of celebrating the Passover. Jesus and the disciples would then also have taken sides with the point of view of the Pharisees, whilst the Sadducees followed their own dating. Consequently the Synoptists are right when they state that Jesus celebrated the Passover according to the Law and was crucified on the 15th Nisan, and John is also correct in stating (e.g. in John xviii. 28) that the Jewish authorities still had to eat

---

[1] Cf. their *Kommentar zum Neuen Testament aus Talmud und Midrasch*, vol. ii, pp. 842 ff.

the paschal repast on the day of the crucifixion seeing that John here follows the dating of the Sadducees.

Quite a number of conservative and other Bible expositors of to-day follow this interpretation introduced by Chwolson and remodelled and developed by Strack-Billerbeck. In this connection we mention Dr. C. Bouma,[1] Ubbink,[2] P. A. E. Sillevis-Smit,[3] and W. M. Christie.[4]

However, this suggested solution of the apparent discrepancy between the Synoptists and John is not without serious objections. Accordingly it is violently opposed on the liberal-critical side,[5] and on the conservative side it is by no means generally accepted.

The following are a number of considerations that make us hesitate to accept Strack-Billerbeck's solution as the correct one.

Firstly. Their theory remains mere guess-work. It has by no means been proved that there ever was a genuine instance *before the fall of Jerusalem and the destruction of the temple* when there was not merely a difference of *opinion*, but also a difference of *action* concerning the day of the celebration of the Passover. It may be true that there was a discussion as to the fixing of the day, but we have no indication that, in connection with such an important matter as the Passover (the feast *par excellence* among the Jews), and a feast held at Jerusalem (the centre of all Jewry at that time), there ever was an occasion before A.D. 70 when one section of the people celebrated the Passover on one day and another section celebrated it on a different day.[6] Indeed, such a thing is unthinkable in the Jerusalem of those days. It may be imagined what confusion would have been created by such a difference in the celebration of the feast.

Take, for example, the slaughtering of the lambs. The service of the temple was mostly under the control of the Sadducees. They had to arrange matters in connection with the slaughtering of the lambs and the shedding of the blood against the altar. Would they have been able to allow the slaughtering to take place two days in succession? For indeed it was regarded as a holy matter, and the priest and the people acted unanimously in such matters. How could it then have been expected that the priests should on two successive days have attended to the

---

[1] *Het Evangelie naar Johannes*, pp. 17–18.
[2] *Inleiding tot den Bijbel, in loc.*
[3] *Handboek voor de Heilige Geschiedenis, in loc.*
[4] " Did Christ eat the Passover with His Disciples? " in *Expository Times*, xliii (1931–2), pp. 515 ff.; reprinted in *Palestine Calling* (1939), pp. 129 ff.
[5] *Inter alia* by Maurice Goguel, *Life of Jesus* (Eng. tran., pp. 432 f.); and Dalman, *Sacred Sites and Ways*, p. 315.
[6] Cf. Strack-Billerbeck, *Kommentar zum Neuen Testament, in loc.*

slaughtering and the accompanying sacred acts?[1] With all the thousands upon thousands attending the feast together in Jerusalem and coming from so many different regions, there would have been no limits to the confusion if the slaughtering of the paschal lambs and the celebration of the Passover had taken place on two successive days, *while all knew that the Law had enacted that this had to take place on one particular day.* Under the circumstances, the Sadducees would never have been able to give a satisfactory explanation of their extraordinary procedure by celebrating the Passover a day later. It can hardly be imagined that the Sadducees, who were known to be rationalistic men, " broad of outlook " and diplomatic in their conduct, and who certainly did not desire to fall into disfavour with the people unnecessarily, would for unimportant reasons such as are adduced by Strack-Billerbeck have created all the confusion and drawn upon themselves the enmity of the broad masses (for the people always followed the Pharisees in practically everything).

Taking everything[2] into consideration, the truth, therefore, seems to be that there may have been some discussion and difference of opinion as to the fixing of the Jewish Passover day, but when it came to the actual determination of the day the Calendar Commission would, after consultation with both parties, have fixed the date officially and would have regulated all matters in connection with the celebrations accordingly, so that the people might take part unanimously in the sacred proceedings.[3]

(*c*) In conclusion, we come to the school that declares that all four Gospels teach unanimously that Jesus instituted the Holy Communion at the actual paschal repast and that He died on the 15th Nisan.

As one of the leading exponents of this view in the nineteenth century we mention Edersheim[4] (a well-known authority in his day on Jewish life at the time of Christ). Together with him Hengstenberg,[5] Lange,[6] S. J. Andrews,[7] David Smith[8] and others were strong supporters of this view.

---

[1] W. M. Christie (*Palestine Calling*, pp. 139 f.) holds that in these circumstances those who followed the Pharisaic reckoning (including Jesus and the Apostles) would have dispensed with the lamb.
[2] Cf. Dalman, *Sacred Sites and Ways*, p. 315.
[3] Cf. Maurice Goguel, *Life of Jesus* (Eng. tran., pp. 432 f.), for further objections to the historical possibility of the double dating.
[4] Cf. *The Life and Times of Jesus the Messiah* and *The Temple, its Ministry and Service.*
[5] Cf. his commentary on John.
[6] Cf. his commentary on John.
[7] Cf. *The Life of Our Lord.*
[8] Cf. *The Days of His Flesh.*

In later times Zahn,[1] J. B. Lightfoot,[2] Ubbink,[3] C. H. Irwin[4] and others accepted this view, and the first two especially defended their point of view with weighty arguments, maintaining that both the Synoptists and John teach that Jesus celebrated the lawful Passover and was crucified thereafter, and that the crucifixion took place on the 15th Nisan.[5]

Our personal conviction is that this is the correct view. However, from the nature of the case, we cannot here enter into all the finer details or advance full arguments. For this we refer to the works of the above-named champions of this solution. The arguments briefly amount to the following:

A. *The evidence of John.*

John xiii. 1 does not teach, as it seems to teach according to the translation of this verse in the A.V. and R.V., that the Saviour instituted the Holy Communion before the Passover. As translated in the A.V. and R.V., this verse mentions as reason why Jesus loved the disciples until the end, (*a*) the fact that He knew that His hour was come, and (*b*) the fact that He loved His own people. No one, however, can maintain that such a translation makes proper sense.

So also, by making " before the feast " refer to " Jesus . . . loved them until the end ", the sense is not clearly expressed. What could John have meant by such a statement?

If, however, we take the expression " before the feast " along with εἰδώς (knowing), the verse immediately reads more naturally, for then we may translate it as follows: " Knowing (already) before the Passover that His hour had come to depart out of this world unto his Father, Jesus, he who loved his own in this world, loved them unto the end (or ' to the uttermost ')."

When thus translated, this verse gives beautiful sense as a prologue or a summarising title to what follows in chapters xiii–xviii. John, therefore, by these words wanted to emphasise two things expressly: (1) Jesus already knew before the Feast of the Passover that His hour was come and that He would die. This emphasis on Christ's prescience is very typical of John (cf. xii. 7, 23, xiii. 3, 11, 18, xviii. 4, xix. 28). (2) Jesus loved His disciples even to the bitter end. Not only the washing of the feet is a proof of this, but the whole of the passion.

---

[1] Cf. his *Introduction to the New Testament* and his commentaries.
[2] Cf. especially his *Biblical Essays.*
[3] Cf. his commentary on John in *Tekst en Uitleg.*
[4] Cf. his *Universal Bible Commentary.*
[5] Cogent evidence for this viewpoint is presented (on the basis of Rabbinical literature) by Professor P. J. Heawood, " The Last Passover in the Gospels ", in *The Expository Times*, 53 (1941-2), pp. 295 ff.

Accordingly this translation gives a deep and glorious meaning to the words of John and is perfectly clear and intelligible.

Moreover, there is nothing to prevent us from translating it thus. On the contrary, " the placing of the time phrase first is just as natural if taken with ' knowing ' (εἰδώς) as with ' He loved ' (ἠγάπησεν), and it is thus given the emphasis which the writer intends . . . ' Even before the feast ' . . . did Jesus know that He was to suffer ".[1] And " since εἰς τέλος must be equivalent to ἕως τέλους, the other temporal expression πρὸ δὲ τῆς ἑορτῆς τοῦ πάσχα cannot be taken with the same phrase, but is to be taken with εἰδώς."[2]

Walter Bauer agrees with this: " As the early exegetes (Chrysostom, Theodore, Cyril of Alexandria) and the Sinaitic Syriac rightly saw, πρὸ δὲ τῆς ἑορτῆς τοῦ πάσχα belongs to εἰδώς. The idea that Jesus foresaw His end and was not surprised by it dominates the whole passion story in John. . . . The current adverbial expression εἰς τέλος can be an indication of time (' at the end ', ' finally ' . . .) or it can also be an expression of degree (' altogether ', ' fully ', ' in a conclusive manner ' . . .). In John both senses really run together: ' to the very end ' and ' in the highest degree of completeness '. The sentence represents a heading to chapters xiii–xviii, or, even better, to chapter xiii–xx."[3]

Even Westcott, who held that John teaches that Jesus was crucified on the 14th, admits that verse 1 " is complete in itself ". In verse 2 " we have a fresh beginning ".[4] So we have no right to make the fixing of the date refer to the meal mentioned in verse 2 or to the washing of the feet.

We are supported in our translation of verse 1 and also in our view that the verse serves as a prologue or title to what follows, by numerous translators and expositors.[5]

The Twentieth Century New Testament, e.g., translates xiii. 1 as follows: " Before the Passover Festival began, Jesus knew that the time had come for Him to leave the world and go to the Father. He had loved those who were His own in the world, and He loved them to the last." Weymouth's translation agrees with this construction, as also does R. A. Knox's.

Ubbink, also, is of the opinion that xiii. 1 forms a short prologue similar to i. 1–18, and that it indicates the scheme of the passion: " Before ' the ' feast . . . Jesus saw His way before

---

[1] Zahn, *Introduction to the New Testament*, vol. iii, p. 289.
[2] *Idem.*
[3] *Das Johannes Evangelium*, p. 162.
[4] *St. John*, p. 189.
[5] Cf. especially Zahn, *Evangelist des Johannes*, pp. 529 ff.

Him—ancient expositors already drew attention to this prescience . . . and now that He goes to the Father, but leaves His
disciples behind in the world . . . it is as though His love becomes
more fervent than before."[1]

In like manner Prof. Dr. A. M. Brouwer in *Het Nieuwe Testament* renders xiii. 1 as follows: " Before the Passover commenced,
Jesus knew that His hour was come to pass over from this world
to the Father. And even as He had always shown love to His
own people who were in the world, so He continues to manifest
His love for them unto the end " (translated from the Dutch).

Translated thus, the verse teaches that what follows in verse 2
is the paschal repast.

Even Moffatt, who rejects the statements of the Synoptists,
translates John xiii. 1 as follows: " Now before the Passover
festival Jesus knew that the time had come for him to pass from
this world to the Father. He had loved his own in this world and
he loved them to the end."[2]

From all this it is quite clear that in xiii. 1 John does not by
any means wish to convey that what follows in verse 2 actually
took place before the Passover. On the contrary, it would rather
appear that his words imply the exact opposite. The main point
at issue is, however, that he wishes to emphasise the fact that as
Jesus habitually knew things beforehand, so He knew in advance
everything connected with His impending death, and knew this
even before the Passover.[3] Accordingly he writes xiii. 1 as a
prologue or title to what follows.

Verse 1, then, forms a separate entity, and in verse 2 we have
a new beginning, in which John proceeds to describe an incident
that took place during the Last Supper. He assumes that his
readers are quite aware of the fact that this meal was the paschal
repast which the Lord celebrated with His disciples on the evening
before His crucifixion, and that He then instituted the Holy
Communion. For this reason he merely refers to it by the single
word δεῖπνον without stating expressly what precise meal it was.
He knew that[4] the first three Gospels and also the Epistles of
Paul gave[5] a full account of the celebration of the paschal repast

---

[1] *Evangelie naar Joh.*, p. 144.
[2] *The Moffatt New Testament.* So also Macgregor, in his volume on John in the
Moffatt New Testament Commentary, accepts this translation although he, too,
rejects the Synoptists' representation of the Last Supper as the Passover Feast.
[3] For a particularly clear exposition of the fact that in xiii. 1 John supports the
Synoptists, cf. Andrews, *The Life of our Lord*, pp. 466–7.
[4] In connection with John's knowledge of the older New Testament writings cf.
Jülicher-Fascher, *Einleitung in das Neue Testament*, p. 384, and also the works of Zahn.
[5] W. Lock in Gore's *New Commentary on Holy Scripture*, in loc., is right in stating:
" The Supper is clearly the same as that in the Synoptists. The evangelist had no

and the institution of the Holy Communion. Consequently he does not repeat the same facts, but mentions a few supplementary occurrences that took place during the meal, as they had made a great impression on him and had not been described in the other Gospels. However, what he adds fits in excellently with their evidence. In Luke xxii. 24, e.g., it is stated that there was an argument among the disciples as to who was the greatest among them. So it would have been a most natural thing for Jesus to wash the disciples' feet in order to teach them amongst other things the lesson of humble readiness to serve and to reveal the folly of their carnal disposition. John's narrative gives added meaning to our Lord's words reported in Luke: " I am in your midst as he that serveth."

In John xiii. 2 ff., also, John by no means contradicts[1] the statements of the Synoptists, but supplements them.

Since John in chapter xiii so clearly shows that he assumes[2] his readers to have a thorough knowledge of and confidence in the accounts of the other three Gospels, we have to be very careful that we do not so readily take it for granted that John in other parts of his Gospel dated the crucifixion of the Lord on the day before the paschal repast.

John xiii. 27–9. It is admitted even by Strack-Billerbeck that it was by no means in conflict with the Jewish laws to bestow alms or to buy food for the feast days during the Passover night.[3]

The expression in John xiii. 29, " Buy those things that we have need of against the feast ", also gives no ground to infer that the supper mentioned in xiii. 2 was not the paschal repast. For here it is not stated, " Buy what we need for the paschal repast ", but " what we need for the feast, i.e. for the seven days' feast which commences to-night and for which still many things are required".[4]

John xviii. 28. This text is of cardinal importance in our investigation. Numerous critics, and especially Strack-Billerbeck,[5] declare that the expression φάγωσι τὸ πάσχα can mean nothing

---

need to repeat the institution of the Eucharist; that had been narrated and was being regularly celebrated. He adds additional facts and discourses which carry forward the main thought of his Gospel."

[1] It should here also be mentioned that even Dr. C. Bouma (who supports the view of Strack-Billerbeck) admits that John xiii. 1 f. contains no contradiction of the Synoptists, but at this point is in perfect agreement with them (cf. *Het Evangelie naar Johannes*, p. 172).

[2] For detailed proof that John did indeed know the other Gospels and assumes such knowledge on the part of his readers, we refer our readers to Zahn, *Introduction to the New Testament*, part iii, pp. 254 ff.; Holtzmann, *Einleitung in das Neue Testament*, pp. 440–1; and numerous others. See also Howard, *The Fourth Gospel*, pp. 144 ff.

[3] *Kommentar zum Neuen Testament*, vol. ii, p. 842 ff.

[4] Cf. Lightfoot, Zahn, Edersheim, Ubbink, Strack-Billerbeck, etc., *in loc.*

[5] *Kommentar zum Neuen Testament*, vol. ii, p. 842 ff.

else than that John here states that the Jews still had to eat the paschal repast and that therefore, according to John, the Lord was already condemned to be crucified the morning before the paschal repast.

In spite of all the arguments adduced in this connection, we nevertheless do not feel convinced that by the expression John definitely meant the eating of the paschal repast *as such*. On the contrary, we are convinced that a mistake is made in expecting from John a too precisely Jewish mode of expression.[1]

For we have to bear in mind that it was many years after the destruction of Jerusalem in A.D.70 and the accompanying termination of the Jewish temple service that John wrote his Gospel. Accordingly we should not lose sight of the possibility that John, when he writes about matters concerning the temple service, uses his terms in a loose manner and does not, e.g., make a fine distinction between the various parts of the feast.

John does indeed show throughout his Gospel that he is fully conversant with Jewish customs, modes of thought and speech, and the like. But, on the other hand, he also shows unmistakable signs of having been influenced by Greek culture, and thus, e.g., he writes his Gospel in Greek.[2] We have, therefore, no right to expect him to imitate the Jewish mode of expression slavishly in everything.

On the contrary, in spite of everything alleged by Strack-Billerbeck and others in opposition to this, we are convinced, with Zahn,[3] Edersheim,[4] Hengstenberg,[5] David Smith,[6] Andrews,[7] Ubbink,[8] and other that the expression φάγωσι τὸ πάσχα in John xviii. 28 does not mean the eating of the paschal repast as such but refers to the seven days' feast of the unleavened loaves (and more especially to the sacrificial meals eaten during the feast). The feast as a whole was at that time currently designated by the people as " the feast of the Passover " or merely " the Passover ", e.g. in Luke xxii. 1, where it is expressly stated: " Now the feast of unleavened bread drew nigh, *which is called*

---

[1] And, as we shall show afterwards, even the Jewish mode of expression is not so precise on this point.

[2] Cf. the words of Filson in *Origins of the Gospels* (p. 200): " In spite of all indebtedness to Judaism and to primitive Palestinian Christianity, the actual setting of John was in the Hellenistic world, among Greek-speaking and overwhelmingly Gentile readers. It was written to create faith in people of the Graeco-Roman world."

[3] His commentary on John, etc.

[4] *The Life and Times of Jesus the Messiah, in loc.*

[5] Commentary on John, *in loc.*

[6] *The Days of His Flesh, in loc.*

[7] *The Life of our Lord, in loc.*

[8] *Evangelist van Johannes, in loc.*

the Passover." Also in Acts xii. 1 τὸ πάσχα is used for the whole feast.[1]

It is indeed generally recognised that τὸ πάσχα had the wider meaning.[2]

It is especially of importance that we should note that John himself frequently uses τὸ πάσχα in this sense, e.g., in John ii. 13, vi. 4, xi. 55, xviii. 39, etc. Thus, apart from any other considerations, it is highly probable that in xviii. 28 he also uses τὸ πάσχα in this wider sense.

Moreover, it was a recognised Jewish[3] custom to speak (in connection with the Passover) of " *eating* the feast " instead of " *celebrating* the feast ". And where also John assigns to τὸ πάσχα a wider meaning, namely, that of the whole seven days' feast it is quite natural that, instead of saying, " celebrate the *feast* ", or " eat the *feast* ", or " eat the *feast of the Passover* ", he would use the expression, " eat the *Passover* ".

Now it is of importance that during the seven days' feast, in addition to the usual offerings, feast offerings had to be brought every day. In John xviii. 28 there is accordingly a special reference to the eating of the various sacrificial meals during the seven days of feasting, and not in this instance to the eating of the paschal repast on the first evening of the feast.[4]

It is plain from the Mishnaic tractate *Pesachim*, ix, 5, that the simple term " passover " was occasionally used to denote the whole seven days' feast.[5] Cf. also Deuteronomy xv. 2: " Thou shalt therefore *sacrifice the passover* unto the Lord thy God, of the flock and the herd ". So that " passover " is here not merely confined to the name of the paschal lamb. So also in 2 Chronicles xxxv. 8–19 small cattle *and* oxen are called passover offerings.

Also the expression in 2 Chronicles xxx. 22 " they did eat throughout the feast seven days ", points to the Jewish custom of using the expression " to eat a feast ", for the Hebrew reading is וַיֹּאכְלוּ אֶת־הַמּוֹעֵד (*wayyōkhĕlū' eth-hammō'ēdh*) literally, " they ate the *festival* "[6] (and not the feast offering) ".

---

[1] Cf. also Josephus, *War*, i, 3, vi, 9, etc.
[2] Cf. Zahn, *Introduction to the New Testament*, vol. iii, p. 293. See also Ezekiel xlv. 21, where " Passover " is made equivalent to the feast of seven days.
[3] Cf. Zahn, *Introduction to the New Testament*, vol. iii, p. 298, and the Hebrew text of 2 Chronicles xxx. 22.
[4] Cf. Zahn, *in loc.*
[5] Cf. Zahn, *op. cit.*, vol. iii, p. 297. Cf. also P. J. Heawood in *The Expository Times*, lix (1947–8), p. 251: " Nor is the phrase ' but that they might eat the passover ' (John xviii. 28), over which commentators have boggled, really out of place on what was the chief feast-day of the whole Paschal period."
[6] It may be, as Kittel's *Bib. Hebr.* says, that we should follow the LXX here and read *wayēkhallū 'eth hammō'ēdh*, " and they completed the festival "; but the Massoretic text represents the traditional reading.

We therefore conclude with Zahn that "the usage of the expression 'to eat the Passover' loosely and popularly for the entire seven days' or, properly, seven and a half days' feast, beginning with the slaughter of the Passover lamb, is adequately attested."[1]

So it is clear, in the light of all this, that John in xviii. 28 means the celebration of the seven days' feast which included the eating of the sacrificial meals during the whole of the seven days' feast, and probably John xviii. 28 refers in particular to the eating of the *Chagigah* ("Festival-offering") which had to be eaten during the forenoon after the first Passover day.[2]

As already indicated, John assumed that his readers were acquainted with the accounts of Mark and the other Gospels and that they accepted the accounts as correct. In particular he was aware that, according to the other Gospels, Jesus was crucified on the 15th Nisan. Therefore he was not afraid that by using the expression φαγεῖν τὸ πάσχα in xviii. 28 they would misunderstand him and gain the impression that by it he meant the eating of the paschal repast, in contradiction to the other Gospels.

The fact is, therefore, that it is not John's actual statements that create a problem in relation to the Synoptists, *but a wrong interpretation of his statements.* This wrong interpretation, as already mentioned, originated about the last quarter of the second century A.D., when the close contact with first-hand knowledge concerning the views of John and the other leaders of the first century became more and more meagre, and expressions in the Gospels were interpreted differently from what the authors had intended.[3]

So the reason why John in xviii. 28 mentions the fact that the Jews did not want to enter the governor's palace is not in order to contradict the data of the Synoptists, but in order to emphasise the hypocrisy of the Jews' behaviour: they are very careful not to break an outward ceremonial regulation, but they do not recoil from the dreadful sin of bringing their innocent Messiah before the pagan governor in their hate and jealousy, in order to have Him condemned to death.

---

[1] *Introduction to the New Testament,* p. 282.

[2] Cf. Edersheim, *Life and Times of Jesus,* ii, pp. 566 ff., also Lightfoot, *Biblical Essays.*

[3] In order to prove how little the champions (in the second and third centuries A.D.) of the so-called Johannine dating of the crucifixion (e.g. Hippolytus and Apollinarius) really understood the data of the Gospels, we need only mention the fact that they again and again alleged that the first three Gospels teach that Jesus was undoubtedly crucified already on the 14th Nisan (cf. the appropriate passages in *Ante-Nicene Christian Library*). Only an extremely superficial reading of the Gospels could have caused them to adopt such a point of view. It was their main object and desire to represent Jesus as the true Paschal Lamb, and therefore they chose the 14th Nisan.

John xix. 14. This verse also is generally adduced as a so-called proof that John teaches that Jesus was crucified already before the Passover. The verse is often interpreted as though it said that the day of the crucifixion was the preparation *for* the Passover: it is even translated so in the American Revised Standard Version. But A.V. and R.V. rightly translate παρασκευὴ τοῦ πάσχα by " the preparation of the passover ".

The fact[1] is, however, that at the time when John wrote the Greek term παρασκευή (" preparation ") was already for a long time the technical term used to indicate " Friday ",[2] the equivalent of the Hebrew עֶרֶב שַׁבָּת (*'ērebh shabbāth*).

Apart from John xix. 14, the word occurs in five other places in the New Testament, namely in Matthew xxvii. 62; Mark xv. 42; Luke xxiii. 54; John xix. 31, 42. In all these instances its meaning is clearly as Mark has defined it: " the preparation . . . *that is the day before the Sabbath* " (προσάββατον) (Mark xv. 42).

The Jews, in order to observe the Sabbath laws fittingly, were accustomed to make preparations for the Sabbath[3] on Friday (the day before their Sabbath). And so the day before the Sabbath gradually came to be called παρασκευή, as to-day in German *Sonnabend* is used as the name for Saturday. In the time of Tertullian, παρασκευή had already for such a long time been the fixed name for Friday, that he even argues that this was the name for Friday ever since creation.[4]

Accordingly παρασκευὴ τοῦ πάσχα in John xix. 14 means that the day of the Lord's crucifixion was the Friday *of* the Passover, the Friday that falls during Passover week, i.e., Passover Friday (Good Friday). It is a grammatically correct rendering and all the evidence is in favour of it.[5]

Dr. Bouma, too, differs here from Strack-Billerbeck and translates " preparation *of* the Passover " and states: " The ' preparation ' had gradually become the customary name for the Friday, Matthew xxvii. 62. Now this Friday fell within Passover week, and was thus the Friday of the preparation *of*, not *for*, the Passover—Passover Friday."[6]

This expression in John xix. 14 was most probably intended

---

[1] Cf. e.g. *Didache*, viii, 1 and *Martyrdom of Polycarp*, vii, where παρασκευή is without doubt used as the technical term for Friday.
[2] Cf. Schlatter, *Markus*, p. 275.
[3] Cf. Exodus xvi. 5.
[4] Cf. *The Writings of Tertullian*, vol. iii, in the series *Ante-Nicene Christian Library*, p. 309.
[5] Cf. Ubbink, *Johannes*, p. 177; Lightfoot, *Biblical Essays*, p. 168; Zahn, *Introduction to the New Testament*, vol. iii, p. 295; Edersheim, *Life and Times of Jesus the Messiah*, ii, p. 381; Hengstenberg, etc.
[6] *Evangelie naar Joh.*, p. 231.

by John as preparatory to his statement in xix. 31, that the
Sabbath after the Lord's crucifixion was "high" day, for (as
we shall see) John calls the Sabbath "high" because *inter alia*
it is the Sabbath which falls in Passover week.

John xix. 31. It is admitted even by Strack-Billerbeck, in view
of the use of the word in the old Jewish writings, that παρασκευή
as a single word could be used as the name for Friday, even
although the Friday was the first day of the Feast.[1]

Now some hold that the words ἦν γὰρ μεγάλη ἡ ἡμέρα
ἐκείνον τοῦ σαββάτου in xix. 31 prove that John counted the
Saturday as the Feast Day, and not the Friday, as the Synoptists
did. According to them, the Sabbath would be called "high"
only when the Passover Day coincides with it. The argument,
however, is refuted by the facts, for it is admitted by Strack-
Billerbeck that the Sabbath could be termed "high" even if
it coincides with the second feast day.[2]

Accordingly Edersheim is right in stating: "The Sabbath
about to open was a 'high day'—it was both a Sabbath and the
second Paschal Day, which was regarded as in every respect
equally sacred with the first—nay, more so, since the so-called
Wave-sheaf was then offered to the Lord."[3]

So in none of John's statements do we find any proof that he
contradicts the synoptic representation concerning the Last
Supper and the crucifixion. On the contrary, we have found that
he confirms and supplements their evidence in everything.

Therefore, together with the first three Gospels, John teaches
that Jesus on the Thursday evening celebrated the lawful Jewish
paschal repast along with His disciples and that He was crucified
on Friday, the 15th Nisan.[4]

Moreover, this representation of the course of events fits in
much better with the spirit of the fourth Gospel than the representation that Jesus suffered already before the Jewish Passover,
and that when the lawful paschal repast was taking place, He
was already in His grave. For who can deny that the paschal
repast was the proper occasion for the institution of the Holy
Communion which in the New Dispensation was to take the place
of the paschal repast, and that Jesus Himself should institute it?

---

[1] Cf. *Kommentar zum Neuen Testament*, vol. ii, pp. 828–32 and vol. iv, p. 76. Cf. also
Edersheim, *Life and Times*, vol. ii, p. 613.
[2] *Kommentar zum Neuen Testament*, vol. ii, 582.
[3] *Life and Times of Jesus the Messiah*, ii, p. 613.
[4] With regard to the objections to date in John as in xix. 41 where it is stated that
Jesus was interred on the Feast Day, and to objections against the statement that the
trial and crucifixion took place on that day, etc., we refer our readers to our discussion
(*infra*) of the date of the Synoptists where all these questions are dealt with.

And was not this the reason why the Lord had stated that He " desired with desire " to celebrate this last paschal repast with His disciples? He had longed for the Old Dispensation with its shadow offerings to pass by, so that the New Dispensation should supersede the old one on the strength of His sacrifice.

Furthermore, the *slaughtering* of the lambs was indeed not the most important part of the Passover, but merely preparatory; it was the paschal repast itself that was of most importance. Why then was it necessary that Jesus, in order to be the true Paschal Lamb, should die just at the very hour when the paschal lambs were slaughtered, and should already be in His grave when the paschal repast commenced?

No, it is far more fitting that, when the paschal lambs were eaten, Jesus Himself as Lord also of the Passover (as He is Lord of the Sabbath) should be present at the paschal repast and should by the institution of the Holy Communion represent Himself as the Sacrificial Lamb of God who in a spiritual sense gives His flesh and blood to us, and should then, after having thus instituted the sign and seal of the New Dispensation, enter upon the way of suffering in order to complete everything. And this is precisely what the first three Gospels and the Gospel of John alike teach us.[1]

B. *The Data of the Synoptists.*

Through the great and thorough work of authorities like Edersheim, Lightfoot and Zahn, and in more recent times of authorities like Dalman, Strack-Billerbeck, Walter Bauer, Grosheide and Schlatter, it has been abundantly and clearly proved that no conclusive objections can be raised against the historical genuineness of the Synoptic narrative in connection with the history and dating of the crucifixion.

Several objections to dating the crucifixion on the 15th Nisan have already been refuted by us in our exposition of Luke xxii and xxiii. In addition, we further wish to deal with the following.

Mark xiv. 2 and Matthew xxvi. 5. It is here stated that the Jews had decided not to arrest and kill Jesus on the feast. Now it is maintained that Jesus must have been already crucified before the feast and that the Gospels here contradict themselves. But this

---

[1] With regard to the Jewish Talmud tradition (T. B., *Sanhedrin*, 43a) which states that Jesus was crucified on the 14th Nisan, no expert will venture to attach much importance to it, since it dates from a very late period and since the writers of the documents concerned were dependent on a weak standard of Christian tradition and writings for their information. Moreover, the Jews in later times would naturally not like to acknowledge that they had caused Jesus to be crucified on the Feast Day. So authorities like Strack-Billerbeck admit candidly that the data supplied by the Talmud are worthless as regards their cogency in such a connection.

view is manifestly too superficial. The authorities as a matter of fact did decide not to arrest the Lord on the feast, but they were not masters of the circumstances! God's will triumphed in spite of their decision, and the Gospels mention it precisely in order to emphasise this fact. Christ's fate was not dependent on the decisions of the Jewish authorities, but the will of His Father had to be carried out and in God's will, as is shown by the Gospels, it was ordained that Jesus should celebrate the lawful paschal repast, institute the Holy Communion, and die on the Feast Day. Thus all the planning of His enemies was overthrown by the providential overruling of God.

The Last Supper. Matthew xxvi. 17–30; Mark xiv. 12–26; Luke xxii. 7–23 and 1 Corinthians xi. 23–9.

By quite a number of critics, as we have already previously observed, it is argued that the Last Supper was not a lawful Jewish paschal repast. Thus they declare that, although the Synoptists profess that it was a paschal repast, their evidence clearly shows that we here have to do with a *Qiddush* meal, an ordinary communal repast or something similar.[1] We have already briefly pointed out the baselessness of these statements. We here mention just a few more proofs that it was indeed the paschal repast. (1) In Mark xiv. 12 the disciples ask: " Where wilt thou that we go and prepare *that thou mayest eat the passover?* " In xiv. 14 Jesus causes the question to be asked: " Where is the guestchamber, where I shall eat *the passover* with my disciples? " Verse 16 states: " they *made ready the passover* ", and then in verses 17 ff. there follows the description of the Last Supper. Now how can one find a clearer insistence that it was indeed the paschal repast? Or would the paschal repast just have been prepared and then have been ignored by Jesus and the disciples to take another meal in its stead? With Mark also the other Synoptists are in agreement. (2) Such words as " brake the bread ", " took the cup", " Take, eat: this is my body ", " This is my blood of the new testament which is shed for many ", and " when they had sung a *hymn* "—all clearly show that here we have to do with no ordinary meal but with a paschal repast.[2]

We are, of course, not entitled to expect a detailed account of the whole meal in the Gospel. Only those portions are mentioned that were of importance for the institution of the Holy Communion. For it is not the purpose of the Gospels to describe every

[1] Cf. e.g. Vincent Taylor, *Jesus and His Sacrifice.*
[2] For a detailed discussion of the subject we refer our readers to Dalman, *Jesus-Jeshua*, pp. 133 ff. and *Sacred Sites and Ways*, p. 318; also to Strack-Billerbeck, *Kommentar zum Neuen Testament*, vol. iv, p. 74; Zahn, *St. Matthew, in loc.*; Edersheim, Lightfoot, etc.

event in the life of Jesus without omitting the minutest details, but to mention the main crises and matters relevant to the evangelists' purpose.

Therefore, to take the fact that the Gospels do not expressly refer to all the various components of the paschal repast as[1] an argument to prove that Jesus did not celebrate the paschal repast, is a quite arbitrary proceeding.

The trial, condemnation and death sentence of Jesus.

In the fact that, according to the Gospels, the Lord was brought before the Jewish Council, was on the following morning tried before the Roman tribunals and sentenced to death, many critics see historical impossibility. But (as Strack-Billerbeck put it) " the rule was not unknown to the old synagogue, that extraordinary circumstances demand extraordinary measures, and it was in accordance with this principle that they proceeded ". They add proofs of this,[2] and express the opinion that in the case of Christ's arrest and condemnation extraordinary circumstances of this nature existed which would cause extraordinary action on the part of the Jews to appear justifiable in their own eyes.[3]

Consequently, when Judas during the Passover night secretly went to inform them that at the garden of Gethsemane there was a splendid opportunity of arresting Him without thereby causing an insurrection among the masses,[4] they seized the chance with both hands and immediately set everything going with feverish haste to arrest Him and to have Him sentenced and executed before a disturbance of the people would be possible. So in the tremendous emotional tension in which they found themselves they felt themselves justified in even transgressing their own laws and enactments in their action against Jesus, where such a course seemed necessary.

With regard to the *death sentence* passed upon our Lord on the Feast Day, there is similarly nothing improbable. Rabbinical pronouncements of that time are adduced in Strack-Billerbeck to show that the death sentence actually could be both passed and executed on the Feast Day under certain circumstances. Thus, e.g., the rabbis taught that if the condemnation and execution of a lawbreaker were necessary to make the people realise the

---

[1] As is done by Luce, Box, Wellhausen, E. Meyer, etc.
[2] *Kommentar zum Neuen Testament*, vol. ii, p. 82.
[3] Cf. *Kommentar zum Neuen Testament*, vol. ii, p. 822.
[4] The Passover night was indeed the most suitable time under existing circumstances to arrest Jesus, since the feast-goers would mostly be quietly at home and there would be no concourse of the masses.

sacredness of the Law, the death sentence could be carried out even on the Feast Day.[1]

Therefore, if we remember that, in the eyes of the Jewish authorities, Jesus was a great transgressor against the Law—not only in respect of such enactments as those governing the observance of the Sabbath but most of all as one adjudged guilty of blasphemy in the highest degree—there is no improbability in His having been condemned and crucified on the Feast Day.

Furthermore, we should bear in mind that it was not the Jews themselves who had Jesus crucified *on that day*, but the Roman governor Pilate and his soldiers. The Jewish rulers were instigators and spectators. In fact, the Roman authorities would have regarded such a well-attended festival as a specially suitable opportunity for the public execution of those convicted of sedition, that the deterrent effect might be as extensive as possible.

The burial of Jesus (Mark xv. 42–6 and parallels).

The action of Joseph of Arimathaea in attending to the burial of Jesus was not forbidden by rabbinical law. The following excerpt from a rabbinical pronouncement of about the time of Christ is quoted by Strack-Billerbeck: " Everything necessary for a dead person may be carried out (on a Feast Day)."[2] On such a day, therefore, a corpse could be attended to, though it was not permitted to dig a grave.[3] And—the Gospels expressly state that Jesus was placed in a sepulchre that had already been hewn out!

To sum up, here is an outline of the conclusions at which we have arrived:

(1) The Last Supper was indeed the regular Passover meal.

(2) The Fourth Gospel by no means contradicts the Synoptic evidence, nor does it suggest a different dating of the day of the crucifixion, but it presupposes, confirms and supplements the Synoptic narrative.

(3) The first three Gospels in no respect contradict themselves or each other, but unanimously teach that Jesus was crucified on the 15th Nisan, after instituting the Holy Communion on the previous evening (during the Passover meal) as the sign and seal of the New Dispensation.

---

[1] *Kommentar zum Neuen Testament*, vol. ii, p. 826.
[2] *Ibid.*, vol. ii, p. 833.
[3] *Ibid.*, vol. iv, p. 53.

(4) It is not the statements of the Gospels, but a misinterpretation of them and an imperfect acquaintance with and understanding of the circumstances surrounding the crucifixion, that create the problems concerning the relation between John and the Synoptists and concerning the historical trustworthiness of the evidence of all four Gospels.

With regard to the precise date of the crucifixion in terms of our calendar, the evidence does not permit us to come to a certain decision; but it is fairly generally accepted that Jesus died on or about the 6th April in A.D. 30.

INDEX OF CHIEF SUBJECTS.

INDEX OF CHIEF SUBJECTS

673

INDEX OF SCRIPTURE REFERENCES

INDEX OF SCRIPTURE REFERENCES

OLD TESTAMENT

APOCRYPHA

NEW TESTAMENT

681